# ONE LAW FOR ALL?

IN MEMORIAM

BERNARD LEO ADELL

1939–2014

# One Law for All?

## *Weber v Ontario Hydro* and Canadian Labour Law

ESSAYS IN MEMORY OF BERNIE ADELL

EDITED BY

*Elizabeth Shilton & Karen Schucher*

IRWIN LAW

One Law for All? *Weber v Ontario Hydro* and Canadian Labour Law


Published in 2017 by

Irwin Law Inc.
14 Duncan Street
Suite 206
Toronto, ON
M5H 3G8
www.irwinlaw.com

ISBN: 978-1-55221-454-1
e-book ISBN: 978-1-55221-455-8

**Cataloguing in Publication available from Library and Archives Canada**

Canada
Ontario
Ontario Media Development Corporation
Société de développement de l'industrie des médias de l'Ontario

Printed and bound by CPI Group (UK) Ltd, Croydon, CR0 4YY

1 2 3 4 5 21 20 19 18 17

# Contents

# Acknowledgements

We are grateful to the Centre for Law in the Contemporary Workplace, Queen's University (CLCW) for sponsoring the *Weber* Symposium which provided the foundation for the essays appearing in this volume. Kevin Banks and Brian Etherington were valuable co-members of the committee that put together the symposium program, and gave helpful advice in assembling and editing this volume. Queen's Law students Dayna Lubelski, Jason Paquette and Alyssa Jagt supplied us with enthusiastic logistical support and skilled research assistance at various stages of the symposium and publication projects. Thanks to the library staff at Queen's Law and the Centre for Industrial Relations and Human Resources, University of Toronto, for their assistance in the editing process. Thanks also to David Mackenzie, a man with a sharp eye for a typo. And a special thank you to Natalie Moniz-Henne, CLCW administrative assistant, whose patience and expertise made a major contribution to the smooth running of the symposium.

We are indebted to the symposium attendees, whose participation in both formal and informal discussions over the symposium weekend contributed useful insights which our contributors have put to good use in revising their draft papers. In addition, we thank the anonymous peer reviewers who generously contributed their time and expertise to improving the quality of the finished product.

We also acknowledge with gratitude the financial support provided by the Social Science and Humanities Research Council of Canada for both the symposium and the publication of this volume.

CHAPTER ONE

# One Law for All? An Introduction

Elizabeth Shilton & Karen Schucher

## A. BERNIE ADELL AND HIS MANY CONTRIBUTIONS TO CANADIAN LABOUR LAW

This volume arises from a symposium in honour of the late Professor Bernard Adell, hosted by the Centre for Law in the Contemporary Workplace at Queen's University (CLCW).[1] The symposium marked the twentieth anniversary of *Weber v Ontario Hydro*,[2] a decision of the Supreme Court of Canada that radically challenged orthodox understandings of the role of arbitration in Canadian labour law. It brought together scholars, practitioners and arbitrators to explore the impact of the decision on labour arbitration and collective bargaining. The themes discussed reflected Bernie Adell's lifelong interest in the intersection between theoretical and practical labour law, and in the institutions that instantiate and enforce that law in Canadian workplaces. This collection of essays is the mature fruit of that symposium.

Bernie Adell left a giant footprint on Canadian labour law. The flood of tributes that followed his unexpected death in 2014 at the age of seventy-five — tributes from former students, academics and members

1 The symposium, entitled *"One Law for All": Has Weber v Ontario Hydro Transformed Collective Agreement Administration and Arbitration in Canada?* [the *Weber* Symposium], was held in Kingston, Ontario on October 30–31, 2015.

2 [1995] 2 SCR 929 [*Weber*].

of the practicing labour law community, both nationally and internationally — contained recurring references to his rigorous and relentlessly scrupulous scholarship, his engaged teaching, his patient and effective mentorship, and his meticulous editorial work. His long career reached back almost to the birth of labour law as an academic discipline in Canadian universities. He was gold medalist in the class of 1961 at the University of Alberta, and went on to Oxford as a Rhodes Scholar to acquire a doctorate in law. His dissertation, a comparative examination of the legal status of collective agreements, was formally supervised by Professor Harold Hanbury, Vinerian Professor of English Law and author of Hanbury's *Modern Equity*. Less formally, Adell was mentored by pioneering UK labour law scholar Otto Kahn-Freund, then at the London School of Economics.[3] A version of his dissertation was subsequently published as *The Legal Status of Collective Agreements in England, the United States and Canada*.[4] In a lengthy review, Professor AWR Carrothers, then President of the University of Calgary, described that book as follows:

> It is a good book, and merits close and careful reading. . . . The author writes with confidence, with courtesy, and with style, eschewing strident criticism for scholarly ratiocination. The text reveals the author's critical understanding not only of the legal materials but also of the cultures of industrial relations in the three countries which he examines.[5]

Adell's academic writing never lost those qualities.

On his return to Canada in 1964, Adell was appointed Assistant Professor at the Faculty of Law at Queen's University in Kingston, Ontario, where he spent his entire academic career, moving up through the academic ranks to full professor and serving both as Associate Dean and as Dean. He took formal retirement in 2004 at a time when mandatory retirement was still a feature of the legal landscape in Ontario. Even as Professor Emeritus, however, he remained actively involved in faculty

---

3 *See* Brian Langille (Speech delivered at the Bora Laskin Award Ceremony, 22 October 2013), online: www.queensu.ca/clcw/sites/webpublish.queensu.ca.clcwwww/files/files/Bernard%20Adell%20Tributes.pdf.

4 BL Adell, *The Legal Status of Collective Agreements in England, the United States and Canada* (Kingston, ON: Queen's University Industrial Relations Centre, 1970).

5 AWR Carrothers, Book Review of *The Legal Status of Collective Agreements in England, the United States and Canada* by BL Adell, (1971) 21:2 *University of Toronto Law Journal* 252 at 256.

life, and was a driving force behind the founding of the Centre for Law in the Contemporary Workplace at Queen's Law in 2010.

Bernie's trademark combination of theoretical rigour and pragmatic analysis is very evident throughout his long curriculum vitae. His interest in workplace dispute resolution informs a 1967 article in the *Canadian Bar Review* which framed a cogent argument that the courts should stay out of the enforcement of collective agreements, leaving that job to the arbitrators.[6] He made notable contributions to labour law scholarship on such topics as collective bargaining rights for university faculty,[7] dispute resolution in collective bargaining (including strikes in essential services)[8] and the workplace pension rights of employees.[9] His continuing preoccupation with the cost-benefit trade-offs of unionization for individual employees is reflected both in this early writing and in scholarly presentations given in the years just prior to his death.[10] In addition, he was

---

6 BL Adell, "Labour Law–Collective Agreement–Right of Individual Employee to Sue Employer" (1967) 45 *Canadian Bar Review* 354.

7 BL Adell & DD Carter, *Collective Bargaining for University Faculty in Canada* (Kingston, ON: Queen's University Industrial Relations Centre, 1972); Bernard Adell, "Establishment of Faculty Collective Bargaining: The Developing Law" in Paul Thomas, ed, *Universities and the Law* (Manitoba: Legal Research Institute of the University of Manitoba,1975) 45; "The Legal Framework of Faculty Collective Bargaining: Some Short Questions and Some Long Answers" in HN Janisch, ed, *The University and the Law* (Halifax: Dalhousie University Faculty of Law, 1975) 121.

8 Bernard Adell, Michel Grant & Allen Ponak, *Strikes in Essential Services* (Kingston: Queen's IRC Press, 2001).

9 Bernard Adell, "Pension Plan Surpluses and the Law: Finding a Path for Reform" in *Task Force on Inflation Protection for Employment Pension Plans, Research Studies Volume* 2 (Toronto: Government of Ontario, 1988) 209; Bernard Adell, "The Canadian System of Retirement Income Support" (Paper prepared for the 12th World Congress of the International Society for Labour Law and Social Security, Madrid, Spain, 20–23 September 1988) (Kingston, ON: Queen's University Industrial Relations, 1988) [Adell, "Retirement Income"]; Bernard Adell, "The Case for Employee Rights in Pension Plan Surpluses" in *New Developments in Employment Law, Meredith Memorial Lectures* (Montreal: Éditions Yvon Blais, 1988) 87.

10 Bernard L Adell, "*International Brotherhood of Teamsters v Therien* and the Suability of Trade Unions in Alberta" (1955–1961) 1 *Alberta Law Review* 571; BL Adell, "The Duty of Fair Representation: Effective Protection for Individual Rights in Collective Agreements?" (1970) 25:3 *Relations industrielles/Industrial Relations* 602 [Adell, "Duty of Fair Representation"]; Bernard Adell, "Collective Agreements and Individual Rights: A Note on the Duty of Fair Representation" (1986) 11:2 *Queen's Law Journal* 251 [Adell," Collective Agreements"]; Bernard Adell, "Establishing a Collective Employee Voice in the Workplace: How Can the Obstacles Be Lowered?" in G England,

consistently and deeply interested in the theory and practice of labour arbitration, an issue about which we will have more to say later in this introduction.

Within the Canadian labour law community, Adell's practical influence went far beyond Queen's. That influence was pervasive in the editing of scholarly journals. For twenty years, including after his formal retirement, he acted as faculty advisor to the *Queen's Law Journal*, training numerous students in the arcane arts of evaluating and editing academic articles. Under Adell's guidance, the *Queen's Law Journal* published many labour and employment law papers. Even more vital to the cultivation of peer-reviewed publication channels for Canadian labour law scholars was his lengthy stint as editor of the *Canadian Labour and Employment Law Journal*. His blue pencil made a deep and abiding impression on the academics and "scholarly practitioners" (Adell's phrase) who submitted their work to his critical review. In introductory remarks to the *Weber* Symposium, CLCW Director Kevin Banks described Adell's editorial approach as a "passion for clarity." Others have used less restrained language to describe the "Bernification"[11] of their work. Brian Langille, speaking on the occasion of Adell's receipt of the prestigious Bora Laskin award in 2013, described that process in these words: "My experiences with Bernie have been like great academic acts of surgery—it is quite something to go under Bernie's knife and have the major organs of your argument re-arranged, rehabilitated and often just removed. And all without anesthetic. You end up much better. But it is not a process for the faint-hearted."[12] And Adell's influence as a legal editor was not confined to Canada. He was an active and highly respected member of the International Association of

ed, *Essays in Labour Relations Law* (Don Mills, ON: CCH Canadian Limited, 1986) 3 [Adell, "Employee Voice"]; Bernard Adell, "The Union's Duty of Fair Representation in Discrimination Cases: The New Obligation to Be Proactive" in Kevin Whitaker et al, eds, (2001–2002) 1 *Labour Arbitration Yearbook* (Toronto: Lancaster House, 2002) 263 [Adell, "The Union's Duty"]; Bernard Adell, "The Duty of Fair Representation: 'a form of words . . .'?," [unpublished]. (PowerPoint delivered at *Adjudicating Human Rights in the Workplace After the Pinto Report, Where Do We Go Next?*, CLCW Workshop, Queen's University, 10 November 2012)) [unpublished].

11 The phrase was coined by David Doorey, one of Adell's many protégés. *See* Doorey's blog tribute at the time of Adell's death: David Doorey, "RIP: Professor Emeritus (Queens U. Law) and Labour Law Giant Bernie Adell," *Law of Work* (blog), online: http://lawofwork.ca/?p=7594.

12 Langille, above note 3.

Labour Law Journals, which paid tribute to his global reputation at its 2014 annual meeting in Dublin, shortly after his death.

Adell's impact as a scholar went far beyond the boundaries of English Canada. He was fluently bilingual, and made key contributions to bridging the "two solitudes" in Canada in the field of labour law, introducing often unilingual anglophone scholars to the important work of scholars in Quebec.[13] In a tribute at the time of his death, Gregor Murray described him as "one of the rare scholars in English-speaking Canada who actually read the francophone scholarship and could place it in context."[14] His international renown is also reflected in the frequency with which he was called upon as the voice of Canada at international labour law workshops and conferences, and the consistency with which he contributed to international comparative labour law publications.[15]

---

13 *See e.g.*, BL Adell, Book Review of *Droit du travail en vigueur au Québec?* by Robert Gagnon, Louis LeBel & Pierre Verge, (1973) 1:2 *Dalhousie Law Journal* 394.

14 Gregor Murray, "Tribute to Bernie Adell" in *Tributes: Professor Emeritus Bernard "Bernie" Adell*, online, www.queensu.ca/clcw/sites/webpublish.queensu.ca.clcwwww/files/files/Bernard%20Adell%20Tributes.pdf.

15 Bernard Adell, "Rights and Functions of Trade Unions and their Representatives at Enterprise Level in Canada" in *Proceedings of 8th International Conference on Labour Law and Social Legislation*, Milan, 1976; Bernard Adell, "Codification of Labour Law in Canada (Common Law Jurisdictions)" in *Proceedings of Ninth International Congress of International Society for Labour Law and Social Security*, Munich, 1978, 772; Bernard Adell, "Country Reports — Canada" in Edward Yemin, ed, *Workforce Reductions in Undertakings: Policies and Measures for the Protection of Redundant Workers in Seven Industrialised Market Economy Countries* (Geneva: International Labour Office, 1982) 37; Bernard Adell, Termination of Employment on the Initiative of the Employer, and Income Security of the Worker Concerned — Canada" in *Proceedings of Tenth International Congress. International Societv for Labour Law and Social Security* (Washington, BNA Inc., 1984) vol. 2, 217; B Adell, "The Canadian System of Industrial Conflict Resolution" in T Hanami & R Blanpain, eds, *Industrial Conflict Resolution in Market Economies: A Study of Canada, Great Britain and Sweden* (Deventer, Netherlands: Kluwer Law and Taxation Publishers, 1987) 25; B Adell et al, "The System of Labour Dispute Resolution in Ontario Hospitals and its Application at Kingston General Hospital" in T Hanami & R Blanpain, eds, *Industrial Conflict Resolution in Market Economies: A Study of Canada, Great Britain and Sweden* (Deventer, Netherlands: Kluwer Law and Taxation Publishers, 1987) 45; Adell, "Retirement Income," above note 9; Roy J Adams & Bernard Adell, "Canada" in Hoyt N Wheeler & Jacques Rojot, eds, *Workplace Justice: Employment Obligations in International Perspective* (Columbia, South Carolina: University of South Carolina Press, 1992) 99; Bernard Adell & Roy J Adams, "Discipline and Discharge for Theft in Ten Countries" in *Proceedings of 45th Annual Meeting* (Anaheim, California:

Throughout his career, Adell was deeply interested in the practical application of the substantive issues discussed and debated at the *Weber* Symposium and now explored in the essays in this volume. Like many labour law professors of his era, he moonlighted as a labour arbitrator from time to time, with over thirty of his decisions reported in *Labour Arbitration Cases*.[16] He was particularly active as an arbitrator in the 1960s

---

Industrial Relations Research Association, 1993) 501; Bernard L Adell & Roy J Adams, "Theft as Cause for Employment Discipline: Some Comparative Observations" (1993) 9:2 *International Journal of Comparative Labour Law and Industrial Relations* 93; Bernard Adell, "Workplace Disciplinary Rules and Procedures in Canada" (1993) 132:5–6 *International Labour Review* 583; Bernard Adell, "The Legal Framework of Collective Bargaining in North America, with Envious Glances at the New Australian Federal Legislation" in Industrial Relations Society of Western Australia, *Occasional Papers*, December 1994.

16 *United Food Processors Union, Local 483 v Canada Starch Co* (1966), 17 LAC 179; *United Automobile Workers, Local 222 v Houdaille Industries* (1966), 17 LAC 420; *United Rubber Workers, Local 232 v Goodyear Tire & Rubber Co of Canada Ltd* (1967), 18 LAC 403; *International Brotherhood of Electrical Workers, Local 1586 v Cansfield Electrical Works Ltd* (1967), 18 LAC 207; *International Union of Office and Professional Employees, Local 165, and Canadian International Paper Co, Re* (1967), 18 LAC 147; *United Automobile Workers, Local 252 v Canadian Trailmobile Ltd* (1968), 19 LAC 227; *United Steelworkers of America, Local 2251 v Algoma Steel Corp* (1968), 20 LAC 15; *Hotels, Clubs, Restaurants, Taverns Employees' Union, Local 261 v Beacon Realty Co* (1968), 19 LAC 227; *United Steelworkers of America v Delta Steel Fabricating Ltd* (1968), 19 LAC 400; *United Automobile Workers, Local 112 v De Havilland Aircraft of Canada Ltd* (1969), 21 LAC 239; *United Steelworkers of America, Local 6962 v Union Carbide Canada Ltd, Gas Products* (1969), 20 LAC 74; *United Brewery Workers, Local 173 v Dare Foods Ltd* (1969), 20 LAC 166; *International Moulders and Allied Workers, Local 362 v Findlays Foundry Ltd* (1970), 22 LAC 48; *TCF of Canada Ltd v Textile Workers Union of America, Local 1332* (1972), 1 LAC (2d) 382; *Weston Bakeries Ltd v Milk & Bread Drivers, Dairy Employees, Caterers & Allied Employees, Local 647* (1973), 5 LAC (2d) 38; *Toronto Parking Authority v Canadian Union of Public Employees, Local 43* (1974), 5 LAC (2d) 150; *University of Toronto v Service Employees Union, Local 204* (1975), 10 LAC (2d) 417; *Collingwood General & Marine Hospital, Re* (1975), 10 LAC (2d) 57; *Hiram Walker & Sons Ltd v Canadian Union of Distillery Workers, Local* (1977), 14 LAC (2d) 412; *Molson's Brewery (Ontario) Ltd v Canadian Union of United Brewery, Flour, Soft Drink, Cereal and Distillery Workers, Local 304* (1979), 23 LAC (2d) 392; *Riverdale Hospital v Canadian Union of Public Employees, Local 43* (1979), 22 LAC (2d) 267; *Eastern Steelcasting v United Steelworkers of America, Local 8794* (1981), 28 LAC (2d) 310; *Ivaco Rolling Mills v United Steelworkers of America, Local 7940* (1981), 1 LAC (3d) 186; *Horton CBI Ltd v United Steelworkers of America, Local 8473* (1982), 4 LAC (3d) 97; *Molson's Brewery (Ontario) Ltd v United Brewery Workers, Local 304* (1983), 12 LAC (3d) 313; *Children's Hospital of Eastern Ontario*

and 70s. By the 1980s, however, his decisions appeared with much less frequency. In 2011, with typical self-deprecating humour, he gave the following account of his arbitration practice in a brief biographical sketch he provided to a CLCW workshop on arbitration: "[Adell] developed the first Canadian law school course in labour arbitration in the 1960s and did some arbitration himself for quite a few years, until both sides realized how unacceptable he was."[17]

Any kernel of truth to Adell's suggestion that he was less than successful as an arbitrator would have had no relation to the quality of his decisions, which are vintage "Bernie," crafted in accessible language reflecting both his mastery of the principles of labour law and his practical commitment to fairness. If employers and unions harboured suspicions about his "acceptability," it may have been because he did not hesitate in his academic writings to raise questions about fundamental principles largely taken for granted by Canada's labour law community. Although he was a firm believer in the utility of unionization, much of his academic output was devoted to a critical examination of the relationship between individual and collective rights and interests within unionized workplaces.[18] Even before the Supreme Court's decision in *Weber*, he questioned whether arbitration was an appropriate forum for dealing with the public law issues then beginning to breach the boundaries of arbitration.[19] In particular, he was concerned about arbitral colonization of "anti-discrimination rights, which are vested in individuals," since

---

*v Ontario Nurses' Association* (1987), 30 LAC (3d) 238; *Montfort Hospital v Ontario Nurses' Association* (1988), 3 LAC (4th) 244; *Canada Post Corp v Canadian Union of Postal Workers* (1990), 15 LAC (4th) 418; *Canada Post Corp v Canadian Union of Postal Workers* (1990), 15 LAC (4th) 77; *Canada Post Corp v Canadian Union of Postal Workers* (1993), 33 LAC (4th) 279; *Ivaco Rolling Mills v United Steelworkers of America, Local 8794* (1997), 67 LAC (4th) 66; *Ivaco Rolling Mills v United Steelworkers of America, Local 7940* (1997), 69 LAC (4th) 1; *Windsor University Faculty Association v University of Windsor* (2002), 112 LAC (4th) 1.

17 The workshop, the first event organized by the CLCW, was entitled *Labour Arbitration as Access to Justice*, 29 April 2011, Toronto, Ontario.

18 *See* articles cited in note 10 above.

19 Bernard Adell, "Overlapping Forums in Collective Agreement Administration" in Gilles Trudeau, Guylaine Vallée & Diane Veilleux, eds, *Études en droit du travail: à la memoire de Claude D'Aoust* (Cowansville, Québec: Éditions Yvon Blais, 1995) [Adell, "Overlapping Forums"] 1 at 12.

arbitration "privileges collective rights."[20] He queried both the normative fairness and the practical necessity of the gatekeeping role played by unions in determining which individual rights claims should be subject to adjudication. He was sceptical that the duty of fair representation could function as an effective tool for monitoring the boundary between individual and collective rights, particularly where public rights were involved.[21] He supported the idea that labour boards should impose a higher standard on unions when grievance claims involved public rights rather than rights generated solely through collective bargaining,[22] but was pessimistic about whether a higher standard would emerge without legislative intervention.

In further defiance of orthodox industrial pluralism, Adell was agnostic about the overall benefit of private over public adjudication of grievances. While he had considerable respect for the flexibility of arbitration as an institution, he was open to considering the merits of substituting equally flexible versions of adjudication by a public tribunal, to which individual employees would have unrestricted access.[23] In a 1991 research report prepared as background for an Ontario Law Reform Commission (OLRC) project on workplace dispute adjudication, he proposed that a public tribunal be established to deal with complaints of unjust discharge by non-unionized employees, employment standards complaints, and grievances under collective agreements. Always a pragmatist, he did not call for the elimination of private arbitration; under his recommendation, parties could opt out of public adjudication as long as they did so through collective bargaining.[24] Despite this "out clause," however, Adell's proposal was greeted with general consternation by the labour law community and did not warrant even a

---

20 Bernard Adell, "Jurisdictional Overlap Between Arbitration and Other Forums: An Update" (2000) 8 *Canadian Labour and Employment Law Journal* 179 at 223 [Adell, "Jurisdictional Overlap"].

21 Adell, "Duty of Fair Representation," above note 10; Adell, "Collective Agreements," above note 10; Adell, "Employee Voice," above note 10; Adell, "The Union's Duty," above note 10.

22 Adell, "The Union's Duty," above note 10 at 266.

23 Bernard Adell, "Law and Industrial Relations: The State of the Art in Common Law Canada" in Gérard Hébert, Hem C Jain & Noah M Meltz, eds, *The State of the Art in Industrial Relations* (Ontario: Queen's University Industrial Relations Centre & University of Toronto Centre for Industrial Relations, 1988) 107 at 134.

24 Bernard Adell, *Adjudication of Workplace Disputes in Ontario: A Report to the Ontario Law Reform Commission* (1991) at Ch 7, 1–9 [unpublished].

passing mention in the report eventually issued by the OLRC.[25] Had it been adopted, many of the *Weber*-related problems discussed in the essays in this volume might well have been avoided.

After watching courts, arbitrators, scholars, individual employees and the parties to collective bargaining struggle with the implications of *Weber* over almost two decades, Adell was greatly intrigued by the idea of reassessing that decision. He was involved in the early planning for the *Weber* Symposium project, and his absence at the symposium was deeply felt.

## B. THE SIGNIFICANCE OF *WEBER* FOR CANADIAN LABOUR ARBITRATION

While *Weber*[26] is one of the most significant decisions ever issued by the Supreme Court of Canada in the field of labour arbitration, it is also one of the most baffling. The case came before the courts as a set of common law tort claims brought by a unionized employee, Murray Weber, against his employer, Ontario Hydro. (Since Ontario Hydro was a public sector employer, Weber added a *Charter* claim to his tort claim to cover all bases.) Despite the fact that tort claims arising in both unionized and non-unionized workplaces had been routinely litigated before Canadian courts for many years, the Supreme Court held that courts had no jurisdiction over Weber's dispute because it arose "in its essential character" from his collective agreement and therefore belonged within the

---

25 *See* Ontario Law Reform Commission, *Report on Avoiding Delay and Multiple Proceedings in the Adjudication of Workplace Disputes* (Toronto: Ontario Law Reform Commission, 1995). Adell took mischievous pleasure in relating this story against himself. It was confirmed by Brian Etherington in his remarks at the *Weber* symposium. Etherington, then a quite junior member of the elite group of practitioners, academics and arbitrators assembled by the OLRC to consult about Adell's research, relates that Adell's proposal to push arbitration off its secure perch as the exclusive mechanism for resolving collective agreement disputes was roundly (and in some cases, quite intemperately) denounced by most attendees.

26 *Weber*'s companion case, *New Brunswick v O'Leary*, [1995] 2 SCR 967 [*O'Leary*], involved a tort claim by an employer, the New Brunswick government, alleging negligence against a unionized employee. The Court dismissed the employer's claim on the same basis as in *Weber*—that the dispute arose "in its essential character" from the collective agreement. Because the primary legal analysis is found in *Weber*, the approach to jurisdictional problems developed by the Court in these decisions has become known as the *Weber* test.

exclusive jurisdiction of a labour arbitrator. It was clear that the collective agreement itself neither created nor directly addressed the tort law rules and *Charter* rights relied on by Weber as the basis of his civil claims. The Court nonetheless held that his dispute arose "inferentially" from that agreement.

In her now-legendary majority judgement, then-Justice Beverley McLachlin held that arbitrators have jurisdiction over any dispute that arises "in its essential character" from a collective agreement, whether directly or indirectly. In her view, adjudicators could identify such disputes by assessing both the nature of the dispute itself and the "ambit of the collective agreement."[27] Her framing of the jurisdictional test did not differ substantially from earlier articulations by the Court of the scope of exclusive arbitral jurisdiction. However, its application in both *Weber* and *O'Leary* arguably removed from the scope of court jurisdiction a variety of legal claims linked more closely to external sources of law than to the language of the collective agreement, and subjected them for good or ill to the institutional constraints of arbitration.

*Weber* thus posed a profound challenge to conventional understandings about the scope of labour arbitration. Brian Etherington has described the Court's decision in *Weber* as "[p]art of a larger trend to privatize and collectivize workplace dispute resolution in the name of efficiency," with profound implications for individual employee rights.[28] Concerned about the impact of union gatekeeping, Etherington argued that "*Weber* appears to raise significant barriers to access to justice, including *Charter* justice, for the organized employee."[29] Etherington and other writers also raised questions about the institutional capacity of arbitration to deal with tort issues, which had typically been litigated using procedures available only to courts.[30] They pointed to new pressures on unions to fund the arbitra-

27 *Weber*, above note 2 at paras 50–58.

28 Brian Etherington, "*Weber* and Almost Everything After: Its Impact on *Charter*, Common Law and Individual Statutory Rights Claims" (Paper delivered at the Charter at Work Conference, University of Western Ontario, 23 October 2004) at 2 [unpublished]. *See also* Brian Etherington, "*Weber*, and Almost Everything After, 20 Years Later: Its Impact on Individual *Charter*, Common Law and Statutory Rights Claims," Chapter 2, this volume at 34–35.

29 Ray Brown & Brian Etherington, "*Weber v. Ontario Hydro*: A Denial of Access to Justice for the Organized Employee?" (1996) 4:1 *Canadian Labour and Employment Law Journal* 183 at 207.

30 Brian Etherington, "*O.P.S.E.U. v. Seneca College*: Deference as a Two-Edged Sword — A Missed Opportunity to Address the '*Weber* Gap'" (2006–2007) 13 *Canadian Labour*

tion of complex claims about such matters as defamation, which might be important to individual employees but were of dubious collective interest.[31] One experienced arbitrator prophesied that labour arbitration could be turned into a "labour court," with plenary jurisdiction over enforcing workplace rights for unionized employees, instead of a private forum for resolving contract disputes.[32] Another expressed "[c]oncern that the good intentions and 'pro-arbitration' bent of [*Weber*] may prove to be a Pandora's box of unforeseen negative consequences for individual rights, as well as for labour arbitration and collective bargaining itself."[33]

In the first decade after it was issued, the Supreme Court's *Weber* decision attracted significant scholarly interest as reflected in special issues of the *Labour Arbitration Yearbook* in 1999–2000, and the *Canadian Labour and Employment Law Journal* in 1999–2000 and again in 2005.[34] At the five-year mark following the *Weber* decision, Donald Carter observed that the "implications of *Weber* are still far from clear."[35] Among other problems, some scholars and practitioners observed an emerging "*Weber* gap" in the post-*Weber* caselaw — a growing discrepancy between the very broad view of arbitral jurisdiction taken by the courts and the much narrower view taken by arbitrators themselves, raising the spectre of rights for which there would be no remedies.[36] Others pointed to the role of *Weber*

---

*and Employment Law Journal* 301 [Etherington, "*O.P.S.E.U. v. Seneca College*"]; Donald D Carter, "An Arbitrator as Human Rights Adjudicator: The Lessons of *Orillia Soldiers Memorial Hospital*" in Kevin Whitaker et al, eds, (1999–2000) 1 *Labour Arbitration Yearbook* (Toronto: Lancaster House, 2000) 55; Donald D Carter, "Looking at *Weber* Five Years Later: Is it Time for a New Approach?" (2000) 8:1 *Canadian Labour and Employment Law Journal* 231 [Carter, "Looking at *Weber* Five Years Later"]; Michel G Picher, "Defining the Scope of Arbitration: The Impact of *Weber*: an Arbitrator's Perspective" in Kevin Whitaker et al, eds, (1999–2000) 1 *Labour Arbitration Yearbook* (Toronto: Lancaster House, 2000) 99; George T Surdykowski, "The Limits of Grievance Arbitration: *Weber* and *Pilon* in Perspective" in Kevin Whitaker et al, eds, (1999–2000) 1 *Labour Arbitration Year Book* (Toronto: Lancaster House, 2000) 67.

31 Picher, above note 30; Adell, "Jurisdictional Overlap," above note 20.

32 Richard MacDowell, "Labour Arbitration — The New Labour Court?" (2000) 8:1 *Canadian Labour and Employment Law Journal* 121.

33 Picher, above note 30 at 109.

34 *Labour Arbitration Yearbook* (1999–2000); Volumes 8 and 12 of the *Canadian Labour and Employment Law Journal*.

35 Carter, "Looking at *Weber* Five Years Later," above note 30.

36 Etherington, "*O.P.S.E.U. v. Seneca College*," above note 30; Andrew Lokan & Maryth Yachnin, "From *Weber* to *Parry Sound*: the Expanded Scope of Arbitration" (2004) 11 *Canadian Labour and Employment Law Journal* 1. *See also* Elizabeth Shilton, "Enfor-

in creating jurisdictional confusion in the resolution of workplace disputes and in exacerbating the problem of multiple duplicative proceedings, particularly in cases involving human rights issues.[37] Decisions of the Supreme Court addressing a variety of post-*Weber* issues have further muddied already troubled waters.[38] The Court's decisions are sometimes difficult to reconcile both with *Weber* and with each other, making the theoretical questions spawned by *Weber* more rather than less complex. The jurisdictional picture has been further complicated by competing Supreme Court decisions on how tribunals with concurrent or over-lapping jurisdiction should deal with disputes and issues that may be, or have already been, litigated both at arbitration and before statutory tribunals or courts.[39] These decisions highlight a range of *Weber*-generated difficulties in identifying the correct forum for the litigation of employment disputes in unionized workplaces — difficulties which create pressures on employer-union relations, contribute to the squandering of public and private

---

cing Workplace Pension Rights for Unionized Employees: Is There a '*Weber* Gap'?" (2015) 19 *Canadian Labour and Employment Law Journal* 135.

37 Brian Etherington, "Promises, Promises: Notes on Diversity and Access to Justice" (2000) 26:1 *Queen's Law Journal* 43; Etherington, "*O.P.S.E.U. v. Seneca College*," above note 30; Craig Flood, "Efficiency v. Fairness: Multiple Litigation and Adjudication in Labour and Employment Law" (2000) 8 *Canadian Labour and Employment Law Journal* 383; Peter A Gall, Andrea L Zwack & Kate Bayne, "Determining Human Rights Issues in the Unionized Workplace: The Case for Exclusive Arbitral Jurisdiction" (2005) 12 *Canadian Labour and Employment Law Journal* 381; Dana F Hooker & Carman J Overholt, "Defending Claims In Different Fora: The Competing Jurisdiction of Arbitrators And Tribunals In British Columbia" (2010) 43:1 *University of British Columbia Law Review* 47; Elizabeth Shilton, "Choice But No Choice: Adjudicating Human Rights Claims in Unionized Workplaces in Canada" (2013) 38:2 *Queen's Law Journal* 461 [Shilton, "Choice But No Choice"].

38 *See Allen v Alberta*, 2003 SCC 13 (jurisdiction over post-termination issues); *Goudie v Ottawa (City)*, 2003 SCC 14 (jurisdiction over pre-termination issues); *Parry Sound (District) Welfare Administration Board v Ontario Public Service Employees Union, Local 324*, 2003 SCC 42 [*Parry Sound*] (jurisdiction over statutory claims); *Québec (Commission des droits de la personne & des droits de la jeunesse) c Québec (Procureur général)*, 2004 SCC 39 [*Morin*] (jurisdiction over human rights issues); *Canada (House of Commons) v Vaid*, 2005 SCC 30 (jurisdiction over human rights issues); *Bisaillon v Concordia University*, 2006 SCC 19 [*Bisaillon*] (jurisdiction over pension claims); *Isidore Garon ltée v Syndicat du bois ouvré de la région de Québec inc*, 2006 SCC 2 (jurisdiction over claims under Quebec's *Civil Code*).

39 *British Columbia (Workers' Compensation Board) v Figliola*, 2011 SCC 52 (tribunals should refuse to deal with such issues); *Penner v Niagara (Regional Police Services Board)* 2013 SCC 19 (tribunals may deal with such issues if it is fair to do so).

resources in duplicative litigation, and inhibit access to adjudication by individual employees.[40] In the aftermath of a decision clearly intended to resolve jurisdictional difficulties by reinforcing the exclusive jurisdiction of arbitrators, such outcomes are both ironic and unfortunate.

## C. THE PERSPECTIVE OF PRACTICING ARBITRATORS

The *Weber* Symposium wrestled with the broad question of whether *Weber* and its progeny have transformed collective agreement administration and arbitration in Canada. At the conclusion of the program, a panel of arbitrators chaired by Susan Stewart, an experienced arbitrator and current chair of Ontario's Public Service Grievance Settlement Board, was invited to comment on that question. Stewart was joined by four other experienced arbitrators: Randi Abramsky (whose arbitration practice has spanned both the US and Canada), Paula Knopf (chair of the arbitration board in the case that subsequently reached the Supreme Court of Canada as *Parry Sound*[41]), Richard MacDowell (former chair of the Ontario Labour Relations Board and long-time arbitrator) and Bruce Archibald (law professor and arbitrator from Canada's east coast). Somewhat to the surprise of symposium participants, who had just heard a series of presentations focusing on the chaotic post-*Weber* picture in the courts, all arbitrators reported that *Weber* has had only minimal impact on their arbitration practices.

Abramsky explained that she arrived in Canada in the 1980s with a background in US arbitration, which at that time focused almost exclusively on collective agreements. She was concerned that *Weber* would bring a host of work-related torts and constitutional issues under the aegis of labour arbitration, increasing the cost and complexity of arbitration and making parties less realistic about mediated settlements. However, despite the fact that tort and *Charter* issues have been raised in grievance documents from time to time, she had never, in the twenty years since the Supreme Court's *Weber* judgment, been asked to issue a decision requiring an interpretation of that decision. While she had been

40 *See* Randi Hammer Abramsky, "The Ontario Law Reform Commission Report on Delay and Multiple Proceedings: A Critique" (1996) 4 *Canadian Labour and Employment Law Journal* 353; Gall, Zwack & Bayne, above note 37; Hooker & Overholt, above note 37; Shilton, "Choice But No Choice," above note 37 at 162–69.

41 Above note 38.

confronted with statutory rights claims, like other arbitrators on the panel she did not see these as *Weber* issues *per se*, since arbitral jurisdiction over statutory claims flows directly from labour statutes.

Knopf provided interesting insight into the evolution of the *Parry Sound* decision. She observed that the legal argument on the jurisdictional issue before the arbitration board took no more than an hour and half, and no one in the room had any idea that the case would ultimately emerge as a precedent-setting decision from the Supreme Court of Canada. As the arbitration board saw the case, it raised the relatively straightforward question of whether a workplace could be run in ways that did not comply with law — to which the commonsense answer was no. She noted that the union or the grievor could have taken the problem to a human rights tribunal; the fact that they did not reflects what she saw as a consistent preference by unionized parties to have their disputes resolved by arbitrators, who understand workplaces, rather than by statutory tribunals, which specialize in human rights issues but may not appreciate workplace realities. In Knopf's view, *Weber* did not represent revolutionary change. Instead, like concepts of fairness and reasonableness which have been embraced by arbitrators over time, *Weber* is simply part of an evolutionary process in which arbitration has become a practical and effective form of "one-stop shopping," from which all parties benefit. Knopf had no doubt that arbitration was well-adapted to provide comprehensive dispute resolution for unionized workplaces. She voiced some skepticism, however, that empirical research would demonstrate the true extent of arbitration's broad role, since arbitrators often resolve more complex cases through mediation rather than adjudication, leaving no paper trail.

MacDowell expressed support for the outcome in *Weber*, but shared the view of other arbitrators that *Weber* has changed neither the theory nor practice of arbitration. From his perspective, *Weber* simply encapsulates section 48(1) of Ontario's *Labour Relations Act*, a version of which has been in place since 1944. MacDowell also emphasized the role of Ontario's *Rights of Labour Act*,[42] which has excluded the jurisdiction of the courts in matters arising out of the collective agreement for many decades. As he saw it, *Weber* did not alter the fundamental rule that collective agreements do not cover all bases; there may be employment disputes in unionized workplaces which are not covered by those agreements and

42 RSO 1990, c R.33.

are therefore not arbitrable. He was therefore critical of the court's reasoning in *Weber* (and *O'Leary*) for unnecessarily muddying jurisdictional waters by suggesting otherwise. At the same time, he expressed interest in giving arbitrators more powers: for example, powers over third parties, which would enable them to address the full range of claims that may arise in connection with the collective agreement. Unlike some of his fellow panel members, he reported that he had been confronted in his arbitration practice with issues and arguments related to *Weber*, and has written decisions addressing some of the conundrums posed by the Supreme Court's decisions.[43]

Archibald expressed qualified support for *Weber*. He rejected the view that *Weber* has unnecessarily complicated a system whose principal virtue was its simplicity. Like Knopf, he characterized *Weber* as part of a general movement within labour arbitration to provide a more complete and systematic approach to dispute resolution in unionized workplaces by increasing the range of options for parties and arbitrators. He emphasized that a more formal approach to adjudication (the "Cadillac" approach) has its place within the system, but so do less formal alternatives. Some alternatives have been less successful — for example, expedited arbitration of statutory issues. But mediation has played a very significant role; its availability (including in the form of med/arb) has increased the ability of arbitration to deal with more complex issues that might otherwise challenge its capacity, of which *Weber*-type tort issues are only one example. Archibald expressed particular interest in the potential of restorative justice approaches to dispute resolution. Rooted in a relational theory of rights, such approaches try to resolve disputes based on values of equality, respect for human dignity and the importance of stability in social relations. In addition, they require decision-makers to take account of the interests of members of the community both within and outside the workplace. He argued that to be effective, however, restorative justice approaches require intervention much earlier than is typically the case with current workplace dispute resolution.

The ideas which emerged from the arbitrators' panel posed some theoretical challenges for both scholars and practitioners participating in the symposium. In addition, the arbitrators threw out a direct practical

43 *Communications, Energy and Paperworkers Union, Local 37-O v Sifto Canada Corp*, [2011] CLAD No 426 (QL); *Canadian Union of Public Employees, Local 133 v Niagara Falls (City)* (2005), 81 CLAS 1; *Greater Essex District School Board and Ontario Secondary School Teachers Federation (OMERS Pension Plan), Re* (2015), 256 LAC (4th) 1.

challenge. They pointed to the obvious institutional fact that arbitrators respond to the problems that are brought before them. If *Weber* and *O'Leary* have indeed granted arbitrators new powers and opened new vistas for arbitral jurisdiction, they asked, why have unions (and employers) not made more creative use of the possibilities suggested by these decisions?

## D. "ONE LAW FOR ALL"?

The title of this volume is an ironic reference to a proposition first articulated by Lord Denning in his 1953 decision in *David Taylor & Son Ltd v Barnett Trading Co*, where he asserted that "[t]here is not one law for arbitrators and another for the court. There is one law for all."[44] Completely without irony, McLachlin J invoked Denning's "one law for all" comment in *Weber* in response to Weber's argument that he would be disadvantaged if forced to resort to arbitration because arbitrators lacked powers conferred on common law judges. In her view, "[t]his concern is answered by the power and duty of arbitrators to apply the law of the land to the disputes before them. To this end, arbitrators may refer to both the common law and statutes."[45] In the context of the *Weber* problem, the meaning of this observation is by no means clear. Indeed, it is this conundrum that has animated two decades of confusing jurisprudence and inconclusive scholarly commentary. In various ways, it is also the key issue animating the essays in this volume.

Lord Denning's assertion that there is "one law for all" was made in a case involving the enforcement of a contract for the purchase and sale of cases of Irish stewed steak. When the seller failed to deliver the product, the buyer claimed damages for breach of contract before an arbitrator, as stipulated by the contract. The seller argued that the contract was illegal and could not be enforced because the sale price violated a statutory price-setting order. Invoking the time-honoured proposition that arbitral jurisdiction is drawn exclusively from the parties' contract, the arbitrator rejected this argument and ordered the seller to pay damages based on the contract price. On appeal, the issue was whether the arbitrator should have refused to enforce an illegal contract. In holding that the price caps applied regardless of whether the contract was enforced by a

44 [1953] 1 WLR 562 (CA) at 570 [*Taylor v Barnett*].

45 *Weber*, above note 2 at para 61.

court or an arbitrator, Denning JA relied on the "one law for all" principle. The Supreme Court of Canada had drawn on this principle in *Douglas/Kwantlen Faculty Assn v Douglas College*,[46] where the substantive issue was whether an arbitrator could address the argument that a mandatory retirement provision in a collective agreement was unenforceable because it violated section 15 of the *Charter*. Quoting Denning JA's conclusion that "[i]f a contract is illegal, arbitrators must decline to award on it just as the court would do," the Court concluded that "[a] fortiori, . . . there cannot be a Constitution for arbitrators and another for the courts."[47] It held that arbitrators had power to apply the *Charter*.

Both *Taylor v Barnett* and *Douglas College* stand for the proposition that statutory and constitutional law may operate to nullify the content of a contract regardless of the forum in which that contract is enforced. That proposition cannot be transposed directly into the very different context in which *Weber* questions arise. On its face, *Weber* was a case about enforcement rather than substantive obligations — about how to manage intersections and overlaps among the multiple legal enforcement processes that might be called upon to resolve a specific workplace rights dispute. Therefore, in holding that Murray Weber's dispute fell within the exclusive jurisdiction of an arbitrator, *Weber* inevitably raised a set of different and deeper questions about the relationship between legal rules and enforcement processes and, in particular, about what legal rules apply to workplace disputes when those disputes are dealt with by an arbitrator. When is an adjudicative body authorized, or required, to "enforce" any and all legal rules that may apply to the dispute it is empowered to resolve? Is the enforcement of some legal rules tied to specific adjudicative bodies? Are all adjudicative bodies created equal, or are there institutional differences among them that are relevant to determining the appropriate scope of their authority? Are there legal rules which are universal, in the sense that they can and should be applied by any adjudicative body with jurisdiction over a particular dispute? If so, what are these rules and what is their source? Are particular legal enforcement mechanisms better suited to applying certain legal rules? Is it fair to limit parties to one legal venue for addressing all potential legal rules that may apply to their situation, particularly if this limitation may in fact deprive either party of some remedies they might otherwise be able to pursue?

---

46 [1990] 3 SCR 570, 77 DLR (4th) 94 [*Douglas College*].

47 *Ibid* at para 76.

Justice McLachlin's cursory references in *Weber* to "one law for all" and the "law of the land" beg all these questions. The plaintiff in *Weber* was clearly more concerned about the content of the legal rules that would apply to his claim than he was about whether his claim would be dealt with by a court or an arbitrator. His desire to go to court after his grievances were settled was a considered attempt to invoke one aspect of "the law of the land" — tort law — which had traditionally been understood not to fall within the jurisdiction of an arbitrator. The core question was therefore whether the common law of torts applied — and if so, how it applied — to unionized employment relationships. Justice McLachlin's decision does not address that question. If we assume that by borrowing Lord Denning's language, she was also borrowing his holding in *Taylor v Barnett* that external legal rules apply to arbitration, we *could* read — and some *have* read — her decision as an affirmation that the same common law rules must apply to both unionized and non-unionized employees. But we know this cannot be what she meant, since the Court has issued multiple decisions over the years highlighting the extent to which the legal framework for collective bargaining has altered the common law of employment both in process and in substance.[48] By 1995, when *Weber* was decided, statutory collective bargaining frameworks had been in place in Canada for half a century, and had irretrievably altered important aspects of the common law relationship between employee and employer, including the bargaining relationship, the terms of the "contract" governing the employment relationship, and the mechanism for resolving disputes in connection with that "contract." But if "one law for all" does not mean that the common law developed in the courts applies unmodified to unionized employees, what does it mean?

48 These decisions include *Syndicat Catholique des Employés de Magasins de Québec Inc v Compagnie Paquet Ltée*, [1959] SCR 206 at para 12, 18 DLR (2d) 346; *McGavin Toastmaster Ltd v Ainscough et al*, [1976] 1 SCR 718 at para 10, 54 DLR (3d) 1; *Ste Anne-Nackawic Pulp & Paper Co Ltd v Canadian Paperworkers Union, Local 219*, [1986] 1 SCR 704 at para 16, 28 DLR (4th) 1; *Canadian Association of Industrial, Mechanical and Allied Workers, Local 14 v Paccar of Canada Ltd*, [1989] 2 SCR 983 at para 38, [1989] 6 WWR 673 [*Paccar*]; *Bisaillon*, above note 38 at para 28; and *Isidore Garon Ltée v Syndicat du bois ouvré de la region de Québec inc*, 2006 SCC 2. They are discussed in Shilton, "*Weber*, The Common Law and Industrial Self-Government," Chapter 3, this volume.

## E. THE ESSAYS IN THIS VOLUME

The essays in this volume all engage with different threads of the "one law" analysis, offering a diverse range of perspectives and approaches to the problems and questions posed by *Weber*. They also suggest a variety of interesting possible answers to the question posed by the arbitrators at the *Weber* Symposium. Brian Etherington's essay opens the discussion with a comprehensive review of how *Weber* and its progeny have been applied by Canadian adjudicators, setting the stage for the essays that follow. Supported by a detailed and thorough examination of the jurisprudence, Etheringon argues that *Weber* and much of its progeny reflect a judicial preference for values of efficiency and finality over values of access to justice and institutional appropriateness. This preference has created gaps in the enforcement of individual rights of unionized employees. These gaps may be jurisdictional, arising when there is no legal forum in which a unionized employee can pursue common law or *Charter* claims. Alternatively, they may arise when a union will not provide access to arbitration for an employee's common law or *Charter* claim. Etherington opposes *Weber*'s presumptive preference for labour arbitration as the exclusive forum for all workplace-related disputes. He concludes by proposing a set of criteria for determining whether tort, *Charter*, and statutory claims are best addressed at arbitration, in the courts or by a statutory tribunal. These criteria are intended to offer "more principled and functional solutions" that more appropriately balance the individual, collective and institutional interests at play, and give priority to access to justice over efficiency.

The essays by Elizabeth Shilton and Brian Langille are efforts to place *Weber* within the larger context of the meaning of collective bargaining for the legal rights of unionized employees. Both reject the conventional critique that the Supreme Court's decisions in *Weber* and *O'Leary* flow from a fundamental misconception of how labour law and labour arbitration work. They see *Weber* not as a jurisdictional contest between courts and arbitrators, but as an important (if far too cryptic) comment on the source and nature of rights and responsibilities in the unionized workplace. Both essays arrive — although by different paths — at the same fundamental conclusion: that *Weber*'s "essential character of the dispute" test affirms (or reaffirms) not just the hegemony of arbitration as the exclusive mechanism for resolving disputes about terms and conditions of employment for unionized employees, but also the centrality of the collective agreement as the source of workplace law (and therefore of workplace rights) for unionized employees. The authors see *Weber* as reinforcing the obligation of arbitrators to draw on basic principles of justice, as do common law judges, to fill the gaps inevitably left by collective bargaining. Shilton's essay develops that argument by going back to first principles, arguing that arbitral exclusivity follows logically from the fact that all terms and conditions of employment are subsumed within collective bargaining frameworks. Langille's "curious little paper" (to borrow his own description) examines the issue through the lens of *O'Leary* rather than *Weber*, arguing that *O'Leary* simply underscores the very basic proposition that within the employment relationship, rights, responsibilities and remedies as between employer and employee must be determined within the context of the collective agreement.

Karen Schucher's essay asks readers to step back from conventional labour law analysis when thinking about the impact of *Weber* both from an institutional perspective, and from the perspective of the welfare of unionized workers. Her essay examines the broad question of *Weber*'s implications for access to justice, and explores that question by addressing fundamental issues about the meaning of "rights," "access" and "justice." Schucher proposes that questions of rights and access to justice should be considered using a relational analysis which examines both the benefits and the burdens of collective bargaining for individual employees, the bargaining unit, and unions. She suggests that within unionized workplaces, rights cannot be conceptualized wholly as individual rights, regardless of whether they are enforced at arbitration, in court or before statutory tribunals; they inevitably have a collective dimension. Accordingly, sweeping the employment rights claims of individual employees under the umbrella of arbitration, or submitting them to union "gatekeeping," does not *per se* violate any fundamental conception of justice. She also asks us to consider some of the practical realities associated with achieving meaningful access to courts and statutory tribunals. While she acknowledges the importance of addressing the needs and interests of individual employees, she argues for an approach that does not pit individuals against the collective good.

Jo-Anne Pickel's essay tackles the question of what impact *Weber* has had on the jurisdiction of *statutory* tribunals, an issue that has been only rarely touched on in the academic literature to date. Focusing on Canadian human rights tribunals and two other Ontario statutory tribunals, she concludes that statutory tribunals are in general much less likely than courts to consign workplace disputes to the exclusive jurisdiction of arbitrators, and much more likely to find concurrent, or even exclusive, jurisdiction for themselves. Pickel argues that concurrent jurisdiction is the norm for statutory human rights tribunals across Canada, with the exception of Quebec. The main concern for these tribunals, then, is not whether they have jurisdiction, but how their jurisdiction should best be exercised to avoid duplication, conserve judicial/administrative resources, and ensure fairness for all parties. Focusing on the Human Rights Tribunal of Ontario (HRTO) where she sits as a Vice-Chair, Pickel explains this tribunal's practice in dealing with disputes that are being pursued in parallel proceedings before the HRTO and in the grievance procedure. Her discussion demonstrates that concurrent jurisdiction does not generally allow unionized employees access to two enforcement venues. Pickel also canvasses a range of complex issues that arise for the HRTO in situations involving parallel proceedings, including those in which grievances have been settled, withdrawn or disposed of through very informal adjudicative procedures, and those in which employees seek to split their cases. Her discussion has potential application beyond the HRTO to other statutory tribunals that assume concurrent jurisdiction with labour arbitration.

The essay by Kevin Banks, Richard Chaykowski and George Slotsve engages through quantitative research with the long-standing concern about delays and inefficiencies in grievance arbitration, a concern that has recently been highlighted by former Chief Justice Warren Winkler.[49] Their work is the first published study that undertakes to quantify the impact of *Weber's* expansion of arbitral jurisdiction on delays and inefficiencies in the arbitration process. In order to conduct this analysis, they compiled a uniquely constructed database of all Ontario arbitration decisions for the year 2010. This database was analyzed with reference to four variables: *Charter* issues, benefit or welfare plan issues, pension plan issues and tort issues. The authors argue that their data supports a conclusion that the expansion of arbitral jurisdiction arising from *Weber* has had little or no impact on arbitral delays and inefficiencies. They also argue that this quantitative finding is consistent with other theoretically-based explanations of arbitral delay and inefficiencies.

49 *See* Warren K Winkler, "Labour Arbitration and Conflict Resolution: Back to Our Roots" (Donald Wood Lecture delivered at the Queen's School of Policy Studies, 30 November 2010), online: www.ontariocourts.on.ca/coa/en/ps/speeches/2010-labour-arbitration-conflict-resolution.htm.

Claire Mummé's essay addresses an issue that has been largely ignored in the scholarly literature: whether *Weber* has had an impact on the representational obligations of unions, particularly in relation to human rights issues. Mummé's essay explores two legal questions pertinent to a collective bargaining climate in which there are still open questions about the relationship between collective agreements and other sources of law. First, Mummé asks whether Supreme Court decisions like *Weber* and *Parry Sound* have altered the standards applied to union conduct in duty of fair representation (DFR) cases involving human rights issues. Second, she asks whether the Court's decisions have broadened the concept of union discrimination to impose human rights liability on unions for failure to promote discrimination grievances. In addition, she raises a series of empirical questions about the impact of arbitral concurrency on union conduct which cannot be answered by examining the jurisprudence alone, but which must be answered to fully address the broad policy issue of how best to adjudicate workplace rights.

Most of the essays in this volume focus on the common law jurisdictions in Canada. Renée-Claude Drouin rounds out the Canadian picture by discussing the application of *Weber* in Quebec. Since *Weber* is a decision from Canada's highest court, the general labour law principles articulated have equal application to the common law and the civil law, despite the fact that the case was governed by Ontario law. As Drouin points out, however, Quebec courts have departed somewhat from courts in the common law provinces in their interpretation and application of the *Weber* principles; indeed, the Supreme Court itself has implied that Quebec's *Civil Code* may raise different questions than the common law for the application of *Weber*. Drouin's essay focuses on two important differences. First, she argues that Quebec adjudicators acknowledge a different conceptual relationship between collective agreements and statutory employment rights than adjudicators in the rest of Canada. Outside of Quebec, adjudicators take a broad "incorporation by reference" approach in which arbitrators simply enforce statutory norms. By contrast, Quebec law calls for a nuanced "hierarchy of sources" approach in which statutory norms may trump provisions of collective agreements, but not in all cases. Second, Drouin argues that in the rest of Canada, adjudicators have interpreted the Supreme Court's jurisprudence as establishing concurrent jurisdiction for arbitrators and human rights tribunals; by contrast, Quebec law acknowledges areas of exclusive arbitral jurisdiction over human rights issues.

The collection closes with an essay by US scholar Alan Hyde, whose analysis of the role of US arbitrators in the enforcement of workplace norms arising outside collective agreements (and in particular, statutory norms) makes Canada's jurisdictional confusion appear relatively benign. Hyde observes that until less than a decade ago, almost all employment-based statutory rights for both unionized and non-unionized employees in the US were enforceable through a "litigation model," in which individual employees pursued their claims in court rather than through administrative procedures, including labour arbitration. He argues that for unionized employees, this model has now been thrown into crisis as a result of a 2009 decision of the US Supreme Court, *14 Penn Plaza LLC v Pyett*.[50] Since the *Pyett* decision, Hyde argues, disputes over whether statutory rights claims should be pursued at arbitration or in court have been commonplace, frustrating employee attempts to secure remedies. The US jurisdictional problem is exacerbated by the fact that statutory employment rights are frequently matters of state law, whereas labour law is federal law. Hyde argues that the litigation model of enforcement in the US is now seriously bogged down and should be replaced, not with a Canadian-style expansion of arbitral jurisdiction, but with an administrative system in which all employees, whether or not they are unionized, would have access without cost to enforcement through a "labour court" or administrative tribunal.

The authors who have contributed these essays do not offer a uniform answer to the question which informed the *Weber* Symposium: has *Weber v Ontario Hydro* transformed collective agreement administration and arbitration in Canada? Nor do they have a uniform prescription for how to extricate ourselves from the tangled post-*Weber* legal world in which we find ourselves. However, their essays are uniformly informative and thought-provoking, providing valuable insights into the practical, theoretical and empirical labour law problems posed by *Weber*, and suggesting useful additional trajectories for further scholarly exploration and policy change.

In the spirit of engaged and scrupulous scholarship to which Bernie Adell dedicated his academic life, we offer this volume in his memory.

---

50 556 US 247 (2009), 129 S Ct 1456.

CHAPTER TWO

# *Weber*, and Almost Everything After, Twenty Years Later: Its Impact on Individual *Charter*, Common Law, and Statutory Rights Claims

Brian Etherington

In *Weber v Ontario Hydro*,[1] the Supreme Court of Canada revisited the issue of judicial deference to labour arbitration as a forum of original jurisdiction for the resolution of disputes between organized employees and their employer. The Court denied Mr Weber access to the courts to pursue claims against his employer based on the common law and the *Canadian Charter of Rights and Freedoms*[2] by adopting a model of exclusive jurisdiction for arbitration over employment disputes arising under a collective bargaining relationship. This model went far beyond the Court's previous calls for judicial deference, and even encompassed employee claims for redress based on violations of their most fundamental, individual rights under the *Charter*.

There has already been a great deal written about the implications of *Weber* and the subsequent decisions of the Supreme Court of Canada and of courts and boards across the country which have tried to apply its reasoning to different contexts of potential overlap in jurisdiction be-

1 [1995] 2 SCR 929, 125 DLR (4th) 583, rev'g (1992), 11 OR (3d) 609 (Ont CA) [*Weber Ont CA*], aff'g (1991) 28 ACWS (3d) 796 (Ont Ct J (Gen Div)) [*Weber*]. See also the companion decision in *New Brunswick v O'Leary*, [1995] 2 SCR 967, 125 (4th) DLR 609 released the same day, which found exclusive arbitral jurisdiction over a negligence claim for damages brought by the employer against a bargaining unit employee.

2 *Canadian Charter of Rights and Freedoms*, Part I of the *Constitution Act, 1982*, being Schedule B to the *Canada Act 1982* (UK) 1982, c 11.

tween arbitration and other forums.[3] For a decision which was so clearly designed to cut down on litigation arising from disputes which were somehow related to the workplace, it has certainly shown great promise in achieving the exact opposite result — at least during the first twenty years after its release.

*Weber* and its progeny, most importantly *Parry Sound (District) Welfare Administration Board v Ontario Public Service Employees Union, Local 324*,[4] have been the key judicial contributions to the transformation of arbitration from an alternative dispute resolution mechanism for the resolution of private, contractual collective bargaining disputes to a *quasi-*

3 Ray Brown and Brian Etherington, "*Weber v. Ontario Hydro*: A Denial of Access to Justice for the Organized Employee?" (1996) 4 *Canadian Labour and Employment Law Journal* 183; David Mullan, "Tribunals and Courts — The Contemporary Terrain: Lessons from Human Rights Regimes" (1999) 24:2 *Queen's Law Journal*. 643; Bernard Adell, "Jurisdictional Overlap Between Arbitration and Other Forums: An Update" (2000) 8 *Canadian Labour and Employment Law Journal* 179; Donald D Carter, "Looking at *Weber* Five Years Later: Is it Time for a New Approach?" (2000) 8 *Canadian Labour and Employment Law Journal* 231; Richard MacDowell, "Labour Arbitration — The New Labour Court?" (2000) 8 *Canadian Labour and Employment Law Journal* 121; George T Surdykowski, "The Limits of Grievance Arbitration: *Weber* and *Pilon* in Perspective" in Kevin Whitaker et al, eds, (1999–2000) 1 *Labour Arbitration Year Book* (Toronto: Lancaster House, 2000) 67; Michel G Picher, "Defining the Scope of Arbitration: The Impact of *Weber*: an Arbitrator's Perspective" in Kevin Whitaker et al, eds, (1999–2000) 1 *Labour Arbitration Year Book* (Toronto: Lancaster House, 2000) 99; Lewis Gottheil, "Defining the Scope of Arbitration: The Impact of *Weber* — A Union Perspective" in Kevin Whitaker et al, eds, (1999–2000) 1 *Labour Arbitration Year Book* (Toronto: Lancaster House, 2000) 157; Eric Durnford, QC, "Defining the Scope of Arbitration: The Impact of *Weber* — A Management Perspective" in Kevin Whitaker et al, eds, (1999–2000) 1 *Labour Arbitration Year Book* (Toronto: Lancaster House, 2000) 149; Kenneth P Swan, "Ships Passing in the Night: Arbitrators and the Courts" in Kevin Whitaker et al, eds, (1999–2000) 1 *Labour Arbitration Year Book* (Toronto: Lancaster House, 2000) 1; William Kaplan et al, "The Scope of Rights Arbitration after *Weber v. Ontario Hydro*" (1999) 7 *Canadian Labour and Employment Law Journal* 249; Valerie J Matthews Lemieux, "The Ongoing Debate Over the Scope of *Weber — Who Has Jurisdiction*?" in Todd Archibald & Michael Cochrane, eds, *Annual Review of Civil Litigation* (Toronto: Carswell, 2001) 141; John-Paul Alexandrowicz, "Restoring the Role of Grievance Arbitration: A New Approach to *Weber*" (2003) 10 *Canadian Labour and Employment Law Journal* 269; Andrew Lokan & Maryth Yachnin. "From *Weber* to *Parry Sound*: the Expanded Scope of Arbitration" (2004) 11 *Canadian Labour and Employment Law Journal* 1.

4 2003 SCC 42 [*Parry Sound*]. This decision held that all collective agreements must be deemed to incorporate the substantive rights and obligations contained in applicable employment-related statutes. *See* below at note 128.

public forum—some have called it a "labour court"[5]—for the enforcement of not only contractual claims but also tort claims and claims under public statutory rights, including constitutional rights. While some have questioned the overall efficiency and policy effectiveness of using such a privately-funded institution to administer and enforce public employment law regimes, I contend that the prime motivations for the transformation were the ascendancy of efficiency and finality concerns during the 1990s and early 2000s, in many cases at the expense of access to justice and institutional appropriateness concerns. *Weber* in particular was not about increasing access to justice or expanding arbitral jurisdiction, but rather about getting the claims of organized workers out of the courts and into privately-funded forums. However, I also contend that the decision of the Supreme Court of Canada in *Québec (Commission des droits de la personne & des droits de la jeunesse) c Québec (Procureur général)*[6] in 2004 provided a turning point, after which courts and administrative law decision-makers, with one or two notable exceptions, became willing to take a more nuanced and balanced approach to deciding jurisdictional issues where the competition is between arbitration and other statutory decision-makers. Thus, while the detrimental effects of *Weber* on access to justice for individual common law and *Charter* claims have not been undone, the single-minded presumption of exclusive arbitral jurisdiction has been almost transformed into an assumption of concurrent jurisdiction for overlaps with other statutory tribunals, allowing for an appropriate and balanced consideration of efficiency, finality, access to justice and institutional appropriateness concerns when dealing with those types of issues.

In this essay I set out my own thoughts on where *Weber* and its progeny have brought us today on the issues relating to multiplicity of proceedings in the adjudication of workplace-related disputes. Throughout the essay, I discuss the hierarchy of values that appears to underlie the single-minded drive towards an exclusive jurisdiction approach in *Weber* and many of its offspring. At various points, I also touch on the impact of the *Weber* movement on unions and grievance arbitration as viable institutions for the successful pursuit of collective bargaining objectives. In Part A, I examine *Weber* in context, looking at its origins and purpose and considering it as part of a larger trend to privatize and collectivize workplace dispute resolution in the name of efficiency. In Parts B, C and D, I assess the extent

5 MacDowell, above note 3 at 144.

6 2004 SCC 39 [*Morin*].

to which *Weber* has affected jurisdiction and access to justice respectively in the areas of common law, *Charter* and statutory rights claims by organized workers, paying attention to the extent to which it has created a gap or shortfall between substantive rights and access to forums to protect or enforce those rights. Finally, in Part E, I offer some thoughts on different approaches that might provide more principled and functional solutions to the problems raised by the interaction between multiple employment law regimes, and a better balancing of the interests at stake.

## A. THE *WEBER* STANDARD IN SOCIAL CONTEXT

The plaintiff, Weber, was an employee of Ontario Hydro and covered under a collective agreement. He was injured at work and began receiving workers' compensation benefits, including a 20 percent disability pension. He then went on an extended leave of absence and received benefits under the collective agreement as well. The employer hired private detectives to conduct a secret surveillance of him, who gained entrance to his home under a pretence. The employer then suspended him for abusing his sick leave, using the information gathered by this entry.

The union filed three grievances on his behalf pursuant to the collective agreement. At the same time, the plaintiff initiated a civil action alleging trespass, nuisance, deceit, invasion of privacy and breaches of his rights under sections 7 and 8 of the *Charter*. A motions judge granted an order dismissing the civil action. The plaintiff appealed and in the meantime the union settled the grievances. The settlement made no reference to the grievor's civil action.

The Court of Appeal for Ontario upheld the dismissal of Weber's tort action. However, the Court reinstated the *Charter* claim, holding that the policy justification for granting exclusive jurisdiction to arbitration could not justify denial of an individual citizen's access to the courts for protection of his most fundamental constitutional rights.[7]

### 1) The Supreme Court of Canada's *Weber* Standard

In the Supreme Court of Canada, the majority opinion authored by McLachlin J (as she then was), joined by L'Heureux-Dubé, Gonthier and

7 *Weber Ont CA*, above note 1.

Major JJ, held that all of Weber's claims fell within the exclusive jurisdiction of the arbitrator, thereby blocking access to the courts. Partially dissenting reasons were delivered by Iacobucci J, joined by La Forest and Sopinka JJ, who agreed with the majority's holding on exclusive arbitral jurisdiction for the common law claims, but would have allowed the *Charter* claims to continue in court.

Justice McLachlin identified three distinct judicial views on the effect of the requirement in Ontario labour legislation that final and binding arbitration clauses be included in the collective agreement. First, the "concurrent jurisdiction" model contemplates concurrent regimes of arbitration and court action: if an action is recognized either at common law or by statute, the action may proceed and the collective agreement cannot deprive the court of jurisdiction. Second, the "overlapping jurisdiction" model allows a civil action to be brought if the issues raised go beyond the traditional subject matter of labour law. Third, the "exclusive jurisdiction" model, the model embraced by the Court, requires labour arbitration to be the exclusive legal venue where the differences between the parties arise from the collective agreement, with no jurisdiction for the courts to entertain an action.

Justice McLachlin relied on the Court's prior decision in *St Anne-Nackawic Pulp & Paper Co v Canadian Paper Workers Union, Local 219*[8] to hold that the jurisdiction to resolve a dispute that arises "expressly or inferentially out of the collective agreement"[9] lies exclusively with the labour arbitrator, regardless of how the dispute may be characterized legally. She also noted that provincial labour relations legislation precluded court action by providing specifically for arbitral resolution of "all *differences* between the parties arising from the interpretation, application, administration or alleged violation of the agreement."[10] To permit concurrent actions would undermine the goal of providing quick and economical resolution of disputes between parties to a collective agreement, with minimum disruption to the parties and the economy. Although McLachlin J accepted that the overlapping jurisdiction model was more attractive, in her view it also failed "to meet the test of the statute, the jurisprudence and policy"

---

8 [1986] 1 SCR 704, 28 DLR (4th) 1 [*St Anne-Nackawic*].

9 *Weber*, above note 1 at para 59.

10 *Ibid* at para 50 (quoting s 45(1) of the Ontario *Labour Relations Act*, RSO 1990, c L2) [emphasis in original].

and would permit parties to evade deference to arbitral resolution of labour disputes by artful and imaginative pleading.[11]

Justice McLachlin concluded that arbitration is the exclusive mechanism if the differences between the parties to the dispute can be said as a factual matter to arise expressly or inferentially out of the collective agreement: "The question in each case is whether the dispute, viewed with an eye to its essential character, arises from the collective agreement."[12] Whether or not a dispute arises out of a collective agreement should be determined by looking at both the essential nature of the dispute and the ambit of the collective agreement. This approach applies to claims alleging a violation of *Charter* rights as well as to claims in contract and tort. Arbitrators have the jurisdiction to apply common law doctrines and remedies when dealing with disputes under the collective agreement,[13] and where they lack power to provide an appropriate remedy the courts may exercise their inherent jurisdiction so that the grievor will not be deprived of an ultimate and effective remedy.[14] Where arbitrators lack expertise in a particular area of law, their errors may be corrected by way of judicial review.[15]

In applying these principles to the facts in *Weber*, the Court found that the benefits of the Ontario Hydro Sick Leave Plan were part of the collective agreement. The Court also relied on the fact that Article 2.2 of the agreement provided that its grievance procedure applied to "[a]ny allegation that an employee has been subjected to unfair treatment or any dispute arising out of the content of" the agreement.[16] In addition, the Court relied on the fact that the agreement provided that the Sick Leave Plan benefits were considered part of the agreement, and that the administration of the "plan and all decisions regarding the appropriateness or degree of its application shall be vested solely in Ontario Hydro."[17] Therefore, any decision concerning the medical plan fell within the purview of the col-

---

11 *Ibid* at para 54.

12 *Ibid* at para 57.

13 *Ibid* at paras 60–61.

14 *Ibid* at para 62.

15 McLachlin J failed to note that only unions are parties to collective agreements, with standing to bring applications for judicial review. The individual grievor has no standing or ability to bring an application for judicial review to correct arbitral errors. *See Société d'énergie de la Baie James c Noël*, 2001 SCC 39.

16 Picher, above note 3 at 114. The author pointed out the irony in the Court's reliance on this provision, because it failed to note that Article 3.1 prevented grievances concerning allegations of unfair treatment from being submitted to arbitration. *Ibid* at 114.

17 *Weber*, above note 1 at para 77.

lective agreement. Since it was alleged that Hydro had acted improperly in making its decision regarding coverage under the medical plan, the arbitrator had exclusive jurisdiction over all aspects of the dispute.

The flood of litigation that followed in the years immediately following *Weber* was, I think, the inevitable consequence of two or three of its most apparent deficiencies. First, and most obvious, was the inherent ambiguity of the purported new "bright line" test for exclusive jurisdiction espoused by the majority. Although the Court articulated a two-factor analysis relying on both the factual nature of the dispute and the ambit of the collective agreement, the patently vague standard of whether the dispute could be said to arise "inferentially" from the collective agreement created an "unprecedented standard upon whose application honest adjudicators will inevitably differ, and in relation to which employers and unions may exercise less contractual control and predictability."[18] Anyone who doubts the wisdom of that observation need only look at the differences of opinion among courts of appeal in various provinces, and between those courts and the various majority and dissenting Supreme Court of Canada opinions in subsequent decisions concerning where jurisdiction resides in cases involving arbitration in competition with courts and other statutory tribunals.[19]

---

18 Picher, above note 3 at 115.

19 *See e.g.*, the history of judicial decisions recounted in *Regina Police Association v Regina (City) Police Commissioners*, 2000 SCC 14 [*Regina Police*]; *Allen v Alberta*, 2003 SCC 13 [*Allen*]; *Goudie v Ottawa (City)*, 2003 SCC 14 [*Goudie*]; *Morin*, above note 6; *Bisaillon v Concordia University*, 2006 SCC 19 [*Bisaillon*]. The most straightforward decision was in *Allen v Alberta*, where the Court held, not surprisingly, that a claim for severance pay under the public service collective agreement, brought by former civil servants whose positions had been privatized, was subject to exclusive arbitral jurisdiction and could not be pursued in court despite the fact the union and government had signed a letter of intent stating that employees who accepted a job with the new private employer would not be entitled to severance pay under the agreement. Although the Alberta Court of Appeal had ruled in favour of court jurisdiction, as Alexandrowicz noted (above note 3), this would likely have been decided the same way based on the caselaw that preceded *Weber*, since it was essentially a claim to enforce a collective agreement clause. By contrast, in *Goudie* the Court held that a civil action by bargaining unit workers could continue where the action was based on a claim that the employer had made pre-hiring representations that they would continue to enjoy the same terms and conditions they had enjoyed while working for their former employer. Although the judge at first instance held that *Weber* precluded court action, the Court of Appeal and Supreme Court of Canada relied on pre-*Weber* jurisprudence to hold that if there was a pre-employ-

Second, although the Court in *Weber* did not expressly address whether its new standard of exclusive jurisdiction would apply to areas of potential overlap between arbitration and statutory tribunals administering employment law statutes, its reasoning certainly invited applications to extend its approach to such cases. The Court's view that the policy concerns of efficiency and not undermining labour arbitration as the legislative choice for resolution of workplace disputes were sufficiently important to override concerns that an individual might be denied access to any forum to protect and enforce fundamental individual constitutional rights and freedoms certainly led some observers to speculate that the same rules should be applied to the arguably less fundamental rights granted to employees under employment law statutes.

And finally, making access to a legal mechanism to seek protection and enforcement of fundamental, individual constitutional rights contingent on union support meant that employees who were unable to gain the required support were likely to seek vindication in court in any event, no matter how likely it appeared that such an avenue would be foreclosed by the principles of *Weber*. The more fundamental the rights involved, the more likely that disaffected employees who are denied union support will turn to litigation, despite the cost and time involved. They simply have nothing to lose at that point.

## 2) Placing *Weber* in Context: Was it the Temper of the Times?

At the time *Weber* was decided, I found it incredible that the Supreme Court of Canada could so cavalierly disregard the concerns expressed by Justice Arbour in the Court of Appeal for Ontario that an individual

ment agreement, the essential character of a dispute over such an agreement could not arise from the collective agreement because the employees were not in the bargaining unit when the agreement was made. I agree with the observations of Lokan and Yachnin (above note 3 at 8–9), that these decisions do little to instruct us about how the essential character of a dispute is determined and that it is "difficult to discern a principled basis for the distinctions drawn by the Court in *Allen* and *Goudie*." As they point out, it is not obvious why a dispute about a pre-employment representation concerning terms of employment that are to apply after hiring under a collective agreement does not arise out of the collective agreement, while issues arising from a letter of intent concerning conditions that are to apply after employees leave the workplace do arise out of the collective agreement, given that arbitrators have in past cases taken jurisdiction over disputes that concerned the effect of pre-hiring representations made to employees.

citizen's access to the courts for protection of her most fundamental constitutional rights should not be made contingent on support from a collective organization like a union.[20] What was most disturbing at the time was the majority's refusal to even address this concern, and instead to address other concerns about the expertise of arbitrators to decide *Charter* issues, as if that had been the Court of Appeal's main concern. How could this refusal be explained, especially when it related to constitutional individual rights? Looking back today on the Court's decision in *Weber*, it is much more easily understood when viewed as part of a larger trend among legislators, administrators and adjudicators to place much more value on concerns about efficiency and avoiding multiplicity of proceedings in a period of significant cutbacks and downsizing of government resources.

By the early 1980s, some commentators had begun to note that the proliferation of statutory individual employment rights in the 1960s and 1970s had led to problems arising from the potential for a multiplicity of proceedings.[21] But if one reads the commentary of that period, there was generally a recognition of the difference between the statutory employment standards processes designed to protect individual public statutory rights, and the processes for enforcing contractual rights in common law courts or in private arbitration mechanisms established by the parties under collective agreements. Suggestions that exclusive jurisdiction should be granted to one forum or the other to avoid overlaps in jurisdiction were generally rejected because this approach might jeopardize access to an appropriate forum for effective enforcement of the various private and public rights at stake. However, commentators were often in favour of some policy of deference to prior decisions by other tribunals in order to avoid the problems arising from multiplicity of proceedings, provided that measures were taken to ensure that the various public and private rights at stake had received due consideration in the prior proceeding. This is similar to the approach taken by the Ontario Labour Relations Board when faced with issues of overlapping jurisdiction between itself and grievance arbitration.[22] Thus, although adjudicators and

---

20 *See* Gottheil, above note 3 at 160, for discussion of this point.

21 *See e.g*,. Katherine E Swinton & Kenneth P Swan, "The Interaction Between Human Rights Legislation and Labour Law" in Kenneth P Swan & Katherine E Swinton, eds, *Studies in Labour Law* (Toronto: Butterworths, 1983) 111.

22 *See e.g.*, *United Food & Commercial Workers International Union, Local Union 175 v Valdi Inc (Valdi Discount Foods),* 1980 CanLII 885 (ON LRB).

commentators were becoming concerned about the potential inefficiencies and costs associated with overlapping jurisdiction, they continued to place significant value on the need to ensure access to justice where it conflicted with efficiency concerns.

However, in the late 1980s and 1990s, in a context of disappearing public resources, several important developments point to a reversal of this hierarchy of values.[23] Most notable was a shift to privatize and collectivize various processes for the administration and enforcement of individual statutory rights. In the case of human rights, for example, individuals faced large backlogs and extensive delays of many years to have their complaints processed by human rights commissions,[24] and turned to alternative processes to seek protection against human rights violations. In the organized sector they increasingly turned to the grievance process to pursue their complaints if they could get the support of their union. Arbitrators had gradually begun to accept jurisdiction to hear grievances alleging a violation of human rights statutes if there was a sufficient nexus with a collective agreement provision. In 1993, this method of asserting arbitral jurisdiction over human rights issues was given legislative recognition in the Ontario *Labour Relations Act*;[25] several other jurisdictions in Canada also give grievance arbitrators an express mandate to interpret and apply human rights legislation. For unorganized employees, the strategy employed by creative counsel was to go back to the common law courts to seek human rights protection under the guise of traditional torts. They were initially blocked by the bar imposed in *Seneca College of Applied Arts & Technology v Bhadauria*.[26] However, in the early 1990s courts began to allow actions based on conduct addressed by human

23 Geoffrey England wrote several articles and books that explore what he saw as a gradual transformation of substantive employment law principles to reflect an increasing tension between a rights paradigm, which had seen its values in ascendancy in the 1960s and 70s, and an efficiency paradigm, which was gaining popularity among judges and policy-makers in the 1980s and 90s. *See e.g.*, Geoffrey England, "Recent Developments in the Law of the Employment Contract: Continuing Tension Between the Rights Paradigm and the Efficiency Paradigm" (1995) 20:2 *Queen's Law Journal* 557.

24 For those not familiar with the extent of these problems and the difficulties they presented for access to justice for members of diverse groups protected by human rights legislation, *see* Ontario Human Rights Code Review Task Force, *Achieving Equality: A Report on Human Rights Reform* (Toronto: Government of Ontario, 1992).

25 *See Labour Relations Act, 1995*, SO 1995, c 1, Schedule A, s 48 (12)(j).

26 [1981] 2 SCR 181, 124 DLR (3d) 193.

rights legislation to continue, as long as the claim also alleged causes of action previously recognized at common law and did not seek damages based on a violation of the human rights legislation.[27]

The tightening of government budgets and the push to make the delivery of government services more efficient led to a further significant move towards privatization and collectivization of human rights processes. Human rights commissions in several jurisdictions, most notably Ontario, adopted a policy of almost complete refusal to take jurisdiction over human rights complaints by employees who worked in an organized workplace and were subject to a collective agreement. In the interests of responding to criticisms of inefficiency and delay, in 1993 the Ontario Human Rights Commission adopted a strict and rigorous policy of deferral to arbitration where the complainant worked under a collective agreement.[28] The Commission's guidelines referred to the important public interest in stable and harmonious labour relations, and expressed concerns that the human rights process should not become a tool to replace the collective bargaining process.[29] The guidelines in place at that time did suggest that the Commission should consider each case on its own basis, and noted that one factor to consider was whether there may also be complaints against the union. Nevertheless, published statistics and anecdotal evidence suggest that a refusal to process complaints submitted by organized employees had become the normal course of operations by the late 1990s.[30]

---

27 See the discussion in Anne L Mactavish & JF Lenz, "Civil Actions for Conduct Addressed by Human Rights Legislation — Some Recent Substantive and Procedural Developments" (1996) 4 *Canadian Labour and Employment Law Journal* 375. In some cases, the courts actually commented on the ineffectiveness of the human rights process as a reason for letting the court action continue.

28 The Commission claimed the authority to adopt this policy under the discretion given to it under the former section 34 of the *Human Rights Code* not to deal with a complaint where it could be more appropriately dealt with under another Act. *Human Rights Code*, RSO 1990, c H.19.

29 Ontario Human Rights Commission, *Guidelines on the Application of Section 34 of the Ontario Human Rights Code* (Ontario: OHRC, September 1996).

30 "Ontario Complaint Guidelines Cause Rejection Rate to Triple" (Jan/Feb. 1999), *Lancaster's Human Rights and Charter Law Reporter*, Vol 15, No 1/2, at 3. Cases in which a decision to decline to process was taken tripled following introduction of the policy in 1993. Union counsel reported that during this period the Commission refused to process cases when they learned the complainant worked under a collective agreement, even in cases where there was concern expressed that the union

Perhaps even more indicative of this shift in values in the 1990s was the outright legislative transfer of exclusive jurisdiction over the adjudication of employment standards complaints to grievance arbitration processes for organized employees in the 1996 amendments to the Ontario *Employment Standards Act*,[31] an express transfer of jurisdiction over statutory individual rights claims from public officials and tribunals to private organizations and procedures — unions and grievance arbitration.

Growing concern about the inefficiencies caused by overlapping jurisdiction and the potential for multiplicity of proceedings was also reflected in academic commentary and government law reform studies published during this period.[32] Interestingly, however, if one looks at the journal articles and law reform commission reports of this period, the exclusive jurisdiction solution adopted by the Court in *Weber* was seldom mentioned and almost never recommended. Instead, most commentators from both the private and government sectors recommended recognition of overlapping jurisdiction and avoidance of unnecessary multiplicity of proceedings by deploying some form of pre-hearing deferral and referral, combined with post-hearing policies of deferral or expanded application of existing

---

would not support a grievance to arbitration and there was a possibility of a claim against the union as well as the employer.

31 *Employment Standards Act, 2000*, SO 2000, c 41 ss 99–101 [*ESA*]. The Act was also amended to prevent the inefficiencies of allowing multiple proceedings involving unorganized employees by putting them to an election between civil proceedings for wrongful dismissal and a complaint under the Act regarding termination and severance payments. *Ibid* at ss 97–98.

32 For examples of academic commentary *see* Randi Hammer Abramsky, "Grievance Arbitration, External Law and the Problem of Multiple Forums" in William Kaplan, Jeffrey Sack & Morley Gunderson, eds, (1994–1995) 1 *Labour Arbitration Year Book* (Toronto: Lancaster House, 1995) 41; Randi Hammer Abramsky, "The Problem of Multiple Proceedings: an Arbitrator's Perspective" in William Kaplan et al, eds, (1996–1997) 1 *Labour Arbitration Year Book* (Toronto: Lancaster House, 2000) 45. In addition, in 1990 the Ontario Law Reform Commission began a long-running project on multiple proceedings in workplace adjudication that culminated in its publication of the *Report on Avoiding Delay and Multiple Proceedings in the Adjudication of Workplace Disputes* (Toronto: Ontario Law Reform Commission, 1995) [OLRC Report]. *See also* the Ontario Ministry of Labour's short-lived 2001 proposal for a new "super" labour tribunal to take over the adjudicative workload of six existing statutory adjudication tribunals, although this proposal did not deal with private sector grievance arbitration: Ontario Ministry of Labour, *Looking Forward: A New Tribunal for Ontario's Workplaces, Consultation Paper* (Ontario: Ministry of Labour, 2001).

doctrines of *res judicata* and issue estoppel.[33] What is clear from reading these articles and reports is that there was both a growing concern that the proliferation of employment law rights under the various statutory regimes required some measures to address the inefficiencies and other problems that can arise from multiple proceedings, and a concern that any measures adopted should ensure that the various rights issues arising were addressed effectively by an appropriate adjudicative body.

Finally, the growing concern over multiplicity of proceedings was also reflected in a flurry of decisions commencing in the early 1990s, dealing with the application of the doctrine of issue estoppel to civil claims for wrongful dismissal based on prior rulings made by administrative bodies in processing claims under employment standards legislation. The move to relax the requirements of issue estoppel to prevent multiple proceedings began with the Court of Appeal for Ontario's ruling in *Rasanen v Rosemount Instruments Ltd*.[34] The majority reasons clearly indicated concern about efficiency in workplace adjudication, with several quotations from decisions urging the need to defer to administrative law decision-makers and treat their decisions as final and binding. The decision in *Rasanen* was followed by a series of decisions on the same issue in the Court of Appeal, in which different panels displayed very different degrees of commitment to the values of efficiency in adjudication when weighed against access to justice for individual employees.[35]

33 *Ibid*. *See especially* OLRC Report.

34 (1994), 17 OR (3d) 267, 112 DLR (4th) 683 [*Rasanen*].

35 The Court of Appeal decision in *Danyluk v Ainsworth Technologies Inc* (1998), 42 OR (3d) 235, 167 DLR (4th) 385 (CA), aff'd 2001 SCC 44 [*Danyluk*] represents the high point in the broad application of issue estoppel. For the conflicting view, which clearly tips the balance in favour of access to justice, *see Minott v O'Shanter Development Co* (1999), 42 OR (3d) 321, 168 DLR (4th) 270 (CA) and *Heynen v Frito-Lay Canada Ltd* (1999), 45 OR (3d) 776, 79 DLR (4th) 317 (CA). For a return to a more efficiency-oriented approach *see Schweneke v Ontario* (2000), 47 OR (3d) 97, 94 ACWS (3d) 927 (CA). However, the priorities relied on in *Rasanen* appear to have been ultimately reversed by the Supreme Court of Canada's decision in *Danyluk*, which held that even where the requirements of issue estoppel are made out by one party, the Court must go on to exercise a broad discretion to decide whether it should nevertheless allow the second proceeding to continue after considering several contextual criteria, the most important of which is the potential injustice to the individual litigant of denying access to proceed. The Supreme Court of Canada's on-going struggle to balance concerns about finality and efficiency with access to justice interests when dealing with multiple forums continued, with what are arguably conflicting results. *See British Columbia (Workers' Compensation Board)*

It is in this context that one can better understand a decision that appeared to place greater weight on efficiency concerns than on the need to ensure access to justice for the protection of fundamental individual *Charter* rights. In its brief attempts to give policy justifications for its adoption of the exclusive jurisdiction model, the majority opinion in *Weber* made express reference to two reasons — efficiency[36] and the need to prevent court actions that might undermine arbitration as the legislative choice for the resolution of workplace disputes.[37] However, it is important to note that no commentator writing on this topic has ever suggested that arbitration was at risk of being undermined by numerous litigants seeking to evade it by going to courts or other tribunals. Arbitration was clearly the forum of choice for most, if not all potential litigants because, provided they could obtain the union support required for access to arbitration, it was generally the least expensive and quickest route to a hearing. If there was any concern about the health of grievance arbitration in the 1990s, it was that it might be the victim of its own success, becoming overburdened by its ever-increasing jurisdiction to decide statutory and *Charter* issues and facing a risk that it might become too complex, slow and expensive to be the dispute resolution success story it had been up to that point.

Of course, to suggest that grievance arbitration was the victim of its own success cannot conceal the fact that its increasing popularity was perhaps more a result of the failures of administrative agencies and adjudicative forums under the statutory regimes to provide timely and effective resolution of claims. Nevertheless, whatever the reasons for the popularity of arbitration, any concerns expressed in *Weber* that grievance arbitration needed to have exclusive jurisdiction over common law and *Charter* claims to prevent it suffering from disuse were disingenuous at best. Of the justifications offered by the majority, the only one that held any water was the adjudication efficiency rationale, and it clearly reflected a value that was in ascendancy during that period.

---

*v Figliola*, 2011 SCC 52 (where finality concerns won out), and *Penner v Niagara Regional Police Services Board*, 2013 SCC 19 (where fairness and access to justice concerns prevailed).

36 *Weber*, above note 1 ("It is important that disputes be resolved quickly and economically, with a minimum of disruptions to the parties and the economy" at para 51).

37 *Ibid*.

## B. *WEBER*'S IMPACT ON COMMON LAW CLAIMS AND THE JURISDICTIONAL DIVIDE BETWEEN ARBITRATION AND COURTS

*Weber* has led to a considerable number of arbitration decisions concerning the extent to which it has increased the jurisdiction of arbitrators to decide common law contract and tort claims by bargaining unit employees, both against employers and against third parties, including co-workers and others, such as insurance companies. There was some initial uncertainty arising from early decisions which suggested that *Weber* expressed an intention to have all workplace disputes that arose in some fashion from the collective agreement resolved exclusively by arbitrators, even where such resolution would require empowering arbitrators to exercise jurisdiction over third parties.[38] However, those issues have been resolved by subsequent judicial and arbitral rulings foreclosing arbitral jurisdiction over third parties.[39] The absence of any arbitral jurisdiction

---

38 The best-known examples in the early years were cases involving contractual claims by employees against third-party insurers under benefit clauses in the collective agreement. The decision of the Court of Appeal for Ontario in *Pilon v International Minerals & Chemical Corp (Canada) Ltd* (1996), 31 OR (3d) 210, 141 DLR (4th) 72 [*Pilon*], seemed to say that *Weber* required arbitrators to take exclusive jurisdiction over claims under benefit plans or policies as long as it could be said that the employee would not have had a claim but for a clause in the collective agreement.

39 In the arbitration decisions in *CAW-Canada v Honeywell Ltd* (1997), 65 LAC (4th) 37 (Arbitrator: Mitchnick), rev'd *sub nom Sun Life Assurance Co of Canada v CAW-Canada* (2000), 135 OAC 115, leave to appeal to SCC refused 147 OAC 200 (note) (1 February 2001) and *Dubreuil Forest Products Ltd v Industrial Wood and Allied Workers of Canada, Local 2693 (Dubreuil Brothers Employees Assn) (Ladouceur Grievance)*, [1998] OLAA No 484 (Arbitrator: Bendel), rev'd *sub nom London Life Insurance Co v Dubreuil Brothers Employees Assn* (1998), 83 ACWS (3d) 4, rev'd (2000), 49 OR (3d) 766, leave to appeal to SCC refused [2001] SCCA No 496 (15 March 2001), the arbitrators took the Court in *Pilon* at its word, and held that they had jurisdiction over a claim against the employer and the insurer. They made it clear, however, that their rulings did not affect the traditional approach to determining liability as between the employer and the insurer based on the four-category approach of Donald JM Brown & David M Beatty, *Canadian Labour Arbitration*, 4th ed (Carswell, 2006) (loose-leaf) at 4:1400. These decisions were later quashed by the Ontario Divisional Court and Ontario Court of Appeal, where the Courts failed to recognize the distinction between issues of forum and liability, ruled that *Pilon* did not intend to change the traditional approach, and further held that arbitrators have no jurisdiction to add third parties without their consent. Since the *Dubreuil Forest Products* decision, many arbitrators have consistently held that they have no jurisdiction to add third parties or to make remedial orders imposing liability against

under *Weber* to add third parties or impose orders against them appears to apply whether they are non-bargaining unit co-workers, insurance companies or other third parties, and appears to apply equally to tortfeasors and to discriminators under human rights legislation.[40] This represents one type of *Weber* gap that has arisen in several arbitration cases in recent years, in which arbitrators have held that they have no jurisdiction to add third parties to the proceeding or impose liability against them, even where they may be co-workers.[41]

In this part of the essay, I examine three aspects of *Weber*'s impact on bargaining unit employees' access to the courts for common law claims:

1) the different approaches that have been taken in applying the *Weber* standard to determine whether or not access to the courts for tort claims should be denied;
2) the Supreme Court of Canada "*Weber* on Steroids" decision; and
3) institutional concerns and "*Weber* gaps" resulting from the application of the *Weber* standard to common law claims advanced by organized employees.

---

third parties. *See e.g.*, *Limojet Gold Express Ltd v Public Service Alliance of Canada, Local 05/21081* (2006), 160 LAC (4th) 314 (Arbitrator: Larson); *Cherubini Metal Works Ltd v United Steel Workers of America, Local 4122* (2008), 172 LAC (4th) 1 (Arbitrator: Christie) [*Cherubini Metal*]; *GDI Services (Canada) LP and United Food and Commercial Workers Union, Local 175 (Aguilar), Re* (2013), 237 LAC (4th) 331 (Arbitrator: Parmar) [*GDI Services*]. For an outlier on this issue *see Rivtow Marine Inc and International Union of Operating Engineers, Local 115* (2004), 78 CLAS 272 (Arbitrator: Glass).

40 Arbitrators have also been asked to rule on whether they have jurisdiction to resolve tort claims by one employee against another — sometimes another who is outside the bargaining unit — where the basis of the action is conduct by the co-worker in the workplace. A good example is *Air Canada Pilots Association v Air Canada*, [1998] LVI 2945-3 (Arbitrator: Mitchnick), in which the arbitrator held that he did not have jurisdiction to decide a defamation claim by a pilot against a flight attendant in another bargaining unit, where the basis of the claim was a memo from the attendant to the employer alleging misconduct by the pilot. Contrast this decision with *Giorno v Pappas* (1999), 42 OR (3d) 626, 170 DLR (4th) 160 [*Giorno*], discussed below, in which the Court of Appeal for Ontario held that *Weber* prevented the Court from taking jurisdiction over such a claim despite the fact it was against another employee who was not in the bargaining unit.

41 *See Cherubini Metal*, above note 39 and *GDI Services* above note 39. It was held that the application of *Weber* and *Parry Sound* do not give an arbitrator applying human rights codes jurisdiction to award remedies against third party discriminators.

### 1) Access to the Courts for Tort Claims by Bargaining Unit Employees

The *Weber* gap created by the inability of arbitrators to add third parties to arbitration proceedings is compounded where the affected employees are barred from access to the courts for claims against those third parties. There have been numerous court decisions concerning the jurisdiction of courts to hear tort claims between employees and employers, and employees and third parties, including co-workers. These decisions have demonstrated a significant degree of confusion and inconsistency amongst courts of appeal across the country in applying the *Weber* standard for exclusive jurisdiction. The confusion inherent in the test itself, combined with inconsistency among attempts to apply the test, can be illustrated by juxtaposing just a few court of appeal decisions from Ontario, British Columbia and Quebec.

The Court of Appeal for Ontario has, albeit with some inconsistency, applied the *Weber* standard in the most expansive fashion to preclude access to the courts for tort claims by unionized employees against third party co-workers, both supervisors[42] and non-managerial co-workers.[43] Perhaps the most remarkable decision in this line of cases is *Giorno v Pappas*.[44] The plaintiff filed a grievance alleging workplace harassment against a co-worker who was not a supervisor and was not in her bargaining unit. The grievance was settled by the union without prejudice to any civil claims by the grievor. The grievor then commenced a defamation action against the co-worker, her employer (the Ministry of Housing) and the Ontario Rent Review Hearings Board. The Court of Appeal upheld an order striking out the claim against all defendants on the basis of *Weber*. The Court held that *Weber* required exclusive jurisdiction for the arbitral forum because the facts giving rise to the dispute were all workplace related. The dispute could be said to arise inferentially from the collective agreement because the agreement contained a broad general clause requiring the employer to provide a safe and healthy workplace. The Court held that it was irrelevant that relief was sought against third parties other than the employer, despite the fact that *Weber* said nothing about claims against third parties.

---

42 *Dwyer v Canada Post Corp*, [1997] OJ No 1575, 70 ACWS (3d) 816 (CA).

43 *Ruscetta v Graham* (1998), 78 ACWS (3d) 297, 114 OAC 320 (CA), leave to appeal to SCC refused, 120 OAC 196 (note) (15 October 1998).

44 *Giorno*, above note 40.

The Court seemed to accept the fact that this result would likely deprive the plaintiff of any forum in which to claim relief for intentional torts committed by the third-party co-worker. It justified this outcome on the basis that the employee could claim some remedy against the employer under the general health and safety clause in the collective agreement. However, this was a questionable assumption at best, particularly as it related to attempts to hold the employer vicariously liable for the intentional torts of co-workers.[45] It is entirely likely that the impugned co-worker's speech could be found defamatory, but not a threat to the plaintiff's health and safety under the terms of the collective agreement.[46] And, as stated in *Weber*, arbitrators do not have independent jurisdiction to grant tort remedies in the absence of finding a violation of the collective agreement. Thus, it seems quite likely that the plaintiff could be denied any "ultimate remedy" for defamation at arbitration. This possibility seems to be ignored by the reasoning in *Giorno*. Nevertheless the broad *Giorno* approach to the use of *Weber* to bar access to courts for tort actions against both employers and third parties continues to be applied with vigour in Ontario and some other provinces.[47]

One also has to question the desirability of requiring unions to be exclusive gatekeepers in deciding whether claims of intentional torts such as defamation should be brought against co-workers, managers and employers in the arbitration process.[48] I would certainly question the desirability of this for good labour relations and ensuring access to justice

45 *See e.g.*, *City of Toronto and Canadian Union of Public Employees, Local 79, Re* (2014), 245 LAC (4th) 439 (Arbitrator: Brown) [*Toronto and CUPE*] which applied *Weber* to deny an employer grievance against the union for fraud and theft by a former member of the bargaining unit because there was no breach of the collective agreement by the union, and the union could not be held liable for the intentional wrongdoing of one of its members. Further, as discussed at note 39 above, Ontario courts have held that arbitrators can never add the co-worker who committed intentional torts as a party to the arbitration proceedings.

46 As far as I am aware, no court has held that you must prove that speech presents a threat to your health or safety to succeed on a defamation claim.

47 *See e.g.*, *Andrews v Air Canada*, 2008 ONCA 37 [*Andrews*], barring actions for both tort and *Charter* claims against the employer and non-bargaining unit co-workers in a case involving false accusations of wrongdoing against the plaintiff. *See also* *Giesbrecht v McNeilly*, 2008 MBCA 22; *Cherubini Metal Works Ltd v Nova Scotia (Attorney General)*, 2007 NSCA 38; *Beaulieu v University of Alberta*, 2014 ABCA 137.

48 *Seneca College v Ontario Public Service Employees Union* (2001), 102 LAC (4th) 298 at paras 40–59 (Arbitrator: P Picher) [*Seneca Arbitration Decision*, rev'd sub nom *OPSEU v Seneca College of Applied Arts and Technology* (2004) 73 OR (3d) 185 (Div

for organized workers. Such concerns may have led the Court of Appeal of Quebec to reject such a broad reading of *Weber* in several decisions released at approximately the same time as *Giorno*. The two notable decisions which stand in stark contrast to the Ontario approach are *Saiano c Côté*[49] and *Nadeau v Carrefour des jeunes de Montréal*.[50] In *Saiano*, the plaintiff sued his employer and his manager for defamation based on what he claimed were false allegations by the manager that he had made sexist remarks about a co-worker. The Court refused to strike out the plaintiff's claim on the basis that the claim was not one that could be characterized as in essence arising from the collective agreement. The Court also distinguished *Weber* on the basis that it did not deal with claims against a third party who is not a party to the collective agreement, and held that *Weber* did not deprive individual workers of their common law rights simply because they were unionized and working under a collective agreement.[51] In *Nadeau*, the plaintiff and thirteen co-workers were fired after allegations of child abuse, followed by a police investigation and criminal charges. All charges were dropped after a preliminary inquiry. The plaintiff then sued her employer, several co-workers and the police for several torts, including bad faith and negligence. The Court struck out the claim against the employer on the basis of *Weber*,[52] but upheld the plaintiff's right to sue her managers and co-workers.[53] On the issue of claims against third parties, the Court affirmed its position in *Saiano* that *Weber* could

Ct) [*Seneca Div Ct Decision*], aff'd (2006) 80 OR (3d) 1 (CA) [*Seneca OCA Decision*], leave to appeal to SCC refused, 228 OAC 396n (16 November 2006).

49 (1998), 82 ACWS (3d) 81, [1998] RJDT 1051 (QC CA) [*Saiano*].

50 (1998), 82 ACWS (3d) 916, [1998] RJDT 1513 (QC CA) [*Nadeau*].

51 *Saiano*, above note 49 at para 30.

52 The Court rejected the Court of Appeal for Ontario's holding in *Piko v Hudson's Bay Co* (1998), 41 OR (3d) 729, 167 DLR (4th) 479 that the involvement of criminal justice system actors changed the essential character of the dispute and deprived the arbitrator of exclusive jurisdiction. *Piko* appears to be the outlier in the Ontario cases, as demonstrated by several further Court of Appeal for Ontario decisions which followed *Giorno* with little or no analysis or reasoning. *See e.g.*, *Bhadauria v Toronto Board of Education*, 174 DLR (4th) 382, 117 OAC 356 (CA) and *Sloan v York Region District School Board*, [2000] OJ No 2754, 98 ACWS (3d) 825 (CA). The Court of Appeal for Saskatchewan also applied *Weber* to bar tort claims by a university professor against the employer and several individual administrators alleging harassment and sabotage of research. *See Hemmings v University of Saskatchewan*, 2002 SKCA 96.

53 *McNeil v Brewers Retail Inc*, 2008 ONCA 405, affirms the *Piko* exception to allow court jurisdiction for the tort of malicious prosecution.

not deprive a court of jurisdiction to hear claims against managers or co-workers, because they are not parties to the collective agreement and not subject as individuals to the mandatory grievance procedure. The Court was unwilling to deprive Nadeau of her *only* opportunity to seek redress against her co-workers.

Contrasting the reasoning in *Giorno* and the Quebec cases reveals a difference in the hierarchy of values held by both courts. Towards the end of his reasons in *Giorno*, Justice Goudge referred to the need to preclude employees from suing co-workers in court because it "prevents the undercutting of the dispute resolution process that is given exclusive statutory jurisdiction over disputes that arise under the collective agreement."[54] On this view, the concerns of efficiency and not undermining the collective bargaining dispute resolution mechanism are clearly paramount to any concerns about access to justice for individual workers. The fact that the worker may be deprived of any forum in which to protect her common law rights against intentional torts is not significant as long as she may have a potential claim of some kind against her employer—despite the fact that this potential claim could go forward only if the union chose to support it to arbitration, and even it if did go forward, a valid defamation claim may not constitute a threat to health and safety under the collective agreement. By contrast, in the Quebec cases the Court clearly placed the need to preserve access to justice for individual workers above efficiency concerns. The decisions emphasized that the plaintiff's only opportunity to seek redress against her co-workers was to invoke court jurisdiction, and that *Weber* should not be used to deprive workers of the opportunity to assert common law rights against intentional torts simply because they are organized.

The juxtaposition of *Giorno* and the decision of the Court of Appeal for British Columbia in *Fording Coal Ltd v United Steel Workers of America, Local 7884*[55] is even more striking. In *Fording Coal*, the employer sued the union and its president for remarks in a local newspaper alleging lax safety practices on the part of the employer. The employer also filed a grievance under the collective agreement. The union pushed to have the grievance heard by the arbitrator and the company sought an adjournment so that it could proceed with its civil action. The arbitrator held that he had jurisdiction based on *Weber*, and on the fact that the dispute con-

54 *Giorno*, above note 39 at para 29.

55 1999 BCCA 38 [*Fording Coal*].

cerned the exercise of management rights in terms of productivity, discipline and safety in the workplace. The union also referred to collective agreement language requiring the parties to promote cordial relations and to co-operate fully in the promotion and achievement of matters set out in the agreement. The Court of Appeal quashed the arbitral ruling, preferring to characterize the dispute as being in essence about the defamatory statements made by the union president and not about production or safety issues.[56] The majority stated that in its opinion, the collective agreement did not contemplate arbitrators adjudicating upon the freedom of speech rights of the union president or the law of defamation. The majority also noted that there are special procedures and rules of evidence applicable to defamation actions in court that could not be easily dealt with in the arbitration process. It concluded that the dispute fell well outside "the normal scope of employer-employee relations" and thus was not contemplated as an appropriate subject for arbitration.[57]

---

56 If a similar approach had been taken in *Weber*, the dispute could easily have been characterized as being in essence about the invasion of privacy by a third party using false pretences, and not about components of the sick leave policy of the employer.

57 An approach similar to *Fording Coal* was taken in *Johnston v Anderson*, 1999 BCCA 66, where the Court held that *Weber* did not prevent a court action for defamation by a workplace supervisor against several bargaining unit employees for derogatory comments published in a newsletter circulated to fellow employees and some non-employees. However, the Court of Appeal for British Columbia has more recently ruled in favour of exclusive arbitral jurisdiction over issues raised in a defamation claim in *Haight-Smith v Neden*, 2002 BCCA 132 [*Neden*], where the Court struck out a defamation claim by a former teacher against a principal, vice-principal, school superintendents, teachers and three members of Canadian Union of Public Employees. The Court held that all claims against board officials and fellow members of the bargaining unit were barred by *Weber* because all the alleged defamatory statements related to the plaintiff's character, history and capacity as an employee and were made to persons who would be expected to be informed of workplace problems. The claims against the non-bargaining unit members were dismissed on the ground of qualified privilege. *See also Blanco-Arriba v British Columbia*, 2001 BCSC 1557 [*Blanco-Arriba*]. By contrast, *Fording Coal* was applied recently with some vigour by an Ontario arbitrator to deny arbitral jurisdiction to hear a claim brought by an employer against a union president for statements made in a newspaper about the employer. *See Renfrew County and District Health Unit and ONA (Letter to Editor), Re*, [2013] OLAA No 429, 116 CLAS 301 (Arbitrator: Keller). The decision contains a good discussion of the defamation jurisdiction of arbitrators, but leaves open the question of whether the employer might be denied access to the courts based on *Giorno* and other Court of Appeal for Ontario decisions that have applied *Weber* broadly to bar tort claims.

When one contrasts the subject matter of the disputes and the collective agreement language at issue in *Fording Coal* and *Giorno*, it is again clear that the different results had little to do with the application of the *Weber* test for exclusive arbitral jurisdiction, and were much more likely determined by the different values placed on efficiency, finality, access to justice, and institutional appropriateness concerns. There appeared to be a much more direct connection or nexus between the alleged defamatory speech and the collective agreement obligations in *Fording Coal* than in *Giorno*, where the grievor would have had to make the contentious and probably untenable argument that critical speech was a threat to her health and safety in order to have any chance for redress.

A recent decision of Chief Justice Hinkson in the British Columbia Supreme Court provides a good example of the courts' ongoing tendency to apply *Weber* in a broad fashion to bar access for tort claims against employers and third parties where there is language in the collective agreement that appears to provide some basis for a grievance. In *Bruce v Cohon*[58] the plaintiff, a star player in the CFL for many years, sued the league, several of his former teams and several third parties, including a "neutral consulting physician" and a retired players' association, for injuries he suffered when he was allegedly allowed to play over two seasons despite suffering from the effects of concussions. The Court struck out all claims on the basis of *Weber* because the collective agreement had several clauses dealing with player health and safety and appeared to allow for grievances to be initiated by players on the basis of negligence by their employers. The Court expressly relied on *Giorno* as standing for the principle that *Weber*'s ruling on exclusive arbitral jurisdiction applied to claims against third parties, whether or not they were acting as agents of the employer. The somewhat unique character of collective bargaining in a professional sports context, which appears to allow for a great deal of individual bargaining by players and agents over issues affecting compensation, was not seen as undermining the policy preference expressed in *Weber* and in the relevant provincial labour codes (British Columbia and Quebec) for the mandatory final and binding resolution of disputes by arbitration.[59]

58 2016 BCSC 419.

59 The Chief Justice was not swayed by the NHL precedents that appeared to recognize the professional sports bargaining context as different, and allowed negligence actions to continue against professional NHL team employers: *see Robitaille v Vancouver Hockey Club Ltd*, [1979] BCJ No 887, 19 BCLR 158 (SC) and *Belanger v*

In the federal sector, the first ten years after *Weber* saw many judicial decisions — which may be described as almost incomprehensible in their diversity of analysis and reasoning — addressing whether *Weber* bars access by federal civil servants to the courts to pursue common law claims against their employers and individual co-workers. The complexity of the issues in this area is significantly enhanced by the somewhat unique and frequently criticized restrictions on access to third-party adjudication built into the federal grievance and adjudication process under sections 91 and 92 of the federal *Public Service Staff Relations Act (PSSRA)*.[60] Prior to 2005, there were numerous and inconsistent decisions of provincial courts of appeal and the Federal Court of Appeal that led to great difficulty in predicting with any degree of certainty when the courts would or would not take jurisdiction over claims made by federal civil servants. While some of the better decisions suggested a strong emerging resistance to the simple-minded application of *Weber*,[61] there were also many provincial and federal court decisions which applied *Weber* to deny access to the courts by civil servants whose access to third-party adjudication to enforce their common law rights was very uncertain.[62]

---

*Pittsburgh Penguins Inc* (1998), 77 ACWS (3d) 238, 17 CPC (4th) 245 (Ont Ct J (Gen Div)). Hinkson CJ's decision appears to raise doubt that either of those cases would be decided in the same manner today.

60 RSC 1985, c P-35. In 2005, the *PSSRA* was replaced by the *Public Service Labour Relations Act*, SC 2003, c 22, s 2 (*PSLRA*), but similar issues arise in that certain types of grievances are barred from referral to arbitration under ss 209 and 236 in a manner that is similar to ss 91 and 92 of the *PSSRA*.

61 Most notable in this regard are *Pleau v Canada (Attorney General)*, 1999 NSCA 159, leave to appeal to SCC refused, [2000] SCCA No 83 (28 September 2000) [*Pleau*] and *Guenette v Canada (Attorney General)* 60 OR (3d) 601, 216 DLR (4th) 410 (CA) [*Guenette*]. *See also Burgess v Ontario (Ministry of Health)* (2001), 55 OR (3d) 507, 199 DLR (4th) 295 (CA), which dealt with concurrent or overlapping jurisdiction between courts and a provincial adjudicative body for non-unionized civil servants in the area of wrongful dismissal. *Burgess* provided a similar analysis in favour of allowing access to courts in areas where the legislation creating the statutory device did not provide a clear and unequivocal ouster, there was considerable uncertainty about whether the claimants would be able to pursue the claims in the statutory adjudicative forum, and the courts were likely to provide a more expert tribunal than the statutory mechanism, given the nature of the claims at issue. *See also Phillips v Harrison*, 2000 MCBA 150.

62 See the numerous decisions cited in *Guenette*, above note 61 at 2. For recent examples *see Jadwani v Canada (Attorney General)* (2001), 52 OR (3d) 660, 141 OAC 22

Then, in 2005 the Supreme Court of Canada issued a decision in *Vaughan v Canada*[63] that applied *Weber* in a broad fashion to foreclose access to the courts by federal civil servants under the *PSSRA*, even where that legislative scheme did not appear to provide them with any access to third-party adjudication. The majority agreed that the legislation was not as clear as the labour relations legislation at issue in *Weber* in expressly ousting court jurisdiction, but nevertheless held that the doctrine of judicial restraint set out in *Weber* should be followed, even where the labour relations scheme did not provide for recourse to independent adjudication. The decision suggested that courts may retain some residual jurisdiction to grant access in cases involving whistle-blowers who were being punished by their employer, and suggested that the cases favouring court access to that point[64] had been based on such an exception. However, it appeared to reject the argument that the determination of when to exercise residual court jurisdiction should be based on the presence of effective redress in the form of access to independent adjudication. Clearly the value of access to justice was not in ascendancy in the majority ruling in *Vaughan*.[65] By contrast, the dissenting judges, McLachlin CJC and Bastarache J, were of the view that the absence of access to an effective independent forum for adjudication pointed away from a finding of exclusive jurisdiction for the labour relations grievance mechanism.

In *Canada (House of Commons) v Vaid*, [66] the Court applied *Weber* and its progeny to hold that an adjudicative body established to hear grievances under the *Parliamentary Employment and Staff Relations Act (PESRA)*[67]

---

(CA) [*Jadwani*] and *Gaignard v Canada (Attorney General)* (2003), 67 OR (3d) 611, 232 DLR (4th) 43 (CA) [*Gaignard*].

63 2005 SCC 11 [*Vaughan*]. The plaintiff had been on leave for four years and working in the private sector when he was notified that he had been declared surplus under the *Public Service Employment Act*, SC 2003, c 22, s 12, and would soon be laid off. He then applied for early retirement incentives that were being made available to employees in the federal civil service, but was denied. This type of decision was grievable under the *PSSRA* but could not be referred to arbitration, so he commenced a civil action based on negligence.

64 *See Guenette* and *Pleau*, above note 61.

65 In *Bron v Canada (Attorney General)*, 2010 ONCA 71, the Court held that, despite *Vaughan*, there was no longer room for any exception to *Weber* exclusive arbitral jurisdiction for tort claims by whistle-blowers because of express provisions in s 236 of the *PSLRA* enacted in 2005.

66 2005 SCC 30.

67 RSC 1985, c 33 (2nd Supp), s 2.

had exclusive jurisdiction over a constructive dismissal claim made by the former chauffeur of the Speaker of the House of Commons, including claims of breaches of the *Canadian Human Rights Act*. The Court held that the parallel jurisdiction of the Canadian Human Rights Commission was ousted by the exclusionary wording of section 2 of the *PESRA*.[68]

### 2) *Weber* on Steroids: *Bisaillon v Concordia University*

The Supreme Court of Canada's focus on keeping workplace disputes arising in an organized setting out of the courts continued with a vengeance in its 2006 decision in *Bisaillon v Concordia University*.[69] The majority reaffirmed what it referred to as "a liberal position according to which grievance arbitrators have a broad exclusive jurisdiction over issues relating to conditions of employment, provided that those conditions can be shown to have an express or implicit connection to the collective agreement."[70] The case involved an application by a university employee who worked under a collective agreement, to institute a class action on behalf of members of the employee pension plan against the university challenging actions taken with respect to the administration and use of the pension fund, including a unilateral contribution holiday. The majority of members of the pension plan were employees who were in nine bargaining units, subject to nine separate collective agreements with nine different unions. One union had agreed to the actions taken by the employer, but eight unions supported the employee's application for a class action. The superior court judge declined to authorize the class action on the basis that the subject matter of the dispute was within the exclusive jurisdiction of grievance arbitration under each of the nine collective agreements because the pension plan was a benefit provided for under the various collective agreements. The Court of Appeal of

---

68 *PESRA*, above note 67 at s 2. This provision states that, ". . . except as provided in this Act, nothing in any other Act of Parliament that provides for matters similar to those provided for under this Act . . . shall apply."

69 2006 SCC 19 [*Bisaillon*].

70 *Bisaillon, ibid* at para 33. This wording could be seen as affirming the kind of broad application imposed by provincial courts in cases like *Giorno*, which appeared no longer to require that the dispute in its essential nature "arose" expressly or inferentially out of the collective agreement, but rather only required a finding of some implicit — one might even use the term "loose" or "tenuous" — connection with the collective agreement.

Quebec reversed the decision on the basis that the pension plan existed independently of any single collective agreement, and a grievance arbitrator appointed under any one agreement would have no jurisdiction over the claims of employees covered by the other eight agreements. As the Court of Appeal recognized, this was a case where real efficiency and finality could only be obtained through access to a court action encompassing all employees.

The majority of the Supreme Court of Canada, in an opinion by LeBel J, reinstated the application judge's decision not to authorize a class action, on the basis that the disputes fell within the exclusive jurisdiction of grievance arbitrators under the various applicable agreements because each of the agreements referred expressly to the pension plan. The parties had decided to incorporate the conditions for applying the pension plan into their collective agreements, and it would be incompatible with the collective bargaining regime, which assigned exclusive representation rights to the nine unions, to grant the status of class representative to the individual plaintiff in a class action. The majority reached this conclusion despite the fact that eight of nine unions supported the application, despite its admission that each grievance arbitrator would have jurisdiction only over the claims of employees who were subject to the collective agreement under which he or she was appointed, and despite the probability that the whole process could lead to multiple proceedings and inconsistent results.[71]

The dissenting opinion, authored by Bastarache J, was of the view that in its essential character, the dispute did not arise out of the interpretation or application or violation of the collective agreement because the pension plan transcended any single collective agreement, making the Superior Court the only forum with jurisdiction to hear these claims. It also noted the presence of a single, indivisible pension fund that pre-existed the multiple collective agreements and employment contracts; although more than one agreement sought to regulate access to this pension fund, no single agreement could purport to alter or affect the fund itself. The dissent was also influenced by the inevitable risk of multiple proceedings and contradictory rulings. This made the vehicle of a class

71 The majority briefly acknowledged the practical problems that would result from its ruling, but then suggested in a cryptic fashion that there were "a number of tools of civil procedure that can be used to resolve the problems caused by multiple proceedings." *Bisaillon, ibid* at para 61. However, no such tools were identified.

action in Superior Court the only principled and practical way to resolve the claims in dispute.

*Bisaillon* stands out as a decision in which blind adherence to the *Weber* preference for keeping disputes involving organized employees out of courts led to a decision that serves absolutely none of the interests at stake in making decisions about exclusive versus concurrent jurisdiction. The values of finality, efficiency, avoiding inconsistent results, institutional appropriateness, and ensuring access to justice are all undermined by the result in *Bisaillon*. That is why I have referred to it as *Weber* on steroids.

### 3) Arbitration as a Forum for Common Law Claims and *Weber* Gaps

Have individual employees found access to justice to seek redress for violation of common law rights through access to grievance arbitration and appropriate arbitral treatment of such claims since *Weber*? Or has application of the *Weber* standard for exclusive jurisdiction allowed for the development of a "*Weber* gap" between rights and access to *fora* for enforcement of those rights?

It is difficult to assess the extent and impact of cases in which employees who seek to enforce common law rights through arbitration are denied access to arbitration because their union has refused to support what is in effect often an individual private rights claim by one worker against other employees or managers — the first possible factor in the creation of a *Weber* gap. In such cases the union may not see any collective benefit to be derived from supporting the grievance and may in fact see risk of causing significant harm to its collective bargaining interests, especially where supporting the grievance may harm its ability to work with management on a day-to-day basis. A careful, comprehensive and costly empirical study would be required to determine with any accuracy the extent to which unions refuse to process such claims, and the impact of their refusal.

However, a brief review of arbitral jurisprudence considering claims for remedies for common law rights allows us to make several observations about their frequency and prospects for success. First, the number of such claims to result in an arbitral award does not appear to have been great.[72] Second, where claims have been made, they are frequently met

72 My research revealed a very small number of awards in which such claims were made before an arbitrator, a result confirmed by my personal experience as an

with strong preliminary objections by employers that they are beyond the jurisdiction of the arbitrator, which may go some way toward explaining the first observation.[73] Third, arbitrators have generally refused to take jurisdiction to consider a claim for damages under a common law right or protection if they are unable to find any violation of the collective agreement.[74] Fourth, where arbitrators do take jurisdiction to consider

---

active grievance arbitrator in Ontario, and by the views expressed by Arbitrators Knopf, MacDowell and Archibald at the Weber Symposium. (See Chapter 1, this volume at 13–16.) The fact that *Weber* is not argued frequently in support of tort claims before arbitrators, and arises more frequently in what have become known as *Weber* motions to strike out common law actions brought in courts by organized employees, leads me to two observations. First, it raises the possibility that unions are frequently acting as junior management in terms of keeping these claims away from arbitration, probably for the collective bargaining reasons suggested earlier in this essay. Second, the court time spent dealing with *Weber* motions to strike, which can be considerable, might be better spent by accepting jurisdiction and dealing with motions to strike on the merits in cases of frivolous and baseless claims.

73 *See e.g.*, *Transit Windsor v Amalgamated Transit Union, Local 616* (2003), 114 LAC (4th) 385 (Arbitrator: Brandt) [*Transit Windsor*]; *Vancouver Hospital & Health Sciences Centre v British Columbia Nurses' Union* (2000), 87 LAC (4th) 205 (Arbitrator: Gordon) [*Vancouver HHSC*]; and *ABT Building Products Canada Ltd v Communication, Energy and Paperworkers Union of Canada, Local 434* (2000), 90 LAC (4th) 1 (Arbitrator: Christie) [*ABT Building*].

74 *See e.g.*, *Ontario Public Service Employees Union v Ontario (Ministry of Correctional Services)* (2002), 113 LAC (4th) 49 (Arbitrator: Brown); *Vancouver HHSC*, *ibid*; *Mount Sinai Hospital v Ontario Nurses Association (Caesar-Small Grievance)*, [2000] OLAA No 475 (Arbitrator: Davie) [*Mount Sinai*]; *Nordic Gaming Corp v Service Employees International Union, Local 2.ON* (2006), 157 LAC (4th) 296 (Arbitrator: OV Gray). This of course is consistent with passages in *Weber* which clearly mandated that arbitrators have no jurisdiction to award common law damages in the absence of a collective agreement violation — something the Courts of Appeal in several jurisdictions appear to have completely overlooked. However, see also the British Columbia decision in *Vancouver Coastal Health Authority v Hospital Employees Union* (2004) 124 LAC (4th) 353 (Arbitrator: McDonald) [*Vancouver Coastal*], where an arbitrator relied on *Weber* to take jurisdiction to consider and decide a defamation claim where the union had not even alleged a violation of the collective agreement — this clearly appears to be an anomaly in the jurisprudence. Interestingly, this case was decided by the same arbitrator who took jurisdiction over a defamation claim by the employer against union officials for comments made in a local newspaper in *Fording Coal*, above note 55, only to have that decision quashed by the BCCA. In *Vancouver Coastal*, the defamation claim was brought by a number of employees for management comments to a local newspaper that the employees had created a security risk by leaving their security guard posts one hour early. It

a common law claim such as defamation, the legal analysis of the common law requirements is often fairly rudimentary[75] — although there are notable exceptions.[76] Fifth, arbitrators who have considered claims for defamation and intentional infliction of mental suffering have in several cases decided not to award damages despite finding the elements of the tort made out;[77] and in most cases where damages were held to be payable, arbitrators have tended to award minimal damages in the range of $1,000 to $5,000.[78] Sixth, although arbitrators have often indicated that

---

appears that the arbitrator was motivated by a concern that the employees might find themselves falling into a *Weber* gap, since after *Fording Coal*, there has been a consistent trend in British Columbia Court of Appeal decisions to apply *Weber* to deny access to the courts to bargaining unit employees (as opposed to the employer or management employees) for pursuing defamation claims. *See e.g.*, *Neden*, above note 57.

75 *See e.g.*, *Surrey (City) v Canadian Union of Public Employees, Local 402 (Weber Grievance)*, [2003] BCCAAA No 243 (Arbitrator: S Beattie) [*Surrey*]; *Clearbrook Grain & Milling Co v United Food and Commercial Workers' Union, Local 1518* (2000), 93 LAC (4th) 312 (Arbitrator: Burke) [*Clearbrook*]; *Snowcrest Packers Ltd and United Food and Commercial Workers' Union (Dhesi), Re* (2005) 80 CLAS 256 (Arbitrator: Jackson); *Bilodeau v New Brunswick NB (Board of Management) (Policy Grievance)*, [2005] NBLAA No 21 (Arbitrator: Bladon) [*Bilodeau*].

76 For a more comprehensive analysis of common law doctrine see *ABT Building*, above note 73; *Transit Winsdor*, above note 97; *York University v York University Faculty Association (Noble Grievance)* (2005), 92 CLAS 117 (Arbitrator: Goodfellow).

77 *See e.g.*, *ABT Building*, above note 73, where the arbitrator concluded there were no damages proven; and *Transit Windsor*, above note 73, where the arbitrator employed both the concepts of qualified privilege and absence of malice to find no damages payable, despite the defamatory nature of the comments. Note also *Ontario and OPSEU, Re* (2015), 253 LAC (4th) 60 (Arbitrator: Briggs) [*Ontario and OPSEU*], in which the arbitrator applied *Parry Sound*, above note 4, to find concurrent jurisdiction to apply the *Freedom of Information and Protection of Privacy Act*, RSO 1990, c F.31 as part of the collective agreement. The arbitrator also applied *Weber* to find that the new tort of "intrusion upon seclusion" was made out by the improper disclosure of confidential medical information by a co-worker. However, the arbitrator held that no damages could be awarded against the employer because vicarious liability did not apply where the tortious actions were intentionally dishonest and not part of scope of duties of the co-worker.

78 *See e.g.*,*Clearbrook*, above note 75; *Canada Post Corp and Canadian Union of Postal Workers*, [1998] CLAD No 658 (Arbitrator: Joliffe) ($1,000); *Bilodeau*, above note 75 ($2000); *Canada Safeway v United Food and Commercial Workers Union, Local 401 (Szautner Grievance)* (2009), 181 LAC (4th) 124 (Arbitrator: Ponak) ($2500 for mental distress): *Harrison Hot Springs (Village) v Canadian Union of Public Employees, Local 458* (2006), 155 LAC (4th) 200 (Arbitrator: Keras) (four weeks wages

they have jurisdiction to award punitive and aggravated damages, in the first decade following *Weber* they generally took the position that such damages would not be available for a breach of the collective agreement unless the union could prove an independently actionable wrong, such as a common law tort, in addition to violation of the collective agreement. Moreover, they often denied claims for such damages even where an independent tort was proven.[79] An independently actionable wrong is no longer a requirement for mental distress damages, following the Supreme Court of Canada's decision in *Honda Canada Inc v Keays*,[80] and arbitrators seem to be somewhat more prepared to seriously consider such claims where they are supported by the evidence. There also appear to have been a few more arbitral decisions awarding significant damages for aggravat-

for intentional infliction of mental distress). Although there have been one or two exceptions to this trend toward minimal damages for common law torts, they tend to involve cases where the behaviour of the employer drove the grievor out of the workplace and there was no claim for reinstatement; the tort damages may have been seen as a way of augmenting compensation to replace reinstatement. Two cases appear to be the only examples of significant damage awards for tortious conduct in the first ten years after *Weber*: *Surrey,* above note 75 ($20,000 for defamation and intentional infliction of mental distress) and *CVC Services v IWA-Canada, Local 1-71* (1997), 65 LAC (4th) 54 (Arbitrator: Lanyon) (the arbitrator awarded damages in the amount of one year's wages — $16,000 — but it is difficult to separate the tort damages from the damages for violation of the collective agreement).

79 *See e.g., Eurocan Pulp & Paper Co v Communications, Energy and Paperworkers Union of Canada, Local 298,* (2003), 67 CLAS 188 (Arbitrator: M Jackson); *Bethany Care Society v United Nurses of Alberta, Locals 91 & 173* (2000), 87 LAC (4th) 216 (Arbitrator: Sims); *Pacifica Papers Inc v Communications, Enegry and Paperworkers Union of Canada Local 76* (2001), 75 CLRBR (2d) 208 (Arbitrator: Pylypchuk); *Seneca Arbitration Decision,* above note 48. The one great outlier in this area is *Province of Newfoundland and Labrador (Treasury Branch) v Newfoundland Public and Private Employees* (unreported decision of Arbitrator Peter Darby, 17 February 2003) in which the arbitrator awarded $100,000 in punitive damages to the grievor. The award appears to be both unique and somewhat peculiar in that, although the arbitrator found an independently actionable tort of intentional infliction of mental suffering, he declined to award aggravated damages on that claim on the basis that the grievor had been adequately compensated for the tort in his award for general damages. However, it is difficult to find in the award any indication of an amount for general damages being awarded for the independent tort, as opposed to the amounts awarded for breaches of the collective agreement.

80 2008 SCC 39.

ed and punitive damages in recent years, although they are still relatively few in number.[81]

Overall, the cases on *Weber* jurisdiction for arbitrators to remedy common law wrongs leave one with the impression that arbitrators are not totally comfortable with the role of making findings of tortious wrongdoing by employers, managers and union officials, or providing significant damage awards to provide redress to particular individuals. This is perhaps understandable when one considers that arbitrators do not enjoy the tenured security of judges and depend for their continued employment as a third-party neutral on their continued acceptance by both the union and employer. As such, their primary criterion for a good decision is more likely to be the impact of their decision on the future labour relations between the two parties to the collective agreement, a criterion that may not be met by considering what remedies best protect the common law rights of individual workers.

The most significant and thoughtful consideration of the impact of *Weber's* intended transfer of jurisdiction over common law tort claims to arbitration is found in the decision of Arbitrator Pamela Picher in *Seneca College*.[82] The arbitration concerned the discharge of a college professor for allegedly sending anonymous, anti-Semitic material in inter-office mail envelopes to a human resources director who was an adherent of the Jewish faith. The arbitration board concluded that the employer had terminated the grievor after an unreasonable delay of seven years follow-

81 *See e.g., Greater Toronto Airports Authority v Public Service Alliance Canada, Local 0004* (2010), 191 LAC (4th) 277 (Arbitrator: Shime) [*GTAA Arbitration Decision*], rev'd in part *Greater Toronto Airports Authority v Public Service Alliance Canada, Local 0004*, 2011 ONSC 487 [*GTAA Div Ct*]. Arbitrator Shime awarded $50,000 for mental distress damages and $50,000 for punitive damages in addition to significant amounts for compensation in lieu of reinstatement. In *GTAA Div Ct*, the Divisional Court quashed both the mental distress and punitive awards and sent the case back to the arbitrator to reconsider appropriate amounts in light of remedial principles requiring adjudicators to pay attention to the amount of other damages awarded, and to justify why a punitive amount was needed. *See also Madill and Spruce Hollow Heavy Haul Ltd*, 2015 CarswellNat 1480 (Arbitrator: Larson) (applied *Weber* to give $50,000 for aggravated and $25,000 for punitive damages); *Canada Post Corp v Canadian Union of Postal Workers* (2012), 217 LAC (4th) 181 (Arbitrator: Peltz) (applied *Weber* and *GTAA* to give mental distress damages of $11,500); *Limojet Gold Express Ltd v Public Service Alliance of Canada Local 05/21081* (2008), 171 LAC (4th) 28 (Arbitrator: Larson) (applied *Weber* to give $100,000 in punitive damages for an unlawful strike).

82 *Seneca Arbitration Decision*, above note 48.

ing the alleged incidents, without any evidence to prove he was responsible for writing the offensive material or sending it to the recipient, and ordered him reinstated. In addition to the usual remedies for discharge without just cause, the union sought aggravated and punitive damages for the torts of defamation and intentional infliction of mental distress, arguing that the employer had acted in bad faith and with malice in moving to discharge without evidence to support just cause.

After first attempting to factually distinguish *Weber* from the case before her, Arbitrator Picher moved on to what can only be described as a scathing but insightful indictment of the failure of the Supreme Court of Canada to consider the labour relations implications of its broad and ambiguous standard for exclusive arbitral jurisdiction over tort claims. She noted that collective agreements include the aspects of their workplace relationship that the parties have decided to regulate under that agreement, and that traditionally they have not chosen to include the regulation of alleged tortious wrongdoing under the common law, although they could of course do so if they wished. She also noted that the parties have traditionally not permitted such matters to be considered in the arbitration process, but have chosen for good reason to leave such matters to the operation of the common law and adjudication by the courts. For Picher, if not for the Supreme Court of Canada, those reasons are obvious: alleged tortious misconduct normally involves heated and emotional personal disputes of a one-time nature, and requiring such disputes to be resolved in the arbitration process is not conducive to nurturing on-going collective bargaining relationships. Making arbitration the forum for pursuing such individual personal disputes and seeking aggravated and punitive damages would actually create an incentive for participants in the process to not bury the hatchet and move forward in the case of the use of strong language to advocate positions, a common feature of collective bargaining. It would divert the energy and resources of the parties away from traditional collective bargaining concerns and would likely create a very heavy financial burden for both employers and unions, depleting their ability to pursue traditional collective agreement claims through arbitration. In addition, under *Weber* and *O'Leary* individual employees could be made liable in negligence for accidents at work and made subject to orders for damages that could ruin them financially for life, without the procedural rights and appeals provided to litigants in courts. Picher concluded that "if all wrongs arising in the workplace, tortious as well as contractual, are indiscriminately placed within the grievance and arbitration procedure, the very efficiency and vitality of that cornerstone of the labour relations system is at risk."[83]

What approach then does Arbitrator Picher recommend? In effect she advocates the adoption of what I will refer to as the "anti-*Weber* presumption." She concluded that because of the inherent dangers in giving arbitrators broad exclusive jurisdiction over tort claims arising in the workplace, we should be loathe to conclude that the parties "would intend by inference to embrace such potentially devastating consequences."[84] Instead we should adopt the following approach: "Absent clear and compelling language in the collective agreement that would give rise to the inference, or absent express legislative authority, the parties should be presumed to intend that such tortious disputes will be resolved, as they have been for centuries, in the courts of common law, not at arbitration."[85] Thus Picher was able to find no arbitral jurisdiction over the tort claims, even though the factual matrix showed a much closer connection between the tort claims of the grievor and the employer's blatant violation of the collective agreement than existed in many of the previous cases in which courts and arbitrators had applied *Weber* to find exclusive arbitral jurisdiction.[86] On Picher's reasoning, the tort claim could proceed to court despite the fact that the arbitrator had jurisdiction to deal with the just cause issues.

Ultimately Arbitrator Picher's award was upheld by the Court of Appeal for Ontario in a decision which confirmed the Court's overall deference to arbitral decision-making. The Court ruled that the patent unreasonableness standard of review was to be applied despite the jurisdictional nature of the issue of arbitral jurisdiction over common law tort claims.[87] The deferential stance of the Court was perhaps surprising, given the extent to which the *Seneca College* award declining arbitral jurisdiction was out of synch with judicial decisions like *Giorno* which applied *Weber* to decline court jurisdiction.[88] However, in reviewing arbitral awards in the last ten years taking exclusive jurisdiction over tort claims asserted under the *Weber* doctrine, it is quite apparent that arbitrators

83 *Ibid* at para 50.

84 *Ibid* at para 52.

85 *Ibid.*

86 *Ibid* at paras 54–57.

87 *Seneca OCA Decision,* above note 48.

88 This latter point was made very clearly by the Divisional Court when it quashed Arbitrator Picher's award. *See Seneca Div Ct Decision,* above note 48.

have declined to adhere to the anti-*Weber* presumption advocated by Picher, and have at least indicated a willingness to deal with these common law issues where there is an arguable violation of the collective agreement to ground their jurisdiction over the dispute. In many cases the arguable violation of the collective agreement is an alleged violation of an employment-related statute, or the new "extended" portion of the collective agreement created by *Parry Sound*.[89] A very eloquent discussion of the expansion of arbitral jurisdiction created by *Weber* and *Parry Sound*, and its application to take jurisdiction over claims of violation of privacy legislation and tort claims based on invasion of privacy, is found in the decision of Arbitrator MacDowell in *Canadian Union of Public Employees, Local 133 v Niagara Falls (City)*.[90]

Although Arbitrator Picher is to be admired for her articulate expression of the harmful impact of the transfer of exclusive jurisdiction over tort claims that has been wrought by *Weber*, the juxtaposition of her "anti-*Weber* presumption" award in *Seneca College* and several perhaps overly broad applications of *Weber* in court decisions like *Giorno* leaves us with the following question. To the extent that more arbitrators were prepared to follow her lead and severely restrict exclusive arbitral jurisdiction, would they widen the *Weber* gap, leaving more individual employees with no forum for protection of common law rights?

## C. *WEBER*'S IMPACT ON *CHARTER* CLAIMS

The judicial decisions applying *Weber* to *Charter* claims arising from the workplace indicate that our courts have taken the Supreme Court of Canada's concern for adjudicative efficiency seriously and have applied the *Weber* standard broadly to bar access to courts to pursue such claims.

89 Above note 4. As discussed below at note 128, *Parry Sound* held that all collective agreements must be deemed to incorporate the substantive rights and obligations contained in applicable employment-related statutes.

90 [2005] OLAA 228, 81 CLAS 1. A similar analysis is offered in two other cases also involving tort claims based on the recently recognized privacy tort of inclusion upon seclusion, in *Kawartha Pine Ridge District School Board v Elementary Teachers' Federation of Ontario* (2008), 169 LAC (4th) 353 (Arbitrator: Luborsky) and *Ontario and OPSEU*, above note 77.

With very few exceptions,[91] almost all *Charter* claims by organized employees to date have been barred by *Weber*,[92] often with only cursory reasons that contain little or no analysis.[93] Its most frequent use has perhaps been to bar access to courts for *Charter* claims by federal civil servants who are subject to the grievance and adjudication procedures provided in the *PSSRA*.[94] The *Charter* cases to date appear to have adhered generally to the *Giorno* position that *Weber* bars actions against not only the employer but also other individual employees (both those who are in the bargaining unit, including union officials,[95] and those who are not).[96]

---

91 One such exception is *Billinkoff v Winnipeg School Division No 1* (1999), 134 Man R (2d) 99, 170 DLR (4th) 50 (CA), involving a claim by both unionized and non-unionized school board employees that their *Charter* rights have been violated by the failure to provide paid time off to observe Jewish holy days. The respondents argued that the unionized employees should have proceeded at arbitration, and the non-unionized employees should have gone to the human rights commission. The Court dismissed these jurisdictional challenges on the pragmatic ground that a court was the only forum which could deal with all the parties and all the grounds involved in the case; it made sense to have all applications decided in one forum to avoid unnecessary costs and inconsistent results. Equally interesting is *Morin v Prince Edward Island School Board, Regional Administrative Unit No 3*, 2002 PESCAD 9, involving a teacher's *Charter* claim that restrictions on his right to show an instructional film violated his freedom of expression. The court had earlier dismissed a challenge to its jurisdiction to deal with the Charter issues, relying on the Ontario Court of Appeal decision in *Weber* (*see Morin v Board of School Trustees of Regional Administrative Unit #3*, 1995 CanLII 3428 (PE SCAD)). A majority of the PEI Court of Appeal upheld the *Charter* claim without any reference to the jurisdictional issue. The dissenting judge, McQuaid JA, expressed concern that the Supreme Court decision in *Weber*, which reversed the Ontario Court of Appeal on the issue of *Charter* jurisdiction, strongly suggested that the matter belonged before an arbitrator, but was nonetheless prepared to proceed on the ground that an arbitrator would not have full remedial authority under the *Charter* (he would, however, have dismissed the *Charter* claim on the merits).

92 *See e.g.*, *Brunet v Ottawa Police Assn* (2004), 131 ACWS (3d) 445, 2005 CLLC 220-009 (Sup Ct J) [*Brunet*]; *Blanco-Arriba*, above note 57; *McCaffery v British Columbia (Solicitor General)*, 2004 BCSC 176; *Petrov v British Columbia Ferry Corp*, 2003 BCSC 270; *Small v Newfoundland (Department of Human Resources and Employment)*, 2003 NLSCTD 90.

93 *See e.g.*, *Bhaduria*, above note 52 and *Andrews*, above note 47.

94 *See e.g.*, *Gaignard*, above note 62; *Jadwani*, above note 62; *Chase v R*, 2004 FC 273 [*Chase*]; *Pieters v R*, 2004 FC 26 [*Pieters*].

95 *Brunet*, above note 92.

96 *Gaignard*, above note 62; *Jadwani*, above note 62; *Brunet*, above note 92.

Perhaps most notable in this group of decisions are the arguments made by the plaintiff in *Chase v R*[97] that in barring his access to court to protect his fundamental *Charter* rights, the operation of the *Weber* standard itself was a violation of his section 7 and section 15 *Charter* rights. A similar argument was made with respect to section 15 rights in *Pieters v Canada*.[98] In both cases the equality rights challenge was dismissed on the ground that, although *Weber* prevented access to the courts to pursue a claim of discrimination under section 15 of the *Charter* on the basis of race or nationality, the *Weber* bar itself operated solely on the basis of whether the claimant was a unionized employee and not on the basis of an enumerated or analogous ground under section 15 of the *Charter*. Unfortunately, the section 7 challenge to *Weber* in *Chase* was dismissed in a one-line rejection of the argument that the *Weber* doctrine threatened the plaintiff's life, liberty or security of the person. It may well be that the access to adjudicative procedures under sections 91 and 92 of the *PSSRA* available in both *Chase* and *Pieters* could undermine a section 7 claim. However, if a *Charter* claim was in issue in a fact situation similar to those found in *Pleau* and *Guenette* (or even *Giorno*), and there was a real threat that the *Weber* gap would leave the employee without access to any legal forum to enforce *Charter* rights, it would be much more difficult for a court to dismiss an argument that security of the person was not threatened.

What has been the impact of *Weber* on how arbitrators treat *Charter* claims? In addressing this question, it is important to remember that in *Douglas/Kwantlen Faculty Association v Douglas College*[99] the Supreme Court of Canada held that arbitrators have the jurisdiction under section 52 of the *Constitution Act 1982* to apply the *Charter* to statutes at issue in disputes before them, and to the collective agreements and actions of parties which are subject to the *Charter*. The Court also held that arbitrators can grant remedies sought for breach of the *Charter*, as long as they are within the remedial powers arbitrators possess under their enabling statute, and they have jurisdiction over the parties and the subject matter of the dispute. Despite recognizing concerns that this outcome might burden arbitration with undue complexity, the Court gave precedence to the advantages of speedy access to justice that would flow from hav-

97 *Chase*, above note 94.

98 *Pieters*, above note 94.

99 [1990] 3 SCR 570, 77 DLR (4th) 94 [*Douglas College*].

ing arbitrators ensure compliance with *Charter* rights at the first level of adjudication.[100]

*Weber* purported to change things in two respects. First, unlike *Douglas College*, it made arbitration the *exclusive* forum for adjudication of *Charter* claims arising inferentially from the collective agreement. In using *Douglas College* as support for a move to exclusive jurisdiction over *Charter* claims, Justice McLachlin effectively turned that prior decision on its head — taking a decision which was expressly intended to expand the *fora* available for access to *Charter* justice, and using it as authority for severely restricting access to courts for *Charter* claims. Second, *Weber* purported to declare that arbitrators were courts of competent jurisdiction to grant remedies under section 24 of the *Charter*. However, McLachlin J immediately qualified this statement by holding that arbitrators would only have jurisdiction to grant remedies for *Charter* violations to the extent that the remedies sought were within the remedial authority granted to arbitrators under their founding statute. Thus, this holding did not appear to expand the jurisdiction of arbitrators to grant *Charter* remedies to any significant extent beyond what had already been recognized in *Douglas College*.[101]

While *Weber* did little to increase the applicability of the *Charter* to arbitration or to expand the *Charter* jurisdiction of arbitrators, one might nevertheless have expected some increase in the number of *Charter* claims brought before arbitrators as a consequence of the denial of access to the courts to pursue individual *Charter* actions.[102] Although there may have been a slight increase in such claims since 1995, it would be

100 *Ibid* at paras 51–55.

101 It is perhaps for this reason that many of the significant *Charter* decisions by arbitrators in the years since *Weber* have placed greater reliance on *Douglas College* than on *Weber* as the basis for their jurisdiction. *See e.g., Mount Sinai Hospital,* above note 74 and *Peel (Regional Municipality) Police Services Board v Peel Regional Police Assn* (2001), 100 LAC (4th) 73 (Arbitrator: Kirkwood) [*Peel*].

102 The lack of significant growth in *Charter* claims at arbitration is perhaps even more curious when we remember that there was also some expansion of the basis for a finding that the *Charter* applies to the actions of a private party, at least where it is acting in furtherance of a government policy or program, which arguably should have led to more *Charter* cases in arbitration. *See Eldridge v British Columbia (Attorney General),* [1997] 3 SCR 624, 151 DLR (4th) 577. For application of this broader standard in arbitration *see Independent Electricity Market Operator v Society of Energy Professionals* (2003), 118 LAC (4th) 385 (Arbitrator: Herman) [*Independent Electricity*].

misleading to suggest that there has been a significant increase or a flood of such claims.[103] Nevertheless, there has been a fairly wide variety in the type of *Charter* claims brought before arbitrators, including the following: a claim that a provision of the Ontario *Employment Standards Act* violated section 15;[104] several claims that a benefits insurance plan discriminated on the grounds of family status, marital status and sex contrary to section 15;[105] a claim that a mandatory retirement policy and the Ontario *Human Rights Code* violated section 15;[106] a claim that the 2006 amendments to the Ontario *Human Rights Code* that abolished mandatory retirement but continued to allow employers to discriminate against persons over age 65 in terms of benefits and insurance plans violated section 15;[107] claims that employer surveillance of employees violates section 8;[108] a claim that an employer dress code that prohibited certain hair and beard styles offended the grievor's privacy rights under section 7;[109] claims that breathalyser evidence acquired in contravention of the

---

103 In the decisions reported from 1996 to 2004 in QL systems, a national computer database for arbitration decisions, I counted approximately twenty arbitral decisions that contained some discussion of a *Charter* claim as part of the matter under adjudication and made some reference to *Weber* as the source of their jurisdiction to apply the *Charter*. In the same search there were approximately 400 cases that made some reference to the *Charter*, of which I would estimate that only about 50 percent or fewer actually found that the *Charter* was relevant and applicable to the case before them. (This estimate is based on an unscientific sampling of the first thirty to forty cases in the search, which were the cases with the most references to the *Charter*.)

104 *Mount Sinai*, above note 74.

105 *Peel*, above note 101; *Calgary Roman Catholic Separate School District No 1 v Alberta Teachers' Association, Local* 55 (1998), 68 LAC (4th) 1 (Arbitrator: Sims) [*CRCSSD*]; *Re Upper Canada District School Board v Ontario Secondary School Teachers' Federation, District* 26 (2004), 126 LAC (4th) 158 (Arbitrator: Keller) [*UCDSB*].

106 *Independent Electricity*, above note 102.

107 *Ontario Nurses Association v Chatham-Kent (Municipality)* (2010), 202 LAC (4th) 1 (Arbitrator: Etherington).

108 *Toronto Transit Commission v Amalgamated Transit Union, Local* 113 (2004), 126 LAC (4th) 353 (Arbitrator: Shime); *Friolet v Treasury Board (Solicitor General of Canada — Correctional Service)*, 2002 PSSRB 85 (Arbitrator: Henry); *Toronto and CUPE*, above note 45.

109 *Employés du transport local et industries diverses c United Parcel Service Canada, local* 931, 2003 CanLII 25824 (QC CS). Note that the collective agreement expressly incorporated the *Charter* by reference. Foisy upheld the *Charter* claim.

*Charter* should be excluded under section 24(2);[110] claims that discipline for statements made by employees violated their freedom of expression under section 2(b);[111] and a claim by an employee that his freedom to not associate under section 2(d) was violated by a union shop security clause.[112] (In this latter case, the employee was given separate standing in the arbitration where the union sought an order forcing the employer to comply with the union shop clause by terminating the employee for refusing to become a union member.)

Two recent arbitration decisions demonstrate the potential significance of arbitral jurisdiction to apply the *Charter* in light of the Supreme Court of Canada's recent expansion of the scope of protection for collective bargaining activity under section 2(d) of the *Charter*. First, in *Alberta v Alberta Union of Provincial Employees*,[113] a three-person arbitration board considered a *Charter* challenge under section 2(d) that the provision of the Alberta *Public Service Employee Relations Act* which excluded many categories of public servants from any bargaining unit violated their freedom of association. It is clear that the grievance was filed after the *Health Services and Support-Facilities Subsector Bargaining Association v British*

110 *See International Brotherhood of Electrical Workers v Edmonton Power Inc* (1997), 69 LAC (4th) 283 (Arbitrator: Malone) and *Cape Breton (Regional Municipality) v Canadian Union of Public Employees, Local* 759 (1999), 84 LAC (4th) 106 (Arbitrator: MacLellan). Interestingly, both arbitrators distinguished *Weber* and held that they were not courts of competent jurisdiction under s 24 of the *Charter* because they were consensual arbitrators appointed under provincial legislation that required the parties to have a provision in the collective agreement to provide for final settlement of disputes without work stoppage, *by arbitration or otherwise*.

111 *Peel Board of Education v Ontario Secondary School Teachers' Federation (Fromm Grievance)*, [2002] OLAA No 154 (Arbitrator: Burkett); *Alberta Union of Provincial Employees v Alberta*, [1998] AGAA No 57, 61 CLAS 357 (Arbitrator: McFetridge); *British Columbia Public School Employers' Assn v British Columbia Teachers' Federation* (2004), 129 LAC (4th) 245 (Arbitrator: Munroe).

112 *Canada Post Corp and Canadian Union of Postal Workers (Safire), Re*, [1996] CLAD No 1156, 46 CLAS 252 (Arbitrator: Christie). There have been other cases, often search or surveillance cases where privacy interests are at issue, where arbitrators have held that although the *Charter* is not applicable to the dispute before them, their interpretation and application of arbitral doctrines should nevertheless take *Charter* values into account. See for example *West Lincoln Memorial Hospital v Christian Labour Association of Canada, Local* 302 (2004), 126 LAC (4th) 52 (Arbitrator: Luborsky).

113 (2011), 212 LAC (4th) 114 (Arbitrator: Jones), aff'd 2013 ABQB 83, rev'd 2014 ABCA 43.

*Columbia*[114] decision was rendered, but before *Fraser v Ontario (Attorney General)*[115] was decided. However, the case was argued and decided in the months immediately following the release of *Fraser*. The arbitrator provided a lengthy consideration of all of the Supreme Court of Canada's jurisprudence on freedom of association, and ultimately dismissed the grievance on the basis that the exclusions did not make it effectively impossible for the excluded employees to join together and make some form of collective representation to their employer, similar to what was upheld in *Fraser*.[116]

Second, in *Canadian Union of Public Employees, Local 835 v South Shore District Health Authority (Acute Health Care Restructuring Grievance) et al*,[117] Arbitrator Dorsey received a special statutory appointment

---

114 2007 SCC 27 [*BC Health*].

115 2011 SCC 20 [*Fraser*].

116 The decision of the arbitration panel on both the jurisdictional and *Charter* issues was initially upheld on judicial review but later quashed by the Court of Appeal for Alberta, above note 113. That court held that the board lacked jurisdiction because the *Charter* challenge was not related to the interpretation, application, administration or violation of the collective agreement, and the union lacked standing to bring the challenge on behalf of the excluded workers, who were not members of the bargaining unit or covered by the collective agreement.

117 [2014] NSLAA No 10 (Arbitrator: Dorsey). A year later in *Canadian Union of Public Employees, Local Unions 835, 1933, 2431, 2525, 4150 et al v South Shore District Health Authority et al*, online: www.nsnu.ca/site/media/nsnu/Health%20Authorities%20Act%20-%20Mediation%20Arbitration%20Decision(1).pdf, Dorsey rejected all of the unions' *Charter* submissions. He held that it was not unconstitutional for legislation to reconfigure bargaining units. In this regard, Dorsey cited the decision of the Court of Appeal of Quebec in *Confédération des syndicats nationaux v Québec (Procureur général)*, 2011 QCCA 1247, which upheld a large reduction in the number of bargaining units in Quebec's health care sector on the basis that the *Charter* does not protect any particular bargaining unit scheme. He concluded that the statutory limitations on union representation did not violate s 2(d) of the *Charter*, stating: "This limitation does not have the 'effect of making it impossible to act collectively to achieve workplace goals.' Nor does it prevent employees from maintaining their union membership or the formation of a union. An amalgamated successor union can be fashioned in a manner that respects employees' associational rights as advocated by the unions. . . .The *Health Authorities Act* does not deny or substantially interfere with employees' ability to associate or their access to engaging in meaningful negotiations with their employer through a collective bargaining process to attain their objectives" (at paras 625–28). His decision did not consider the January 2015 trilogy of Supreme Court of Canada decisions (below note 118, in particular *MPAO)*, that arguably significantly added to protections for freedom in

as a "mediator-arbitrator" to assist the government and four unions in implementing the restructuring of the nine existing district health care authorities into one single provincial authority, with only four, large province-wide bargaining units. The affected unions brought several *Charter* challenges before him, involving claims that the new regime violated the freedom of association of the affected workers in several different respects. The most far reaching claim, brought by only one union — the Nova Scotia Government Employees Union (NSGEU) — effectively sought an order or declaration that the entire restructuring process, including the powers given to the arbitrator to create new units, was inoperative as inconsistent with the section 2(d) rights of the affected workers, because it destroyed their existing bargaining rights. Arbitrator Dorsey rejected the argument that he had authority to grant the remedy sought by NSGEU — a declaration that the statutory provisions that established his authority were inoperative. However, he held that the Supreme Court of Canada's decisions on arbitral authority, including *Weber*, recognized his jurisdiction to determine the constitutional validity of a provision in the enabling statute and to grant specific *Charter* remedies of the type sought by the Canadian Union of Public Employees in relation to the interpretation and application of the enabling statute in a manner that balanced *Charter* values and statutory objectives.

These two decisions may foreshadow an increase in the number of arbitral cases dealing with freedom of association under the *Charter*, based on the Supreme Court of Canada's 2015 trilogy of decisions that increase the scope of *Charter* protection for concerted collective activity in pursuit of collective bargaining objectives.[118] For example, it is quite foreseeable that the broad recognition of the right to strike contained in the *Saskatchewan Federation of Labour v Saskatchewan* decision could allow a union to raise *Charter* issues in an arbitration dealing with discipline or damage claims arising from illegal strike activity.

---

the choice of union representation under s 2(d) of the *Charter*. A few months later, after an additional ruling by Arbitrator Dorsey on bargaining unit composition and representation rights, the Nova Scotia government (no doubt motivated by the trilogy) bargained an acceptable "council of unions" bargaining structure that basically allowed the four existing unions to retain their existing members and representation rights under the new provincial bargaining unit structure.

118 *Mounted Police Association of Ontario v Canada (Attorney General)*, 2015 SCC 1 [*MPAO*]; *Royal Canadian Mounted Police v Canada (Attorney General)*, 2015 SCC 2 [*Meredith*]; *Saskatchewan Federation of Labour v Saskatchewan*, 2015 SCC 4 [*SFL*].

## D. *WEBER*'S IMPACT ON THE JURISDICTIONAL DIVIDE BETWEEN ARBITRATION AND OTHER ADMINISTRATIVE TRIBUNALS

The decision in *Weber* left litigants with great uncertainty over whether it was intended to apply to potential overlaps in jurisdiction between arbitration and other administrative tribunals. Although the Court made no reference to this area of concern, its ruling on *Charter* claims made it inevitable that litigants would attempt to use it to argue for exclusive jurisdiction for arbitration over other statutory tribunals as well. If employees could be denied access to courts for claims concerning their fundamental *Charter* rights, why not for claims involving human rights or other employment-related statutes?

The spectre of an "exclusive jurisdiction" approach to determining jurisdiction as between arbitration and a statutory tribunal was raised by the Supreme Court of Canada's 2000 decision in *Regina Police*.[119] The case concerned a dispute over whether a police officer should be allowed to withdraw a resignation given in the face of threats of disciplinary action by the police chief. The union filed a grievance under the collective agreement which went to arbitration, but the arbitrator held that she lacked jurisdiction because the dispute was in essence about discipline, and matters of discipline and discharge were governed by the provincial *Police Act* and dealt with by adjudicative bodies created under that Act. The arbitrator's decision was upheld at the first level of review, but reversed by the Court of Appeal for Saskatchewan, which held that *Weber* meant exclusive jurisdiction should rest with arbitration.

The Supreme Court of Canada reversed the appeal decision and reinstated the arbitrator's ruling. In doing so, it held that the exclusive jurisdiction model adopted in *Weber* should be applied to determine jurisdictional disputes between two competing statutory regimes as well. If the essential character of the dispute as a factual matter arises explicitly or implicitly from the interpretation, application, administration or violation of the collective agreement, then exclusive jurisdiction rests with arbitration. However, where the competing forum is another statutory regime, the Court must ultimately decide whether the essential character of the dispute falls within the ambit of the collective agreement or within the other statutory scheme, and in doing so it must consider

119 Above note 19.

the intention of the legislature in creating that legislative scheme.[120] The decision did not appear to contemplate the possibility of concurrent or overlapping jurisdiction between the two statutory regimes.[121]

Although there were several attempts, both before and after *Regina Police*, to have courts recognize exclusive arbitral jurisdiction in the area of overlapping jurisdiction with other administrative tribunal processes, for the most part courts of appeal across the country declined to apply *Weber* to hold that arbitrators have exclusive jurisdiction where the legislature has given a statutory mandate to a public tribunal created under the statutory regime to enforce the legislation. Canadian courts have been particularly consistent in ruling in favour of concurrent jurisdiction in the case of overlaps with human rights tribunals. In several cases the courts pointed to access to justice concerns that could result from making access to a forum to enforce human rights contingent on union support.

Most notable of these early appellate court decisions, because it was issued shortly after *Regina Police*, was the Court of Appeal for Ontario decision in *Naraine v Ford Motor Co of Canada*.[122] The Court's reasons seriously challenged the applicability of *Weber's* exclusive jurisdiction approach in cases of overlap between arbitration and statutory human rights tribunals. The case involved a former employee, whose discharge for cause in 1985 was upheld by an arbitrator who did not apply the *Human Rights Code* or make any express findings on the grievor's allegations of discrimination. When a human rights board of inquiry upheld the grievor's complaint of discrimination in 1996 and ordered the employee reinstated, the employer appealed on the grounds that the arbitrator had exclusive jurisdiction over the dispute and claimed issue estoppel. Justice Abella expressed doubt about whether *Weber* was intended to apply to human rights disputes because of the fundamental, *quasi*-constitutional nature of human rights legislation. She went on to pay lip service to *Weber*

120 *Ibid* at paras 23–24.

121 The binary choice between exclusive jurisdiction for either arbitration or a *Police Act* tribunal set out in *Regina Police* continues to be the rule of the day in numerous subsequent arbitration awards dealing with whether an arbitrator or the applicable tribunal created under police legislation has exclusive jurisdiction. *See e.g., Durham Regional Police Association v Durham Regional Police Service (Turpin Grievance)*, [2009] OLAA No 411 (Arbitrator: Albertyn); *Toronto Police Services Board v Toronto Police Association* (2011), 202 LAC (4th) 113 (Arbitrator: Knopf); *Toronto Police Association v Toronto Police Services Board*, 2015 ONCA 188; *Edmonton (City) v Edmonton Police Association* (2012), 216 LAC (4th) 291 (Arbitrator: DP Jones).

122 (2001), 209 DLR (4th) 465, 110 ACWS (3d) 517 (Ont CA) [*Naraine*],

and *Regina Police* by holding that the essential character of the dispute before the arbitrator and the human rights commission "were separate and distinct, warranting consideration by separate adjudicative bodies."[123] In her view, the essence of the grievance related to the grievor's discharge and discipline, while the essence of the human rights complaint related to racial discrimination and harassment. This appeared to be little more than an attempt to recast *Weber* to allow for concurrent or overlapping jurisdiction in the human rights area.[124]

More importantly, Abella JA openly questioned the appropriateness of applying *Weber* in cases involving fundamental human rights because of the danger of making access to a forum to enforce individual rights contingent upon support by a collective entity. She noted that in an arbitration proceeding only the employer and the union have party status, and decisions to proceed rest with the union, and not the grievor. She also noted that human rights violations may be alleged against the union as well. She concluded that giving exclusive jurisdiction to arbitrators in that context could render chimerical the human rights of individual organized employees.[125]

---

123 *Ibid* at para 57.

124 *Ibid* at paras 57–60. The Court also noted that by giving authority to the Commission not to deal with a complaint where it felt it was appropriate to defer to processes available under another Act, the Ontario *Human Rights Code* demonstrated a legislative intent to favour a model of concurrent jurisdiction. This type of provision has been a common feature of human rights legislation in other jurisdictions in Canada.

125 *Ibid* at para 62. Justice Abella stated, "The unionized employee's interests are advanced by and through the union, which necessarily decides how the allegations should be represented or defended. Applying *Weber* so as to assign exclusive jurisdiction to labour arbitrators could therefore render chimerical the rights of individual unionized employees. This does not mean, however, that the availability of jurisdictional concurrency should be seen as encouraging 'forum' shopping. The jurisdictional outcome will depend upon the circumstances of each case, including the reasonableness of the union's conduct, the nature of the dispute, and the desirability of finality and consistency of result." The analysis in *Naraine* is similar to and draws on *Cadillac Fairview Corp v Saskatchewan (Board of Inquiry)* (1999), 173 DLR (4th) 609, [1999] 7 WWR 517 (CA), leave to appeal to SCC refused, [1999] SCCA No 492 (30 March 2000) [*Cadillac Fairview*], a case decided before *Regina Police*. That decision similarly appeared to pay lip service to *Weber* by describing the dispute before it as one concerning a human rights violation in its essential character. However, the Court placed greater significance on the fact that human rights have been recognized by the courts as *quasi*-constitutional rights which are fundamental, more important than other laws, do not have to be bargained and cannot be undermined

In *Naraine*, the Court of Appeal appeared to approve the adoption of a model of concurrent jurisdiction and to rely on a policy of deferral, based on the nature of the dispute and the conduct and results of the prior proceeding, to avoid undue multiplicity of proceedings. But perhaps most significant, the rationale adopted by the Court to support this approach mirrored the concerns expressed by the Court of Appeal for Ontario in *Weber* as the reason for not making *Charter* claims subject to the exclusive jurisdiction approach. As noted by other commentators, if the *quasi*-constitutional nature of individual human rights is important enough to require that individual employees have access to a separate forum to enforce those rights, then how can they be denied similar individual access for the enforcement of their even more fundamental constitutional *Charter* rights?[126]

Although the issue of the application of *Weber* to human rights disputes was argued by the Ontario Human Rights Commission before the Supreme Court of Canada in *Parry Sound*, the Court expressly declined to consider whether its conclusion that the arbitrator had jurisdiction to apply the *Human Rights Code* ousted the jurisdiction of the statutory commission.[127] The Court's ruling that all collective agreements henceforth must be deemed to incorporate the provisions of employment-related statutes that impose rights and obligations was clearly more significant than *Weber*, in terms of expanding arbitral jurisdiction and transforming the role of arbitration from private adjudication to a forum for enforcement of public statutory rights.[128] However, although that same expansion

---

by contract. The Court also noted the special procedures that applied to complaints under the public statutory regime, giving the human rights commission carriage of the complaint before the tribunal. These features of the statutory regime indicated that the legislature did not intend to grant exclusive jurisdiction to arbitration where such complaints could be made subject to support by the union as a precondition to having any access to a forum to protect human rights.

126 Alexandrowicz, above note 3.

127 *Parry Sound*, above note 4 at para 15.

128 This assessment of the significance of *Parry Sound* arises from both practice experience and a look at the volume of arbitral decisions that refer to and apply *Parry Sound*. In the last ten years there were 400 to 500 reported arbitral awards that referred to *Weber*. In that same time period there were between 800 and 900 awards that referred to *Parry Sound*. It should also be noted, however, that the Court's decision in *Isidore Garon ltée v Syndicat du bois ouvré de la region de Québec inc*, 2006 SCC 2 [*Isidore Garon*] created an important limitation on *Parry Sound*'s extension of arbitral jurisdiction. In *Isidore Garon*, the Court dealt with the decisions of two

of arbitral jurisdiction also significantly expanded the scope for overlapping jurisdiction between arbitration and statutory employment tribunals, the Court chose to postpone the decision on whether to apply the *Weber* approach to this area to a future case.[129]

The answer arrived a year later in somewhat dramatic fashion in *Morin*.[130] This decision appears to represent a considerable retreat from the position set out in *Regina Police*—that one should apply an exclusive jurisdiction approach in all cases where there is a potential for overlap between two statutory regimes.[131] *Morin* involved a 1997 agreement by the provincial teachers' unions to an amendment to provincial collective agreements with Quebec, under which teaching experience gained in 1996–97 would not receive credit for wage grid purposes. This amendment had a negative impact on the financial compensation to be received by a minority group comprised of younger and less experienced teachers. The younger teachers filed a complaint with the Quebec Human Rights

---

Quebec arbitrators that they had jurisdiction to consider claims for reasonable notice of termination under the *Civil Code of Quebec* (*CCQ*). Both employers had closed down their operations and simply provided the notice required under the Quebec *Act Respecting Labour Standards* (*ALS*). In both cases, the collective agreements did not include a plant closing provision. One agreement did have a clause requiring the employer to pay notice required under the *ALS* if employees were laid off for longer than six months; the other had no language concerning payment of termination payments. Although there was a split at the Superior Court level on the correctness of these two decisions, the Quebec Court of Appeal upheld the arbitrators' findings of jurisdiction in both cases, largely on the strength of *Parry Sound*. The Supreme Court of Canada held that substantive rules or rights from a statutory scheme that is incompatible with the collective labour relations regime cannot be incorporated into the collective agreement, and therefore do not come within the jurisdiction of a grievance arbitrator appointed under the agreement. If a rule in a statutory provision governing the individual employment relationship is compatible with the collective bargaining regime, and it is a supplementary or mandatory norm, then the arbitrator will have jurisdiction to apply it. Thus, not everything set out in the *CCQ* or other employment-related statutes is implicitly incorporated into collective agreements—only those parts of the statute that are compatible with the collective agreement scheme.

129 Some commentators have suggested that the decision implicitly supports a concurrent jurisdiction approach. *See* Lokan & Yachnin, above note 3, at 24. The decision of the Court of Appeal for British Columbia in *Canpar Industries v International Union of Operating Engineers, Local 115* (2003), 2003 BCCA 609, tends to support that view.

130 *Morin*, above note 6.

131 This is certainly the position taken by Bastarache J in a strong dissenting opinion supported by Arbour J.

Commission claiming that the amendment discriminated against them on the basis of age contrary to the Quebec *Charter of Human Rights and Freedoms*.[132] The Commission referred the complaint to the Quebec Human Rights Tribunal, where the Attorney General of Quebec, the school boards, and the teacher unions and their federations asked the Tribunal to find that it had no jurisdiction because the dispute was within the exclusive jurisdiction of labour arbitration pursuant to *Weber* and *Regina Police*. The Court of Appeal of Quebec ruled in their favour, but its decision was reversed by the Supreme Court of Canada in a majority decision authored by Chief Justice McLachlin.

The very different tenor of the *Morin* decision is signalled by the following quotation from the early part of McLachlin CJC's opinion. After setting out the overlapping, concurrent and exclusive jurisdiction models discussed in *Weber*, she observed:

> *Weber* holds that the model that applies in a given situation depends on the governing legislation, as applied to the dispute viewed in its factual matrix. . . . However, *Weber* does not stand for the proposition that labour arbitrators always have exclusive jurisdiction in employer-union disputes. Depending on the legislation and the nature of the dispute, other tribunals may possess overlapping jurisdiction, concurrent jurisdiction, or themselves be endowed with exclusive jurisdiction.[133]

The chief justice went on to caution that we should not start with a presumption of exclusive jurisdiction for arbitrators when dealing with other statutory regimes. Rather, in each case we must ask "whether the relevant legislation applied to the dispute at issue, taken in its full factual context, establishes that the labour arbitrator has exclusive jurisdiction over the dispute."[134] And to answer this question we must perform a two-step analysis, first examining the relevant legislation and what it says about arbitral jurisdiction, and second looking at the nature of the dispute to see whether the legislation suggests that it falls exclusively to the arbitrator. Taking the first step, McLachlin CJC looked at the provisions of both the labour legislation and the human rights statute and noted that the Quebec *Charter* openly acknowledged the possibility of concurrent jurisdiction with other tribunals. Moving on to the second step, she noted that the focus should be on "whether the dispute, viewed in its essen-

132 *Charter of human rights and freedoms*, CQLR, c C-12 [Quebec *Charter*].

133 *Morin*, above note 6 at para 11. The majority opinion was supported by five justices.

134 *Ibid* at para 14.

tial character and not formalistically, is one over which the legislature intended the arbitrator to have exclusive jurisdiction."[135] The analysis in McLachlin CJC's reasoning at this second step is notable for a glaring omission. When comparing the essential nature of the dispute in *Weber* with the dispute in *Morin*, she referred twice to the dispute in *Weber* as one concerning a claim for tort arising from the employer's alleged trespass on the employee's land in the course of a dispute about sick-leave under the collective agreement. On both occasions she failed to mention that *Weber* was also a claim for damages for breach of privacy rights under sections 7 and 8 of the *Charter*.[136] I can only assume that the failure to mention the *Charter* claims in *Weber* anywhere in her opinion was deliberate, given the similarities with the *Morin* case in terms of claims for violation of fundamental individual rights. It was also central to her analysis, because she described the critical difference between *Weber* and *Morin* as lying within the factual context that gave rise to the disputes, and not in the labour relations legislation governing arbitration in the two provinces. She described the *Morin* dispute as being essentially a dispute as to how the collective agreement should allocate decreased resources among union members, which gave rise to the issue of whether it was discriminatory to negotiate and agree to a term that adversely affected only younger and less experienced teachers. Although this would clearly appear to fall within subject areas with which arbitrators are familiar,[137]

135 *Ibid* at para 20.

136 *Ibid* at paras 21–22. McLachlin CJC's omission to mention the *Charter* issue in *Weber* appears quite disingenuous, given that the Court of Appeal for Ontario had upheld exclusive arbitral jurisdiction over the common law claims but reinstated the plaintiff's action based on *Charter* rights. This meant that the main impact of the Supreme Court of Canada's ruling in favour of the employer was the striking out of the plaintiff's *Charter* claim. This was the only issue on which the Supreme Court of Canada differed from the Court of Appeal, which made totally implausible any suggestion that the Supreme Court of Canada's decision in *Weber* was not about the right of an individual organized worker to enforce *Charter* rights in the courts. Bastarache J made this point very clearly in his dissent. He also noted that the collective agreement at issue in *Morin* contained a typical human rights clause guaranteeing to the teachers the full exercise of rights under the *Quebec Charter*.

137 Arbitrators frequently have to look at negotiation history evidence to settle disputes about the meaning of agreement language or whether one party should be estopped from enforcing contractual rights. They also have been asked on many occasions to determine whether collective agreement language violated human rights legislation or *Charter* guarantees of equality. *See e.g.*, *Peel*, above note 101; *CRCSSD*, above note 105; *USDSB*, above note 105.

the Chief Justice concluded that this was not a dispute over which the arbitrator had exclusive jurisdiction because it did not arise out of the operation of the collective agreement so much as out of the pre-contractual negotiation of that agreement.[138] This led her to conclude that the dispute, viewed in its essential nature,

> [p]ertain[s] more to alleged discrimination in the formation and validity of the agreement, than to its "interpretation or application," which is the source of the arbitrator's jurisdiction under the *Labour Code*, s. 1(f). The Human Rights Commission and the Human Rights Tribunal were created by the legislature to resolve precisely these sorts of issues.[139]

These attempts to distinguish *Morin* from *Weber* as a factual matter are unconvincing in almost every respect. As Bastarache J noted in his dissent, *Weber* also included a claim for violation of fundamental constitutional rights under sections 7 and 8 of the *Charter*.[140] As Bastarache J also noted, it was *the result* of the negotiations—the offending amended clause in the collective agreement—that was challenged by the complaint, not the talks themselves. The essential character of the dispute concerned pay and whether teaching experience during the 1996–97 school year should be taken into account to determine pay levels, which is part of the foundation of collective agreement terms setting out working conditions.

What then really led the majority to retreat from an exclusive jurisdiction approach in this case? The explanation for this apparent about-face

---

138 McLachlin CJC relied on *Goudie* for the proposition that disputes that arise out of prior contracts or the formation of the collective agreement itself may raise issues that do not fall within the scope of arbitration. As discussed at note 19 above, *Goudie* is clearly a case which could have been decided either way, given what arbitrators have traditionally been asked to do in terms of resolving disputes arising from pre-collective agreement representations. By contrast, the type of dispute at issue in *Morin*, namely whether the actions of one party or another in negotiations should make a clause in question unenforceable, has long been a matter on which arbitrators are asked to rule.

139 *Morin*, above note 6 at para 25. Interestingly, in the next paragraph the Chief Justice held that the nature of the dispute did not lend itself to characterization as a grievance under the collective agreement because the claim was that the agreement itself was discriminatory. Yet the arbitration reports are full of just this type of grievance and, as noted by Bastarache J. in his dissent, the collective agreement at issue contained a typical human rights clause guaranteeing to the teachers the full exercise of rights under the *Quebec Charter*.

140 *Ibid* at para 56.

comes in the last two pages of the majority's decision, providing three additional reasons for declining to find exclusive arbitral jurisdiction. First, after noting that the unions in this case were possibly opposed in interest to the complainants because they were affiliated with the federations that agreed to the offending amendment, the majority expressly adopted the concerns stated by the Court of Appeal for Ontario in *Naraine*: that the individual claimant employees could be left without meaningful legal recourse to enforce their individual statutory rights if the union chose not to refer a grievance to arbitration on their behalf.[141] Second, the majority expressed concerns that even if a grievance reached arbitration, the teacher federations and government ministry that negotiated the amendment at the provincial level would not be subject to the jurisdiction of the arbitrator, as the parties to such arbitration would be the local unions and school boards. Given the numerous decisions involving tort and *Charter* claims by unionized employees in which the courts have said they are not concerned that third parties responsible for the harm may not be made subject to arbitral jurisdiction as long as the grievor may be able to claim redress against some employer entity, this seems like a tremendous change of heart. Finally, the majority also held that because the complaints involved a general challenge to the collective agreement that could affect hundreds of teachers, the provincial Human Rights Tribunal "was a 'better fit' for this dispute than the appointment of a single arbitrator to deal with a single grievance" under the *Labour Code*.[142] However, this can be said to be a common feature of many *Charter* claims. It was also true of the issues at stake in the class action dealt with in *Bisaillon* two years later, but that did not help the plaintiffs in that case to gain access to the courts.[143]

It is most significant that the last three reasons offered for the Court's change in direction appear to be directed to concerns about *access to justice* and *institutional appropriateness* for the effective enforcement of the rights in issue — the very interests the Court refused to acknowledge in *Weber* in its single-minded pursuit of adjudicative efficiency. These differences are graphically displayed by contrasting the majority's reasons with the dissenting opinion of Bastarache J, which once again insisted

141 *Ibid* at para 28. In making this point, the majority quoted the passages from *Naraine* that are set out in note 125 above.

142 *Ibid* at para 30.

143 See discussion at note 70 above.

that in all cases we must "determine the essential character of the issue and find one single entity to handle it."[144] In the dissenting judges' view, even if the problem in *Morin* could be characterized exclusively as a human rights violation, it would still be subject to the arbitrator's exclusive jurisdiction because it was an issue that was expressly or inferentially linked to the collective agreement.[145] In essence, the dissenting position was that in any case where the arbitrator would have had jurisdiction to rule on the grievance if it had been brought in that forum, it should be found to be the subject of exclusive arbitral jurisdiction. This point of view speaks only to the pursuit of adjudicative efficiency and the concern that allowing for concurrent jurisdiction would do violence to the comprehensive statutory scheme and undermine arbitration.

The extent of the emerging rift among members of the Court on its application of *Weber* to potential overlap between statutory regimes was further revealed in the decision in *Quebec (Attorney General) v Quebec (Human Rights Tribunal),*[146] released the same day as *Morin*. Although this case did not deal with a collective agreement or arbitration as one of two possible forums for the pursuit of legal rights, it nevertheless illustrates radically different approaches to questions of overlap in jurisdiction between two statutory regimes. The majority position was comprised of two separate opinions, each supported by two justices, and appeared to endorse a return to the *Weber/Regina Police* approach in holding that the provincial Commission des affaires sociales (CAS) had exclusive jurisdiction over a claim that a feature of the low-income social benefits program discriminated against women on maternity leave and thus discriminated on the basis of sex and pregnancy contrary to the *Quebec Charter*. The majority held that the Quebec Human Rights Commission lacked jurisdiction to consider a complaint in connection with the denial of benefits to the complainant by the CAS. The dissenting opinion, written by McLachlin CJC, was consistent with her reasons in *Morin* and supported by two members of the majority in that case. These dissenting reasons provided an even more open endorsement of a concurrent or overlapping jurisdiction approach when the dispute can be characterized as also raising clear human rights issues, despite statutory language in

144 *Morin*, above note 6 at para 71.
145 *Ibid* at para 67.
146 2004 SCC 40 [*CAS*].

the *Income Security Act* indicating an intention to give exclusive jurisdiction to the CAS.[147]

The conflicting opinions of different groupings of the members of the Court in *Morin* and *CAS* appear to indicate different perspectives on the importance of adjudicative efficiency concerns, as opposed to access to justice and institutional appropriateness concerns. For those of us who have criticized *Weber* and its progeny for failing to give adequate weight to the latter two concerns, the majority opinion in *Morin* and the dissent in *CAS* offer some hope that the debate has been reopened. This already appears to have been true in the case of overlapping jurisdiction with human rights tribunals and one would think that, by analogy, this should also provide an opportunity to reconsider the appropriateness of an exclusive jurisdiction approach to claims under the *Charter*.

In the years since *Morin* was decided, concurrency has clearly been accepted across Canada as the general approach to be followed in dealing with human rights issues.[148] Several court of appeal decisions in differ-

---

147 This was also the position of the dissent, in spite of the fact that there was no union or other collective that might render it impossible for the complainant to access the CAS appeal processes. This latter difference from *Morin*, and the fact there were no third parties involved that would not be subject to CAS jurisdiction, led two members of the *Morin* majority to agree with Bastarache J that the CAS had exclusive jurisdiction, despite the expertise of the Human Rights Commission on such issues. *Ibid* at paras 42–43.

148 I recognize that Elizabeth Shilton has taken the position that *Morin*, properly interpreted, does not suggest a presumption in favour of concurrency for arbitrators and human rights tribunals but rather leaves us with a multi-factor inquiry that has to be applied on a case-by-case basis to decide whether arbitrators or tribunals have exclusive jurisdiction. *See* Elizabeth Shilton, "Choice, but No Choice: Adjudicating Human Rights Claims in Unionized Workplaces in Canada" (2013) 38:2 *Queen's Law Journal* 461. I disagree with her on this point, mainly because, if you apply the factors identified in *Morin* to any human rights legislation in effect in Canada, you are left with a conclusion of concurrency. I also contend that the proof of my analysis is in the decisions of courts, tribunals and arbitrators across the country that have applied *Morin* to find concurrency in all cases. But I of course share the concerns she expresses about the problems that can arise for human rights complainants in a situation of concurrency, where there is reliance on deferral and tribunal authority to refuse to deal with a human rights claim on the grounds that it has been appropriately dealt with in arbitration. *See* Shilton at 495–502. I would also note that the Human Rights Tribunal of Ontario decisions in *Paterno v Salvation Army*, 2011 HRTO 2298 (CanLII) and *Paterno v Governing Council of the Salvation Army in Canada*, 2012 HRTO 205 (CanLII) appear to be outliers, in that they are the only cases I am aware of where the arbitrator accepted the employer's argument that he

ent provinces have applied *Morin* as endorsing concurrent jurisdiction between arbitrators and human rights processes.[149] In some cases, the courts indicated that one should start with a presumption of concurrent or overlapping jurisdiction in the case of competition between arbitral and statutory tribunal jurisdiction unless there is express statutory language to rebut that presumption.[150] In other cases they have pointed to the fundamental *quasi*-constitutional nature of human rights law as a further justification for concurrent jurisdiction, again unless there is very clear and express language to indicate otherwise.[151] Many human rights statutes across the country clearly contemplate concurrent jurisdiction with other tribunals, such as arbitration, in that they provide mechanisms for the deferral and dismissal of a complaint where it has already been dealt with appropriately in another forum.[152] And clearly

---

had to take jurisdiction over the human rights issues attached to the discharge of the grievor, over the objections of the union and the grievor.

149 *See e.g.*, *Amalgamated Transit Union, Local 583 v Calgary (City)*, 2007 ABCA 121. The Court cited *Morin*'s approval of the holding in *Naraine* that exclusive arbitral jurisdiction was not appropriate for human rights complaint matters, as discussed at note 125 above.

150 In *Calgary Health Region v Alberta (Human Rights & Citizenship Commission)*, 2007 ABCA 120, the Court of Appeal once again ruled in favour of concurrent jurisdiction. Here the grievor was terminated during her probationary period. The union filed a grievance alleging violation of the collective agreement, bad faith and discrimination contrary to the anti-discrimination clause in the agreement. Ten days later the grievor filed a human rights complaint claiming that the employer discriminated against her on the grounds of physical disability (Chronic Fatigue Syndrome) and mental disability (depression). The employer argued exclusive arbitral jurisdiction; the union argued concurrent jurisdiction and requested that the arbitration board defer the hearing pending the outcome of the human rights complaint. The arbitrator applied *Morin* to rule in favour of concurrent jurisdiction but refused to defer to the human rights process because he thought the arbitration process was a better fit given the nature of the dispute. On judicial review the Superior Court held that this was a case for exclusive arbitral jurisdiction. The Court of Appeal for Alberta endorsed the arbitrator's rulings and in effect appears to have created a presumption, relying on *Morin*, that one of the non-exclusive jurisdictional outcomes would generally apply in the absence of legislative language pointing clearly to exclusivity. In that case, concurrency was the proper approach.

151 *Nova Scotia (Human Rights Commission) v Halifax (Regional Municipality)*, 2008 NSCA 21 (relying on *Cadillac Fairview*, above note 125 on this point).

152 *See e.g.*, Ontario *Human Rights Code*, RSO 1990, c H-19, ss 34, 45.1. The Tribunal has jurisdiction to dismiss an application under s 45.1 on the basis of other proceedings only if it finds that the substance of the application has been appropriately

this is the manner in which Ontario arbitrators and Human Rights Tribunal of Ontario (HRTO) vice-chairs have interpreted these provisions and the *Morin* decision. When confronted with motions to adjourn and defer to the other process with concurrent jurisdiction, arbitrators have looked at very pragmatic considerations concerning access to justice, fairness, efficiency, expertise of the decision-makers, prejudice to the parties, the likelihood of inconsistent results and duplication of efforts, the status of the proceeding in each forum and which forum has the broader jurisdiction to resolve all of the issues at play.[153] Similarly, there are numerous decisions of HRTO vice-chairs considering motions to defer to grievance and arbitration procedures. Once again all of these decisions approach

---

dealt with by another proceeding. Both of these discretionary powers, deferral and dismissal, are provided for in a way that contemplates concurrent jurisdiction in another proceeding, and there is nothing in the legislation that appears to contemplate that another proceeding or tribunal would have exclusive jurisdiction so as to oust the HRTO.

153 *See e.g., Ontario Public Service Employees Union v Ontario (Ministry of Community Safety and Correctional Services) (Therrien Grievance)* (2008), 173 LAC (4th) 193 (Arbitrator: Lynk); *Ontario Public Service Employees Union v Ontario (Ministry of Finance) (O'Connor Grievance),* [2010] OGSBA No 156 (Arbitrator: Lynk); *Ontario Public Service Employees Union v Ontario (Ministry of Community and Social Services) (Barllari Grievance),* [2008] OGSBA No 54 (Arbitrator: Carrier); *Ontario Public Service Employees Union v Ontario (Liquor Control Board of Ontario) (Crowley Grievance) (Re),* [2010] OGSBA No 124 (Arbitrator: Kirkwood); *Kawartha Pine Ridge District School Board v Ontario Secondary School Teachers' Federation, District 14* (2010), 197 LAC (4th) 83 (Arbitrator: Knopf); *Paragon Health Care Inc (Receiver and Manager of) v Service Employees International Union, Local 1 (Markland Grievance),* [2011] OLAA No 313 (Arbitrator: Kaplan); *University Health Network v Ontario Nurses' Association (Vedd Grievance)* (2007), 159 LAC (4th) 298 (Arbitrator: Marcotte). In the latter case the arbitrator expressly rejected the employer submission that he take exclusive jurisdiction over the human rights issues, holding that the law did not allow him to oust concurrent HRTO jurisdiction. *See also Bayshore Home Health v Service Employees International Union, Local 1 (Pidgeon Grievance),* [2011] OLAA No 3 (Arbitrator: Randall) and *British Columbia (Ministry of Provincial Revenue) v British Columbia Government and Servie Employees Union) (Chang)* (2009), 181 LAC (4th) 278 (Arbitrator: Hope). In the latter case the arbitrator accepted the employer's motion to dismiss the grievance on the basis that the British Columbia Human Rights Tribunal had ruled against the grievor's human rights complaint, which dealt with the same facts and issues. He relied on the principle of collateral attack from *Toronto (City) v Canadian Union of Public Employees, Local 79*, 2003 SCC 63. In all cases it was recognized that the arbitrators shared concurrent jurisdiction with human rights tribunals.

the case from the premise of concurrent jurisdiction, and make deferral decisions based on pragmatic considerations of fairness, expedition, efficiency and the avoidance of duplication and inconsistent results.[154]

Rulings in favour of concurrent jurisdiction are also common in many, if not most, areas of overlap with other statutory processes. Arbitrators have frequently held that they have concurrent jurisdiction in cases involving issues arising under legislation concerning occupational health and safety,[155] pay equity,[156] labour relations,[157] privacy[158] and pensions. [159] In the area of pensions, however, when the pension dispute arose out of the collective agreement in some fashion, as suggested by *Bisaillon*, there has been a significant lack of consensus among the decisions on arbitral jurisdiction. This may indicate a lack of familiarity and comfort in dealing with some of the complexities of the laws regulating pensions.[160]

---

154 *See e.g., Aubin v Waterloo (Regional Municipality)*, 2008 HRTO 214 (CanLII). "The tribunal will generally defer an application where there is an ongoing grievance under the collective agreement based on the same facts and issues. However, the Tribunal must also consider, in light of the particular circumstances of each case, whether deferral is the most fair, just and expeditious way of proceeding with the application." *Ibid* at para 4. The application in this case was deferred because the union had referred the grievances to arbitration.

155 *See e.g., Central Care Corp v Service Employees International Union, Local 1.on*, 2006 CarswellOnt 4182 (WL Can) (Arbitrator: Levinson); *Valard Construction LP and Canadian Union of Skilled Workers (De Vries), Re*, [2014] AWLD 1267, 117 CLAS 230 (Arbitrator: Alexander-Smith).

156 *See e.g., Chatham-Kent Board of Health and Ontario Nurses' Association, Re* (2006), 85 CLAS 144 (Arbitrator: Crljenica).

157 *See e.g., Millwrights & Machine Erectors, Local 2309 v International Brotherhood of Electrical Workers, Local* 353, [2005] CLAD No 175, 81 CLAS 146 (Arbitrator: MacDowell); *Expertech Network Installation Inc and Community, Energy and Paperworkers Union of Canada* (2006), 87 CLAS 361 (Arbitrator: Surdykowski).

158 *Ontario and OPSEU*, above note 77; *Canadian Union of Public Employees, Local 133 v Niagara Falls (City)*, [2005] OLAA No 228, 81 CLAS 1, MacDowell; *Kawartha Pine Ridge District School Board v Elementary Teachers' Federation of Ontario*, above note 90.

159 *Greater Essex District School Board and Ontario Secondary School Teachers Federation (OMERS Pension Plan), Re* (2015), 256 LAC (4th) 1 (Arbitrator: MacDowell). *See also PPG Canada Inc v Ontario (Superintendent Financial Services)*, 2015 ONFST 10. The latter ruling is really one that recognizes partial concurrency, holding that the pension legislation at issue gave the pension regulator exclusive jurisdiction over some issues, such as the approval of the pension plan wind up report.

160 *See e.g., West Parry Sound Health Centre and Ontario Nurses' Association (Pension Contributions), Re*, [2008] OLAA No 705, 96 CLAS 122, 2008 CanLII 66136 (ON

Workers' compensation involves similar difficulties in that most legislation in this area establishes exclusive jurisdiction for workers' compensation tribunals over the issues of whether there has been a workplace injury or illness. However several arbitrators have indicated that they may have concurrent jurisdiction over related issues, such as harassment arising from the reporting of a workplace injury or illness.[161]

## E. CONCLUSION

What *Weber* and most of its offspring could and should have done was to develop a principled, yet pragmatic and functional, approach to deciding questions of appropriate forum in cases of concurrent and overlapping jurisdiction. The single-minded drive displayed in *Weber*, *Regina Police* and *Bisaillon* to apply an "exclusive jurisdiction" approach to all areas of potential overlap focused almost exclusively on considerations of adjudicative efficiency and finality. Although there was also reference to concerns about not undermining arbitration as the legislative choice for resolving workplace disputes under the collective bargaining regime, there was no real threat of this happening at the time *Weber* was decided,

---

LA) (Arbitrator: Parmar); *Grand River Hospital Corp v Ontario Nurses' Association* (2010), 200 LAC (4th) 363 (Arbitrator: Howe); *Rouge Valley Health System and Ontario Nurses' Association*, [2013] OLAA No 57, 114 CLAS 77, 2013 CanLII 8011 (ON LA) (Arbitrator: Stout). In all three cases the arbitrators declined to take jurisdiction over grievances claiming that the employer had failed to make appropriate pension contributions for part-time nurses based on certain types of hours that attracted premium rates, despite the fact that the collective agreement referred to the pension plan and gave part-time nurses the option to enroll in it or receive a percentage in lieu. All three arbitrators held that they did not have jurisdiction because the dispute in its essential nature arose from the pension plan, not from the collective agreement. Even in the *Greater Essex DSB and OSSTF* case referred to at note 159 above, although arbitrator MacDowell held that he had concurrent jurisdiction, he chose to defer to the expertise of the decision-makers under the *Pension Benefits Act*, RSO 1990, c P.8 and the *Ontario Municipal Employees Retirement System Act*, RSO 1990, c 0.29, remaining seized in the event that the union was not able to get an appropriate hearing in the other process.

161 See *e.g.*, *Manitoba and Manitoba General Employees Union (St Hilaire), Re* (2010), 102 CLAS 126 (Arbitrator: Gibson); *Valard Construction LP and Canadian Union of Skilled Workers (De Vries), Re*, [2014] AWLD 1267, 117 CLAS 230 (Arbitrator: Alexander-Smith); *Edmonton Police Service v Edmonton Police Association*, 2015 CanLII 39179 (AB GAA) (Arbitrator: Sims).

or at any time since. Even prior to *Weber*, arbitration was already becoming the chosen — and in the view of some, too popular — forum to pursue *Charter*, human rights and other employment-related statute claims. The reasons for that popularity are obvious given the cost, expense and delay for the average individual to pursue those claims elsewhere on her own. So there was no need to bolster the demand for resort to arbitration to resolve workplace rights disputes.

Nor would I ever suggest that we should attempt to prevent arbitration from having jurisdiction to play the important role it has played in recent years as an available forum for the resolution of such rights.[162] The advantages of allowing the parties to have recourse to arbitration to have their disputes decided in a manner that reflects our most fundamental rights and freedoms remain as true today as they did in 1990 when the Supreme Court of Canada recognized those advantages in *Douglas College*. The problems arose when the intent of expanding jurisdiction over *Charter* issues recognized in that decision was turned on its head by *Weber*'s attempt to limit the adjudicative *fora* available to hear the *Charter* claims of individual, organized workers.

The problem with the *Weber* approach from the outset was its failure to consider the access to justice and institutional appropriateness concerns that arise from making collective bargaining institutions — designed for the effective pursuit of collective interests — the exclusive mechanism for the enforcement of fundamental, individual constitutional and statutory rights, and certain common law rights. The access to justice and institutional concerns raised by imposing on organized workers a system that makes unions the gatekeepers to enforcement of these rights have been recognized by some courts, despite *Weber*'s failure even to mention them. The Court of Appeal for Ontario's decisions in *Weber* and *Naraine*, and perhaps most importantly the Supreme Court of Canada majority opinion in *Morin*, represent the most significant judicial recognition of the need to balance these concerns with adjudicative efficiency interests in order to allow for concurrent or overlapping jurisdiction in appropriate cases. Similarly, the reasons of Arbitrator Picher in *Seneca College* gave articulate expression to the access to justice and institutional appropriateness

162 I have never felt otherwise, despite the reservations I have expressed elsewhere that the privatization and collectivization of the enforcement of public individual rights presents significant concerns about access to justice, and effective protection and enforcement of such rights. See Brian Etherington, "Promises, Promises: Notes on Diversity and Access to Justice" (2000) 26:1 *Queen's Law Journal* 43.

concerns that should be considered in determining whether arbitrators should be granted exclusive jurisdiction over tort claims by employees. That decision is invaluable for stating the very real dangers to the future viability and long-term success of unions and grievance arbitration as institutions to resolve collective bargaining disputes if the *Weber* approach to exclusive jurisdiction is followed blindly.

In my view these decisions, and in particular *Morin*, have provided the springboard for a rethinking of our approach to dealing with issues of potential overlaps in jurisdiction, especially in the area of *Charter* claims. What is required is a multi-factored analysis to determine whether a particular type of dispute should be subject to exclusive arbitral jurisdiction or should allow for overlapping or concurrent jurisdiction.[163] I propose that the following factors should be addressed in approaching issues of overlapping or concurrent jurisdiction if we are to have a truly principled, functional and pragmatic approach that also addresses access to justice and institutional appropriateness concerns.

1) *The nature of the rights at issue*. Are the rights being asserted primarily of a private and collective nature? Or are they primarily individual statutory or constitutional rights? If the rights are fundamental, public individual rights of a constitutional or *quasi*-constitutional nature, then we probably should not make their protection or enforcement subject to exclusive control by private collective procedures such as union-controlled grievance procedures, or arbitration processes controlled by unions and employers.[164] In such cases concurrency should be the rule of the day, as we have seen in the human rights area of overlap.
2) *The intention of the parties*. Looked at both subjectively and objectively, is it the kind of dispute that the parties would have contemplated as being dealt with exclusively by arbitration?[165] In this respect, I cannot imagine that before *Weber* any employers or unions contemplated the possibility that agreeing to collective agreement language concerning harassment in the workplace would preclude all employees in the unit from access to courts to protect their *Charter* rights and freedoms.

163 I note in this respect that even before *Morin* was decided, other commentators called for development of a policy of deferral to replace the exclusive jurisdiction approach. *See especially* Alexandrowicz, above note 3 at 281–82.

164 *See e.g.*, the decisions of Arbour J in the Court of Appeal for Ontario in *Weber Ont CA*, above note 1, Abella J in *Naraine*, above note 122, and McLachlin J in *Morin*, above note 6 and the discussion of these decisions above.

165 *See Seneca Arbitration Decision*, above note 48.

Similarly, I cannot imagine that before *Giorno* any employer or union could say, with any honesty, that they contemplated the possibility that agreeing to a health and safety clause could bar employees from access to courts to pursue defamation actions against third party employees not in the bargaining unit or in a managerial capacity.

3) *The essential character of the dispute.*[166] Is the dispute of a kind that bargaining concerns are, or should be, central to its resolution? Is it the type of issue that is normally addressed in collective bargaining or grievance and arbitration proceedings?[167] Is it essentially a dispute about terms and conditions of employment, or the enforcement and application of terms of the collective agreement, or representations by one party to the other?[168]
4) *Access to justice concerns.* What are the implications for access by the claimant to a forum with the jurisdiction and authority to grant effective redress for the enforcement of the rights at issue of granting exclusive jurisdiction to arbitration? Will a grant of exclusive jurisdiction raise a real threat of denial of access to justice to protect individual rights of the organized employee? In *Giorno*, for example, as discussed earlier, the Court seemed to ignore the prospect that the employee might fail on a grievance because she could not prove a threat to health and safety despite the fact she had been the subject of defamation, with the result that she was denied any forum for vindication of her common law rights.

---

166 I note that this continues to be one of the most easily manipulated criteria from the original *Weber* test and leads to result-oriented or declaratory reasoning. Examples are McLachlin CJC's ability to characterize Mr Weber's concerns about the invasion of his and his wife's privacy in their home by a third party as arising from the collective agreement, but subsequently finding in *Morin* that a human rights complaint that a collective agreement was discriminatory did not arise from the collective agreement, but rather from the negotiations preceding the agreement. Similarly, in *Bisaillon* the majority found that concerns about employer contributions to the pension plan in their essential nature arose from the collective agreement, while the dissent found they were essentially issues that arose from the pension plan. However, I think it remains a relevant criterion.

167 It has long been accepted that arbitrators should have exclusive jurisdiction over these types of disputes as a central feature of an industrial pluralist approach to our collective bargaining regime. *See McGavin Toastmaster Ltd v Ainscough*, [1975] 1 SCR 718, 54 DLR (3d) 1 [*McGavin Toastmaster*] and *St Anne-Nackawic*, above note 8.

168 *See* the discussion of *Goudie* at note 19 above. *See also Canadian National Railway v Beatty* (1981), 34 OR (2d) 385, 28 DLR (3d) 236 (Div Ct).

5) *Institutional appropriateness concerns*. Are the claims in dispute of a type that arbitrators are accustomed to dealing with and have the necessary expertise and resources to resolve successfully? Is the forum capable of dealing with procedural problems raised by the type of claims being made in the dispute, such as adding parties?[169] In this regard, we should also question whether we want arbitrators, who are essentially private adjudicators dependent for their future employment on their continued mutual acceptability with the parties to collective bargaining — employers and unions — to have exclusive jurisdiction in the first instance over the development of fundamental, individual public rights.[170]
6) *The impact on the long term health and viability of collective bargaining institutions like arbitration and unions of giving them exclusive jurisdiction to deal with the type of individual rights dispute at issue*. Most unions are not enamoured with the prospect of having exclusive jurisdiction to decide whether to proceed with defamation or other intentional tort actions against employers, managers or co-workers, especially workers in the same bargaining unit. They are similarly not enamoured with being turned into private tort law commissions or private *Charter* commissions that provide the only means of bringing a tort claim or *Charter* claim forward for all employees in the unit. For most unions, the burden of ensuring the enforcement of collective agreement rights is seen as more than sufficient to demand all of their financial and personnel resources. The downloading of sole responsibility for the costs of enforcing public statutory rights, from government institutions to unions, is a serious concern for most unions.[171]
7) *Adjudicative efficiency concerns and finality*. What are the implications of allowing a concurring or overlapping jurisdiction approach in terms of adjudicative and party resources, including cost, delay and other

169 *See* the majority reasons in *Morin*, above note 6.

170 Note that Donald Carter expressed similar concerns about the *Weber* approach and proposed a more functional approach that takes into account institutional appropriateness concerns. Carter, above note 3.

171 These developments would also seem to reinforce the concerns expressed by many critical legal scholars in the 1970s and 1980s that unions were at risk of being co-opted as junior management in the workplace through their control over the grievance arbitration process. *See* Harry Glasbeek, "Voluntarism, Liberalism, and Grievance Arbitration: Holy Grail, Romance, and Real Life" in Geoffrey England, ed, *Essays in Labour Relations Law* (Don Mills, ON: CCH, 1986) 57.

multiplicity of proceeding concerns? Can such concerns be dealt with or managed effectively by applying a policy of deferral and issue estoppel premised on the type of context-based approach to balancing access to justice and efficiency concerns found in the Supreme Court of Canada's decision in *Danyluk v Ainsworth Technologies Inc*?[172]

8) *Concerns about undermining arbitration as the primary method of resolving workplace disputes in a collective bargaining context.* Would allowing concurrent or overlapping jurisdiction provide a serious threat to the future viability and acceptance of arbitration as the primary dispute resolution mechanism? This concern probably could be dropped altogether given the current preferences of the parties to collective agreements to use arbitration to deal with a wide range of disputes, but one cannot always predict the future.

While a multi-factored approach of this type may appear to present problems of complexity and uncertainty, the "bright line" *Weber* approach has done little to eliminate confusion and inconsistency, has continued to produce considerable litigation and has simultaneously presented the dangers of *Weber* gaps and the potential for harm to our collective bargaining institutions. I venture that the application of these factors would in most cases result in a finding of concurrent jurisdiction between arbitrators and *statutory* tribunals where there is overlapping jurisdiction under employment-related statutes. And in the interests of certainty and predictability, I would not be averse to the courts recognizing a general assumption or presumption of concurrent jurisdiction in areas of overlap between arbitrators and *statutory* regimes, subject of course to rebuttal where the legislators use express language to denote an intention to give one body exclusive jurisdiction. I see nothing wrong with requiring legislators to make it clear that they intend to grant exclusive jurisdiction to arbitrators when they create a statutory tribunal and give it a clear mandate to administer and enforce the law at issue. They appear to know how to do this when it is their actual intention.[173]

I would also make *Charter* claims subject to concurrent jurisdiction between arbitration and courts, thereby returning us to the law as it existed under *Douglas College* immediately before *Weber* was decided. If there ever was any justification for making such claims subject to

172 *Danyluk,* above note 35.

173 Of course legislatures have experience with how to do this clearly. *See e.g., ESA,* above note 31 at s 99.

exclusive arbitral jurisdiction, in *Weber*, that justification has been undone by the majority recognition in *Morin* that access to justice concerns must override efficiency concerns when we are dealing with fundamental, individual human rights, for which access to a forum for enforcement should never be made contingent on collective support.

The application of such a multi-factored approach would result in continued exclusive arbitral jurisdiction over almost all common law claims. That was for the most part where the law was before *Weber* was decided.[174] I do not think there is any appetite in the labour relations community for undoing the Supreme Court of Canada's recognition in *McGavin Toastmaster* of the fundamental transformation of the employment relationship that was brought about with the introduction of a state-recognized collective bargaining regime to subsume and replace the common law contract of employment.[175] To re-open access to the courts for individual claims based on the common law of contract or tort when dealing with issues that are commonplace to the modern employment relationship would undoubtedly be viewed as undermining the compromise between individual and collective rights adopted as a central feature of the *Wagner Act* regime. Nothing in this essay should be read as calling for any kind of presumption of concurrency for common law claims.

However, the approach advocated here would require our courts to reassess how they deal with unique or unusual claims that appear not to have anything to do with the everyday workings of the employment relationship or collective bargaining, and are beyond anything the parties might have contemplated being governed by the collective agreement or the competence and capacity of arbitration to deal with in an effective and practical manner.[176] An appropriate balancing of interests does not support the unquestioned adherence to exclusive jurisdiction for all *Charter* and common law claims espoused in *Weber*.

---

174 *See* above note 164.

175 And much earlier in *Syndicat catholique des employées de magasins v Paquet Ltée*, [1959] SCR 206, 18 DLR (2d) 346.

176 I would include tort claims against third parties as examples of the first type of claim, and cases like *Bisaillon* for the second category, where, as Bastarache J recognized, the majority decision to deny all employees under the plan access to the courts to deal with pension plan issues because they were covered by nine different collective agreements meant there was no forum available that could give an effective remedy against the employer should claims of pension plan misbehavior by the employer be made out.

CHAPTER THREE

# *Weber*, the Common Law, and Industrial Self-Government

Elizabeth Shilton

*Words of an agreement which speak loudly and liberally to one arbitrator may be palls of silence to another.*[1]

The decision of the Supreme Court of Canada in *Weber v Ontario Hydro*[2] has often been read as requiring arbitrators to take jurisdiction over claims that have their source in the common law. Based on this reading, the decision has been denounced as subverting the foundational purpose of labour arbitration as a tool for enforcing the parties' private law.[3] In

1 Bora Laskin, "Problems of Procedure and Proof in Labour Arbitration" (1962) 5 *Canadian Public Administration* 76 at 85 [Laskin, "Problems of Procedure"].

2 [1995] 2 SCR 929 [*Weber*].

3 *See e.g.*, Ray Brown & Brian Etherington, "*Weber v Ontario Hydro*: A Denial of Access to Justice for the Organized Employee?" (1996) 4 *Canadian Labour and Employment Law Journal* 183; Bernard Adell, "Jurisdictional Overlap Between Arbitration and Other Forums: An Update" (2000) 8 *Canadian Labour and Employment Law Journal* 179; Donald D Carter, "Looking at *Weber* Five Years Later: Is it Time for a New Approach?" (2000) 8 *Canadian Labour and Employment Law Journal* 231; Brian Etherington, "*OPSEU v Seneca College*: Deference as a Two-Edged Sword — A Missed Opportunity to Address the '*Weber* Gap'" (2007) 13:3 *Canadian Labour and Employment Law Journal* 301; Michel G Picher, "Defining the Scope of Arbitration: The Impact of *Weber*: An Arbitrator's Perspective" in Kevin Whitaker et al, eds, (1999–2000) 1 *Labour Arbitration Year Book* (Toronto: Lancaster House, 2000) 99.

*Seneca College v Ontario Public Service Employees Union*,[4] Arbitrator Pamela Picher identified a number of "potentially devastating consequences" flowing from a requirement that arbitrators enforce the common law, including the overloading of grievance procedures, the exacerbation of interpersonal conflicts in the workplace, and the squandering of collective resources on disputes without collective dimensions.[5] Picher concluded that "[i]f all wrongs arising in the workplace, tortious as well as contractual, are indiscriminately placed within the grievance and arbitration procedure, the very efficiency and vitality of that cornerstone of the labour relations system is at risk."[6] In her view, such disputes should be resolved "as they have been for centuries, in the courts of common law, not at arbitration."[7] Arbitrator Michel Picher summed up the views of many scholars, arbitrators and practitioners in his widely-quoted observation that "the good intentions and 'pro-arbitration' bent of [*Weber*] may prove to be a Pandora's box of unforeseen negative consequences for individual rights, as well as for labour arbitration and collective bargaining itself."[8]

In this essay, I challenge the view that *Weber* requires arbitrators to enforce the common law, and the related conclusion that *Weber* undermines the role of labour arbitration as a mechanism for enforcing the parties' private law. I argue, on the contrary, that *Weber*'s liberal vision of arbitration attempts to restore arbitration to its original role as the "judicial branch" of industrial self-government. The theory of arbitration espoused in *Weber* closely tracks that of the "industrial pluralist" arbitrator-scholars whose work was so influential in shaping the arbitration model enshrined in Canadian collective bargaining statutes. For industrial pluralists, unionized workplaces were private enclaves regulated by a law autonomously generated through collective bargaining. That law displaced the common law rules which would have otherwise governed the employment relationship.

---

4 (2001) 102 LAC (4th) 298, (Arbitrator: P Picher) [*Seneca Arbitration Decision*], rev'd sub nom *OPSEU v Seneca College of Applied Arts and Technology* (2004) 73 OR (3d) 185 (Div Ct), aff'd (2006) 80 OR (3d) 1 (CA), leave to appeal to SCC refused, 228 OAC 396n (16 November 2006).

5 *Seneca Arbitration Decision*, above note 4 at para 52.

6 *Ibid* at para 50.

7 *Ibid* at para 52.

8 M. Picher, above note 3 at 109.

In its ideal form, the pluralist conception depended for its coherence on the idea that employers and unions were equal partners in "making" the law of the unionized workplace. That conception was never very stable, since it was in constant competition with the fundamental conception of the employment relationship as one of domination and subordination, and with deeply embedded ideas about the nature and incidents of property rights. It was ultimately corrupted by a generation of arbitrators unwilling to translate the formal equality reflected in collective bargaining statutes into a substantively equal distribution of power in the workplace. Those arbitrators opted for a more employer-friendly distribution of power rooted in the common law, under which unionized employers retained their common law power to control and direct the workforce *except* to the extent that unions were able to fetter that power through limitations reflected in the collective agreement. Their approach became known as "reserved rights" theory.

Arbitrators influenced by reserved rights theory applied narrow and literalist "readings" of collective agreements that created a gap between employment rights and arbitral remedies. This gap left room for the emergence of the idea that terms and conditions of employment in unionized workplaces could subsist outside the perimeter of the collective agreement, governed by the common law of employment and enforceable — if they were enforceable at all — in the ordinary civil courts. *Weber's* liberal approach to the jurisdiction of arbitrators eliminates (or at least shrinks) that gap, bringing disputes about terms and conditions of employment in unionized workplaces back into the industrial pluralist world in which they are addressed within the framework of the collective agreement. Within this framework, disputes are resolved according to their "essential character" rather than their common law classification, and the common law plays no role *per se*. Understood thus, *Weber* poses no challenge to such core pluralist principles as the autonomy of the parties to make their own law through collective bargaining, or the integrity of arbitration as the judicial branch of industrial self-government. Indeed, the centrality given to the collective agreement by the Supreme Court of Canada's decision goes a considerable way towards reclaiming these principles from the desuetude to which reserved rights theory had consigned them.

I develop my argument as follows. Part A examines the influence of the pluralist idea of industrial self-government on the role of arbitrators within the collective bargaining model established by the US *Wagner*

*Act.*[9] Part B explores what happened to this idea when it was imported into Canada, which adopted the basic structure of the *Wagner Act* but modified that structure to give arbitration a more central role. Part C identifies the emergence of a "reserved rights" theory of arbitration that undermined the ideal of industrial self-government by creating room for terms and conditions of employment governed by management prerogative and the common law. Part D explains how reserved rights theory took root in Canada, despite the valiant exertions of a minority of pluralist arbitrators. Part E identifies some of the contradictions generated by reserved rights theory for a collective bargaining model in which all terms and conditions of employment fall within the scope of bargaining. Part F argues that the Supreme Court of Canada's decision in *Weber* helps to resolve those contradictions by directing arbitrators away from formalism and forcing them to focus on the "essential character of the dispute." Part G concludes that *Weber* restores the collective agreement to its intended place as the repository of the governing law of the unionized workplace and the fundamental substratum of employment rights. However, *Weber*'s reassertion of the primacy of the agreement may ultimately be unsustainable in the modern world of employment relations in which public rights, as well as third-party rights and interests, constantly encroach on the private world of industrial self-government imagined by industrial pluralist theorists.

## A. INDUSTRIAL SELF-GOVERNMENT AND THE ROLE OF ARBITRATION

The role of collective bargaining as a mode of establishing terms and conditions of employment evolved slowly in unionized workplaces. Early collective agreements consisted of rudimentary wage schedules, bearing little resemblance to the thick and detailed documents we now call by that name.[10] Where workplace disputes arose — whether they were "rights disputes" (i.e., disputes about how to apply the collective agreement) or "interest disputes" (i.e., disputes over matters not addressed in the agreement) — the parties had a variety of tools available to resolve them. The

9 *National Labor Relations Act*, 29 USCA §151-169 [*Wagner Act*].

10 Dennis R Nolan & Roger I Abrams, "American Labor Arbitration: The Early Years" (1983) 35:3 *University of Florida Law Review* 373 at 411–13.

employer and the union might sit down and bargain *ad hoc* or permanent solutions. The union might strike to enforce its position. Or the parties might agree to submit the dispute to a third party, sometimes a permanent umpire and sometimes an arbitrator chosen to deal with a single issue. In addition, from time to time unionized parties might end up in court over workplace disputes. In this simpler world, arbitration played a relatively minor role in dispute resolution. As industry expanded and became more bureaucratized, collective agreements became both more complex and more comprehensive, and industrial conflict became more costly. Arbitration gradually emerged as the preferred mechanism for resolving rights disputes. By 1934, just prior to the passage of the *Wagner Act*, 66 percent of US collective agreements contained some form of arbitration clause.[11]

The *Wagner Act* did not directly address dispute resolution. It imposed a duty on employers to recognize and bargain with a majority union "in respect to rates of pay, wages, hours of employment, or other conditions of employment."[12] But its legislative history reveals that "[t]he Wagner Act was not concerned, except incidentally, with what took place after the proper union had been recognized by the employer and negotiations got underway."[13] Issues of dispute resolution were left to be addressed through collective bargaining, with the parties free to choose from the same menu of tools which had been available to them prior to the passage of the Act, regardless of whether the dispute involved rights or interests.

Out of this laissez-faire approach evolved an even stronger preference for arbitration for use in resolving rights disputes.[14] There was no job description for arbitrators, however, and as employers, unions and arbitrators made their way within the new world of regulated collective bargaining, the proper role of arbitrators was a matter of continuing

11 *Ibid* at 411. Alan Hyde points out that the arbitration clauses of this era were very diverse, and many did not distinguish between rights and interest disputes: see Hyde, "The Crisis in the US Litigation Model of Labour Rights Enforcement," Chapter 10, this volume.

12 *Wagner Act*, above note 9 §159.

13 Archibald Cox & John T Dunlop, "Regulation of Collective Bargaining by the National Labor Relations Board" (1950) 63:3 *Harvard Law Review* 389 at 389 [Cox & Dunlop, "Regulation of Collective Bargaining"].

14 By 1942, 76 percent of US agreements had arbitration clauses. *See* Nolan & Abrams, above note 10 at 411. Currently more than 95 percent of US agreements contain such clauses. *See* William B Gould IV, *A Primer of American Labor Law*, 5th ed (New York: Cambridge University Press, 2013) at 256.

debate. That debate was strongly influenced by the industrial pluralist school of industrial relations,[15] exemplified in the influential writings of scholar-arbitrators Harry Shulman, Archibald Cox and John T. Dunlop.[16] In "Reason, Contract and Law in Labor Relations," published in 1955 in the *Harvard Law Review*,[17] Shulman expounded the core pluralist idea of collective bargaining as "industrial self-government" — a system in which individual unionized workplaces are governed by a private "rule of law and reason" established by the parties. Industrial pluralists saw unionized workplaces functioning as self-contained zones in which the parties made and enforced their own governing law, with minimal interference from the state. Within this autonomous system, arbitration played a role roughly analogous to the judicial branch of public democratic government.[18]

Pluralists did not insist that arbitrators should decide *all* workplace disputes. Since arbitration clauses were optional in US agreements, the parties could bargain about which disputes would be submitted to an arbitrator and which would remain subject to other forms of dispute resolution. Both before and after the passage of the *Wagner Act*, arbitration clauses could be custom-designed to be as broad or as narrow as the parties chose to make them. But in general, pluralists took a very liberal view

---

15 In her iconic critique of industrial pluralism, "The Post-War Paradigm in American Labor Law" (1981) 90:7 *Yale Law Review* 1509 at 1511, Katherine Van Wezel Stone defines the term as follows:

> Industrial pluralism is the view that collective bargaining is self-government by management and labor; management and labor are considered to be equal parties who jointly determine the conditions of the sale of labor power. The collective bargaining process is said to function like a legislature in which management and labor, both sides representing their separate constituencies, engage in debate and compromise, and together legislate the rules under which the workplace will be governed. The set of rules that results is alternatively called a statute or a constitution — the basic industrial pluralist metaphors for the collective bargaining agreement.

16 These men all had long and distinguished careers as academics, public servants and arbitrators. Shulman served as Dean of Yale Law School. Cox, a professor at Harvard Law School, was Solicitor-General in the Kennedy administration and also served as Watergate Special Prosecutor. Dunlop, a labour economist and Harvard professor, was US Secretary of Labor in the Ford administration.

17 Harry Shulman, "Reason, Contract and Law in Labor Relations" (1955) 68:6 *Harvard Law Review* 999.

18 *Ibid* at 1016.

of the role of the arbitrator. For them, collective agreements were frameworks for an on-going relationship rather than compendia of discrete rights; both the negotiation and the administration of the agreement were simply points on a continuum whereby the parties continuously defined and refined their governing law.[19] It followed that, despite the analogy to the judicial branch, arbitrators did not function like common law judges. They answered to the parties rather than to external law. Their job was to resolve the problems which had been put before them. They were expected to respond flexibly and pragmatically to disputes for which legal rules could not be explicitly laid down in the collective agreement, given the practical limitations of the bargaining process and the dynamism of the workplace. Their task required them not only to apply the language of the agreement, but also to draw upon what Cox called the "common law of the shop," defined as a set of principles which were "not judge-made principles of the common law, but the practices, assumptions, understandings, and aspirations of the going industrial concern."[20] Cox provided a non-exhaustive list of normative sources for this "common law of the shop": "legal doctrines, a sense of fairness, the national labor policy, past practice at the plant and perhaps industrial practice generally."[21] The parties remained in control of the content of "their" law, since they could tie the arbitrator's hands through collective bargaining if they chose to do so. But where they left gaps and ambiguities, or where they employed general phraseology — "just cause" is a recurring example in pluralist literature — arbitrators must nonetheless solve the problems before them. As Cox put it, "the labor arbitrator necessarily pours meaning into the

19 *Ibid*; Archibald Cox, "Rights under a Collective Agreement" (1956) 69:4 *Harvard Law Review* 601 at 625. *See also* Archibald Cox, "Individual Enforcement of Collective Bargaining Agreements" (1957) 8:12 *Labour Law Journal* 850; Archibald Cox, "Current Problems in the Law of Grievance Arbitration" (1958) 30 *Rocky Mountain Law Review* 247; Charles B Craver, "Labor Arbitration as a Continuation of the Collective Bargaining Process" (1990) 66:3 *Chicago-Kent Law Review* 571 at 571–78, 624–29.

20 Archibald Cox, "Reflections Upon Labor Arbitration" (1959) 72:8 *Harvard Law* Review 1482 at 1500 [Cox, "Reflections Upon Labor Arbitration"]. Shulman declined to specify the criteria arbitrators could and should look to, emphasizing the role of "wise judgement," as fully informed as possible about context and implications. Above note 17 at 1016–18.

21 *Ibid* at 1500.

general phrases and interstices of a document written somewhat in the generalities of basic regulatory legislation."[22]

This highly flexible conception of the role of the arbitrator alarmed some scholars of the day, who argued for a more rights-based approach to the enforcement of collective agreements. They expressed particular concerns about the implications of subjecting individual employee claims to union gate-keeping and sought a more prominent role for individual employees in enforcing their own claims, particularly when they involved critical job interests.[23] Despite such concerns, however, the pluralist view triumphed in the US courts. In a set of cases decided in 1960 which has become known as the *Steelworkers Trilogy*,[24] the US Supreme Court embraced the pluralist metaphor of "industrial self-government." The Court acknowledged that a collective agreement is "more than a contract; it is a generalized code to govern a myriad of cases which the draftsman cannot wholly anticipate."[25] In addition, the Court endorsed arbitration as "part and parcel of the collective bargaining process itself,"[26] and accepted that

---

22 Archibald Cox, "The Legal Nature of Collective Bargaining Agreements" (1958) 57:1 *Michigan Law Review* 1 at 23 [Cox, "Legal Nature of Collective Bargaining"].

23 *See e.g.*, Clyde W Summers, "Union Powers and Workers' Rights" (1951) 49:6 *Michigan Law Review* 805; Clyde W Summers "Individual Rights in Collective Agreements and Arbitration" (1962) 37:3 *New York University Law Review* 362; Alfred W Blumrosen, "Group Interests in Labor Law" (1958–1959) 13:3 *Rutgers Law Review* 432; Alfred W Blumrosen, "Legal Protection for Critical Job Interests: Union-Management Authority versus Employee Autonomy" (1959) 13:4 *Rutgers Law Review* 631; Alfred W Blumrosen, "The Worker and Three Phases of Unionism: Administrative and Judicial Control of the Worker-Union Relationship" (1963) 61:8 *Michigan Law Review* 1435.

24 *United Steelworkers of America v American Manufacturing Co*, 363 US 564 (1960); *United Steelworkers of America v Warrior & Gulf Navigation Co*, 363 US 574 (1960) [*Warrior & Gulf Navigation*]; *United Steelworkers of America v Enterprise Wheel & Car Corp*, 363 US 593 (1960) [*Enterprise Wheel & Car*]. The *Steelworkers Trilogy* established that where there is an arbitration clause in a collective agreement, the role of the courts was to issue an order compelling the parties to arbitrate, rather than dealing with the dispute on the merits. The decisions quote both Cox and Shulman. The *Steelworkers Trilogy* is discussed in Stone, "The Post-War Paradigm," above note 15 and in Katherine VW Stone, "The Steelworkers' Trilogy: The Evolution of Labor Arbitration" in Laura Cooper and Catherine Fisk, eds, *Labour Law Stories: An In-Depth Look at Leading Labor Law Cases* (New York: Foundation Press, 2005). *See also* David E Feller, "A General Theory of the Collective Bargaining Agreement" (1973) 61:3 *California Law Review* 663.

25 *Warrior & Gulf Navigation*, above note 24 at 578.

26 *Ibid.*

"[t]he processing of disputes through the grievance machinery is actually a vehicle by which meaning and content are given to the collective agreement."[27] Arbitrators charged with enforcing collective agreements must do more than simply apply express contract language: "The labor arbitrator's source of law is not confined to the express provisions of the contract, as the industrial common law—the practices of the industry and the shop—is equally a part of the collective bargaining agreement although not expressed in it."[28] The Court acknowledged that this role puts pressure on arbitrators, but observed:

> The labor arbitrator is usually chosen because of the parties' confidence in his knowledge of the common law of the shop and their trust in his personal judgment to bring to bear considerations which are not expressed in the contract as criteria for judgment. The parties expect that his judgment of a particular grievance will reflect not only what the contract says but, insofar as the collective bargaining agreement permits, such factors as the effect upon productivity of a particular result, its consequence to the morale of the shop, his judgment whether tensions will be heightened or diminished.[29]

The *Steelworkers Trilogy* assented to the pluralist idea that in the process of arbitration, the private law of the workplace is both made and enforced. This idea has parallels in the symbiotic relationship between courts and the common law, through which judges simultaneously make and enforce legal rules. The analogy is incomplete, of course, since the parties to collective bargaining are accorded a more complex and continuing role in the law-making process than are users of the common law courts. But it is nonetheless important in understanding the scope afforded to arbitrators by the courts. Arbitrators are not simply "readers" of the collective agreement; to give meaning to the bare language, they must also interpret and apply it, a process calling for creativity and a deep sensitivity to workplace dynamics.

---

27 *Ibid* at 581.

28 *Ibid* at 581–82.

29 *Ibid*. The gendered pronouns are apt, since the ideal arbitrator in pluralist writings is unquestionably a "wise man."

## B. ARBITRATION UNDER THE CANADIAN COLLECTIVE BARGAINING MODEL

Under the industrial pluralist approach which evolved in the US, collective bargaining occupied the field previously occupied by the common law. However, while arbitration was the preferred mechanism for resolving disputes arising out of the collective "bargain," US arbitrators did not automatically have jurisdiction over the full fruits of that bargain. Arbitration was not mandated by the *Wagner Act*, and the issues to be resolved by arbitration (if any) were determined by the parties through collective bargaining. It was open to unions and employers to custom-design their arbitration clauses to cover all, part or none of the rights and responsibilities addressed in the agreement. However, a finding that an issue was not arbitrable did not create space for private bargains between employer and employee, or for the unilateral exercise of management rights. Even where issues were not arbitrable, they continued to be governed by the over-riding obligation to recognize the union as bargaining agent. US law held that the statutory duty to bargain was continuous as long as the union was bargaining agent. This meant that employers could be required to bargain over matters not already addressed in the agreement not only during formal negotiations, but also during the term of the agreement.[30] In addition, the *Wagner Act* placed no limitations on the right to strike,[31] and disputes not covered by an arbitration clause could be resolved by industrial action unless the union had agreed at the bargaining table to forgo the right to strike during the life of the collective agreement. Accordingly, in the US the consequences of a finding that a workplace rights claim was inarbitrable (i.e., not subject to the arbitra-

30 *See* Archibald Cox & John T Dunlop, "The Duty to Bargain Collectively During the Term of an Existing Agreement" (1950) 63:7 *Harvard Law Review* 1097 [Cox & Dunlop, "Duty to Bargain Collectively"]. A limitation on the US duty was that employers could not be compelled to bargain over a very narrow category of matters regarded as inherent prerogatives of management, which were regarded as "permissive" rather than "mandatory" subjects of bargaining: for example, the pricing of products. *See* James B Atleson, *Values and Assumptions in American Labor Law* (Amherst: University of Massachusetts Press, 1983) at 111–35; *NLRB v Wooster Division of Borg-Warner Corporation* 356 US 342 (1958).

31 While the *Wagner Act* did not mandate arbitration, courts tended to read no-strike commitments into collective agreements with broad arbitration clauses. *See Local 174, Teamsters, Chauffeurs, Warehouseman & Helpers of America v Lucas Flour Company*, 369 US 95 (1962); Stone, "The Post-War Paradigm," above note 15 at 1538–41.

tion clause) were not fatal to that claim; if a matter was inarbitrable, the union had other options for resolution.

In Canada, the situation was different. As is well-known, Canada generally adopted the *Wagner Act* model as its legal framework for collective bargaining. However, post-war Canadian statutes took a somewhat different approach to dispute resolution. For our purposes, there were three critical and interlocking distinctions.[32] First, in contrast to the US where both the existence and the scope of no-strike clauses were negotiable, Canadian labour statutes carefully regulated work stoppages and did not permit strikes during the life of the collective agreement.[33] Accordingly, unions could not lawfully resort to industrial action to resolve mid-contract rights disputes. Second and closely related, Canadian statutes directed that collective agreements provide mechanisms for dispute resolution.[34] Many statutes specifically mandated arbitration; others appeared to leave more options by requiring "arbitration or otherwise." In practice, however, arbitration was almost invariably the choice. Statutory mandates were reinforced by arbitration clauses "deemed" to be included in collective agreements where the parties had failed to provide for comprehensive dispute settlement, or by provisions which gave power to labour boards to impose arbitration clauses.[35] Statutes also dictated the *scope* of arbitration clauses. For example, the Ontario *Labour Relations Act* mandated arbitration for the resolution of "all differences between the parties arising from the interpretation, application, administration or

32 These differences are discussed in James K Hayes, *Perspectives on management rights: the curious logic of the argument for reducing industrial discord by removing the mid-term strike bar from labour relations legislation* (Don Mills: Ontario Federation of Labour, 1974) at 39–52.

33 Saskatchewan was the exception; it did not initially have a statutory strike ban, but has since fallen into line with other provinces. Hayes provides a cross-Canada review of the provisions of provincial and federal labour codes related to the strike ban. *Ibid* at 66–79.

34 For a detailed review of early statutory provisions dealing with rights dispute resolution in Canada, *see* Alfred William Rooke Carrothers, *Labour Arbitration in Canada: A Study of the Law and Practice Relating to the Arbitration of Grievance Disputes in Industrial Relations in Common Law Canada* (Toronto: Butterworths, 1961) at 18–36. *See also* Bora Laskin, "Problems of Procedure and Proof in Labour Arbitration" (1962) 5:1 *Canadian Public Administration* 76 at 77–79. Laskin dates the introduction of compulsory arbitration in Canada to PC 1003, the federal war-time Order in Council which set the stage for *Wagner Act*-type collective bargaining in Canada.

35 Carrothers, *ibid* at 26. Typical of these "deeming" provisions is the language now found in s 48(2) of *Labour Relations Act, 1995*, SO 1995, c 1, Schedule A.

alleged violation of the agreement, including any question as to whether a matter is arbitrable."[36] Subsequent caselaw made it clear that parties could not bargain to exclude certain "differences" from the scope of arbitration; if a "difference" arose from the collective agreement an arbitrator had exclusive jurisdiction to resolve it, even if the parties had expressly provided otherwise in their agreement.[37] In contrast to the US, then, in Canada the scope of arbitration could never be narrower than the scope of the collective agreement. Third, under Canadian law the duty to bargain applied only when the collective agreement was "open," whereas under US law, the duty continued during the life of the agreement.[38] This meant that while parties were permitted to make changes by mutual consent while the agreement was in effect, the statute did not lend a party any aid if the other party refused to come to the table.

These differences significantly altered the meaning of a finding that a rights dispute was inarbitrable. Under US law, a finding of inarbitrability was simply a finding that arbitration was not the forum chosen by the parties for resolving that particular type of dispute. Under Canadian law, it was a finding that such a dispute could not be resolved at all within the statutory framework for collective bargaining, at least until the next round of bargaining. Such a finding has serious consequences for the distribution of power in the workplace. It is unlikely that Canadian legislatures intended that their statutes would place some terms and conditions of employment outside the system of private law created by collective bargaining. In fact, the evidence is all to the contrary. In deviating from the *Wagner Act* model, Canadian legislatures almost certainly intended to make the boundaries of industrial self-government even more impermeable, and thus impose even stricter limits on industrial conflict than the US had seen fit to impose.[39] However, as we shall see,

---

36 *Labour Relations Act, 1995*, SO 1995, c 1, Schedule A. Other provinces adopted similar language. *See* Carrothers, *supra* note 34 at 25.

37 This principle was confirmed by Supreme Court of Canada in *Parry Sound (District) Welfare Administration Board v Ontario Public Service Employees Union, Local 324*, 2003 SCC 42 at para 35 [*Parry Sound*], but it had been recognized much earlier by arbitrators and lower courts. *See e.g.*, *Toronto Hydro-Electric System v CUPE, Local 1* (1980), 29 OR (2d) 18, 111 DLR (3d) 693, aff'd 30 OR (2d) 64, 113 DLR (3d) 512, leave to appeal to SCC refused, 35 NR 210n (15 December 1980).

38 The Honourable George W Adams, *Canadian Labour Law*, 2d ed (Canada Law Book: 1993) (loose leaf) at 10.1660.

39 *See* Laurel Sefton MacDowell, "The Formation of the Canadian Industrial Relations System During World War Two" (1978) 3 *Labour/Le Travail* 175 at 194; Judy Fudge

reserved rights arbitrators operating within Canadian statutory frameworks adopted a narrow and restrictive approach to arbitrability that had the potential to open space for individual bargaining, and permit terms and conditions of employment to flourish outside the statute. We shall now trace how that occurred.

## C. RESERVED RIGHTS THEORY AND THE POWER OF MANAGEMENT

The *Steelworkers Trilogy* did not end the US debate about the proper role of arbitration in resolving workplace disputes. But it did answer a number of important questions. It established the primacy of arbitration over the civil courts as the preferred mechanism for resolving disputes arising under collective agreements. It established the principle that where there are disputes over arbitrability, that issue should be decided by an arbitrator, and not by a court. It created a presumption in favour of arbitrability: "An order to arbitrate a grievance should not be denied unless it may be said with positive assurance that the arbitration clause is not susceptible of an interpretation that covers the asserted dispute. Doubts should be resolved in favour of coverage."[40] But despite that presumption, the *Trilogy* acknowledged that not every workplace dispute was arbitrable.

In addition, the debate continued about what tools arbitrators should use to resolve disputes, even where they were clearly arbitrable. In a 1963 article, legal philosopher Lon Fuller laid out two opposing conceptions of that role: the "arbitrator as judge," and the "arbitrator as labour relations physician" (the latter a thin disguise for the pluralist arbitrator embraced by the *Trilogy*).[41] Fuller did not approve of the "labour relations physician"; indeed, he described key passages of the *Trilogy* as relieving "by a single stroke . . . the arbitrator-physician . . . both of the restraints of judicial office and of any undue concern to find justification for what he does

& Eric Tucker, *Labour Before the Law: The Regulation of Workers' Collective Action in Canada, 1900–1948* (Toronto: Oxford University Press, 2001) at 300–1; Judy Fudge & Harry Glasbeek, "The Legacy of PC 1003" (1994) 3 *Canadian Labour and Employment Law Journal* 357.

40 *Warrior & Gulf Navigation*, above note 24 at 587–88.

41 Lon L Fuller, "Collective Bargaining and the Arbitrator" (1963) *Wisconsin Law Review* 3.

in the words of the agreement."[42] Fuller accepted—indeed lauded—the idea of industrial self-government,[43] but rejected the more free-wheeling elements of the pluralist model, including what he called "the indiscriminate use of the tripartite form"[44] and "[t]he mediating form-free arbitrator."[45] Ultimately, he believed that "[t]he morality of arbitration lies in a decision according to the law of the contract."[46]

But abstract adherence to "the law of the contract" does not take us far towards resolving the problem of the contents of the contract, or the collective "bargain." The territory that separated the "arbitrator as judge" from the "arbitrator as labour relations physician" often consisted more of opposing conceptions of how to give content to "the law of the contract" than of opposing conceptions of adjudicative style. At its core was the question of what arbitrators should do when faced with matters for which the collective agreement did not provide an explicit set of rules set out in the agreement or, as arbitrators often framed it, what they should do when faced with "silence" in the collective agreement. On the menu of available options, silence could mean that management was free to act unilaterally unless the union could prevent that outcome through industrial action. Silence could mean that the status quo should govern (and logically be deemed part of the agreement of the parties) until it was changed through collective bargaining. It could also mean that the arbitrator should determine an acceptable outcome through some version of "interest arbitration."

This last option was precluded by the *Steelworkers Trilogy*, in which the Court firmly asserted that "an arbitrator is confined to interpretation and application of the collective agreement. He does not sit to dispense his own brand of industrial justice. He may of course look for guidance from many sources, yet his award is legitimate only as it draws its essence from the collective bargaining agreement."[47] This left the other two options. Inevitably, in choosing between them, arbitrators brought to the task certain preconceptions and assumptions about the broader meaning of collective bargaining frameworks and the distribution of power under collective bargaining regimes. In the abstract, these assumptions and preconceptions

42 *Ibid* at 6.

43 According to Fuller, "our system of industrial self-government is one of the finest expressions of the American genius for political arrangements." *Ibid* at 45.

44 *Ibid* at 38.

45 *Ibid* at 44. Fuller also castigated the "stiffly literal judge."

46 *Ibid* at 23–24.

47 *Enterprise Wheel & Car*, above note 24 at 597.

can be grouped into two broad categories: the "reserved rights" school, and the "joint sovereignty" or "equal partnership" school.[48] Hard-line reserved rights theorists saw collective bargaining not as an exercise in joint law-making, but as a struggle over whether and what limitations should be placed on management's plenary power. The starting point for their analysis was the distribution of workplace power at common law; a union arguing for restrictions on management conduct had to meet the burden of establishing through clear language in the agreement that the employer intended to cede some of its pre-existing powers (which they tended to call "rights"). For reserved rights theorists, terms and conditions not directly reflected in the language of the agreement remained under the unilateral control of management. Accordingly, they typically held that unilateral management changes to the *status quo* in these areas were not subject to arbitral review. By contrast, "joint sovereignty" theorists saw collective bargaining as establishing a new regime of governance in which unions and employers were partners in the process of creating the legal rules that would govern the workplace. For them, silence about an issue did not mean that power defaulted automatically to management; instead, the meaning of silence must be determined on a case-by-case basis, applying a range of tools developed by arbitrators for teasing meaning out of context.

Consistent with their theory of industrial self-government, industrial pluralists generally aligned themselves with versions of the joint sovereignty view.[49] More attuned to meanings implied by the collective bargaining

---

48 For a discussion of these general arbitral philosophies, see Brian Langille, "Equal Partnership in Canadian Labour Law" (1983) 21:3 *Osgoode Hall Law Journal* 496 [Langille, "Equal Partnership"]; David M Beatty, "The Role of the Arbitrator: A Liberal Version" (1984) 34:2 *The University of Toronto Law Journal* 136; David Beatty & Brian Langille, "Bora Laskin and Labour Law: From Vision to Legacy" (1985) 35:4 *University of Toronto Law Journal* 672; and Andrew Goldsmith, "The Management-Control Collective Bargaining Relationship: Three Models" (1986) 24:4 *Osgoode Hall Law Journal* 775. These philosophies exist on a continuum, and some scholars view the middle ground as constituting a third "school." For example, Goldsmith labels the three schools Unitary, Pluralist and Radical, taking the pluralists at their word that they occupy a moderate middle ground. There were certainly theorists who used the language of joint sovereignty in a more radical sense than the pluralists, although the pluralists themselves were far from consistent in their practical applications of joint sovereignty.

49 Pluralist literature uses the phrases "joint sovereignty," "joint government" and "joint responsibility" apparently interchangeably, and less often the term "equal partnership."

framework, pluralist arbitrators were less likely to find agreements "silent." To paraphrase Canadian pluralist Bora Laskin, words of an agreement which might be "palls of silence" to a reserved rights arbitrator might "speak loudly and liberally" to an arbitrator who approached a dispute from a pluralist perspective.[50] For example, on the question of existing rights and benefits not directly addressed in the agreement, Cox and Dunlop argued for a default rule that "[a] collective agreement should be deemed, unless a contrary intention is manifest, to carry forward for its term the major terms and conditions of employment which prevailed when the agreement was executed."[51] By contrast, a reserved rights arbitrator would dismiss a grievance challenging unilateral changes to existing benefits unless those benefits were guaranteed in the collective agreement.

While the theoretical positions staked out by reserved rights and pluralist arbitrators suggested substantial differences between the two schools, those differences were often less substantial in practice. For the pluralists, equal *partnership* did not necessarily mean equal *power* in the workplace. It only meant that how power would be shared was a matter for collective bargaining. It was up to the parties to agree on which matters would lie exclusively in the hands of the employer, and which would lie within the realm of joint responsibility. Each agreement might draw that boundary differently; part of the task of the arbitrator was to locate the boundary and determine on which side a particular dispute fell.[52] As Cox put it, arbitrators must examine the collective agreement and determine what model of governance the parties had chosen: "Is it a monarchy except insofar as the employer has assumed the obligations explicitly stated or fairly implied from the contract? Or has the whole realm of matters of mutual concern to employer and employees been brought within the joint authority of the company and union . . . ?"[53] Cox and Dunlop slotted bargaining issues into conventional categories, with some (for example wages, hours and seniority) generally understood to be "matters for joint-union management determination," while others (for example, type of product, pricing policies, the location of plants, and somewhat puzzlingly, "the assignment of workers") were matters about which "it is

50 Laskin, "Problems of Procedure," above note 1.

51 Cox & Dunlop, "Duty to Bargain Collectively," above note 30 at 1116–1117.

52 Cox, "Legal Nature of Collective Bargaining," above note 22 at 25–36.

53 *Ibid* at 30.

generally agreed that management shall have exclusive responsibility."[54] They accepted that the boundaries between these categories were "being continuously defined by the give-and-take of collective bargaining,"[55] and would vary from shop to shop and industry to industry. But they also accepted that where the agreement placed matters within the area of management prerogative, the arbitrator's writ did not run. Cox readily conceded in his writings that "[i]n this sense, the management-rights theory seems sound."[56]

For pluralists, then, the language of the agreement played an important role in determining the scope of management rights. It was likewise important for reserved rights theorists. Although they viewed management rights as inherent in the employment relationship, they acknowledged that this "natural" distribution of power could be disturbed by collective bargaining; indeed, this was the essence of their theory. In response to evolving arbitral jurisprudence, unions and employers typically attempted to negotiate management rights clauses which defined the boundaries between employee rights and management prerogatives with some precision. They sometimes added so-called "zipper clauses" for good measure, which declared that the written agreement constituted the "full agreement" between the parties. Such clauses narrowed the differences between the two schools still further, and US arbitrators of both schools could and did enforce areas of reserved management rights without abandoning their very different theoretical postulates.

## D. RESERVED RIGHTS THEORY WITHIN THE CANADIAN MODEL

While the practical differences between the two schools may have been relatively narrow, those differences nevertheless had real impact on the distribution of power within the workplace. As Brian Langille explains it, reserved rights theory "weigh[s] the scales in favour of employers . . . grant[ing them] a head start in negotiations by guaranteeing that em-

---

54 Cox & Dunlop, "Regulation of Collective Bargaining," above note 13 at 401–2. They also posited a third category, "matters within the exclusive control of the union," which included internal union membership issues.

55 *Ibid* at 406.

56 Cox, "Reflections Upon Labor Arbitration," above note 20 at 1506. *See also* Cox, "Legal Nature of Collective Bargaining," above note 22 at 34–35.

ployers [are] given certain rights for free."[57] In the world of reserved rights, the onus is always on the union to prove that management has ceded power and never on the employer to prove that it has retained power. Unquestionably, even under US law this onus made a difference to how arbitrators resolved threshold questions of arbitrability, as well as how they went about resolving disputes that made it over that threshold. However, the differences between the US and Canadian collective bargaining frameworks meant that it had even harsher implications in Canada. In a study of the role of arbitrators published in the late 1960s, Paul Weiler denounced Canada's mid-contract strike ban and time-limited duty to bargain as "radically deficient because they do not allow the interests of union and employees a fair access to the decision-making process."[58] Weiler argued that "the legal regime must be changed to require effective bargaining about employer-instituted changes in working conditions."[59] He made a strong plea for law reform in Canada which would make the duty to bargain continuous, and relieve unions of the no-strike bar during the life of the agreement if the parties were unable to negotiate solutions for problems on which the existing agreement was silent. That law reform did not come.

Within the existing legal framework, however, Canada had distinguished arbitrators who pushed back against reserved rights theory. Most prominent among them was Bora Laskin, law professor, arbitrator and ultimately Chief Justice of the Supreme Court of Canada. Laskin was a student at Harvard Law School at the same time as Archibald Cox, and had clearly absorbed a similar philosophy of collective bargaining. His debt to the US pluralists is visible in the 1953 decision in *International Chemical Workers Union, Local 279, in Re Rexall Drug Company Limited, Toronto,*[60] in which he chaired a board of arbitration dealing with four termination grievances challenging the employer's mandatory retirement policy. The union argued that forced retirement violated the seniority and just cause provisions of the agreement.[61]

---

57 Langille, "Equal Partnership," above note 48 at 534–35.

58 Paul C Weiler, "The Role of the Labour Arbitrator: Alternative Versions" (1969) 19:1 *University of Toronto Law Journal* 16 at 44.

59 *Ibid* at 44.

60 (1953), 4 LAC 1468 (Arbitrator: Laskin) [*Rexall*].

61 The decision makes no reference to the management rights clause except to note that the agreement contained "the usual provisions respecting Management rights." *Ibid* at para 3.

The employer's retirement policy was part of a workplace pension plan that pre-dated collective bargaining and was not part of the collective agreement. As we have seen, the pluralist approach gave pre-existing benefits like this a measure of co-existence with the collective agreement. An issue very like the *Rexall* issue had been analysed by Cox and Dunlop in a 1949 article in which they discussed a range of theoretical perspectives on how arbitrators should treat pension and benefit plans which had been unilaterally established by the employer and were not formally reflected in the collective agreement.[62] They promoted the view that, "the parties to a comprehensive collective bargaining agreement, in the absence of contrary evidence, are to be presumed to have executed the agreement upon the understanding that major conditions of employment not covered by the agreement will continue 'as they were' unless changed by mutual agreement."[63] This presumption harmonized the pre-collective bargaining *status quo* with the agreement, and left room for plans which pre-dated collective bargaining to continue. However, an important component of the Cox and Dunlop approach was the understanding that pre-existing plans could be terminated or changed only through collective bargaining.

Although Cox and Dunlop's article is nowhere cited, Laskin's *Rexall* decision applied their presumption virtually to the letter. Laskin rejected the union's position that the terms of the pension plan should be disregarded because it had not been collectively bargained. In his view, since it was "known to the employees and to the Union prior to the execution of the first Collective Agreement between Union and Company,"[64] it should be presumed that the collective agreement was intended to allow for its terms, provided those terms were not inconsistent with the terms of the agreement.[65] He found mandatory retirement consistent with the job security provisions of the agreement as it applied to two of the four employees — those who had received pensions on their retirement. He found it *not* consistent, however, for the two remaining employees, who had not qualified for pension. Accordingly, they were entitled to reinstatement.[66] The decision noted that the pensioned employees too would have been

62 Cox & Dunlop, "Duty to Bargain Collectively," above note 30 at 1117–18.

63 *Ibid* at 1118. They characterized this as a middle ground between extreme reserved rights and joint sovereigntist positions.

64 *Rexall*, above note 60 at para 8.

65 *Ibid*.

66 *Ibid* at paras 7–10.

entitled to reinstatement if they had been subjected to unjust or unreasonable treatment. Very importantly, the decision adopted the view that a search for consistency between employer-imposed terms and conditions of employment and the terms of the collective agreement should be undertaken only with respect to initiatives that *pre-date* collective bargaining. Employer unilateral action *after* the union has acquired bargaining rights has no such protection: "[i]f the company had sought to introduce a compulsory retirement policy unilaterally after the advent of the Union, then clearly no force could be given to it."[67]

Laskin laboured doggedly to sell this approach to Canadian arbitrators. In *United Electrical, Radio & Machine Workers of America, Local 527 in Re Peterboro Lock Mfg Co Ltd,* he articulated his pluralist philosophy: "[I]t is a very superficial generalization to contend that a Collective Agreement must be read as limiting an employer's precollective bargaining prerogatives only to the extent expressly stipulated. Such a generalization ignores completely the climate of employer-employee relations under a Collective Agreement." He insisted that "[t]he change from individual to Collective Bargaining is a change in kind and not merely a difference in degree. The introduction of a Collective Bargaining regime involves the acceptance by the parties of assumptions which are entirely alien to an era of individual bargaining. Hence, any attempt to measure rights and duties in employer-employee relations by reference to pre-collective bargaining standards is an attempt to re-enter a world which has ceased to exist." It was not appropriate, Laskin argued, to transpose the old rules of the common law into the new world of collective bargaining: "Just as the period of individual bargaining had its own 'common law' worked out empirically over many years, so does a Collective Bargaining regime have a common law to be invoked to give consistency and meaning to the Collective Agreement on which it is based." [68] In *Peterboro Lock* itself, this philosophy led him to conclude that the employer had violated the agreement by failing to honour an incentive rate worked out in accordance with a negotiated procedure, even though the rate itself was not reflected in the agreement.

Five years later, in *Re Sudbury Mine, Mill and Smelter Workers, Local 598 & Falconbridge Nickel Mines Ltd,* Laskin reiterated his *Peterboro Lock* credo. He emphasized that collective agreements must be interpreted in light of their purposes, in the context both of the statutory framework for

67 *Ibid* at para 8.

68 (1954) 4 LAC 1499 (Arbitrator: Laskin) at 1502 [*Peterboro Lock*].

collective bargaining (which he described as "the policy umbrella sheltering collective agreements") and an industrial "common law" gradually evolving "to give meaning and consistency to a collective agreement."[69] In *Falconbridge*, which posed a contracting out problem, his approach led to a dismissal of the grievance, not because he found the agreement silent but because he found within it a mutual understanding that contracting out was permissible except in certain circumstances specified in the agreement.

However, Laskin's efforts to stem the tide of reserved rights theory in Canadian arbitration practice ran up against some powerful adversaries, including the editors of the *Labour Arbitration Cases*. Their headnotes to published decisions contained editorial addenda featuring such fundamentalist pronouncements as, "[g]enerally speaking management rights which must extend to delimiting the duties of the various classes of employees are paramount and only to be restricted in so far as the collective agreement effectively cuts them out";[70] "contracting out is a normal and customary management function in operating and managing a business and, therefore, to take it out of that category an exception must be shown to exist in the terms of the bargaining agreements";[71] and "[w]here management rights are restricted in a collective agreement the words of limitation must be unequivocal."[72] Since Laskin's decisions did not conform to this orthodoxy, they attracted particularly acerbic commentary. Typical is the note to *Falconbridge*, in which the editor's exasperation with Laskin's persistent refusal to "get with the program" is palpable beneath the turgid prose:

> The elaborate philosophical dissertation, entirely *obiter*, on the theories upon which these contracting-out situations have been worked out in awards which, despite careful analysis, still seem to be irreconcilable, is no doubt interesting. Nevertheless this *obiter* still seems to be merely another voice supporting what appears to be a minority position. Perhaps what appears to be an apologia for an abortive attempt to introduce

---

69 (1958) 8 LAC 276 (Arbitrator: Laskin) at para 16 [*Falconbridge*].

70 *Re Oil, Chemical & Atomic Workers, Local 16-351 & Fiberglas Ltd* (1956), 6 LAC 322 (Arbitrator: Laskin).

71 *Re United Automobile Workers, Local 222 & General Motors Ltd* (1958), 8 LAC 90 (Arbitrator: Cross).

72 *Re United Automobile Workers, Local 676 & Hayes Steel Products Ltd* (1958), 8 LAC 149 (Arbitrator: Cross).

> nebulous principles such as the climate of labour-management relations and a common law of labour arbitration awards, may afford a reason for the elaboration of the *obiter*. We doubt, however, whether it will win many converts among the chairmen who, by their awards, have demonstrated dissentient views.[73]

As is now notorious, Laskin's purposive approach was ultimately driven underground, if not killed off entirely, by Harry Arthurs, chairing the arbitration board in *Re United Steelworkers of America and Russelsteel Ltd.*[74] *Russelsteel* was a contracting out case, under a collective agreement which was "silent" on the practice. The decision outlined the two poles of the debate over the meaning of "silence" in contracting out cases—the reserved rights approach under which contracting out was permissible unless expressly prohibited in the agreement, and the Laskin/pluralist approach which insisted that the "climate of collective bargaining" must be taken into account when determining the implications of "silence."[75] After a careful numerical tabulation of existing Canadian arbitration decisions on the contracting out issue, Arthurs declared the debate closed and announced a winner: the reserved rights approach. Deftly usurping Laskin's famous phrase, he found that the tide among Canadian arbitrators had turned so decisively against Laskin's position that the reserved rights view on contracting out must now be regarded as part of "the climate of collective bargaining." Accordingly, parties must be deemed to negotiate in the knowledge that as a practical matter, arbitrators will permit contracting out unless there is express language in the agreement to the contrary. Applying that logic, Arthurs dismissed the grievance.[76]

---

73 *Falconbridge*, above note 69 at 276.

74 (1966), 17 LAC 253 (Arbitrator: Arthurs) [*Russelsteel*].

75 *Ibid* at paras 7–8. The decision acknowledged that the view expressed by Laskin was "widely accepted in labour arbitration in the United States."

76 The decision concluded on the cautious note that "no argument was advanced to us that the violation might consist in failing to bargain with the union beforehand, rather than in the very act of contracting out, cf. *Fibreboard Paper Products v NLRB* (1964), 379 US 203." *Ibid* at 260. In *Fibreboard*, the US Supreme Court had held that contracting out is a mandatory subject of bargaining under the statute, and an employer's unilateral decision to contract out without bargaining violates its duty to bargain.

## E. SOME CONTRADICTIONS POSED BY RESERVED RIGHTS THEORY

*Russelsteel* met a highly receptive audience among Canadian arbitrators. In a 1985 article, Gordon Simmons asserted with only slight exaggeration that after *Russelsteel*, "[a]rbitrators, without exception, apply the management rights theory notwithstanding frequent attempts by union counsel and representatives to have it sidetracked in favour of the equal rights theory."[77] *Canadian Labour Arbitration*, the arbitrators' *vade mecum*, confirmed this conclusion.[78] But reserved rights theory is not easy to reconcile with core principles of Canadian labour law. By acknowledging that aspects of the unionized employment relationship may exist ungoverned by the collective agreement, management rights theory fostered the idea that aspects of that relationship may continue to be governed by common law. This idea clashes head-on with the principle that industrial self-government is a substitute for the common law, and likewise with the closely-related principle that once a union is in place, all aspects of the employment relationship are mediated by collective bargaining.

The principle that the law of the collective agreement displaces the common law of employment has long been understood by the Supreme Court of Canada. That principle lies at the core of *Syndicat Catholique des Employés de Magasins de Québec Inc v Compagnie Paquet Ltée*, in which Judson J rejected a challenge to the union's authority to bargain for a dues check-off without authorization from each individual employee, holding that where a union is the lawful bargaining agent, "[t]here is no room left for private negotiation between employer and employee."[79] It is the bedrock of Laskin CJC's holding in *McGavin Toastmaster Ltd v Ainscough et al* that "the common law as it applies to individual employment contracts is

77 Gordon Simmons, "Arbitral *Stare Decisis*: An Unheralded but Important Doctrine in Canadian Arbitral Jurisprudence" (1986) 11:2 *Queen's Law Journal* 347 at 347. Interestingly, if perhaps somewhat disingenuously, the *Russelsteel* decision itself claims to "take no general position on the 'reserved rights' controversy." Above note 74 at 259.

78 Donald JM Brown & David M Beatty, *Canadian Labour Arbitration*, 4th ed (Carswell, 2006) (loose-leaf) ("Indeed, it is now generally conceded that whether or not an express provision giving management the power to initiate such changes is included in the agreement, management nevertheless possesses this power or ability to initiate such changes. Very simply, arbitrators have recognized that such authority flows from management's responsibility to manage the enterprise" at 5:0000).

79 [1959] SCR 206 at para 12, 18 DLR (2d) 346.

no longer relevant to employer-employee relations governed by a collective agreement,"[80] and therefore contract doctrines such as fundamental breach and repudiation do not apply to collective agreements. It is reflected in Estey J's observation in *Ste Anne-Nackawic Pulp & Paper Co Ltd v Canadian Paperworkers Union, Local 219* that despite ample precedent for permitting employers to bring civil suits against unions, "[t]he more modern approach is to consider that labour relations legislation provides a code governing all aspects of labour relations."[81] It underlies La Forest J's observation in *Canadian Association of Industrial, Mechanical and Allied Workers, Local 14 v Paccar of Canada Ltd.* that "employer-employee relations governed by a collective agreement displaced the common law of individual employment," and that "the tripartite relationship of union, employer and employee brought about by the Code displaces common law concepts" as long as the employer continues to be subject to a duty to bargain with the union. [82]

Reserved rights theory is equally difficult to reconcile with the requirement that an employer must recognize the union as the exclusive bargaining agent with respect to all terms and conditions of employment — a principle I have elsewhere called the "recognition rule."[83] Canada has not followed the US in adopting a duty to bargain that continues throughout the life of a collective agreement. The Supreme Court has nevertheless made it very clear that under Canadian legislative frameworks, the recognition rule applies to *all* terms and conditions of employment, regardless of whether or not they are reflected in the collective agreement. As LeBel J put it in *Bisaillon v Concordia University*, the union's bargaining authority is "not limited to the context of the collective agreement but extends to all aspects of the employee-employer relationship . . . [A]ny negotiations regarding conditions of employment that are not mentioned in the current collective agreement must be conducted by the certified

80 [1976] 1 SCR 718 at para 10, 54 DLR (3d) 1.

81 [1986] 1 SCR 704 at para 16, 28 DLR (4th) 1. This passage was cited by the minority in *Irving Pulp & Paper Ltd v Communications, Energy and Paperworkers Union of Canada, Local* 30, 2013 SCC 34 at para 67 in support of its concurrence with the majority that arbitrators are entitled to deference on judicial review.

82 [1989] 2 SCR 983 at para 38, [1989] 6 WWR 673 [*Paccar*].

83 *See* Elizabeth Shilton, "Enforcing Workplace Pension Rights for Unionized Employees: Is There a '*Weber* Gap'?" (2015) 19 *Canadian Labour and Employment Law Journal* 135 at 140–44 [Shilton, "Pension Rights"].

union."[84] This principle leaves no scope for individual bargaining within areas marked out by arbitrators as governed by management prerogative. And if there can be no individual bargaining, it logically follows that there can be no unilateral imposition of new terms and conditions of employment, since terms unilaterally imposed by the employer outside the union context are understood to be contractual (i.e., agreed-upon), notwithstanding that agreement may be a legal fiction.

To be sure, when the Supreme Court has enunciated these principles, it has typically done so when looking at collective bargaining from an abstract height. The Court has been far from consistent in applying them to concrete situations. That inconsistency is well illustrated by its pre-*Weber* jurisprudence in cases involving pension plans and mandatory retirement. In *Bell Canada v OPEIU, Local 131*,[85] the Court quashed a carefully reasoned decision by arbitrator Paul Weiler, who had held that a clause providing that "[t]he Company may dismiss or suspend an employee for sufficient and reasonable cause" was broad enough to govern compulsory retirement, since compulsion to retire was a form of dismissal for all practical purposes.[86] In brief and question-begging reasons, the Court held that "[d]ismissal, suspension and retirement on pension are three different and distinct concepts," and therefore forced retirement could not be reviewed by an arbitrator under language which mentioned only dismissal and suspension.[87] Such decisions created conundrums for well-meaning arbitrators attempting to harmonize the Court's reserved rights jurisprudence with the recognition rule. For example, in *Re Palm Dairies and Retail, Wholesale and Department Store Union, Local 580*,[88]

84 2006 SCC 19 at para 28 [*Bisaillon*]. *See also Isidore Garon Ltée v Syndicat du bois ouvré de la region de Québec inc*, 2006 SCC 2 at paras 9–16 [*Isidore Garon*].

85 [1974] SCR 335 at para 3, 37 DLR (3d) 561. *See also Canadian Car & Foundry Co v Dinham*, [1960] SCR 3, 21 DLR (2d) 273. For a similar narrow and legalistic approach to remedial issues, see *e.g.*, *Union Carbide Canada Ltd v Weiler*, [1968] SCR 966, 70 DLR (2d) 333 and *Port Arthur Shipbuilding Co v Arthurs*, [1969] SCR 85, 70 DLR (2d) 693.

86 Although Weiler's arbitration decision is not reported, it is quoted extensively by George W Adams in "Bell Canada and the Older Worker: Who Will Review the Judges?" (1974) 12:2 *Osgoode Hall Law Journal* 389 at 408.

87 Bora Laskin (by then a justice of the Supreme Court of Canada) dissented, in what Adams describes as "the first thoroughly reasoned judicial opinion outlining the appropriate standards of judicial review in private labour arbitration matters." Adams, above note 86 at 395–96.

88 (1980), 26 LAC (2d) 414 (BC) (Arbitrator: Hope).

a board of arbitration dismissed a grievance challenging the employer's right to impose mandatory membership in a contributory pension plan without negotiating with the union. The board accepted the basic proposition that employers are not permitted to *negotiate* with individual employees, but concluded that collective bargaining statutes did not prohibit them from *imposing* terms and conditions of employment. The board registered both doctrinal and normative discomfort with this conclusion, but claimed to have no choice: "the Supreme Court of Canada has decreed that employers retain certain residual rights that can be lost or compromised only through collective bargaining itself," making residual rights theory the "law of the land."[89]

The contradictions generated by reserved rights theory have also created problems for determining the legal status of terms and conditions of employment which exist outside the collective agreement. Are such "orphan" rights enforceable, and if so, where and how can they be enforced if arbitrators claim to have no jurisdiction to enforce them? For employees who are not unionized, terms of the individual contract of employment are enforceable in the civil courts. But for unionized employees, individual contracts of employment cannot be enforced as long as the union continues to hold bargaining rights. The Supreme Court of Canada made this clear in *Paccar* when it rejected the argument that individual contracts of employment are suspended during the life of the collective agreement but "pop up" again to become effective as soon as that agreement expires.[90] It was made even clearer in the Court's decision in *Isidore Garon,* which expressly confirmed that individual contracts of employment are legally inoperative as long as the union holds bargaining rights.[91] As Deschamps J put it, the individual contract "cannot be relied on as a source of rights" as long as a union is the bargaining agent.[92] She linked the eclipse of the individual contract not to the existence of a collective agreement, but to the union's exclusive bargaining authority. To the question of, "[w]hat rights are supplanted by the collective scheme?", her response was unequivocal: "[i]f the right claimed can be characterized as

---

89 *Ibid* at para 114.

90 Above note 82.

91 *Isidore Garon*, above note 84 at para 27. For a discussion of this case, see Renée-Claude Drouin & Gilles Trudeau, "What Does *Isidore Garon* Mean for Arbitral Jurisdiction in Quebec?" (2006–2007) 13 *Canadian Labour and Employment Law Journal* 347.

92 *Isidore Garon, ibid.* Deschamps J was speaking for the majority.

a condition of employment, it cannot be negotiated individually by the employer and the employee. The union alone performs this task, and it must do so for the employees collectively."[93] If unionization has this effect regardless of whether or not there is a subsisting collective agreement, it inexorably follows that it also has this effect regardless of the content of that agreement.

The Supreme Court of Canada's numerous explicit holdings that the common law and the individual contract of employment have no application to employees in unionized workplaces leave in legal limbo terms and conditions of employment created by employer fiat. If the application of reserved rights theory places such terms and conditions outside arbitral jurisdiction, courts cannot logically step in to apply the common law without violating important principles of labour law flowing directly from the statutory framework. This does not mean that courts *do not* in fact step in. Prior to *Weber* they did so with some regularity, particularly with respect to issues involving pension and benefit plans, which courts had historically enforced in unionized workplaces in much the same way as in non-unionized workplaces.[94] Judicial jurisdiction was rarely challenged in such cases, and courts were consequently not called upon to explain the anomaly. However, it was inevitable that at some point, the Supreme Court would have to confront the conceptual gap between the abstract idea of collective bargaining as a substitute for the common law of employment, and the concrete reality that narrow approaches to arbitral jurisdiction left some terms and conditions unenforceable within the mechanisms created by the collective bargaining framework.

## F. *WEBER* AND THE "ESSENTIAL CHARACTER OF THE DISPUTE"

*Weber* and its companion case, *New Brunswick v O'Leary*,[95] were the Supreme Court of Canada's effort to close that conceptual gap. In interestingly symmetrical decisions, the Court held that attempts by both employee and employer to bring common law tort claims before the courts were inconsistent with the statutory collective bargaining framework, Canadian labour policy and evolving jurisprudence which promoted arbitration

---

93 *Ibid* at para 25.

94 This issue is discussed in more detail in Shilton, "Pension Rights," above note 83 at 144–46.

95 [1995] 2 SCR 967. The Court's main reasons are found in *Weber*.

as the preferred mechanism for resolving disputes in unionized workplaces.[96] The Court held that the disputes underlying the claims in both cases arose in their essential character from the collective agreement and belonged within the exclusive jurisdiction of an arbitrator, despite the fact that the plaintiffs had framed them as tort claims (and in the case of *Weber*, as a *Charter* claim as well).

Other essays in this collection have reviewed in detail the facts and legal histories of the *Weber* and *O'Leary* cases and I will not replough that ground. For my purposes, I want to make three simple points about what the Supreme Court of Canada did and did not decide in these cases. First, the foundation of the Court's holding is simply that substance should triumph over form in drawing jurisdictional boundaries between courts and arbitrators. Justice McLachlin commenced her *Weber* decision with this question: "When may parties who have agreed to settle their differences by arbitration under a collective agreement sue in tort? That is the issue raised by this appeal, and its companion case, *New Brunswick v O'Leary* . . . ."[97] In responding to that question, McLachlin J held that neither employees nor employers may evade the dispute resolution procedures established under collective agreements (and collective bargaining statutes) by filing pleadings which characterize their disputes as common law causes of action. As LeBel J put it in a later decision, *Weber* held that jurisdictional issues must be addressed using a "flexible and contextual method which seeks to avoid formalistic classifications."[98]

Second, the Court held only that the substantive disputes in the two cases should be dealt with by arbitrators rather than courts. Nowhere in either decision does the Court so much as hint at what the outcomes of such arbitrations would or should be. *Weber* critics have expressed dismay at the prospect that individual employees might be required to pay significant monetary damages for behavior that has traditionally been treated in unionized workplaces as a disciplinary matter only. They have also expressed concern that exposing employers to potential liability for damages for defamation may have a "chilling effect" on routine workplace interactions.[99] But neither of those outcomes follows inexorably — or even probably — from the Court's conclusion that these disputes fall

96 *Weber*, above note 2 at paras 40–46.

97 *Ibid* at para 32.

98 *Allen v Alberta*, 2003 SCC 13 at para 14.

99 *See e.g.*, *Seneca Arbitration Decision*, above note 4 at para 51; M. Picher, above note 3 at 122–25.

within the exclusive jurisdiction of an arbitrator. In both cases, an arbitrator might well dismiss the grievances on the ground that the remedy sought was inappropriate under the governing legal rules. In other words, the plaintiffs could lose their claims on the merits, a not-uncommon outcome even in cases in which there is no dispute about jurisdiction.

Third, in neither case does the Court hold that arbitrators have the jurisdiction to enforce the common law of torts. In fact, the reverse is true. The decisions are very clear that it is the disputes or "differences" which the Court locates within the exclusive jurisdiction of an arbitrator. What happens to those disputes will depend on what legal rules are found to govern at arbitration. The decisions do not purport to expand the range of arbitral authority or add to the powers arbitrators have been given by the statutory framework and the collective agreements they are asked to enforce. Justice McLachlin could scarcely have been clearer on this point:

> This does not mean that the arbitrator will consider separate "cases" of tort, contract or *Charter*. Rather, in dealing with the dispute under the collective agreement and fashioning an appropriate remedy, the arbitrator will have regard to whether the breach of the collective agreement also constitutes a breach of a common law duty, or of the *Charter*.[100]

Standing alone, none of these points should have been particularly controversial. Why then has there been so much scholarly and arbitral resistance to their implications? If the plaintiffs in *Weber* and *O'Leary* had packaged their claims as contract claims — as they well could have, given the nature of the claims — the Court's conclusion that the disputes should be dealt with by an arbitrator would not likely have created controversy in the labour law community even though contract claims are rooted in the common law. In principle, we accept that for unionized employees the collective agreement occupies the space that would otherwise be occupied by the terms of individual contracts of employment — not just *some* of that space, but *all* of that space. We understand that rights structuring the employment relationship which we would have called contract rights at common law must now be located in the collective agreement if they are to be enforceable. That reality rubs up against reserved rights doctrine, as we have seen in Part E, but it is nevertheless understood and accepted in its general contours.

100 *Weber*, above note 2 at para 60.

What is less intuitively obvious is that the collective bargaining regime also substitutes for *tort* claims arising from the employment relationship. It is this proposition, fundamental to the *Weber* and *O'Leary* holdings, that has attracted the strongest criticism. But this proposition logically follows from the premise that collective bargaining governs legal relations between employer and employee in unionized workplaces. Tort and contract are two sides of the same coin. They are simply convenient categories in which to place common law rules regulating relationships, and they have always been fairly porous categories within relationships primarily defined by contract. Tort principles and contract principles constantly overlap and merge. In the mid-1970s, commercial law scholar Grant Gilmore famously announced "the death of contract." He argued that contract law was in the process of being subsumed by tort law, and proposed somewhat facetiously that instead of torts and contracts, law schools should now teach their first year students a new subject: "contorts."[101] Gilmore wrote before the "law and economics" movement gained serious momentum, and it is arguable that the trend he identified has now been reversed, with contract law swallowing tort law within contractual relationships. The point is the same, however: while contract and tort are distinct in the abstract, clear boundaries are difficult to locate in concrete relationships such as the employment relationship.

When Canadian courts deal with employment relationships in which no union is involved, they maintain constant vigilance to avoid duplication and overlap with respect to contract and tort remedies. They show extreme reluctance to develop novel tort remedies, preferring to do remedial justice on the safer and better-trodden ground of contract law.[102] Their reasons are clearly articulated in *Piresferreira v Ayotte*,[103] in which the Court of Appeal for Ontario declined to impose a general tort duty on employers to avoid the negligent infliction of mental suffering. Applying the conventional two-part test for identifying a legal duty of care, the Court held that the employment relationship was sufficiently proximate to give rise to such a duty, but nevertheless found strong counter-

101 Grant Gilmore, *The Death of Contract* (Columbus: Ohio State University Press, 1974) at 87–90.

102 *See Wallace v United Grain Growers Ltd*, [1997] SCR 701 at paras 75–77, 152 DLR (4th) 1, where the Court rejected a tort of "breach of a good faith and fair dealing obligation with regard to dismissals." See also *Honda Canada Inc v Keays*, 2008 SCC 39 at paras 57–58.

103 2010 ONCA 384, leave to appeal to SCC refused, 282 OAC 399n (20 January 2011).

vailing policy reasons for refusing to give it legal recognition. The Court expressed concern that within employment relationships, a duty to avoid the infliction of mental suffering would largely duplicate the law of constructive dismissal, and would disrupt settled principles of "employment law" — not tort law or contract law, but "employment law." The Court was also concerned that giving legal recognition to a tort duty of this type would involve courts in monitoring employee performance and supervision. To quote the judgment:

> It is unnecessary and undesirable to expand the court's involvement in such questions. It is unnecessary because if the employees are sufficiently aggrieved, they can claim constructive dismissal. It is undesirable because it would be a considerable intrusion by the courts into the workplace, it has a real potential to constrain efforts to achieve increased efficiencies, and the postulated duty of care is so general and broad it could apply indeterminately.[104]

The bottom line is that the common law of both tort and contract regulate terms and conditions of employment.[105] In unionized workplaces, terms and conditions of employment are governed by collective bar-

104 *Ibid* at para 62. The Court in *Piresfeirrara* confirmed that employers and supervisors may be liable in tort for *intentional* infliction of mental suffering on an employee but rejected an objective standard for determining intention because such a reduced standard would also "unduly interfere with the settled principles of employment law." *Ibid* at paras 62, 76.

105 This point is implicitly conceded by arbitrators and scholars who insist that tort rights and remedies *may* fall within the jurisdiction of arbitrators, but only if the parties to collective bargaining have explicitly said so in their collective agreements. *See e.g.*, *Seneca Arbitration Decision,* above note 4 at para 41:

> If the parties to a collective agreement wanted, they could choose to include clauses prohibiting tortious misconduct. They could expressly prohibit defamatory conduct by either the employer or employee; they could expressly prohibit negligent conduct by either the employer or the employee; they could expressly prohibit the intentional infliction of mental distress; they could expressly provide that complaints of this nature could be not only grieved but also brought to arbitration. If the parties choose to regulate the potential torts that might arise in their workplace interactions, then the commission of these torts would become a breach of their contractual arrangement and damages flowing from the tortious conduct would then properly flow directly from the collective agreement.

In fact, the parties could *not* bargain about these issues if they were not terms and conditions of employment, since they would not fall within the scope of bargaining.

gaining and collective agreements, and it is neither practical nor legally coherent to attempt to compartmentalize them into tort claims and contract claims and deal with them in different fora. *Weber* quite logically directs decision-makers to ignore how the common law has categorized employment-related legal rights, and focus instead on the essential character of the dispute. It is simply not relevant whether a dispute would be a contract dispute or a tort dispute if the employment relationship were not unionized. Since the relationship *is* unionized, the issue is whether "the dispute in its essential character arises from the interpretation, application, administration or violation of the collective agreement." If employers and employees have reciprocal rights and responsibilities arising from the employment relationship, it is in the collective agreement that they will be found, and not in the external common law that would apply if they were not unionized.

This point is strongly underlined in the 2006 decision of the Supreme Court of Canada in *Bisaillon*,[106] in which the Court applied *Weber* to hold that disputes involving the university's employer-sponsored pension plan belonged within the exclusive jurisdiction of an arbitrator and could not be pursued through a civil class action. While the nine collective agreements involved referred to the pension plan, their language fell well short of the "incorporation by reference" standard established in Canadian arbitral jurisprudence for treating pension plan issues as falling within the jurisdiction of arbitrators.[107] The Concordia plan began to accumulate a significant surplus, which the university accessed to take contribution holidays, pay plan expenses and fund early retirement packages, unilaterally amending the plan text to authorize its use of the funds, and to spell out that any surplus would revert to the university on plan termination.[108] Eight out of the nine Concordia unions collaborated to challenge these moves by way of a class action. The ninth union, the faculty association, moved (with Concordia's backing) to have the action dismissed, claiming that pension matters belonged within the exclusive jurisdiction of an arbitrator. The majority of the Supreme Court of Canada agreed, holding that permitting the class action to proceed would be "incompatible with the exclusive jurisdiction of grievance arbitrators and the representative function of certified unions."[109]

106 *Bisaillon*, above note 84.

107 See Brown & Beatty, above note 78 at 4:1440.

108 *Bisaillon*, above note 84 at para 8.

109 *Ibid.*

In support of this conclusion, LeBel J, author of the majority decision, focused primarily on the intimate connections between the recognition rule, i.e., the union's "monopoly of representation," and the exclusive jurisdiction of an arbitrator.[110] Justice LeBel directly linked the recognition rule to the scope of exclusive arbitral jurisdiction, as determined by the *Weber* test. He noted that in *Weber* and subsequent cases, the Court "has clearly adopted a liberal position according to which grievance arbitrators have a broad exclusive jurisdiction over issues relating to conditions of employment, provided that those conditions can be shown to have an express or implicit connection to the collective agreement."[111] He was clear that once there is a collective agreement in place, regardless of its content, that agreement becomes "the regulatory framework governing relations between the union and the employer, as well as the individual relationships between the employer and employees."[112]

Both *Weber* and *Bisaillon* are not without their ambiguities. In *Weber*, McLachlin J refused to rule out the possibility that employers and employees may find themselves involved in civil litigation with each other, conceding that the "fact that the parties are employer and employee may not be determinative" of the jurisdictional question, and the *Weber* approach "does not preclude all actions in the courts between employer and employee."[113] However, she provided no useful clues as to how such claims could arise out of the employment relationship.[114] In addition, she made reference from time to time to the common law as if it might still have some vitality at arbitration.[115] The title of the symposium which gave rise to this volume is based on one such reference in which McLachlin J,

110 *Ibid* at paras 23–28.

111 *Ibid* at para 33.

112 *Ibid* at para 25.

113 *Weber*, above note 2 at paras 52–53.

114 The cases McLachlin J cited in her reasons in *Weber* in support of this proposition are unhelpful in teasing out her meaning. *Weber*, above note 2 at para 54. *Butt v USWA* (1993), 106 Nfld & PEIR 181 was essentially a duty of fair representation claim against the union. In *Bourne v Otis Elevator Co* (1984), 45 OR (2d) 321, the court dismissed the plaintiff's wrongful dismissal claim for lack of jurisdiction. In a single case, *Elliott v De Havilland Aircraft Co of Canada Ltd* (1989), 13 ACWS (3d) 409, 32 OAC 250, a court did take jurisdiction over a unionized employee's common law claim. Ironically, this case — a claim in bailment against a unionized employer for loss of an employee's tools — would almost certainly be dismissed by a post-*Weber* court on the ground that the dispute arose out of the collective agreement.

115 *Weber*, above note 2, paras 55–56, 61.

quoting Lord Denning, reminded us that arbitrators are bound to apply the "law of the land": "There is not one law for arbitrators and another for the court, but one law for all."[116] These ambiguities are compounded by her insistence that disputes fall within the exclusive jurisdiction of an arbitrator only where they pass the *Weber* test, which requires assessment of *both* the "nature of the dispute" and the "ambit of the collective agreement." While the word "ambit" signals a capacious approach to interpretation going beyond the express wording of the agreement, the *Weber* test nevertheless demands *some* link between the dispute and the agreement—although the outcomes in *Weber* and *O'Leary* themselves suggest that the link may be quite tenuous.[117] The requirement of a link suggests that disputes which by their "nature" are arbitrable under some agreements may yet by inarbitrable under others, a result that appears to confuse the question of "arbitrability" with the quite different question of whether the grievance will succeed or fail on the merits under the language of the particular agreement.

In *Bisaillon*, too, the Court hedged its bets, declining from an abundance of judicial caution to articulate a definitive rule that court jurisdiction will always be ousted where disputes relate to terms and conditions of employment. Justice LeBel cited, with apparent approval, appellate case law holding that a pension plan was "an integral part of the collective agreement" simply because it "formed part of the employees' remuneration and conditions of employment."[118] He also cited scholarly authority that "the inclusion in a collective agreement of very general clauses, such as the classic clause recognizing the employer's management rights, could confer jurisdiction over issues regarding the application and implementation of benefits plans, including pension plans."[119] He was clearly drawn to this approach, which would make the scope of arbitration co-extensive with the scope of bargaining. However, since the

116 *Ibid* at para. 61.

117 Experienced arbitrators who have examined the provisions of the agreements at issue in *Weber* and *O'Leary* more closely than the Court did have identified elementary errors of collective agreement interpretation in the Court's decisions, and expressed serious skepticism that the links the Court found reflect any "intention of the parties" to open arbitration to these types of claims. *See* Picher, above note 3 at 108–118; Richard MacDowell, "Labour Arbitration—The New Labour Court?" (2000) 8 *Canadian Labour and Employment Law Journal* 121 at 150–1.

118 *Bisaillon*, above note 84 at para 38.

119 *Ibid.*

Concordia collective agreements all made at least some reference to the pension plan, LeBel J could and did resolve the case on the narrower, if still unorthodox, ground that references to the plan in the Concordia agreements were sufficient to bring the plan within the ambit of the agreement for jurisdictional purposes.[120] His articulation of the Court's "liberal position" — that arbitrators have "a broad exclusive jurisdiction over issues relating to conditions of employment, provided that those conditions can be shown to have an express or implicit connection to the collective agreement" — begs the question of what "connection" means in this context, and how it is to be identified.

Despite their ambiguities, however, these decisions leave no room for enclaves of employment "rights" unilaterally established by the employer outside the collective agreement, enforced outside the arbitration process and governed by the common law. Instead, they confirm — with only a few rough edges — that within unionized workplaces, rights arising out of the employment relationship are governed by the procedures and outcomes of collective bargaining within the framework of collective bargaining statutes. It follows that reserved rights theory in the form conventionally applied by Canadian arbitrators cannot survive *Weber*.

## G. CONCLUSION: A RETURN TO INDUSTRIAL SELF-GOVERNMENT?

The lesson of *Weber* is not that arbitrators have jurisdiction over the common law. The lesson is that the common law does not have direct relevance to disputes that involve terms and conditions of employment in unionized workplaces. *Weber*, further glossed by *O'Leary* and *Bisaillon*, reminds us that the fruit of collective bargaining consists not only of the express terms of the agreement but also the rights implied by that agreement within the legal framework regulating collective bargaining and labour arbitration. These decisions confirm the industrial pluralist principle that the private law governing the unionized workplace is the law of the collective agreement. They do not instruct arbitrators to bring the common law into that agreement. Instead, they instruct arbitrators

120 *Ibid* at paras 50–51. The orthodox position is that "maintenance of benefit" provisions are not sufficient to constitute "incorporation by reference." *See* Brown & Beatty, above note 78 at 4:1440.

to do what arbitrators have always understood to be their core task — to enforce the agreement. But they also remind arbitrators that the agreement consists of more than its express wording, and that they must take a liberal — indeed a Laskinesque — perspective when determining the "essential character" of workplace disputes and the "ambit" of collective agreements.

What does this mean for unionized employees? A liberal approach means that arbitrators may look to the common law, as they always could and often did, for analogies and persuasive policy reasons for importing or rejecting concepts and approaches to problem-solving in applying collective agreements. It does not mean that they may apply the common law *per se*; it is what the pluralists called the "common law of the shop," derived from the "climate of collective bargaining," that puts flesh on the bones of collective agreements. But a liberal approach leaves no room for the "strict constructionist" approach characteristic of reserved rights theory.

This is the good news for unionized employees, since it ensures a forum for resolving workplace disputes that might otherwise have fallen into reserved rights limbo. But *Weber* also has some not-so-good news for unionized employees, as Murray Weber learned the hard way. It effectively makes collective agreements the only source of private employment-based rights, and arbitration the only port of call for their enforcement. In rejecting a narrow conception of arbitral jurisdiction, the Court has made it clear that unionized employees (and employers) cannot "have their cake and eat it too." It has dispelled the illusion that employment-based claims found to be inarbitrable may be resolved as common law claims in the courts. The option proposed by the arbitration board in *Seneca College* to the grievor whose claim for aggravated/punitive damages it denied — the option of "pursu[ing] his claims in tort in the appropriate civil forum"[121] — is simply not available.

*Weber*'s restatement of the relationship between the collective agreement and the common law, reflected also in *O'Leary* and subsequently applied in *Bisaillon*, resolves the contradictions identified in Part E which flow from importing reserved rights doctrine into the Canadian collective bargaining model. The decisions confirm that in unionized workplaces, collective bargaining occupies the field formerly occupied by the common law of employment. They restore the primacy of the recognition

121 *Seneca Arbitration Decision*, above note 4 at para 61.

rule by insisting that all employment-based rights in unionized workplaces must be negotiated with the union; they cannot be simply imposed by the employer. This means that any rights grounded in the "private law" relationship flowing between employer and employee will arise from the collective agreement, if not directly then indirectly. All such rights claims will therefore be arbitrable. Not all will succeed, of course, since the content of private rights will vary from workplace to workplace, and will depend, as it always has, on the relative strength of the parties' bargaining power. But after *Weber*, employment-based rights can no longer be consigned to enclaves of inarbitrability.

*Weber* has thus reclaimed territory arbitrators had ceded to the courts in defiance of the policy behind the statutory framework for collective bargaining. In doing so, it has provided a theoretical road map for undoing much of the injury inflicted on the pluralist conception of industrial self-government by reserved rights theory. It must be acknowledged, however — indeed it is a key message of Etherington's essay in this volume[122] — that both courts and arbitrators have had some difficulty in following that road map. *Weber* has had only partial success in restoring arbitration to its central role as an autonomous mechanism for settling disputes in unionized workplaces, and has failed entirely in eliminating the jurisdictional contests that have plagued employment litigation.

At least part of the continuing problem lies within the industrial pluralist vision itself. That vision depends on two propositions which, if indeed they were ever true, are certainly not true in twenty-first century workplaces: that there is a clear conceptual and practical divide between private law and public law, and that employment law is private law. Since the days of the early pluralist theorists, there has been a massive intrusion of public law into the realm of labour arbitration.[123] While arbitral jurisdiction to enforce public law is not always exclusive, the Supreme Court of Canada has made it clear that when arbitrators are required to apply public law, they are carrying out a public responsibility which may well clash head on with the intention of the parties.[124] Ironically, in reasserting the centrality of the parties' private enforcement mechan-

---

122 Brian Etherington, "*Weber*, and Almost Everything After, 20 Years Later: Its Impact on Individual *Charter*, Common Law and Statutory Rights Claims," Chapter 2, this volume.

123 See Elizabeth Shilton, "Labour Arbitration and Public Rights Claims: Forcing Square Pegs into Round Holes," (2016) 41 Queen's Law Journal 275.

124 *Parry Sound*, above note 37.

isms, *Weber* itself weaves the *Constitution* — that most public of all public laws — ever more closely into the fabric of the collective agreement. The fact that labour arbitration now plays an incontestably public role calls into serious question the legitimacy of its continued autonomy from public enforcement systems.

The autonomy of arbitration is also under siege from claims which clearly "arise out of the collective agreement" in the sense that they involve rights generated through collective bargaining, but may be polycentric in that they have important implications for third party rights and interests. Examples include disputes involving insured benefit plans. They also include many pension disputes, which may involve multi-employer pension plans or raise issues which have direct impact on retirees, spouses and non-employee beneficiaries who are not represented by the union. Third-party rights and interests may also arise with some frequency in quite routine cases involving claims of workplace discrimination and harassment which implicate employees who are not members of the bargaining unit. Claims for reasonable accommodation may also cross bargaining unit boundaries.

Claims arising out of public law and claims that directly affect rights and interests beyond the confines of the bargaining unit generate pressures that cannot be fairly and efficiently contained within the perimeter of a process designed to enforce private law. Such claims take arbitrators well beyond the sheltered world of the industrial pluralists, and challenge both the legitimacy and the efficacy of autonomous dispute resolution controlled by the parties to collective bargaining. Despite the Supreme Court's best efforts in *Weber* and subsequent cases, rehabilitating the pluralist/Laskin vision of arbitration as an organ of industrial self-government may no longer be a feasible or worthwhile project. Instead, it may be time to open a new debate about whether the adjudication of rights claims in unionized workplaces should become a public responsibility, and if so, what a public enforcement system would look like.

But that is a topic for another symposium.

CHAPTER FOUR

# Burning Down the (Boat) House: How the Common Law Helps Make Sense of *Weber*

Brian Langille

## INTRODUCTION — "IT WAS TWENTY YEARS AGO TODAY"

This is a curious little paper. I like little papers — but I am not so sure I like them to be curious, at least at this stage of the game. But here it is.

First, a few words about what this paper is not. This paper is not an attempt to have the final say about *Weber v Ontario Hydro*,[1] nor to reconcile all of the jurisprudence which has followed. I have not read all of the post-*Weber* decisions that try to make sense of the case. (I have read a few but not all). However, having a complete grasp of that material is not critical in this instance because I am not interested, at least for the purposes of this paper, in what I see as the common view of *Weber* and the problems it presents to the labour law community. Nor am I interested in the way many arbitrators and Courts have responded to *Weber* — for example, by actually dealing with, or deciding not to deal with defamation claims as such.[2] So this is not a paper which seeks to make a contribution to the mainstream debate about *Weber* and its legal legacy.

Rather, I wish to pursue the idea that the mainstream debate, as far as I have had to deal with it and as far as I can understand it, is often, in

1 [1995] 2 SCR 929 [*Weber*].

2 See the discussion of Innis Christie's well known decision in *ABT Building Products Canada Ltd v Communications, Energy and Paperworkers Union of Canada, Local 434* (2000), 90 LAC (4th) 1 [*ABT Building*] below at Part D.

my view, misconceived and unhelpful. I seek another stream into which to divert the *Weber* debate. I think that alternative stream exists and has been available from the beginning. It can be seen more clearly if we take the time to read the much shorter and "to the point" decision in *Weber's* companion, *New Brunswick v O'Leary*[3] and to appreciate the rather basic and common law-based ideas it deploys. It is in light of such a reading that the standard "Weber discourse" can be seen as largely misconceived. Not only misconceived, but also unhelpful, in that it adds credence to the stinging critique of the current state of health of Canadian labour arbitration set out in Warren Winkler's 2010 Donald Wood Lecture.[4] In that lecture, Winkler expresses deep concern that because we are losing sight of the broad contours of Canadian labour law, we are "at risk of becoming dysfunctional and irrelevant,"[5] and that as a result our decisions are not only legally misguided, but come at greater expense and delay to the parties — exactly the opposite of what labour arbitration was intended to do. Lacking a comprehensive labour law vision in which to position the *Weber* decision also makes it less likely that we will get "back to our roots"[6] as Winkler rightly wishes we could do.

The basic point, as I hope will become clear, is that the standard view of *Weber* starts in the wrong place. It is what may be called an "institutional" or "arbitration-centric" or "process" view. On this view, the place to start thinking about *Weber* is to see the problem as one of "jurisdiction" (to deploy what is in my view a really useless term in almost all labour law contexts in which it is invoked): the jurisdiction of arbitrators to apply sources of law external to the collective agreement and the competing "jurisdiction" of other adjudicators; or the exclusive "jurisdiction" of either to do so. I think this starts too close to the legal ground. To frame *Weber* properly, we need to draw our lens back to see the *Weber* issue as an instance of a broader, basic, less technical, but also more familiar, substantive legal problem. To get *Weber* in view. This is the main, and perhaps "curious" point of this paper.

---

3 [1995] 2 SCR 967 [*O'Leary*].

4 Warren Winkler, "Labour Arbitration and Conflict Resolution: Back to Our Roots" (2010 Don Wood Lecture delivered at the School of Policy Studies, Queen's University, 30 November 2010), (Kingston: Queen's Industrial Relations Centre, 2010), online: http://irc.queensu.ca/articles/labour-arbitration-and-conflict-resolution-back-our-roots [Winkler].

5 *Ibid* at 1.

6 *Ibid*.

This paper argues that *Weber* stands for an entirely sound proposition in basic legal thinking—that the work contract, whether individual or collective, speaks to and alters the normal set of rights, responsibilities, and remedies that apply between strangers. *Weber* instructs arbitrators that they are responsible for workplace disputes and that when a union official criticizes the employer's safety record, or when an employee says some very unfortunate things about the boss, then what would otherwise be a defamation case if the parties had been two strangers has to be seen and dealt with very differently, because the parties in this dispute are not strangers. This paper's claim is that this line of thought has been available since the very day that *Weber* was decided. This is because of the much briefer decision in *Weber's* companion, *O'Leary*, which was issued on the same day. In my view *O'Leary* holds the key to a much simpler view of *Weber*.

In what follows, I first examine the common perception of *Weber*, and why it misses this critical legal point (Part A). I then move on to the decision in *O'Leary*, and why it is the key to understanding *Weber* (Part B). In Part C I take a brief look at the old, and it seems forgotten, but still ongoing common law debate about our issue. This debate reminds us that current and recent cases on "third parties" may look, at first blush, to be about general contract law, but actually turn out to part of this puzzle. Part D draws together these considerations with a view to letting us see *Weber* as we should. *Weber*, it turns out, is not so much a technical decision case about arbitrators' exclusive "jurisdiction"—i.e., a case which says some very alarming things about arbitrators hearing common law suits for defamation. Rather, it is better seen as primarily a substantive case about the content of collective agreements, which relies upon some very basic legal ways of thinking, rooted in the common law. As such it makes a lot of sense and tells arbitrators to get on with the job they have been doing all along.

## A. THE PROBLEM WITH THE RECEIVED VIEW OF WEBER

The reaction of the Canadian arbitration community, and much of the labour relations community, to the Supreme Court of Canada's decision in *Weber* was one of amazement, disbelief, and, at least in private, apoplexy. Twenty years and much jurisprudential confusion later, it seems that this is still the case. That is why we are having this very symposium.

The commonly-held view established by *Weber* is that in workplaces under collective agreements arbitrators are not only to interpret and apply those agreements and related workplace laws, such as human rights codes or employment standards laws, but, further, can hear tort, constitutional (i.e., *Charter*) and other claims if they arise in the workplace context. This proposition has left many scratching their heads, if not gasping for breath. On this view, *Weber* means that an employer cannot sue an employee (and vice-versa) in the Courts for wrongs like defamation, but rather must pursue defamation claims before an arbitrator. If it is true that arbitrators are now empowered to hear defamation law suits, then *Weber* certainly marks a very unfortunate turn of legal events and is a legitimate source of consternation.

Some, who are very well placed to do so, have tried to patiently explain to the world all that is wrong with *Weber* on this view of what the case stands for.[7] But, as explained above, this paper takes a different and, hopefully more positive approach. My basic argument, only briefly developed here, is also I think bolder. I challenge the conventional interpretation of *Weber*, arguing that *Weber* says something quite different from what people think it says, and something actually helpful and non-threatening. I argue that *Weber* is simply a modern playing out of a very old labour problem, one which has long antecedents in the common law of the contract of employment. This is the problem of the relationship, in the most common sort of case, of tort and contract.

But that puts the matter too abstractly. To be more specific, we can put this point in terms of the following example: if a unionized employee (negligently) hits the plant wall with a fork lift, isn't there something odd about the employer suing that employee in tort for the resulting damage? A warning, or a one-day suspension, or some other form of discipline is understandable. But a law suit? On the view taken here it is vital to see that this discomfort with this approach does not arise from any technical matter concerning an arbitrator's "exclusive" jurisdiction under our statutory schemes. It is a substantive matter, not a procedural one,

7 *See i.e.*, Richard MacDowell, "Labour Arbitration—The New Labour Court?" (2000) 8 *Canadian Labour and Employment Law Journal* 121; Bernard Adell, "Jurisdictional Overlap Between Arbitration and Other Forms: An Update" (2000) 8 *Canadian Labour and Employment Law Journal* 179 at 179; Donald D Carter, "Looking at *Weber* Five Years Later: Is it Time for a New Approach?" (2000) 8 *Canadian Labour and Employment Law Journal* 231; Brian Etherington, "Promises, Promises: Notes on Diversity and Access to Justice" (2000) 26:1 *Queen's Law Journal* 43 at 60–62; Michel

and it relates to the very issue of what the collective agreement actually says — both explicitly and implicitly.

And a central point in this brief paper is that our discomfort would be equally strong at common law — maybe the employer can dismiss, or even, now, perhaps, discipline the fork lift driver — but to sue an employee in tort, that seems very odd. Indeed, as we shall see, this issue has been the subject of long debate at common law.

It is odd, but why? Well, as is suggested below, for the same sort of reasons that have led the Supreme Court of Canada to hold that it would be odd if a third party suffering damages because of an employee's negligence can sue the employee, and not just the employer.[8] Or to complete the trio of issues actually in play here — for the same sort of reasons that a third party who is injured by the employee's negligence *can* sue the employer.[9]

At the heart of our instinct in these cases is a sound idea — that the work contract, whether individual or collective, speaks to and alters the normal set of tort rights, responsibilities, and remedies that apply between strangers. Seen this way *Weber* is not telling arbitrators to hear defamation suits — nor to tack on a negligence claim to the discipline handed out by the employer to the fork lift driver in our example. Rather, *Weber* is instructing arbitrators that they are responsible for workplace disputes — that when a union official criticizes the employer's safety record, or when an employee says some very unfortunate things about the boss (or vice-versa), what would otherwise be a defamation case between two strangers has to be seen and dealt with very differently. In short, it

---

G Picher, "Gilmer in the U.S. and Weber in Canada: Workplace Arbitration Exalted — And Assaulted" 1 *Labour Arbitration Year Book* (Toronto: Lancaster House, 1999) 1 [Picher]; Ray Brown and Brian Etherington, "*Weber v. Ontario Hydro*: A Denial of Access to Justice for the Organized Employee?" (1996) 4 *Canadian Labour and Employment Law Journal* 183; William Kaplan et al, "The Scope of Rights Arbitration after Weber v. Ontario Hydro" (1999) 7 *Canadian Labour and Employment Law Journal* 249; Michel G Picher, "Defining the Scope of Arbitration: The Impact of *Weber*: an Arbitrator's Perspective" (1999–2000) 1 *Labour Arbitration Year Book* 148. *See also* the excellent discussion of the defamation problem in M Philip Tunley & Brian PLJ Smeenk, "Defamation in a Labour and Employment Context" (2006–2007) 32 *Advocate's Quarterly* 83.

8 *London Drugs Ltd v Kuehne & Nagel International Ltd*, [1992] 3 SCR 299, 97 DLR (4th) 261 [*London Drugs*].

9 In the standard vicarious liability case, the law is dealing with three sides of a triangle: employer-employee-third party. And the law must, and does, get the sides to line up.

has to be dealt with within the web of terms and understandings, explicit and implicit, which are appropriate and have been developed to deal with workplace issues. The parties to these disputes are not strangers — they live in a world governed by a large and complex set of understandings, rules, and now detailed arbitral jurisprudence. So these cases are not to be seen as "mere" tort cases anymore. Rather, they raise discipline issues, administration of the collective agreement issues. They should not be thought of as raising tort issues at all, perhaps. Understood in this way, *Weber* belongs with other decisions that address one of the most complex questions of our law — the relationship of contract and tort. The general answer has to be — and is — that contract trumps tort. What *Weber* is doing is reminding us of this truth.

It is true that there are pragmatic considerations here — for instance, the employer has insurance for damage to the workplace and the employee does not. But these considerations are best understood as informing and being reflected in the terms and norms which have long governed all but the most unusual workplaces, and long restrained human resource professionals in most circumstances from breaking the "rules of the game" and seeking to do an end run around them via tort (or now constitutional) law. If we keep our eyes on the contractual reality arbitrators will never hear tort or constitutional claims "straight up." They will hear them as they always have — as part of reasonable contract administration within a thick set of workplace contractual norms. What would have been a straight-up negligence case between strangers is now part of a process of progressive discipline. Because that is what the parties have agreed to do.

## B. *NEW BRUNSWICK v O'LEARY*

If *O'Leary* had not come along we would have had to invent it. But because *O'Leary* did come along we can dispense with my fork lift example, and deal with real facts. In the Court's words: "O'Leary was employed by the Province of New Brunswick as a traffic counter operator. His work required him to travel throughout the province. The Province alleges that O'Leary drove its leased vehicle with a flat tire, necessitating repairs amounting to $2,815.54. The Province brought an action against O'Leary for this amount."[10] Mr O'Leary filed a motion to strike the employer's claim,

10 *O'Leary*, above note 3 at para 1.

arguing that it arose out of a collective agreement and thus fell within an arbitrator's "exclusive jurisdiction." The New Brunswick courts dismissed that motion, holding that the negligence claim did not fall under the collective agreement. Quite correctly, our Supreme Court rejected that view. It reached its conclusion by actually reading the agreement and noting two separate terms that were called into play — the general power to discipline and, in this particular agreement, an express term under which employees are responsible for "the safety and dependability of the employer's property and equipment." Thus, even though "negligence" was not explicitly mentioned in the collective agreement, it was dealt with "impliedly."

The case is brief and the reasoning bare — it relies upon *Weber* to carry the freight. Yet because it is so starkly decided, this case gives us our best window on *Weber*. There is nothing in the language of the decision, nor its logic, which permits the conclusion that what the court is doing here is instructing the arbitrator to hear the common law negligence case filed by the employer. Just the opposite. The key to the decision is that the collective agreement governs such matters. The logic is very basic, very legal, and very correct: the accident that transpired and the resulting claim are precisely the sorts of events that the collective agreement has addressed. The employer was seeking to do an end run around those contractual provisions by acting as if the parties were strangers, and suing in tort in a common law court. That is, there is not merely a procedural point here (who gets to hear the employer's case?); there is a substantive point (no matter who decides, what rules are in play?). And here there are very powerful rules in play, which transmogrify what would otherwise have been a straightforward tort claim — a non-employee of New Brunswick negligently damages the province's truck — into a very different sort of claim. The most important of these rules in most employment contexts will be the rules regarding discipline. Under those rules, what happens to Mr O'Leary at arbitration will depend on whether he had done this sort of thing before, his general disciplinary record, and all of the familiar arbitral considerations. This does not mean that Mr O'Leary receives a "get out of jail free" card. Far from it. Mr O'Leary is much more exposed than the ordinary New Brunswicker. This is because, unlike the ordinary citizen of New Brunswick, Mr O'Leary might, depending on all of the familiar considerations, lose his job for damaging the truck. Other New Brunswickers are merely on the hook for $2,815.54. Furthermore, and as the Court notes, it might be open to an arbitrator to make Mr O'Leary pay for the damage. But that would be a remedy constructed against a very different background and set of rules than would govern a "normal" negligence case at common law. As the Court put it in *Weber*: "This does not mean that the arbitrator will consider separate "cases" of tort, contract or *Charter*. Rather, in dealing with the dispute under the collective agreement and fashioning an appropriate remedy, the arbitrator will have regard to whether the breach of the collective agreement also constitutes a breach of a common law duty or of the *Charter*."[11]

This point about *Weber* being both a procedural and a substantive case is very important. It is true that these two issues overlap but we can analytically separate them, as we must when we look next at the common law. There the substantive point stands alone. But the traditional view of *Weber*, that it is only a procedural case about "jurisdiction," misses the much more important substantive point.[12]

## C. BURNING DOWN THE (BOAT) HOUSE: *WEBER* AND *O'LEARY* "AT COMMON LAW"

The issue at the heart of *Weber*—the relationship between the contract of employment (or collective agreement) and otherwise applicable law—has a long history at common law. For some time, employers have tried to do to employees under an individual contract of employment what New Brunswick in *O'Leary* tried to do to its unionized worker. And it has always been controversial. The issue can come up in three basic ways:

1) When an injured third party sues the employer as vicariously liable for the employee's negligence. (Standard vicarious liability).
2) When an employer directly sues an employee for losses caused by the employee's negligence, or seeks indemnity/subrogation after a vicarious liability finding. (This is *Douglas*[13] and *O'Leary*.)
3) When a third party sues a negligent employee directly, instead of, or in addition to, suing the employer. (This is *London Drugs*[14]—and the stevedoring cases.)

---

11 *Weber*, above note 1 at para 60.

12 This may be understandable in light of the structure of the *Weber* litigation; the main issue there was the exclusion of the courts, not how an arbitrator should approach the problem.

13 *Douglas v Kinger (Litigation Guardian of)*, 2008 ONCA 452 [*Douglas*].

14 Above note 8.

There is no real need to distinguish these circumstances, for they resolve to the same basic issue—the impact of contract, and specifically the contract of employment, on otherwise straightforward negligence liability.

So although it is interesting and important to note that all the cases get to the same result, and for the same reason, let us focus on situation number two. While it is possible to trace this very interesting debate back to the controversial decision of the House of Lords in *Lister v Romford Ice and Cold Storage Co Ltd*,[15] and then to a well-known and terrific dissent by Seaton JA in *Overmeyer Co v Wallace Transfer Ltd*,[16] we are now blessed in Ontario with a comprehensive and thoughtful 2008 Court of Appeal decision in *Douglas v Kinger*[17] which reviews all of this, and comes to a sound way of thinking about the issue.

What characterizes these cases is the legal instinct that the plaintiff-employer or third party was trespassing, in a way most employers simply did not do, upon a basic understanding about the limits of employee liability. But understanding where this instinct comes from has taken some time. *Douglas* does by and large correctly articulate the reasons behind the instinct. In an important sense, *Douglas* is a common law version of *Weber*.

The facts of the case are wonderful. A thirteen year-old employee was hired to do chores at the employer's cottage. He could not tell if the lawn mower gas tank had any gas in it—so he did the obvious thing—he lit a match to take a look. . . . Don't worry, he did not get hurt. But he did burn down the boathouse, costing his employer $285,000. The employer, in a subrogated claim brought by his insurer, sued the employee for the loss. It was held that the employer could not recover in either tort or contract. This is the right result and for the same reasons, I argue, as the result in *Weber* and *O'Leary*, with the procedural point about arbitrator's jurisdiction not involved at all. Although the judgement is overtly written in tort terms, it is clear that it could have been written, and in real terms *was* written, in contract law terms—because the issue is the relationship between the two. To have "law and order" here, the story must be the same from the two sides of this coin, albeit expressed in slightly different legal terminology. Thus, although here expressed in the language of tort law, and tests of foreseeability

15 (1956), [1957] AC 555 (HL).

16 (1975), 65 DLR (3d) 717, [1976] WWR 656 (BCCA).

17 *Douglas*, above note 13.

and proximity, the essence of the decision is more plainly expressed in the language of contract law: the reason the employer cannot sue the employee is that the contract between them says so. This is what employers and employees (and third parties for that matter) have agreed. To let the employer sue would violate the parties' reliance interests and reasonable expectations. The instinct that this employer, unlike the vast majority of employers, is attempting an end run around something is here made clear — the something that it is trying to avoid is the contract. Interestingly, the Court in *Douglas* makes the following observation, which completes the parallel to *Weber*:

> In addition, while employees are implicitly, if not explicitly, expected to exercise reasonable care in their employment, there are other means to encourage that care without burdening the employee with an impossible financial judgment. While the appellant argued that a finding of liability against the respondent will promote responsibility in all workers, I am not persuaded that is so. Discipline and dismissal are often cited as more useful tools to promote deterrence without the need to impose financial responsibility. Thus, a policy that supports good industrial relations weighs against the imposition of a duty of care.[18]

Expressed in very economical terms, that is the point of this short paper.

So where does that leave us? Pretty much where we should be and where we started, if only we had noticed.

But we do face a certain number of problems. Among these is the fact that "*Weber* discourse" has expanded so that it is now seen as critical to issues beyond the sorts raised in *Weber* and *O'Leary* — and in *Douglas*. So a large number of cases in which *Weber* is invoked are now cases about competing statutory regimes.[19] Insofar as *Weber* and *O'Leary* are relevant, they are relevant for the same reasons — that whoever hears the case should not do an end run around the collective agreement in a way which gets the substantive law of the relationship between the parties wrong.

---

18 *Ibid* at para 60.

19 *See i.e., Regina Police Assn v Regina (City) Police Commissioners*, 2000 SCC 14; *Québec (Commission des droits de la personne et des droits de la jeunesse) v Québec (Procureure générale)*, 2004 SCC 39.

## D. AN EXAMPLE OF MY THINKING IN PRACTICE

Now a word about a wonderful arbitration decision,[20] *ABT Building Products Canada Ltd. and C.E.P., Loc. 434 (Shatford)*, written by my mentor, Innis Christie. In that carefully reasoned decision Innis was confronted with the classic *Weber* issue put to him in the standard manner. Did he have "jurisdiction" to decide a defamation case? He answered this question with a considered "yes." He then went on to "seemingly" do just that — to apply the law of defamation and decide that case on that basis. But I say "seemingly" and I put that in "scare quotes" for a reason. My reading of the case is that what Innis actually did was to act as a labour arbitrator, dealing with things said by the employer about an employee (alleging, to use a general way of putting it, misuse of sick leave — as in *Weber*) in the context of the reasonable administration of the collective agreement. He therefore treats the matter sensibly, given that complex context with all its nuances and necessary considerations of the ways of doing business. His decision contains a full and frank discussion of disciplinary matters, the necessity of management making disciplinary judgement calls, but also of the unreasonableness of some of the employer's conduct on the facts — here, making unusual public allegations before fully investigating and so on — all leading to a situation in which an apology from the employer was appropriate. As in *Douglas* the legal language, on the surface, is the language of defamation law (in *Douglas* it was negligence law), rather than contract law. But what carries the day is the analysis of the way those general parts of our law are modified both by contract law, and also by the statutory regime of which arbitration of collective agreement disputes is an integral part. On my reading, *ABT Building Products* is about reasonable contract administration. This is, I think, exactly what McLachlin J meant in *Weber* when she said: "This does not mean that the arbitrator will consider separate "cases" of tort, contract or *Charter*. Rather, in dealing with the dispute under the collective agreement and fashioning an appropriate remedy, the arbitrator will have regard to whether the breach of the collective agreement also constitutes a breach of a common law duty or of the *Charter*."[21]

In order to follow this instruction, one has to read the collective agreement in context and determine what the contract and the regime

20 *ABT Building*, above note 2.

21 Above note 1 at para 60.

for enforcement of collective agreements through arbitration have done to redefine employees' general tort rights and remedies (as in *O'Leary*), or their *Charter* rights (to free speech, for example), or their privacy rights.

A perfect example of my general point is found in the *ABT Building Products* decision. Innis begins by invoking Justice Tom Berger's discussion of the role of qualified privilege in employment relationships:

> The only Canadian case cited by counsel for the Employer, *Fisher v Rankin*, is an even better example of how qualified privilege should operate in an employment context, more particularly a unionized one. It involved allegedly otherwise defamatory statements in the report of a joint union-management committee made in the course of grievance proceedings. Berger J. elaborated his reasons for concluding that such proceedings were the subject of qualified privilege . . . ;
>
>> The provisions of the collective agreement relating to the resolution of grievances are founded on the premise that there will be frank explanation by management of the reasons for the disciplinary action it has taken, and an opportunity for the union to put the case for the employee concerned. To hold that what is said at a meeting of the Joint Standing Committee may subject those present to a suit for defamation would nullify the whole proceeding.
>>
>> The company and the union had a collective agreement. That collective agreement was required by law to include a provision for the resolution of grievances. . . .
>>
>> No system for resolving grievances provided for under s. 22 of the Act would function at all if the reasons for discharge were not put before the union as the representative of the employees. I think that to deny to the company's representatives the defence of qualified privilege would have a chilling effect upon their willingness to state fairly and frankly the reasons for an employee's discharge.
>>
>> I think that society has an interest in seeing that the machinery established under s. 22 of *The Labour Relations Act* functions effectively: . . . The union's interest is clear. It is the employee's bargaining agent. The union in a sense acts as the advocate for the disciplined member. That duty is, rightly, cast upon it by the judgment in *Fisher v Pemberton et al.* . . . . It cannot adequately represent him unless it knows the case it has

> to meet. The union also has an interest, as the representative of all the employees, in knowing the grounds upon which the company has acted. To offer only one illustration, it has an interest in seeing that an objectionable precedent for disciplinary action is not set. The reasons for allowing qualified privilege to be asserted as a defence seem to me to be compelling.[22]

Innis applied Berger's reasoning to reach his own conclusion that qualified privilege did not apply in the circumstances before him:

> I find that the Employer here, having by-passed its own arrangements for checking on the validity of the Grievor's medical certificate, compounded its failure to respect established processes by not going through the Union in attempting to deal with what it thought would be a difficult labour relations incident. In communicating its concerns to the Union, statements about the Grievor in the same terms as those made to the meetings clearly would have attracted qualified privilege. So too might have statements to other employees as the situation unfolded, but in my opinion the highly unusual process adopted by the Employer on August 7, 1998, of going straight to the employees as a group about a matter in which the Union was supposed to represent them did not attract qualified privilege.[23]

This, in my view, is all just "normal" arbitration thinking about reasonable contract administration — which places the constraint of contextual reasonableness on both sides — expressed with an overlay of terms borrowed from defamation law. I think it is clear that it is the contextual demands of the collective agreement (i.e., contractual demands) which decide the case. This is what *O'Leary* instructs us all to do. It is remarkable that the common law can provide illumination in this regard. But so can arbitrators like Innis Christie.

## CONCLUSION — "BACK TO OUR ROOTS"

This reading of *Weber* may strike many, perhaps all, as naïve. It seems to put a lot of faith in arbitrators to bring very basic ideas to bear, and posits that labour arbitration cases are usually not "rocket science." It may also strike others as being out of touch with the complexities of modern

---

22 *ABT Building*, above note 2 at 41–42.

23 *Ibid* at 42.

labour arbitration. But perhaps the view expressed here is just one way of seeing the truth in Winkler's remark that "labour arbitration as we know it . . . has lost its course . . . its trajectory . . . its vision."[24]

This comment, in turn, points to a pedagogical point that I feel is important. This paper started after I wrote down, very quickly, some remarks after a labour law class in 2010. The class in which I had these thoughts was not one in which we were discussing *Weber*. In fact, we were not discussing labour arbitration. We were not even in the collective bargaining part of the course. Rather, we were discussing *Douglas* in the common-law portion of the class. It was precisely because of the comprehensive and integrated teaching approach that we advance in the *Labour Law Casebook*, in which we teach "all" of the law of work, all at once, that I was able to make the connection between *Douglas* and *Weber*. This in turn caused me to reflect that we really did make the right choice in the 1980s to go for an "integrated" approach to the teaching of labour law and employment law. Without this approach, we will fail to grasp a lot of basic and important ideas which all labour lawyers need to have taken on board. This little paper is, in my view, another "proof" of that thesis.

Recently I have come to the conclusion that this integrated approach is also necessary to grasp the legal and constitutional concept of freedom of association. A proper framing of that issue requires starting with the common law of freedom of association. Only then can we appreciate what the *Wagner Act* model really achieved from a legal point of view: it redistributed the common-law apportionment of rights and duties that had previously been laid out by common law judges. Once we appreciate that, we are in a position to understand our *Charter* cases, which are arguments about what the legislature cannot do, or must do, or can be free to choose to do or not do, in terms of altering the underlying common law distribution of rights and freedoms. Further, by starting with the common law, we can comprehend the role of international labour law in assisting courts to determine when the *Charter* requires legislatures to alter the common law complex of rights/duties and freedoms which constitute our freedom of association, and when it requires that they do not.

Without this comprehensive understanding, we will, as Winkler noted, not only have lost our course but also lack the vision to find our way back. Winkler offers his remedy in the last paragraph of his speech: "We have to get back to the basics, reformulate, and recalibrate the system to get it

24 Winkler, above note 4 at 1.

back on track. The changes can be made so that we return to the notion of a decision on the merits and not on some esoteric technicality — to a process that is timely, and that is affordable."[25]

On the view taken here the standard reaction to *Weber* was made available, perhaps inevitable, by the course of the developments that Winkler describes and deplores. Only from within that legalistic reality would we read *Weber* as a recipe for more and worse of the same. If we do not accept that reality as inevitable or desirable, we can read *Weber* — with the help of *O'Leary* (and *Douglas*) — as an invitation, or perhaps even an instruction, from the Supreme Court to labour arbitrators to get back to their real business of understanding and applying the "common law of the shop." And maybe that is what good arbitrators, such as Innis Christie, have really been doing all along.

25 *Ibid* at 10.

CHAPTER FIVE

# More Glue than Cracks? Rethinking *Weber* Gaps and Access to Justice for Unionized Employees

Karen Schucher

*In the liberal-individualist approach that has dominated American thought about legal procedure (and so much else), the purpose of law is to protect rights, and the purpose of rights is to empower the self. . . . Since the liberal theory of justice isolates the self from its social context and relationships, it considers that protection against others is sufficient for empowerment.*[1]

*Focusing on human relations is consistent with the traditional project of law. Law is deeply implicated in creating, interpreting, rationalizing, applying and enforcing rules of social interaction between individuals and groups. Though not always acknowledged in relational terms, law is integrally connected to the nature, quality and character of human relationships. It is in this capacity that law has contributed to the absence of caring and the widespread existence of relations of permanent inequality. Ironically, this same capacity also gives law the potential to promote more caring relationships and thereby enhance equality.*[2]

1 David M Trubek, "Critical Moments in Access to Justice Theory: The Quest for the Empowered Self" in Allan C Hutchinson, ed, *Access to Civil Justice* (Toronto: Carswell, 1990) 107 at 112.

2 Colleen Sheppard, "Caring in Human Relations and Legal Approaches to Equality" (1992–1993) 2 *National Journal of Constitutional Law* 305 at 329.

One potential outcome of the Supreme Court's decision in *Weber v Ontario Hydro*,[3] as Brian Etherington has argued in this volume and elsewhere, is that individual unionized employees may be denied access either to the courts or to labour arbitration to pursue common law or *Charter*[4] claims relating to their employment. Etherington sees this outcome as constituting a denial of access to justice for unionized employees.[5] I agree that where an individual is precluded from advancing a legal claim through formal legal enforcement processes, this raises an access-to-justice question that merits careful examination.[6] However, I have concluded that such an examination provides considerable reason to doubt that by consigning common law and *Charter* issues to labour arbitration, *Weber* has resulted in a denial of access to justice. I have similarly concluded that consigning statutory issues to labour arbitration does not result in a denial of access to justice. In this paper, I explain why I have reached these conclusions.

Etherington's particular concern is that *Weber* produces what he calls "*Weber* gaps": situations where unionized employees have no access to a legal forum in which to enforce common law or *Charter* rights claims relating to the workplace. He identifies two types of *Weber* gaps created by *Weber* and its application in subsequent cases. The first occurs where neither a court nor a labour arbitrator will accept jurisdiction to address

---

3 [1995] 2 SCR 929 [*Weber*].

4 *Canadian Charter of Rights and Freedoms*, Part I of the *Constitution Act, 1982*, being Schedule B to the *Canada Act 1982* (UK), 1982, c 11.

5 Brian Etherington, "*Weber* and Almost Everything After: 20 Years Later — Its Impact on *Charter*, Common Law, and Individual Statutory Rights Claims," Chapter 2, this volume [Etherington, "20 Years Later"]; Brian Etherington, "*O.P.S.E.U. v. Seneca College*: Deference as a Two-Edged Sword — A Missed Opportunity to Address the '*Weber* Gap'" (2006–2007) 13 *Canadian Labour and Employment Law Journal* 301 [Etherington, "*O.P.S.E.U. v. Seneca College*"]; Brian Etherington, "Promises, Promises: Notes on Diversity and Access to Justice" (2000) 26:1 *Queen's Law Journal* 43 [Etherington, "Promises, Promises"]; Ray Brown & Brian Etherington, "*Weber v Ontario Hydro*: A Denial of Access to Justice for the Organized Employee" (1996) 4:1 *Canadian Labour and Employment Law Journal* 183.

6 This argument was at the heart of the debate over replacing the Ontario Human Rights Commission enforcement process with direct access by individuals to the human rights tribunal. *See e.g.*, Michael Gottheil & Katherine Laird, "Direct Access to a Specialized Tribunal: The Ontario Experience" in Le Tribunal des droits de la personne et le Barreau du Québec, eds, *L'accès direct à un tribunal spécialisé en matière de droit à l'égalité: l'urgence d'agir au Québec?* (Cowansville, Québec: Éditions Yvon Blais, 2008) 145.

a unionized employee's common law or *Charter* claim. This could occur where a court concludes that the claim is connected with a matter covered by a collective agreement, and therefore falls within the exclusive jurisdiction of an arbitrator, but an arbitrator can find nothing in the agreement which would permit meaningful adjudication of the claim.[7] This type of *Weber* gap is a true gap, in that valid common law or *Charter* claims may exist, but employees cannot advance these claims in any formal legal process, with or without the support of the union.

The second type of gap is perhaps better described as a barrier rather than a gap. It occurs where a rights claim clearly falls within the exclusive jurisdiction of an arbitrator, but the union will not support the employee's grievance to arbitration.[8] In other words, there is an enforcement process available, but the unionized employee does not have independent access to this process and the union — the gatekeeper — will not provide access. This type of gap was not, of course, *created* by *Weber*; it has always existed with respect to employment rights flowing directly from the collective agreement and has long been a concern to liberal commentators such as Bora Laskin[9] and Bernie Adell, who argued that unions should not control access to arbitration.[10] But Etherington suggests that by sweeping

7 Etherington, "20 Years Later," above note 5 at 39–41. *See also* Elizabeth Shilton, "Enforcing Workplace Pension Rights for Unionized Employees: Is There a '*Weber* Gap'?" (2015) 19 *Canadian Labour and Employment Law Journal* 135.

8 Etherington, "20 Years Later," above note 5 at 51–55.

9 As far back as 1963, Bora Laskin argued that "[i]f collective bargaining is to be viewed as helping to fulfill an employee's claim to decent working conditions, then he should be given access to the machinery by which they may be vindicated if his bargaining agent chooses to refuse its support." Bora Laskin, "Collective Bargaining and Individual Rights" (1963) 6 *Canadian Bar Journal* 278 at 287.

10 BL Adell, "The Duty of Fair Representation: Effective Protection for Individual Rights in Collective Agreements?" (1970) 25:3 *Relations industrielles/Industrial Relations* 602; Bernard Adell, "Collective Agreements and Individual Rights: A Note on the Duty of Fair Representation" (1986) 11:2 *Queen's Law Journal* 251 [Adell, "Collective Agreements"]; Bernard Adell, "Establishing a Collective Employee Voice in the Workplace: How Can the Obstacles Be Lowered?" in G England, ed, *Essays in Labour Relations Law* (Don Mills, ON: CCH Canadian Limited, 1986) 3; Bernard Adell, "The Union's Duty of Fair Representation in Discrimination Cases: The New Obligation to Be Proactive" in Kevin Whitaker et al, eds, (2001–2002) 1 *Labour Arbitration Yearbook* (Toronto: Lancaster House, 2002) 263 [Adell, "Union's Duty"]; Bernard Adell, "Jurisdictional Overlap Between Arbitration and Other Forums: An Update" (2000) 8 *Canadian Labour and Employment Law Journal* 179 at 223; Bernard Adell, "The Duty of Fair Representation: 'a form of words . . .'?", (PowerPoint delivered at *Adjudicating*

common law and *Charter* claims under the exclusive aegis of labour arbitration, *Weber* has not just exacerbated the problem of union control, but has qualitatively changed its nature by subjecting rights that are quintessentially individual rights to a gate-keeping process that can only be justified for rights which have been generated through collective processes. Adell expressed similar concerns with respect to the trend towards giving arbitrators exclusive jurisdiction over employment-related statutory claims. While Adell did not frame his argument in the currently popular language of access to justice, the issue he raised was the same: whether individual employment "rights-bearers" would be denied legal channels within which to enforce those rights simply because they were unionized.

In this essay, I examine formal legal enforcement processes as an aspect of access to justice in general, and as a component of access to justice for unionized employees. I accept the general proposition that access to formal legal enforcement processes is a component of access to justice. I also accept that there are cases in which unionized employees have been denied access to justice when they were not able to pursue certain common law or *Charter* claims in any legal process.[11] However, I do not accept the larger claim that unionized employees as a class are denied access to justice because there may be cases in which individual employees have been unable to pursue common law or *Charter* claims in court or at arbitration. In my view, access-to-justice issues need to be addressed not only with reference to individual situations but also with reference to the larger social context in which these situations arise. Accordingly, in order to assess the extent to which limits on employee control over access to formal legal enforcement processes constitute a denial of access to justice, those limits must be examined in the larger context of the benefits and burdens of collective bargaining. In my view, Etherington's access-to-justice critique of *Weber* places excessive value on the opportunity to pursue common law and *Charter* claims. When examined in the broader context of the overall benefits that unionized employees generally enjoy, a claim that individual, unionized employees are denied access to justice—either absolutely, or in comparison with non-unionized employees—when they cannot pursue common law and *Charter* claims either in the courts or at arbitration cannot be sustained, in my view.

---

*Human Rights in the Workplace After the Pinto Report, Where Do We Go Next?*, CLCW Workshop, Queen's University, 10 November 2012)) [unpublished].

11 Etherington, "20 Years Later," above note 5 41–48 .

In Part A of the essay, I argue that concerns about unionized employees' access to formal, legal enforcement processes should be analyzed in a broader access-to-justice context. Such analysis suggests that unions, unionization and collective bargaining are access-to-justice institutions, offering access-to-justice benefits that outweigh any concern about individual employee access to formal, legal enforcement processes. In Part B, I propose an analysis of individual rights claims more layered than the one that underlies the Etherington/ Adell critique of union control over access to labour arbitration. In Part C, I extend and apply this analysis to the "*Weber* gap" concerns relating to common law and *Charter* claims, as well as to *Weber*'s potential extrapolation to statutory rights claims. In Part D, I offer some concluding reflections about why the arguments I develop in this essay should form part of future discussions about dispute resolution within unionized workplaces.

## A. UNIONS AS ACCESS-TO-JUSTICE INSTITUTIONS

### 1) The Many Meanings of Access to Justice

Access to justice is often equated with access to law, which in turn is often equated with formal enforcement processes, popularly conceptualized as court battles.[12] However, formal enforcement of formal legal rules is only one of many understandings of what access to justice means and requires. Access to justice can also be understood as access to concrete, social benefits. These benefits may or may not be explicitly or necessarily connected with law, although law may provide tools for seeking to achieve them. As Colleen Sheppard has written:

> "Justice means children with full bellies sleeping in warm beds under clean sheets." I have often reflected upon the wisdom of Mari Matsuda's words, which remind us of the importance of articulating the meaning of human rights concepts in concrete, everyday terms. For if we cannot translate the rhetoric of justice, democracy, human rights and equality

12 The courtroom scenes in *To Kill a Mockingbird* and the many law-related television dramas are classic examples of this popular understanding.

> into the concrete contexts of everyday injustices, we will not be able to build upon these norms to effect social change.[13]

It is also useful to remember that access to justice is not a static concept but is, as Marc Galanter described it, a "moving frontier."[14] Our understandings of what justice means and requires evolve and change over time and, as they do, so do our understandings of what constitutes access to justice: "[j]ustice is the negation or correction of injustice. But there is not a fixed sum of injustice that is diminished by every achievement of justice. The sphere of perceived injustice expands dynamically with the growth of human knowledge, with advances in technical feasibility, and with rising expectations of amenity and safety."[15]

In the same way as access to justice means many different things, so does access to law or access to justice through law.[16] Law itself is many things. It is legal rules, which may be set out in legislation, caselaw and "private" instruments such as contracts. It is law-making institutions authorized to develop legal rules: both public institutions such as legislatures, courts and tribunals, and private institutions, such as the collective bargaining relationship. It is the processes by which law-making institutions develop legal rules. And it is formal legal enforcement institutions and their processes. Each aspect of law can be analyzed through an access-to-justice lens, to assess the extent to which it functions to facilitate or to limit access to justice.

Legal rules have significant impact on virtually every aspect of our lives. Therefore, both the content of legal rules and access to the institutions that make and change legal rules are access-to-justice issues. Enforcement of legal rules is critical to ensuring that legal rules are followed and have impact; therefore, access to legal enforcement processes is an

---

13 Colleen Sheppard, *Inclusive Equality: The Relational Dimensions of Systemic Discrimination in Canada* (Montreal & Kingston: McGill-Queen's University Press, 2010) at 3 [Sheppard, *Inclusive Equality*].

14 Marc Galanter, "Access to Justice as a Moving Frontier" in Julia H Bass, WA Bogart, & Frederick H Zemans, eds, *Access to Justice for a New Century: The Way Forward* (Toronto: Law Society of Upper Canada, 2005) 147 at 155.

15 *Ibid* at 154.

16 For an extensive inventory of different perspectives on the meaning of access to justice through law, *see* Roderick A MacDonald, "Access to Justice in Canada Today: Scope, Scale, Ambitions" in Julia H Bass, WA Bogart, & Frederick H Zemans, *Access to Justice for a New Century: The Way Forward* (Toronto: Law Society of Upper Canada, 2005) 19.

access-to-justice issue. In order for there to be meaningful and effective access to legal rules and legal enforcement processes, most people will require at least some assistance by way of legal services; therefore, access to legal services and legal representation is an access-to-justice issue.[17]

Turning to more social conceptions of justice, there are also many different understandings of what access to justice means and requires. If we see justice as including social goods, access to justice can include access to employment, access to income security, access to housing, access to food, access to public transportation, etc. Claims to expand access to these social goods can be and often are conceptualized as raising issues of justice, and the shortfall between the claim and the realization of those claims can be described as a denial of justice. Thus, for example, it can be argued that a society that fails to support full employment, or to provide a guaranteed annual income, or to provide robust social housing, or to provide access to healthy food, or to support public transportation, is a society that fails to provide access to justice. These social conceptions of justice may often involve or implicate law, when individuals and groups seek to further their social justice goals through legislative change or through litigation.

Resources are required to address all the access-to-justice issues described above. Access-to-justice questions are, therefore, also questions about the allocation and distribution of always-limited resources. As Galanter observed, "[i]n a world of expanding capabilities and rising expectations, where claims of injustice proliferate, we cannot avoid the necessity of rationing justice. Justice is not free. It uses up resources — money, organization, and not least the limited supply of attention. And every expenditure of these involves corresponding opportunity costs."[18]

### 2) Unions, Collective Bargaining, and the Development of Substantive Legal Rules

Applying this expanded and multi-faceted approach to access to justice, a broad range of access-to-justice benefits flow from unions, unionization, and collective bargaining when these institutions are functioning

17 *See e.g.*, Julie MacFarlane, *The National Self-Represented Litigants Project: Identifying and Meeting the Needs of Self-Represented Litigants, Final Report* (May 2013), online: www.lsuc.on.ca/uploadedFiles/For_the_Public/About_the_Law_Society/Convocation_Decisions/2014/Self-represented_project.pdf.

18 Galanter, above note 14 at 155–56.

well. Indeed, I argue that unions, unionization and collective bargaining are themselves access-to-justice measures, which generally create significantly greater substantive and procedural justice for unionized employees than is experienced by non-unionized employees. I do not claim that unions are without flaws, or that they always properly address the needs and interests of individual unionized employees, or that the duty of fair representation is perfectly calibrated to monitor union control over the enforcement of collective agreement provisions. I accept that there have been, and will be, cases where individual, unionized employees are denied access to justice because they have not been permitted to pursue common law and *Charter* claims in a formal enforcement process. However, unionized employees are not alone in finding themselves unable to pursue claims in formal legal process. In my view, the implications of particular denials of access to justice to unionized employees must be assessed in their broader context to determine what remedial responses, if any, may be appropriate.

From the perspective of employees, collective action is the defining function of unions and unionization. One of the underlying premises of the Canadian collective bargaining model is that collective action enables employees to increase their bargaining power and engage in negotiations for terms and conditions of employment on a more equal footing with the employer.[19] Unionized employees generally enjoy better working conditions, better salaries and greater job security than non-unionized employees in the same or similar sectors.[20] The legal rules which create

---

19 *See, e.g.*, Paul Davies & Mark Freedland, *Kahn-Freund's Labour and the Law*, 3d ed (London: Stevens & Sons, 1983) at 12–28, 65–70 and the sources at note 20, below.

20 Susan Hayter, "Unions and Collective Bargaining" in Janine Berg, ed, *Labour Markets, Institutions and Inequality: Building Just Societies in the 21st Century* (Geneva: International Labour Organization, 2015); Lynne Fernandez, *Unions Boost Democracy and Prosperity for All* (Winnipeg: Canadian Centre for Policy Alternative, 2015) at 4–6, online: www.policyalternatives.ca/sites/default/files/uploads/publications/Manitoba%20Office/2015/11/Unions_Boost_Democracy.pdf; Garry Sran *et al*, "Why Unions Matter: Unions, Income Inequality and Regressive Labour Laws" in Matthew Behrens, ed, *Unions Matter: Advancing Democracy, Economic Equality, and Social Justice* (Toronto: Between the Lines, 2014) 13; Andrew Jackson, *Work and Labour in Canada: Critical Issues*, 2d ed (Toronto: Canadian Scholars' Press Inc, 2010) ch 9 at 195–221; Morley Gunderson & Douglas Hyatt, "Union Impact on Compensation, Productivity and Management of the Organization" in Morley Gunderson & Daphne Taras, eds, *Canadian Labour and Employment Relations*, 6d ed (Toronto: Pearson Addison Wesley, 2009) 383 at 389–92; Jelle Visser & Daniele Checchi, "In-

these concrete benefits are set out in the collective agreement negotiated by the union and the employer. A more equal balance of power between workers and the employer also creates the potential for more democratic workplaces, in which there are opportunities for workers to be treated with more respect and to participate in decision-making that affects their work lives.[21] Non-unionized employees bear the entire burden as individuals of negotiating their contractual agreement with their employer. Most non-unionized employees other than senior executives will be at a significant power disadvantage in employment contract negotiations. They will also rarely have access to legal advice or representation to assist them in these negotiations. As an institution for the development of substantive workplace legal rules, collective bargaining generally produces a better package of concrete benefits than the packages available to individual, non-unionized employees. It is therefore an access-to-justice institution for unionized employees.

The substantive legal rules that unions achieve through collective bargaining are considered "private law" because they are negotiated by the parties to collective bargaining relationships and directly apply only to the parties to those relationships.[22] However, the substantive legal rules set out in collective agreements can also have public impact by providing spillover benefits for employees outside the collective bargaining relationship.[23] The texts of collective agreements are often available to the public, offering precedents that may in some circumstances provide

---

equality and the Labor Market: Unions" in Wiemer Salverda, Brian Noland & Tim M Smeeding, eds, *The Oxford Handbook of Economic Inequality* (Oxford: Oxford University Press, 2009) 230.

21 Nathalie Des Rosiers, "Unions and Democratic Governance: Empowering Participatory Citizenship" in Matthew Behrens, ed, *Unions Matter: Advancing Democracy, Economic Equality, and Social Justice* (Toronto: Between the Lines, 2014) 93; Christopher Schenk, "Unions and Democracy," online: (2014) *Canadian Centre for Policy Alternatives* www.policyalternatives.ca/sites/default/files/uploads/publications/2014/04/unions_and_democracy.pdf.

22 For a helpful and interesting discussion of the historical roots of the "pluralist" approach to the collective bargaining relationship and collective agreement enforcement see Elizabeth Shilton, "Labour Arbitration and Public Rights Claims: Forcing Square Pegs into Round Holes" (2016) 41:2 *Queen's Law Journal* 275 [Shilton, "Square Pegs into Round Holes"].

23 Scott Walsworth, "What do Unions do to Innovation? An Empirical Examination of the Canadian Private Sector" (2010) 65:4 *Relations industrielles/Industrial Relations* 543 at 544.

negotiating leverage.[24] Many grievance arbitration decisions, which complement the substantive rules set out in collective agreements by interpreting these rules and applying them to concrete situations, are also publicly available and may similarly provide bargaining leverage.[25] While differences among the language and practice of collective agreements are always important, this body of arbitral jurisprudence, like the general common law, has a public dimension in its potential application beyond the specific dispute and the specific collective agreement that results in a specific decision. Thus, both the "private law" set out in collective agreements, and the corresponding body of arbitral jurisprudence, have social justice dimensions within and beyond the boundaries of the bargaining unit.

Unions also play a direct access-to-justice role in developing legal rules beyond the collective bargaining relationship by engaging in social action, and participating in legislative processes designed to seek changes in legislation and government programs that will benefit all employees. Canadian law has recognized these activities as a legitimate supplementary use of union dues, even though the impact and benefits of these activities extend beyond the bargaining unit.[26]

In all these ways, unions contribute significantly to the development of legal rules that are components of access to justice.

### 3) Unions and Enforcement of Substantive Legal Rules

Once concrete benefits have been achieved through the collective bargaining process, unions are typically responsible for enforcing those benefits through the procedures set out in the collective agreement. Here again, unionized employees are in a privileged position compared

24 In Ontario, for example, the Ministry of Labour maintains a collective agreement library that is open to the public. Some unions also publish their collective agreements on their websites, *e.g.*, the Ontario Public Service Employees Union.

25 Hard copies of grievance arbitration decisions published in the *Labour Arbitration Cases* reporter are available in libraries open to the public. Digital copies of many grievance arbitration decisions are available on the Canadian Legal Information Institute [CanLII], an open-access database of legislation and caselaw. A comprehensive collection of grievance arbitration decisions is available on LexisNexis Quicklaw, a subscription database that is sometimes accessible to the public through law libraries.

26 *Lavigne v Ontario Public Service Employees Union*, [1991] 2 SCR 211 at para 277 *per* La Forest J.

to non-unionized employees because they have access to the grievance arbitration enforcement process and to union representation throughout that process. It is true that this union representation is not a simple advocacy relationship. The union typically has carriage of the grievance and, therefore, significant control over whether a grievance will be filed, whether it will be settled or referred to arbitration, and how it will be presented if it goes forward to arbitration. However, while unions do not support every grievance, unless a union completely fails to fulfill its collective agreement administration responsibilities, unionized employees will generally have more ability to enforce their workplace benefits and protections than do non-unionized employees.

Civil courts are the legal venue for pursuing non-unionized employment contract disputes. While senior-level employees may have access to legal assistance with disputes arising from their employment contract, non-unionized employees typically cannot afford legal assistance or representation in contract disputes with their employers.[27] Individuals who do not have access to legal assistance must either abandon their disputes or try to handle them on their own. Predictably, outcomes for individuals who pursue legal claims without professional assistance are generally less positive than outcomes for individuals who have professional representation.[28]

Collective agreement grievance procedures typically involve both informal and formal dispute resolution processes. Formal legal enforcement processes are most often engaged at the end of a spectrum which provides opportunities for informal enforcement. Even where formal legal enforcement processes are engaged in efforts to develop or change legal rules, resort to formal process usually occurs only after efforts to engage political and other less formal processes. Informal dispute resolution processes under collective agreements long pre-dated the now-widespread use of "alternative" dispute resolution as an access-to-justice strategy in civil cases. Such less formal processes for resolving disputes

---

27 McFarlane, above note 17; Department of Justice Canada, *The Legal Problems of Everyday Life: The Nature, Extent and Consequences of Justiciable Problems Experienced by Canadians,* by Ab Currie (Government of Canada, 12 May 2009), online: www.justice.gc.ca/eng/rp-pr/csj-sjc/jsp-sjp/rr07_la1-rr07_aj1/index.html; Pascoe Pleasence & Nigel J Balmer, "Caught in the Middle: Justiciable Problems and the Use of Lawyers" in Michael Trebilcock, Anthony Duggan & Lorne Sossin, eds, *Middle Income Access to Justice* (Toronto: University of Toronto Press, 2012) 27.

28 *Ibid.*

are now considered a hallmark of access to justice, in part because they provide opportunities for the parties to engage directly in the resolution of disputes and to have more control over outcomes.[29]

The collectivity that is formed through unionization, and resourced through union dues, also creates the potential for unions to assist workers with problems that are not covered by the collective agreement but may intersect with the workplace. Unions often provide support and resources to employees applying for employment insurance benefits, long-term disability benefits[30] or workplace safety and insurance benefits. Unions may provide support and resources to professional employees such as health care professionals and teachers, whose professional licences may be in jeopardy because of concerns about conduct, competence, or fitness to practice. Unions may provide support and resources to employees facing criminal and quasi-criminal law problems when their employment may be affected by the outcome of the criminal or quasi-criminal legal process.

My point is not that unions and collective bargaining are the only method, or even the best method, of achieving strong workplace benefits and protections. There may indeed be better approaches, including legislating uniform employment benefits and conditions for all employees. However, as long as employment benefits and protections remain a combination of legislated minimum standards and negotiated standards, collectively negotiated standards will provide greater benefits and protections than individually negotiated standards. Similarly, I do not argue that the grievance arbitration process is the only, or the best, institutional method of enforcing employment rights for unionized employees. However, it provides significantly more effective access to dispute resolution than is currently available to non-unionized employees. For these reasons, unions and unionization as institutions facilitate access to justice. It is against that backdrop that the access-to-justice impact of limitations on individual employee access to formal legal enforcement processes must be analysed. In the next part of this essay, I begin that analysis by examining the nature of individual rights within collective agreements and the union-controlled enforcement process.

---

29 *See e.g.*, MacDonald, above note 16 at 79–85; Galanter, above note 14 at 148–52.

30 I am referring here to long-term disability benefits disputes that are not arbitrable under the collective agreement.

## B. INDIVIDUAL RIGHTS AND SOCIAL RELATIONS IN ENFORCEMENT PROCESSES

The core of the concern raised by Etherington and Adell is that there are inappropriate limits on the ability of unionized employees to enforce their individual, substantive rights. Adell argued that "whenever the law gives a substantive right to someone, as it does to an individual employee to enjoy the fruits of collective bargaining as contained in a collective agreement, it ought (in the absence of compelling reasons to the contrary) to provide a procedural means of enforcing that substantive right."[31] Adell saw union control over access to grievance arbitration as an unnecessary limitation even for routine agreement-based disputes. When the rights at issue were generated outside the agreement, controlled access was even less legitimate, in his view.[32] For Etherington, *Weber* has widened the "gap or shortfall between substantive rights and access to forums to protect or enforce those rights."[33]

These arguments rest on two assumptions: that unionized employees "have" or "possess" the rights at issue as individuals, and that they should therefore have channels, as individuals, to enforce them. In this part of the essay, I seek to unpack these assumptions. I argue that the rights of unionized employees have both an individual and a collective dimension, and that both dimensions need to be considered in any assessment of whether and to what the extent limits on the ability of employees to make individual enforcement decisions deny them access to justice. I develop my argument by first examining different approaches to the meaning of legal rights generally. I then explore the relationship between unionized employees as individuals and the collectivity through which their individual rights are achieved, within a context in which rights are understood not simply as "property" but as having a social/relational dimension.

### 1) Legal Rights and Social Relations

The language of "rights" is deeply embedded in legal discourse. We use the term "legal rights" as shorthand both for legal rules intended to govern social conduct—often referred to as "substantive rights"— and legal

31 Adell, "Collective Agreements," above note 10 at 255.

32 Adell, "Union's Duty," above note 10 at 263–66.

33 Etherington, "20 Years Later," above note 5 at 28.

rules intended to govern the processes for enforcing substantive rights—often referred to as "procedural rights." Although substantive rights and procedural rights are two distinct categories, they are often synergistically related, each one both affecting and affected by the other.[34] Appeals to legal rights are often made by individuals and groups challenging social inequalities and invoking "rights" as a means to seek redress. They may call, for example, for rights to greater income equality, rights to non-discriminatory treatment, rights to fair wages and fair conditions of work, and rights to safe and affordable housing. However, legal rights are "equal opportunity" instruments. Consistent with rule-of-law values of universality and neutrality, legal rights can be invoked by any individual or group to support any claim that individual or group wishes to advance through law. Thus, appeals to rights can be advanced to support arguments from any position on a political spectrum; just as rights can be invoked in relation to claims to eliminate discrimination or poverty, they can be invoked to support claims to be free from government regulation, to be exempt from paying taxes, to own and use firearms, or to impose terms and conditions of employment on workers.

There are many critiques of rights discourse. I suggest that just as rights are shorthand for legal rules and legal enforcement processes, critiques of rights discourse are similarly often shorthand for critiques of the role of law in governing social conduct. Politically left-leaning critics of rights discourse often argue that legal rights, at best, deliver formal rather than substantive change,[35] that they wrongly focus only on individ-

34 Colleen Sheppard, "The Promise and Practice of Protecting Human Rights: Reflections on the Quebec *Charter of Human Rights and Freedoms*" in Faculté de droit de l'Université McGill, ed, *Mélanges Paul-André Crépeau*, (Cowansville, Québec: Éditions Yvon Blais, 1997) 641 at 641–42.

35 For example, Alan David Freeman wrote: "As surely as the law has outlawed racial discrimination, it has affirmed that Black Americans can be without jobs, have their children in all-black, poorly funded schools, have no opportunities for decent housing, and have very little political power, without any violation of antidiscrimination law." Alan David Freeman "Legitimizing Racial Discrimination through Antidiscrimination Law: A Critical Review of Supreme Court Doctrine" (1978) 62:6 *Minnesota Law Review* 1049 at 1050. Jeanne Gregory similarly expressed the argument: "[Anti-discrimination legislation] is on the statute book in order to protect, not threaten, the fundamental structures of capitalist society, and therefore cannot by itself constitute the vehicle for achieving a non-racist, non-sexist society." Jeanne Gregory, "Sex Discrimination, Work and the Law" in Bob Fine et al, eds, *Capitalism and the Rule of Law: From Deviancy Theory to Marxism* (London:

uals at the expense of groups and communities,[36] and that they wrongly weaken political discourse and engagement.[37] Politically right-leaning critics of rights discourse often accuse activists of attempting to use law to circumvent political processes in order to redistribute social power and social goods.[38]

Although I share many of the concerns raised by the left-leaning critics of rights discourse, I continue to believe there is a role for law in seeking to achieve greater social equality. However, I prefer a social relations approach to legal rights, which offers a relational and more dynamic analysis. Rights discourse tends to describe rights in the language of ownership, as "things" or "possessions" which people "have" or "own." This property-like characterization masks the nature of the relationship between substantive rules and enforcement processes, by implying that simply being a "rights holder"—in itself a passive state or status—should be sufficient by itself to produce results. A social-relations approach to legal rights characterizes rights not as property but rather as claims which call for a response from others: "[a] legally enforceable set of expectations as to how others . . . should behave . . . ."[39] This approach underscores the relational nature of rights, which have concrete effect only when the action they require is fulfilled.

---

Hutchinson & Co, 1979) 137 at 150. *See also* Judy Fudge, "What do We Mean by Law and Social Transformation?" (1990) 5 *Canadian Journal of Law and Society* 47; Judy Fudge, "The Paradoxes of Pay Equity: Reflections on the Law and the Market in *Canada* and *PSAC*" (2000) 12 *Canadian Journal of Women and the Law* 313; Eric Tucker, "Renorming Labour Law: Can We Escape Labour Law's Recurring Dilemmas?" (2010) 39:2 *Industrial Law Journal* 99.

36 *See e.g.*, Trubek, above note 1.

37 *See e.g.*, Allan Hutchinson & Patrick Monahan, "Democracy and the Rule of Law" in Allan C Hutchinson and Patrick Monahan, eds, *The Rule of Law: Ideal or Ideology* (Toronto: Carswell, 1987) 97; Judy Fudge, "The Canadian Charter of Rights: Recognition, Redistribution, and the Imperialism of the Courts" in Tom Campbell, KD Ewing & Adam Tomkins, eds, Sceptical Essays on Human Rights (Oxford: Oxford University Press, 2001) 335.

38 *See e.g.* Rainer Knopff & Thomas Flanagan, *Human Rights & Social Technology: The New War on Discrimination* (Ottawa: Carleton University Press, 1989).

39 Anthony Woodiwiss, *Human Rights* (London and New York: Routledge, 2005) at xi. For more discussion of social relations approaches to law, *see e.g.*, Sheppard, *Inclusive Equality*, above note 13 and Jennifer Nedelsky, *Law's Relations: A Relational Theory of Self, Autonomy, and Law* (Oxford: Oxford University Press, 2011).

## 2) Legal Rights and Enforcement

I use the expression "legal rights" to mean the prescriptions that are set out in legal rules and norms that have been established by legislation, common law and "private" legal documents, and can be asserted through legal claims. As I have argued elsewhere, these prescriptions take a variety of forms; they can require conduct, prohibit conduct, impose duties, confer benefits, etc.[40] The language in which "rights" are prescribed can also range from the highly concrete[41] to the more general and abstract.[42] All "legal rights," however, acquire concrete meaning in their application to specific social conduct. And regardless of how concretely prescriptive the language may appear, there is almost always room for argument about what the legal norm means, whether it should apply to a particular situation and if so, how it should apply to that situation: "legal rules are not self-evident and self-applying characterizations of human behavior" and "there can be more than one appropriate legal characterization of human conduct."[43] The meaning and scope of all legal norms is continually shaped when they are placed "at the level of the debate concerning a specific application"[44] — sometimes to be expanded and sometimes to be narrowed.

Under collective agreements, substantive legal rules would include provisions governing wages, employment benefits and job security. At

40 Karen Schucher, *Coercing Justice? Exploring the "Aspirations and Practice" of Law as a Tool in Struggles Against Social Inequalities* (PhD Dissertation, Osgoode Hall Law School of York University, 2014) at 14–17, online: http://digitalcommons.osgoode.yorku.ca/cgi/viewcontent.cgi?article=1008&context=phd.

41 For example: "18(1) An employer shall give an employee a period of at least 11 consecutive hours free from performing work in each day." *Employment Standards Act, 2000*, SO 2000, c 41, s 18(1).

42 For example: "5(1) Every person has a right to equal treatment with respect to employment without discrimination because of race, ancestry, place of origin, colour, ethnic origin, citizenship, creed, sex, sexual orientation, gender identity, gender expression, age, record of offences, marital status, family status or disability." *Human Rights Code*, RSO. 1990, c H.19, s 5(1).

43 Ontario Law Reform Commission, *Study Paper on Prospects for Civil Justice*, by Roderick A Macdonald (Toronto: OLRC, 1995) at 47–48. *See also* Pierre Bourdieu, "The Force of Law: Toward a Sociology of the Juridical Field" (1987) 38:5 *Hastings Law Journal* 814 at 821: "The practical meaning of law is really only determined in the confrontation between different bodies (e.g., judges, lawyers, solicitors) moved by divergent specific interests."

44 Bourdieu, *ibid* at 823.

common law, substantive legal rules would include rules that define tortious conduct: for example, defamation, invasion of privacy and negligence. Under the *Charter*, substantive rules are set out in the provisions guaranteeing democratic freedoms (such as freedom of speech and association), the provisions governing legal rights (such as life, liberty and security of the person), and the provisions governing equality rights. Substantive legal rules under employment-related statutes include anti-discrimination provisions in human rights legislation, minimum standards provisions in employment standards legislation covering areas such as wages, hours of work and overtime, leaves of absence and layoffs, and provisions in occupational health and safety legislation governing health and safety in the workplace.

The articulation of expectations, whether by way of contract or common law or legislation, is an essential first step. But if those expectations are not fulfilled, and if there is no way of requiring them to be fulfilled, they have little or no concrete meaning for workers. Substantive legal rules can be implemented without dispute, and where disputes arise about the interpretation or application of these rules, it is always open to the parties to the dispute to come to an informal resolution. Access to formal legal enforcement processes becomes necessary only where the parties cannot reach agreement on how to resolve disputes about the meaning or application of substantive rules.

### 3) Individual Rights and Collective Agreement Enforcement

The collective action that is the defining feature of unionization produces a unique legal construct, within which there are multiple social and legal relations. The union and the employer are the parties to the collective bargaining relationship, to the collective agreements that are negotiated within this relationship, and to the grievance arbitration proceedings under the collective agreement. The employees whose employment relationship and work are regulated by the collective agreement are not parties to this agreement, but are bound by the agreement.

The union is the bargaining agent for all employees in the bargaining unit. In some workplaces, employees can be required to become members of the union as a condition of employment. In others, employees have a choice about becoming members of the union and participating in the governance of the union; in such workplaces, a typical bargaining unit includes employees who are members and employees who are not members of the union. In its representational capacity as bargaining agent, the union has a statutory duty of fair representation to all employees in the bargaining unit, including employees who are not members of the union. Institutionally, the union also has a legal relationship with employees who take out union membership.[45] The legal relationship between the union and its members is typically governed by its constitution, and either the common law principles that apply to voluntary associations or the legal principles that apply to non-profit corporations if the union is incorporated.

The employer has an employment relationship with all employees in the bargaining unit. The employment relationship between the employer and the employees is regulated by the collective agreement, and any additional statutory obligations. The employer is not permitted to negotiate terms and conditions of employment directly with any individual employee(s) or group(s) of employees; individual employees and groups of employees are likewise not permitted to negotiate terms and conditions of employment with the employer.

In principle, a collective agreement can authorize individual employees to make their own decisions about whether to file a grievance, whether to accept a resolution arrived at through the grievance procedure, and whether to take a grievance to arbitration. In practice, employees may be permitted to initiate grievances, but the union generally retains exclusive authority to decide whether to accept a settlement (with or without the grievor's agreement) or to refer a grievance to arbitration.[46] The union's conduct in exercising this exclusive authority is publicly governed by a statutory duty of fair representation.[47] However, it is generally accepted that the duty of fair representation sets a low bar for unions, and that labour relations boards rarely overturn union decisions.[48]

What do individual employee rights mean within this context? At a fundamental level, the needs and interests of the collective of employees in the bargaining unit are the *raison d'étre* for having a union. Without individual employees coming together and choosing to be collectively represented by a union, there would be no union. And although the union

45 *Berry v Pulley*, 2002 SCC 40.

46 Shilton, "Square Pegs into Round Holes," above note 22 at 288.

47 The union's conduct in making decisions about grievances and arbitration can also be privately governed by the membership and the union constitution.

48 Adell, "Union's Duty," above note 10 at 267; Morgana Kellythorne, "Toward a Theory of the Duty of Fair Representation" (2003) 9 *Appeal* 32.

is the party to the collective agreement, the terms and conditions of that agreement are primarily for the benefit of the employees. In this sense, it is reasonable to characterize the benefits flowing from collective agreements as individual employee rights.

As noted earlier, there is an obvious and intuitive appeal to the argument that if the rights at issue are individual employee rights, individuals should have control over decisions to pursue claims through formal legal process if they believe those rights are not being implemented. Even for rights created exclusively by collective bargaining, Adell (and Laskin before him) argued that the current regime does not provide adequate enforcement rights for employees, and that individual employees should be able to pursue grievances on their own through formal legal processes if the union will not take their claims to arbitration.[49] However, the argument that simply removing the union as gatekeeper to arbitration would be sufficient to create access to justice ignores the many other gatekeepers that would surface if unions were to lose their gatekeeping role. These other gatekeepers include access to information, access to advice, access to support and access to representation. New gatekeepers might also emerge in the form of preliminary determination screening processes of the type implemented by statutory tribunals inundated by individual claims.[50]

Reflecting on the potential for negative consequences if individual grievors were able to proceed to arbitration on their own, Adell speculated

49 Adell, "Collective Agreements," above note 10; Adell, "Union's Duty," above note 10; Laskin, above note 9.

50 For example, the Human Rights Tribunal of Ontario, Rule 19A "Summary Hearing," authorizes the Tribunal to hold a "summary hearing" to determine "whether an Application should be dismissed in whole or in part on the basis that there is no reasonable prospect that the Application or part of the Application will succeed." This rule is used extensively, both at the request of respondents and on the Tribunal's own initiative. Social Justice Tribunals Ontario, "Human Rights Tribunal of Ontario: Rules of Procedure," Rule 19A: Summary Hearings (Ottawa: SJTO, 10 May 2016), online: www.sjto.gov.on.ca/documents/hrto/Practice%20Directions/HRTO%20Rules%20of%20Procedure.html. The Ontario Labour Relations Board often employs "consultations" to screen out claims in relation to duty of fair representation complaints and employment standards review applications. Rule 39.1 of the Board's Rules of Procedure also authorizes the Board to dismiss an application without a hearing or a consultation "where it considers that an application does not make out a case for the orders or remedies requested." Ontario Labour Relations Board, "Rules of Procedure" (Ottawa: OLRB, March 2016), online: www.olrb.gov.on.ca/english/Rules_of_Procedure.pdf.

that "no union which does a reasonably conscientious and competent job of screening grievances should have much fear that its rejects would be warmly received by arbitrators."[51] The suggestion is that requiring unions to give up exclusive control over access to arbitration might create more incentives for them to maintain a "conscientious and competent" decision-making process than does the public scrutiny currently provided by the statutory duty of fair representation. This may be true. However, it is also possible that permitting individual employees to pursue grievances on their own might have the opposite effect, creating incentives for unions to shift on to employees some of the responsibility and costs they would otherwise have assumed themselves.

Individual employees who proceed to arbitration on their own might also find themselves facing the union as an adversary in the arbitration proceeding, particularly if the employee seeks to advance a position with which the union does not agree. Laskin pointed out that if individuals were able to pursue grievances to arbitration on their own, unions would have "stand-by rights" which would allow them to protect the collective dimension of the collective agreement and the collective interest of the bargaining unit in how that agreement is interpreted and applied.[52] Even if we accept that unionized employees have individual rights under collective agreements, they have achieved those rights by virtue of the collectivity. There is therefore a collective interest as well as an individual interest at stake in situations where there are differing opinions about what the collective agreement provisions mean or how they should be applied in concrete situations. There is also, of course, a collective interest in decisions about the allocation and expenditure of union resources on collective agreement enforcement.[53]

The specific factual context must therefore be considered when assessing what exactly is being denied to an individual unionized employee who has been precluded from pursuing formal legal process. In *Weber*, the employer hired a private investigator to surveil Murray Weber while he was on sick leave and receiving benefits under the employer's sick-leave

51 Adell, "Collective Agreements," above note 10 at 257. At the same time, Adell acknowledged that individual access to arbitration has the potential to undermine unions in societies where the legitimacy of unions is less widely accepted by employers. He placed Canada in this category, as compared to western European countries. *Ibid* at 258.

52 Laskin, above note 9 at 291.

53 *Ibid.*

plan. The union filed three grievances relating to Ontario Hydro's surveillance, seeking the following remedies: an undertaking that the surveillance practice would be discontinued; an undertaking that absences from work would be monitored by Health Services as provided in the collective agreement; an order requiring Ontario Hydro to pay damages to Weber, his wife and his family for mental anguish and suffering; rescission of the suspension with compensation; and full compensation for any damages caused by management's conduct. The grievances were ultimately settled after at least twelve days of hearing. The union then appears to have supported Weber's efforts to pursue his common law and *Charter* claims.[54] It is impossible to assess the quality of the settlement because the public record does not include any information about its content. However, it does seem fair to say that the union expended significant resources pursuing remedies for Weber, and that Weber likely experienced greater access to justice than would the average, non-unionized employee.

Thus, the question of what it means for an individual unionized employee to have access to justice in relation to enforcing substantive employment rights is a more complex question than appears on the surface. In relation to rights under the collective agreement, unionized employees are never *just* individuals with individual rights; they are also parts of the collective, with the benefits as well as the burdens of that status. It is possible that the same is true for unionized employees in relation to individual rights acquired *outside* the collective agreement, under common law, the *Charter* and employment-related statutes. I now turn to a consideration of that issue.

## C. RELATIONSHIPS AMONG RIGHTS: COLLECTIVE AGREEMENT, COMMON LAW, *CHARTER*, AND STATUTORY RIGHTS

The question that arose directly from *Weber* is whether unionized employees can pursue common law and *Charter* claims in a civil action against their employers, where these claims arise from a factual context that also raises a violation of the collective agreement. Although *Weber* focused specifically on common law and *Charter* claims, the Supreme

54 The court decisions do not record whether the union provided Weber with legal resources to initiate his civil action; however, on the face of the record it appears that union counsel represented Weber on the motion to strike his civil action and in the subsequent appeals from this motion.

Court of Canada's analysis in *Weber* also has obvious implications for statutory rights claims. In this Part, I first propose a common framework for analyzing the interaction between collective agreement rights and these other categories of legal rights, and for addressing questions about whether these other categories of rights should be treated differently because they are "public" rights rather than "private" rights. I then consider unique issues that relate specifically to each of the three categories of rights, i.e., common law, *Charter* and statutory rights. Finally, I reflect on some of the pros and cons of a concurrent jurisdiction model in addressing *Weber* gaps.

### 1) Common Conceptual Framework for the Interaction between Collective Agreement Rights and "Public" Legal Rights

In the preceding Part, I argued that individual legal rights under collective agreements have both an individual and a collective dimension, and that the collective dimension is always relevant to how individual rights are interpreted and applied. In my view, the same can be said for the employment-related rights of unionized employees under common law, the *Charter* and employment-related statutes. In factual situations that support a common law, *Charter* or statutory rights claim as well as a grievance under the collective agreement, both the individual employee and the bargaining unit as a whole have an interest in how all the legal rights at issue will be interpreted and applied.[55] Thus, where a workplace situation gives rise both to a grievance and to legal claims based in common law, the *Charter*, or statutory rights, these other legal claims are not purely individual rights, but have a collective dimension as well. Put another way, I suggest that there are no purely individual rights in employment relationships governed by a collective agreement.

Applying this reasoning to the *Weber* context, Weber's tort and *Charter* claims were not simply individual claims but claims that had a collective dimension as well that should not be ignored. The union and the bargaining unit had an interest in how the employer managed the sick

55 The analysis I propose may be another route to reaching Elizabeth Shilton's conclusion that *Weber v Ontario Hydro* brings ". . . disputes about terms and conditions of employment in unionized workplaces back into the industrial pluralist world in which they are dealt with inside the framework of the collective agreement." *See* Elizabeth Shilton, "*Weber*, the Common Law and Industrial Self-Government," Chapter 3, this volume at 89.

leave plan, and an interest in knowing whether employer surveillance was a violation not only of the collective agreement but also of tort law and *Charter* law. If an arbitrator ruled that the employer's conduct violated tort and *Charter* law as well as the collective agreement, this ruling could provide a precedent for future grievances and affect the dynamic of collective bargaining. The same analysis would apply if Weber's claims had been grounded in employment-related statutes. How statutory rights are interpreted and applied in a particular workplace has implications not only for individual employees but also for the collective bargaining relationship between the union and the employer, and the bargaining unit as a whole. If unionized employees pursue a statutory benefit through a statutory enforcement process, the positions they take within the statutory process may have potentially beneficial or potentially negative implications for others in the bargaining unit. Where individual employees wish to advance positions that are adverse in interest to the bargaining unit, the union will have a legitimate interest in participating in the individual proceeding.

I anticipate two objections to this analysis. The first is grounded in the view that common law, *Charter* and statutory rights are rights that attach personally to unionized employees, separate and apart from their status as employees in a bargaining unit covered by a collective agreement. For the reasons set out above, I am not persuaded by this argument. I also disagree with this objection because it ignores the fact that the legal rights at issue are intended to have impact in a specific social context: in this case, the workplace. The workplace context embeds individuals in a fabric of social relations, where the exercise of legal rights has implications not only for them as individuals but also for their bargaining unit co-workers. In my view, therefore, where the common law, *Charter* or statutory claims of unionized employees overlap with collective agreement claims, the legal rights supporting those claims are not simply individual rights.

The second objection is that the analysis I propose fails to respect the fact that common law, *Charter* and statutory rights are "public" rights (almost always linked with public enforcement processes), and that public rights have a different status from "private" collective agreement rights. I agree that common law, *Charter* and statutory rights are public rights, in the sense that they are established by public institutions (courts, legislatures and tribunals) and are, therefore, available to the public at large. However, I do not share the view that public rights have a higher status, or more importance, simply because they are established in this way.[56] The argument that public rights are more important because their source is legislative or judicial rather than contractual reflects an abstract analysis of rights as free-standing legal constructs. I prefer an approach that focuses on the social impact of rights rather than on their abstract status. Employment rights, regardless of how they are established, are intended to function in their "private" social contexts, and to regulate "private" employment social relations by, for example, prohibiting discrimination, establishing minimum standards for work conditions, and requiring protection against unsafe and unhealthy working conditions in the "private" workplace. A social impact approach acknowledges that employees will attach value to legal rights based on whether and how those rights address the particular workplace problem or dispute the employee faces.

Similarly, I accept that there is a public interest and an access-to-justice interest in keeping open the channels to public enforcement processes: the courts for common law and many *Charter* claims, and statutory tribunals for statutory rights claims. Again, though, I suggest that the importance of these interests should be examined not only from a theoretical perspective but also with reference to what happens to individuals in practice. Access to the bare option of being able to initiate a civil action or file an application with a statutory tribunal does not constitute access to justice. Whether or not it facilitates access to justice depends on other contextual factors, such as whether the employee has access to resources sufficient to match the resources the employer will bring to the litigation.

I acknowledge, of course, that access to legal enforcement processes is an element of access to justice. As a complement to the above analysis, therefore, I suggest that access-to-justice values are best respected when unions, employers and arbitrators take a liberal approach to making connections between collective agreements and other legal rights. I reject an "anti-*Weber* presumption" of the type described in Etherington's essay, which would direct arbitrators to resist drawing connections between collective agreement protections and common law legal claims unless the parties expressly agree to include these claims in the collective

---

56 For a discussion of Québec jurisprudence on the implications of difference sources of workplace rights *see* Renée-Claude Drouin, "Some Unique Features of *Weber*'s Application in Quebec: The Treatment of Statutory Labour Rights and Human Rights Claims," Chapter 9, this volume.

agreement.[57] While I would not necessarily characterize the approach I am suggesting as a pro-*Weber* presumption, I am persuaded that a generous attitude towards making connections between collective agreement rights and other legal rights is most consistent with the relational understanding of legal rights that I advocate. Under a relational approach, labour arbitrators would be asked to look at collective agreements to find connections between those agreements and common law, *Charter* or statutory rights claims. A generous approach to making connections among legal rights reflects *Weber*'s instruction that, "[w]hat matters is not the legal characterization of the claim, but whether the facts of the dispute fall within the ambit of the collective agreement."[58] Connecting all legal rights that attach to a particular fact situation allows for a focus on the social function of these rights, instead of abstracting them and treating them as distinct from their social function. As Dianne Pothier has argued:

> Legal analysis tends to proceed by the framing of questions which give rise to the creation of legal categories in pursuit of answers to these questions. In the process, the framing of questions is often given scant attention, and legal categories are taken for granted. Legal analysts often forget that the answer they obtain may depend a great deal on how the question is asked. It is an all too familiar habit to separate legal issues into discrete categories, ignoring the possibility of connection.[59]

It is true, of course, that how unions or employers or arbitrators will respond to an invitation to make connections will be informed, at least in

---

57 Etherington, "20 Years Later," above note 5 at 57–58. Etherington locates such an anti-*Weber* presumption in arbitrator Pamela Picher's analysis in *Seneca College v Ontario Public Service Employees Union* (2001), 102 LAC (4th) 298 (Arbitrator: P Picher), rev'd sub nom *OPSEU v Seneca College of Applied Arts and Technology* (2004) 133 LAC (4th) 193, 73 OR (3d) 185 (Div Ct), aff'd (2006) 150 LAC (4th) 385, 80 OR (3d) 1 (CA), leave to appeal to SCC refused, 228 OAC 396n (16 November 2006). Although Etherington commends Picher's analysis, he is concerned that adopting an anti-*Weber* presumption could widen the *Weber* gap. He argues for a presumption in favour of concurrent jurisdiction over *Charter* and statutory claims, but states: "Nothing in this paper should be read as calling for any kind of presumption of concurrency for common law claims." *Ibid* at 89.

58 *Weber*, above note 3 at para 49.

59 Dianne Pothier, "Developments in Employment Law: The 1994–95 Term" (1996) 7 *Supreme Court Law Review, Second Series* 293 at 293. *Weber v Ontario Hydro* and *New Brunswick v O'Leary* are two of the cases Pothier discusses in this piece.

part, by their orientation to the question of whether arbitration is an appropriate forum for addressing broad legal rights. This question raises general considerations, which I have addressed above. It can also raise more specific issues that should be considered in evaluating limits on unionized employees' access to the courts for common law and *Charter* issues, and to statutory tribunals for statutory rights issues, which I now turn to examine.

### 2) Common Law Rights and Labour Arbitration

In assessing the relationship between common law rights and collective agreements, Etherington argues that the grievance arbitration process is not well-suited to addressing tort claims. First, he argues that efforts to assert tort claims at arbitration can produce *Weber* gaps, particularly where an arbitrator finds a link between the common law claim and the collective agreement, but cannot address the common law claim without the participation of a third party who cannot be added to the proceeding for jurisdictional reasons.[60] Second, he argues that because tort claims often involve emotionally-charged, interpersonal conflicts, dealing with them within the arbitration process can inflame workplace relationships, with negative effects on the workplace and the collective bargaining relationship. In addition, he argues that arbitrators are "not totally comfortable with the role of making findings of tortious wrongdoing by employers, managers and union officials or providing significant damage awards to provide redress to particular individuals," speculating that their lack of "comfort" may flow from their lack of tenure.[61]

In my view, there are ways to address all these concerns relating to the interaction between common law claims and the collective agreement. Arbitrators could be given the power to add third parties, either by judicial ruling or by legislation. The concern about interpersonal and emotionally-charged disputes does not arise only in relation to conflicts that might involve tort claims. Garden variety discharge and discipline cases, the meat-and-potatoes of labour arbitration, often involve interpersonal conflicts. Likewise, workplace harassment claims, whether sexual harassment or other forms of harassment, are often emotionally charged. But such cases are not excluded from collective agreement enforcement

60 Etherington, "20 Years Later," above note 5 at 55–57.

61 *Ibid* at 51–55.

for this reason. And finally, if arbitrators are indeed more reluctant than courts to find tort violations and award high levels of damages (assuming that they are),[62] arbitrators should be encouraged to examine the foundations for their reluctance. Such reluctance may indeed be a response to concerns about "job security," as Etherington suggests; but there may also be sound labour relations reasons for taking a different approach to tort and damage principles within unionized workplaces than courts have traditionally taken in non-unionized workplaces.[63]

### 3) *Charter* Rights and Labour Arbitration

In relation to claims flowing from *Charter* rights, some commentators have expressed indignation that unionized employees might be denied access to the courts and individual carriage of enforcement proceedings. This indignation is associated with the idea that *Charter* rights are the most important—almost sacred—rights. As Etherington put it:

> It must have come as no little surprise to Murray Weber to learn that, simply by becoming part of a bargaining unit that was represented by a trade union, he would forfeit the rights normally enjoyed by other citizens, including non-unionized employees, to vindicate their common law rights in a court of law. . . . *But perhaps Weber was even more astounded to learn that he could be denied access to the courts to seek redress for violations of his most fundamental* Charter *rights by virtue of his inclusion in a bargaining unit that was covered by a collective agreement.*[64]

For reasons I have explained above, I do not share the underlying view that *Charter* rights are more important than other rights in relation to an individual employee's workplace situation. To provide just one example, if employees are exposed to unsafe or unhealthy work conditions, their rights under occupational health and safety legislation (e.g., the right to refuse unsafe work and access to an expedited process for addressing work refusals), or under the collective agreement (which might include

---

62 While Etherington implies that courts are—or would be— more disposed than labour arbitrators to find tort violations and make high damages awards, he does not provide authority for that proposition.

63 Implicit in the Langille and Shilton essays (Chapters 3 and 4 in this volume) is the argument that the considerations shaping tort-like rules might differ as between unionized and non-unionized workplaces.

64 Brown & Etherington, above note 5 at 184 [emphasis added].

both substantive and procedural rights in excess of statutory minima) will likely be more valuable to them than any rights they may have under section 7 of the *Charter*, even assuming that the *Charter* applies to their employment, and that section 7 rights to life and security of the person include the right to a safe and healthy workplace.

### 4) Statutory Rights and Labour Arbitration

Statutory enforcement processes raise important questions about the distribution of public resources for legal enforcement. Although the civil courts are a form of public enforcement because they are established and resourced by the government, they are still driven by private litigants whose ability to participate effectively is highly dependent on their private resources. Statutory enforcement processes, by contrast, are generally designed to offer more support to claimants, often by providing government investigators with power to make orders that can then be challenged through an administrative law process. Therefore, there is in principle more cause for concern if workers and their unions are denied access to statutory enforcement processes. However, while there is an important interest in the fair distribution of public enforcement resources, in practice statutory tribunals do not always, or necessarily, provide a better enforcement option than labour arbitration.

Public enforcement of human rights codes is an important case in point. Problems with public enforcement through human rights commissions are well-documented, and ultimately led in Ontario and British Columbia to the substitution of an enforcement model that provides "direct access" to the human rights tribunal. However, direct access has proved to be far from perfect as a solution to the access-to-justice problem. The five-year review of Ontario's direct access system reported strong concerns about lack of access to legal support and representation, similar to concerns about lack of legal support and representation in the civil justice system.[65] Concerns have also been raised that Ontario's public

65 Ontario Ministry of the Attorney General, *Report of the Ontario Human Rights Review 2012*, by Andrew Pinto (Ottawa: MAG, November 2012) at 46, 108. On the issue of legal representation, Pinto reported that on average 35 percent of applicants had legal representation in proceedings at the HRTO (both mediation and adjudication), as compared to 85 percent of respondents. Pinto correlated data on applicants succeeding at the tribunal with data on applicant representation, and concluded that applicants with some form of legal representation were successful

enforcement system for employment standards claims does not provide adequate enforcement rights for non-unionized workers.[66]

The *Weber* exclusive jurisdiction model has not spread to statutory enforcement processes. Concurrent jurisdiction is currently the norm for human rights statutory enforcement in all provinces other than Quebec. In some contexts, other statutory tribunals in Ontario have themselves assumed exclusive jurisdiction over claims involving unionized workers when those claims overlap with statutory rights.[67] Therefore, the concern about *Weber* implications for statutory rights is perhaps less pressing than for common law and *Charter* rights. However, the formal existence of concurrent jurisdiction does not necessarily mean that an individual employee's attempts to bring a claim through the statutory enforcement process will be successful. Statutory human rights tribunals have discretion to defer to grievance arbitration. More significantly, these tribunals may also have statutory authority to dismiss an application if its substance has been appropriately dealt with in another proceeding. Statutory provisions which permit dismissal in these circumstances have been interpreted to mean that a human rights application by a unionized employee will often be dismissed where both a grievance and a human rights claim were filed based on the same facts, and the grievance was resolved either through settlement (with or without the employee's consent) or arbitration.[68]

---

in 66 percent of the cases; without representation, they succeeded in only 44 percent of cases.

66 *See e.g.*, Leah F Vosko, "'Rights without Remedies': Enforcing Employment Standards in Ontario by Maximizing Voice among Workers in Precarious Jobs" (2013) 50:4 *Osgoode Hall Law Journal* 845. Unionized workers are required to enforce employment standards provisions through grievance arbitration under their collective agreements.

67 Jo-Anne Pickel, "Statutory Tribunals and the Challenges of Managing Parallel Claims," Chapter 6, this volume.

68 *Ibid* at 191–99, for discussion of how the Human Rights Tribunal of Ontario (HRTO) exercises this dismissal power. As Pickel notes, in some situations HRTO Vice-Chairs are willing to parse the facts and find that some portion of the human rights claim can proceed. Pickel also notes that where a grievance is settled without the employee's consent, the HRTO may permit the application to proceed, depending on the circumstances of the settlement. *See also* Elizabeth Shilton, "'Everybody's Business': The Employer-Union Co-Liability Model in Workplace Human Rights Enforcement" (2014) 18:1 *Canadian Labour and Employment Law Journal* 209 at 232–40.

Thus, where a workplace problem that is covered by a collective agreement has a human rights dimension, unionized employees and unions have to make difficult choices about whether the human rights issue can be separated from the collective agreement issue and, even if it can be separated, whether it should be separated. Moreover, even where the union and employee believe they are excluding the human rights issue from the grievance arbitration process, there is always a risk that the human rights tribunal will take a different view and find that the human rights issue was appropriately dealt with under the collective agreement. Under a direct access human rights model, then, unionized employees generally have to make a choice between pursuing a grievance and pursuing a human rights application, with the attendant risks of making the "wrong choice" and being left with no forum in which to advance their claim.[69]

### 5) *Weber* Gaps and Concurrent Jurisdiction

It will come as no surprise after the above discussion that I favour an enforcement model in which all employment-related issues are dealt with in a single forum. In the absence of a real alternative that addresses the limitations of arbitration,[70] I am not persuaded that arbitration is unsuitable to be that forum, and in general, I am comfortable with unions continuing to play the role as gatekeeper. I do remain troubled, however, by the fact that exclusive arbitral jurisdiction leaves no room for alternative options in appropriate circumstances. If a concurrent jurisdiction model were acknowledged for civil actions and statutory enforcement, it would probably address, at least in a formal sense, the *Weber* gap that results when an employee does not receive union support to pursue a grievance or to include civil claims in a grievance. It would also leave room for employees who simply prefer to pursue a civil action rather than a grievance. In addition, such a model might address the *Weber* gap that results when an arbitrator is not able to address a civil claim because third parties cannot be added to the proceeding.

69 Elizabeth Shilton, "Choice, but No Choice: Adjudicating Human Rights Claims in Unionized Workplaces in Canada" (2013) 38:2 *Queen's Law Journal* 461 at 494–502 [Shilton, "Choice, but no Choice"].

70 For discussion of an alternative approach *see* Shilton, "Square Pegs into Round Holes," above note 22.

However, as the experience with concurrent jurisdiction between statutory tribunals and collective agreement enforcement demonstrates, concurrent jurisdiction raises its own set of access-to-justice issues.[71] In the factual context of *Weber*, it is not clear that Weber would have been able to pursue his civil action even if the Supreme Court of Canada had adopted a concurrent or overlapping jurisdiction model. Ontario Hydro might well have persuaded a court to dismiss the action on the ground of *res judicata*. Concurrent jurisdiction may clear an avenue that it is currently blocked, but the dispute will remain subject to the policy imperatives against duplicative proceedings and case splitting that sometimes work to deprive employees of access to the formal legal process of their choice.

Moreover, I am equally troubled by the potential impact of concurrent jurisdiction on the relationship between the union and the bargaining unit. I question whether access to justice for unionized employees would have been better served if the Supreme Court of Canada had adopted a model of concurrent or overlapping jurisdiction. In particular, I am concerned about the possibility that concurrent jurisdiction would create incentives for unions to encourage employees who believe they have grounds for a civil claim against the employer to pursue a civil action on their own, instead of pursuing a grievance. That outcome would generally not be in the best interests of either individual employees or the bargaining unit as whole.

## D. CONCLUDING REFLECTIONS ON ACCESS TO JUSTICE IN UNIONIZED WORKPLACES

Engaging with law to advance social goals inevitably raises broad questions about relationships between law and justice, and relationships between access to law and access to justice. These broad questions in turn raise further questions about relationships between individual and collective interests and about relationships between public and private domains. Reflecting on the *Weber* decision and its impact over the past two decades is an opportunity to reflect on these questions as they relate to workers, unions and collective bargaining.

71 For further discussion, see Pickel, above note 67 at 8 and Shilton, "Choice, but No Choice," above note 69.

Etherington's access-to-justice critique of *Weber* focuses on cracks in the Canadian collective bargaining edifice, as does the Laskin/Adell critique of union control over access to arbitration. I have argued that there is much glue surrounding and stabilizing these cracks, resulting in a relatively strong collective bargaining system that provides unionized employees with significantly more meaningful access to justice than is available to non-unionized employees. The challenge of balancing individual and collective interests is a core issue for the collective agreement enforcement model. The approach I propose rests on the conclusion that there are no purely individual rights in the context of collective agreements. I am untroubled by this conclusion, because in my view there are no purely individual rights in any social context. All rights are the products of social relations. Where there are social relations, there are interdependencies between individuals and collectives. These interdependencies call for on-going balancing and adjustment of individual and collective concerns. In unionized workplaces, there will be both common and competing interests in the relations among individual employees, the bargaining unit, the union and the employer. Understanding and evaluating access to justice in this context calls for a process in which all of these interests are carefully assessed and addressed, with reference both to the legal rights in play and to the social impact of decisions on individuals and the collective. Access to justice will sometimes require that priority be given to the individual and sometimes to the collective. I have argued that unions, unionization, and collective bargaining have social benefits that are both private and public in nature, and those benefits enhance access to justice for workers. Unions, unionization and collective bargaining are part of our current social context, but we cannot take for granted their continued existence and beneficial impacts on workers.[72] The overall rate of unionization in Canada declined by about 8 percent during the 1980s and 1990s, from 38 percent to 30 percent.[73] In 2014, the rate of unionization in Ontario was 27

72 For an analysis of the erosion of the current collective bargaining model in Canada, *see* Eric Tucker, "Shall Wagnerism Have No Dominion?," online: (2014) 21 *Just Labour: A Canadian Journal of Work and Society* 1, www.justlabour.yorku.ca/index.php?page=toc&volume=21.

73 Statistics Canada, "Long Term Trends in Unionization," by Diane Galarneau & Thao Sohn, Catalogue no 75-006-X (Ottawa: Statistics Canada, 2013) at 2, online: www.statcan.gc.ca/pub/75-006-x/2013001/article/11878-eng.pdf.

percent.[74] It is said that the rate of unionization has remained relatively steady during the 2000s; however, further decline is always possible. In my view, policy debates about collective agreement administration and the interaction between collective agreement provisions and related common law, *Charter* and statutory legal provisions must take into account both the potential impact on unions today and in the short-term, and also the potential impact on the future of unions, unionization, and collective bargaining.

Was Bernie Adell right that the current model does not appropriately balance individual and collective rights? If so, can this imbalance be redressed by imposing a higher duty of fair representation? or by requiring unions to support certain kinds of individual claims? or by permitting individual employees to pursue their own claims to arbitration? Would conducting more empirical research give us a better picture of the specific impacts of the current system on individual employees? Or is it sufficient to know, as we already do, that unions do not pursue all the claims that individuals would like them to pursue? My analysis does not answer these questions. It does, however, suggest that in our discussions about options for establishing and enforcing workplace benefits and protections, we take care not to devalue and potentially jeopardize the collective power and benefits of unions. The enforcement system fostered by *Weber* and its progeny certainly has its cracks, but as part of the Canadian collective bargaining system it also provides individual unionized employees with access-to-justice benefits that almost certainly outweigh unfettered access to the courts for the pursuit of common law or *Charter* claims.

74 Ontario Ministry of Labour, "Collective Bargaining, Agreements and Negotiations: FAQ" (Ottawa: OML, 7 October 2015), online: www.labour.gov.on.ca/english/lr/faqs/lr_faq1.php. *See also* Employment and Social Development Canada, "Union Coverage in Canada—2014" (Ottawa: ESDC, 30 November 2015), online: www.labour.gc.ca/eng/resources/info/publications/union_coverage/UnionCoverage_EN.pdf.

CHAPTER SIX

# Statutory Tribunals and the Challenges of Managing Parallel Claims

Jo-Anne Pickel*

It has now been twenty years since the Supreme Court of Canada rendered its decisions in *Weber v Ontario Hydro*[1] and its companion case *New Brunswick v O'Leary*.[2] In those decisions, the Court adopted an exclusive jurisdiction model to hold that arbitrators have exclusive jurisdiction to deal with tort and constitutional claims where the essential character of a dispute arises from the interpretation, application, administration or violation of a collective agreement.

Numerous articles were published shortly after the release of *Weber* and *O'Leary*, primarily addressing what this exclusive jurisdiction model meant for labour arbitration, unions, employers, and individual employees. In the decade following *Weber*'s release, many articles continued to appear, focusing on the impact of *Weber* on labour arbitration in the intervening years.[3] There has been comparatively less scholarship exam-

---

* Any opinions expressed in this essay are those of the author and should not be taken to reflect the views of the HRTO or its Vice-Chairs.

1 [1995] 2 SCR 929 [*Weber*].

2 [1995] 2 SCR 967 [*O'Leary*].

3 *See e.g.*, Bernard Adell, "Jurisdictional Overlap Between Arbitration and Other Forums: An Update" (2000) 8 *Canadian Labour and Employment Law Journal* 179 179; Ray Brown & Brian Etherington, "*Weber v Ontario Hydro*: A Denial of Access to Justice for the Organized Employee?" (1996) 4 *Canadian Labour and Employment Law Journal* 183; Donald D Carter, "Looking at *Weber* Five Years Later: Is it Time for a New Approach?" (2000) 8 *Canadian Labour and Employment Law Journal* 231;

ining what impact, if any, *Weber* and associated cases have had on the jurisdiction of statutory tribunals.[4]

As many scholars have described, *Weber* has had a significant impact on labour arbitration because courts have declined jurisdiction over a range of contract and tort claims which have then been diverted into the arbitral forum.[5] The discussion in the scholarship has focused mainly on just how frequently courts have declined jurisdiction over the claims of unionized employees on the basis of the reasoning in *Weber*. In this essay, I suggest that *Weber's* impact on the jurisdiction of statutory tribunals has, in contrast, been comparatively minor, because statutory tribunals have been much less likely than courts to decline jurisdiction on the basis of exclusive arbitral jurisdiction.

In Part A of the essay, I review the approach taken to *Weber* by Canadian human rights tribunals and two other statutory tribunals in Ontario. I focus on human rights tribunals because the most frequent area of overlap between arbitrators and statutory tribunals has been in relation to human rights. As I discuss, human rights tribunals and reviewing courts in Canadian jurisdictions other than Quebec have held that human rights tribunals have concurrent jurisdiction with labour arbitrators

---

Donald Carter, "An Arbitrator as Human Rights Adjudicator: The Lessons of *Orillia Soldiers Memorial Hospital*" (1999–2000) 1 *Labour Arbitration Year Book* (Toronto: Lancaster House, 2000) 55; Andrew Lokan & Maryth Yachnin. "From *Weber* to *Parry Sound*: the Expanded Scope of Arbitration" (2004) 11 *Canadian Labour and Employment Law Journal* 1; Richard MacDowell, "Labour Arbitration — The New Labour Court?" (2000) 8 *Canadian Labour and Employment Law Journal* 121; Michel G Picher, "Defining the Scope of Arbitration: The Impact of *Weber*: An Arbitrator's Perspective" in Kevin Whittaker et al, eds, (1999–2000) 1 *Labour Arbitration Year Book* (Toronto: Lancaster House, 2000) 99.

4 Some exceptions are the following articles, which deal in whole or in part with the delineation of jurisdiction between arbitrators and statutory tribunals, especially human rights tribunals: Elizabeth Shilton, "Choice, but No Choice: Adjudicating Human Rights Claims in Unionized Workplaces in Canada" (2013) 38:2 *Queen's Law Journal* 461; Dana F Hooker & Carman J Overholt, "Defending Claims In Different Fora: The Competing Jurisdiction of Arbitrators And Tribunals In British Columbia" (2010) 43:1 *University of British Columbia Law Review* 47; Craig Flood, "Efficiency v Fairness: Multiple Litigation and Adjudication in Labour and Employment Law" (2000) 8 *Canadian Labour and Employment Law Journal* 383; Lokan & Yachnin, *ibid*; Sonia Regenbogen Luciw, "*Parry Sound* and Its Successors in the Supreme Court of Canada: Implications for the Scope of Arbitral Authority" (2004) 11 *Canadian Labour and Employment Law Journal* 365.

5 See articles in note 3 above.

over human rights claims brought by unionized employees. In Ontario, it appears that only two statutory tribunals other than the Human Rights Tribunal of Ontario (HRTO) have had to analyze the impact of *Weber* on their jurisdiction. Both tribunals distinguished *Weber* to conclude that they had exclusive jurisdiction over claims filed by unionized employees. In Part B, I focus more specifically on the HRTO. As I discuss, the main issue that arises at the HRTO is not *whether* the Tribunal has jurisdiction over applications filed by unionized employees, but *how* it deals with situations where unionized employees file both applications with the Tribunal and grievances under their collective agreement. I review how the Tribunal puts into practice some of the more general principles underlying the *Weber* decision—that is, the avoidance and/or effective management of multiple overlapping proceedings dealing with substantially the same facts and issues. I discuss two of the main features of the *Human Rights Code*[6] (*Code*) that assist the HRTO in dealing with parallel proceedings: the power to defer consideration of an application and the power to dismiss an application where another proceeding has appropriately dealt with the substance of the application. Although these powers assist in dealing with parallel proceedings, various issues and situations arise that complicate the management of parallel claims which I discuss in Part C of the essay. Lastly, in Part D, I provide concluding remarks on the impact of the *Weber* line of cases on the work of statutory tribunals.

## A. APPROACH TAKEN BY STATUTORY TRIBUNALS TO *WEBER*

A full review of how all statutory tribunals in Canada have applied *Weber* falls beyond the scope of this essay. Instead, I focus primarily on human rights tribunals across Canada, because human rights has been the most frequent area of overlap between arbitrators and statutory tribunals. I also include two other statutory tribunals in Ontario that appear to have addressed the application of *Weber*.

The governing statutes of most statutory tribunals do not expressly address whether the tribunal has concurrent, exclusive or overlapping jurisdiction with labour arbitrators over the claims of unionized employees.[7]

6 RSO 1990, c H 19.

7 Some employment standards statutes do expressly address the jurisdiction of employment standards adjudicators over claims filed by unionized employees. *See e.g.*, the Ontario *Employment Standards Act, 2000*, SO 2000, c 41, s 99 and the British

The caselaw reviewed below suggests that, in spite of *Weber*, statutory tribunals generally have been much more likely than courts to find that they have either concurrent or exclusive jurisdiction over the claims of unionized employees. One reason for this may be the fact that, when making jurisdictional determinations, statutory tribunals must analyze not only the provisions relating to arbitral jurisdiction in the applicable labour relations statutes, but also the provisions of their own governing statutes. Statutory tribunals have been established by legislatures to carry out a certain statutory mandate, which may be regulatory in character or may involve enforcing certain basic rights. When examining their statutory mandate, many tribunals have determined that the legislature intended them to have either concurrent or exclusive jurisdiction over all claims that fall within their mandate, even if these claims are filed by unionized employees.

### 1) Human Rights Tribunals across Canada

No human rights statutes specifically address whether the tribunals or commissions established by them have concurrent, exclusive or overlapping jurisdiction with labour arbitrators over the claims of unionized employees. Human rights tribunals and reviewing courts have been called upon to make jurisdictional determinations by examining the statutory mandate of the tribunal or commission in question against the background of applicable caselaw, including *Weber* and associated cases.[8]

---

Columbia *Employment Standards Act*, RSBC 1996, c 113, s 3(7). In addition, the 2013 federal budget legislation included as-yet-unproclaimed amendments to prevent the Canadian Human Rights Commission from handling complaints filed by federal public service employees against their employer: *Economic Action Plan 2013 Act*, No 2, SC 2013, c 40. If proclaimed, these amendments will require employees of the federal public service who wish to make claims of employment-related discrimination to file grievances with the Public Service Labour Relations and Employment Board.

8 At least one province (British Columbia) has adopted legislative provisions that expressly address whether statutory tribunals have the jurisdiction to apply human rights legislation. *See Administrative Tribunals Act*, SBC 2004, c 45 ss 46.1, 46.2, 46.3. However, this statute does not directly address the delineation of jurisdiction between statutory tribunals and labour arbitrators.

### a) Supreme Court of Canada's Analysis

The Supreme Court of Canada has been called upon to consider the jurisdiction of human rights tribunals over claims filed by unionized employees in at least two decisions: *Quebec (Commission des droits de la personne et des droits de la jeunesse) v Quebec (Attorney General)*, which arose out of Québec,[9] and *Canada (House of Commons) v Vaid*, which arose out of the federal jurisdiction.[10] It is fair to say that these decisions call for the application of a contextual approach to determining jurisdiction over human rights claims. In both cases, the Court held that the legal characterization of a claim is not determinative, that there is no presumption of arbitral exclusivity, and that adjudicators must determine "whether the relevant legislation applied to the dispute at issue, taken in its full factual context, establishes that [a] labour arbitrator has exclusive jurisdiction over the dispute."[11]

*Morin* involved a claim filed by unionized teachers claiming that a legislated freeze on experience increments discriminated against them contrary to Quebec's human rights legislation. The majority rejected the respondents' submission that the dispute fell within exclusive arbitral jurisdiction on the basis of *Weber*, and held that the Quebec Human Rights Commission/Tribunal had concurrent jurisdiction with a labour arbitrator over the claim. They gave a number of reasons for this conclusion, including their view that the claim did not lend itself to characterization as a grievance since it was a challenge to the decision to include certain provisions in the collective agreement, rather than a challenge to the application of these provisions.[12]

*Vaid* involved a human rights complaint filed by a unionized House of Commons employee whose complaint alleged that he was constructively dismissed at least in part because of his race. The Court held that an adjudicator under the *Parliamentary Employment and Staff Relations Act*[13] (*PESRA*) had exclusive jurisdiction over the claim, relying on two factors to support its conclusion. First, the Court held that the claim was

---

9 2004 SCC 39 [*Morin*].

10 2005 SCC 30 [*Vaid*]. See the very thorough review of these decisions in Shilton, "Choice, but No Choice," above note 4 at 471–75, 477–83.

11 *Morin*, above note 10 at para 14. This passage from *Morin* is quoted with approval by the Court in *Vaid*, above note 11 at para 92.

12 For a critique of this distinction see Bastarache J's dissent in *Morin*. *See also* Shilton, above note 4 at 481 and Regenbogen Luciw, above note 4.

13 RSC 1985, c 33 (2nd Supp), s 2.

essentially one of wrongful dismissal, in spite of the employee's discrimination and harassment allegations.[14] According to the Court, there was nothing to "lift [the] complaints out of their specific employment context."[15] Second, the Court relied upon a provision in the *PESRA* which states that the Act prevails over other federal legislation that provides for matters similar to those provided for under the *PESRA*. For these reasons, the Court held that the Canadian Human Rights Commission (CHRC) did not have jurisdiction over the complaint.

In both of these decisions, the Supreme Court of Canada carefully examined the full factual and legislative context of the cases. However, as will be discussed below, the Court's contextual analysis has not always been closely applied by human rights tribunals in Canadian jurisdictions other than Quebec.

**b) Human Rights Tribunals in Canadian Common Law Jurisdictions**

Human rights tribunals in Canadian common law jurisdictions have held that they have concurrent jurisdiction over human rights claims made by unionized employees who are covered by a collective agreement. In so doing, these tribunals have implicitly assumed blanket concurrent jurisdiction over all claims filed by unionized employees.

In Ontario, the jurisdictional issue was addressed for the first time post-*Weber* in *Naraine v Ford Motor Co of Canada*.[16] In that case, a Board of Inquiry (the precursor to the HRTO) held that it had jurisdiction over a human rights complaint challenging an employee's discharge as discriminatory on the basis of race. The employee had filed grievances under his collective agreement. The arbitrator appointed to hear the grievances dismissed the discharge grievance, ruling that the grievor's discharge was justified. Although the arbitrator heard some evidence relating to the alleged discrimination, he held that the evidence was irrelevant to the altercation that had resulted in the discharge.

The Board of Inquiry distinguished *Weber* to hold that it had jurisdiction to hear a parallel complaint that the employee had filed with the Ontario Human Rights Commission (OHRC). Central to the Board of In-

14 *Vaid*, above note 10 at para 98.

15 *Ibid* at para 94.

16 (2001), 209 DLR (4th) 465, 110 ACWS (3d) 517 (Ont CA) [*Naraine*], rev'g 209 DLR (4th) 465, 110 ACWS (3d) 517 (Ont Div Ct), rev'g 24 CHRRD/466 (Ont Board of Inquiry), rev'g 27 CHRRD/230 (Ont Board of Inquiry), rev'g 28 CHRRD/267 (Ont Board of Inquiry).

quiry's analysis was its conclusion that it was not clear at the time of the arbitration (in 1986) that the arbitrator had jurisdiction to apply the *Code*. The arbitration occurred prior to the inclusion of section 48(12)(j) in the Ontario *Labour Relations Act*[17] (*LRA*), a provision that specifically grants arbitrators the power to interpret and apply human rights and other employment-related statutes.

Both the Ontario Divisional Court and the Court of Appeal upheld the Board of Inquiry's decision. The Court of Appeal relied upon the same reasoning as the Board of Inquiry to distinguish *Weber*. The Court held that, at the time Mr Naraine filed his grievance, the OHRC in fact had *exclusive* jurisdiction over his human rights claims since, according to the Court, the arbitrator did not have jurisdiction to deal with the *Code* allegations. The Court also referred to what it described as "symmetrical amendments" to the *LRA* and the *Code* that provided for concurrent jurisdiction over human rights claims arising in the unionized context. These amendments were the former section 34(1)(a) of the *Code*, which gave the OHRC statutory authority to decline to deal with complaints which in its opinion could or should be more appropriately dealt with under another Act, and section 48(12)(j) of the *LRA*, which as noted earlier provides arbitrators with clear authority to apply the *Code*.[18] The Court of Appeal held that the goal of these provisions was consistent with the goal at the heart of *Weber*—to avoid the proliferation of proceedings to the greatest extent possible:

> The underlying goal of these symmetrical amendments is to avoid the gratuitous bifurcation or proliferation of proceedings, especially when the arbitrable grievance and the human rights complaint emerge seamlessly from the same factual matrix. That goal was also, I think, at the heart of *Weber*. In my view, *Weber* stands for the proposition that when several related issues emanate from a workplace dispute, they should all be heard by one adjudicator to the extent jurisdictionally possible,

---

17 *Labour Relations Act, 1995*, SO 1995, c 1, Schedule A, s 48(12)(j).

18 I note that although the Court of Appeal referred to these as symmetrical "amendments," s 48(12)(j) was not added to the *LRA* at the same time as s 34(1)(a) was added to the *Code*. Section 34(1)(a) was included in the *Code* from 1982 until the substantial revisions to the *Code* that came into force in 2008, whereas section 48(12)(j) was added to the *LRA* in 1995. Therefore, it would be more appropriate to speak of symmetrical or complementary "provisions" rather than symmetrical "amendments."

> so that inconsistent results and remedies, such as those in Mr. Naraine's case, may be avoided.[19]

The HRTO has relied upon the Court of Appeal's decision in *Naraine* in subsequent decisions to hold that it has concurrent jurisdiction over human rights claims filed by unionized employees.[20] The underlying assumption in the Tribunal's caselaw is that it has a blanket concurrent jurisdiction over all human rights claims filed by unionized employees, regardless of the degree of connection between the claim and the collective agreement.[21] I also note that the 2008 amendments to the *Code* arguably reinforce the Tribunal's conclusion on the issue of concurrent jurisdiction. Under the pre-2008 *Code*, the OHRC had discretion to decide not to deal with a complaint if the allegations "could" or "should" more appropriately have been dealt with under another Act. This provision was repealed in 2008. Now, the Tribunal has the power to dismiss applications under 45.1 of the *Code* only if, in its opinion, the substance of the application "has been" appropriately dealt with in another proceeding. These amendments reinforce the Tribunal's conclusion that the legislature intended the Tribunal to have concurrent jurisdiction over human rights claims, even if they could have been raised in other forums such as the arbitral forum.

---

19 *Naraine*, above note 16 at para 60.

20 *See Monck v Ford Motor Company of Canada*, 2009 HRTO 861 (CanLII) at para 8 [*Monck*] and *Snow v Honda of Canada Manufacturing*, 2007 HRTO 45 (CanLII) at para 14. The Tribunal has also held that it has concurrent jurisdiction when an applicant has filed a parallel claim under other statutory schemes such as the *Workplace Safety and Insurance Act*. *See Snow*, *ibid* and *Frankson v Workplace Safety and Insurance Board*, 2011 HRTO 2107 (CanLII). One circumstance in which the Tribunal does not have concurrent jurisdiction is in a situation where an employee commences a parallel civil proceeding in court in which the person is seeking a remedy with respect to an alleged *Code* infringement. Subsection 34(11) of the *Code* bars the Tribunal from taking jurisdiction in such a case.

21 *See e.g.*, *Nash v Ottawa-Carleton District School Board*, 2012 HRTO 2299 (CanLII) [*Nash*]. Here, the Tribunal assumed jurisdiction over an application where an employee who had filed a grievance asked her union to withdraw the grievance early in the arbitration. *See also Asiamah v Olymel SEC/LP*, 2009 HRTO 1750 (CanLII) at paras 22–24 [*Asiamah*]. In this decision, a presumption of blanket jurisdiction was also evident where an applicant filed a parallel grievance that dealt with some, but not all, of the allegations raised in his or her application to the Tribunal. The Tribunal's assumption of blanket jurisdiction is also implicit in the many cases where it has assumed jurisdiction over applications based on facts analogous to those in *Vaid*.

Human rights tribunals and reviewing courts in all the other common law jurisdictions that have addressed this issue have used a similar analysis to conclude that human rights tribunals have concurrent jurisdiction over claims filed by unionized employees.[22] For example, the Canadian Human Rights Tribunal (CHRT) and the Federal Court of Canada have held that the CHRT has concurrent jurisdiction over human rights claims filed by unionized employees.[23] Both the CHRT and the Federal Court relied heavily on section 41 of the *Canadian Human Rights Act* (*CHRA*) to support this conclusion. This section, which is the equivalent of the former section 34(1)(a) of the Ontario *Code*, gives the CHRC the discretion to decline to deal with complaints where it appears to it that the complainant ought to exhaust the grievance process. In the view of the CHRT and the Federal Court, this provision clearly gives the CHRC, and implicitly the CHRT, concurrent jurisdiction to deal with any complaint arising from a collective agreement, unless the CHRC itself decides that the grievance procedure ought to be exhausted.

What is striking about this caselaw is that it has not applied the contextual analysis used by the Supreme Court of Canada in *Morin* and *Vaid*. Human rights tribunals and courts in all jurisdictions outside Quebec have not distinguished between disputes that arise from the insertion of a particular clause in a collective agreement and disputes over the application of the collective agreement, as the Court did in *Morin*. They have also not examined the factual context of applications to determine whether any factors serve to "lift [the] complaints out of their specific employment context," as the Court did in *Vaid*.[24]

---

22 *Bannister v Best Facilities*, 2008 BCHRT 438 (CanLII); *Nova Scotia (Human Rights Commission) v Halifax (Regional Municipality)*, 2008 NSCA 21, leave to appeal to SCC refused, 390 NR 391(note) (18 September 2008); *Calgary Health Region v Alberta (Human Rights & Citizenship Commission)*, 2007 ABCA 120, leave to appeal to SCC refused, 390 NR 396(note) (25 October 2007); *Price v Fredericton (City) Chief of Police*, [2004] NBHRBID No 1; *Cadillac Fairview Corp v Saskatchewan (Board of Inquiry)* (1999), 173 DLR (4th) 609, [1999] 7 WWR 517 (Sask CA).

23 *See e.g.*, *Canadian Broadcasting Corp v Paul* (1998), 168 DLR (4th) 727, 85 ACWS (3d) 36 (FCTD) and *Eyerley v Seaspan International Limited*, 2000 CanLII 28898 (CHRT).

24 Above note 10 at para 94.

### 2) Quebec's Human Rights Tribunal and Courts

The Quebec Human Rights Tribunal (QHRT), and reviewing courts in Quebec, have taken a different approach to analyzing the impact of the *Weber* line of cases on the QHRT's jurisdiction. Unlike the approach taken by adjudicators in other jurisdictions, the QHRT and courts in Quebec have more strictly applied the contextual analysis set out in *Morin*. In a number of decisions, the QHRT and courts have distinguished between disputes that arise from the insertion of a particular clause in a collective agreement and disputes over the application of the collective agreement.[25] They have found that the QHRT shares concurrent jurisdiction with arbitrators over the former category of cases, but that the latter category of cases falls within the exclusive jurisdiction of arbitrators.

In one sense this difference in approach is perhaps not surprising—since *Morin* dealt specifically with the jurisdiction of the QHRT, courts and the QHRT are strictly bound to apply the analysis set out in the decision. By contrast, courts and human rights tribunals in other jurisdictions have either distinguished *Morin* based on minor differences in statutory wording or glossed over it altogether. However, there is no obvious reason why the jurisdiction of the QHRT should differ from that of human rights tribunals in other jurisdictions. Therefore, we are left with a somewhat paradoxical situation in which human rights tribunals in the rest of Canada have taken jurisdiction over types of claims over which the QHRT has declined jurisdiction in Quebec.

### 3) Other Statutory Tribunals in Ontario

Only two other statutory tribunals in Ontario appear to have addressed the impact of *Weber* on their jurisdiction to deal with claims filed by unionized employees: the Financial Services Tribunal (FST) and the Information and Privacy Commissioner of Ontario (IPCO). Both held that they had exclusive jurisdiction over the claims made in the cases in which they were called upon to address the impact of *Weber* on their jurisdiction.

---

25 See e.g., *Université de Sherbrooke c Québec (Commission des droits de la personne et des droits de la jeunesse)*, 2015 QCCA 1397 at para 27; *Québec (Commission des droits de la personne et des droits de la jeunesse) c Université de Montréal*, 2006 QCCA 508 at para 67; *Québec (Commission des droits de la personne et des droits de la jeunesse) c Université Laval*, 2005 QCCA 27 at paras 42–46.

**a) Financial Services Tribunal**

The FST was called upon to address a preliminary objection to its jurisdiction based on *Weber* in *PPG Canada Inc v Ontario (Superintendent Financial Services)*.[26] The case dealt with the question of whether two wind-up reports filed by PPG Canada Inc (Company) complied with the provisions of the *Pension Benefits Act* (*PBA*).

The FST noted that, unlike the Court in *Weber*, it was required to consider the legislative intent behind two statutes — its own governing statute, the *PBA*, as well as the provisions relating to arbitral jurisdiction contained in the *LRA*. After examining both statutes, the FST had no doubt that the legislature intended the Superintendent of Financial Services, and by extension the FST, to have exclusive authority to determine whether to approve wind-up reports for all pension plans registered under the *PBA*, regardless of whether these plans are incorporated into collective agreements.

Among other things, the FST emphasized the Superintendent's broad institutional expertise in interpreting the complex statutory requirements found in the *PBA*. It also stressed its authority to protect the best interests of pension plan members, former members, retired members and other persons entitled to benefits under a pension plan. The FST noted that not all of these individuals may be members of a bargaining unit covered by a collective agreement. For these reasons, the FST concluded that an arbitrator was not institutionally equipped to "stand in the statutory shoes of the Superintendent."[27] It held that the *PBA* sets out a clear and comprehensive scheme that assigns exclusive jurisdiction to the Superintendent and the FST to determine whether to approve a wind-up report and address any other related issues.

The Company in *PPG* argued, in the alternative, that even if the FST had jurisdiction, it should defer consideration of the wind-up report issue to an arbitrator. The FST held that the *PBA* did not permit it to defer its statutory duties to another body. However, it did note that an arbitrator may have a role to play in certain cases that come before the FST. Where interpretive issues relevant to a wind-up report have already been arbitrated, for example, the Superintendent and FST may have to apply doctrines such as *res judicata*, abuse of process and issue estoppel. As well, the FST noted that, in some cases, it may be appropriate for the

26 2015 ONFST 10 [*PPG*].

27 *Ibid* at para 46.

Superintendent and FST to suspend their proceedings to await the outcome of an on-going grievance arbitration.

It should be noted that the FST's decision in *PPG* dealt only with the wind-up report issue before it. It is not clear what the FST's analysis would be in relation to other issues arising under the *PBA*.[28]

**b) Information and Privacy Commissioner of Ontario**

The IPCO has similarly distinguished *Weber* to assume exclusive jurisdiction over at least two claims filed by unionized employees.[29] Both cases involved freedom of information requests under the *Freedom of Information and Protection of Privacy Act* (*FIPPA*). In both cases, the IPCO framed the essential character of the disputes as whether *FIPPA* provides a right of access to the government-held information at issue. In one decision, the IPCO stressed that *FIPPA* provides a detailed code for establishing and determining public rights of access to information.[30] It noted that *FIPPA* establishes the IPCO as an independent arbiter of those rights, and an essential part of the legislative scheme, as expressed in the purposes of the Act. In the other decision, the IPCO noted that the collective agreement did not purport to oust the IPCO's jurisdiction and that it would be contrary to public policy if it did.[31] The IPCO also stressed the strong public accountability purposes served by *FIPPA* in ensuring that citizens have access to information held by public institutions. It noted that, unlike an arbitrator, the IPCO is invested with wide-ranging powers under *FIPPA* to deal with access to information requests. As well, the IPCO noted that there is no provision in the *LRA* for a requester to participate in an arbitration. Based on this reasoning, the IPCO held that it had ex-

---

28 Meanwhile, arbitrators have taken different views as to the scope of their jurisdiction over claims relating to the *PBA*. *See e.g.*, *West Parry Sound Health Centre and Ontario Nurses' Association (Pension Contributions), Re,* [2008] OLAA No 705, 96 CLAS 122, 2008 CanLII 66136 (ON LA); *Rouge Valley Health System v Ontario Nurses' Association*, 2013 CanLII 8011 (ON LA), in which the arbitrators reached different conclusions on the issue.

29 *See Ontario (Ministry of Community and Social Services)*, [2010] OIPC No 125 [*Ontario (MCSS)*] and *University of Ottawa (Re)*, 2011 CanLII 74312 (ON IPC) [*University of Ottawa*].

30 *Ontario (MCSS), ibid.*

31 *University of Ottawa*, above note 30.

clusive jurisdiction over the claims in both cases, even though they arose in the unionized context.[32]

While the IPCO has not expressly assumed a blanket exclusive jurisdiction over all access to information requests filed by unionized employees, such a conclusion may well be implicit in the cases discussed above. In light of the IPCO's reference to the "complete code" provided under *FIPPA*, as well as its public accountability mandate, one would be hard pressed to imagine an access to information claim over which it would not take exclusive jurisdiction. However, given the lack of IPCO caselaw dealing with other *FIPPA*-related issues, it is unclear whether the IPCO would assert exclusive jurisdiction over other types of claims made under *FIPPA*.

The FST and IPCO cases reviewed above call to mind the observations of Andrew Lokan and Maryth Yachnin who, in examining the jurisdiction of arbitrators in relation to statutory tribunals, argued that it is difficult to make a credible case that legislatures intended arbitration to completely supplant the jurisdiction of statutory tribunals established specifically to carry out different policy initiatives or to enforce certain rights.[33] Their view appears to have been shared by the statutory tribunals which have been called upon to consider whether the reasoning in *Weber* should be applied to them as well, and have determined, instead, that they have either concurrent or exclusive jurisdiction over claims filed by unionized employees. Thus, as the caselaw reviewed above demonstrates, statutory tribunals have been more likely than courts to find that they have jurisdiction over claims filed by unionized employees.

## B. HRTO'S GENERAL APPROACH TO PARALLEL CLAIMS

I now move from the more general review of *Weber*'s implications for statutory tribunals to focus more specifically on the HRTO. In light of the HRTO's assumption of concurrent jurisdiction over claims filed by

---

32 Although the IPCO has held that it has exclusive jurisdiction over at least certain issues arising under *FIPPA*, arbitrators have assumed jurisdiction over the interpretation and application of privacy legislation provided that a grievance raising such issues also has a connection to a collective agreement. *See Kawartha Pine Ridge District School Board v Elementary Teachers' Federation of Ontario* (2007), 169 LAC (4th) 353 and *Canadian Union of Public Employees, Local 133 v Niagara Falls (City)*, [2005] OLAA 228, 81 CLAS 1.

33 Lokan & Yachnin, above note 3.

unionized employees, the main issue that arises at the HRTO is not *whether* the Tribunal has jurisdiction over such claims, but *how* it deals with situations where an applicant has filed parallel claims. Situations involving multiple claims raise various issues for the Tribunal. Two main issues arise in HRTO cases: (1) whether it is appropriate for the Tribunal to proceed with consideration of an application if there exists an ongoing parallel proceeding, and (2) whether it is appropriate for the Tribunal to proceed with an application if a parallel proceeding has already dealt with the substance of an application.

### 1) HRTO Power to Defer its Proceedings

The *Code* provides the Tribunal with the power to defer consideration of an application.[34] Deferral is a discretionary measure that the Tribunal exercises on the basis of the circumstances in each case. Some factors the Tribunal has identified as relevant to deciding whether it is appropriate to defer consideration of an application are the following: (1) the subject matter of the other proceeding, (2) the nature of the other proceeding, (3) the types of remedies available in the other proceeding and (4) whether it would be fair overall to the parties to defer, having regard to the status of each proceeding and the steps that have been taken to pursue them.[35] Deferral does not affect a party's substantive rights. Instead, it suspends the Tribunal's process pending the outcome of another proceeding. Deferral is aimed at avoiding duplication of legal processes. It reflects the recognition that a variety of tribunals have the jurisdiction to deal with human rights matters[36] and that the facts underlying Tribunal applications may also form the basis of other proceedings.

The Tribunal has stated that it will typically defer an application when there is an ongoing grievance under a collective agreement based on the same facts and/or issues. In doing so, the Tribunal generally has not relied on the reasoning in *Weber* as a factor for granting deferral requests. Instead, the Tribunal relies upon the following factors:

---

34 *Human Rights Code*, above note 6 at s 45; Ontario, Human Rights Tribunal of Ontario, *Rules of Procedure*, 30 April 2014, rule 14.

35 *See Baghdasserians v 674469 Ontario*, 2008 HRTO 404 (CanLII).

36 *See Tranchemontagne v Ontario (Director of Disability Support Program, Ministry of Community and Social Services)*, 2006 SCC 14.

1) the fact that labour arbitrators have jurisdiction to apply the *Code* and to award *Code* remedies,
2) the desire to avoid the potential for inconsistent decisions that might occur if claims proceed in parallel, and
3) a recognition of the unfairness that may arise if parties are required to litigate more than one proceeding dealing with substantially the same issues in two different forums at the same time.

The Tribunal has also relied upon institutional factors relating both to labour arbitration and to its own processes, which it set out most fully in *Melville v Toronto (City)*.[37] In that case, the applicant was an employee of a long-term care home operated by the City of Toronto. She filed an application with the HRTO against her employer and her union in which she alleged systemic discrimination by her employer against racialized employees. She also alleged that the respondents discriminated against her personally, including allegations of discrimination through the imposition of improper discipline.

The applicant had filed at least two grievances that related to the issues in her application: a grievance alleging harassment and another alleging unjust discipline for a certain workplace incident. Both respondents requested that the Tribunal defer the application pending the conclusion of the grievance and arbitration process. The Tribunal granted the respondents' deferral requests. In his reasons as to why deferral was appropriate, the Tribunal's then-Associate Chair articulated an analysis that implicitly underlies many other deferral cases, stating as follows:

> An individual working under a collective agreement has a choice — he or she can choose not to file or proceed with a grievance and to pursue the application at the Tribunal instead. If the applicant chooses the grievance process and what comes with it, including representation by the union and the enforcement of particular rights under the collective agreement, he or she cannot also proceed with a Tribunal application at the same time. Deferral avoids two simultaneous proceedings that may result in conflicting determinations, ensures that the respondent need not be actively defending the same matter in two legal proceedings at the same time, and focuses the Tribunal's limited resources on cases where it is the only process being pursued. In my view, it is consistent with the Tribunal's mandate to interpret its rules in a fair, just

37 2012 HRTO 22 (CanLII).

> and expeditious manner to defer a case when a grievance is ongoing, whether or not that grievance has yet been referred to arbitration. The grievance process is a stage in dispute resolution before the matter is referred to an independent third party, but that does not mean that there is no proceeding ongoing. Fairness supports avoiding the duplication of proceedings.[38]

In support of his conclusion, the Associate Chair cited *Weber* and stated that, in general, the law gives exclusive jurisdiction to labour arbitrators where a matter arises expressly or inferentially from the collective agreement. He then noted that the *Code* "departs from those principles by allowing a unionized applicant to file a Tribunal application."[39] However, he held that it was not unfair to require an applicant to pursue only one recourse at a time.

The Tribunal has deferred consideration of applications even when an employee has filed grievances only *after* filing their application.[40] The Tribunal has also deferred applications where there is substantial or significant, but not complete, overlap between the issues raised in the application and an employee's grievance(s).[41] However, despite its general practice of deferring applications where there exist parallel grievances, the Tribunal has refused to defer consideration of an application, or has re-activated a deferred application where the grievance process was not moving forward in a timely manner.[42] Therefore, it is open to an applicant whose case has been deferred to request reactivation of an application on the basis that a grievance process has been unreasonably slow. As the Tribunal noted in *Melville*, it is also always open to an employee to withdraw his or her grievance entirely and proceed before the Tribunal.

As noted earlier, deferral by itself does not affect an applicant's substantive rights, and it is always open to an applicant whose HRTO application was deferred to seek to proceed with his or her application before the Tribunal once the grievance/arbitration proceeding is complete. However, where an application has been deferred, the applicant's ability to proceed

---

38 *Ibid* at para 8.

39 *Ibid* at para 11.

40 *See e.g., McCartney v Toronto (City)*, 2012 HRTO 175 (CanLII).

41 *See e.g., Webster v University Health Network — PMH*, 2010 HRTO 2186 (CanLII) and *Ferenczy v Conseil des écoles publiques de l'Est de l'Ontario*, 2014 HRTO 1636 (CanLII).

42 *See e.g., Monck*, above note 21, and *Gomez v Grand River Foods*, 2011 HRTO 2106 (CanLII).

after a grievance/arbitration proceeding is complete will be subject to the Tribunal's power to dismiss the application under section 45.1 of the *Code,* which does affect an applicant's substantive rights, as I discuss in the next section.

## 2) HRTO Power to Dismiss Applications under Section 45.1 of the *Code*

The second *Code* provision that comes into play in situations involving multiple proceedings is section 45.1, which grants the Tribunal the power to "dismiss an application, in whole or in part, in accordance with its rules if the Tribunal is of the opinion that another proceeding has appropriately dealt with the substance of the application." In applying section 45.1, the Tribunal does not consider the procedural or substantive correctness of the other proceeding or decision when deciding whether an application may proceed.[43] Instead, section 45.1 is the statutory reflection of the collective principles underlying the doctrines of issue estoppel, collateral attack and abuse of process.[44] As stated by the Divisional Court, in applying section 45.1 the Tribunal seeks to strike a balance between the related concerns of finality, judicial economy, consistency and the need to ensure that justice is done in a particular case.[45] The Tribunal does so by following the analysis set out in two Supreme Court of Canada decisions: *Figliola*[46] and *Penner v Niagara (Regional Police Services Board).*[47]

The Tribunal first considers whether there has been another proceeding within the meaning of section 45.1. The Tribunal has stated that a "proceeding" implies that an impartial third person has applied an objective legal standard to a certain set of facts and reached a conclusion.[48] Therefore, the Tribunal has ruled that an employer's decision to deny a

---

43 *Gomez v Sobeys Milton Retail Support Centre*, 2011 HRTO 2297 (CanLII) at para 4 [*Gomez*].

44 See *British Columbia (Workers' Compensation Board) v Figliola*, 2011 SCC 52 at para 24 [*Figliola*] and *Gomez, ibid* at para 24.

45 For the Tribunal's general approach to the application of s 45.1, see *Claybourn v Toronto Police Services Board*, 2013 HRTO 1298 (CanLII) and *KM v Kodama*, 2014 HRTO 526 (CanLII). Both of these decisions were upheld by the Ontario Divisional Court in *Ontario (Community Safety and Correctional Services) v De Lottinville*, 2015 ONSC 3085.

46 *Figliola*, above note 44. 2011 SCC 52.

47 2013 SCC 19 [*Penner*].

48 *Maxwell v Cooper-Standard Automotive Canada Limited*, 2013 HRTO 1482 (CanLII) at paras 37–38.

grievance at Step 2 of a grievance procedure is not a proceeding within the meaning of section 45.1.[49] Likewise, a union's mere withdrawal of a grievance is not a proceeding under section 45.1.[50] However, the Tribunal has held that a settlement may amount to a proceeding under section 45.1 of the *Code*.[51]

If the Tribunal finds that there has been another proceeding, it goes on to consider whether, in its opinion, the other proceeding appropriately dealt with the substance of the application. In doing so, it applies the factors set out in *Figliola*:

1) whether there was concurrent jurisdiction in the other proceeding to decide human rights issues,
2) whether the previously decided issues were essentially the same as what is being complained of to the Tribunal, and
3) whether there was an opportunity for the complainants or their privies to know the case to be met and have the chance to meet it, regardless of how closely the previous process procedurally mirrored the one the Tribunal prefers or uses itself.[52]

The Tribunal also considers whether it would be unfair to use the results of another proceeding to dismiss an application under section 45.1. This consideration arises from the decision in *Penner* on the application of the doctrine of issue estoppel.[53] In *Penner*, the Court dealt with a situation where an individual filed a complaint of misconduct against a police officer under the *Police Services Act*.[54] Following the exhaustion of that procedure, the individual filed a civil action claiming compensation arising out of the same incident and allegations. The Court had to determine whether the doctrine of issue estoppel applied to bar the civil action, and concluded that the doctrine should not be applied if its application would be unfair in the circumstances of the case.

---

49 *Wang v Hilton Toronto*, 2015 HRTO 1131 (CanLII) at paras 19–32.

50 *See e.g.*, *Soni v Hilton Suites Toronto/Markham Conference Centre and Spa*, 2015 HRTO 713 (CanLII) at para 6 and *Jean v Résidence St Louis*, 2011 HRTO 1800 (CanLII) at para 19.

51 *Dunn v Sault Ste. Marie (City)*, 2008 HRTO 149 (CanLII) at para 37 [*Dunn*]. For a discussion of the HRTO's approach to settlements entered into in prior proceedings: see Part C(2) below.

52 *Figliola*, above note 44 at para 37.

53 *Penner*, above note 47.

54 RSO 1990, c P.15.

The majority stated that unfairness in applying the doctrine of issue estoppel may arise in one of two main ways. First, the unfairness of applying issue estoppel may arise from the unfairness of the prior proceedings. Second, even where the prior proceedings were conducted fairly and properly having regard to their purposes, it may nonetheless be unfair to use the results of that process to preclude the subsequent claim. Applying this analysis to the facts in *Penner*, the majority concluded that it would be unfair to prevent the plaintiff from proceeding with his civil action for a number of reasons. These reasons included the reasonable expectations of the parties, the fact that the plaintiff had no personal or financial stake in the disciplinary proceeding and the fact that the application of issue estoppel against the plaintiff would have the effect of permitting the chief of police to become the judge of his own case.

The HRTO has applied this unfairness assessment to all section 45.1 cases decided since *Penner*, including cases where the previous proceeding took the form of an arbitration proceeding. However, a review of this caselaw shows that the Tribunal has so far only once found that it would be unfair to use the results of a previous arbitral proceeding to dismiss an application.[55]

### 3) Does the Combined Effect of Deferral and Section 45.1 Amount to *De Facto* Exclusive Arbitral Jurisdiction?

As a result of the Tribunal's approach to its deferral power and its dismissal power under section 45.1 of the *Code*, when an employee files both an application with the HRTO and a grievance in relation to the same facts, their application is likely to be deferred by the HRTO. They then face the possibility that their application will be dismissed under section 45.1 if an arbitrator has appropriately dealt with the substance of their application.

Some readers may conclude that this amounts to a *de facto* system of exclusive arbitral jurisdiction over human rights claims in the province. However this is not the case, since unionized employees who wish to proceed before the Tribunal are always free to do so if they have not filed a grievance under their collective agreement or if their union has decided

55 In the case in question the Tribunal held that it would be unfair to use the results of a previous mediation-arbitration to dismiss an application since it was not clear that the process had dealt with the substance of the application. See *Beausoleil v Ontario (Community Safety and Correctional Services)*, 2013 HRTO 1553 (CanLII) [*Beausoleil*]. See a more detailed review of *Beausoleil* in Part C below.

not to act upon their grievance — for example by not resolving the grievance or not referring it to arbitration. Even employees who have filed grievances may have a right to proceed before the Tribunal if they withdraw their grievances or if their union is not processing their grievance in a timely way.[56] Therefore, the system is one of concurrent jurisdiction, albeit one which in practice may see most claims being decided in the arbitral forum.

The HRTO's power of deferral and power to dismiss applications under section 45.1 of the *Code* are important tools to deal appropriately with situations where employees file multiple parallel claims. The use of these tools to manage and deal with parallel claims does require time and resources on the part of the Tribunal. However, the time and resources dedicated to deferrals and/or preliminary hearings under section 45.1 are significantly less than the time and resources that would be spent on matters if duplicative litigation were permitted. It is also quite possible that the Tribunal would be required to spend even greater resources making jurisdictional determinations if it were to apply the *Morin* contextual approach to determining jurisdiction on a case by case basis. Nevertheless, while the powers of deferral and of dismissal under section 45.1 assist in dealing with parallel proceedings, various issues and situations arise that complicate the management of parallel claims, as I discuss in the next section.

## C. COMPLICATED ISSUES ARISING AT THE HRTO IN RELATION TO PARALLEL PROCEEDINGS

In this section, I discuss various issues that have arisen in cases where unionized employees filed both an application with the HRTO and a grievance under their collective agreement.

### 1) Settlements of Grievances

Interestingly, Mr Weber, who sought to bring the civil claim in *Weber*, had filed a grievance under his collective agreement which was settled at arbitration. This scenario arises with some regularity at the HRTO. The Tribunal is fairly frequently called upon to address situations where an

56 See cases cited at note 42 above.

applicant's grievance has been settled by their union and employer but they nevertheless wish to proceed with their application before the Tribunal. In such cases, the Tribunal must consider whether the application should be dismissed under section 45.1 of the *Code* and/or pursuant to one of the principles animating section 45.1, such as abuse of process.

As a matter of labour law, unions have carriage of grievances and thus the authority to settle grievances on behalf of their members. However, the Tribunal does not automatically dismiss an application if the applicant's union has entered into a settlement on their behalf. *Code* rights are individual rights and, therefore, individuals have a right to enforce these rights before the Tribunal unless they themselves have explicitly or implicitly voluntarily agreed to settle their *Code*-related claims.[57] At the same time, the Tribunal has recognized the public interest in enforcing settlements that were freely arrived at by the parties in other forums, especially in the area of labour relations.[58] The Tribunal has thus held, for example, that a settlement may constitute a "proceeding" for the purposes of section 45.1 the *Code*.[59] In addition, the Tribunal has held that it would be an abuse of process for parties to seek to litigate settled matters unless there are compelling reasons to continue to process the application despite the settlement.

In general, the Tribunal examines the circumstances surrounding the settlement to determine whether the applicant explicitly or implicitly voluntarily consented to it and accepted its terms. In doing so, the Tribunal has generally dismissed applications as an abuse of process where an applicant has signed a settlement that covers the allegations in the application and it is apparent that the parties intended to resolve all outstanding issues between them through the settlement.[60] This is the outcome unless there are compelling reasons to proceed despite the existence of the settlement. It is exceedingly rare for the Tribunal to proceed with an application if the applicant already has signed a settlement that covers the issues raised in the application. The few cases where the Tribunal has proceeded with an application in the face of such a settlement have

57 *See Lemieux v Guelph General Hospital*, 2010 HRTO 1267 (CanLII) at paras 18–20 and *Ma v University of Toronto*, 2015 HRTO 1551 (CanLII) at paras 49–51 [*Ma*].

58 *Dunn*, above note 51.

59 *Ibid.*

60 *Dickson v General Motors of Canada Limited*, 2013 HRTO 1347 (CanLII) at para 18; *Solcan v Kitchener (City)*, 2011 HRTO 2205 (CanLII) at paras 41–42 and the cases cited therein.

involved a finding that the applicant's consent to the settlement was vitiated due to the presence of a mental disability.[61] The Tribunal has also stated that it may be appropriate to proceed with an application if an applicant's consent to a previous settlement was vitiated by duress.[62] However, although applicants who seek to proceed with applications despite having signed a settlement frequently allege duress, no applicant at the HRTO has yet succeeded in making out the very high threshold for a finding of duress.

In situations where a grievor/applicant has not signed a settlement, the Tribunal generally considers whether other factors establish that he or she implicitly accepted the terms of settlement. The Tribunal has generally found that it is not an abuse of process to proceed with an application if an applicant has not signed a settlement agreement and there are no other signs that the applicant has voluntarily accepted the settlement. This would be the case, for example, if the applicant's union and employer arrived at a settlement without the applicant's knowledge and from which the applicant derived no benefit. Cases where an applicant derived a benefit from the agreement are more complicated and turn on their precise facts. In some cases, the Tribunal has distinguished between an applicant's receipt of a benefit and his or her implicit acceptance of the settlement terms. The overriding question is whether the surrounding circumstances establish that the applicant implicitly accepted the terms of the settlement, even if he or she refused to sign the settlement agreement.[63]

### 2) Alternative Forms of Dispute Resolution

Another complicated scenario may arise in situations where parties have agreed to employ alternative forms of dispute resolution during a grievance arbitration proceeding. This may arise especially in situations where a union and employer are in a mature bargaining relationship and the collective agreement allows the parties to use expedited forms of dis-

---

61 *See Anamguya v Intercon Security*, 2010 HRTO 2464 (CanLII) and *Walkinshaw v Complex Services Inc*, 2011 HRTO 1977 (CanLII).

62 See discussion of this threshold in *Nolan v Royal Ottawa Health Care Group*, 2014 HRTO 1604 (CanLII) and *Perricone v Fabco Plastics Wholesale*, 2010 HRTO 1655 (CanLII).

63 *See, e.g,. Ma,* above note 57; *Melendez v City of Toronto*, 2012 HRTO 403 (CanLII) at paras 19–20; *Healey v McMaster University*, 2010 HRTO 1874 (CanLII) at paras 49–51.

pute resolution such as mediation-arbitration to process grievances. In such cases, the Tribunal's decision-making under section 45.1 of the *Code* may be less straightforward than it would be if the prior proceeding takes the form of a standard arbitration.

In applying section 45.1 of the *Code* to such situations, the Tribunal does not require that prior proceedings mirror the Tribunal's process or traditional litigation processes.[64] The Tribunal has also been prepared to apply section 45.1 to dismiss applications where a prior mediation-arbitration resulted in a bottom line decision with no reasons.[65] However, there is a risk that the Tribunal will not dismiss an application if it is not satisfied that a prior proceeding has dealt with the substance of an application.[66]

For example, the Tribunal refused to dismiss the application in *Beausoleil.*[67] The applicant in the case had filed a grievance that raised the same issues as her application. Her union and employer agreed to deal with her grievance, along with ten others she had filed, through a form of mediation-arbitration provided for under the collective agreement. At the end of the process, a Vice-Chair of the Grievance Settlement Board issued a short decision which stated, "some of the grievances have no merit and should be dismissed, others are (sic) questionable merit and others may have some merit."[68] In the section 45.1 decision under the *Code*, the HRTO Vice-Chair recognized that the mediation-arbitration process at issue was designed to be an expeditious and efficient manner of resolving workplace disputes between the parties. However, she held that it would be unfair to use the results of the mediation-arbitration process to bar the applicant from proceeding with her application, given the arbitrator's brief reasons and the absence of evidence concerning what was put before the arbitrator.

---

64 See *Georgievska v Kingdom Hotels Limited*, 2013 HRTO 818 (CanLII); *Clarke v Kingdom Hotel Toronto Ltd*, 2013 HRTO 2002 (CanLII); *Beausoleil,* above note 55; *Marshall-Wilkinson v Ontario (Community Safety and Correctional Services)*, 2014 HRTO 1154 (CanLII) [*Marshall-Wilkinson*].

65 *See Marshall-Wilkinson, ibid.*

66 *See Beausoleil,* above note 57.

67 *Ibid.*

68 *Ibid* at para 16.

### 3) Employees Who Withdraw Grievances during the Arbitration Process

Yet another type of complicated issue that arises for the HRTO is how to deal with a situation where an employee who has filed both a grievance and an application decides to withdraw their grievance during the arbitration process. In such a scenario, a respondent may request that the Tribunal dismiss the applicant's HRTO application as an abuse of process. The Tribunal has dealt with this scenario in at least two cases: *Nash v Ottawa-Carleton District School Board*[69] and *Hicks v Hamilton-Wentworth Catholic District School Board*.[70]

In determining whether to proceed with an application before the Tribunal would amount to an abuse of process, the Tribunal will consider all the surrounding circumstances. The factors considered by the Tribunal have included the following:

1) the stage of the grievance process at which the grievance was withdrawn,[71]
2) whether the arbitrator made an abuse of process finding at arbitration,[72] and
3) whether any other factors exist that would make it an abuse of the Tribunal's process to proceed with consideration of the application.

### 4) Case Splitting

One final complicated issue arises when applicants seek to split their cases by seeking to advance non-human rights claims relating to a certain incident or incidents in one forum, and also filing an application in relation to the same set of facts before the Tribunal.

In a number of cases the Tribunal has dismissed applications under section 45.1 if the prior proceeding raised the same facts and the applicant should have, but failed, to advance their human rights claims in the prior

---

69 *Nash*, above note 21.

70 2015 HRTO 1702 (CanLII) [*Hicks*].

71 In *Nash*, above note 21, the Vice-Chair held that it was not an abuse of process to permit the applicant to proceed with her application before the Tribunal in part because she withdrew her grievance early in the arbitration process and before any evidence was heard by the arbitrator.

72 In *Hicks*, above note 70, the Vice-Chair held that it would amount to an abuse of process to permit an application to proceed in part because an arbitrator had dismissed the applicant's grievance on the basis of abuse of process.

proceeding.[73] The Vice-Chairs in some of these cases have held that an applicant should not be permitted to restrict the *Code* arguments made in a grievance so that he or she can pursue them later before the HRTO. In a similar vein, some Vice-Chairs have held that it would be an abuse of process for the Tribunal to permit an applicant to re-litigate the same case based on a different legal theory. By contrast, other Vice-Chairs take a less global approach and parse out which allegations have been appropriately dealt with in the arbitral proceeding and which have not.[74]

As the situations described above illustrate, the HRTO must address a number of complicated issues in dealing with parallel proceedings where employees file a *Code* application at the same time as they pursue grievances under their collective agreement. These issues add to the complexity of considerations that can arise for the HRTO in determining how to exercise its powers of deferral and of dismissal under section 45.1 of the *Code*.

## D. CONCLUDING REMARKS

While there may be "one law for all" (or one set of laws), there continue to be different fora in which that law/set of laws may be applied. In this essay, I have explored the impact of *Weber* on statutory tribunals, with a particular focus on human rights tribunals and other statutory tribunals in Ontario. Based on the caselaw reviewed, statutory tribunals have held that they have concurrent — or even exclusive — jurisdiction over claims filed by unionized employees. Thus, it may be argued that *Weber*'s impact on statutory tribunals has been relatively minor as compared to its impact on civil claims filed by unionized employees, despite the *Weber* line of cases and despite the authority of arbitrators to apply human rights and other employment-related statutes.

Where statutory tribunals conclude that they have concurrent jurisdiction with arbitrators, the main issue they face is not a jurisdictional one, but instead a more practical one, namely how best to manage multiple, parallel claims in a manner that balances the desire for finality and

73 *See Paterno v Salvation Army*, 2011 HRTO 2298 (CanLII); *Manhas v AO Smith Enterprises*, 2010 HRTO 659 (CanLII); *Cunningham v CUPE 4400*, 2011 HRTO 658 (CanLII); *Sutton v United Food and Commercial Workers Canada, Local 175*, 2010 HRTO 935 (CanLII).

74 *See e.g., Asiamah,* above note 21 at paras 22–23.

economy with considerations of fairness to the parties. As illustrated by the experiences of the HRTO described above, this balance is not always straightforward or easy to achieve.

CHAPTER SEVEN

# Did *Weber* Affect the Timeliness of Arbitration?

Kevin Banks, Richard Chaykowski, & George Slotsve*

In two recent papers, Ontario's then Chief Justice Warren Winkler described the present system of grievance arbitration as one which "can be slow, expensive and detached from the realities of the workplace."[1] He argued that it "has lost its course, has lost its trajectory, has lost its vision," and "is at risk of becoming dysfunctional and irrelevant."[2]

Justice Winkler was calling for a new urgency in response to an old problem. Researchers and commentators have argued since the early 1970s that the system is prone to unnecessary delay.[3] Empirical research on time delay in arbitration shows a steady increase in the average time from initiating a grievance to the rendering of an arbitration award in all Canadian jurisdictions studied.[4] Moreover, studies have shown that

---

* The authors gratefully acknowledge support from the National Academy of Arbitrators Research and Education Fund for this research.

1 Warren K Winkler, "Arbitration as a Cornerstone of Industrial Justice" (Kingston, ON: Queen's University School of Policy Studies, 2011) [Winkler, "Industrial Justice"].

2 Warren K Winkler, "Labour Arbitration and Conflict Resolution: Back to Our Roots" (Donald Wood Lecture delivered at the Queen's School of Policy Studies, 30 November 2010), online: www.ontariocourts.on.ca/coa/en/ps/speeches/2010-labour-arbitration-conflict-resolution.htm.

3 Howard Goldblatt, *Justice Delayed: The Arbitration Process in Ontario* (Toronto: Labour Council of Metropolitan Toronto, 1974).

4 Goldblatt, *ibid*; Joseph B Rose, "Statutory Expedited Grievance Arbitration: The Case of Ontario" (1986) 41:4 *Arbitration Journal* 30 at 30–35; John Fricke, *An Empirical*

delay in labour arbitration can harm contract negotiations, cause financial loss to the employer, harm the quality of the arbitration hearing itself as memories of the material events dim with the passage of time, inhibit productivity by generating both employee restiveness and uncertainty among supervisors and impose injustice on employees whose rights under collective agreements are less likely to be fully vindicated as time elapses.[5]

Given the persistence and the stakes of the problem, it is important to understand its root causes. One prominent argument, advanced by Chief Justice Winkler and echoed by others in the labour relations community, is that the expansion of arbitral jurisdiction has fostered delay by increasing both the potential for litigation over the scope of arbitral jurisdiction and the complexity of legal issues with which arbitration must deal.[6] Among the most notable expansions of arbitral jurisdiction was that effected by the Supreme Court of Canada's decision in *Weber v Ontario Hydro*.[7] In *Weber*, the Supreme Court of Canada ruled that arbitrators have exclusive jurisdiction with respect to "disputes which expressly or inferentially arise out of the collective agreement."[8] *Weber*'s definition of arbitral jurisdiction is notoriously ambiguous, giving rise to extensive commentary and repeated litigation over which issues fell within arbitral jurisdiction and which did not. It also effectively gave the Supreme Court's blessing to a considerable expansion of arbitral jurisdiction beyond the four corners of rights and obligations contained in collective agreements. *Weber* and subsequent jurisprudence applying it have found tort actions by employees against employers, issues related to pension plans and benefit and welfare plans not expressly incorporated into collective agreements, and claims of violation of the *Canadian Charter of Rights and Freedoms*, to fall within the exclusive jurisdiction of labour arbitrators. *Weber* thus presented labour arbitration with a host of new

---

*Study of the Grievance Arbitration Process in Alberta* (Edmonton: Alberta Labour, 1976); Allen Ponak & Corliss Olson, "Time Delays in Grievance Arbitration" (1992) 47:4 *Industrial Relations* 690; Kenneth W Thornicroft, "Accounting for Delay in Grievance Arbitration" (1993) 44:9 *Labor Law Journal* 543; Gilles Trudeau, "The Internal Grievance Process and Grievance Arbitration in Quebec: An Illustration of the North American Methods of Resolving Disputes Arising from the Application of Collective Agreements" (2002) 44:3 *Managerial Law* 27.

5 Allen Ponak et al, "Using Event History Analysis to Model Delay in Grievance Arbitration" (1996) 50:1 *Industrial and Labor Relations Review* 105.

6 Winkler, "Industrial Justice," above note 1.

7 [1995] 2 SCR 929 [*Weber*].

8 *Ibid* at para 59.

and potentially quite complex legal and factual issues that had the potential to increase delay within the system.

To be sure, this is not the only theory that may account for increased delay in Canadian labour arbitration. Others are briefly reviewed in Part A below. But, like most other theories of the problem, the *Weber* delay hypothesis has not been empirically tested. Previous studies have focused on proximate rather than underlying causes of delay. There has been no published quantitative research into the timeliness of labour arbitration procedures in Canada since 2002, and none that could capture the effects of arbitral jurisdiction on delay. In this paper we present results from a comprehensive statistical study attempting to analyse quantitatively the impacts on efficiency and delay in arbitration of the subjects added to arbitral jurisdiction by the Supreme Court's decision in *Weber*. We find that the subject matter jurisdiction added by *Weber* has had little or no impact, and argue that there are good reasons in theory to believe that this finding is correct. The causes of delay in labour arbitration likely lie elsewhere. Whatever the flaws of the *Weber* decision, systemic effects on delay are not among them.

We begin in Part A with a framework of hypotheses with respect to potential causes of delay in labour arbitration. This framework makes clear that the theory of delay consequent upon expanded jurisdiction is simply one of several that could account for increasing delay. It also clarifies the conceptual bases of our research methods. Part B briefly sets out our methods of data collection and analysis. Part C presents a quantitative analysis, for the year 2010, of the incidence of *Weber* issues within Ontario labour arbitration awards and the relationship between decisions on those issues and time elapsed at each stage of the arbitration process. Part D presents our conclusions, along with their policy and research implications.

## A. POSSIBLE CAUSES OF INEFFICIENCY AND DELAY IN LABOUR ARBITRATION

Arbitration is a form of private dispute resolution provided through a competitive market. In principle, therefore, the parties should be able to control the process so as to ensure its efficiency. The policy premises of the Canadian labour arbitration system assume that efficiency is in the interests of both parties. Cases involving serious matters of discipline or discharge have tended to be handled more quickly, suggesting that arbitration can in fact operate more rapidly where the parties want it to do so.[9]

On its face, the apparent persistence and growth of delay in that system therefore presents something of a puzzle. But upon closer examination of labour arbitration as an institution and of the literature on delay, one can identify several types of potential explanations. First, legislation or wider legal culture may impose demands and constraints upon arbitration that lie outside the control of the parties. Second, the stable preferences of one or more of the parties may undermine demand for expeditious dispute resolution. Third, even where both parties have stable general preferences for expeditious dispute resolution, incentive or coordination problems in the short term may prevent them from demanding it effectively. Finally, it is possible that institutional or cultural factors impede or undermine the willingness of arbitrators to supply expeditious dispute resolution. We briefly consider each type of potential explanation in turn.

### 1) Exogenous Demands and Constraints

Exogenous demands and constraints upon arbitration that result in increasing delay might arise from one or more of four sources.

#### a) Increased Frequency of Complexity Due to the Expansion of Jurisdiction

First, expansion of arbitral jurisdiction by legislation or court decision might have increased the proportion of cases raising numerous or complex legal or factual issues that must be decided through labour arbitration.[10] In legally and factually complex cases, the goal of timeliness has always existed in tension with the over-riding imperative to provide a forum in which legal and factual issues can be fully and fairly adjudicated. Since the *Weber* decision in 1995, arbitrators in Ontario and elsewhere have been tasked with interpreting and applying a wide variety of laws beyond the terms of collective agreements. As a consequence of *Weber*, arbitrators can be called upon to interpret and apply tort law, the *Charter*, and rights under pension, benefit and welfare plans. The Supreme

9 Ponak et al, above note 5; Ponak & Olson, above note 4; Kenneth W Thornicroft, "Sources of Delay in Grievance Arbitration" (1995) 8:1 *Employee Responsbilities and Rights Journal* 57 [Thornicroft, "Sources of Delay"].

10 Winkler, "Industrial Justice," above note 1; Trudeau, above note 4.

Court of Canada's decision in *Parry Sound (District) Welfare Administration Board v Ontario Public Service Employees Union Local 324*[11] in 2003 confirmed, in addition, that arbitrators have jurisdiction to interpret and apply human rights codes as though they formed part of collective agreements. *Charter*, common law, human rights and pension and benefit claims arguably tend to raise issues of greater factual or legal complexity than do claims raised under terms and conditions negotiated into collective agreements. Such non-collective agreement claims may also raise issues of fact and law that are not as familiar to the arbitrator or party representatives and may therefore require more time to address.

#### b) Increased Frequency of Lengthy Cases as an Unintended Consequence of Increased Use of Mediation-Arbitration

In Ontario, these effects might be compounded by the unintended consequences of increased use of mediation-arbitration (med-arb). Med-arb might successfully resolve a high proportion of simpler disputes, leaving relatively more cases presenting complex legal or factual issues for arbitration and placing greater demands on arbitration at a system-wide level. It might thus change the composition of the population of cases decided at arbitration and increase delay within that population, despite making resolution of the overall population of disputes referred to arbitration more efficient. It should be noted, however, that this hypothesis is unlikely to account for the full extent of increased delay, as the tendency towards increased delay predates the increased use of med-arb by at least two decades.

#### c) Increased Litigation of the Scope of Jurisdiction

As both the prior literature and the essays in this volume make clear, *Weber* might have contributed to delay by leaving the scope of arbitral jurisdiction ambiguous, thus increasing the proportion of cases raising jurisdiction issues that must be decided prior to dealing with the merits of a dispute. Overlapping jurisdiction may also produce delay, as arbitration proceedings are deferred pending outcomes in other forums.[12]

---

11 2003 SCC 42 [*Parry Sound*].

12 Randi Hammer Abramsky, "The Ontario Law Reform Comission Report on Delay and Multiple Proceedings: A Critique" (1996) 4 *Canadian Labour and Employment Law Journal* 353; Bernard Adell, "Jurisdictional Overlap Between Arbitration and Other Forums: An Update" (2000) 8 *Canadian Labour and Employment Law Journal* 179; Carter, "Looking at *Weber* Five Years Later," above note 5; Craig Flood, "Efficiency

#### d) Culture of Legalism

Some have argued that a culture of legalism has infected labour arbitration, leading to greater use of tactics such as procedural objections, unnecessarily lengthy presentation of witness evidence, unduly extensive cross-examination of witnesses and a tendency on the part of arbitrators to issue legally rigorous and extensive reasons not necessarily of direct interest to the parties.[13] Consistent with these contentions, previous research has found that the use of lawyers as representatives can increase delay.[14] Furthermore, arbitrators as a group may be caught up in a culture of legalism, producing awards with a level of detail in legal and factual analysis that is out of proportion to the matter under consideration.[15]

### 2) Demand Factors: Party Preferences

Arbitrators are appointed by agreement of the parties. While they obtain their formal powers to manage the arbitration process from the *Labour Relations Act*, the practical extent of the mandate of an arbitrator to manage the process often also flows from the agreement, or at least the implicit expectations, of the parties. Arbitration is generally *ad hoc* and the continuing work of arbitrators depends upon their continuing acceptability within the labour relations community. In the absence of clearly communicated expectations to the contrary, arbitrators will often default to case management practices that are widely accepted. These in turn are likely to reflect the common and stable preferences of parties within a given geographic or industrial sector.

There is generally nothing to prevent parties from streamlining the entire arbitration process to provide for rapid appointment of arbitrators and scheduling of hearings, limited presentation of oral evidence, compressed time for the presentation of legal argument and short deadlines for rendering arbitral awards. Ontario has provided all collective agreement parties with access to a publicly-operated expedited arbitrator appointment system since 1979, a system which has been shown to

v. Fairness: Multiple Litigation and Adjudication in Labour and Employment Law" (2000) 8 *Canadian Labour and Employment Law Journal* 383.

13 Winkler, "Industrial Justice," above note 1.

14 Thornicroft, "Sources of Delay," above note 9.

15 Winkler, "Industrial Justice," above note 1.

reduce delay.[16] Privately-developed expedited arbitration systems have reduced case handling times in industries such as garment, rail and longshoring for many years.[17] Such procedures can be expected to reduce delay.[18] Grievance mediation systems have also proven effective at reducing backlogs of cases that can clog arbitration schedules.[19]

There is some evidence that parties are moving to reduce delay in arbitration in Ontario. Earlier studies have shown a shift from three-person arbitration boards to the appointment of single arbitrators, a shift which stands to reduce delay.[20] Furthermore, as noted above, the shift in Ontario from traditional arbitration procedures towards med-arb may also increase rates of pre-hearing settlement.

Yet there is little evidence of widespread change in the way that parties choose or design arbitration proceedings themselves. Privately-administered expedited arbitration systems remain uncommon.[21] While the use of three-person panels has continued to decline in the last two decades, so has the use of Ontario's expedited arbitration system.[22] This suggests that parties either prefer traditional arbitration proceedings, or have trouble agreeing upon or implementing alternatives. Furthermore, if one party is more interested in timeliness than the other, it will likely only agree to use expedited procedures where the more interested party makes negotiating concessions on other matters.

---

16 Rose, above note 4; Kevin Banks, Richard Chaykowski & George Slotsve, "Arbitration as Access to Justice: An Update on the Profile of Labour Arbitration Cases in Ontario" (Presentation delivered at the 2011 Industrial Relations Conference "Building and Maintaining Healthy Workplace Relationships," 16–17 June 2011) [unpublished].

17 Mark Thompson, "Expedited Arbitration: Promise and Performance" in William Kaplan, Jeffery Sack & Morley Gunderson, eds, (1992) 1 *Labour Arbitration Year Book* (Toronto: Lancaster House, 1992) 41; David C McPhillips, Peter R Sheen & Wayne Moore, "Expedited Arbitration: A New Experience for British Columbia" in William Kaplan et al, eds, (1996–1997) 1 *Labour Arbitration Year Book* (Toronto: Lancaster House, 1996) 29.

18 Rose, above note 4; Thompson, above note 17.

19 Elizabeth Rae Butt, "Grievance Mediation: The Ontario Experience" in *School of Industrial Relations Research Essay Series No 14* (Kingston, ON: Industrial Relations Centre Queen's University, 1988); Mitchell S Birken, *Grievance Mediation: The Impact of the Process and Outcomes on the Interests of the Parties* (Kingston, ON: IRC Press, 2000).

20 Ponak & Olson, above note 4; Thornicroft, "Sources of Delay," above note 9.

21 Thompson, above note 17; Winkler, "Industrial Justice," above note 1.

22 Banks, Chaykowski & Slotsve, above note 16.

Having first considered why one party or both parties might have stable preferences for processes associated with delay, we next turn to consider how short-run incentives or coordination problems may impede agreement on expeditious processes.

### a) Greater Value Placed on Perceived Fairness or Correctness

Parties may attach greater value to the fairness or perceived fairness of arbitration proceedings, or the substantive correctness of the decision, than to timeliness. In one study, employers ranked quality of arbitral awards as a greater concern than timeliness.[23] Unions may seek to minimize the risk that grievors will perceive the process to be unfair, if grievors tend to place greater weight on procedural fairness than on substantive outcome in deciding whether they are satisfied with grievance processes.[24] Unions may also take a cautious approach to procedural formalities in order to minimize the risk of the legal costs and political problems associated with a duty of fair representation complaint by a dissatisfied grievor, even though expedited arbitration procedures generally do not violate legal duties of fair representation.[25]

### b) Minimizing the Risk of Unpredictable Outcomes

For the same reason, unions may take a cautious approach to arbitrator selection. Employers may seek to minimize downside risks as well. Previous analysts have hypothesized that the tendency of collective agreement parties to prefer a small number of the busiest and most experienced arbitrators may reflect an effort to minimize risk of an unpredictable and negative outcome.[26] For similar reasons, a party or both parties may hire a preferred lawyer as a representative despite the potential for delay in scheduling a hearing in order to accommodate his or her schedule.[27]

---

23 Arthur Eliot Berkeley, "The Most Serious Faults in Labor-Management Arbitration Today and What Can Be Done to Remedy Them" (1989) 40:11 *Labor Law Journal* 728.

24 Michael E Gordon & Roger L Bowlby, "Propositions About Grievance Settlements: Finally, Consultation with Grievants" (1988) 41:1 *Personnel Psychology* 107.

25 Clarence R Deitsch & David A Dilts, "Case Characteristics Affecting the Method of Grievance Dispute Settlement" (1988) 1:2 *Employee Responsibilities and Rights Journal* 113; Thompson, above note 15; Donald D Carter, "Grievance Arbitration and the Charter: The Emerging Issues" (1989) 44:2 *Industrial Relations* 337.

26 Trudeau, above note 4.

27 Ponak et al, above note 5.

#### c) Allowing Time for Public Sector Decision-Making Processes

Earlier research suggests that the presence of public sector employers and unions is associated with greater delay.[28] One possible explanation for this may be that public sector actors may place less emphasis on speed and may have more cumbersome decision-making processes for grievance resolution.

#### d) Allowing Time for Healing

In some cases, delaying the resolution of a dispute may benefit one or both parties by allowing time to repair personal relationships in a non-adversarial forum, to find alternative job opportunities in order to separate antagonists, or to enable persons suffering from illnesses such as addiction to seek treatment sufficient to obtain a favourable prognosis. Increased awareness of such problems may have led to increased delay across the system.

### 3) Incentive or Coordination Problems

There are a number of ways in which cost, information or coordination problems may prevent the use of more timely arbitration procedures, even where parties generally consider timeliness a priority of the highest order.

#### a) Lack of Information

First, lack of information about the workings of expedited arbitration procedures may create uncertainty about whether it will pay off to make the investment of time and political or institutional capital in negotiating, obtaining support for and administering such procedures.

#### b) Transaction costs

Second, the transaction costs of negotiating and implementing expedited procedures, other than *ad hoc* measures such as agreed statements of fact, may exceed the costs of delay where the parties have a single case or a small number of cases going to arbitration. For example, the costs of negotiating agreements for rapid scheduling of hearings by mutually acceptable arbitrators, or for case management processes providing for early disclosure, identification of issues, and agreement on undisputed facts, may exceed their return on investment.

---

28 Ponak & Olson, above note 4; Thornicroft, "Sources of Delay," above note 9.

### c) Up-Front Costs

Third, moving to a system in which arbitration cases are dealt with expeditiously may require clearing a backlog of earlier cases. If the backlog of cases is sufficiently large, one or more of the parties may be unwilling or unable to allocate sufficient resources to do so.

### d) Agency Problems

Fourth, the incentives of agents may be misaligned—those dealing with arbitration of grievances may not have incentives to resolve grievances expeditiously. This may be the case, for example, where the remuneration or career advancement of counsel does not depend upon timely resolution of a particular case or set of cases, where timely resolution of disputes may simply increase counsel's workload but not his or her remuneration, where counsel's future income is not significantly dependent upon the particular client in question, or where the client does not sufficiently monitor and emphasize timeliness in awarding further work. There may also be agency problems between the union and the grievor. The grievor may care very much about timely resolution, but the union (like counsel) may have a full slate and large backlog of grievances, with no particular incentive to expedite most grievances.

### e) Risk of Defection

Fifth, particular kinds of cases will often present parties with reasons for tactical delay. For example, an employer with a relatively weak case but internal political problems with a likely remedy may seek to delay resolution. Alternatively, an employer might choose delaying tactics in order to raise costs for a union and weaken its position within the overall bargaining relationship. For termination grievances where the employee is likely to be reinstated, the employer may have a strong incentive to delay in order to avoid that outcome. A union may advance a grievance for internal political reasons, despite its weakness as a legal claim, and choose to delay resolution in the hopes of reaching a negotiated settlement or at least delaying political fallout resulting from the likely dismissal of the grievance. In each situation, short-term incentives may trump longer-term interests in expeditious dispute resolution.

Resisting incentives to delay in such a case is a form of cooperation that depends on trust that the other party will similarly do so. Some important aspects of expedited procedures, such as early disclosure, the negotiation of agreed statements of fact or the willingness to use arbitrator selection systems that limit party control over which arbitrator is chosen in a given case, also require such cooperation. Without some form of assurance that the other party will not seek to seize immediate advantage where such procedures present it, and then later resile from expedited procedures where they no longer do so, a party may correctly judge that it should not pursue expedited procedures. This will be so even where such procedures would make the party better off, if implemented on an ongoing basis. The stability of any commitment to expeditious dispute resolution may be further weakened where a lack of trust or a history of conflict undermines the confidence of parties that cooperation to implement expedited procedures will overcome incentives to strategically defect.

### 4) Supply of Expeditious Dispute Resolution

One study found some arbitrators to be associated with greater delay in a statistically significant way.[29] Recent research suggests, however, that procrastination is unlikely to be widespread among arbitrators, and that as a group arbitrators are less prone to procrastination than the general population.[30] On the other hand, it might be hypothesized that leading arbitrators are often too busy to write awards in a timely manner, while less experienced but more available arbitrators often lack the skills and experience required by the parties. As a result, there might effectively be a shortage in the supply of expeditious dispute resolution.

## B. RESEARCH METHODOLOGY

This paper reports results from a comprehensive statistical study of efficiency and delay in Ontario, Canada's largest jurisdiction. This is the first published study to attempt to quantify the impacts on efficiency and delay of subject matters added to the scope of arbitral jurisdiction. To do this, we have compiled a unique database to which we apply a range of statistical analyses.

---

29 Thornicroft, *ibid.*

30 Allen Ponak, Daphne G Taras & Piers Steel, "Personality and Time Delay Among Arbitrators" in Paul D Staudohar & Mark I Lurie, eds, *Arbitration 2010: The Steelworkers Trilogy at 50: Proceedings of the Sixty-Third Annual Meeting, National Academy of Arbitrators, Philadelphia, Pennsylvania, May 26–29 2010* (Arlington, VA: BNA, 2011).

### 1) The Database

The database for our analysis contains the main characteristics of every publicly reported arbitration decision in Ontario in 2010. Arbitrators are required by law in Ontario to file their awards with the Ontario Ministry of Labour. The Ministry makes those awards publicly available. They are also published in Quicklaw's Ontario Labour Arbitration Awards (OLAA) database. This provides access to a complete census of awards, in keyword searchable full text format.

Using a coding frame for the arbitration decisions piloted in initial research conducted in the spring and summer of 2011, detailed information regarding the characteristics of the arbitration decisions was recorded using the decision as the unit of observation. For each decision, the database includes the date intervals at each of the following three stages of the arbitration process:

1) event giving rise to the grievance and/or the initiation of the grievance to the commencement of hearings;
2) the commencement of hearings to the close of hearings; and
3) the close of hearings to the rendering of an award.

This information formed the basis for the construction of the dependent time variables utilized in the analysis, including: Event to First Hearing Time; Grievance to First Hearing Time; Hearing Days; Hearing Time; and Award Time (refer to Appendix Table 1, Panel B for definitions of these variables).

The database also included detailed information about the characteristics of the case and the parties involved, including the following ten data:

1) the arbitrator;
2) the type of arbitration board (sole arbitrator or three person panel);
3) the gender of the arbitrator;
4) the gender of the grievor;
5) whether the employer is in the government, health, education or private sector;
6) whether the award was issued under expedited arbitration or med-arb provisions of the *Ontario Labour Relations Act*;
7) whether the parties used an agreed statement of fact;
8) whether the arbitrator decided a contested issue of fact;
9) whether the employer or union was represented by counsel; and

10) award outcomes (grievance dismissed or upheld).

The database also included the procedural and substantive subject matters decided in the award, which formed the basis of case subject matter variables that are a main focus of this analysis. Each subject was constructed as a dichotomous variable (coded 1 if a subject of the case and 0 if not). A detailed list of the subjects is provided in Appendix Table 1, Panel B.

In *Weber*, the Supreme Court of Canada held that arbitrators have jurisdiction to decide any dispute that in its essential character arises expressly or inferentially out of the interpretation, application, administration or alleged violation of a collective agreement. In subsequent jurisprudence applying *Weber*, the scope of arbitral jurisdiction was extended beyond disputes concerning legal rights and obligations contained in the collective agreement. Arbitrators have assumed jurisdiction to interpret and apply legal rights and obligations created outside of the collective agreement and not incorporated into the collective agreement, where necessary to resolve disputes with a sufficient factual nexus to subject matters governed by collective agreements. Such external sources of law include most notably tort law, the *Charter*, and pension and benefit plans not incorporated into a collective agreement but which nonetheless specifically provide for the payment of benefits in certain circumstances. The Supreme Court itself acknowledged that arbitrators may lack expertise in matters such as tort law or the *Charter*, and said that the answer to such concerns was judicial review.[31] This answer might assist in ensuring the correctness of outcomes, but fails to respond to the concern that adding unfamiliar and potentially contentious issues to the docket of the arbitration system might increase delay. The ambiguity of the nexus to the collective agreement also, in the eyes of many commentators, increased the likelihood of litigation over the scope of arbitral jurisdiction itself.

To examine the effects of *Weber* jurisdiction on delay, we examined four subject matter variables. Specifically, we examined whether or not pension plans, benefit or welfare plans, *Charter* and tort issues were addressed in the arbitration cases and, if so, what effects they had on delay. In order to further assess the potential impact of *Weber*, we also constructed a combined *Weber* variable (refer to Appendix Table 1, Panel C for the definition) that captures whether any of these four subjects are addressed in a given case. We do note that while arbitral jurisdiction

31 *Weber*, above note 7, at para 55.

to decide tort claims must be founded on *Weber*'s interpretation of the *Labour Relations Act*, the same is not true of all cases related to the other "*Weber* subjects" identified above. We do not, however, attempt to quantify the number of cases in which arbitrators took jurisdiction based on *Weber*. This is for a number of reasons. Given the ambiguity of *Weber* jurisdiction, and the fact that it may not be raised as an issue for decision and therefore not discussed in all cases in which jurisdiction must be legally founded on *Weber*, this would be a complex task. We therefore first seek to identify the prevalence of subject matters with respect to which *Weber* increases the likelihood that arbitrators will take jurisdiction, and to analyze what effects, if any, deciding such issues has on delay. In this way we can identify whether *Weber* is likely to have any impact on delay. If we found that deciding such issues causes delay, we might then undertake a qualitative review of such cases to try to quantify more precisely the prevalence of decisions that expressly, or by necessary implication, were based upon *Weber* jurisdiction. As we indicated in the introduction, it turned out that we did not find such effects and therefore did not need to undertake further qualitative review of these awards.

We also sought to measure the effects that *Weber* might have had on delay within the system by increasing litigation over the scope of jurisdiction. There are many potential jurisdiction issues in addition to whether the dispute bears a sufficient nexus to the collective agreement under the *Weber* test. This makes it likely that many, if not most, jurisdiction issues are not *Weber*-related. Our coding frame did not distinguish *Weber* jurisdictional issues from other such issues. Because we did find statistically significant effects of deciding matters of jurisdiction on delay (one of our control variables — see Appendix Table 1), we undertook a qualitative review of all awards coded as deciding a jurisdiction issue to identify any that decided *Weber*-related ones.

Interim and consent awards were identified so that they could be excluded from the population of final awards subject to analysis.

### 1) Statistical Methods

We begin our analysis with a descriptive profile of the distribution of arbitration cases by subject. This permits us to assess the overall incidence of issues. We then examine *Weber* issues and elapsed time at each stage of the arbitration process in order to determine, at a descriptive level, whether cases that address *Weber* issues are associated with longer times.

In the second stage of the analysis, using multivariate regression analysis, we examine the relationship between each of the time variables identified above and the type and number of legal issues associated with *Weber* jurisdiction and decided in arbitral awards. Our approach is to estimate formal hazard models where the dependent variable of interest is the duration of a process, or the time to exit from a state; in this analysis, the variable is the elapsed time between the close of arbitration hearings to the rendering of an award.[32] The duration distribution function represents the probability of exit from the state after a specified amount of time has elapsed. An alternative representation is the probability of survival in a given state to a given point in time. The basic building block in duration modelling is the exit rate or hazard function at some given point in time. For example, in discrete terms, the hazard function is the probability that a grievance for which the hearing has been concluded for "x" days will have an award rendered in the near future (short time interval of length x + y days). The survival function, or the duration density, can be completely described in terms of the hazard function.

The characteristics of the hazard function have important implications for the pattern of the probability of exit from some state over time. Negative (positive) duration dependence represents a situation in which the probability of exit decreases (increases) as the elapsed time increases. The potential patterns of duration dependence depend on the form of the hazard function rate. For example, the hazard rate may first increase with elapsed time before decreasing, as the elapsed time increases.

The hazard rate can also be allowed to depend on observed characteristics of the grievance process. It is useful to distinguish between two classes of covariates.[33] The first class of covariates are termed time-invariant covariates, where the values of the covariates do not depend on the period of duration in a state; for example, the gender of the grievor. In the case of time-invariant characteristics, the duration in a state does not influence the value of the covariate since it does not change with time–therefore one would treat these covariates as exogenous to the duration process.

On the other hand, for time-varying covariates, for example, arbitrator case load, the level of the covariate depends on the duration in the state in question. There are various parametric and non-parametric

32 John D Kalbfleisch & Ross L Prentice, *The Statistical Analysis of Failure Time Data*, 2d ed (Hoboken, NJ: Wiley & Sons, Inc, 2002).

33 Mario A Cleves et al, *An Introduction to Survival Analysis Using Stata*, 2d ed (College Station, TX: Stata Press, 2008).

specifications to introduce covariates into duration and survival analysis.[34] For example, an oft-used mechanism is the proportional hazard specification, which adjusts the conventional hazard specification by assuming that a baseline hazard is proportional to a covariate function, where the covariates are thought to influence the duration in a state and the exit rate. The specific mechanism(s) to introduce covariates is an empirical issue and will be determined when we analyze the data.[35]

In our analysis, we first estimated each model as a Cox proportional hazard and tested the proportional-hazards assumption using the Schoenfeld residuals. If the model Cox proportional hazard was rejected, we then estimated an accelerated failure time (ATF) model for each of the following distributions: exponential, loglogistic, weibull, lognormal, and gamma. We chose the preferred distribution based on a Likelihood Ratio test in cases where the distributions were nested, and based on the Akaike's information criteria[36] in cases where the distributions were not nested. We also estimate each model as a frailty model (a model with unobservable heterogeneity), using both gamma and inverse-gamma distributions. In all cases the frailty models were rejected based on a likelihood ratio test.

Our statistical analysis enables us to determine whether litigating jurisdictional or particular substantive legal issues, and whether the number of legal issues litigated, increases the likelihood of delay at each stage of the arbitration process in a given case.

## C. DOES *WEBER*'S EXPANSION OF JURISDICTION CAUSE DELAY?

Our analysis demonstrates that *Weber*-related issues were neither frequent nor likely to be a cause of delay in the year under study. This strongly suggests that *Weber*'s expansion of jurisdiction has had no system-wide effects on delay in labour arbitration in Ontario.

---

34 Marc Nerlove & S James Press, *Univariate and Multivariate Log-Linear and Logistic Models* (Santa Monica, CA: Rand Corporation, 1973).

35 Nicholas M Kiefer, "Economic Duration Data and Hazard Functions" (1988) 26:2 *Journal of Economic Literature* 646.

36 *See* Hirotugo Akaike, "Information Theory and an Extension of the Maximum Likelihood Principle" in BN Petrov & F Csaki, eds, *2nd International Symposium on Information Theory* (Budapest: Akadémia Kiadó,, 1973) 267; Hirotugo Akaike, "A New Look at Statistical Model Identification," online: (1974) 19:6 *IEEE Transactions on Automatic Control* 716 http://ieeexplore.ieee.org; Hirotugo Akaike, "Likelihood of a Model and Information Criteria" (1981) 16 *Journal of Econometrics* 3.

### 1) The Frequency and Incidence of *Weber* Issues

The four substantive areas related to *Weber* jurisdiction accounted, collectively, for only approximately 4.3 percent of all arbitration cases in 2010. Among the four main subject areas related to *Weber* jurisdiction, those with the greatest case frequency were benefit or welfare plans (3.4 percent of cases), followed by pension plans (0.8 percent); the *Charter* was associated with only 0.1 percent of cases and no cases were associated with tort law.

FIGURE 1: DISTRIBUTION OF CASES BY SUBJECT

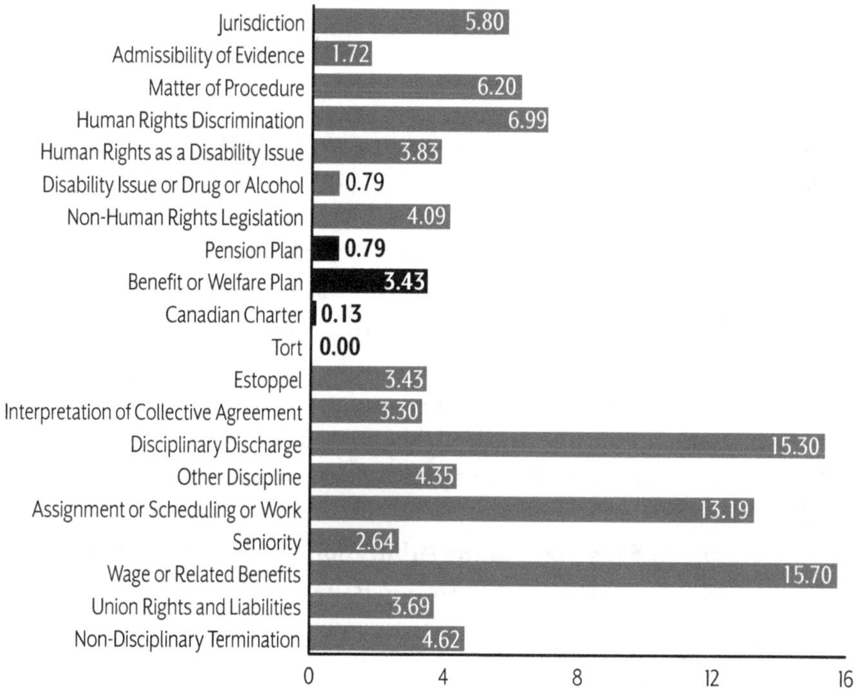


These small percentages stand in contrast to the continuing prevalence of traditional subjects of labour arbitration. The distribution of arbitration cases, by subject, is presented in Figure 1. In descending order, the subjects most frequently dealt with at arbitration were wages or related benefits (15.7 percent), disciplinary discharge (15.3 percent of cases), the assignment or scheduling of work (13.2 percent), human rights or other discrimination (7 percent) and matters of procedure (6.2 percent).

Arbitrators decided issues of jurisdiction in 5.8 percent of cases. As discussed above, our coding frame did not distinguish *Weber* jurisdictional issues from other such issues. Accordingly, we reviewed each case in which a jurisdictional issue arose to identify the nature of the issue. That review found no case in which an arbitrator was called upon to determine whether he or she had jurisdiction to decide a matter on the basis of *Weber*'s recognition of exclusive arbitral jurisdiction to decide disputes arising expressly or inferentially from a collective agreement.

## 2) *Weber* Issues and Elapsed Time at Each Stage of the Arbitration Process

In this section we consider whether or not *Weber* issues are associated with increased time lapses in each of the three periods under study: (a) event or grievance to first hearing, (b) hearings and (c) completion of hearings to award.

### a) Time Lapse at Each Stage of the Arbitration Process

We begin by considering the average time lapse at each stage of the arbitration process, shown in Figure 2, below. The most striking feature of this profile is that the time between event and arbitration far exceeds the time required for the arbitration process from first hearing to the rendering of an award. This finding is consistent with previous studies.[37] Across all cases, the average time from the event to first hearing is 307 days (see Figure 2). By contrast, hearing time averages 86 days, award time averages 46 days and total time for the arbitration process (hearing time plus award time) averages about 136 days.

### b) Time Lapse at Each Stage of the Arbitration Process: *Weber* Issues versus Traditional Labour Arbitration Issues

In order to provide a more nuanced perspective on time lapse and subject matter, for each stage of the arbitration process we examined the average time, and the proportion of cases completed over various time intervals, by detailed subject. This detailed assessment by case subject matter permits us to consider the time lapses in cases associated with *Weber* jurisdiction subjects in relation to the times associated with subjects that fall squarely within the historic scope of labour arbitration, and still constitute the bulk of the labour arbitration case load.

The proportions of cases completed at various intervals, by key subject, are provided in Table 1. Note that the table includes only two of the

37 Ponak et al, above note 5.

FIGURE 2: TIME LAPSE, DISCIPLINE AND NON-DISCIPLINE

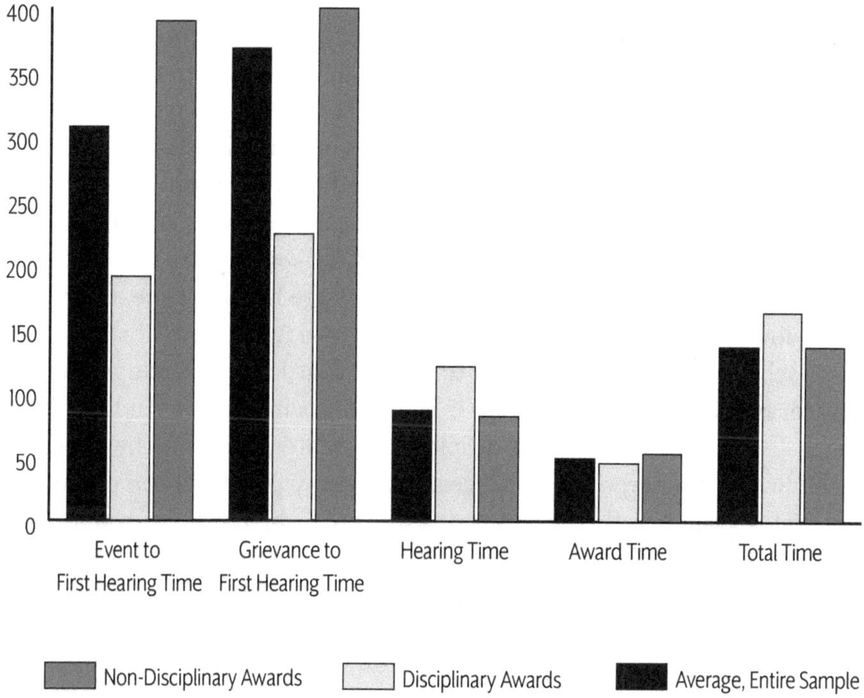


four areas under *Weber* jurisdiction — pension plans and benefit/welfare plans — because there were too few cases in the sample that addressed the *Charter* and no cases that addressed tort law issues.

*i) Time to First Hearing*

One might hypothesize that the legal or factual complexity of *Weber*-related issues would increase preparation time and therefore lead to delay in scheduling hearings. However, times from grievance to first hearing for *Weber*-related subjects fall within the range of times for other more traditional subjects of arbitration.

It is noteworthy that times from event to first hearing for benefit and welfare plan issues were considerably longer than for other subjects shown in Table 1. Given the relatively short average time from grievance to hearing for benefit and welfare plan issues, the most likely explanation for the long delay from event to first hearing is that such issues are ongoing rather than discrete events that either may be raised as grievances following a long period during which they were not brought to the attention of the union, or were the subject of informal resolution discussions between the union and employer.

There is thus little basis in average times to first hearing upon which to conclude that *Weber* jurisdiction leads to delay. However, there is some evidence suggesting that the time interval from event to first hearing is governed by party prioritization of access to arbitration to a far greater extent than by the requirements to prepare for arbitration. The average time lapse from event to first hearing for discipline cases is roughly half (at 190 days) that of non-disciplinary cases (at 389 days). This is despite the fact that such cases show the longest average hearing time and a relatively low proportion of cases completed in 90 days or less (at 58 percent for discharge cases). It is logical to expect that longer hearings require greater preparation. This finding is consistent with earlier studies.[38] The much faster time to hearing, despite the greater length of hearings in disciplinary discharge cases, suggests that party prioritization exerts significantly greater influence over delay prior to hearings than does the complexity of the matter to be heard.

*ii) Hearing Time*

The two subject matter areas related to *Weber* jurisdiction with respect to which there were more than one decision observed—pension plans and benefit/welfare plans—had relatively low average hearing times at 54 and 103 days, respectively, with 80 percent and 72 percent respectively of cases completed in 90 days or less.

*iii) Award Time*

Benefit/welfare plan issues and jurisdiction issues had an average award time of about 60 days and 54 days respectively, which was lower than the award time for cases dealing with the interpretation of collective agreements (at 97 days) or work assignment or scheduling cases (at 88 days).

On the other hand, *Weber* jurisdiction cases dealing with pension plans had by far the highest average award time, at 403 days. However, given the small number of observations (five cases), this result may not be generalizable. Two of the five pension cases awards were rendered in thirty days or less, indicating that the long average time was due to a mere three decisions. It is possible that these decisions would be outliers in a larger sample population.

38 *Ibid.*

TABLE 1 TIME DURATION OF FINAL AWARDS

| | Subject Matter | | | |
|---|---|---|---|---|
| | Pension Plan | Benefit/ Welfare Plan | Wages and Related Benefits | Jurisdiction |
| **Hearing Time** | | | | |
| Average | 54.20 | 103.60 | 52.75 | 83.47 |
| % with hearing time of 30 days or less | 80.00 | 72.00 | 75.70 | 71.88 |
| % with hearing time of 60 days or less | 80.00 | 72.00 | 79.44 | 75.00 |
| % with hearing time of 90 days or less | 80.00 | 72.00 | 82.24 | 81.25 |
| % with hearing time of 120 days or less | 80.00 | 72.00 | 82.24 | 81.25 |
| Number of Observations | 5 | 25 | 107 | 32 |
| **Award Time** | | | | |
| Average | 403.40 | 60.20 | 45.19 | 53.56 |
| % with award time of 30 days or less | 40.00 | 48.00 | 60.75 | 50.00 |
| % with award time of 60 days or less | 40.00 | 64.00 | 80.37 | 65.63 |
| % with award time of 90 days or less | 40.00 | 72.00 | 85.98 | 81.25 |
| Number of Observations | 5 | 25 | 107 | 32 |
| **Event to First Hearing Time** | | | | |
| Average | 345.00 | 577.71 | 382.41 | 500.75 |
| % completed within 30 days | 0.00 | 0.00 | 0.00 | 0.00 |
| % completed within 60 days | 0.00 | 0.00 | 2.27 | 0.00 |
| % completed within 90 days | 0.00 | 7.14 | 6.82 | 8.3 |
| % completed within 180 days | 0.00 | 21.43 | 22.73 | 8.3 |
| % completed within 270 days | 0.00 | 35.71 | 45.45 | 16.67 |
| % completed within 360 days | 100.00 | 50.00 | 56.82 | 33.33 |
| % completed within 540 days | 100.00 | 57.14 | 77.27 | 50.00 |
| % completed within 700 days | 100.00 | 71.43 | 86.36 | 83.33 |
| Number of Observations | 1 | 14 | 44 | 12 |
| **Grievance to First Hearing Time** | | | | |
| Average | 452.00 | 287.25 | 376.05 | 546.81 |
| % completed within 30 days | 0.00 | 0.00 | 5.00 | 0.00 |
| % completed within 60 days | 0.00 | 0.00 | 7.50 | 9.5 |
| % completed within 90 days | 0.00 | 12.50 | 17.50 | 14.29 |
| % completed within 180 days | 50.00 | 50.00 | 30.00 | 19.05 |
| % completed within 270 days | 50.00 | 62.50 | 47.50 | 28.57 |
| % completed within 360 days | 50.00 | 87.50 | 57.50 | 42.86 |
| % completed within 540 days | 50.00 | 87.50 | 77.50 | 71.43 |
| % completed within 700 days | 50.00 | 87.50 | 82.50 | 80.95 |
| Number of Observations | 2 | 8 | 40 | 21 |

| | Subject | | |
|---|---|---|---|
| | Interpret. of Coll. Agt. | Discharge for Discipline | Work Assign./ Sched. |
| **Hearing Time** | | | |
| Average | 96.61 | 140.44 | 88.08 |
| % with hearing time of 30 days or less | 52.17 | 45.45 | 65.11 |
| % with hearing time of 60 days or less | 52.17 | 54.55 | 69.77 |
| % with hearing time of 90 days or less | 65.22 | 57.58 | 79.07 |
| % with hearing time of 120 days or less | 69.57 | 65.66 | 79.07 |
| Number of Observations | 23 | 99 | 86 |
| **Award Time** | | | |
| Average | 89.09 | 47.73 | 57.01 |
| % with award time of 30 days or less | 39.13 | 44.55 | 50.00 |
| % with award time of 60 days or less | 60.87 | 66.34 | 74.42 |
| % with award time of 90 days or less | 69.57 | 83.17 | 84.88 |
| Number of Observations | 23 | 101 | 86 |
| **Event to First Hearing Time** | | | |
| Average | 453.3 | 177.56 | 363.69 |
| % completed within 30 days | 0.00 | 1.17 | 0.00 |
| % completed within 60 days | 0.00 | 10.23 | 0.00 |
| % completed within 90 days | 0.00 | 19.32 | 3.44 |
| % completed within 180 days | 0.00 | 67.05 | 13.79 |
| % completed within 270 days | 20.00 | 84.09 | 41.38 |
| % completed within 360 days | 50.00 | 93.18 | 58.62 |
| % completed within 540 days | 80.00 | 97.73 | 79.31 |
| % completed within 700 days | 90.00 | 98.86 | 96.55 |
| Number of Observations | 10 | 88 | 29 |
| **Grievance to First Hearing Time** | | | |
| Average | 284.75 | 183.56 | 316.41 |
| % completed within 30 days | 0.00 | 5.56 | 0.00 |
| % completed within 60 days | 8.33 | 16.67 | 11.76 |
| % completed within 90 days | 16.67 | 22.22 | 17.65 |
| % completed within 180 days | 50.00 | 72.22 | 23.53 |
| % completed within 270 days | 58.33 | 77.78 | 47.06 |
| % completed within 360 days | 66.67 | 83.33 | 70.59 |
| % completed within 540 days | 91.67 | 100.00 | 88.24 |
| % completed within 700 days | 100.00 | 100.00 | 94.12 |
| Number of Observations | 12 | 18 | 34 |

### 3) Results of Regression Analysis

We employ regression methods to investigate more rigorously the question of whether there are time delays in *Weber*-related cases. Following the statistical methods outlined above, we estimated regressions for each of the following dependent variables:

1) event to first hearing time;
2) hearing time;
3) award time; and
4) hearing days.

Each regression included each of the *Weber* subject variables (i.e., pension plan; benefit or welfare plan; and *Charter*) that are the main focus of the analysis, as well as a complete set of control variables (refer to Appendix Table 1, Panel C for a list of these variables).

The regression results for the disaggregated *Weber* issue variables are presented for each of the dependent variables in Panels A through D of Table 2. In addition, the results for the combined *Weber* variable are presented in Panel E. Overall, we find that the *Weber* issue variables are not statistically significant. Therefore, we find no empirical evidence to support a conclusion that there are meaningful impacts of the extension of arbitral jurisdiction arising from *Weber* on delay and, hence, on efficiency in labour arbitration.

The results suggest that *Weber* cases do not markedly differ from other cases dealing with jurisdictional issues. This would therefore also suggest that there are no significant impacts on delay of the extension of arbitral jurisdiction arising from *Weber*. We would caution, however, that these results are based upon a relatively small population of *Weber* jurisdiction issues, which makes it difficult to draw generalizable inferences from these observations.

TABLE 2 WEBER VARIABLE REGRESSION RESULTS

| | Coefficient | Robust Standard Error | Z | P > \|z\| | 95 % Confidence Interval | |
|---|---|---|---|---|---|---|
| **Panel A: Event to First Hearing Time** | | | | | | |
| Pension Plan | 0.4450 | 0.4162 | 1.07 | 0.285 | -0.3706570 | 1.2607570 |
| Benefit or Welfare Plan | -0.3859 | 0.2865 | -1.35 | 0.178 | -0.9475191 | 0.1756382 |
| Charter | . | . | . | . | . | . |
| | | | Logistic regression; Number of observations = 336 | | | |
| **Panel B: Hearing Time** | | | | | | |
| Pension Plan | -0.7984 | 0.8838 | -0.90 | 0.366 | -2.5305400 | 0.9337593 |
| Benefit or Welfare Plan | -0.7741 | 0.5800 | -1.33 | 0.182 | -1.9108270 | 0.3625798 |
| Charter | 1.7237 | 1.0928 | 1.58 | 0.115 | -0.4182048 | 3.8655620 |
| | | | Lognormal regression; Number of observations = 482 | | | |
| **Panel C: Award Time** | | | | | | |
| Pension Plan | 1.0769 | 1.1037 | 0.98 | 0.329 | -1.0862490 | 3.2399820 |
| Benefit or Welfare Plan | -0.5309 | 0.4035 | -1.32 | 0.188 | -1.3218240 | 0.2599981 |
| Charter | 0.9506 | 0.7094 | 1.34 | 0.180 | -0.4397474 | 2.3408670 |
| | | | Lognormal regression; Number of observations = 484 | | | |
| **Panel D: Hearing Days** | | | | | | |
| Pension Plan | -0.2174 | 0.1329 | -1.64 | 0.102 | -0.4778954 | 0.0430855 |
| Benefit or Welfare Plan | -0.2025 | 0.1019 | -1.99 | 0.047 | -0.4022951 | -0.0026889 |
| Charter | 1.0280 | 0.6730 | 1.53 | 0.127 | -0.2911211 | 2.3469430 |
| | | Generalized Gamma regression; Number of observations = 503 | | | | |
| **Panel E: Event to First Hearing Time** | | | | | | |
| Weber | -0.1670 | 0.2774 | -0.60 | 0.547 | -0.7106936 | 0.3766729 |
| | | Generalized Gamma regression; Number of observations = 336 | | | | |

## D. CONCLUSIONS

Taken together, the results of the regression analysis and the qualitative examination of the *Weber* cases support the conclusion that there are no statistically significant impacts of the extension of arbitral jurisdiction arising from *Weber* on delay and efficiency in labour arbitration. The total number of cases raising issues within new jurisdiction is relatively small in relation to the total number of legal issues decided. When *Weber* issues do arise, they do not appear to cause delay. We conclude that *Weber* issues are unlikely to have a significant impact on efficiency and delay within Ontario's labour arbitration system. These results point to the need to investigate the importance of other potential explanations for delay in labour arbitration in future research.

## APPENDIX TABLE 1: VARIABLE DEFINITIONS

| **Panel A: Duration Variables** | | |
|---|---|---|
| **Duration Variable** | **Variable Definition** | **Code Value** |
| Event to First Hearing Time | Days (duration) between event and first hearing dates | Number |
| Grievance to First Hearing Time | Days (duration) between grievance and first hearing dates | Number |
| Hearing Days | Number of hearing days | Number |
| Hearing Time | Days (duration) between first hearing and last hearing dates | Number |
| Award Time | Days (duration) between last hearing and award dates | Number |

| **Panel B: Subject Variables** | |
|---|---|
| **Subject Variable Definition** | **Code Value** |
| Jurisdiction | 0 "No" 1 "Yes" |
| Admissibility of Evidence | 0 "No" 1 "Yes" |
| Matter of Procedure | 0 "No" 1 "Yes" |
| Human Rights or Other Discrimination | 0 "No" 1 "Yes" |
| Human Rights is a Disability Issue | 0 "No" 1 "Yes" |
| Disability Issue is Drug or Alcohol Dependence | 0 "No" 1 "Yes" |
| Non-Human Rights Legislation | 0 "No" 1 "Yes" |
| Pension Plan | 0 "No" 1 "Yes" |
| Benefit or Welfare Plan (whether insured or not) | 0 "No" 1 "Yes" |
| Canadian Charter | 0 "No" 1 "Yes" |
| Tort | 0 "No" 1 "Yes" |
| Estoppel | 0 "No" 1 "Yes" |
| Interpret. of Collective Agreement | 0 "No" 1 "Yes" |
| Discharge for Discipline | 0 "No" 1 "Yes" |
| Other Discipline (Non-Discharge) | 0 "No" 1 "Yes" |
| Assignment or Scheduling of Work | 0 "No" 1 "Yes" |
| Seniority | 0 "No" 1 "Yes" |
| Wages or Related Benefits | 0 "No" 1 "Yes" |
| Union Rights and Liabilities | 0 "No" 1 "Yes" |
| Non-Disciplinary Termination | 0 "No" 1 "Yes" |

| **Panel C: Weber Variable** | |
|---|---|
| Weber = Pension Plan + Benefit or Welfare Plan + Canadian Charter + Tort | Number |

| Panel D: Regression Control Variables | |
|---|---|
| **Variable Definition** | **Code Value** |
| Award Dealt with ONLY subjects NOT LISTED | 0 "No" 1 "Yes" |
| Award ALSO dealt with other issues | 0 "No" 1 "Yes" |
| Industry of Firm/Employer | 0 "Government" 1 "Health" 2 "Education" 3 "Other" |
| Sole arbitrator or tripartite | 0 "Sole Arbitrator" 1 "Tripartite Board" |
| Award issued under the expedited arbitration provisions | 0 "No" 1 "Yes" |
| Total number of Subjects Dealt With in the Award Number | Number |
| Did the parties provide the Arbitrator with an agreed statement of fact? | 0 "No" 1 "Yes" |
| Total Number of grievances in Award Number | Number |
| Employer Represented by Legal Counsel | 0 "No" 1 "Yes" 2 "Unknown" |
| Union Represented by Legal Counsel | 0 "No" 1 "Yes" 2 "Unknown" |
| Total Word Count | Number |

CHAPTER EIGHT

# Questions, Questions: Has *Weber* Had an Impact on Unions' Representational Responsibilities in Workplace Human Rights Disputes?

Claire Mummé

## INTRODUCTION

Union representation in Canada is premised on strength in numbers — the collective makes each member stronger. But collective representation, by its nature, can also produce tension between collective and individual rights and interests. A recurring theme of Bernie Adell's scholarship was a concern for how best to balance this tension.[1] He was, in particular, critical of the union's veto over access to labour arbitration,

* My sincere thanks to the organizers and participants in the CLCW's *Weber* Conference for a great few days of conversation, and useful comments on this essay. Thanks in particular to anonymous reviewers for some very helpful nuances, to Renée-Claude Drouin for providing me with a better sense of the legal context in Quebec, to Aaron Bhogossian and Tori-Lee Jenkins for helpful research assistance, and to Elizabeth Shilton for her ongoing support and intellectual engagement.

1 BL Adell, "The Duty of Fair Representation — Effective Protection for Individual Rights in Collective Agreements?" (1970) 25:3 *Relations industrielles/Industrial Relations* 602; Bernard Adell, "Collective Agreements and Individual Rights: A Note on the Duty of Fair Representation" (1986) 11:2 *Queen's Law Journal* 251 [Adell, "Collective Agreements"]; Bernard Adell, "Jurisdictional Overlap Between Arbitration and Other Forums: An Update" (2000) 8 *Canadian Labour and Employment Law Journal* 179 [Adell, "Jurisdictional Overlap"]; Bernard Adell, "The Duty of Fair Representation: 'a form of words . . .'?," (PowerPoint delivered at *Adjudicating Human Rights in the Workplace After the Pinto Report, Where Do We Go Next?*, CLCW Workshop, Queen's University, 10 November 2012)) [unpublished].

suggesting in 1985 that the veto provided unions with too much power over important personal rights.[2] For this reason, he suggested, members ought to have the right to bring forward a grievance to arbitration at their own cost if the union refused to do so. Adell reiterated that concern after the Supreme Court of Canada's 1995 decision in *Weber* which, he thought, served to compound the tensions unions must manage between individual and collective rights.[3]

There has been much commentary on *Weber*, and on the Supreme Court's subsequent 2004 decision in *Parry Sound (District) Welfare Administration Board v Ontario Public Service Employees Union Local 324*.[4] Concerns raised include the impact of these decisions on the institution of labour arbitration, the more general implications of merging legal regimes focused on individual rights into a system premised on collective representation, the potential for diminution of the individual rights of unionized employees, and the costs to unions associated with expanded arbitral jurisdiction.[5] Human rights issues have been at the centre of

---

2 Adell, "Collective Agreements" at 255–58.

3 Adell, "Jurisdictional Overlap," above note 1 at 224–29; *Weber v Ontario Hydro* [1995] 2 SCR 929 [*Weber*].

4 2003 SCC 42 [*Parry Sound*].

5 Some of these issues are discussed in other chapters in this volume. *See also* Ronald Pink & DC Wallbridge, "The Future of Labour Arbitration" (Paper delivered at The 2010 Administrative, Labour and Employment and Privacy and Access Conference, Ottawa, 26–27 November 2010) (2010) *Canadian Bar Association*; Fay Faraday, "The Expanding Scope of Arbitration: Mainstreaming Human Rights Values and Remedies" (2005) 12 *Canadian Labour and Employment Law Journal* 355; Andrew K Lokan & Maryth Yachnin, "From *Weber* to *Parry Sound:* The Expanded Scope of Arbitration" (2004) 11 *Canadian Labour and Employment Law Journal* 1; John-Paul Alexandrowicz, "Restoring the Role of Grievance Arbitration: A New Approach to *Weber*" (2003) 10 *Canadian Labour and Employment Law Journal* 269; Adell, "Jurisdictional Overlap," above note 1; Richard MacDowell, "Labour Arbitration — The New Labour Court?" (2000) 8 *Canadian Labour and Employment Law Journal* 121; Brian Etherington, "Promises, Promises: Notes on Diversity and Access to Justice" (2000) 26:1 *Queen's Law Journal* 43; Donald Carter, "Looking at *Weber* Five Years Later: Is it Time for a New Approach?" (2000) 8 *Canadian Labour and Employment Law Journal* 231; Michel G Picher, "Defining the Scope of Arbitration: The Impact of *Weber*: An Arbitrator's Perspective" in Kevin Whitaker et al, eds, (1999–2000) 1 *Labour Arbitration Year Book* (Toronto: Lancaster House, 2000) 99; Raymond Brown & Brian Etherington. "*Weber v Ontario Hydro*: A Denial of Access to Justice for the Organized Employee" (1996) 4 *Canadian Labour and Employment Law Journal* 183. For a defence of exclusive arbitral jurisdiction, see Peter Gall, Andrea Zwack and Katie Bayne, "Determining Human Rights Issues in the Unionized Workplace: The

much of both the debate and the jurisprudence concerning expanded arbitral jurisdiction. But one problem that has received less attention is the impact of *Weber* and *Parry Sound* on the nature and extent of unions' human rights *representational* obligations in the administration of the collective bargaining agreement.[6] Examining how unions are handling their representational role in regards to members' human rights requires, for the most part, answering a series of empirical questions — questions that are not easily resolved through a study of caselaw.

This essay attempts to put forward a research agenda for properly evaluating the changing nature of unions' human rights representational obligations since *Weber*. I begin by investigating two legal questions: first, whether unions are held to a more stringent duty of fair representation (DFR) standard in regards to members' discrimination grievances than prior to *Weber* and *Parry Sound*, and second, whether there has been a broadening of the concept of union discrimination under human rights codes, such that unions may be held liable for failing to bring forward discrimination grievances. With the legal picture in place, I then set out a series of empirical questions that need further research to properly assess whether, and to what extent, *Weber* and *Parry Sound* have altered unions' human rights obligations in the administration of collective agreements, and more generally, their approaches to dealing with human rights issues in the workplace. The essay intentionally raises more questions than it answers, with the objective of provoking further research on important issues regarding labour law in action.

---

Case for Exclusive Jurisdiction" (2005) 12 *Canadian Labour and Employment Law Journal* 381.

6 For one notable exception, see Yves-Christian Ménard, *La discrimination en milieu de travail et le devoir juridique de représentation syndicale: une analyse socio-juridique* (LLM Thesis, Université de Montréal Faculté des études supiérieures, 2011) [unpublished]. *See also* Elizabeth Shilton, " 'Everybody's Business': Human Rights Enforcement and the Union's Duty to Accommodate" (2014) 18:1 *Canadian Labour and Employment Law Journal* 209, which touches upon unions' human rights responsibilities in the negotiation of collective agreements, an issue I do not examine here.

## A. THE IMPACT OF *WEBER* AND *PARRY SOUND* ON THE BALANCE BETWEEN INDIVIDUAL AND COLLECTIVE RIGHTS OF UNIONIZED WORKERS

The details of the SCC's decisions in *Weber* and *Parry Sound* are addressed elsewhere in this volume,[7] and will not be repeated here. Much of the early discussion on the significance of *Weber* focused on the practical strains placed on unions and on the labour arbitration process by the expansion of exclusive arbitral jurisdiction.[8] The concerns triggered by *Weber* were magnified after the SCC's decision in *Parry Sound*, which, for a time at least, seemed to significantly expand arbitrators' exclusive jurisdiction as regards statutory employment rights, and in particular human rights claims.[9]

*Weber* and *Parry Sound* provided clear benefits to employers. Expanded exclusive arbitral jurisdiction reduced the number of fora in which an employer could be sued. And because the principle of exclusivity endows unions with control over access to labour arbitration, the employer could now deal with only one party (the union) to negotiate settlements over a broader swath of legal claims. Moreover, the union would likely exercise a disciplining force in deciding which grievances were brought forward, thereby reducing the number of weak and frivolous claims faced by the employer.

For employees, *Weber* was a mixed bag. On the one hand, a single decision-maker could now resolve most of their work-related claims. Moreover, workers would now have the benefit of union representation and cost-free

---

7 *See e.g.*, Brian Etherington, "*Weber*, and Almost Everything After, 20 Years Later: Its Impact on Individual *Charter*, Common Law and Statutory Rights Claims," Chapter 2.

8 See sources above note 5.

9 The outcome in *Parry Sound* itself can be explained relatively uncontroversially as a simple application of s 48(12)(j) of the Ontario *Labour Relations Act, 1995*, SO 1995, c 1, Schedule A [*OLRA*], which grants arbitrators the power "to interpret and apply human rights and other employment-related statutes, despite any conflict between those statutes and the terms of the collective agreement." But the Court went farther to hold that statutory human rights obligations are effectively incorporated as terms of the collective agreement. Combined with the Supreme Court's expansive understanding in *Weber* of what constitutes matters that "in their essential character, arise from the interpretation, application, administration or violation of the collective agreement" (*Weber*, above note 3 at para 57), *Parry Sound* appeared to significantly increase the scope of exclusive arbitral jurisdiction over employment-related statutes that had previously been enforceable in other forums.

(at least to individuals) legal proceedings rather than paying for the costs of legal action and legal representation themselves. They would also have the strength of the collective at their backs. On the other hand, because the union decides which grievances to bring forward to arbitration, unionized employees would now not have carriage over important individual rights claims, with the potential that those claims would not be resolved at all. For commentators such as Adell, this last concern was particularly acute as regards workplace discrimination issues.

The impact of *Weber* on unions differed depending on their size and individual histories. Long before *Weber* and *Parry Sound*, some unions had bargained human rights provisions into their collective agreements. And it was clear since *McLeod v Egan*[10] that employment-related statutes could be applied at arbitration to the interpretation of collective bargaining agreements, a principle further solidified in Ontario by the addition of section 48(12)(j) to the *Labour Relations Act* in 1995.[11] What *Weber* and *Parry Sound* changed was the scope of what would be considered a matter arising out of a collective bargaining agreement, and therefore subject to exclusive arbitral jurisdiction. This mattered, amongst other reasons, because the twin principles of majoritarianism and exclusivity serve to appoint unions as the exclusive representative of the bargaining unit, with control over access to the grievance process and arbitration.[12] To the extent that labour arbitration now appeared to be the exclusive forum for adjudicating an increasing number of members' individual rights claims, scholars wondered whether unions would now face heightened scrutiny under the DFR, and thus face pressure to account more stringently for the ways they determined the appropriate balance between individual and collective interests.[13]

To be clear, tensions between individual and collective interests were not new. Collective representation requires managing disparate and sometimes conflicting interests amongst members. The new question was whether *Weber* would serve to heighten such tensions, particularly

---

10 (1974), [1975] 1 SCR 517, 46 DLR (3d) 150 [*McLeod*].

11 *OLRA*, above note 9.

12 How this works is well explained in *Judd v Communications, Energy and Paperworkers Union of Canada Local 2000*, [2003] BCLRBD No 63, 2003 CLLC 220-055 [*Judd*].

13 Bernard Adell, "The Union's Duty of Fair Representation in Discrimination Cases: The New Obligation to be Proactive" in Kevin Whitaker et al, eds, (2000–2001) 1 *Labour Arbitration Year Book* (Toronto: Lancaster House, 2002) 263 at 264 [Adell, "The Union's DFR"].

for smaller, less well-funded unions, by directing an increasing number of disputes concerning statutory and common law workplace rights to labour arbitration, access to which was determined by the union. Would the union now face greater scrutiny in regards to its duty of fair representation when, for instance, the only way to accommodate a member with a disability was to disregard the seniority list, thereby displacing the rights of other members? Would it change the way unions dealt with situations where one member accused another of discrimination, and the union had to represent the interests of both? And what would be the cost implications of the expanding zone of member rights to be resolved at labour arbitration? In an article on *Weber* penned in 2000, Adell noted:

> The increasingly frequent links between anti-discrimination rights, which are vested in individuals, and the collective agreement administration process, which privileges collective rights, threaten to put very heavy pressure on the DFR both in theory and in practice. Those pressures are further aggravated by the various lines of jurisprudence stemming from *Weber v. Ontario Hydro* . . . [T]hat jurisprudence is giving unions and the grievance arbitration process an as yet ill-defined range of new responsibilities for enforcing employee rights (and duties) previously enforced in other forums . . . .[14]

*Weber* addressed itself to the jurisdictional relationship between common law courts and statutory tribunals. The issue of competing jurisdiction between statutory tribunals was addressed a few years later in *Québec (Commission des droits de la personne et des droits de la jeunesse) v Québec (Procureur général)*.[15] There the majority of the Court modified the *Weber* analysis in the context of competing statutory tribunals, holding that it was first necessary to examine the nature of the jurisdictional grant of authority to each tribunal to determine whether one or other held exclusive jurisdiction, or whether their jurisdiction was concurrent. If jurisdiction was concurrent, one should then determine which tribunal was the best fit in the circumstances. The *Morin* majority was attracted to this more flexible approach at least in part from a concern that unions may, in some circumstances, be opposed in interest to some of their members.[16] The decision implied (although it did not decide) that where the union deter-

14 Adell, "Jurisdictional Overlap," above note 1 at 223.
15 2004 SCC 39 [*Morin*].
16 *Ibid* at para 28.

mined that the balance tipped in favour of collective rather than individual interests, a path to adjudication other than labour arbitration should be available to individual employees.

Two years after *Morin*, the Supreme Court of Canada held in *Tranchemontagne v Ontario (Director, Disability Support Program)* that all statutory decision-makers endowed with the power to decide questions of fact and law have the authority to interpret and apply human rights codes.[17] Although *Morin* still formally controls, after *Tranchemontagne 1* most decision-makers no longer engage in the second step of the *Morin* analysis, concluding *a priori* that labour arbitrators and human rights tribunals share concurrent jurisdiction over the human rights claims of unionized employees. Instead, most decision-makers focus on attempting to control multiple proceedings before concurrent tribunals through issue estoppel and *res judicata* principles.[18]

One might have thought that the adoption of a concurrency model would lessen the weight of unions' representational obligations. In theory, the concurrency model allows for a unionized employee either to pursue a grievance through the union to arbitration, or to bring her claim independently to a human rights commission or tribunal. In practice, in Ontario at least, that choice has been realizable since the abolition of the Ontario Human Rights Commission's gatekeeping function, and the institution of direct access to the Human Rights Tribunal in 2006.[19] But as Elizabeth Shilton has convincingly argued, there are strong pressures

---

17 2006 SCC 14 [*Tranchemontagne 1*].

18 The Supreme Court issued two recent decisions on the application of issue estoppel in the context of competing statutory tribunals; *British Columbia (Workers' Compensation Board) v Figliola*, 2011 SCC 52, and *Penner v Niagara (Regional Police Services Board)*, 2013 SCC 19. There continues to be uncertainty in the caselaw, and within the Court, about how to balance the principles of fairness and of finality when dealing with overlapping tribunal jurisdiction. For a short but interesting analysis of the relationship between these two decisions, see Paul Daly, "Does *Penner* Overrule *Figliola*? What's the Canadian Law on Issue Estoppel?" (11 April 2013) *Administrative Law Matters* (blog), online, www.administrativelawmatters.com/blog/2013/04/11/does-penner-overrule-figliola-whats-the-canadian-law-on-issue-estoppel. For an analysis of *Figliola*'s labour impact see Shilton, above note 6 at 236–239. For a consideration of *Figliola* from a human rights perspective, *see* Laverne Jacobs, "*Figliola*: Competing Jurisdiction, Shared Governance, and Protecting Human Rights in the Canadian Administrative State," online: (2013) *Social Science Research Network* http://papers.ssrn.com/sol3/papers.cfm?abstract_id=2184585.

19 Shilton, above note 6 at 234–35; Etherington, above note 5 at 51–62.

that push unionized employees to arbitration rather than human rights tribunals.[20] In many instances collective bargaining agreements may offer greater rights and protections than human rights codes. For example, the collective agreement may provide stronger accommodation language than the undue hardship standard imbedded in the human rights code. Or the agreement's "just cause" and progressive discipline requirements may impose greater obligations on the employer than provided by the code. Or there may be issues at play in addition to the discrimination claim which would be resolvable at arbitration, but over which a human rights tribunal does not have jurisdiction. For a host of reasons, therefore, it may be more beneficial for a unionized employee to proceed to arbitration than to bring a human rights claim to a tribunal.[21] The benefits of arbitration are attested to by the fact that the number of discrimination grievances decided by arbitrators does not appear to have diminished since *Morin* and *Tranchemontagne 1*.[22] What, then, are the legal principles that animate unions' obligations towards their members' human rights disputes?

## B. UNIONS' POST-*WEBER* LEGAL OBLIGATIONS REGARDING WORKPLACE DISCRIMINATION

As already mentioned, it was clear prior to *Weber* that unions had important human rights obligations in the workplace. Since *McLeod*, arbitrators have been required to consider human rights principles in their interpretation of collective bargaining agreements.[23] In Ontario, this power was given explicit statutory support in 1994 with the addition of section 48(12)(j) of the *OLRA*.[24] And in 1992, in *Central Okanagan District School No 23 v Renaud*, the Supreme Court held that in addition to employers, unions

20 Shilton, *ibid* at 235–40.

21 *See* Shilton, *ibid*, for a discussion of a unionized employee's options and their differing consequences under a system of concurrency between labour arbitration and human rights tribunals. Of course employees' decision-making in such instances is not always well informed, and there is always a risk of making forum choices without the benefit of a clear sense of the consequences.

22 Bernie Adell observed at the Inaugural Innis Christie Symposium at Dalhousie University in 2010 that the 4th Series of the LACs should be known as the "human rights series." *See* Pink & Wallbridge, above note 5 at 5.

23 *McLeod*, above note 10.

24 *OLRA*, above note 9.

also owe a duty to accommodate workers in the workplace under human rights legislation.[25] Although it is the employer that is primarily responsible for ensuring a discrimination-free workplace, the Court in *Renaud* held that in limited circumstances a union could also be directly liable for discrimination under human rights codes. This could occur where the union participated with the employer in negotiating discriminatory collective bargaining provisions, or where the union impeded employers' legitimate attempts to accommodate a union member. Finally, through the duty of fair representation, unions were required to represent all members in good faith, and in a non-arbitrary and non-discriminatory manner.[26]

The first question then is whether, since *Weber* and *Parry Sound*, unions have faced greater scrutiny of their duty of fair representation when deciding not to bring forward, or to settle, a human rights grievance. The second is whether there has been greater scope for unions' direct liability under human rights codes in such situations.

### 1) The Post-*Weber* DFR Standard

At the time *Weber* was decided, the Supreme Court's most current statements on the DFR were contained in two cases decided in 1990, *Gendron v Supply & Services Union of Public Service Alliance of Canada, Local 50057*,[27] and *Centre hospitalier Régina Ltée v Québec (Tribunal du travail)*.[28] Since then, the Court has issued only one decision on the DFR, and the principles have remained constant.[29]

The duty of fair representation acts as a check on the principle of exclusivity. The union's role as the exclusive representative of the employees in the bargaining unit endows it with the discretion to determine which matters to take forward to arbitration, and to determine when and on what terms to settle disputes with the employer. But that discretion must be exercised in good faith, without discrimination or arbitrariness. In *Gendron* the Court explained that "while the union's status as exclusive bargaining agent operates to counteract the economic power of the employer, and therefore works to the benefit of those represented, it was

---

25 [1992] 2 SCR 970, 95 DLR (4th) 577 [*Renaud*].

26 *OLRA*, above note 9, s 74.

27 [1990] 1 SCR 1298, 21 ACWS (3d) 289 [*Gendron*]

28 [1990] 1 SCR 1330, 69 DLR (4th) 609 [*Centre Hospitalier*].

29 *Noël v Société d'énergie de la Baie James*, 2001 SCC 39 [*Noel*].

nevertheless necessary to ensure that unions wielded their power fairly."[30] The DFR is therefore a protective legal mechanism afforded to individual members to hold unions accountable for the ways in which they determine the needs of the collective, and when to pursue matters on behalf of individual members.

Bad faith arises where there is hostility or animus towards the employee.[31] Arbitrariness arises where unions' decisions are not based on a thorough study of the facts and the content of the agreement, where the significance of the grievance and of the consequence for the employee are not taken into consideration, and/or where serious negligence mars the decision-making process.[32] Discrimination is defined as differential treatment without a legitimate labour relations purpose; for the purposes of the DFR, discrimination therefore encompasses both grounds prohibited by human rights statutes and other types of non-justifiable differential treatment.[33] The DFR, however, does not impose a standard of perfection, or even of reasonableness. The Boards and the courts acknowledge that when they are balancing the interests of many, unions cannot function with constant scrutiny over every decision. They have the right to be wrong and to make mistakes, so long as their decisions are reasoned, not arbitrary, in bad faith or discriminatory.[34]

The DFR principles have remained relatively unchanged since *Rayonier*, and the SCC's approval of the *Rayonier* principles in *Gagnon* in 1984.[35] Nonetheless, in 2001 Adell identified some decisions suggesting that labour boards had begun to assess the DFR standard more stringently in regards to unions' decisions not to bring forward discrimination grievances. He suggested that there was an increasing jurisprudential move

---

30 *Gendron*, above note 27 at para 28.

31 *Rayonier Canada (BC) Ltd v International Woodworkers of America, Local 1-217*, [1975] BCLRBD no 42, [1975] 2 Can LRBR 196 at paras 15–17 [*Rayonier*].

32 *Judd*, above note 12 at paras 58–70.

33 *Rayonier*, above note 31 at para 17.

34 *Ibid* at para 24. In *Chrysler Canada Ltd*, [1999] OLRB Rep July/August 757, [1999] OLRD No 2454 [*Switzer Grievance*] the Ontario Labour Relations Board, discussing the DFR standard, stated, "So long as it acts honestly, objectively and gives due consideration to matters which fall within the ambit of its responsibility as exclusive bargaining agent, a union will not be held to account if it makes a mistake or a simple error in judgment. A union has a sort of limited 'right to be wrong'." *Ibid* at para 21.

35 *Canadian Merchant Service Guild v Gagnon*, [1984] 1 SCR 509, 9 DLR (4th) 641.

towards requiring unions to be more proactive in their representation when a member raised a human rights issue in the workplace.[36]

In a number of DFR proceedings in the late 1990s, labour boards suggested that unions may have a duty to be more proactive in their representation of members with psychological disabilities. The first such case, as Adell noted, was *H(K) v Communications, Energy and Paperworkers Union, Local 1-S*,[37] a decision issued by the Saskatchewan Labour Relations Board in 1997. There a grievor was subject to escalating discipline for a series of incidents that were the product of a depression from which he suffered. There were serious disagreements between his physician and that of the employer, which led the employer to request an independent third examination. The Board noted that while there was no provision in the collective bargaining agreement requiring a third party examination in this type of situation, the union had nevertheless agreed to the employer's request and pushed the grievor to submit despite his doctor's concerns. The Board also found problematic the union's failure to challenge the appropriateness of a progressive discipline framework for dealing with the grievor's situation. The Board ultimately concluded that while the union's approach might have been acceptable in general, by not taking into account the specific circumstances of the grievor's disability the union discriminated against him in violation of its duty of fair representation.

The Board's concern in *H(K)* was that the union failed to recognize the effects of the psychological disability on the grievor, and the disability's relationship both to the alleged misconduct, and to the grievor's interactions with the union or employer. In other words, the union's obligation to be more proactive in its representation arose because of the nature of the grievor's illness, and not because his dispute with the employer involved a discrimination claim or other "critical job interest." However, other cases have applied a duty to be proactive in cases simply on the basis that the dispute involved a disability.[38] Most notably, in 2004 in *Bingley v Teamsters, Local 91*,[39] the Canadian Industrial Relations Board (CIRB) imposed an obligation on the union to be proactive in a case involving a courier who suffered from a form of skin cancer, and who sought a reduction in the hours of her shift as a temporary accommodation to minimize sun

36 Adell, "The Union's DFR," above note 13.

37 [1997] Sask LRBR 476, 98 CCLC 220-020 [*H(K)*].

38 *Haggith v Canadian Union of Public Employees, Local 401*, [2001] BCLRBD No 273, [2001] LVI 3212-6 [*Haggith*].

39 [2004] CIRB No 291, [2004] CIRBD No 32 [*Bingley*].

exposure. When she was denied the accommodation, her union filed a grievance that was ultimately resolved prior to arbitration. Bingley thereafter sought to bring a second grievance to secure back pay for wages lost during the period without accommodation. The union refused to bring forward the second grievance, and she brought a DFR claim against the union.

The CIRB began its analysis by noting that the duty of fair representation and the human rights duty to accommodate are related but distinct duties. It then examined a number of cases, including *H(K)*, which suggested that where a DFR complaint arises from a union's failure to bring forward an accommodation grievance, a more searching analysis of the union's decision-making is appropriate:

> Due to the sensitive and important issues associated with the accommodation of disabled workers in the workplace, labour boards also look to see whether unions have given disabled employees' grievances greater scrutiny. The cases generally concur that the usual procedure applied to other members of the bargaining unit may be insufficient in representing a grievor with a disability, mainly because the member's situation will require a different approach.[40]

The union must not, therefore handle a disability grievance in the "ordinary" manner. "[I]t must be proactive and more attentive in its approach."[41] The CIRB effectively assessed the union's actions and decisions on a standard of reasonableness, a standard labour boards have assiduously avoided in applying the DFR more generally.[42] So long as the union was "reasonably careful and reasonably assertive," the Board stated, it would not "worry about whether [its] decision not to pursue a grievance is correct on the language of the collective agreement, or even on the language of the applicable human rights statute."[43] The CIRB then went on to list a number of criteria to consider when assessing the DFR in disability discrimination cases: (a) whether the union's intervention was reasonable where the employer failed to implement appropriate accommodation measures; (b) whether the quality of the process that allowed the union to come to its conclusion was reasonable; (c) whether the union went beyond its "usual" procedures and applied an extra measure of

40 *Ibid* at para 64.

41 *Ibid* at para 74.

42 *Rayonnier*, above note 31.

43 *Bingley*, above note 39 at para 83.

care in representing the employee; and (d) whether the union applied an extra measure of assertiveness in dealing with the employer. These criteria seem to combine concern that grievors with both physical and psychological disabilities might suffer specific difficulties in undertaking the grievance process itself, and concern about the serious nature of discrimination-related claims. Applying this approach, the CIRB concluded that the union had not been sufficiently proactive or assertive. Accordingly, it had discriminated against Bingley and thus violated its duty of fair representation. The CIRB ordered the union to pay the employee's costs. It also ordered the parties to attempt to settle the matter, remaining seized if no settlement was reached.

In general, the CIRB attempted to preserve the distinction between the DFR (over which it has jurisdiction) and the union's duty to accommodate (over which it does not). However, in discussing the principles applicable to the duty to accommodate, it arguably expanded on the principles enunciated by the Supreme Court of Canada in *Renaud* by suggesting that unions could be directly liable simply for failing to bring forward a discrimination grievance. As previously noted, the Court in *Renaud* identified two scenarios in which a union could be liable for discrimination under human rights codes: where the union has agreed to a discriminatory practice or where it unreasonably impedes employer accommodation. As the Court explained, the "union's responsibility is engaged when it causes or takes part in the work policy that is the source of the discriminatory act against the employee, such as a provision contained in the collective agreement."[44] In *Bingley*, however, the Board appeared to contemplate a third scenario in which unions may be liable: "The union's responsibility may also be engaged when it does not address the discrimination even though it did not cause or take part in the discriminatory work policy. . . . A union may be held responsible for the discriminatory effects of an employment policy decision by not seeking to put an end to the discrimination."[45] This observation was clearly obiter in *Bingley*, and to date, does not appear to have been embraced either federally or in any province; indeed, as discussed below, it has been specifically disavowed in Ontario.[46]

---

44 *Renaud*, above note 25.

45 *Bingley*, above note 39 at para 59, 61.

46 See the discussion of *Gungor v Canadian Auto Workers Local 88*, 2011 HRTO 1760 (CanLII) [*Gungor*], below.

*Bingley* has been discussed in a number of DFR cases since it was issued, but only rarely applied.[47] The principles enunciated in *Bingley* have received the most thorough treatment in a 2010 decision called *Schwartzmann v Manitoba Government and General Employees' Union.*[48] In *Schwartzmann*, the Manitoba Labour Board expressed approval of the principles set out in *Bingley*, and went on to refine them. It linked human rights issues with the existing DFR jurisprudence regarding "critical job interests," and added discrimination disputes to the existing categories of issues, such as terminations, which deserve special attention because of their particular significance to employee interests: "[i]n the circumstance of a disabled employee alleging a violation of statutory anti-discrimination rights, the employment interests are serious and any associated grievance may have enormous consequences for the employee."[49] Because human rights issues are critical job interests, the Board held, unions need to take a more proactive role in assisting employees to understand their rights and responsibilities, and in obtaining the necessary medical reports, particularly where their disability makes doing so more difficult.[50] On the facts before it, however, the Board found that the union had met this more exacting standard, and thus lived up to its duty of fair representation.

Drawing upon the Supreme Court of Canada's decision in *Parry Sound*, the Commission des Relations du Travail of Quebec has also held that unions must undertake a more proactive approach in assisting members with human rights issues in the workplace.[51] In *Chuuon c Association des*

---

47 *Oliver and Nape, Re*, [2012] LRBD No 10; *Schwartzman v Manitoba Government and General Employees' Union*, [2010] MLBD No 49, 190 CLRBR (2d) 184 [*Schwartzman*]; *Gough v United Steelworkers of America, Local 1976*, 2010 CIRB 534, [2010] CIRBD No 39; *Pepper v Teamsters, Local 879*, 2009 CIRB 453, [2010] CIRBD No 22; *Jakutavicius v Public Service Alliance of Canada*, 2005 PSLRB 70; *Mallet v Canadian Brotherhood of Railway, Transport and General Workers*, 2014 CIRB 730, 259 CLRBR (2d) 257 [*Mallet*]; *Phillips & Temro Co (Re)*, [2013] MLBD No 31, 235 CLRBR (2d) 195 [*Phillips*].

48 *Schwartzman*, *ibid.*

49 *Ibid* at para 117.

50 *Ibid* at para 119. *See also Gendron*, above note 27, for a discussion of the role of critical job interests in assessing the union's DFR; and *Banks v Canadian Union of Public Employees, Local 4828*, [2013] SLRBD No 20, where the employee unsuccessfully argued that harassment (not based on a prohibited ground) constitutes a critical interest.

51 Nancy Martel & Pierre E Moreau, *Le devoir de juste représentation* (Montréal: LexisNexis Canada, 2009) at 87–88. On January 1, 2016, the Commission des relations du travail of Quebec was renamed the Tribunal administratif du travail.

*employés du Groupe Holiday Inc* the Commission held that when a grievance concerns a members' discrimination claim, the union is obliged to intervene, to be proactive, to deploy additional efforts and to be particularly sensitive in the manner of representation.[52]

Ontario, however, has not experimented with a heightened DFR standard in regards to human rights claims. As Adell noted in 2001, the Ontario Labour Relations Board issued two decisions around the same time as *H(K)* suggesting that unions had a right to be wrong in regards to discrimination grievances, just as with any other grievance. In *Gen-Auto Shippers* the Board held that the union did not violate the DFR when it refused to grieve the application of a rule that placed workers at the bottom of a seniority list when they temporarily moved job classifications. The employee in this case had moved to another classification because of an injury that interfered with his ability to perform the duties of his assigned classification. The Board found that the union was justified in deciding in favour of the interests of the collective that benefited from the rule, because it was not plainly obvious that the rule violated the *Human Rights Code*.[53] The Board applied the same reasoning in the same year in *Thunder Bay Hydro*, in which it upheld a union's decision not to challenge a "last chance" agreement on human rights grounds, again because it was not clear on its face that the agreement violated the code.[54] The issue of whether or not there is a higher DFR standard in discrimination cases has not received significant treatment in Ontario since the late 1990s.[55]

There is therefore some general support for the idea that unions must be particularly proactive in dealing with members' disability-related grievances. Manitoba and Quebec appear to recognize such an obligation,

---

52 2005 QCCRT 115 at para 46. *See also Maltais c Section locale 22 du syndicat canadien des communications, de l'énergie et du papier (SCEP)*, 2006 QCCRT 316; *Syndicat des fonctionnaires municipaux de Montréal (SCFP) c Commission des relations du travail*, 2009 QCCS 4456.

53 *Mason v Gen-Auto Shippers &Teamsters, Local 938*, [1999] OLRB 242, [1999] OLRD No 664 [*Mason*].

54 *Creed v International Brotherhood of Electrical Workers, Local 339*, [1999] OLRD No 3422 [*Creed*].

55 Both *Mason* and *Creed* were recently cited in *Sysco Food Services of Toronto*, [2016] OLRD No 465. However, in that case the OLRB concluded that even if a duty to be proactive applied, the union had met the higher standard applicable in termination scenarios of providing a "persuasive account" of its reasoning, based on the well-founded nature of the legal opinion and the union's careful review of the merits of the case.

and *Bingley* has received some positive treatment elsewhere,[56] but Ontario has not followed suit. Outside of Quebec, the duty to be proactive, where it is accepted, is recognized only in disability cases, although some of its analysis is arguably applicable to other grounds of discrimination. At a general level, then, a higher standard of investigation may be required in regards to disability discrimination, but no overall change has otherwise occurred in the DFR caselaw since *Weber* and *Parry Sound* in the standards applied to union handling of human rights issues.

### 2) Human Rights Claims against Unions before Human Rights Tribunals

The abolition of "gatekeeper" human rights commissions in a number of provinces since the early 2000s, and the adoption of direct access models, has opened a wider door to claims made by employees against unions before human rights tribunals (HRTs).[57] In theory, claims of union discrimination could have proceeded through the human rights system prior to the adoption of direct access models. In practice, however, Commissions typically deferred or dismissed applications from unionized workers, such that very few claims of union discrimination reached human rights tribunals.[58] The implementation of direct access tribunals has thus increased the possibility of overlapping discrimination claims against a union, before both a labour board (LRB) and an HRT.

Discrimination claims come before an LRB through a DFR claim that the union discriminated against the claimant, often in tandem with additional arguments that the union acted arbitrarily or in bad faith. Because LRB jurisdiction is broader than that of HRTs, there is some scope for parallel proceedings. Where there is overlap, however, it has typically been recognized as a zone of concurrent jurisdiction, dealt with through principles of *res judicata* and its legislative equivalents.[59] LRBs and HRTs

---

56 See cases above note 47.

57 In Ontario, British Columbia and Nunavut, claimants may file claims directly with human rights tribunals. In other jurisdictions, claimants must first bring a claim to a human rights commission, which usually investigates the matter and decides whether to bring the claim forward to adjudication before the tribunal. The Commissions in those jurisdictions thus act as gatekeepers.

58 Etherington, above note 5 at 51–62.

59 In Ontario the HRTO approaches multiple proceedings through s 45 of the *Human Rights Code*, which empowers the Tribunal to defer applications, and s 45.1, which permits it to dismiss applications where the underlying substance has been appro-

also recognize, however, that each has a core of expertise and often defer to each other in those areas.

In *Gungor*, the Human Rights Tribunal of Ontario (HRTO) explained the differences in jurisdiction and role between LRBs and HRTs. LRBs have "direct and immediate jurisdiction" to assess the adequacy of a union's representation regarding member's potential grievances, including discrimination grievances.[60] LRBs rule only on the process of union conduct and decision-making as regards particular grievances, and can order that grievances be taken to arbitration for conclusive analysis of their merits. But they do not rule on the issue of whether union conduct contravened the human rights code. By contrast, HRTs are capable of dealing directly with underlying human rights code-related issues raised by both the conduct of the employer, and by the conduct of the union in providing or failing to provide representation.[61]

The Saskatchewan LRB has adopted similar descriptions of its jurisdiction in comparison with the Saskatchewan Human Rights Commission and Tribunal.[62] In *Metz* the Board identified questions such as whether the employer's efforts to accommodate the grievor, and whether the settlement of a grievance complied with the human rights code as matters within the primary jurisdiction of the Human Rights Commission. The Board retained jurisdiction, however, over the procedural issues relating to the quality of the union's representation in dealing with the accommodation issues.[63]

---

priately dealt with by another proceeding. See Jo-Anne Pickel, "Statutory Tribunals and the Challenges of Managing Parallel Claims," Chapter 6, this volume. The Tribunal considers DFR proceedings, and the settlement of DFR claims, to be "another proceeding" for the purposes of s 45.1. *See Human Rights Code,* RSO 1990, c H 19, s 45.1; *Dunn v Sault Ste Marie (City)*, 2008 HRTO 149 (CanLII).

60 *Gungor,* above note 46 at para 53.

61 *Ibid* at paras 54–55.

62 Although there are numerous DFR cases that refer to parallel human rights claims by the employee, there are only a few in which the human rights claim is still under way or has been completed by the time of the DFR hearing, and thus very few in which the Board needs to undertake a *res judicata* and/or jurisdictional analysis. *See e.g., O'Flaherty v Vancouver Community College Faculty Association*, [2011] BCLRBD No 7, [2011] BCWLD 2372; *DM (Re),* [2006] SLRBD No 30, 130 CLRBR (2d) 132 [*DM*]; *Metz (Re),* [2003] SLRBD No 5 [*Metz*].

63 *Metz, ibid* at paras 38–63 The Board followed a similar process in *DM, ibid,* but deferred both the substantive and procedural issues to the Tribunal, on the basis that an evaluation of the union's processes required a determination as to whether the employee suffered from a disability and the nature of that disability, which the

Employees may, of course, opt to by-pass the LRB altogether and bring a claim regarding discrimination by their union solely to the HRT. There are two types of human rights claims that can be made against unions. The first is that the union discriminated against an employee "in employment" (in Ontario, a violation of section 5 of the *Code*), or "in membership" (in Ontario, a violation of section 6). In *Gungor* the HRTO explained that in claims involving union representation, a union can be found to have violated section 5 only if the impugned conduct falls within the two scenarios outlined in *Renaud*.[64] In other words, unless a union has participated in the creation of a discriminatory term in a collective agreement, or has failed to accommodate by impeding an employer's legitimate accommodation efforts, its conduct is not governed by section 5. However, claims that the union has represented a member in a discriminatory fashion may constitute a violation of section 6, which prohibits discrimination in respect of membership in a trade union.

The HRTO has been very clear, however, that mere failure to bring forward a grievance is not in itself sufficient to find a violation of the *Code*, even where the matter at issue is an allegation of discrimination. To make out a prima facie case of discrimination, the employee must demonstrate that the union's decision not to act was at least in part based on a prohibited ground of discrimination. In *Traversy* the HRTO put it this way: "[A] claim that the union violates the *Code* must be based on an assertion of differential treatment, and not simply a failure to act. The failure or refusal to take forward a human rights issue such as accommodation of a disability in the workplace is not, in and of itself, a breach of the *Code*. . . .There must be a claim, and a factual foundation for the claim, that the failure to act was based on discriminatory factors."[65]

---

Commission was better suited to provide. In *DM* the Board observed that since the employee's complaints were deferred rather than dismissed, the employee could return to the Board if any of the DFR issues were not addressed by the Commission (but noted that it may be bound by the Commission's findings if this occurred). In *Mallet*, above note 47, the CIRB similarly deferred a complaint to the Canadian Human Rights Commission, but re-opened it after the Commission had closed the file because the applicant did not return calls.

64 *Traversy v Mississauga Professional Firefighters' Association*, 2009 HRTO 996 (CanLII) [*Traversy*]. *See also Baylet v Universal Workers Union*, 2009 HRTO 700 (CanLII); *Gungor*, above note 46; *Holowka v Ontario Nurses Association*, 2010 HRTO 2171 (CanLII); *Crosby v United Food and Commercial Workers Canada*, 2012 HRTO 1158 (CanLII).

65 *Traversy*, *ibid* at para 33.

In *Gungor* the Tribunal was urged to adopt the standards for union conduct outlined by the CIRB in *Bingley*. The HRTO emphatically declined to do so. Vice-Chair Mark Hart explained that *Bingley* concerned the nature of a union's representation, not the validity of the underlying discrimination grievance sought by the employee. Vice-Chair Hart went further to expressly distance the HRTO from the comments made in *Bingley* which suggested that unions may be liable under human rights codes simply for failure to challenge employer discrimination.[66] In his view, the decision of the Supreme Court of Canada in *Renaud* clearly limited a union's duty to accommodate to situations in which it had participated in the creation of a discriminatory workplace rule or term of the collective agreement, or impeded the implementation of a reasonable accommodation; the Court did *not* hold that unions could be held liable for failing to take steps to address discrimination in which they did not participate in one of these ways.

Thus preliminary examination of the caselaw suggests that employees are no more successful before HRTs than they are before LRBs in arguing that their union has discriminated against them. The cases heard by HRTs are usually simply claims of unfairness in union decision-making, and do not identify a prohibited ground of decision-making. Accordingly, they are usually dismissed as being outside the Tribunal's jurisdiction.

## C. FURTHER EMPIRICAL RESEARCH IS NEEDED

The previous analysis barely scratches the surface of the questions that arise in considering unions' representational responsibility for human rights in the workplace. Although legal principles regarding the DFR (except as regards disability) and unions' direct liability for discrimination do not appear to have changed significantly since *Weber* and *Parry Sound*, there is the general sense that unions have become increasingly sensitized to their human rights obligations over the last few decades. How unions approach their representational responsibilities regarding workplace discrimination, and whether their behaviour has changed since *Weber* and *Parry Sound*, are questions that cannot be answered except by a series of empirical inquiries which I outline in more detail below.

66 *Gungor*, above note 46.

## 1) The Effects of Concurrency

### a) Finality

There are two general justifications for the union veto. The first arises from the union's position as exclusive bargaining representative. The veto allows the union control over which issues to negotiate and which issues to grieve, giving the union authority to make final decisions in the interest of the collective. It also provides the employer with a single party capable of making settlements over all workplace disputes, thus allowing the parties to circumscribe the scope of, and bring final resolution to their differences. One question that therefore arises under a concurrency model is whether, in practice, the concept of finality has become effectively illusory.

Where multiple tribunals have concurrent jurisdiction, courts must balance values of finality and fairness. Conflicts between these values are typically addressed through the doctrines of *res judicata* and issue estoppel, and/or their statutory counter-parts. [67] The caselaw reveals numerous situations in which a union has brought forward but then settled a member's human rights grievance with the employer. The member then brings both a DFR claim against the union to an LRB, and a human rights claim against the employer, the union, or both, to an HRT. In other cases, the union carries the grievance to arbitration, but the affected employee nonetheless brings a simultaneous DFR claim against the union, and a human rights claim against both the union and the employer, on the basis of the same or related issues.[68] In many DFR cases the employer is considered an interested party, and may make submissions. Similarly, unions or employers are often invited to make submissions as intervenors in claims at the HRTO in which they have not been named as respondents. Where a grievance or DFR case is ongoing, the HRTO may defer the application until the other proceeding is concluded, and vice versa. However, the existence of concurrent jurisdiction among these tribunals means that the three parties — the employee, the union and the employer — are forced to deal with a number of different decision-makers over the same series of issues.

---

67 *See* sources above note 18.

68 *See e.g.*, *Ontario Public Service Employees Union v Ontario (Ministry of Community Safety and Correctional Services) (Therrien Grievance)* (2008), 173 LAC (4th) 193 (Arbitrator: Lynk).

Even though issue estoppel and *res judicata* principles act to curb the full re-litigation of a claim before a second decision-maker, all three parties are often required to make argument in a number of fora. In this situation, is finality in decision-making still effective? Does it therefore continue to be a strong justification for the union veto over the filing and processing of grievances? Do unions benefit, or are they harmed by the pressures put on them by the union veto in the context of concurrency? Would unions instead benefit from simply allowing individual employees to bring forward certain types of grievances to arbitration at their own cost, as Adell advocated, and let an arbitrator resolve them as between the employee and the employer? As discussed, employees can often proceed directly to human rights decision-makers where the union refuses to take forward their discrimination grievance.[69] However, in doing so, they may forego other collective bargaining entitlements. Examining the parties' experiences in the federal public sector may be instructive here, as the *Public Sector Labour Relations Act* currently permits employees to bring certain types of grievances forward to arbitration without their union's assistance.[70] A preliminary review suggests that cases brought forward by individuals without the support of the union are rarely successful.[71] But the success rate may ultimately not be the sole criteria to assess. Individual employees may also derive intangible benefits from being given the agency to act on their own behalf where the union chooses not to do so. DFR and human rights claims against the union might thereby be reduced, with a consequent improvement in feelings of satisfaction with the union's representation.

Further empirical research is required in order to determine whether the potential for harm in depriving unions of control, and introducing further volatility into relationships with the employer, outweighs the po-

69 This is true in most provinces, although Quebec is an exception. *See* Renée-Claude Drouin, "Some Unique Features of *Weber*'s Application in Quebec: The Treatment of Statutory Labour Rights and Human Rights Claims," Chapter 9, this volume.

70 *See Public Sector Labour Relations Act*, SC 2003, c 22, s 2, s 209 [*PSLRA*].

71 Actual tabulation is somewhat difficult because the decisions are not always clear as to whether the union declined to support the grievance, or whether the employee was not unionized at all. The *PSLRA* permits non-unionized workers access to the arbitration process under ss 209(b)–(d). In the federal public sector there is a standing tribunal that adjudicates grievances, and employees are therefore not required to pay half of the arbitrator's fee. In the private sector, a requirement to contribute to arbitrators' fees would almost certainly be a significant deterrent to individual employees proceeding without union support.

tential benefits achieved by allowing individuals to bring forward grievances on their own. Assessing the potential of such a reform would require a qualitative study of union, employer and employee experiences to assess whether and to what extent finality in decision-making has been weakened by concurrency, what impact any potential weakening has on the parties' relationships, what benefits might flow to individual employees, and what effects direct access to arbitration for human rights grievances might have on the institution of arbitration, and those involved in it.

### b) Union Choices Regarding Adjudication Fora

Decisions in human rights cases brought before HRTs by unionized employees against employers sometimes imply that unions have been involved at least in a background capacity. Sometimes the union brings the claim itself. In other cases it acts as an intervenor on questions related to the impact of the decision on the rest of the bargaining unit. Union activity may also be visible in cases where, for example, there is an attempt to split a claim, where the union brings a grievance to arbitration which does not raise a human rights issue, and the worker then brings a separate human rights claim to the Tribunal. (At least in Ontario, such strategies have not been successful.[72]) But in other cases the union's role is less clear, because the decision does not address whether the employee is proceeding to the Tribunal against the union's wishes, or with its tacit and/or financial support.

Another topic for study is therefore the question of when and why unions might suggest that a member forego arbitration and instead proceed directly to the Tribunal. On what basis would a union decide to take a claim on a member's behalf to the Tribunal? Does it do so primarily in regards to systemic discrimination claims? Do unions simply act as a facilitating resource? Or do they pay for counsel to represent employees before the Tribunal? If so, when and how often do they do so? Finally, is there a difference in the number of claims brought against unions to the HRTs in direct access-model provinces, as compared to those where commissions play a gatekeeping function?

---

72 *Paterno v Salvation Army*, 2011 HRTO 2298 (CanLII). *See also* Shilton, above note 6 at 236.

### 2) The DFR

As described above, the predicted heightening of the DFR standard post-*Weber* has occurred only in regard to disability discrimination claims, and only in some provinces. But questions still remain. Are there more DFR claims now than prior to *Weber*? And if so, is any causal relationship discernible between expanded arbitral jurisdiction and a rise in DFR claims? Even if the legal standards by which union decision-making are judged have not greatly changed post-*Weber* and *Parry Sound*, have unions changed the ways in which they make decisions about whether to bring discrimination grievances? Do they, in fact, treat discrimination claims as critical job interests, and subject them to a more searching analysis than in other types of claims? Have unions placed a higher standard on themselves as regards their representational obligations for members' human rights issues over the years? If they do so now, did they also do so prior to *Weber* and *Parry Sound*? What factors do they consider? And if they do, how does this affect their ability to balance the individual rights of members and the collective interests of the bargaining unit?

### 3) Unions' Obligations in Intra-member Discrimination Scenarios

Finally, how are unions dealing with their representational responsibilities where the discrimination alleged arises between and among union members? What do unions do, and what should they do, when one member accuses another of sexual harassment, or racism? These problems have been under-studied, but pose grave difficulties for unions who are obliged to represent members with directly conflicting individual interests,[73] and sharply highlight the difficulties unions face in determining what is in the collective interest when significant individual rights issues are involved.

Here the issue is not the union veto per se; both the "accuser" and the "accused" may have access to a decision-making forum. The issue is the nature of the union's representational obligations during the process of investigation and any subsequent adjudication. In most cases the accuser will bring a complaint of discrimination by another employee to her employer (although she may also seek the union's aid in convincing the

73 Lori Park has written the only study I have located on this issue. *See* Lori L Park, "Fair Representation and Conflict of Interest: Sexual Harassment Complaints Between Co-Workers" (1997) 6 *Dalhousie Journal of Legal Studies* 121.

employer to take appropriate action). Because it is the employer's legal responsibility to provide a discrimination-free workplace, the employer should investigate, and may then take disciplinary action against the accused employee. If disciplinary action is taken, the union must then determine how to apportion its representational duties to both the accuser and accused. If no disciplinary action is taken, it must then determine whether it will launch a human rights grievance on behalf of the accuser, and how it will represent the accused in that scenario.

Practices seem to vary widely among unions and within collective agreements. Some unions have processes in place to appoint a representative for each employee, with a firewall between the representatives to ensure confidentiality. In some instances, unions will pay for one party to secure independent counsel, while directly representing the other. Other unions have negotiated for the creation of joint union-management investigation processes, in which each party appoints an external representative to investigate the allegations. In some situations, however, the union will represent only the disciplined member, on the assumption that the accuser's interests are aligned with the employer's. This last approach has serious pitfalls, since the employer's interest is ultimately to avoid liability. Unless specific policies or contract terms so provide, the employer is not obliged to keep employees informed of more than the very broad outlines of the progress of the complaint. If the union does not provide representational services, the employee who has lodged the complaint will have no mechanism to contest the process of the investigation, and will be beholden solely to the employer for information about who is appointed to investigate, who is contacted for information, what material has been provided to the accused, etc. — all information the employer may not wish to share. She may find therefore find herself effectively in the dark, as a process unfolds that directly affects her. In addition, given that discrimination claims are usually brought by members with lesser socioeconomic power — women, racialized workers, sexual minority employees, etc. — the union may be perceived as disinterested in the experiences of its more vulnerable members, which may in turn give rise to serious morale issues within the bargaining unit.

Very little research has been done investigating union practices in intra-member discrimination claims, and these practices are rarely visible in the caselaw. Given the potential difficulties in such cases, however, further investigation of unions' experiences with different models would be highly instructive in determining what practices are currently used, and what "best practices" should be promoted and developed.

## CONCLUDING THOUGHTS

This essay has raised questions for further study of the ways in which unions undertake their representational obligations in regards to human rights disputes in the workplace since *Weber* was issued. As the preceding discussion suggests, the relevant caselaw is not greatly instructive. At a general level, it arguably establishes a higher standard for applying the DFR in regards to disability discrimination, but not beyond. And the human rights tribunals have remained faithful to the limited scope of union liability elaborated in *Renaud*.

The reported decisions of LRBs and HRTs suggest little reason for concern that unions are not doing their job in connection with enforcement of employee human rights. Most claims filed against unions appear unmeritorious. Their facts usually reflect employees who are frustrated and unhappy with all parties in the workplace, but do not usually reveal any inappropriate action (or inaction) by the union. In these cases, unions appear to take seriously their obligations to investigate and assess the merits of a grievance, and its effects on the collective. But we know little about the underlying reasons why the caselaw reflects this picture. It may simply be that unions have, by and large, internalized and expanded their human rights obligations and are properly representing their members as regards workplace discrimination issues. Or it may be that where a union has acted arbitrarily or discriminatorily in refusing to bring forward a discrimination grievance, the case settles prior to adjudication, in either forum. Finally, it may also be that unionized workers who experience inappropriate recalcitrance by their unions in regards to a discrimination grievance are too powerless or too disillusioned to bring additional claims.

I suspect all three scenarios have some validity. Most unions are cognizant of the weight of their obligations in regards to important individual rights held by their members, and have been so at least since *Weber*, if not before. Most unions try to balance individual human rights interests against the needs of the collective. When meritorious claims arise, it is likely that the parties often settle prior to adjudication, whether the claims are framed as DFR claims or human rights claims. But there are also likely to be some workplaces that continue to be characterized by a culture of systemic discrimination. We simply do not know from the caselaw how well employees in those workplaces have been served by expanded arbitral jurisdiction.

It remains to be assessed, however, whether concurrent jurisdiction among arbitrators, LRBs and HRTs is the answer. If parallel cases are permitted in multiple forums on essentially the same issue, we need further empirical study on whether finality continues to have meaning, whether it continues to have value for workplace parties, and whether it justifies the union veto. Thus a host of questions remain to be answered to discover whether and to what extent *Weber* and *Parry Sound* have had real impact on unions' approaches to their representational obligations regarding workplace discrimination. If, as the Supreme Court of Canada has noted, human rights in the workplace are "everybody's business," there is still much we do not know about the effects of *Weber* and *Parry Sound* on the ways in which unions are managing their part of that business.[74]

74 *Renaud*, above note 25 at para 44. *See also* Shilton, above note 6 for an analysis of *Renaud* and its impact on unions.

CHAPTER NINE

# Some Unique Features of *Weber's* Application in Quebec: The Treatment of Statutory Labour Rights and Human Rights Claims

Renée-Claude Drouin

In the landmark case of *Weber v Ontario Hydro*,[1] the Supreme Court of Canada held that labour arbitrators generally have exclusive jurisdiction to resolve disputes arising from the implementation and interpretation of a collective agreement. Faced with deciding whether an employee could sue his employer in court on the ground of tort rules and alleged violations of *Charter* rights, the Court discarded concurrent[2] and overlapping jurisdictional models,[3] and concluded that Weber's action could not be tried. Clearly favouring a "one-stop shop" approach to deciding all aspects of a single dispute arising in a unionized workplace, the Court held that the question of jurisdiction did not depend on the way the parties had legally framed their claims. Instead, the central jurisdictional question was "whether the dispute, in its essential character, arises from the interpretation, application, administration, or violation of the collective agreement."[4]

1 1995 SCC 108 [*Weber*].

2 *Ibid* (Under such a model,"[w]here an action is recognized by the common law or by statute, it may proceed, notwithstanding that it arises in the employment context" at para 44).

3 *Ibid* ("On this approach, notwithstanding that the facts of the dispute arise out of the collective agreement, a court action may be brought if it raises issues which go beyond the traditional subject matter of labour law" at para 52).

4 *Ibid* at para 57.

Since the answer was affirmative, the dispute belonged within the exclusive jurisdiction of an arbitrator.

The *Weber* decision is part of a long judicial and doctrinal reflection on the role and function of grievance arbitration in the context of evolving labour laws. Historically, the development of collective labour relations institutions was at odds with the common law, in particular given the liberal approach of the latter regarding contractual matters, which clashed with workers' need for protection. Collective autonomy, or the right of the parties in labour relations—unions and employers—to develop and implement their own normative system in the workplace,[5] was traditionally seen as the most desirable way for workers to access better working conditions and to establish a degree of industrial democracy.[6] From the perspective of industrial pluralism,[7] grievance arbitration, the judicial branch of the workplace governance system, was seen as a resolutely private mode of justice, ensuring that the will of the parties, as expressed in the collective agreement, would be implemented.

The legal context in which grievance arbitration initially appeared has been profoundly transformed in recent decades by increasingly strong state intervention in the field of labour relations, aimed at ensuring a number of common protections for all workers with regard to occupational health and safety, minimum labour standards or more general human rights and freedoms.[8] As a result of these legislative interventions, statutory rights are now just as likely to be the source of working conditions for unionized workers as the collective bargaining agreement itself. This development has necessarily raised questions regarding the relationship between statutory rights, the collective agreement, and grievance arbitration. Two issues in particular appear to be fundamental: whether arbitrators have the power to decide a grievance not only on the basis of the content of the collective agreement, but also on the basis of statutory employment rights; and how that power to resolve disputes is

---

5 Pierre Verge, "L'affirmation constitutionnelle de la liberté d'association: une nouvelle vie pour l'autonomie collective?" (2010) 51 *Cahiers de droit* 353 at 355.

6 Guylaine Vallée & Dalia Gesualdi-Fecteau, "La constitutionnalisation du droit du travail: une menace ou une opportunité pour les rapports collectifs de travail?" (2007) 48 *Cahiers de droit* 153 at 165-6.

7 See Elizabeth Shilton, "*Weber*, The Common Law and Industrial Self-Government," Chapter 3, this volume.

8 Vallée & Gesualdi-Fecteau, above note 6 at 169.

divided among the arbitrator, the common law courts and the other specialized bodies.[9]

*Weber* fits into a line of cases in which the Supreme Court takes a liberal approach to the jurisdiction of labour arbitrators, extending the arbitrator's more traditional domain. Hence, the mixed reactions to the ruling: "The decision and its aftermath have had a great impact on Canadian doctrine, with some observers seeing in it a dangerous trend toward a form of privatization of justice while others have rejoiced at the Court's recognition of the integrity of the arbitral forum."[10] On a practical level, despite clues provided by courts, in Quebec, as in other Canadian provinces, delineating the frontiers of arbitral jurisdiction after *Weber* has proved to be a challenge in many instances. One of the reasons for this lies in the fact that the exclusive jurisdiction model put forward in *Weber* derived from a case in which the competing jurisdictions at play were arbitration on the one hand, and the general courts on the other. Since this binary divide does not fully grasp the complex architecture of modern labour law, *Weber* left many questions unanswered or only partially answered. One of these relates to the proper way to integrate different sources of law—primarily the collective agreement and statutory rights—in the context of arbitral jurisdiction. Another relates to the role of arbitration in resolving human rights disputes arising in unionized workplaces. On these questions, the caselaw from Quebec is to some extent at odds with the rest of Canada, in part because of the civil law tradition applicable in the province for matters of private law.

In Part A of this essay, I examine the first of these questions: the relationship between collective agreements and statutory law. I argue that as a result of the decisions of the Supreme Court in *Isidore Garon ltée v Tremblay; Fillion et Frères (1976) inc. v Syndicat national des employés de garage du Québec inc*[11] and *Syndicat de la fonction publique du Québec v Quebec (Attorney General),*[12] the rule developed by the Court in *Parry Sound (District) Welfare Administration Board v Ontario Public Service Employees Union, Local 324*[13]—that human rights and other employment-related

9 Gilles Trudeau, "L'arbitrage des griefs au Canada: plaidoyer pour une réforme devenue nécessaire" (2005) 84:2 *Canadian Bar Review* 249 at 256 [Trudeau, "L'arbitrage des griefs"].

10 *Ibid* at 250. [translated by author].

11 2006 SCC 2 [*Isidore Garon*]

12 2010 SCC 28 [*SFPQ*].

13 2003 SCC 42 [*Parry Sound*].

statutory rights are implicitly incorporated into every collective agreement—has been discarded in favour of a "hierarchy of relevant sources of labour law approach." Part B of the essay examines the second question, on which Quebec again appears to stand alone: the identification of the appropriate forum to adjudicate human rights disputes in unionized workplaces. In *Québec (Commission des droits de la personne et des droits de la jeunesse) v Québec (Attorney General)*,[14] McLachlin CJC revisited and applied her ruling in *Weber*, and stressed that there was no *a priori* exclusive arbitral jurisdiction in cases of apparent conflicts of jurisdiction between two specialized tribunals. Tribunals and review courts outside of Quebec have interpreted this decision as conferring concurrent jurisdiction on labour arbitrators and human rights tribunals when adjudicating the human rights claims of unionized employees.[15] I argue that in Quebec, a more restrictive approach has been adopted which recognizes that arbitrators have privileged and exclusive jurisdiction when the dispute does not challenge the content of the agreement, but instead relates to the interpretation and application of a collective agreement. I analyze the possible reasons underlying Quebec's peculiarity in this regard.

## A. FROM THE IMPLICIT CONTENT OF THE COLLECTIVE AGREEMENT TO THE HIERARCHY OF RELEVANT SOURCES OF LABOUR LAW

One of the important lessons deriving from *Weber* is that the arbitrator's jurisdiction is exclusive when the nature of the dispute falls within the ambit of the collective agreement.[16] Hence, the boundaries of labour arbitration are intrinsically linked with the explicit or implicit content of the collective agreement. Yet, as previously mentioned, many employment standards applicable to unionized employees are established by statutes and are not the product of the collective bargaining process. How "permeable" is the collective agreement to these outside norms?[17] To what

14 2004 SCC 39 [*Morin*].

15 Elizabeth Shilton, "Choice, but No Choice: Adjudicating Human Rights Claims in Unionized Workplaces in Canada" (2013) 38:2 *Queen's Law Journal* 461 [Shilton, "Choice, but No Choice"].

16 *Weber*, above note 1 at para 49.

17 This expression is taken from Denis Nadeau, "La perméabilité du droit au sein des rapports collectifs du travail et la compétence arbitrale: nouveau regard sur la

extent does a labour arbitrator have jurisdiction over cases contesting the apparent violation of such standards? Since *McLeod v Egan*[18] in 1974, it is clear that the arbitrator has jurisdiction to apply a statute and disregard a stipulation of a collective agreement that goes against mandatory rules. While this may appear obvious today, in its own time this decision stood in sharp contrast with the commonly-held view of the labour arbitrator as the interpreter of the parties' will. Prior to this ruling, grievance arbitrators had granted particular legitimacy to the law of the parties over statutory rights.[19] The decision thus "signalled a break with 30 years of a legislative scheme based on the quasi indelible principle of the contractual autonomy of the parties to a collective agreement."[20] With *McLeod*, labour arbitration took a decisive turn from a purely private adjudication mode to one that included a public dimension.

This orientation was reinforced in *Parry Sound*, where the majority of the Supreme Court implicitly incorporated human rights and statutory labour rights into the content of collective agreements. However, the implicit incorporation argument did not provide a satisfying answer to some problems related to the relationship among relevant sources of law in the unionized workplace. In the last decade, the Supreme Court has been profoundly divided on this issue in a number of cases. In the Quebec context, the most important of these, in addition to *Parry Sound*, are *Isidore Garon* and *SFPQ*. The split decisions of the Court in these cases can be regarded as a conflict between two distinct visions of the collective labour relations regime.[21] On the one hand, there is an aim to preserve the traditional vision centred on the collective autonomy of the parties, which favours respect for the parties' will as expressed in the collective agreement. The competing vision, on the other hand, recognizes the plurality of labour law sources and strives to find ways to articulate the relationship among

---

valse-hésitation de la Cour suprême du Canada" (2010) 69 *Revue du Barreau* 219 [Nadeau, "La perméabilité du droit"].

18 (1974), [1975] 1 SCR 517, 46 DLR (3d) 150 [*McLeod*].

19 Vallée & Gesualdi-Fecteau, above note 6 at 169–70.

20 Denis Nadeau, "L'arbitrage des griefs: vecteur d'intégration des droits de la personne dans les rapports collectifs du travail," in Le Tribunal des droits de la personne et le Barreau du Québec, *La Charte des droits et libertés de la personne: Pour qui et jusqu'où?* (Cowansville: Éditions Yvon Blais, 2005) 153 at 157 [Nadeau, "L'arbitrage des griefs"] [translated by author].

21 Nadeau, "La perméabilité du droit," above note 17 at 223.

these different sources within the collective labour relations scheme, including labour arbitration.

### 1) *Parry Sound* and the Implicit Incorporation of Employment-Related Statutory Rights into the Collective Agreement

After *McLeod,* labour arbitrators generally used their power to apply statutes not only in the course of the interpretation of the collective agreement, but also to ensure respect for employees' statutory rights.[22] Studies show that they were nevertheless reluctant to apply a statute on a specific issue when the collective agreement did not address that issue.[23] These hesitations were swept away by the Supreme Court's judgment in *Parry Sound*, in which the majority held that "substantive rights and obligations of employment-related statutes are implicit in each collective agreement over which an arbitrator has jurisdiction."[24]

The main question in this Ontario case was whether the grievance of a probationary employee who had been discharged soon after her return from maternity leave was arbitrable, despite a provision in the applicable collective agreement which excluded probationary discharges from the types of issues that could be submitted to the grievance and arbitration procedures. Since the agreement did not expressly prohibit discrimination and gave the employer "sole discretion" to terminate the employment of workers on probation, the union relied on section 5(1) of the Ontario *Human Rights Code* in challenging the employee's dismissal. This raised the question of whether the grievance was within the ambit of the collective agreement and came under arbitral jurisdiction.[25]

Iacobucci J, writing for the majority, answered this question in the affirmative. He held that the management rights of the employer were constrained not only by the explicit provisions of the collective agreement, but also by the employee's statutory rights:

> A collective agreement might extend to an employer a broad right to manage the enterprise as it sees fit, but this right is circumscribed by

22 In Quebec, this power is expressly provided in the *Labour Code*, CQLR, c C-27, s 100.12(a) [*Labour Code*].

23 Vallée & Gesualdi-Fecteau, above note 6 at 164.

24 *Parry Sound*, above note 13 at para 28.

25 Or, as expressed in the majority judgment: "whether or not the substantive rights and obligations of the *Human Rights Code* are incorporated into each collective agreement over which the Board has jurisdiction." *Parry Sound*, *ibid* at para 21.

> the employee's statutory rights. The absence of an express provision that prohibits the violation of a particular statutory right is insufficient to conclude that a violation of that right does not constitute a violation of the collective agreement. Rather, human rights and other employment-related statutes establish a floor beneath which an employer and union cannot contract.[26]

As the Court underlined, "there are certain rights and obligations that arise irrespective of the parties' subjective intentions."[27] Consequently, a grievance arbitrator has both the power and duty to enforce employment-related statutory rights.

In *Parry Sound*, the majority went further than the Court had ever gone before in including statutory rights within the realm of labour arbitration. This decision appears to stand in sharp contradiction to the traditional vision of the collective autonomy of the parties on a number of points. It limits the ability of the parties to freely determine the terms of their relations as they see fit, since they can no longer exclude human rights or other employment-related statutory norms from their agreement.[28] It also changes the traditional view that a collective bargaining agreement is a purely private contract. As affirmed in the majority judgment, the collective agreement has both a private and public function, which is to ensure "the peaceful resolution of labour disputes."[29] Most importantly, the implicit incorporation argument changes the *power* of labour arbitrators to apply statutory rights into a *responsibility* to do so.[30] *Parry Sound*, building on the reasons of the Court in *McLeod*, therefore radically altered the traditional nature of labour arbitration as the private judicial system of the parties founded on the "spirit of autonomy and self-government which pervades collective bargaining relationships."[31]

The dissenting judges, on the other hand, took a radically different approach which accorded much greater autonomy to the parties in defining

---

26 *Ibid* at para 28. *See also* para 23.

27 *Ibid* at para 36.

28 As Fernand Morin puts it: "En somme, la liberté des parties à la convention collective est contenue et déterminée par les lois de l'emploi". Fernand Morin, "Fragilité des limites conventionnelles à l'arbitrage de grief: l'arrêt *Parry Sound*" (2003) 58:4 *Relations industrielles* 690 at 701.

29 *Parry Sound*, above note 13 at para 30.

30 *Ibid* at para 40.

31 Paul C Weiler, *Reconcilable Differences: New Directions in Canadian Labour Law* (Toronto: Carswell, 1980) at 94.

the terms of their collective agreement. While they recognized that the collective agreement could not contain a provision contrary to mandatory norms, they considered that the parties had the right to exclude certain categories of employees from the arbitral procedure. Major J (with LeBel J concurring) wrote:

> [E]xplicit statutory directions override conflicting provisions of collective agreements, but they do not affect the parties' ability to define the limits of their agreement. Parties remain free to exclude certain classes of employees, such as probationary, part-time, or temporary employees, from some of the provisions of the agreement, just as they remain free to exclude certain kinds of disputes from the jurisdiction of the arbitrator.[32]

Therefore, the dissenters would have held that the arbitration board had no jurisdiction and the human rights commission was the appropriate forum to deal with the dispute. As Nadeau has noted, this approach restricts the exclusive jurisdiction of the arbitrator to the application and interpretation of the collective agreement as negotiated by the parties, and excludes from the arbitral domain working conditions or work-related protections that originate from statutes.[33] The dissociation this entails between the collective bargaining sphere and statutory rights is not likely to induce a coherent and harmonious integration of different sources of law into the labour relations system.[34]

While the majority decision appears to be conducive to a more coherent interplay between conventional and statutory workplace rules, some observers have underlined that the implicit incorporation theory must be understood as a legal fiction or metaphor, since it "can neither allow nor provide justification for the parties to appropriate these rules of public order and treat them as if they were rules of their own making, to the point where they could use them as they so wished, and dismiss them as they saw fit."[35] The better approach, as notably suggested by Fernand

32 *Parry Sound*, above note 13 at para 94.

33 Nadeau, "La perméabilité du droit," above note 17 at 227–28 (paras. 11-2)

34 Fernand Morin, "Pertinence, cohérence et conséquences de l'arrêt *Parry Sound*" in Barreau du Québec, Développements récents en droit du travail (Cowansville: Éditions Yvon Blais, 2004) 29 at 40 [Morin, "Pertinence, cohérence et conséquences"].

35 *Ibid* at 37 [author's translation]. As underlined by Morin, although the Canadian Constitution has a prominent character over statutes, one does not say that the Constitution is "incorporated" into statutes. In Quebec, the same argument can be

Morin, is that *Parry Sound* should be understood as promoting the harmonization of rules from different sources of law based on the hierarchy of norms in the legal system.[36]

On a practical level, given the relatively broad number of statutory standards in Quebec, the decision in *Parry Sound* raised questions about the exact scope of the implicit content of the collective agreement. In the civil law context, the general law in the *Civil Code of Quebec*[37] (*CCQ*) can be viewed as codified statutory law, in the sense that it is established through a statute which expresses the explicit will of the legislature. An entire chapter of the *CCQ* is dedicated to the contract of employment. This chapter goes beyond merely establishing a contractual framework, and sets out a number of substantive standards concerning the employment relationship.[38] As a result, the parties' obligations in relation to the contract of employment are partly imposed by the legislature through the general law, rather than being entirely subject to the parties' private will. The *CCQ* itself establishes an essential connection between the terms of statutory labour law and those of the *CCQ*, which makes their harmonization necessary. The nature of that harmonization is complex, however. While the preamble of the *CCQ* asserts that it is "the foundation of all other laws," it goes on to state that "other laws may complement the Code or make exceptions to it." As Pierre Verge has explained: "A conceptual harmonization between the Code and other laws is necessarily subject to any particular aims of the latter, which must otherwise show a clear intention to depart from the Code, in order to ensure coherence and stability in the legal order."[39] Thus, general law principles should be used to complement and interpret statutory labour laws and collective agreements, unless there is a clear legislative intention to disregard them.

---

made regarding the *Civil Code of Quebec*, which is not considered to be implicitly incorporated into contracts.

36 *Ibid* at 38–39.

37 SQ 1991, c 64.

38 For instance, the employer's obligation to protect the health, safety and dignity of the employee (art 2087 *CCQ*); the employee's obligation to act faithfully and honestly (art 2088 *CCQ*); the right to notice of termination (arts 2091 and 2092 *CCQ*); the imposition of restrictions on non-competition clauses (arts 2090 and 2095 *CCQ*); and the affirmation that a contract of employment is not terminated by alienation of the enterprise (art 2097 *CCQ*).

39 Pierre Verge, "Les lois du travail sous le prisme du nouveau code civil: Les premiers intervenants," in *Le Code civil et les relations de travail* (Québec: Département des relations industrielles de l'Université Laval, 1993) at 13. [translated by author].

The majority judgment in *Parry Sound* led many observers to conclude that the "public order" provisions of the *CCQ* were an implicit part of any collective agreement. However, not all actors adhered to this position, which led to contradictory decisions from labour arbitrators and conflicting judgments from the Superior Court. Confusion regarding the new contours of arbitral jurisdiction also came from sharp disagreements over whether some provisions of the *Act Respecting Labour Standards*[40] (*ALS*) should be implicitly incorporated into the collective agreement. Only a few provisions of the *ALS* are *expressly* incorporated into collective agreements. However, like most employment-related statutes in Quebec, the *ALS* states that its content is a matter of public order, and that any contrary provisions in an individual contract or collective agreement are void.[41]

In *Isidore Garon*, the Supreme Court took on the issue of whether and when provisions of the *CCQ* were incorporated into collective agreements. The majority addressed the question by enunciating a "compatibility test": if a statutory provision is compatible with the regime of collective labour relations and is a supplementary or mandatory norm, an arbitrator has the power to apply it. However, this decision did not dissipate the confusion, but rather added to it: the jurisdiction of the arbitrator now appeared even blurrier since it was not clear what the compatibility test really meant and whether it was relevant only insofar as the *CCQ* was concerned.

## 2) *Isidore Garon* and the Compatibility Test[42]

In *Isidore Garon*, the Supreme Court had to decide whether article 2091 *CCQ*, requiring reasonable notice on termination of employment was implicitly incorporated into a collective agreement.[43] The case dealt with

40 CQLR, c N-1.1.

41 *Ibid*, ss 93–94. A similar provision can be found in *An Act Respecting Occupational Health and Safety*, QCLR, c S-2.1, s 4, and in *An Act Respecting Industrial Accidents and Occupational Diseases*, CQLR, c A-3.001, s 4.

42 This section draws from Renée-Claude Drouin & Gilles Trudeau, "What Does *Isidore Garon* Mean for Arbitral Jurisdiction in Quebec?" (2007) 13:2 *Canadian Labour and Employment Law Journal* 347.

43 Arts 2091 and 2092 *CCQ*, which are relevant for the analysis, read as follows:

> 2091. Either party to a contract for an indeterminate term may terminate it by giving notice of termination to the other party.
>
> The notice of termination shall be given in reasonable time, taking into account, in particular, the nature of the employment, the specific circumstances in which it is carried on and the duration of the period of work;

the decisions of two separate employers, Isidore Garon ltée and Fillion et Frères, to close their businesses and dismiss their employees. Both employers gave notice of termination as required by the *ALS*, but the union in each case filed a grievance claiming additional compensation pursuant to the requirement set out in article 2091 *CCQ*. The collective agreement covering the employees of Isidore Garon ltée provided that section 82 *ALS* would apply in the event of a layoff of six months or more. The collective agreement establishing the conditions of employment for employees working for Fillion et Frères was silent on the subject. In both cases, the employer filed a preliminary objection challenging the jurisdiction of the arbitrator to hear grievances alleging violations of the *CCQ*. The arbitrators in both cases decided that they had jurisdiction to hear the grievance. On judicial review, however, the Superior Court affirmed the arbitrator's jurisdiction in one case but quashed the award in the other on the basis that the dispute did not arise from the interpretation or application of the collective agreement. These judgments were rendered before the Supreme Court decision in *Parry Sound*.

The Quebec Court of Appeal heard the *Isidore Garon* and *Fillion* appeals at the same time. Referring to *Parry Sound* and section 62 of the *Labour Code*, which states that a collective agreement "may contain any provision respecting conditions of employment which is not contrary to public order or prohibited by law," the Court of Appeal held that because of their public order character, articles 2091 and 2092 *CCQ*, were implicitly incorporated into the collective agreements. Thus, the Court of Appeal concluded that the arbitrators had jurisdiction to deal with the grievances.

By a 4:3 majority, the Supreme Court of Canada granted the employers' appeal, holding that articles 2091 and 2092 *CCQ* did not apply to the collective labour law regime. In the majority judgment, Deschamps J identified two different trends in the caselaw. The first pertains to the relationship between the collective labour law regime and the individual contract of employment, an issue that has been a subject of debate in Quebec for many years. Embodied in the *Paquet-McGavin Toastmaster* judgments, this line of cases "recognizes the autonomy of labour law, which is statute law of a social nature and which, as a result, supplants

---

2092. The employee may not renounce his right to obtain an indemnity for any injury he suffers where insufficient notice of termination is given or where the manner of resiliation is abusive.

the general law."[44] As interpreted by the majority, it stands for the proposition that individual freedom of contract between the employer and an employee, and the related law of general application, does not survive the coming into play of the collective labour relations scheme. The second line of cases, referred to by Deschamps J as the *Weber-Parry Sound* line, recognizes the jurisdiction of arbitrators to apply the substantive rights and obligations provided for in employment-related statutes and human rights legislation, which are implicitly incorporated into collective agreements.

Deschamps J sought to reconcile the apparently inconsistent principles put forward in these two lines of cases by enunciating a compatibility test: "if a rule is incompatible with the collective labour relations scheme, it cannot be incorporated [into the collective agreement] and must be disregarded. . . . If the rule is found to be compatible and if it is a supplementary or mandatory norm . . . the arbitrator will have jurisdiction to apply it."[45] However, she did not lay down a concrete and pragmatic test to be used to determine whether or not a legal norm is compatible with the regime of collective labour relations, nor did she identify which categories of legal norms had to be assessed for their compatibility. She limited herself to giving three reasons, based on the nature of notice of termination, for why article 2091 *CCQ* is not compatible with the regime of collective labour relations. First, "[n]otice of termination is essentially agreed to on an individual basis when employment is terminated, whereas collective conditions of employment are necessarily agreed to in advance by the union and the employer."[46] Second, notice of termination is a *quid pro quo* for the employer's right to sever the employment relationship at any time and without cause, whereas the collective agreement "seeks to preserve the continuity of the employment relationship,"[47] and limits the employer's right accordingly. And third, the legislative history of article 2091 *CCQ* highlights the legislature's intent not to require notice of termination in the context of collective labour relations. Based on these reasons, she held that the arbitrators did not have jurisdiction to hear either the Isidore Garon or Fillion grievances.

In the dissenting judgment, LeBel J agreed with the majority that the *Paquet-McGavin Toastmaster* line of cases precludes individual contracts

44 *Isidore Garon*, above note 11 at para 10.

45 *Ibid* at para 24.

46 *Ibid* at para 32.

47 *Ibid* at para 48.

of employment from contradicting the provisions of a collective agreement in a way that would undermine the collective labour relations scheme and the union's exclusive representation rights. However, he also stressed that

> the parties' ability to freely negotiate the substantive standards that will govern them is limited by the obligation to respect or incorporate into the agreement, the rights and values protected by the charters and the legal rules imposed by the legislature, including certain general principles of law, particularly those that are of public order.[48]

Further, he underlined the fact that section 62 of the *Labour Code* already provided for the implicit incorporation of substantive employment-related rights into any collective agreement, as enunciated in *Parry Sound*.[49] Without discarding the implicit incorporation argument and its usefulness, he stressed that in the context of the *CCQ*, "the use of the term 'incorporate'" might not be "entirely accurate."[50] For the first time, he put forward the "harmonization" concept, emphasizing the need to harmonize the various sources of labour law by establishing a hierarchy among them. Pointing out that a collective agreement cannot be contrary to public order, he held that articles 2091 and 2092 *CCQ* were provisions of public order.

Despite his emphasis on the public order character of articles 2091 and 2092 *CCQ*, however, LeBel J then went on to weigh the compatibility of these provisions with the collective labour relations scheme:

> The *C.C.Q.* contains provisions of public order that apply directly to labour relations. Under arts 2091 and 2091 *C.C.Q.*, an employee is entitled to reasonable notice of termination and may not renounce that right. *It must therefore be determined whether the right is incompatible with the collective labour relations scheme, in which case the union could not assert the right for the benefit of the employees it represents.*[51]

It was with regard to the compatibility of articles 2091 and 2092 *CCQ* with the collective labour law regime that the two sets of reasons really diverge.

48 *Ibid* at para 141.

49 *Ibid* at para 152.

50 *Ibid* at para 168.

51 *Ibid* at para 177 [emphasis added].

Unlike Deschamps J, LeBel J did not consider articles 2091 and 2092 to be incompatible with the collective labour relations scheme. In his words:

> There is nothing to prevent employees governed by a collective agreement from being entitled to reasonable notice under the *C.C.Q.* Far from being incompatible with the collective labour law scheme, arts 2091 and 2092 *C.C.Q.* supplement it and provide a remedy to employees who lose their jobs without being adequately compensated by their employer.[52]

He concluded by upholding the jurisdiction of the arbitrator to entertain the grievances in the cases at hand.

With regard to the first line of cases referred to by Deschamps J in the majority opinion, the decision settled the doctrinal disagreement over whether there is a residual right of individual negotiation on matters not covered by a collective agreement. Both the majority and dissenting reasons in *Isidore Garon* make it clear that, under the collective labour relations scheme, there is no room for employees to directly negotiate any condition of employment with the employer, whether or not the condition in question is addressed in the collective agreement. In addition, the Court explicitly spelled out that individual contracts of employment are not abolished in the collective labour law context, but *simply suspended*.[53] Finally, the entire Court recognized that the general law can be used to interpret the terms of a collective agreement. Since the *Labour Code* and the collective agreement do not contain all of the rules governing collective labour relations, referral to some provisions of the *CCQ* may be essential in order to establish the parties' rights and obligations.[54]

However, while both the majority and dissenting judgments recognized the role of the *CCQ* as a supplement to the collective agreement, they disagreed in part on how to determine which takes precedence. For the majority, Deschamps J rejected the view that the collective agreement

52 *Ibid* at para 189.

53 *Ibid* at para 27. On this issue, the dissenting judgment said: "there remains, at the very least, an individual act under which the employee is hired, and its effect, in any case, survives should the certification and the collective agreement cease to have effect." *Ibid* at para 133.

54 For instance, the employee's duty of loyalty, and the employer's obligation to pay the remuneration agreed upon can only be explained by reference to notions of general law. *See* Gilles Trudeau, "Synthèse des délibérations," in *Le Code civil et les relations de travail* (Québec: Département des relations industrielles de l'Université Laval, 1993) 79 at 85 [translated by author].

is superimposed onto the individual contract of employment,[55] preserving all rights which would be part of the individual contract except to the extent that they are incompatible with collective labour relations. Rather, she concluded that, "the collective agreement provides a framework into which mandatory norms are incorporated,"[56] and only those provisions of the *CCQ* that are compatible with the collective labour relations scheme are implicitly incorporated into collective agreements. LeBel J took a different view of the interplay between the rules arising from the collective agreement and the principles of general law. He pointed to the preliminary provision of the *CCQ* which establishes the nature of the Code as the *jus commune* of Quebec and the foundation of other laws. Since both the *CCQ*[57] and the *Labour Code*[58] give precedence to rules of public order over negotiated norms, he concluded that "a juridical act, such as a collective agreement, cannot derogate from the rules of the *C.C.Q.* that are of public order."[59] In other words, he applied a hierarchy of sources of law to determine precedence. (Nevertheless, LeBel J ultimately appeared to recognize, without explanation, the need to determine whether a statutory rule applicable to individual employment contracts is compatible with the collective labour law regime.)

Although the majority judgment raised the issue of the implicit incorporation of statutory rights into the collective agreement, it nonetheless represented a return to an approach whereby the contractual autonomy of the parties may prevail over the rules of public order.[60] The reasoning of the majority assumes that the establishment of collective labour relations in an enterprise restores a balance of power between the employees and their employer: "To say that an employee is isolated or vulnerable when he or she is represented by a union would be an affront to organized labour."[61] According to this perspective, union representation enables workers to obtain working conditions that are necessarily fair, and

---

55 This view, based on the preliminary provision of the *CCQ*, was promoted by Fernand Morin in Fernand Morin, "Effets combinatoires de deux codes: Code du travail et Code civil du Québec" (1994) 49:2 *Relations Industrielles* 227.

56 *Isidore Garon*, above note 11 at para 29.

57 *See* art 9 *CCQ*; art 1373 *CCQ*.

58 Above note 22 at s 62.

59 *Isidore Garon*, above note 11 at para 170.

60 Nadeau, "La perméabilité du droit," above note 17 at 229–230 (para.16).

61 *Isidore Garon*, above note 11 at para 59. *See* Vallée & Gesualdi-Fecteau, above note 6 at 186.

therefore the collective agreement, the result of negotiations between the parties, should prevail.[62] The end result of this case, however, shows the flaw in that line of reasoning; the laid-off employees here would have been better off not being unionized, as they would then have been entitled to reasonable notice under the *CCQ*!

The approach of the majority was largely met with disapproval in Quebec,[63] in particular because it goes against the principle of legislative supremacy, which requires the courts to fully apply any valid legislation. It seems illegitimate for the courts to second-guess the legislature by submitting a statute to a test — other than one of constitutional validity — before applying it. In Quebec, the relationship among the *Labour Code*, collective agreements negotiated pursuant to the *Code*, and other statutory law has always been governed by the principle of public order, and the underlying hierarchy of sources of law. According to section 62 of the *Labour Code* referred to earlier, the regime of collective labour relations must give way to any legislated rule that is explicitly or implicitly a matter of public order. The majority in *Isidore Garon* appeared to ignore this basic principle, or at least to set it aside in an effort to protect the integrity of the regime of collective labour relations. Yet, it is difficult to explain why a court should require arbitrators to disregard an employment standard that the legislature has made mandatory through the enactment of a specific employment statute.

The new approach adopted in *Isidore Garon* did not clarify the implicit incorporation argument established by *Parry Sound*. Rather, it raised further questions. What was the meaning of the compatibility test? What type of legal norms were subject to the test? With regard to the first question, the test was sometimes misread by labour arbitrators as a narrow test of compatibility between the particular provision of an employment-related statute and the specific terms of the collective agreement, rather than as a global test of whether the provision was compatible with the regime of collective labour relations. With regard to the second question, *Isidore Garon* related specifically to the interplay between the collective agreement and the *CCQ*, an issue that could not have been discussed in *Parry Sound* since that case originated in Ontario. This left room for the interpretation

62 Nadeau, "La perméabilité du droit," above note 17 at 230 (para.16).

63 *See e.g.*, Fernand Morin, "Être et ne pas être à la fois salarié! Ou les arrêts *Garon/Fillion* et le Code civil du Québec — Suites et poursuites," in Barreau du Québec, ed, *Développements récents en droit du travail 2006, volume 245* (Cowansville: Éditions Yvon Blais, 2006) 21; Drouin & Trudeau, above note 42.

that the compatibility test had only narrow application. However, some statements in the majority judgment appeared to imply that the Court had in fact revisited *Parry Sound*: "The principle that emerges from [*Parry Sound*] is that, if a rule is incompatible with the collective labour relations scheme, it cannot be incorporated and must be disregarded."[64] Following the ruling in *Isidore Garon*, most arbitrators applied the compatibility test broadly. It was acknowledged early that the compatibility test did not apply to the Quebec *Charter of Human Rights and Freedoms*.[65] However, other employment-related statutes were generally subjected to it by arbitrators and Superior Court judges alike, until the Quebec Court of Appeal stepped in to rule that *Isidore Garon* applied only to the *CCQ*.[66]

On a practical level, arbitrators have applied the test set out in *Isidore Garon* to a number of different provisions of the *Civil Code*. For example, article 2094 *CCQ* provides that "[o]ne of the parties may, for a serious reason, unilaterally resiliate the contract of employment without prior notice." Not surprisingly, this provision has been assimilated to articles 2091 and 2092 *CCQ* and thus declared incompatible with the collective labour relations regime. This means that an employee cannot rely on article 2094 *CCQ* to challenge his or her dismissal before a grievance arbitrator.[67] By contrast, articles 6 and 7 *CCQ*, which state that any right must be exercised in good faith, have been uniformly deemed to be implicitly incorporated into collective agreements. Arbitrators have ruled that these provisions impose a general standard of behaviour that applies to everyone and constitute matters of public order.[68] This means,

---

64 *Isidore Garon*, above note 11 at para 24.

65 CQLR, c C-12.

66 *Syndicat Canadien de la Fonction Publique (Section locale 4296) SCFP-FTQ c Seigneurie-des-Milles-Îles (Commission scolaire)*, 2006 QCCA 1646 [*SCFP-FTQ*]. See the analysis of this judgment and its implications in Vallée & Gesualdi-Fecteau, above note 6.

67 *SCFP-FTQ, ibid.* See also *Marguerite-Bourgeoys (Commission scolaire) c Choquette*, 2006 QCCS 3083 [*Choquette*]. Interestingly enough, most collective agreements contain a provision prohibiting the employer from dismissing an employee without just cause, a test very close to that set out in art 2094 *CCQ*.

68 *See e.g., Choquette, ibid*; *Syndicat des travailleuses et travailleurs en petite enfance de la Montérégie — CSN et Centre de la petite enfance les joyeux calinours* (2006), AZ-50352934, DTE 2006T-183; *Commission scolaire du Fer et Syndical de l'enseignement de la région du Fer*, AZ-55000191, DTE 2006T-940; *Laval (Ville de) et Syndicat des cols bleus de la Ville de Laval inc, section locale 4545 (SCFP)*, AZ-50381725, DTE 2006T-735.

for instance, that a probationary employee whose collective agreement precludes the right to grieve dismissal could nevertheless do so by claiming that the dismissal was in bad faith.[69]

Prior to the Court of Appeal's clarification regarding the breadth of the compatibility test in *SCFP-FTQ*,[70] the test had been applied to provisions of the *ALS*. The possible incorporation into collective agreements of section 124 *ALS*, which provides protection against unjust dismissal for employees with two or more years of continuous service in the same enterprise, gave rise to sharp debates and contradicting decisions. The Supreme Court was eventually called upon to address this question. In resolving the issue, the majority departed from the implicit incorporation argument and adopted yet another approach regarding the interplay between the collective agreement and employment-related statutory norms: the hierarchy of relevant sources of labour law.

### 3) *SFPQ* and the Hierarchy of Relevant Sources of Labour Law

The *Act Respecting Labour Standards*,[71] adopted by the Quebec legislature in 1979, is one of the cornerstones of Quebec's labour and employment law. It establishes minimum working conditions that cannot be set aside, for both unionized and non-unionized employees. These minimum standards relate to several aspects of work: wages, hours of work, holidays, family or parental leave, psychological harassment, termination of employment, etc. The *ALS* also provides for different kinds of recourse to ensure its proper implementation.[72] Until recently, the Commission des normes du travail was the public body in charge of overseeing the implementation of the *ALS*, receiving complaints related to the violation of the Act and representing employees in disputes against their employer.[73] Complaints under the *ALS* were heard by the Commission des relations du travail (CRT), an administrative tribunal created under the *Labour Code*, which also had jurisdiction to solve disputes arising from the implementation of the latter.

69 See cases cited above note 68. For an analysis of the application of the good faith principle in relation to the dismissal of probationary employees, *see* Sophie Cloutier & Jacques Provencher, "L'arrêt *SFPQ*: une mise à jour s'impose!," in La Conférence des arbitres du Québec, *Débats d'actualité, Volume 2* (Montréal: Wilson & Lafleur, 2014) 147 at 161–68.

70 *SCFP-FTQ*, above note 66.

71 *ALS*, above note 40.

72 *See* Chapter V of the *Act*.

73 *See e.g.*, *ALS*, above note 40, ss 39, 98–99.

Since January 1, 2016, the Commission's functions have been exercised by the newly created Labour Standards, Equity, Occupational Health and Safety Commission,[74] and the CRT has been replaced by the Administrative Labour Tribunal.[75]

The mandatory nature of the standards contained in the *ALS* flows from section 93 *ALS*:

> Subject to any exception allowed by this Act, the labour standards contained in this Act and the regulations are of public order.
>
> In an agreement or decree, any provision that contravenes a labour standard or that is inferior thereto is absolutely null.

There is no general provision incorporating the minimum standards it sets into every collective agreement, although a few provisions of the *ALS* are expressly incorporated into collective agreements.

The protection against unfair dismissals provided for in section 124 *ALS* is one of the specificities of Quebec's labour and employment law. It departs from the liberal approach to the termination of the employment contract embodied in articles 2091 and 2092 *CCQ*[76] and provides relative job security to employees who can prove that they have two years of uninterrupted service in an enterprise:

> 124. An employee credited with two years of uninterrupted service in the same enterprise who believes that he has not been dismissed for a good and sufficient cause may present his complaint in writing to the Commission des normes, de l'équité, de la santé et de la sécurité du travail or mail it to the address of the Commission des normes, de l'équité, de la santé et de la sécurité du travail within 45 days of his dismissal, except where a remedial procedure, other than a recourse in damages, is provided elsewhere in this Act, in another Act or in an agreement.
>
> If the complaint is filed with the Administrative Labour Tribunal within this period, failure to have presented it to the Commission des normes, de l'équité, de la santé et de la sécurité du travail cannot be set up against the complainant.[77]

Although section 124 *ALS* is found in Chapter V of the Act (referring to recourses) it has long been recognized as both a substantive and proced-

74 *An Act to Establish the Administrative Labour Tribunal*, CQLR, c T-15.1, s 239.

75 *Ibid*, s 1.

76 Art 2091 *CCQ*; art 2092 *CCQ*.

77 *ALS*, above note 40, s 124.

ural standard. This normative duality was affirmed by the Quebec Court of Appeal in *Produits Pétro-Canada Inc c Moalli*, almost thirty years ago.[78] On the substantive level, section 124 forbids the dismissal of an employee without just cause after the required two years of uninterrupted service. On the procedural level, it sets up a process for employees to contest an unfair dismissal—i.e., a dismissal that does not respect the substantive norm—and obtain reinstatement in the workplace or monetary compensation. The recourse provided for in section 124 is residual in nature; if there is an equivalent remedial procedure elsewhere in the *ALS*, another statute, or an agreement (including a collective agreement) which is available to the dismissed employee, this recourse is not accessible.

In *SFPQ*, the Supreme Court was required to determine whether an arbitrator could hear an unlawful dismissal complaint based on section 124 *ALS*. In two separate grievances, the union challenged the termination of a casual employee and a probationary employee of the Quebec government, pleading that they had been dismissed without good and sufficient cause. The collective agreement governing the parties expressly prevented employees in both these categories from grieving a termination of employment, thus denying them any job security. Both employees, however, had completed the two years of uninterrupted service required by section 124. While the employer acknowledged that the employees were subject to the protection granted by this provision, it disagreed with the union on the appropriate forum to hear the unlawful dismissal complaints. The union submitted that the arbitrator had jurisdiction over the matter, since section 124 was implicitly incorporated into the collective agreement. The employer argued that the CRT had exclusive jurisdiction to hear the cases.

The labour arbitrators hearing the two grievances came to differing conclusions. The Superior Court, on judicial review, adopted the position that section 124 was implicitly incorporated into the collective agreement, and held that the arbitrators had exclusive jurisdiction over the dismissal grievances. The Court of Appeal, however, rejected this approach. In its judgment, the Court stressed the importance of determining the legislature's intention where issues of jurisdiction were concerned. For the Court of Appeal, it appeared to be clear from the text of the *ALS* that the legislature had chosen a specialized tribunal, the CRT, rather than the grievance arbitrator, to hear complaints under section 124.

78 [1987] RJQ 261, JE 87-135.

Once again, the Supreme Court was strongly divided on the issue of arbitral jurisdiction. A majority of five judges granted the appeal, while four dissented. LeBel J, writing this time for the majority, set the background of his analysis by pointing out from the start of his reasons that the collective agreement at play must be considered in light of the overall legislative regime put in place in the province to oversee workplace relations.[79] Surprisingly, since the parties had centred their arguments on the question of whether section 124 *ALS* was implicitly incorporated into the collective agreement, LeBel J questioned the relevance of this approach for the cases under review:

> The parties are asking this Court to determine whether the substantive standard of public order set out in s. 124 A.L.S., which prohibits the dismissal without good and sufficient cause of an employee who has two years of uninterrupted service, is implicitly included in every collective agreement. In my view, the issue is framed incorrectly and does not reflect the true question raised by the appeals. To me, the issue is not whether the provisions of the A.L.S. are incorporated into the collective agreement or how jurisdiction is formally conferred on the C.R.T. *Rather, these appeals raise a question about the hierarchy of sources of Quebec labour law and more specifically about how the A.L.S., as a statute of public order, affects the content of the collective agreements and thus the jurisdiction conferred on the grievance arbitrators responsible for interpreting and applying such agreements.*[80]

After reviewing in detail the respective positions of the parties, LeBel J rejected the implicit incorporation argument on the ground that it was inconsistent with the drafting techniques used by the Quebec legislature to incorporate certain provisions of the *ALS* into collective agreements. Since some provisions of the *ALS* are expressly "deemed to be an integral part of every collective agreement,"[81] it appeared that the legislature did not intend that *all* provisions were implicitly incorporated. In particular, if the legislature had intended to incorporate section 124 into all collective agreements, it would have explicitly said so, using the same drafting technique that it used in other provisions of the Act.

79 *SFPQ*, above note 12 at para 5.

80 *Ibid* at para 25 [emphasis added].

81 *See ALS*, above note 40, ss 81.18, 81.19, 123.7, 123.15, & 123.16.

In LeBel J's view, the issue therefore had to be considered through the lens of the hierarchy of relevant sources of labour law:

> In my opinion, the perspective from which the status of the *A.L.S.* as a statute of public order must be considered here is not really that of whether the provisions of the *A.L.S.* are implicitly incorporated into collective agreements, but that of how the hierarchy of relevant sources of labour law affects the content and implementation of such agreements. Only by examining the agreement from the perspective of the adaptations flowing from this public order status can it be determined whether the grievance arbitrator or the C.R.T. has jurisdiction to rule on the challenges of the employees and their union against the employee's dismissal.[82]

Since section 124 *ALS* is a public order provision, the clauses of a collective agreement that deprive an employee who has accumulated two years of relevant service with an employer from protection against unfair dismissal must be "read out" of the agreement. It is the content of the collective agreement as modified by the impact of public order provisions that must be analyzed when deciding whether there is an equivalent recourse in the collective agreement for the purpose of section 124.

Applying this reasoning to the case before him, LeBel J went on to say that when the clauses prohibiting seasonal and probationary employees from contesting their dismissals are "read out" of the agreement, the general clause that provides for the right to file a grievance remains intact. The arbitration procedure is therefore open to all employees who have completed two years of uninterrupted service with the employer.[83] Furthermore, the arbitration procedure must be considered equivalent to a complaint before the CRT since both decision-makers have "similar powers of intervention and similar guarantees of independence and impartiality."[84] From this, LeBel J concluded that the arbitrators had jurisdiction to hear the complaints.

In her dissenting opinion, Deschamps J also rejected the argument put forward by the union that section 124 *ALS* was implicitly incorporated into the collective agreement. Referring to the majority judgment of the Supreme Court in *Morin*, she framed the issue as a question of legisla-

82 *SFPQ*, above note 12 at para 39.

83 *Ibid* at paras 50–53.

84 *Ibid* at para 52.

tive intention. In her view, since *Morin* had established that there was no exclusive arbitral jurisdiction "*in abstracto*," the relevant statutes had to be analyzed to determine whether the arbitrator or the CRT was the appropriate forum.[85] She concluded that in the case at hand, the legislature had chosen to entrust the dispute to a specialized tribunal, the CRT.[86] Although Deschamps J recognized that the parties could not deny an employee the protection against unfair dismissal granted by section 124 *ALS*, she held that they could place limitations on access to a grievance procedure under the collective agreement: "[t]hey cannot of course agree that an employee will not be protected. But there is no obligation to make a forum available to *all* employees under the agreement."[87] In her view, the language of section 81.20 *ALS* clearly acknowledged the possibility that substantive protection could be provided without access to a remedial process:

> The provisions of sections 81.18, 81.19, 123.7, 123.15 and 123.16, with the necessary modifications, are deemed to be an integral part of every collective agreement. An employee covered by such an agreement must exercise the recourses provided for in the agreement, insofar as any such recourse is available to employees under the agreement.[88]

Since the parties to the collective agreement had chosen *not* to give jurisdiction to a labour arbitrator on the matter, the collective agreement did not provide an "alternative recourse." Deschamps J concluded:

> An analysis of the legislature's intention shows that s. 124 A.L.S. cannot be incorporated implicitly into collective agreements. Reading words in is neither required nor even authorized by the A.L.S., the LC or the collective agreement. Reading words out is no more appropriate. Restrictions on the arbitration procedure are not contrary to public order, since they do not deprive employees of the protection afforded by the standard and recourse provided for in the A.L.S. To rewrite the collective agreement, it would have to be assumed that the legislature drafted the A.L.S. incoherently. It would also have to be assumed that the Quebec legislature adopted the model of exclusive arbitral jurisdiction for all disputes relating to the application of mandatory legislative stan-

85 *Ibid* at para 66.
86 *Ibid* at para 57.
87 *Ibid* at para 97.
88 *Ibid* at para 95.

> dards. These assumptions are unfounded. Parties to a collective agreement can choose to incorporate an adequate protection, and if they do so, the alternative forum provided for in s. 124 ALS will not be available. However, the parties did not choose to do so in respect of the employees concerned in these appeals.[89]

Deschamps J therefore would have protected the autonomy of the parties to negotiate access to the grievance procedure for certain categories of employees.

The *SFPQ* judgment, like its predecessors, illustrates how profoundly divided the Court can be on the arbitrator's jurisdiction to hear grievances based on employment-related statutory norms that cannot strictly be based on provisions of the collective agreement as negotiated by the parties. Although Deschamps J had concurred with the majority judgment in *Parry Sound*, she has subsequently become a fierce advocate of the autonomist approach to the interplay between the collective agreement and the plurality of norms applicable to the employment relationship. Her opinions (for the majority in *Isidore Garon* and the dissenters in *SFPQ*) manifest a deep respect for the parties' will and the working conditions they have actually negotiated in the collective agreement. They also display a certain caution, if not wariness, towards the incorporation of "foreign" norms — statutory norms that have not been negotiated by the parties — into the collective agreement. However, as mentioned above, this approach can lead to incongruous decisions, such as the exclusion of public order norms from the legal framework relevant to collective labour relations and arbitral jurisdiction. In *SFPQ*, Deschamps J distinguished the case under review from *McLeod*, *Parry Sound* and *Isidore Garon* on the ground that "the forum responsible for enforcing the rights in question was not in issue in any of those cases. Rather, what was in issue was the application of the substantive protection."[90] While this reasoning is solid with regard to the *McLeod* and *Isidore Garon* cases, it is much less convincing with regard to the judgment in *Parry Sound*, where not only the substantive protection was discussed, but also the choice of the appropriate forum — the arbitration board or the Human Rights Commission. In fact, Deschamps J's reasons in *SFPQ* are very close to the dissenting reasons of Major J in *Parry Sound*: both have the effect of placing the implemen-

89 *Ibid* at para 115.
90 *Ibid* at para 105.

tation of human rights or employment-related statutory norms outside the realm of arbitral jurisdiction based on the parties' intention to do so.

Curiously enough, while LeBel J had concurred with Major J's minority opinion in *Parry Sound*, his position evolved starting with *Isidore Garon*, followed by *SFPQ*, towards an approach that was much more akin to the majority judgment in the former case. In retrospect, LeBel J may have concurred with the dissenting opinion in *Parry Sound* in part because he had difficulty adhering to the implicit incorporation argument. His uneasiness with the implicit content of the collective agreement, already alluded to in *Isidore Garon*, appeared clearly in *SFPQ*, in which he favoured the hierarchy of different sources of labour law as his analytical approach. This conceptual framework is an interesting combination of legal pluralism and industrial pluralism since it recognizes the necessity to take into account the multiple sources of labour law — private as well as public — while placing the responsibility to articulate the interactions between these different sources in the hands of collective labour relations actors, including labour arbitrators. While this approach appears to have replaced the implicit incorporation argument in Quebec, the practical implications of this shift may be limited, as will be explained in the following section.

### 4) The Demise of the Implicit Incorporation Argument?

Not long after the Supreme Court's ruling in *SFPQ*, the Quebec Court of Appeal heard another case concerning the interplay between the collective agreement and the *ALS*.[91] This time, the issue centred around the jurisdiction of the arbitrator to hear a grievance based on sections 82 and 83 *ALS*. The collective agreement between the parties provided for one week's notice in the case where the company had to lay off one or several employees. Section 82 *ALS* provides for a period of notice in the case of a lay off for more than six months that varies in accordance with the number of years of uninterrupted service credited to each employee in the enterprise. Since the plaintiffs had accumulated more than ten years of service, they were entitled to eight weeks of paid notice under the *ALS*.[92] While the arbitrator designated by the parties to hear the case decided

91 *Syndicat des métallos, section locale 2843 (Métallurgistes unis d'Amérique section locale 2843) v 3539491 Canada inc*, 2011 QCCA 264 [*Syndicat des métallos*].

92 *ALS*, above note 40, s 82.

that he had jurisdiction to hear the grievance on the basis that sections 82 and 83 were implicitly incorporated into the collective agreement, the Superior Court took the opposite view and granted the judicial review of the arbitral award. The Court of Appeal, in its analysis, stressed that both the arbitrator and the Superior Court had heard the case before the Supreme Court judgment in *SFPQ*, "*which unanimously rejected the implicit incorporation argument* and favoured, by a majority, an approach based on 'how the hierarchy of relevant sources of labour law affects the content and implementation of such agreements.'"[93]

Both parties had modified their claims before the Court of Appeal in light of the new approach established in *SFPQ*. The union argued that the majority judgment in the latter had consecrated the arbitral jurisdiction to apply sections 82 and 83 *ALS*. The employer pleaded that if a clause in a collective agreement is considered null, then the issue is not within the ambit of the collective agreement and there is no ground for arbitral jurisdiction. In its reasons, the Court of Appeal recalled that, in accordance with *SFPQ*, it is the content of the collective agreement as modified by public order provisions that must be analyzed. Referring to *Weber* and *Bisaillon v Concordia University*,[94] the Court stressed that, in order to determine whether the arbitrator had jurisdiction, it had to ask whether the issue, in its essence, derived from the collective agreement. Since the parties had established provisions relating to paid notice in the case of a lay-off, the matter was deemed to be related to the interpretation and application of the collective agreement. The collective agreement deprived the employees of the protection afforded by a minimum standard of the *ALS*. Hence, the arbitrator had jurisdiction to apply sections 82 and 83, and to read the relevant clause of the collective agreement in accordance with these public order provisions.

In a subsequent case based on similar facts and arguments, the Quebec Court of Appeal reaffirmed its conclusion that the Supreme Court had dismissed the implicit incorporation argument in *SFPQ*.[95] One may ask whether this shift in approach has any conceptual or concrete implications. At first sight, the difference between the implicit incorporation argument and the hierarchy of different sources of law is slight, since

93 *Syndicat des métallos*, above note 91 at para 11 [translated by author].

94 2006 SCC 19.

95 *AGC Flat Glass North America Ltd c Syndicat national de l'automobile, de l'aérospatiale, du transport et des autres travailleuses et travailleurs du Canada (TCA-Canada)*, 2013 QCCA 381 at para 33.

both approaches lead to the nullity of provisions that are deemed contrary to human rights or employment-related norms of public order. Nevertheless, as Denis Nadeau clearly demonstrates,[96] there are, at a conceptual level, important differences between the two. In a thoughtful piece on the subject, Professor Nadeau argues that the hierarchy of sources is more in line with the "ordering" of different sources of law in the legal system. While the implicit incorporation argument implies a certain form of "collage" between the explicit and implicit content of the collective agreement through the migration of exterior norms into the collective agreement, the hierarchy of sources is more compatible with the collective autonomy of the parties. According to this latter approach, the intention of the parties will be respected as long as it is not contrary to "superior norms," i.e., those that have been prioritized by the legislature. Therefore, the content of the collective agreement will be modified only when such modification is necessary to ensure the harmonization of different sources of law.[97]

Before *SFPQ*, this approach had also been advocated by Guylaine Vallée. Her views on the matter were endorsed by LeBel J in the majority judgment:

> As Professor Guylaine Vallée correctly points out, [TRANSLATION] "[i]n the collective labour relations context, it is up to the parties to give effect to the hierarchy of sources under the collective agreement or during the grievance process. The interplay among the rules deriving from those sources in a unionized environment must be determined by collective labour relations authorities and not outside such authorities."[98]

As noted earlier, this approach preserves the collective autonomy of the parties, while taking into account the plurality of labour law sources.

In light of this change in approach in envisioning the interplay between the collective agreement and public order norms, some earlier

96 Nadeau, "La perméabilité du droit," above note 17 at 236–37 (para 32).

97 *See* Carole Sénéchal, "Le contenu explicite de la convention collective, un leurre?" (2013) 43 *Revue Générale de Droit* 89 at 122–24.

98 *SFPQ*, above note 12 at para 44, citing Guylaine Vallée, "Les lois de l'emploi et la convention collective," in Dominic Roux & Anne-Marie Laflamme, eds, *Rapports hiérarchiques ou anarchiques des règles en droit du travail: Chartes, normes d'ordre public, convention collective, contrat de travail, etc.* (Montréal : Wilson & Lafleur Ltée, 2008) 81 at 88. This was also advocated by Fernand Morin, as previously mentioned: Morin, "Pertinence, cohérence et conséquences," above note 34.

findings concerning arbitral jurisdiction have been called into question. For instance, the arbitrator's jurisdiction to hear the grievance of a probationary employee contesting his or her dismissal on the basis of good faith requirements, which had been recognized by courts and arbitrators prior to *SFPQ*, was challenged again on the ground that articles 6 and 7 *CCQ* were no longer implicitly incorporated into the collective agreement. Both the Superior Court and, subsequently, the Court of Appeal for Quebec rejected this point of view,[99] reasoning that public order provisions overrule a collective agreement that deprives an employee of his right to grieve a dismissal on the ground of employer abuse or bad faith, regardless of whether or not those provisions are incorporated into the collective agreement. Therefore, it appears that the shift from the implicit incorporation argument to the hierarchy of different sources of labour law argument does not lead to contradictory solutions in practice. In fact, as one author suggested, the two arguments might be regarded as "functionally equivalent."[100]

There is no clear indication in the caselaw that courts and arbitrators in other provinces have embraced the new approach set out by LeBel J in *SFPQ*. In fact, *Isidore Garon* and *SFPQ* are seldom referred to outside of Quebec. The distinctive legal character of the *CCQ* might explain the lack of attention *Isidore Garon* has received in Canadian provinces with a common law tradition. The principles established in *SFPQ* appear of a more general application, especially since the framework for collective labour relations is very similar in all provinces. Still, *SFPQ* reflects a bias in favour of arbitral jurisdiction that seems stronger in Quebec than in the rest of Canada, as the analysis in the next part will show.

## B. DO HUMAN RIGHTS TRIBUNALS AND LABOUR ARBITRATORS HAVE CONCURRENT JURISDICTION OVER HUMAN RIGHTS ISSUES?

The lessons from *Weber* have been applied in multiple contexts, including situations where it has been necessary to determine which of two com-

99 *See Société de transport de l'Outaouais c Dumoulin*, 2011 QCCS 6025; *Centre de santé et de services sociaux de Bécancour-Nicolet-Yamaska c Sexton*, 2013 QCCA 233.

100 Michel Coutu, "Les décisions récentes de la Cour suprême du Canada sur l'article 124 de la Loi sur les normes du travail: la quadrature du Cercle?" in *Arbitrage de griefs*, Cowansville, Éditions Yvon Blais, La Collection Blais, volume 8-2011, 223 at 246.

peting statutory regimes should hear a dispute.[101] One of the most enduring questions in this regard has been whether labour arbitrators and human rights tribunals have concurrent jurisdiction over human rights issues arising in unionized workplaces. Arbitral jurisdiction over human rights claims has largely been recognized since *Weber*, but whether these claims fall within the exclusive domain of the labour arbitrator has been subject to debates and conflicting views. One aspect of the question, of course, pertains to the specific provisions granting apparently competing jurisdiction to a human rights body. In Quebec, the enforcement system for human rights established by the *Charter of Human Rights and Freedoms*[102] is a "gatekeeper" model. Complaints of statutory violations are filed with the Human Rights Commission, which filters the cases, offers mediation services and makes decisions about which disputes will go before the Human Rights Tribunal for adjudication.[103] The jurisdiction of the Commission and the Tribunal are not exclusive, and there is a civil recourse through which human rights violations can be brought before the general courts.[104]

The Quebec Human Rights Tribunal has historically considered itself competent to hear disputes related to equality rights in unionized workplaces and has developed its own caselaw on the matter.[105] The intrusion of the Tribunal into a field generally considered to be the realm of labour arbitrators has provoked mixed reactions.[106] Some observers have denounced the "usurpation" of the arbitrator's jurisdiction by the Tribunal on the ground that it could jeopardize the integrity of the collective labour relations regime, and argued that arbitrators are well-equipped to deal with equality rights specific to unionized workplaces, an issue on which

---

101 *See e.g., Regina Police Association v Regina (City) Police Commissioners*, 2000 SCC 14.

102 *Quebec Charter of Rights and Freedoms*, above note 65.

103 *See ibid*, ss 71–85.

104 *Ibid*, s 77.

105 Denis Nadeau, "Le tribunal des droits de la personne du Québec et le principe de l'exclusivité de l'arbitrage de grief ou l'histoire d'une usurpation progressive de compétence" (2000) 60 *Revue du Barreau* 387 [Nadeau, "Le tribunal des droits"]; Marc Mancini, "Les droits et libertés de la personne en milieu syndical: l'arbitre de grief ou le Tribunal des droits de la personne, quel est le forum compétent?" (2009) 68 *Revue du Barreau* 327.

106 For an overview of different opinions, *see* Guylaine Vallée et al, *Le droit à l'égalité: les tribunaux d'arbitrage et le Tribunal des droits de la personne* (Montréal, Les Éditions Thémis, 2004).

they have developed a specific expertise.[107] Others have argued that concurrent jurisdiction is essential to avoid the development of two different regimes of equality rights, and to ensure that each individual employee is not deprived of his fundamental rights and has access to an adjudicative body.[108] Studies have analyzed how these two different adjudicative bodies have applied the right to equality in unionized workplaces.[109]

Since the Supreme Court judgments in *Parry Sound*[110] and *Morin*, however, the Quebec Court of Appeal has adopted a more restrictive view of the degree to which the Tribunal has concurrent jurisdiction to deal with complaints arising in unionized workplaces, taking the view that only cases deemed to raise questions pertaining to the "negotiation" of the collective agreement, as opposed to its "application and interpretation," attract concurrent jurisdiction. However, as noted in the introduction, human rights tribunals and courts in the rest of Canada take a different approach, generally considering that tribunals and arbitrators have broad concurrent jurisdiction.[111] Therefore Quebec's more restrictive approach to the jurisdiction of the provincial Human Rights Tribunal stands virtually alone. This situation appears to result from discrepancies in the application of the two-step approach to solving conflicts of jurisdiction between two specialized tribunals, as outlined by the Supreme Court in *Morin*.

---

107 *See* Nadeau, "Le tribunal des droits," above note 105; Diane Veilleux, "Tribunal des droits de la personne du Québec, arbitre de griefs: quel doit être le forum compétent?" in Guylaine Vallée et al, eds, *Le droit à l'égalité: les tribunaux d'arbitrage et le Tribunal des droits de la personne* (Montréal, Les Éditions Thémis, 2004) 215.

108 François Lamoureux, "Commentaires" in Guylaine Vallée et al, eds, *Le droit à l'égalité: les tribunaux d'arbitrage et le Tribunal des droits de la personne* (Montréal, Les Éditions Thémis, 2004) 121.

109 *See* Vallée et al, above note 106; Chantal Robert and Guylaine Vallée, "Le traitement des plaintes concernant la discrimination en matière d'emploi par l'arbitre et par le Tribunal des droits de la personne du Québec: une étude comparative exploratoire" (2000) 41 *Les Cahiers de Droit* 95.

110 Note that in *Parry Sound* the majority considered it "unnecessary" to determine at this point in time whether this jurisdiction was concurrent with that of the Ontario Human Rights Commission. *Parry Sound*, above note 13 at para 15.

111 Shilton, "Choice, but No Choice," above note 15. *See also* Elizabeth Shilton, "Labour Arbitration and Public Rights Claims: Forcing Square Pegs into Round Holes" (2016) 41:2 *Queen's Law Journal* 275 [Shilton, "Square Pegs into Round Holes"].

### 1) *Morin* and the Two-Step Approach

*Morin* concerned the identification of the proper forum to hear a discrimination complaint arising from modifications made in 1997 to the collective agreement of teachers in Quebec. At that time, in order to reach its zero deficit target, the government had planned a broad range of cost-saving measures. As part of these measures, it had negotiated with the teachers' union an amendment to the collective agreement imposing a one-year freeze on the accumulation of experience for teachers who had not reached the top of the salary grid. A group of younger teachers impacted by the amendment filed an age discrimination complaint with the human rights commission, arguing that their right to equality had been violated since they were being treated less favourably than older teachers. The respondents — the parties who had negotiated the contested modifications — asked the Human Rights Tribunal to decline jurisdiction on the basis that the issue fell within the exclusive jurisdiction of grievance arbitration. The Tribunal rejected the respondents' motion to dismiss. This decision was initially reversed by the Court of Appeal, but finally upheld by the Supreme Court. Writing for the majority, McLachlin CJC framed the issue in light of the earlier judgment of the Court in *Weber*: "*Weber* does not stand for the proposition that labour arbitrators always have jurisdiction in employer-union disputes. Depending on the legislation and the nature of the dispute, other tribunals may possess overlapping jurisdiction, concurrent jurisdiction, or themselves be endowed with exclusive jurisdiction."[112]

Having established that there was "no legal presumption of exclusivity *in abstracto*"[113] for arbitral jurisdiction, she outlined a two-step approach for determining whether arbitral jurisdiction over a specific type of dispute was exclusive: "The first step is to look at the relevant legislation and what it says about the arbitrator's jurisdiction. The second step is to look at the nature of the dispute, and see whether the legislation suggests it falls exclusively to the arbitrator."[114] Applying the first step, the Chief Justice looked first at the relevant provisions of the *Labour Code*, which she interpreted as establishing exclusive jurisdiction for arbitrators over issues pertaining to the interpretation and application of the collective agreement. She then analyzed the Quebec *Charter of Human*

112 *Morin*, above note 14 at para 11.

113 *Ibid* at para 14.

114 *Ibid* at para 15.

*Rights and Freedoms* and stressed that while the Quebec Human Rights Tribunal had a broad mandate "for interpreting and applying the *Charter* in a wide range or circumstances,"[115] its jurisdiction was not exclusive.

Turning to the second step, McLachlin CJC recalled the instructions given by the majority in *Weber* to determine whether the arbitrator has exclusive jurisdiction over a given dispute: "We must look at the dispute in its full factual context. Its legal characterization — whether it is a tort claim, a human rights claim, or a claim under the labour contract — is not determinative."[116] Examining the case under review, she characterized the conflict between the protagonists as a problem related to the inclusion of a discriminatory clause in the text of the collective agreement. The "essence of the dispute" therefore lay in "the process of the negotiation"[117] of the collective agreement, rather than in its operation. Since the issue could not strictly be regarded as a matter of the interpretation and application of the collective agreement, arbitral jurisdiction could not be exclusive. Therefore, the Human Rights Tribunal could exercise its own jurisdiction over the complaint.

Chief Justice McLachlin recognized that the claim could have been brought before an arbitrator, but concluded that the latter would only have had concurrent jurisdiction over the matter. She gave four reasons to justify this holding. First, "the nature of the question does not lend itself to characterization as a grievance *under* the collective agreement, since the claim [was] not that the agreement ha[d] been violated, but that it [was] itself discriminatory."[118] Second, if the union had refused to grieve the dispute because it had conflicting interests with the plaintiffs, the latter would have been left without recourse.[119] Third, if a grievance had been lodged, "the arbitrator would not have [had] jurisdiction over all the parties to the dispute" since the arbitral process provided for in the collective agreement was directed at the local parties, and the amendment had been negotiated at the provincial level between the *Centrale des syndicats du Québec* and the Minister.[120] Finally, given the breadth of the

115 *Ibid* at para 18.
116 *Ibid* at para 20.
117 *Ibid* at para 23.
118 *Ibid* at para 27.
119 *Ibid* at para 28.
120 *Ibid* at para 29.

dispute and the number of teachers involved, the Human Rights Tribunal appeared to be a "better fit."[121]

Bastarache J, dissenting, also stressed the need to "identify the essential character of the dispute in its factual context and ignore the possible legal characterization of that dispute."[122] Like McLachlin CJC, he took the position that the jurisdictional question must be answered by applying the *Weber* test: in other words, by analysing and determining "the nature of the dispute and the ambit of the collective agreement."[123] However, he strongly disagreed with McLachlin CJC as to the outcome of that analysis in the case before the Court. In Bastarache J's view, the issue, in its essence, concerned the reimbursement of lost salary and experience.[124] These subjects "form the very foundation of a contract and working conditions,"[125] and therefore fall within the ambit of the collective agreement. Thus, in his view, the arbitrator had exclusive jurisdiction over the claim.

Accordingly, the disagreement between McLachlin CJC and Bastarache J focused on what constituted the "essential character" of the dispute. In *Weber*, referring to *St Anne Nackawic Pulp & Paper Co v Canadian Paper Workers Union, Local 219*,[126] the majority had underlined the factual context as the central element in determining whether an arbitrator had exclusive jurisdiction: "one *must look not* to the legal characterization of the wrong, but to the facts giving rise to the dispute."[127] While Bastarache J strictly followed this approach in his dissenting opinion, McLachlin CJC subtly opened the door to considering the legal characterization of the issue as an element of the analysis. As some authors have noted, identifying the dispute as pertaining more to the negotiation of the collective agreement than to its interpretation is not simply a matter of factual context, but also of legal characterization.[128]

---

121 *Ibid* at para 30.

122 *Ibid* at para 33.

123 *Ibid* at para 46.

124 *Ibid* at para 57.

125 *Ibid* at para 57.

126 [1986] 1 SCR 704, 28 DLR (4th) 1 [*St Anne-Nackawic*].

127 *Weber*, above note 1 at para 49 [emphasis added].

128 Christian Brunelle and Mélanie Samson, "Les conflits de compétence entre tribunaux spécialisés: une question de textes ou de contextes?" (2008-2009) 39 *Revue de droit de l'Université de Sherbrooke* 223 at 246. *See also* the strong criticisms raised in Denis Nadeau, "L'arrêt *Morin* et le monopole de représentation des syndicats: assises d'une fragmentation" (2004) 64 *Revue du Barreau* 161.

A similar shift in the approach to determining the essential character of the dispute has been noticeable in judgments of appellate courts outside Quebec, which have both concluded that labour arbitrators and human rights tribunals have concurrent jurisdiction over human rights claims arising in unionized workplaces. Conversely, an analysis of the Quebec Court of Appeal's judgments following *Morin* shows that Court applying the two-step approach in a manner that is much more consistent with the previous ruling of the Supreme Court in *Weber* than the judgments of its provincial counterparts. These differences are discussed below.

### 2) The Follow-Up to *Morin* in Quebec

Since the decision of the Supreme Court in *Morin* more than a decade ago, the Quebec Court of Appeal has had to intervene on a number of occasions to solve conflicts of jurisdiction in cases concerning allegations of discrimination in unionized workplaces. In these cases, the Court has respectfully followed the majority ruling in *Morin*. In assessing the factual context of discrimination claims, it has made a clear distinction between issues concerning the negotiation process and those related to the operation of the collective agreement. Two decisions rendered on the topic by the Court of Appeal not long after the judgment in *Morin* concerned the validity of agreements reached by unions and employers to fulfill the requirements of the *Pay Equity Act*.[129] Like other similar legislation in Canada, this statute aims to "redress differences in compensation due to the systemic gender discrimination suffered by persons who occupy positions in predominantly female job classes."[130] Differences in compensation must be evaluated and pay equity plans must be put in place in the enterprise to remedy wage inequalities. In *Université Laval c Commission des droits de la personne et des droits de la jeunesse*,[131] the Court of Appeal concluded that the Human Rights Tribunal was the appropriate forum to hear a systemic discrimination complaint lodged by several office workers who alleged that the pay equity agreement reached by their union and their employer under the provisions of the *Pay Equity Act* violated their equality rights under the Quebec *Charter of Human Rights and Freedoms*. The Court concluded that, in its factual context, the dispute related to

129 CQLR, c E.12-001.

130 *Ibid*, s 1.

131 2005 QCCA 27.

allegations of systemic wage discrimination ensuing from the negotiation of the pay equity agreement between the union and the employer.[132] Hence, in direct line with *Morin*, the Court of Appeal found that the question pertained to the process of negotiation leading to the adoption of the pay equity agreement alleged to be discriminatory, and its insertion into the collective agreement.[133] These facts supported recognition that the Human Rights Tribunal had concurrent jurisdiction.[134]

In a subsequent similar case,[135] the Court of Appeal had to decide whether the Human Rights Tribunal had jurisdiction to hear a complaint from employees challenging the validity of a pay equity agreement once the union had submitted a grievance to a labour arbitrator on the same ground. The case revolved around the application of sections 49 and 77[136] of the *Quebec Charter*, and the question of whether the plaintiffs had exercised an alternative recourse leading to the remedies provided for

---

132 *Ibid* at para 41.

133 *Ibid* at para 42.

134 *Ibid* at para 45.

135 *Université de Montréal c Commission des droits de la personne et des droits de la jeunesse*, 2006 QCCA 508 [*Université de Montréal*].

136 These sections read as follows:

> s 49. Any unlawful interference with any right or freedom recognized by this Charter entitles the victim to obtain the cessation of such interference and compensation for the moral or material prejudice resulting therefrom.
>
> In case of unlawful and intentional interference, the tribunal may, in addition, condemn the person guilty of it to punitive damages.
>
> s 77. The commission shall refuse or cease to act in favour of the victim where
>
> (1) the victim or the complainant so requests, subject to the commission›s ascertaining that such request is made freely and voluntarily;
>
> (2) the victim or the complainant has, on the basis of the same facts, personally pursued one of the remedies provided for in sections 49 and 80.
>
> The commission may refuse or cease to act in favour of the victim where
>
> (1) the complaint is based on acts or omissions the last of which occurred more than two years before the filing of the complaint;
>
> (2) the victim or the complainant does not have a sufficient interest;
>
> (3) the complaint is frivolous, vexatious or made in bad faith;
>
> (4) the victim or the complainant has, on the basis of the same facts, personally pursued a remedy other than those provided for in sections 49 and 80.
>
> The decision of the commission shall state in writing the reasons on which it is based and indicate any remedy which the commission may consider appropriate; it shall be notified to the victim and the complainant.

in the *Charter*, in which case, the Human Rights Commission and the Tribunal were entitled to dismiss the case.[137] The Court concluded that the Tribunal was not required to dismiss the case since, as in *Morin*, arbitral jurisdiction was not exclusive. Moreover, the Court declared that the Tribunal was a more appropriate forum in this context since it could grant some remedies to ensure respect for the provisions of the *Pay Equity Act* that were not within the powers of the arbitrator, including an order to develop and put in place a new pay equity plan.[138]

In *Résidences Laurendeau, Légaré, Louvain c Tribunal des droits de la personne*,[139] the employer, a long-term care facility, had established a gender-oriented job allocation policy—with which the union had concurred—whereby positions and duties in connection with intimate care were assigned to employees based on the beneficiaries' gender preferences. A number of employees filed sex discrimination complaints, and the issue arose as to whether the Human Rights Tribunal or arbitration was the appropriate forum to settle the dispute. The Court of Appeal concluded that while the Tribunal and the labour arbitrator had concurrent jurisdiction to hear the case, the Tribunal was the "better fit" to resolve the dispute, since the union had agreed to the challenged policy.[140] In her examination of the essential character of the dispute, Rayle J, writing for the Court, stressed that the factual context had to be analyzed in its entirety. In this instance, this meant considering not only the equality rights issues raised by the employees, but also the beneficiaries' fundamental rights to dignity and privacy.[141] Taking into account all these elements, the Court concluded that the Human Rights Tribunal was the appropriate forum.

*Montréal (Ville de) c Audigé*[142] raised a somewhat different problem. The case challenged an article of the collective agreement providing that when "two employees had the same general seniority date, the determining factor was the birth date."[143] Due to this provision, the plaintiff, M Audigé, had lost three seniority ranks in favour of colleagues who were older than he was but had been hired after him. The unique feature of the case was

137 *Université de Montréal*, above note 135.

138 *Ibid* at paras 69, 72.

139 2005 QCCA 572.

140 *Ibid* at para 19.

141 *Ibid* at para 37.

142 2013 QCCA 171 [*Audigé*].

143 *Ibid* at para 12.

that the provision in question had not been negotiated between the union and the employer, but imposed through interest arbitration.

The union refused to file a grievance and the plaintiff therefore initiated a complaint before the Human Rights Commission, which considered the allegations of discrimination sufficient, but nevertheless exercised its discretionary power not to submit an application to the Human Rights Tribunal.[144] Quebec law gives individual employees the right to proceed directly to court in these circumstances, a right which the plaintiff exercised in this case. The employer filed a motion to dismiss, alleging that the issue concerned the application of the collective agreement, and the plaintiff's only recourse was a duty of fair representation (DFR) complaint against his union. The lower court's decision to dismiss the employer's motion was confirmed by the Court of Appeal, which held that the allegations raised by the plaintiff were related to the inclusion of a discriminatory clause in the collective agreement, a situation for which arbitral jurisdiction is not exclusive, as established by *Morin*. The Court held that a DFR complaint would likely be illusory[145] since the employee would have to prove that the union had acted "in bad faith or in an arbitrary or discriminatory manner or show[ed] serious negligence."[146] The Court distinguished the case from *SFPQ*, on the ground that the issue was not the ambit of the collective agreement or how it should be interpreted, but the existence of a clause alleged to be discriminatory. It held that the court therefore had jurisdiction to hear the plaintiff's claim in damages.[147]

By contrast, claims of discrimination in the workplace related to the application and interpretation of the collective agreement have been considered to fall under the exclusive jurisdiction of the arbitrator. In *Golzarian c Québec (Procureur général)*,[148] the Court of Appeal had to decide the proper forum to hear the complaint of a former Sûreté du Québec employee who claimed that he had been the victim of discrimination and harassment in the workplace because of his Iranian origins. His employment was terminated after he had been absent on sick leave for more than four years. While the union representing him had filed a grievance on his behalf to challenge his dismissal, Mr Golzarian had also filed a

144 See *Quebec Charter of Human Rights and Freedoms*, above note 65, s 84.

145 *Audigé*, above note 142 at paras 44–45.

146 *Labour Code*, above note 22, s 47.2.

147 *See also Université de Sherbrooke c Commission des droits de la personne et des droits de la jeunesse*, 2015 QCCA 1397.

148 *Golzarian c Québec (Procureur général)*, 2006 QCCA 1571.

lawsuit with the Superior Court and a complaint with the Human Rights Commission. In its judgment, the Court of Appeal held that while the allegations of discrimination and bullying raised by the plaintiff were very serious, they pertained to workplace relations and fell under the statutory grievance mechanism. The Court concluded that the plaintiff should have followed the procedure provided for in his collective contract of employment rather than pressing on to bring a claim before the Superior Court.[149] Unfortunately in this case, Mr Golzarian's lawyers had instructed the union to abandon the proceedings before the arbitrator.

Similarly, in *Québec (Procureur général) c Désir*,[150] the Court of Appeal had to decide whether the arbitrator had sole jurisdiction over a dispute concerning the dismissal of an employee who alleged that her termination was abusive and discriminatory. In this case, the collective agreement contained a provision that deprived the arbitrator of the power to grant damages when deciding a dispute. The union had grieved the dismissal and reached a settlement with the employer, but not to the employee's satisfaction. The employee therefore sued her former employer in the Court of Quebec for compensatory and punitive damages under section 49 of the Quebec *Charter*. The Court of Appeal concluded that the dispute was purely a matter of employment relations and derived from the exercise by the employer of his management rights under the collective agreement. The Court of Appeal acknowledged that the provision of the collective agreement depriving the arbitrator of the power to award damages might prevent the award of a remedy in cases where equality rights were violated. However, the Court of Appeal held that the validity of this provision, in the factual context, would have to be analyzed by the arbitrator, who had exclusive jurisdiction to settle the issue, in line with the Supreme Court ruling in *Parry Sound*. As the Court saw it, the arbitrator's power to interpret statutes would give him or her power to apply section 49 of the Charter, which provides for the award of compensatory and punitive damages in cases of discrimination.

This latter case illustrates just how difficult it can be to draw a clear line, as the Quebec Court of Appeal has consistently attempted to do, between cases involving inclusion in the collective agreement of a clause that violates human rights protections and cases involving the application and interpretation of the collective agreement. These judgments

---

149 *Ibid* at para 54.

150 2008 QCCA 1755.

clearly show, however, that the exclusive jurisdiction of labour arbitrators over issues related to the operation of the collective agreement is uncontested, even when those cases raise human rights issues. The difficulty lies in identifying the essential character of the dispute.

### 3) The Legal Ground for Concurrent Jurisdiction over Human Rights Issues between Human Rights Tribunals and Labour Arbitrators in other Canadian Provinces

The concurrent jurisdiction of labour arbitration boards and human rights tribunals has been affirmed by at least three provincial Courts of Appeal outside Quebec: the Saskatchewan Court of Appeal, the Alberta Court of Appeal and the Nova Scotia Court of Appeal. The decision of the Saskatchewan Court of Appeal on the matter in *Cadillac Fairview Corp Ltd v Saskatchewan (Human Rights Commission)*[151] came a few years after the judgment of the Supreme Court in *Weber*, but before the judgments in *Parry Sound* and *Morin*. It concerned two complaints filed with the Saskatchewan Human Rights Commission dealing with sexual harassment and discrimination in a unionized workplace, and raised the question of the appropriate jurisdiction to hear the claims. The Saskatchewan Court distinguished the case from *Weber*, pointing out that the latter "dealt with circumstances where a party to a collective agreement has tried to assert a concurrent common law right" rather than with "circumstances where there is a parallel competing statutory right of a public interest nature which arises out of the employment relationship."[152] Even though the relevant collective agreement expressly prohibited discrimination, including on grounds of sex, the Court held that the essential nature of the dispute was a human rights violation. In the Court's view "the fact the parties have included a covenant to comply with the Code in the collective agreement cannot change the essential character of the dispute."[153] The Court underlined that the complaint procedure provided for in the *Saskatchewan Human Rights Code* was the only "method of enforcement of the substantive rights" within the code, and that it "foreclose[d] any cause of action at common law."[154] The Court therefore concluded that the specialized human rights tribunal was competent to deal with the

151 (1999), 173 DLR (4th) 609, [1999] 7 WWR 517 [*Cadillac Fairview*].
152 *Ibid* at para 22.
153 *Ibid* at para 30.
154 *Ibid* at para 32.

matter. In stark contradiction to the lessons from *Weber*, the Court analyzed the "essential nature" of the dispute in light of its legal characterization, rather than considering its factual context and whether it related to the interpretation and application of the collective agreement. The Court also implied that the jurisdiction of a human rights tribunal was exclusive, a conclusion which, in my view, can no longer be considered valid after *Parry Sound.*

For its part, the Alberta Court of Appeal, in two different judgments released concurrently in 2007, held that the jurisdiction of a labour arbitrator to settle a dispute over allegations of discrimination and human rights violations in the course of a grievance was not exclusive, but rather was concurrent with the jurisdiction of the Alberta Human Rights and Citizenship Commission. The factual background of both cases was very similar. Considering that they had been discharged on discriminatory grounds (physical and mental disability), the employees had filed both a grievance and a human rights complaint to challenge their terminations. In *Amalgamated Transit Union, Local 583 v Calgary (City)*,[155] the union grieved the dismissal on the ground that there were "insufficient warnings and notice prior to the termination." Although the collective agreement contained a clause prohibiting discrimination, that clause was not expressly mentioned in the grievance. By contrast, the employee's human rights complaint alleged discrimination on several grounds. At the arbitration hearing, the employer asked the arbitration board to deal with the human rights aspects of the employee's complaint. The Union objected that it had chosen not to challenge these aspects of the dispute through the grievance procedure, electing instead to let the employee pursue them through a complaint to the Commission. The arbitration board decided that it had exclusive jurisdiction over the entire dispute.

The Court of Appeal ruled that since there was a question of competing jurisdiction between two specialized tribunals, the exclusivity of arbitral jurisdiction could not be presumed, and the two-step approach outlined by the majority of the Supreme Court in *Morin* had to be applied. Looking at the intent of the Alberta legislature in enacting the *Labour Relations Code*[156] and the *Human Rights, Citizenship and Multiculturalism Act*,[157] the Court considered the wording used in sections 135 and 136 of the

155 2007 ABCA 121 [*ATU*].

156 RSA 2000, c L-1.

157 RSA 1985, c H-11.7, as repealed by *Alberta Human Rights Act*, RSA 2000, c A-25.5.

former, which conferred jurisdiction on labour arbitrators. Comparing the relevant provisions with those used in the Ontario statute considered in *Weber* and the Quebec statute analyzed in *Morin*, the Court observed that: "the language in the Alberta statute is arguably weaker than either of them."[158] It insisted that "clearer and more explicit language would be needed to oust the jurisdiction of the Commission over all human rights issues that arise in a unionized workplace."[159] The Court also stressed an additional difference between the statutory frameworks in Quebec and Alberta: "unlike the Quebec legislation at issue in *Morin*, the Alberta *Human Rights Act* does not contain a deferral clause that would allow the Commission to stop acting on behalf of a complainant in circumstances where the complainant has sought a remedy elsewhere."[160]

Turning then to the nature of the dispute, the Court found that there were actually two separate disputes because of the way the union had framed its grievance. Oddly, rather than analyzing the essence of these disputes as prescribed in *Morin*, the court went on to discuss the latitude accorded to the union in framing its grievances, and its duty of fair representation. The Court took the view that even if the arbitration board were considered to be the appropriate forum to hear the discrimination allegations, the union would not be compelled "to put forward evidence and argument in support of the discrimination allegations" unless it chose to do so. Thus, in the Court's words, "[T]he application of the exclusive jurisdiction model is not appropriate here, as it would effectively leave the unionized employee without a forum in which to air her discrimination allegations." The Court therefore concluded that the legislature intended jurisdiction in such cases to be concurrent. Although this might lead to multiple proceedings, as it had in this case, the Court ruled that "efficiency alone is not a reason to restrict access to the human rights complaints process."[161]

In *Calgary Health Region v Alberta (Human Rights & Citizenship Commission)*,[162] the human rights issues raised by the employee's dismissal were expressly mentioned in the grievance referred to the arbitration board by the union. They were also, of course, raised in the complaint filed by the employee with the Commission. In deciding which of the two

158 *ATU*, above note 155 at para 55.

159 *Ibid* at para 57.

160 *Ibid* at para 60.

161 *Ibid* at para 69.

162 2007 ABCA 120.

forums had jurisdiction over the dispute, the Court of Appeal applied the same approach as in *ATU*, recalling the conclusion it had reached in that case that "each of the competing tribunals has *prima facie* jurisdiction over the subject matter of the dispute."[163] Turning to the nature of the dispute, the Court rejected the conclusion of the arbitration board that arbitration was the "best fit" to handle a termination dispute: "With respect, we do not agree that an analysis of 'best fit' can lead to a finding of exclusive jurisdiction in this case. The intent to grant exclusive jurisdiction must be found in the legislation. The interplay of the two legislative schemes at issue here indicates that neither body was intended to have exclusive jurisdiction over all human rights issues that arise in a unionized workplace environment."[164] The Court decided that the arbitration board had concurrent jurisdiction and could therefore hear the discrimination claim arising from the grievance. The Court concluded, however, that the Commission also had jurisdiction and had properly continued to process the complaint.

The Nova Scotia Court of Appeal adopted a similar approach in *Halifax (Regional Municipality) v Nova Scotia (Human Rights Commission)*[165] when asked to decide whether a unionized employee was prevented from filing a race-based complaint with the Nova Scotia Human Rights Commission because his collective agreement contained an anti-discrimination clause. Like its Alberta counterpart, the Nova Scotia Court of Appeal analyzed the issue in line with the principles enunciated by the majority in *Morin*, applying the two-step approach. The Court observed that the *Trade Union Act*[166] conferred a broad mandate on the arbitrator with regard to issues pertaining to the interpretation or application of the collective agreement. It found it significant, however, that section 42 of the Act provided for the final settlement of disputes by arbitration *or otherwise.* It also highlighted the fact that the clause in the collective agreement which permitted grievances pertaining to the violation of employment and human rights-related statutes expressly provided that "[t]he effect of this clause shall not be to reduce the rights of the employee or the Union as prescribed by the legislation."[167] The Court observed that the *Trade Union Act* "does not undermine the parties' intent to enhance rather than

163 *Ibid* at para 34.

164 *Ibid* at para 37.

165 2008 NSCA 21 [*Nova Scotia (HRC)*].

166 RSNS 1989, c 475.

167 *Nova Scotia (HRC)*, above note 165 at para 33.

to reduce access to human rights remedies in cases of alleged violation of statutorily protected human rights."[168] The Court concluded that the jurisdiction of the Human Rights Commission was "broad in scope," providing for "a mechanism for the investigation and enforcement of human rights." It found nothing in the *Human Rights Act* which suggested that this jurisdiction was in any way limited. Therefore the legislative context did not reveal an intention to grant exclusive jurisdiction over this issue to an arbitrator.

The Court then turned to the analysis of the second step, the essential character of the dispute. It took the view that the "heart of the dispute" was related to racial discrimination. Although the discriminatory incidents of which the plaintiff complained had taken place in the workplace, the dispute did not, in the Court's view, "arise explicitly or implicitly from the interpretation, application or administration of the Collective Agreement."[169] The Court found support for its conclusion that the arbitrator's jurisdiction was concurrent rather than exclusive in the fundamental and quasi-constitutional character of the *Human Rights Act*.[170]

Both the Alberta and Nova Scotia Courts of Appeal applied the two-step approach outlined by McLachlin CJC in *Morin* in a similar fashion. In the first step, they distinguished their provincial labour legislation from the *Quebec Labour Code* and the *Ontario Labour Relations Act*. They found the Alberta and Nova Scotia statutes conferring jurisdiction on the labour arbitrator to be "weaker" than those in Quebec and Ontario. It is interesting to note that neither Court expressly discarded the proposition that arbitrators have exclusive jurisdiction over issues pertaining to the application or interpretation of the collective agreement, as affirmed in *Weber*. They simply considered that the language used in the relevant statutes was insufficiently strong to prevent human rights tribunals from exercising their own statutory jurisdiction. This approach is simply not available in Quebec, since *Morin* itself originated in Quebec, and the Supreme Court made it very clear in that decision that arbitral jurisdiction is exclusive for all matters concerning the operation of the collective agreement, including human rights issues. There can also be no question regarding the non-exclusive character of the jurisdiction of Quebec's Human Rights Tribunal over human rights claims, since plaintiffs have

168 *Ibid* at para 40.

169 *Ibid* at para 52.

170 *Ibid* at paras 71 and 79.

the well-established choice under the Quebec *Charter* to opt for another forum.

The Saskatchewan, Alberta and Nova Scotia Courts of Appeal have distanced themselves from the instructions given by the Supreme Court in *Weber* as to the characterization of the essential nature of the dispute. In Saskatchewan's *Cadillac Fairview* case, the complaints were related to sexual harassment and discrimination in the workplace. In the other cases analyzed in this section, the employees' claims were related to dismissal. In their factual context, the questions raised should have been considered to be issues arising from the application of the collective agreement. Yet the courts refused to characterize them as such, and instead dealt with them as human rights or discrimination claims. This is especially obvious in *Nova Scotia (HRC)*, where the Court, in the second step of the approach set out in *Morin*, delineated the issue as "racial discrimination."[171] Here, the Court was clearly considering the legal characterization of the claim, rather than whether it concerned a matter covered by the collective agreement. The departure by other provincial appellate courts from the strictures in *Weber* explains at least in part why these courts reached conclusions different from those of the Quebec Court of Appeal on the concurrent jurisdiction of labour arbitrators and human rights tribunals over human rights disputes arising in unionized workplaces.

## C. CONCLUSION

Statutory and judicial evolutions have transformed labour arbitration from an essentially private mode of dispute resolution into one that has an important public dimension. The initial function of labour arbitrators — to interpret and apply collective agreements — is now combined with a power, and often a duty, to take statutory norms into account when seeking the appropriate solution to a grievance. Hence, sorting out the interplay between the different relevant sources of law in the collective labour relations context, and harmonizing them based on their inherent hierarchy in the legal system has become a central responsibility for labour arbitrators. However, there continues to be much debate over whether labour arbitration as an institution — with its peculiar features,

171 *Nova Scotia (HRC)*, above note 165 at para 51.

reflecting its originally private nature[172] — is properly equipped to handle the implementation of public order norms, particularly those stemming from human rights statutes.[173]

In Canada, outside of Quebec, courts have tended to restrict the exclusive jurisdiction of arbitrators over disputes deriving from the interpretation and application of the collective agreement, as affirmed in *Weber,* and have striven to preserve the domain of human rights tribunals over the implementation of equality rights, even in unionized workplaces. This orientation is largely driven by a concern that fundamental individual rights — and in the case of human rights, quasi-constitutional individual rights — will be lost if their enforcement is assigned exclusively to a procedure in which unions have a monopoly of representation and ultimate decision-making power over the administration of the collective agreement.[174] By contrast, in Quebec, the perceived necessity to safeguard the integrity of the collective labour relations regime, of which labour arbitration is a central component, has led to the adoption of a liberal approach to the jurisdiction of labour arbitrators, as affirmed by the Supreme Court in judgments such as *St Anne Nackawic, Weber* and *Bisaillon*, even in disputes related to human rights. Despite the will of the Quebec Human Rights Tribunal to affirm its jurisdiction over equality rights claims in all workplaces, including unionized ones, cases where the dispute concerns the interpretation or application of the collective agreement remain within the exclusive jurisdiction of arbitrators; only those that pertain to the "negotiation" of the agreement, as set out in *Morin*, are subject to concurrent jurisdiction between the human rights tribunal and labour arbitrators. Applying the two-step approach outlined in *Morin* entails its own difficulties, as the judgments of the Quebec Court of Appeal analyzed in this essay illustrate. On a practical level, however, the Quebec approach has a number of potential advantages. It avoids a multiplicity of proceedings, and possible conflicting decisions. More importantly, keeping the adjudication of human rights claims within the labour arbitration realm avoids the possible dissociation between

172 For instance, the arbitrator is chosen by the parties, who are also responsible for his remuneration.

173 *See* Trudeau, "L'arbitrage des griefs," above note 9; Gérard Notebaert, "Faut-il réformer le système l'arbitrage de grief au Québec?" (2008) 53:1 *McGill Law Journal* 103; Jean Bernier, "L'arbitrage de grief: un système de justice privé ou public?" (2012) 53:1 *Les Cahiers de droit* 161.

174 *See* Shilton, "Choice, but No Choice," above note 15; Shilton, "Square Pegs into Round Holes," above note 111.

workers' fundamental rights and the collective labour law regime. Labour arbitration can therefore act as a "vector" of human rights implementation in the workplace.[175]

The Quebec approach entails enhanced responsibilities for the different actors within the collective labour relations regime. The transformation of the power of the arbitrator to apply human rights and statutory labour rights of public interest into a *responsibility* to do so was underlined in *Parry Sound,* a decision that also emphasized the obligation of the employer to comply with human rights in exercising its reserved management rights. Moreover, unions are subject to a more stringent standard with regard to their duty of fair representation when dealing with human rights issues, as they must take into account the fundamental nature of such rights.[176] By attributing to collective labour relations actors the responsibility of ensuring respect for human rights, the integrity of the regime based on the ideal of self-government is preserved. At the same time, public interest norms, rather than being isolated from the parties' system of governance, are integrated into that system, thereby helping to maintain their relevance and legitimacy.[177]

175 *See* Nadeau, "L'arbitrage des griefs," above note 20.

176 Nancy Martel & Pierre E Moreau, *Le devoir de juste représentation* (Montréal : LexisNexis, 2009) at 87–89. But see Claire Mummé, "Questions, Questions: Has *Weber* had an Impact on Unions' Representational Responsibilities in Workplace Human Rights Disputes?," Chapter 8, this volume at 249–69, where Mummé questions whether this more stringent standard has uniform application across Canada.

177 Vallée & Gesualdi-Fecteau, above note 6 at 187.

CHAPTER TEN

# The Crisis in the US Litigation Model of Labour Rights Enforcement

Alan Hyde

To each individual classified as an "employee," the United States guarantees a suite of legal rights that, in international comparison, is noteworthy primarily for its (1) paucity and (2) extraordinary difficulty of enforcement. The US maintains what Canadians call a "litigation model," under which statutory claims for labour standards and anti-discrimination claims must normally be brought to court for enforcement. This US model is what Canada's *Weber* doctrine is seeking to avoid.[1] I am sincerely grateful to the organizers of this symposium for the opportunity to reflect on this litigation model, something taken for granted in the extensive and outstanding literature on the current crisis in US labour rights enforcement. My preliminary conclusions are that the origins of the litigation model are obscure and its maintenance poorly-defended; that it is rapidly approaching crisis; that the Canadian practice of encouraging arbitration of statutory claims is unlikely to work well in the US; but that it is long past time for the US to design administrative agencies with full authority to reinstate and compensate victims of labour standards violations and workplace discrimination.

Recent scholarship on statutory labour rights enforcement in the US reflects a sense of crisis, yet this extensive, illuminating literature takes for granted the litigation model that is the very source of the crisis. Other

1 I owe this insight to Chris Dassios, who chaired the symposium panel where I initially presented this paper.

aspects of enforcing statutory labour rights have been much discussed. The growth of the temporary-help sector and other labour market intermediaries has created complex structures in which many employees are, for legal purposes, ostensibly employed by small, undercapitalized entities, rather than the more powerful ultimate purchasers of labour services.[2] Increasingly, this problem is being addressed through more liberal findings of "joint employment," under which the worker is jointly employed by more than one beneficiary of his or her work.[3] In addition, state statutes increasingly impose legal responsibilities on ultimate purchasers of labour even where relations of joint employment cannot be found. This concept of "responsibility" for labour conditions should be, I have argued, the preferred framework for discussion of the problem.[4] There has been much concern about misclassification: that is, denying working people their statutory rights by describing them, for example, as independent contractors or student interns. For federal statutes, the definition of "employee" involves one of a number of multi-factor factual inquiries into the control of work, and generalization is difficult. (While most federal statutes are interpreted to adopt a common law definition of employee, state law is permitted to adopt a more-inclusive definition of employee.[5]) Also

2 See David Weil, *The Fissured Workplace: Why Work Became So Bad for So Many and What Can Be Done to Improve It* (Cambridge MA: Harvard University Press, 2014); Alan Hyde, "To What Duties Do Global Labour Rights Correlate? Responsibility for Labor Standards Down the Production Chain" ["To What Duties"] in Yossi Dahan, Hanna Lerner & Faina Milman-Sivan, eds, *Global Justice and International Labour Rights* (Cambridge UK: Cambridge University Press, 2016) 209.

3 For example, see *Browning-Ferris Industries of California Inc*, 362 NLRB No 186, 204 LRRM 1154 (2015) (recycling plant and labour supply firm joint employers); *Cano v DPNY Inc*, 287 FRD 251 (SDNY 2012) (franchisor and franchisee; triable issue of fact whether they are joint employers); *Lin Nan Zheng v Liberty Apparel Co*, 617 F 3d 182 (2d Cir 2010) (the garment needle shop and garment label for whom garments were produced are joint employers).

4 Cal Lab Code §2810 and 2810.3 (responsibility of those who contract for labour through intermediary; no finding of joint employment required); NY Lab Law §§240, 241-a, 241(6) (various "non-delegable duties" of landowners who hire construction labour through intermediaries; no finding of joint employment required). See generally *Hyde*, "To What Duties," above note 2.

5 See *e.g.*, *O'Connor v Uber Technologies Inc*, 82 F Supp 3d 1133 (ND Cal 2015) (labour standards suit by on-call drivers, denying summary judgment to employer); *Alexander v FedEx Ground Package Sys*, 765 F 3d 981 (9th Cir 2014) (FedEx drivers are statutory employees and not self-employed, relying in part on California law); *Hargrove v Sleepy's LLC*, 106 A 3d 449 (NJ Sup Ct 2015). An individual is presumed to be statu-

much-discussed is the practice of having employees who are not represented by unions—that is, the overwhelming majority of employees in the US—sign boilerplate clauses agreeing not to sue their employers, but instead to submit claims to arbitrators.[6] US courts normally uphold such clauses,[7] at least where they refer to the right to sue that they purport to waive,[8] and bind the employer as well as the employee.[9] The heavy proportion of immigrant workers—many in the US without authorization, and many concentrated in the worst jobs—creates practical difficulties in effective enforcement of labour rights, despite the fact that such workers are statutory employees covered by labour law and labour standards law.[10] Finally, Janice Fine and Jennifer Gordon have criticized the passive role given to worker organizations in labour standards enforcement, and advocated a more active role in cooperation with administrative agencies.[11]

---

tory employee for purposes of labour standards, unless the putative employer shows that he or she is either "free from control or direction" and the service provided is "outside the usual course of business" or "in an independently established . . . business." This is sometimes called the "ABC test" and is used in several US states. *Ibid* at 458. But see *Glatt v Fox Searchlight Pictures Inc*, 791 F 3d 376 (2d Cir 2015) (claims of interns to wages depend on assessment of comparative benefit to the intern and the putative employer). In my opinion, there is a decided trend toward classifying disputed individuals as employees rather than independent contractors.

6 Margaret Jane Radin, *Boilerplate: The Fine Print, Vanishing Rights, and the Rule of Law* (Princeton NJ: Princeton University Press 2014); Katherine Van Wezel Stone, "Mandatory Arbitration of Individual Employment Rights: The Yellow Dog Contract of the 1990s" (1996) 73 Denv U L Rev 1017; Imre Szalai, *Outsourcing Justice: The Rise of Modern Arbitration Laws in America* (Durham NC: Carolina Academic Press 2013) (showing clear original understanding not to apply federal *Arbitration Act* to contracts of employment).

7 *Gilmer v Interstate/Johnson Lane Corp.*, 500 US 20 (1991); *Circuit City Stores Inc v Adams*, 532 US 105 (2001).

8 *Atalese v US Legal Services Group LP*, 99 A3d 306 (NJ Sup Ct 2014), cert denied 135 S Ct 2804 (2015).

9 *Armendariz v Foundation Health Psychcare Services, Inc*, 24 Cal 4th 83 (Cal Sup Ct 2000).

10 *Sure-Tan Inc. v NLRB*, 467 US 883 (1984) (unauthorized migrants are statutory employees covered by federal labour laws); *Hoffman Plastic Compounds Inc v NLRB*, 535 US 137 (2002) (reaffirming holding that unauthorized migrants are statutory employees, but holding that Board remedial powers may be limited by their unauthorized status); *Lucas v Jerusalem Café LLC*, 721 F 3d 927 (8th Cir 2013) (unauthorized migrants must be paid statutory wages).

11 Janice Fine, "Solving the Problem from Hell: Tripartism as a Strategy for Addressing Labour Standards Non-Compliance in the United States" ["Solving the Problem from

It is seldom if ever observed, however, that all these problems presuppose that the enforcement of labour rights will occur in courts, and will be decided using common-law standards and litigation methods for finding facts, defining employment, and enforcing contracts. This essay will examine that assumption.

Part A will describe the current multiplicity of decision-makers involved in the enforcement of statutory labour rights, and the resultant jurisdictional morass. Part B will describe the historical evolution of this crisis, emphasizing how each of the prominent institutions enforcing labour rights was, by the time it emerged from a hostile Congress, designed to fail. I shall discuss three models of labour rights enforcement, in chronological order of their historical appearance: the "administrative model" of the National Labor Relations Board (NLRB), an agency empowered to grant reinstatement and compensatory damages, subject to limited judicial review; the "litigation model" of the *Fair Labor Standards Act* (*FLSA*) and subsequently various antidiscrimination statutes, in which administrative agencies have no such remedial power and claimants must eventually sue in general courts of law; and the "arbitration model" under collective bargaining agreements.[12] Part C will discuss the collision of these institutions in recent years, in which a foolish Supreme Court decision has led to the crisis identified in Part A, in which no claim of labour law is too simple to be immune from extensive jurisdictional conflict.[13] The conclusion offers preliminary speculation on reform of the system,

Hell"] (2013) 50:4 Osgoode Hall LJ 813; Janice Fine & Jennifer Gordon, "Strengthening Labor Standards Enforcement through Partnerships with Workers' Organisations" ["Strengthening Labor Standards Enforcement"] (2010) 38:4 Politics & Society 552; Janice Fine, "Co-Production: Bringing Together the Unique Capabilities of Government and Society for Stronger Labor Standards Enforcement" ["Co-Production"]. *Labor Innovations for the 21st Century (LIFT) Fund,* online: theliftfund.org/wp-content/uploads/2015/09/LIFTReportCoproductionOct_ExecSumm-rf_4.pdf.

12 In this essay, "arbitration" refers exclusively to grievance arbitration under collective bargaining agreements. I do not deal with the quite different systems mentioned above (see sources in above notes 6–9), also called "arbitration," which cover employees without union representation and are imposed by boilerplate contracts of employment; nor do I deal with commercial arbitration.

13 I refer to *14 Penn Plaza LLC v Pyett*, 556 US 247 (2009) [*Pyett*], in which the Court ordered dismissal of an employee's suit alleging age discrimination on the grounds that the applicable collective bargaining agreement called for submission of such claims to grievance arbitration. While this result is unsurprising to Canadians, it represents an abrupt change in US practice and has led to the jurisdictional confusion illustrated in Parts A and C of this essay.

suggesting that enforcement of labour standards and anti-discrimination legislation could occur at the state level without federal legislation.[14] This makes reform at least plausible, since there has been no labour legislation of this scope at the federal level in half a century. However, it would come at the price of creating significant differences among the US states.

## A. THE PROBLEM: "ANFRACTUOUS" LITIGATION[15]

Reference to a crisis in enforcement is not hyperbole. To illustrate that fact, consider the following recent sequence of decisions. I would not describe this sequence as typical — it is among the worst I have recently encountered — but it arises from a simple factual situation and, as we shall see, could easily arise in many similar scenarios. It has also occasioned unusually critical language from the courts.

Richard Wawock is an electrician in Los Angeles County, employed by CSI Electrical Contractors and represented by the International Brotherhood of Electrical Workers. His employer required him and others to attend mandatory training courses on topics such as safety, first aid, and preventing harassment. The employer did not pay wages for time spent at such courses. Wawock filed suit in California state court in September 2012, claiming that such time must be compensated under the *California*

14 US Federal legislation requiring minimum wage and premium pay for overtime hours (*FLSA*, 29 USC §§201–219, and the various federal statutes prohibiting discrimination in employment: *Civil Rights Act of 1964*, Title VII (race, color, religion, sex, national origin), 42 USC §§2000e to 2000e-17 [Title VII]; *Age Discrimination in Employment Act of 1967*, 29 USC §§621–633a; *Americans with Disabilities Act of 1990*, 42 USC §§12101–12212; *Family and Medical Leave Act*, 29 USC §2601 et seq. All these statutes set national minimum levels of protections. States are permitted to provide more protection to employees, and many have. The classic treatment of the economics of diverging state minima is David Card & Alan B Krueger, *Myth and Measurement: The New Economics of the Minimum Wage* (Princeton NJ: Princeton University Press, 1995). By contrast, for private sector employees, rights to collective action under *the National Labor Relations Act*, 29 USC 151–169 [*NLRA*], and rights concerning pensions and benefit plans (*Employee Retirement Income Security Act* or ERISA, 29 USC §§1001) may not be supplemented by additional state rights, since the federal statute has been held to preempt any such state law.

15 *Wawock v CSI Elec Contractors Inc* (Oct 10, 2014), Case No. 2:14-cv-06102 SVW-MAN (United States District Court, CD Cal) at 2 (order denying in part defendant's motion to dismiss Wawock's application to vacate arbitration award). This decision reviews much of the procedural history of Wawock's claim for wages.

*Labor Code*. He raised no claims under federal labour standards law or under the applicable collective bargaining agreement.[16]

The applicable law is not in dispute. The federal law (which Wawock chose not to invoke) is found in regulations of the US Department of Labor that require payment of wages to employees attending training courses unless four criteria are met: (a) attendance is outside of the employee's regular working hours; (b) attendance is voluntary; (c) the course, lecture, or meeting is not directly related to the employee's job; and (d) the employee does not perform any productive work during such attendance.[17] Applicable California state law generally requires wage payment for work and lacks any distinct regulation of training courses.[18] The employer has at no time suggested any substantive reason why wages are not required. If the course content is as Wawock claims, the employer will be unable to show that the courses lack direct relation to the job. Resolution of this simple factual question, could it be obtained, should result in back wages paid to Wawock and other members of the class.[19]

Instead of challenging the claim on its merits, the employer has instead engaged in vigorous litigation on the jurisdictional issue. First, the employer petitioned the state trial court to send Wawock's wage claim to arbitration by the joint Labor-Management Committee that hears grievances arising under the collective bargaining agreement.[20] Wawock, of course, had raised no claim under his collective bargaining agreement. However, in 2009 the US Supreme Court, in an abrupt change from prior federal law, held in *14 Penn Plaza LLC v Pyett* that a trial court might

16 Most lawyers representing individual employees in suits under labor standards law prefer state court over federal court where possible, particularly in jurisdictions like California and New Jersey. Procedures are often less formal; the substantive law may be more favorable; and there is much more willingness in state court to let disputes go to a jury in situations in which a federal court would likely grant summary judgment to the defendant.

17 *FLSA*, 29 CFR §§785.27

18 Wawock claimed under the general provisions of *California Labor Code* §510, requiring payment for hours worked.

19 Not all courts would agree. One Court of Appeals, applying the federal *FLSA*, has held that a safety course required by the employer as a condition of employment was "voluntary" if employees could schedule it at their convenience: *Chao v Tradesmen International, Inc*, 310 F 3d 904 (6th Cir 2002). This decision is hard to fathom.

20 Such joint committees often replace arbitration in Teamsters contracts and in the building trades. See generally Clyde Summers, "Teamster Joint Grievance Committees: Grievance Disposal Without Adjudication" (1985) 7:3 Berkeley J Emp & Lab L 313.

dismiss an individual claim under federal age discrimination legislation if the claimant is covered by a collective bargaining agreement which clearly waives the employees' right to sue and provides for resolution of their statutory claims in grievance arbitration.[21] Applying *Pyett*, the state trial court sent Wawock's state law wage claim to arbitration by the Joint Committee.[22]

The California trial courts order ignored at least three potentially significant distinctions from the claim sent to arbitration in *Pyett*. First, and most importantly, the trial court made no finding that the dispute resolution clause in the collective bargaining agreement waived the employees' right to sue under California wage law. Instead, it directed the Joint Committee to determine the question of whether Wawock's claim was within its jurisdiction (i.e., was arbitrable). (In *Pyett*, the US Supreme Court had made a finding of waiver a prerequisite to a district court's sending a statutory claim to arbitration. In addition, an earlier case, undisturbed by *Pyett*, held that the federal district court must decide statutory claims for itself where the arbitration clause in the applicable collective bargaining agreement did not clearly cover them.[23]) Second, the trial court did not consider whether California courts applying California state law should apply the federal dismissal standard, or instead provide more protection, as California frequently does. Third, the trial court did not consider whether a joint committee should be treated as the equivalent of the neutral arbitrator in *Pyett*.[24] Wawock appealed the dismissal and the order to arbitrate, but the Court of Appeals (in California, an intermediate appellate level between trial courts and the Supreme Court of California) denied review.[25]

The Joint Committee found that Wawock's claim was arbitrable, and rejected that claim on its merits, denying any compensation for the time spent in class. Wawock then filed suit in federal court, seeking to vacate the award on the grounds that the Committee's finding that the claim

---

21 *Pyett*, above note 13.

22 *Wawock v Superior Court*, 197 LRRM (BNA) 2056, 2013 WL 5273230 (Cal. Ct App, Sept 17, 2013)

23 *Wright v Universal Maritime Service Corp*, 525 US 70 (1998)

24 For federal labour law purposes, a joint committee is normally treated as equivalent to arbitration. *See* e.g., *General Drivers, Warehousemen and Helpers, Local Union No 89 v Riss & Co*, 372 US 517 (1963), though some courts have questioned this (for example, *Taylor v NLRB*, 786 F 2d 1516 (11th Cir 1986)). *See* also *Summers*, above note 20.

25 *Wawock v Superior Court*, above note 22.

was arbitrable manifestly disregarded federal labour law.[26] At the same time, the employer sued in state court, seeking to confirm the award in its favour. Wawock's federal suit was heard first. The federal court vacated the Joint Committee's award, finding that the Joint Committee had disregarded federal law in finding that Wawock's claim was within its jurisdiction. The court found that since the collective bargaining agreement made no mention of statutory claims (let alone clearly commit them to private dispute resolution), it did not represent the clear and unmistakable waiver that *Pyett* has established as a prerequisite to a court's refusal to decide a statutory claim.[27] The employer appealed this decision to the US Court of Appeals for the Ninth Circuit, where it languishes as of this writing for reasons that Wawock's counsel cannot determine (I asked).

The parties then returned to state court to deal with the employer's suit to confirm the award. Wawock now argued that the suit to confirm should be dismissed, because the state court was required to give full faith and credit to the federal decision that the suit was not arbitrable. The state court, however, refused to dismiss the suit, retaining jurisdiction pending the decision of the federal appeals court. Wawock's application to the state appellate court for a writ of mandamus to the state trial court was successful; the appellate court issued the writ, holding that after the federal decision, the state court should have dismissed, rather than adjourned, the employer's suit to confirm the award.[28]

Thus, as I write this essay in April 2016, Wawock's simple factual claim has, in three and a half years, engendered two state trial court decisions, a decision by a Joint Committee, two decisions by the state intermediate court of appeals, and a federal court decision on appeal to the federal

26 A suit raising substantive claims that arise only under state law may not be removed to federal court by the defendant. However, a suit to confirm a labor arbitration award, like any suit to enforce a collective bargaining agreement, necessarily arises under federal law; accordingly, if the plaintiffs do not file the suit in federal courts, it may be removed there by the defendants: *Avco Corp v Aero Lodge No 735, Intern Ass'n of Machinists and Aerospace Workers*, 390 US 557 (1968); *Local 174, Teamsters, Chauffeurs, Warehouseman & Helpers of America v Lucas Flour Co*, 369 US 95 (1962).

27 *Wawock v CSI Elec Contractors Inc*, 2014 BL 170,439, 2014 WL 5420900 (USDC, CD Cal). The court had previously denied the employer's motion to dismiss Wawock's suit: see above note 15.

28 *Wawock v Superior Court*, 2015 LRRM (BNA) 180683, 2015 WL 1577428 2015 BL 99732 (Cal Ct App, Apr 8, 2015). One of the factors contributing to the dysfunction of the US litigation model is the baseline lack of clarity in US employment law over the division between federal and state jurisdiction.

appeals court. His claim is still unresolved. This is the sign of a system for enforcing labour standards that has reached almost total breakdown.

How did the US arrive at this farcical carnival of litigation?[29] More importantly, what should replace it? The confusion in Wawock does not represent "bad lawyering." Nor does it represent temporary confusion, as courts adjust to the 2009 *Pyett* decision. Instead, it reflects an employer who has decided to exploit strategic moves potentially open in many ordinary cases in which unionized employees claim that their statutory rights have been violated. A Canadian reader might be tempted to support arbitration as the preferred institution for resolution of statutory claims like Wawock's, since this approach has proven largely successful in Canada. I believe that Wawock's case instead demonstrates that the Canadian approach of promoting arbitration would not be a good solution in the US. Wawock received a *sort* of arbitration, but it was by a Joint Committee, not an arbitrator. The Committee was inexperienced in addressing statutory claims. It was flatly wrong in assuming jurisdiction over the controversy, and fairly clearly wrong in its understanding of the substantive law of labour standards. Designing an effective system for US labour rights enforcement is a problem without an obvious solution. But first, let us understand the origins of the current crisis.

## B. LABOUR RIGHTS ENFORCEMENT IN THE US: UNCOORDINATED INSTITUTIONS

Part B introduces the confusing multiplicity of institutions that enforce labour rights, such as the right to be paid for work (Wawock's goal), the right to form unions or take collective action, and the right to be free of discrimination on the basis of race, color, national origin, religion, sex, age, or disability. It does not rest on archival research and contains no information that will surprise the reader familiar with US law. Nevertheless, the story is never told this way. American lawyers take for granted that each of the developments discussed here has its own trajectory and does not coordinate with others. There has been little emphasis in the literature on the way each individual enforcement scheme was deliberately

---

29 The federal district court used words like "tortuous," "labyrinth," "anfractuous": *Wawock v CSI Elec Contractors Inc*, Order Denying Defendants' Motion to Dismiss (CD Cal, Oct 10, 2014).

created to fail. And there has been little appreciation of how simple problems like Wawock's can generate quantities of useless litigation, threatening the breakdown of the entire system.

Viewed as a system, US statutory labour rights carry one or more of three distinct enforcement models: administrative, litigation, and arbitration. Administrative enforcement applies to rights to take group action under the *National Labor Relations Act* (*NLRA* or *Wagner Act*); the aggrieved worker lodges a claim with an administrative agency, which thereafter takes it over. There is no charge to the worker, and the agency is empowered to award full reinstatement and compensation.[30] The litigation model is used for claims of violation of labour standards legislation such as the *FLSA*,[31] and for all of the federal laws prohibiting employment discrimination;[32] a worker may be required to complain to an agency, such as the US Department of Labor or Equal Employment Opportunity Commission, or their state analogs. However, that agency has no authority to adjudicate his or her claim. Instead, either the agency, or more usually the worker, will have to litigate the claim in state or federal court. Finally, workers covered by collective bargaining agreements—that is, 6.6 percent of workers in the private sector[33]—usually have an option to file a grievance for violations of their collective bargaining agreements. Such grievance may eventually reach a neutral decision-maker: typically a labour arbitrator, although joint boards like Wawock's are not uncommon. However, grievances belong to the union, not the worker; the worker has no right to compel the union to take up his or her grievance. When the union does so, there is no cost to the worker, but should the union refuse, there is little practical way of reviving the grievance unless the union has violated its duty of fair representation. That duty is rarely enforced by the courts.[34] Arbitration is limited to claims that the collective agreement

30 29 USC §§151–69.

31 29 USC §§201–19.

32 Principally the *Civil Rights Act of 1964*, Title VII (race, color, religion, sex, national origin), 42 USC §§2000e to 2000e-17; *Age Discrimination in Employment Act of 1967*, 29 USC §§621–633a; *Americans with Disabilities Act of 1990*, 42 USC §§12101–12212.

33 US Department of Labor: Bureau of Labor Statistics, News Release: "Union Members—2014" (USDL-15-0072) (January 23, 2015), online: www.bls.gov/news.release/archives/union2_01232015.pdf.

34 Michael J Goldberg, "The Duty of Fair Representation: What the Courts Do in Fact," (1985) 34:1 Buff L Rev 89.

has been violated. Collective agreements in the US, unlike Canada, do not incorporate by reference the entire suite of statutory labour standards.[35]

It is an easy matter to explain why (unlike in Canada) arbitration has played a limited role in the enforcement of statutory individual labour rights in the US. Grievance arbitration as we know it barely existed at the origin of federal enforcement of minimum wages and premium pay for overtime work, provided by the *FLSA* of 1938. When the *Civil Rights Act of 1964* recognized individual rights to be free from workplace discrimination, unions were often defendants in such claims, along with employers, since many unions were discriminators.[36] Turning discrimination claims over to arbitrators responsible to unions and employers would effectively have eliminated those rights. Finally, the legal framework for arbitration, established in a series of Supreme Court cases brought by unions in the 1950s and 1960s, emphasized and perhaps exaggerated the gulf between public law claims and institutions, and private law claims and institutions under collective bargaining agreements. Arbitration was clearly identified with the latter.[37] As a result, American grievance arbitrators have little experience with statutory claims and have never contributed anything significant to the development of statutory labour law.[38]

It is much more difficult to explain why statutory labour rights have never been consolidated into a single federal agency (or labour court) with enforcement powers, but are instead parcelled out among a variety of agencies and tribunals, none particularly effective. Some themes recur.

---

35 *Wright v Universal Maritime Service Corp*, above note 23 (federal district court must decide statutory claims for itself where the arbitration clause in the applicable collective bargaining agreement did not clearly cover them).

36 *Civil Rights Act of 1964*, §703(c), 42 USC §2000e-2(c).

37 *United Steelworkers of America v American Manufacturing Co*, 363 US 564 (1960) (enforcing executory promise to arbitrate; court not to find facts); *United Steelworkers of America v Warrior & Gulf Navigation Co*, 363 US 574 (1960) (enforcing executory promise to arbitrate; court not to construe any substantive provisions of collective agreement); *United Steelworkers of America v Enterprise Wheel & Car Corp*, 363 US 593 (1960) (enforcement of arbitrator's award without review of the merits). Collectively, these cases are known as the *Steelworkers Trilogy*. See generally David Feller, "The Coming End of Arbitration's Golden Age," (1976) 29 The Proceedings of the National Academy of Arbitrators 97, online: NAARB http://naarb.org/proceedings/pdfs/1976-97.PDF.

38 Ariana R Levinson defends arbitral competence with fact-finding and application of known law, but fails to identify any way in which arbitrators have contributed to the development of the underlying law ("What the Awards Tell Us about Labor Arbitration of Employment Discrimination Claims," (2013) 46:3 Mich JL Reform 790).

Passage of any labour legislation is extraordinarily difficult in the US, normally requiring years of Congressional effort, overcoming intense opposition from employers, messy compromises, and enforcement schemes deliberately designed to fail. However, there appears to have been little attention to the precise problem of jurisdictional conflict that has become such a significant (if unnoticed by scholars) feature of statutory labour rights enforcement in recent years.

### 1) Administrative Model: National Labor Relations Board (NLRB)

While this essay does not deal with collective labour rights, I start here because the NLRB, while far from perfect, is a model that might well have been, but was not, emulated in subsequent statutes.

New Deal labour law actually began with a different model—the industry boards of the *National Industrial Recovery Act*, designed to limit competition and raise wages. This statute was held by the Supreme Court to be an unconstitutional delegation of government power to private interests.[39] The second model—the administrative model—has proved more enduring. Since 1935, charges of employer or union interference with employee rights to collective action may be brought to an independent administrative agency with power to issue complaints, try cases, and award legal and equitable relief subject to minimum judicial review.[40] These procedures were specifically held to be constitutional, along with the Act generally.[41] The Board from its inception has been entirely focused on enforcing statutory rights, and is forbidden by statute from employing individuals for conciliation or mediation.[42] Since 1947, prosecutorial and adjudicatory functions are separate. The NLRB maintains doctrines (too complex to explain here) for deferral to grievance arbitration where appropriate, but these affect a relatively small portion of the NLRB caseload, since that caseload deals mainly with workplaces where no union yet represents employees. It is interesting that this administrative model has not been employed again in federal labour legislation in the eighty years since passage of the *Wagner Act*.

---

39 *ALA Schechter Poultry Corp v United States*, 295 US 495 (1935).

40 *NLRA*, 29 USC §§151–169.

41 *National Labor Relations Board v Jones & Laughlin Steel Corp*, 301 US 1, 46–49 (1937).

42 NLRA §4(a), 29 USC §154(a).

## 2) Litigation Models

### a) *Fair Labor Standards Act* of 1938

When newly-elected President Franklin Roosevelt asked Frances Perkins in 1933 to serve as Secretary of Labor, she advised him that her acceptance was conditional on the administration introducing legislation requiring a national minimum wage, a cap on working hours, and the abolition of child labour. Drafts of such legislation had been prepared during the constitutional crisis over the *National Industrial Recovery Act*[43] but, as Perkins told Roosevelt at the time, they had been "locked in the lower left-hand drawer of my desk against an emergency." Roosevelt laughed and said: "There's New England caution for you. . . . You're pretty unconstitutional, aren't you?"[44] In March 1937, the Supreme Court, in the famous "switch in time that saved the Nine," (from Roosevelt's plan to expand the size of the Court, permitting new, progressive appointments), upheld a state minimum wage law.[45] Roosevelt reportedly asked Perkins, "What happened to that nice unconstitutional bill you had tucked away?"[46] Less than two months later, Roosevelt sent a version of Perkins' *FLSA* to Congress, where it encountered strong opposition from Republicans and southern Democrats but ultimately passed a year later, after amendments weakening its substantive provisions. The *FLSA* is generally regarded as the final piece of New Deal legislation.

It also appears to be, as nearly as I can figure out, the origin at the federal level of what Canadians call the "American litigation model." Ruth O'Brien argues that adoption of a litigation model represents Congress's weakening of the original draft *FLSA* as prepared by Benjamin Cohen and

43 See above note 39. Before 1937, New Deal and state employment legislation was frequently found unconstitutional by the US Supreme Court as an interference with liberty of contract, unconstitutional delegation to private bodies, or (in the case of federal legislation) beyond federal power to regulate interstate commerce.

44 Kirstin Downey, *The Woman Behind the New Deal: The Life of Frances Perkins, FDR'S Secretary of Labor and His Moral Conscience* (New York: Anchor, 2010) at 265–69; Jonathan Grossman, "Fair Labor Standards Act of 1938: Maximum Struggle for a Minimum Wage," (1978) 101:6 Monthly Lab Rev 22 at 24.

45 *West Coast Hotel Co v Parrish*, 300 US 379 (1937). *Jones & Laughlin Steel Corp*, above note 41, expanding the federal government's power to regulate interstate commerce (and, as we have noted, upholding a powerful administrative agency), followed *Parrish* by two weeks.

46 Grossman, above note 44 at 24.

Thomas Corcoran for Attorney General Robert Jackson.[47] That original draft proposed a Labor Standards Board, an independent "quasi-judicial" agency modeled on the Federal Trade Commission and NLRB, with power to establish and enforce labour standards after public hearings. [48] That Board would have had investigatory and rule-making powers. Congress eliminated the board, largely because of union opposition (the American Federation of Labor (AFL) and the Congress of Industrial Organizations (CIO) each fearing it would assist the other), and replaced it with a division within the Department of Labor that lacked independent power to issue wage orders. [49] In the intense battle over the legislation, there seems to have been no discussion of the merits of opting for a litigation model.[50] (In fact, even the independent Board, had it emerged, would have had to resort to litigation to enforce its orders, as is true of the Division eventually reflected in the statute.[51]) Congress kept for itself the power to set minimum wage and maximum hours standards, which it retains to this day. The elimination of an independent, evidence-focused Labor Standards Board is part of what I am describing as a system designed to fail.

As a result, no agency of the federal government may order wage payment. Either the aggrieved employee (like Wawock), or the Department of Labor must sue in federal court.[52] The Department also lacks power to issue administrative interpretations, a deficiency noted at the time.[53] The *FLSA* makes no provision for the use of grievance arbitration, as I shall discuss in the next section.

---

47 Ruth O'Brien, "A Sweat Shop of the Whole Nation: The *Fair Labor Standards Act* and the Failure of Regulatory Unionism," (2001) 15:1 Studies in Am Polit Devel 33 at 38–43. The original bill was S 2475, 75th Congress, 1st Session, introduced on May 24, 1937 by Senator (later Supreme Court Justice) Hugo Black.

48 S 2475, Sec 3.

49 O'Brien, above note 47 at 38–43.

50 See generally Willis J Nordlund, *The Quest for a Living Wage: The History of the Federal Minimum Wage Program* (Westport CT: Greenwood Press, 1997) at 46–52. Nordlund summarizes the Congressional debates but does not report any debate about the requirement of enforcement litigation.

51 S 2475, Sec 16 authorized the Labor Standards Board to sue for equitable relief in federal district courts. Section 21 would have authorized suits by employees.

52 *FLSA* §16(b), 29 USC §216(b).

53 "[P]erhaps the outstanding difficulty, from the point of view of employer compliance, has been the lack of an administrative rule-making power": Samuel Herman, "Administration and Enforcement of the *Fair Labor Standards Act*: The *Wage and Hour Law*" (1939) 6:3 Law & Contemp Probs 368 at 378.

No doubt several factors combined to create the federal litigation model. First, some states had parallel wage and hour legislation before 1938 which involved a variation on a litigation model, under which either an aggrieved employee or a government official could go to court;[54] it is likely that the federal legislation drew on these precedents. However, there was surely no well-established tradition in the US prior to 1938 of employees suing under state wage legislation; many state statutes lacked enforcement of any kind, while others had failed to go into effect.[55] Congress in any case was not compelled to follow pre-1938 state law models. Second, enthusiasm in Congress for administrative agencies specifically, and the New Deal generally, had cooled by Roosevelt's second term. Congress's elimination of an independent Board suggests that it would have been equally or more hostile to administrative determination of wage claims, though in theory this responsibility could have been given to the Department of Labor. Third, both the AFL and CIO, each convinced by 1937 that the NLRB was favoring the other, welcomed the elimination of the Board. In addition, they had succeeded in clarifying that collectively-bargained wages could exceed the statutory level.[56] With good reason, the US labour movement hated and distrusted the courts.[57] But once they had exempted themselves from judicial interference with their own wage bargains, they had no objection to such a litigation model for employees unrepresented by unions.

With hindsight, the *FLSA*'s litigation model is at best an enormous opportunity missed, a capitulation to a Congress uncommitted to the success of the program.[58] In a case such as Wawock's claim to payment for training, enforcement options today are artificially limited to state court, federal court, or grievance arbitration, when most effective for Wawock's purpose — and frankly, his employer's — would be a swift administrative ruling from a state or federal Department of Labor.

---

54 Ronnie Steinberg, *Wages and Hours: Labor and Reform in Twentieth-Century America* (New Brunswick NJ: Rutgers University Press, 1982) at 25.

55 Frank T deVyver, "Regulation of Wages and Hours Prior to 1938" (1939) 6:3 Law & Contemp Probs 323 at 327.

56 Howard D Samuel, "Troubled Passage: The Labor Movement and the Fair Labor Standards Act," (2000) 123:12 Monthly Labor Review 32.

57 William E. Forbath, *Law and the Shaping of the American Labor Movement* (Cambridge MA: Harvard University Press 1991) at 37–57.

58 Equally damaging were Congress's elimination of the independent agency and serious legislated restrictions on the Act's coverage: Fine & Gordon, "Strengthening Labor Standards Enforcement," above note 11; O'Brien, above note 47.

### b) Civil Rights Legislation

There are two chief statutory sources of labour rights held primarily by individual US workers. The first, as noted, is the *FLSA* and parallel state legislation. The second is the series of anti-discrimination statutes enacted by Congress between 1963 and 1993.[59] All of these anti-discrimination statutes share two broad structural similarities among themselves and with the *FLSA*. First, they provide minimum levels of coverage; states may, and often do, extend additional protections. Second, they adopt a litigation model. For simplicity we examine the most important, *Title VII of the Civil Rights Act of 1964*. Like the *FLSA*, its passage through Congress was protracted and difficult, opposed by southern Democrats, necessitating negotiations with Republicans who focused most intensely on details of enforcement. Like the *FLSA*, it was set up by Congress to fail, specifically by stripping a proposed administrative agency of any power and instead requiring litigation for enforcement.

Title VII does create an administrative agency, the Equal Employment Opportunity Commission (EEOC). Later statutes expanded that agency's jurisdiction to age and disability cases. By design, the EEOC does not promulgate regulations because it has no statutory authority to do so. Nor does it decide cases, which means that it cannot makes rules as part of the decision-making process, a method employed by the NLRB throughout its history.[60] Its circumscribed powers were the Republican price for support of the legislation, another example of deliberate Congressional creation of an agency designed to fail, as was fairly obvious at

---

59 *Equal Pay Act of 1963*, 29 USC §206(d): equal pay for men and women who perform "equal work" in the same "establishment"; *Civil Rights Act of 1964*, Title VII (race, color, religion, sex, national origin), 42 USC §§2000e to 2000e-17 (no employment discrimination by race, color, religion, national origin, or sex); *Age Discrimination in Employment Act of 1967*, 29 USC § 621–633(a); *Americans With Disabilities Act of 1990* (amended 2008), 29 USC §12101–12212; *Family and Medical Leave Act of 1993*, 29 USC §2601 et seq (held to have been enacted by Congress under its power to legislate equal protection and thus binds state governments. *See Nevada Department of Human Resources v Hibbs*, 538 US 721 (2003)).

60 The Supreme Court has approved the Board's usual practice of announcing rules as part of decided cases, which thereafter serve as precedent: *NLRB v Bell Aerospace Company Division of Textron Inc*, 416 US 267 at 294 (1974). It also approved the only substantive use by the Board of its rule-making power: *American Hospital Association v NLRB*, 499 US 606 (1991). In each case employers argued unsuccessfully that the alternative method was required. The EEOC cannot employ either procedure.

the time.[61] Sovern described it as a "poor enfeebled thing,"[62] while Blumrosen predicted that it would actually be effective.[63] Time has proven Sovern correct.

What does the EEOC do if it doesn't enact regulations or decide cases? Precious little. Filing a discrimination claim with the EEOC or its state analog is a jurisdictional prerequisite to filing a suit to enforce the statutes. The EEOC can conciliate or mediate, a little-studied process. It can litigate the case itself, representing simultaneously the interests of the individual or group complainant and the independent interest of the public in ridding workplaces of discrimination.[64] The EEOC does not characteristically take the broadest or most cutting-edge cases. Most of the cases it litigates are fairly routine, and often seem selected to give junior lawyers training and practice in employment litigation before they are hired by private law firms.[65] Not surprisingly, the EEOC is not an effective litigator; most individuals would be better represented by private counsel, who accept compensation on a contingent-fee basis and achieve higher damage verdicts than the EEOC.[66] In the vast majority of complaints, the EEOC neither conciliates effectively nor takes the case to litigation. It instead issues a "right to sue letter." This is a jurisdictional prerequisite enabling a complainant to sue in federal or state court, but normally means only that the EEOC has not evaluated the case.

This enforcement method was designed to be ineffective, and has proven so over time. If the EEOC were abolished tomorrow, no one would miss it except for private law firms forced to train their own litigators. As with the *FLSA*, its creation was an opportunity missed. Congress should have created an administrative agency like the NLRB, with administra-

---

61 Alfred W Blumrosen, *Modern Law: The Law Transmission System and Equal Employment Opportunity* (Madison: University of Wisconsin Press, 1993) at 47–49.

62 Michael I Sovern, *Legal Restraints on Racial Discrimination in Employment* (NY: Twentieth Century Fund, 1966) at 205.

63 Alfred W Blumrosen, *Black Employment and the Law* (New Brunswick NJ: Rutgers University Press, 1971).

64 *Employment Opportunity Commission v Waffle House Inc*, 534 US 279 (2002) (EEOC may seek all appropriate relief under statute, possibly including damages and reinstatement for individual employees who had agreed to arbitrate their claims, since the EEOC vindicates both public and individual rights).

65 Michael Selmi, "The Value of the EEOC: Reexamining the Agency's Role in Employment Discrimination Law" (1996) 57:1 Ohio St LJ 1

66 *Ibid.*

tive law judges to compile factual records, and a board in Washington to decide cases and set policy.

By contrast, however, the failure of Title VII to refer to grievance arbitration is not an opportunity missed, but instead a reflection of the sad reality of race discrimination in 1964 America. Of course there were unions that played a crucial role in the civil rights coalition. But there were far too many that discriminated along with employers. Unions in the building trades and maritime industries limited access to their trades to the legitimate sons of their white membership. They did not admit African-Americans to membership, conduct that was legal until passage of the *Civil Rights Act of 1964*.[67] By 1964, most collective agreements had established grievance systems that ended in arbitration. However, conspicuous exceptions included unions in the building trades and the Teamsters, whose grievance systems then (and, as Wawock's case shows, now), typically terminated in joint boards that were (and are) the vehicle for union-employer horse-trading, not protection of individual rights.[68] There has thus never been any interest in the civil rights community in channelling discrimination claims to private union-management dispute resolution.

### 3) The Arbitration Model: Rise of Grievance Arbitration during World War II

While the history of grievance arbitration under collective bargaining agreements in the US is fairly well-known, it is worth pointing out a few features that historically made it undesirable as a location for statutory grievances.

First, US grievance arbitration is a creature of World War II labour policy. It was not well-established as a coherent system of labour rights enforcement at the time of the passage of the *FLSA* in 1938, and in any event, that statute, on the insistence of the labour unions, focused on

67 At the insistence of the labour movement, union control of membership admission was specifically protected by the Taft-Hartley amendments to *the National Labor Relations Act*, §8(b)(1)(A), 29 USC §158(b)(1)(A)(proviso permitting unions to prescribe rules for acquisition and retention of membership), and the *Labor-Management Reporting and Disclosure Act of 1959* (LMRDA) §3(o), 29 USC §402(o), limiting its protections to union members who have complied with the union's membership criteria.

68 Ralph C James & Estelle Dinerstein James, *Hoffa and the Teamsters: A Study of Union Power* (Princeton NJ: Van Nostrand, 1965) at 167–85.

workers without union representation. United States Steel had recognized the United Steelworkers, but the other steel employers ("Little Steel") had violently and successfully resisted recognition.[69] General Motors had recognized the United Automobile Workers but Ford had not, and even at GM, arbitration was not institutionalized.[70] The term "arbitration" was commonly used but covered a wide range of institutions.[71] It is idle to speculate what system of workplace justice would have developed had war not come, but it is undeniable that modern grievance arbitration — arbitration before a professional arbitrator empowered to decide rights claims under the collective bargaining agreement, but not new interest claims — became widespread only under the orders of the National War Labor Board.[72]

Second, grievance arbitration achieved legal status and autonomy by emphasizing a rigid split between statutory rights, and rights under a collective bargaining agreement. By the end of the war, large employers and unions were comfortable with the standard wartime agreement

---

69 See generally Ahmed White, *The Last Great Strike: Little Steel, the CIO, and the Struggle for Labor Rights in New Deal America* (Berkeley: University of California Press, 2016).

70 In 1938, grievors at General Motors were required to sign the grievance and present it to the foreman before presenting it to the grievance committeeman. National UAW officials could not be involved for the first twenty-four hours. After Walter Reuther became director of the UAW's GM department in March 1939, he worked to rebuild grievance processes, which became established in the June 1940 collective bargaining agreement, with detailed provisions for resolving disputes, ending in decisions by a permanent umpire. Nelson Lichtenstein observes that "the UAW-GM arbitration experiment was a remarkable innovation, for it represented the very first such permanent mechanism established in heavy industry": "Great Expectations: The Promise of Industrial Jurisprudence and its Demise, 1930–1960," in Nelson Lichtenstein & Howell John Harris eds, *Industrial Democracy in America: The Ambiguous Promise* (Cambridge UK: Cambridge University Press, 1993) 113 at 126–29.

71 Dennis R. Nolan & Roger I. Abrams, "American Labor Arbitration: The Early Years," (1983) 35 U Fla L Rev 373. While Nolan and Abrams argue that American labour arbitration was mature by 1941 and correspondingly owed less than is often claimed to the World War II experience (420–21), their examples in fact show the wide variety of institutions labelled "arbitration" in the 1930s, including mechanisms in anthracite coal and garment production that made little distinction between rights and interest claims. They also show how much changed between 1938, the year the *FLSA* was enacted, and 1941.

72 James B. Atleson, *Labor and the Wartime State: Labor Relations and Law During World War II* (Urbana: University of Illinois Press, 1998) at 60–85.

prohibiting strikes during the life of the contract, and instead referring rights disputes to arbitration. Arbitration law, however, was rickety state law often hostile to arbitration, and the *Federal Arbitration Act* excluded contracts of employment.[73] Unions began a concerted and successful litigation campaign to establish ready enforcement of promises to arbitrate (without judicial scrutiny of either the facts or merits of the claim), and minimal judicial review of the dispute either pre- or post-arbitration. This campaign culminated in the so-called *Steelworkers Trilogy* of 1960.[74] It succeeded by convincing (or perhaps scaring) the Supreme Court that "[t] he labor arbitrator performs functions which are not normal to the courts; the considerations which help him fashion judgements may indeed be foreign to the competence of courts."[75] Chief among these considerations was the avoidance of industrial strife,[76] which empowered the arbitrator to render rulings that drew on the "common law of the shop" and other unarticulated "needs and desires of the parties." The Court perhaps exaggerated the supposed incompatibility of private arbitration and public law.[77] But the very premise of the successful campaign to remove labour arbitration from judicial scrutiny was the assumption that such arbitration deals only with rights under labour agreements, and not statutory claims; the Court's hypothesized "common law of the shop" and "needs and desires of the parties" hardly seem like appropriate vehicles for statutory interpretation.

In a series of thirteen decisions between 1974 and 1998, the Supreme Court consistently maintained this sharp conceptual and practical distinction between (on the one hand) claims under collective bargaining agreements, appropriate for union-management dispute resolution with minimal judicial review, and (on the other hand) statutory claims, for

---

73 9 USC §1. See generally *Szalai*, above note 6.

74 See above note 37.

75 *United Steelworkers v Warrior & Gulf Navigation Co*, above note 37 at 581

76 "In the commercial case, arbitration is the substitute for litigation. Here arbitration is the substitute for industrial strife": *ibid* at 578. For the reference to the "needs and desires of the parties," *see ibid* at 81.

77 In *United Steelworkers v Enterprise Wheel & Car Corp*, above note 37 at 596 n2, the Court quoted Charles R Walker's "Life in the Automotive Factory," (1958:1) 36 Harv Bus Rev 111 at 117: "Persons unfamiliar with mills and factories — farmers or professors for example — often remark upon visiting them that they seem like another world." The *Steelworkers Trilogy* is peppered with similar quotes emphasizing — perhaps overemphasizing — the distinct world of the workplace and the distance between its normative universe, and that of the general law.

which access to public courts and agencies must always be preserved.[78] Of course, these cases arose because the very same incident may easily give rise to both kinds of claims. An individual who believes that his or her discharge represents illegal racial discrimination may be said, with no stretch of the imagination, to be simultaneously and necessarily alleging a discharge without "just cause," normally prohibited by collective bargaining agreements, as both Canadians and Americans well know. Nevertheless, the Court held consistently that the two claims must be kept conceptually distinct. An arbitrator's decision that the employee was discharged for cause did not preclude his or her suit under civil rights statutes, and was admissible in the civil rights suit only for whatever weight the court chose to give it.[79] This conceptual wall between private claims under collective bargaining agreements, and public claims under statutes, so different from the Canadian conceptualization, rested on

1) the unions' insistence in the *Steelworkers Trilogy* and other cases from the 1950s and 60s that arbitration reached only claims under collective agreements — as the phrase at the time went, it was "the substitute for industrial strife," not "the substitute for litigation";[80]
2) Congress's presumed intention to make statutory rights effective;[81] and

---

78 See generally Alan Hyde, "Labor Arbitration of Discrimination Claims After *14 Penn Plaza v Pyett*: Letting Discrimination Defendants Decide Whether Plaintiffs May Sue Them," (2010) 25 Ohio St J on Dispute Resolution 975 at 983–98 ["Labor Arbitration of Discrimination Claims"]

79 *Alexander v Gardner-Denver Com*, 415 US 36 (1974)(employee may sue employer under Title VII despite arbitrator's finding that his discharge was for cause). See also, *e.g.*, *Barrentine v Arkansas-Best Freight System Inc*, 450 US 728, 745) (1981) (allowing employee to sue employer in federal court under the *FLSA* seeking compensation for time spent inspecting trucks, despite collective bargaining agreement requiring compensation for all time spent in employer's service, and adverse ruling by joint employer-union grievance committee); *Lingle v Norge Div of Magic Che Inc*, 486 US 399, 407–10 (1988) (employee may sue in state court alleging that her discharge was retaliation for filing workers compensation claim, despite arbitral finding that she was discharged for cause, because state law remedy is independent of the collective bargaining agreement).

80 *United Steelworkers v Warrior & Gulf Navigation Co*, *above* note 37

81 See, for example, *Atchison, Topeka & Santa Fe Ry Co v Buell*, 480 US 557, 567 (1987) ("It is inconceivable that Congress intended that a worker who suffered a disabling injury would be denied recovery under the [*Federal Employer Liability Statute*] simply because he might also be able to process a narrow labor grievance under the [*Railway Labor Act*] to a successful conclusion.")

3) practical aspects of the arbitration process which make it unacceptable as a forum for statutory claims.[82]

## C. THE CURRENT CRISIS OF THE LITIGATION MODEL

The Court has recently cast doubt on how much of this wall remains intact. In 2009, it held, abruptly reversing course, that a federal trial court should dismiss an individual employee's discrimination suit where the applicable collective bargaining agreement between his union and employer specifically gave arbitrators jurisdiction to decide claims of discrimination.[83] The Court failed to take into account that the union had already decided not to submit the employee's claim to arbitration, despite the fact that the lower courts had expressly noted that key fact. Accordingly, the Court's decision effectively killed the claim. The Court did not attempt to reconcile its decision with, or even mention, the previous thirty years of precedent insisting on a sharp demarcation between an individual's public law claim to be free of discrimination, and the same individual's parallel (but distinct) private law claims under his collective bargaining agreement.[84]

Understandably, the lower federal courts have since been quite confused about their role in similar disputes in which individual employees (or groups of employees) want to litigate a statutory claim, while their employers want it dismissed from court and sent to actual or hypothetical arbitration. Some courts send all statutory claims by employees represented by unions to labour arbitration.[85] Some send such claims to

82 *Alexander v Gardner-Denver Com*, above note 79 at 56–58, noted the legal incompetence of many US arbitrators; the limited fact-finding in arbitration; the usual practice of arbitrators, approved by the Court, of failing to give reasons for awards; the general informality of procedures; the union's exclusive control over whether and how to present a claim to arbitration; and potential lack of harmony between the interests of an individual claimant and the majority of the bargaining unit

83 *Pyett*, above note 13

84 Hyde, "Labor Arbitration of Discrimination Claims, above note 78

85 See, for example, *Portis v Ruan Transp Mgt Sys*, 2015 BL 205580 (WD Va, June 26, 2015) (suit under state whistle-blower statute stayed pending arbitration; applicable collective bargaining agreement made no reference to statutory claims and provide for arbitration of any dispute "arising under the agreement"); *Hodges v All Transit LLC*, 198 LRRM 2513, 2014 BL 37580 (ED NY, Feb. 7, 2014)(dismissing *FLSA* claim for compensation for hours worked because employee was covered by a collective bargaining

arbitration (or equivalent) with instructions to the arbitrators to determine their own jurisdiction.[86] Some carefully scrutinize the arbitration clause of the collective bargaining agreement to see whether it expressly commits statutory claims to arbitration; these courts disagree about what presumptions, if any, they should apply to this contractual construction.[87] Some make distinctions among statutes.[88] Some act as if *Pyett* never existed.[89] The one point that is clear is that arbitrators, who now hear statutory claims that they would never have seen pre-*Pyett*, have not yet risen to the challenge. There are simply no interesting post-*Pyett* opinions by US labour arbitrators on important questions of statutory or other public labour law.

It is idle to wonder whether, had the US gone down the *Weber* path at an earlier time, it might have evolved a Canadian-style cadre of arbitrators

---

agreement with a grievance procedure; agreement made no reference to statutory rights; no attempt to determine "clear and unmistakable" waiver of right to sue).

86 *Wawock v Superior Court*, above note 22.

87 See, for example, *Gilbert v Donahoe*, 751 F3d 303 (5th Cir 2014). Plaintiff claimed that the employer violated rights under disability rights law and the *Family and Medical Leave Act*. Held, the disability bias claim should have been dismissed for want of jurisdiction since the applicable collective bargaining agreement required the employer to comply with discrimination statutes. However, the court should have retained the claim under the *Family and Medical Leave Act*, as the employer's obligation of compliance was found only in an employee manual, not in the text of the collective bargaining agreement.

88 *Manning v Boston Medical Ctr Corp*, 725 F3d 34, 52 (1st Cir 2013) (questioning whether *FLSA* claim may ever be waived by a collective bargaining agreement, noting that the *FLSA*, unlike Title VII or the *Americans with Disabilities Act*, lacks language encouraging arbitration; holding that an arbitration clause applying to "any dispute" is not an effective waiver of the right to sue: "Something closer to specific enumeration of the statutory claims to be arbitrated is required").

89 *US v Brennan*, 650 F3d 65 at 122–23 and n56 (2d Cir 2011) (claim under Title VII: "It is, we emphasize, well established that collective-bargaining remedies are separate and independent from Title VII remedies. . . . When an employee believes that she has suffered discrimination, she may proceed with the grievance procedure, under Title VII, or both, but the fact that the employee has one of these independent types of rights does not entitle her to anything with respect to the other . . . [N]othing in *Pyett* suggests any wavering in the Court's commitment to the traditional separation between contractual collective bargaining agreement rights and statutory Title VII rights."); *Bell v Southeastern Pa. Transp. Auth.*, 733 F3d 490 at 496 (3d Cir 2013) ("Here, where the Operators rely solely on their statutory, rather than their contractual, rights to recovery, district courts have had no difficulty concluding that such plaintiffs may proceed on their *FLSA* claims without first seeking arbitration.")

adept at statutory analysis. (Path dependence has its problems.) On my side of the border, we still have the arbitration system described by the Supreme Court in the *Steelworkers Trilogy* in 1960: "Arbitration is the means of solving the unforeseeable by molding a system of private law for all the problems which may arise and to provide for their solution in a way which will generally accord with the variant needs and desires of the parties [i.e., unions and employers]."[90] For determining whether a given employee was discharged or disciplined for cause, this system works fine. But US arbitrators are almost never called upon to deal with claims of statutory rights, a reality confirmed in the scant literature on the role of arbitration in statutory enforcement, which makes it clear that where unions can choose between arbitral and administrative processes, they take statutory claims to public law institutions for enforcement.[91] Unions simply do not regard arbitration as a viable avenue of enforcement for statutory rights, and US labour arbitration law has yet to contribute anything to the development of statutory labour law.

## D. CONCLUSION

I regard the current jurisdictional confusion in the enforcement of statutory labour rights as a threat to workplace standards every bit as big as the more-commented-upon problems of diversion of unrepresented employees' claims to individual arbitration; employer off-loading of statutory responsibilities to less-capitalized staffing agencies and subcontractors; misclassification of employees; securing effective labour rights enforcement for the large population working in the US without legal authorization; and exclusion of worker organizations from participating in statutory rights enforcement.

Even more fundamentally, I take the view that enforcement through litigation leading to judicial decisions contributes mightily to these other problems. Litigation is expensive, unpredictable, lacks mechanisms to

---

90 *United Steelworkers v Warrior & Gulf Navigation Co*, above note 37 at 581

91 See Levinson, above note 38. See also Pauline T Kim, *"Collective and Individual Approaches to Protecting Employee Privacy: The Experience with Workplace Drug Testing,"* (2006) 66 La L Rev 1009 (dealing with legal strategies for challenging drug testing); David Weil, "Regulating the Workplace: The Vexing Problem of Implementation," (1996) 7 Advances in Indus & Lab Rel 247 (dealing with the enforcement of federal employment regulation in unionized workplaces).

overcome inequality of resources, and frequently resorts to common law analogies of dubious relevance, such as the common law definitions of employee or vicarious liability. Despite my respect for the Canadian experience, however, I do not believe that the solution to this problem in the US lies in channeling statutory claims to labour arbitrators. US arbitrators have historically failed this task. In addition, enforcement through labour arbitration would benefit only the 6.6 percent of private sector workers in the US currently represented by a labour union;[92] most US employees would have no access to arbitration of this type.

Rather, I believe that experts in labour rights should have "sitting in the drawer," just as Frances Perkins had the draft *Fair Labor Standards Act*, legislation creating a unified labour court or agency that could, without cost to employees, investigate and remedy violations of such employment-related statutes as labour standards and antidiscrimination legislation. Should the occasion arise for enactment of such a statute at the federal level, it could be pulled from the drawer. Such an agency could profitably adopt the tripartite model advocated by Janice Fine and Jennifer Gordon, who provide detailed examples of best practices.[93] It could also make much more effective use of mediation than the existing EEOC, Department of Labor, or state analogs.

Vastly more likely, however, is the creation of such agencies in states such as California, New York, New Jersey, or Massachusetts, or cities like San Francisco or New York, which already provide substantive labour standards and protection against discrimination far superior to the federal minima. Effective enforcement will then become just one more dimension of the dissolution of federal labour law in the US and the rise, familiar to a Canadian audience, of primary state (provincial) responsibility for standards in the labour market.

---

92 US Department of Labor, above note 33.

93 See Fine, "Solving the Problem from Hell"; Fine & Gordon, "Strengthening Labour Standards Enforcement through Partnerships with Workers' Organisations"; Fine, "Co-Production," all above note 11. For such an enforcement agency to supplant the litigation model, it would have to be considerably more responsive than even the best existing US labour standards enforcement. In a personal communication on February 2, 2016, Janice Fine said: "I hear over and over again from organizations that they prefer to go the private right of action route, rather than filing complaints, because it allows them to maintain much greater control over the cases as they progress. They hate the cone of silence that descends so often when they help workers file wage claims with state departments of labor or the USDOL."

# About the Contributors

**Kevin Banks** is an Associate Professor and Director of the Centre for Law in the Contemporary Workplace, Faculty of Law, Queen's University. He holds an LLB and a degree in Economics from the University of Toronto, and a doctorate from Harvard Law School. Prior to taking up an academic career, Kevin practised labour law (representing unions and individual workers), and served in a number of senior positions in the federal public service. He has published widely on domestic, international and comparative labour law in national and international academic journals and collected papers, advised governments and government task forces, and sat as an arbitrator under the North American Free Trade Agreement (NAFTA). Succeeding his mentor Bernie Adell, he is currently editor-in-chief of the *Canadian Labour and Employment Law Journal*.

**Richard Chaykowski** received his PhD from Cornell University. He is currently Director of the MIR Program at Queen's University, cross-appointed to Queen's Faculty of Law. He is a member of the Advisory Board of the Queen's Centre for Law in the Contemporary Workplace. He has also been a visiting scholar at MIT, University of Toronto and McGill University. His public service includes a stint as Visiting Chair at Human Resources and Skills Development Canada, and as Research Director for the federal Expert Panel on Older Workers. His teaching and research interests include labour policy, the intersection of labour policy and law, labour relations and collective bargaining, North American labour markets, implications of the aging workforce, employee accommodation in the workplace, and workplace innovation and the impacts of technological change in the workplace. He has published over fifty papers in national and international journals, edited volumes and periodicals, as well as other professional and technical reports.

**Renée-Claude Drouin** is an Associate Professor at the Faculty of Law, University of Montreal, and a researcher with both the Interuniversity Research Centre on Globalization and Work (CRIMT) and the Centre de droit des affaires et du commerce international (CDACI). She has been a member of the Quebec Bar since 1996, and obtained her PhD in law from Cambridge University in 2006. Her scholarly work focuses on domestic and international labour law, with a particular focus on human rights and corporate social responsibility. She has published numerous articles in both French and English on these topics. She is also the Quebec Editor of the *Canadian Labour and Employment Law Journal.*

**Brian D. Etherington** is Professor Emeritus at the Faculty of Law, University of Windsor, where he taught labour law, labour arbitration, personal employment law and criminal law. He holds degrees from McMaster University, Queen's University and Yale University. He is co-author of *Labour Law in Canada*, 5th ed. (Kluwer/Butterworths, 2002), *Leading Cases on Labour Arbitration* (Lancaster House, 2002), and *Labour Arbitration in Canada* (Lancaster House, 2006), and has also published scholarly articles on labour and employment law issues. He belongs to the Canadian Labour Law Casebook Group, served for almost a decade as editor-in-chief of the *Canadian Labour and Employment Law Journal*, and is a member of the Advisory Committee of the Queen's Centre for Law in the Contemporary Workplace. In addition to his scholarly activities, he has been a member of the Law Society of Upper Canada since 1984, and has maintained an active labour arbitration practice for many years.

**Alan Hyde** is Distinguished Professor of Law and Sidney Reitman Scholar at Rutgers School of Law. Before coming to Rutgers, he was an instructor at New York University School of Law and represented the National Labor Relations Board in federal courts of appeals. He has been a visiting professor at Yale, Columbia, Cornell, New York University, Cardozo, Fordham, Brooklyn, the University of Michigan, and the University of

Toronto. He is a member of the American Law Institute and consultant to its current *Restatement of Employment Law*. His research interests focus on the globalization of labor markets and the economics of labor mobility. He also studies the changing meaning of citizenship and low naturalization rates among immigrants to the US. His numerous publications include *Working in Silicon Valley: Economic and Legal Analysis of a High-Velocity Labor Market* (2003) and *Bodies of Law* (1997). He is a director of the Association for Union Democracy, and writes briefs on labor and employment cases on behalf of the Association and other employee rights organizations.

**Brian Langille** is a Professor of Law at the University of Toronto, where he teaches labour and employment law as well as contract law. His research and writing is mainly about labour law, labour law theory, international labour law, and constitutional labour law. He has been a Visiting Professor at the International Institute for Labour Studies (ILO, Geneva), the Graduate Institute for International Studies, University of Geneva, the European University Institute (Florence), the Centre for Transnational Legal Studies (London), the Universitat Pompeu Fabra (Barcelona), and the law school at Dalhousie University, where he was Innis Christie Visiting Professor in Labour and Employment Law. He has been a Fellow of the Institute for Advanced Studies, Nantes, France (2012), a Senior Fellow at Melbourne Law School (2013), and a Visiting Professor at the Hebrew University, Jerusalem (2015). He has advised Canadian governments, the ILO, the OECD and others including public and private sector unions and employers. He is also an experienced labour arbitrator.

**Claire Mummé** is an Assistant Professor at the Faculty of Law, University of Windsor, where she teaches contracts, labour law and employment law. She holds graduate degrees from the University of Toronto and New York University, and a doctorate from Osgoode Hall Law School, where she was a SSHRC Joseph-Armand Bombardier CGS Doctoral Scholar, and a McMurtry Fellow of the Osgoode Legal History Society. She is also a member of the Law Society of Upper Canada. Her research interests focus on law's distributional effects and its role in structuring institutions of the market, as examined through the legal regulation of waged employment. She is currently pursuing research on the legal regulation of supply chains and their effects on labour organizing, and on the common law's responses to changing forms of work in the post-Fordist era. She sits on the Board of Directors of the Windsor Sexual Assault Crisis Centre. Her scholarly articles on employment law, labour law and human rights law have been published both nationally and internationally.

**Jo-Anne Pickel** is a full-time Vice-Chair with the Human Rights Tribunal of Ontario. Prior to her appointment to the Tribunal, she was a partner in a labour law firm where she focused on written advocacy and research in the areas of labour, human rights, constitutional and administrative law. She holds a doctorate in law from the University of Toronto, a Masters of Social Work, and civil law and common law degrees from the Faculty of Law, McGill University. She has taught law at Carleton University and was a Senior Advisor at the National Judicial Institute.

**Karen Schucher** is a Professor at Humber College, where she teaches in the Paralegal Degree and Diploma programmes. She holds a PhD from Osgoode Hall Law School, authoring a dissertation which focuses on the history of human rights code enforcement in Ontario. Prior to entering academic life, she was a partner in the Toronto law firm of Cavalluzzo Shilton McIntyre & Cornish LLP, where she practiced labour and human rights law and headed up the firm's research group. Karen has published widely in areas related to workplace human rights and labour arbitration in a variety of scholarly journals, including the *Supreme Court Law Review*.

**Elizabeth Shilton** is a Senior Fellow with the Centre for Law in the Contemporary Workplace at Queen's, and a McMurtry Visiting Clinical Fellow at Osgoode Hall Law School. She holds a doctorate in law from the University of Toronto, as well as law degrees from Dalhousie (Schulich) and Harvard. She was a founding partner of Cavalluzzo Shilton McIntyre & Cornish LLP, a Toronto-based law firm specializing in union-side labour law. She has taught labour, employment, collective bargaining law and workplace human rights law as an adjunct professor at the University of Toronto, Osgoode Hall (York University) and Queen's University, and has been a Visiting Scholar at Osgoode's Institute for Feminist Legal Studies. She also sat for a number of years as a member and Vice-Chair of Ontario's Financial Services Tribunal/Commission. Her current research focuses on gender and work, pension reform and workplace dispute resolution. Her most recent book is *Empty Promises: Why Workplace Pension Law Doesn't Deliver Pensions* (McGill-Queen's University Press, 2016).

**George Slotsve** received his PhD from the University of Wisconsin-Madison in 1989. He has a BA in Economics from Queen's University (1981) and an MA in Economics from the University of Western Ontario (1982). Dr. Slotsve is currently a faculty member in the Department of Economics at Northern Illinois University. Prior to joining NIU, he held faculty appointments at Vanderbilt University and Dalhousie University, and has been a Visiting Professor at the University of the Philippines (Diliman, Quezon), and a Visiting Scholar and Visiting Professor at Queen's University.

# Bibliography

Abramsky, Randi Hammer. "Grievance Arbitration, External Law and the Problem of Multiple Forums" in William Kaplan, Jeffrey Sack & Morley Gunderson, eds. (1994–1995) 1 *Labour Arbitration Year Book* (Toronto: Lancaster House, 1995) 41.

———. "The Ontario Law Reform Commission Report on Delay and Multiple Proceedings: A Critique" (1996) 4 *Canadian Labour and Employment Law Journal* 353;

———. "The Problem of Multiple Proceedings: an Arbitrator's Perspective" in William Kaplan et al, eds. (1996–1997) 1 *Labour Arbitration Year Book* (Toronto: Lancaster House, 2000) 45.

Adams, George W. "Bell Canada and the Older Worker: Who Will Review the Judges?" (1974) 12:2 *Osgoode Hall Law Journal* 389.

Adams, The Honourable George W. *Canadian Labour Law*, 2d ed (Canada Law Book: 1993) (loose leaf) at 10.1660.

Adams, Roy J & Bernard Adell. "Canada" in Hoyt N Wheeler & Jacques Rojot, eds. *Workplace Justice: Employment Obligations in International Perspective* (Columbia, South Carolina: University of South Carolina Press, 1992) 99.

Adell, B. "The Canadian System of Industrial Conflict Resolution" in T Hanami & R Blanpain, eds. *Industrial Conflict Resolution in Market Economies: A Study of Canada, Great Britain and Sweden* (Deventer, Netherlands: Kluwer Law and Taxation Publishers, 1987) 25.

Adell, BL. "Labour Law–Collective Agreement–Right of Individual Employee to Sue Employer" (1967) 45 *Canadian Bar Review* 354.

———. "The Duty of Fair Representation — Effective Protection for Individual Rights in Collective Agreements?" (1970) 25:3 *Relations industrielles /Industrial Relations* 602.

———. *The Legal Status of Collective Agreements in England, the United States and Canada* (Kingston, ON: Queen's University Industrial Relations Centre, 1970).

———. Book Review of *Droit du travail en vigueur au Québec?* by Robert Gagnon, Louis LeBel & Pierre Verge (1973) 1:2 *Dalhousie Law Journal* 394.

Adell, Bernard. "The Duty of Fair Representation: 'a form of words . . .'?." PowerPoint delivered at *Adjudicating Human Rights in the Workplace After the Pinto Report, Where Do We Go Next?*, CLCW Workshop, Queen's University, 10 November 2012)) [unpublished].

———. "Establishment of Faculty Collective Bargaining: The Developing Law" in Paul Thomas, ed. *Universities and the Law* (Manitoba: Legal Research Institute of the University of Manitoba, 1975) 45.

———. "Collective Agreements and Individual Rights: A Note on the Duty of Fair Representation" (1986) 11:2 *Queen's Law Journal* 251.

———. "Pension Plan Surpluses and the Law: Finding a Path for Reform" in *Task Force on Inflation Protection for Employment Pension Plans, Research Studies Volume* 2 (Toronto: Government of Ontario, 1988) 209.

———. "The Canadian System of Retirement Income Support" (Paper prepared for the 12th World Congress of the International Society for Labour Law and Social Security, Madrid, Spain, 20–23 September 1988) (Kingston, ON: Queen's University Industrial Relations, 1988).

———. "The Case for Employee Rights in Pension Plan Surpluses" in *New Developments i n Employment Law, Meredith Memorial Lectures* (Montreal: Éditions Yvon Blais, 1988) 87.

———. "The Legal Framework of Faculty Collective Bargaining: Some Short Questions and Some Long Answers" in HN Janisch, ed. *The University and the Law* (Halifax: Dalhousie University Faculty of Law, 1975) 121.

———. "Workplace Disciplinary Rules and Procedures in Canada" (1993) 132:5–6 *International Labour Review* 583.

———. "Collective Agreements and Individual Rights: A Note on the Duty of Fair Representation" (1986) 11:2 *Queen's Law Journal* 251.

———. "Establishing a Collective Employee Voice in the Workplace: How Can the Obstacles Be Lowered?" in G England, ed. *Essays in Labour Relations Law* (Don Mills, ON: CCH Canadian Limited, 1986) 3.

———. "Jurisdictional Overlap Between Arbitration and Other Forums: An Update" (2000) 8 *Canadian Labour and Employment Law Journal* 179.

———. "Law and Industrial Relations: The State of the Art in Common Law Canada" in Gérard Hébert, Hem C Jain & Noah M Meltz, eds. *The State of the Art in Industrial Relations* (Ontario: Queen's University Industrial Relations Centre & University of Toronto Centre for Industrial Relations, 1988) 107.

———. "Overlapping Forums in Collective Agreement Administration" in Gilles Trudeau, Guylaine Vallée & Diane Veilleux, eds. *Études en droit du travail: à la mémoire de Claude D'Aoust* (Cowansville, Québec: Éditions Yvon Blais, 1995).

———. "The Union's Duty of Fair Representation in Discrimination Cases: The New Obligation to Be Proactive" in Kevin Whitaker et al, eds, (2001–2002) 1 *Labour Arbitration Yearbook* (Toronto: Lancaster House, 2002) 263.

———. *Adjudication of Workplace Disputes in Ontario: A Report to the Ontario Law Reform Commission* (1991) [unpublished].

———. "The Legal Framework of Collective Bargaining in North America, with Envious Glances at the New Australian Federal Legislation" in Industrial Relations Society of Western Australia, *Occasional Papers*, December 1994.

———. "Rights and Functions of Trade Unions and their Representatives at Enterprise Level in Canada" in *Proceedings of 8th International Conference on Labour Law and Social Legislation*, Milan, 1976.

———. "Codification of Labour Law in Canada (Common Law Jurisdictions)" in *Proceedings of Ninth International Congress of International Society for Labour Law and Social Security*, Munich, 1978, 772.

———. "Termination of Employment on the Initiative of the Employer, and Income Security of the Worker Concerned — Canada" in *Proceedings of Tenth International Congress, International Society for Labour Law and Social Security* (Washington, BNA Inc., 1984) vol. 2, 217.

———. "Country Reports — Canada" in Edward Yemin, ed. *Workforce Reductions in Undertakings: Policies and Measures for the Protection of Redundant Workers in Seven Industrialised Market Economy Countries* (Geneva: International Labour Office, 1982) 37.

Adell, Bernard L. "*International Brotherhood of Teamsters v Therien* and the Suability of Trade Unions in Alberta" (1955–1961) 1 *Alberta Law Review* 571.

Adell, BL & DD Carter. *Collective Bargaining for University Faculty in Canada* (Kingston, ON: Queen's University Industrial Relations Centre, 1972).

Adell, Bernard & Roy J Adams. "Discipline and Discharge for Theft in Ten Countries" in *Proceedings of 45th Annual Meeting* (Anaheim, California: Industrial Relations Research Association, 1993) 501.

———. "Theft as Cause for Employment Discipline: Some Comparative Observations" (1993) 9:2 *International Journal of Comparative Labour Law and Industrial Relations* 93.

Adell, B et al, "The System of Labour Dispute Resolution in Ontario Hospitals and its Application at Kingston General Hospital" in T Hanami & R Blanpain, eds. *Industrial Conflict Resolution in Market Economies: A Study of Canada, Great Britain and Sweden* (Deventer, Netherlands: Kluwer Law and Taxation Publishers, 1987) 45.

Adell, Bernard, Michel Grant & Allen Ponak, *Strikes in Essential Services* (Kingston: Queen's IRC Press, 2001).

Akaike, Hirotugo. "A New Look at Statistical Model Identification," online: (1974) 19:6 *IEEE Transactions on Automatic Control* 716 http://ieeexplore.ieee.org.

———. "Information Theory and an Extension of the Maximum Likelihood Principle" in BN Petrov & F Csaki, eds. *2nd International Symposium on Information Theory* (Budapest: Akadémia Kiadó, 1973) 267.

———. "Likelihood of a Model and Information Criteria" (1981) 16 *Journal of Econometrics* 3.

Alexandrowicz, John-Paul. "Restoring the Role of Grievance Arbitration: A New Approach to *Weber*" (2003) 10 *Canadian Labour and Employment Law Journal* 269.

Atleson, James B. *Labor and the Wartime State: Labor Relations and Law During World War II* (Urbana: University of Illinois Press, 1998).

———. *Values and Assumptions in American Labor Law* (Amherst: University of Massachusetts Press, 1983).

Banks, Kevin, Richard Chaykowski & George Slotsve. "Arbitration as Access to Justice: An Update on the Profile of Labour Arbitration Cases in Ontario" (Presentation delivered at the 2011 Industrial Relations Conference "Building and Maintaining Healthy Workplace Relationships," 16–17 June 2011) [unpublished].

Beatty, David M. "The Role of the Arbitrator: A Liberal Version" (1984) 34:2 *University of Toronto Law Journal* 136.

Beatty, David & Brian Langille. "Bora Laskin and Labour Law: From Vision to Legacy" (1985) 35:4 *University of Toronto Law Journal* 672.

Berkeley, Arthur Eliot. "The Most Serious Faults in Labor-Management Arbitration Today and What Can Be Done to Remedy Them" (1989) 40:11 *Labor Law Journal* 728.

Bernier, Jean. "L'arbitrage de grief: un système de justice privé ou public?" (2012) 53:1 *Les Cahiers de droit* 161.

Birken, Mitchell S. *Grievance Mediation: The Impact of the Process and Outcomes on the Interests of the Parties* (Kingston, ON: IRC Press, 2000).

Blumrosen, Alfred W. "Group Interests in Labor Law" (1958–1959) 13:3 *Rutgers Law Review* 432.

———. "Legal Protection for Critical Job Interests: Union-Management Authority versus Employee Autonomy" (1959) 13:4 *Rutgers Law Review* 631.

———. "The Worker and Three Phases of Unionism: Administrative and Judicial Control of the Worker-Union Relationship" (1963) 61:8 *Michigan Law Review* 1435.

———. *Black Employment and the Law* (New Brunswick NJ: Rutgers University Press, 1971).

———. *Modern Law: The Law Transmission System and Equal Employment Opportunity* (Madison: University of Wisconsin Press, 1993).

Bourdieu, Pierre. "The Force of Law: Toward a Sociology of the Juridical Field" (1987) 38:5 *Hastings Law Journal* 814.

Brown, Donald JM & David M Beatty. *Canadian Labour Arbitration*, 4th ed (Carswell, 2006) (loose-leaf).

Brown, Ray & Brian Etherington, "*Weber v. Ontario Hydro*: A Denial of Access to Justice for the Organized Employee?" (1996) 4 *Canadian Labour and Employment Law Journal* 183.

Brunelle, Christian & Mélanie Samson. "Les conflits de compétence entre tribunaux spécialisés: une question de textes ou de contextes?" (2008–2009) 39 *Revue de droit de l'Université de Sherbrooke* 223.

Butt, Elizabeth Rae. "Grievance Mediation: The Ontario Experience" in *School of Industrial Relations Research Essay Series No 14* (Kingston, ON: Industrial Relations Centre Queen's University, 1988).

Card, David & Alan B Krueger. *Myth and Measurement: The New Economics of the Minimum Wage* (Princeton NJ: Princeton University Press, 1995).

Carrothers, AWR. Book Review of *The Legal Status of Collective Agreements in England, the United States and Canada* by BL Adell, (1971) 21:2 *University of Toronto Law Journal* 252.

Carrothers, Alfred William Rooke. *Labour Arbitration in Canada: A Study of the Law and Practice Relating to the Arbitration of Grievance Disputes in Industrial Relations in Common Law Canada* (Toronto: Butterworths, 1961).

Carter, Donald D. "An Arbitrator as Human Rights Adjudicator: The Lessons of *Orillia Soldiers Memorial Hospital*" in Kevin Whitaker et al, eds. (1999–2000) 1 *Labour Arbitration Yearbook* (Toronto: Lancaster House, 2000) 55.

———. "Grievance Arbitration and the Charter: The Emerging Issues" (1989) 44:2 *Industrial Relations* 337.

———. "Looking at *Weber* Five Years Later: Is it Time for a New Approach?" (2000) 8 *Canadian Labour and Employment Law Journal* 231.

Carter, Donald. "An Arbitrator as Human Rights Adjudicator: The Lessons of *Orillia Soldiers Memorial Hospital*" (1999–2000) 1 *Labour Arbitration Year Book* (Toronto: Lancaster House, 2000) 55

Cleves, Mario A et al. *An Introduction to Survival Analysis Using Stata*, 2d ed (College Station, TX: Stata Press, 2008).

Cloutier, Sophie & Jacques Provencher. "L'arrêt *S.F.P.Q.*: une mise à jour s'impose!" in La Conférence des arbitres du Québec, *Débats d'actualité, Volume 2* (Montréal: Wilson & Lafleur, 2014) 147.

Coutu, Michel. "Les Décisions Récentes de la Cour Suprême du Canada sur L'article 124 de la *Loi sur les Normes du Travail*: La Quadrature du Cercle?" in *Arbitrage de griefs, Volume 8* (Cowansville: Éditions Yvon Blais, La Collection Blais, 2011) 223.

Cox, Archibald. "Current Problems in the Law of Grievance Arbitration" (1958) 30 *Rocky Mountain Law Review* 247.

———. "Individual Enforcement of Collective Bargaining Agreements" (1957) 8:12 *Labour Law Journal* 850.

———. "Reflections Upon Labor Arbitration" (1959) 72:8 *Harvard Law Review* 1482.

———. "Rights under a Collective Agreement" (1956) 69:4 *Harvard Law Review* 601.

———. "The Legal Nature of Collective Bargaining Agreements" (1958) 57:1 *Michigan Law Review* 1.

Cox, Archibald & John T Dunlop. "Regulation of Collective Bargaining by the National Labor Relations Board" (1950) 63:3 *Harvard Law Review* 389.

———. "The Duty to Bargain Collectively During the Term of an Existing Agreement" (1950) 63:7 *Harvard Law Review* 1097.

Craver, Charles B. "Labor Arbitration as a Continuation of the Collective Bargaining Process" (1990) 66:3 *Chicago-Kent Law Review* 571.

Daly, Paul. "Does *Penner* Overrule *Figliola*? What's the Canadian Law on Issue Estoppel?" (11 April 2013) *Administrative Law Matters* (blog), online, www.administrativelawmatters.com/blog/2013/04/11/does-penner-overrule-figliola-whats-the-canadian-law-on-issue-estoppel.

Davies, Paul & Mark Freedland. *Kahn-Freund's Labour and the Law*, 3d ed (London: Stevens & Sons, 1983).

Deitsch, Clarence R & David A Dilts. "Case Characteristics Affecting the Method of Grievance Dispute Settlement" (1988) 1:2 *Employee Responsibilities and Rights Journal* 113.

Department of Justice Canada. *The Legal Problems of Everyday Life: The Nature, Extent and Consequences of Justiciable Problems Experienced by Canadians*, by Ab Currie (Government of Canada, 12 May 2009), online: www.justice.gc.ca/eng/rp-pr/csj-sjc/jsp-sjp/rr07_la1-rr07_aj1/index.html.

Des Rosiers, Nathalie. "Unions and Democratic Governance: Empowering Participatory Citizenship" in Matthew Behrens, ed. *Unions Matter: Advancing Democracy, Economic Equality, and Social Justice* (Toronto: Between the Lines, 2014) 93.

deVyver, Frank T. "Regulation of Wages and Hours Prior to 1938" (1939) 6:3 *Law & Contemporary Problems* 323.

Doorey, David. "RIP: Professor Emeritus (Queens U. Law) and Labour Law Giant Bernie Adell." *Law of Work* (blog), online: http://lawofwork.ca/?p=7594.

Downey, Kirstin. *The Woman Behind the New Deal: The Life of Frances Perkins, FDR'S Secretary of Labor and His Moral Conscience* (New York: Anchor, 2010).

Drouin, Renée-Claude & Gilles Trudeau. "What Does *Isidore Garon* Mean for Arbitral Jurisdiction in Quebec?" (2007) 13:2 *Canadian Labour and Employment Law Journal* 347.

Durnford, Eric, QC. "Defining the Scope of Arbitration: The Impact of *Weber* — A Management Perspective" in Kevin Whitaker et al, eds. (1999–2000) 1 *Labour Arbitration Year Book* (Toronto: Lancaster House, 2000) 149.

Employment and Social Development Canada. "Union Coverage in Canada — 2014" (Ottawa: ESDC, 30 November, 2015), online: www.labour.gc.ca/eng/resources/info/publications/union_coverage/UnionCoverage_EN.pdf.

England, Geoffrey. "Recent Developments in the Law of the Employment Contract: Continuing Tension Between the Rights Paradigm and the Efficiency Paradigm" (1995) 20:2 *Queen's Law Journal* 557.

Etherington, Brian. "*O.P.S.E.U. v. Seneca College:* Deference as a Two-Edged Sword — A Missed Opportunity to Address the '*Weber* Gap'" (2006-2007) 13 *Canadian Labour and Employment Law Journal* 301.

———. "Promises, Promises: Notes on Diversity and Access to Justice" (2000) 26:1 *Queen's Law Journal* 43.

———. "*Weber* and Almost Everything After: Its Impact on *Charter*, Common Law and Individual Statutory Rights Claims" (Paper delivered at the Charter at Work Conference, University of Western Ontario, 23 October 2004) at 2 [unpublished].

Faraday, Fay. "The Expanding Scope of Arbitration: Mainstreaming Human Rights Values and Remedies" (2005) 12 *Canadian Labour and Employment Law Journal* 355.

Feller, David E. "A General Theory of the Collective Bargaining Agreement" (1973) 61:3 *California Law Review* 663.

Feller, David. "The Coming End of Arbitration's Golden Age" (1976) 29 The Proceedings of the National Academy of Arbitrators 97, online: NAARB http://naarb.org/proceedings/pdfs/1976-97.PDF.

Fernandez, Lynne. *Unions Boost Democracy and Prosperity for All* (Winnipeg: Canadian Centre for Policy Alternative, 2015), online: www.policyalternatives.ca/sites/default/files/uploads/publications/Manitoba%20Office/2015/11/Unions_Boost_Democracy.pdf.

Fine, Janice. "Co-Production: Bringing Together the Unique Capabilities of Government and Society for Stronger Labor Standards Enforcement," *Labor Innovations for the 21st Century (LIFT) Fund*, online: theliftfund.org/wp-content/uploads/2015/09/LIFTReportCoproductionOct_ExecSumm-rf_4.pdf.

———. "Solving the Problem from Hell: Tripartism as a Strategy for Addressing Labour Standards Non-Compliance in the United States" (2013) 50:4 *Osgoode Hall Law Journal* 813.

Fine, Janice & Jennifer Gordon. "Strengthening Labor Standards Enforcement through Partnerships with Workers' Organisations" (2010) 38:4 *Politics & Society* 552.

Flood, Craig. "Efficiency v Fairness: Multiple Litigation and Adjudication in Labour and Employment Law" (2000) 8 *Canadian Labour and Employment Law Journal* 383.

Forbath, William E. *Law and the Shaping of the American Labor Movement* (Cambridge MA: Harvard University Press 1991).

Freeman, Alan David. "Legitimizing Racial Discrimination through Antidiscrimination Law: A Critical Review of Supreme Court Doctrine" (1978) 62:6 *Minnesota Law Review* 1049.

Fricke, John. *An Empirical Study of the Grievance Arbitration Process in Alberta* (Edmonton: Alberta Labour, 1976).

Fudge, Judy. "The Canadian Charter of Rights: Recognition, Redistribution, and the Imperialism of the Courts" in Tom Campbell, KD Ewing & Adam Tomkins, eds, *Sceptical Essays on Human Rights* (Oxford: Oxford University Press, 2001) 335.

———. "The Paradoxes of Pay Equity: Reflections on the Law and the Market in *Canada* and *PSAC*" (2000) 12 *Canadian Journal of Women and the Law* 313.

———. "What do We Mean by Law and Social Transformation?" (1990) 5 *Canadian Journal of Law and Society* 47.

Fudge, Judy & Eric Tucker. *Labour Before the Law: The Regulation of Workers' Collective Action in Canada, 1900-1948* (Toronto: Oxford University Press, 2001).

Fudge, Judy & Harry Glasbeek. "The Legacy of PC 1003" (1994) 3 *Canadian Labour and Employment Law Journal* 357.

Fuller, Lon L. "Collective Bargaining and the Arbitrator" (1963) *Wisconsin Law Review* 3.

Galanter, Marc. "Access to Justice as a Moving Frontier" in Julia H Bass, WA Bogart & Frederick H Zemans, eds. *Access to Justice for a New Century: The Way Forward* (Toronto: Law Society of Upper Canada, 2005) 147.

Gall, Peter A, Andrea L Zwack & Kate Bayne. "Determining Human Rights Issues in the Unionized Workplace: The Case for Exclusive Arbitral Jurisdiction" (2005) 12 *Canadian Labour and Employment Law Journal* 381.

Gilmore, Grant. *The Death of Contract* (Columbus: Ohio State University Press, 1974).

Glasbeek, Harry. "Voluntarism, Liberalism, and Grievance Arbitration: Holy Grail, Romance, and Real Life" in Geoffrey England, ed. *Essays in Labour Relations Law* (Don Mills, ON: CCH, 1986) 57.

Goldberg, Michael J. "The Duty of Fair Representation: What the Courts Do in Fact," (1985) 34:1 *Buffalo Law Review* 89.

Goldsmith, Andrew. "The Management-Control Collective Bargaining Relationship: Three Models" (1986) 24:4 *Osgoode Hall Law Journal* 775.

Gordon, Michael E & Roger L Bowlby. "Propositions About Grievance Settlements: Finally, Consultation with Grievants" (1988) 41:1 *Personnel Psychology* 107.

Gottheil, Lewis. "Defining the Scope of Arbitration: The Impact of *Weber* — A Union Perspective" in Kevin Whitaker et al, eds. (1999-2000) 1 *Labour Arbitration Year Book* (Toronto: Lancaster House, 2000) 157.

Gottheil, Michael & Katherine Laird. "Direct Access to a Specialized Tribunal: The Ontario Experience" in Le Tribunal des droits de la personne et le Barreau du Québec, ed. *L'accès direct à un tribunal spécialisé en matière de droit à l'égalité: l'urgence d'agir au Québec?* (Cowansville, Québec: Éditions Yvon Blais, 2008) 145.

Gould IV, William B. *A Primer of American Labor Law*, 5th ed (New York: Cambridge University Press, 2013).

Gregory, Jeanne. "Sex Discrimination, Work and the Law" in Bob Fine et al, eds. *Capitalism and the Rule of Law: From Deviancy Theory to Marxism* (London: Hutchinson & Co, 1979) 137.

Grossman, Jonathan. "Fair Labor Standards Act of 1938: Maximum Struggle for a Minimum Wage" (1978) 101:6 *Monthly Labor Review* 22.

Gunderson, Morley & Douglas Hyatt. "Union Impact on Compensation, Productivity and Management of the Organization" in Morley Gunderson & Daphne Taras, eds. *Canadian Labour and Employment Relations*, 6d ed (Toronto: Pearson Addison Wesley, 2009) 383.

Hayes, James K. *Perspectives on management rights: the curious logic of the argument for reducing industrial discord by removing the mid-term strike bar from labour relations legislation* (Don Mills: Ontario Federation of Labour, 1974).

Hayter, Susan. "Unions and Collective Bargaining" in Janine Berg, ed. *Labour Markets, Institutions and Inequality: Building Just Societies in the 21st Century* (Geneva: International Labour Organization, 2015).

Herman, Samuel. "Administration and Enforcement of the *Fair Labor Standards Act*: The *Wage and Hour Law*" (1939) 6:3 *Law & Contemporary Problems* 368.

Hooker, Dana F & Carman J Overholt. "Defending Claims In Different Fora: The Competing Jurisdiction of Arbitrators and Tribunals In British Columbia" (2010) 43:1 *University of British Columbia Law Review* 47.

Howard Goldblatt. *Justice Delayed: The Arbitration Process in Ontario* (Toronto: Labour Council of Metropolitan Toronto, 1974).

Hutchinson, Allan & Patrick Monahan. "Democracy and the Rule of Law" in Allan C Hutchinson and Patrick Monahan, eds. *The Rule of Law: Ideal or Ideology* (Toronto: Carswell, 1987) 97.

Hyde, Alan. "Labor Arbitration of Discrimination Claims After *14 Penn Plaza v Pyett*: Letting Discrimination Defendants Decide Whether Plaintiffs May Sue Them." (2010) 25 *Ohio State Journal on Dispute Resolution* 975.

———. "To What Duties Do Global Labour Rights Correlate? Responsibility for Labor Standards Down the Production Chain" in Yossi Dahan, Hanna Lerner & Faina Milman-Sivan, eds. *Global Justice and International Labour Rights* (Cambridge UK: Cambridge University Press, 2016) 209.

Jackson, Andrew. *Work and Labour in Canada: Critical Issues,* 2d ed (Toronto: Canadian Scholars' Press Inc, 2010).

Jacobs, Laverne. "Figliola, Competing Jurisdiction, Shared Governance, and Protecting Human Rights in the Canadian Administrative State," online: (2013) *Social Science Research Network* http://papers.ssrn.com/sol3/papers.cfm?abstract_id=2184585.

James, Ralph C & Estelle Dinerstein James. *Hoffa and the Teamsters: A Study of Union Power* (Princeton NJ: Van Nostrand, 1965).

Kalbfleisch, John D & Ross L Prentice. *The Statistical Analysis of Failure Time Data,* 2d ed (Hoboken, NJ: Wiley & Sons, Inc, 2002).

Kaplan, William et al. "The Scope of Rights Arbitration after *Weber v. Ontario Hydro*" (1999) 7 *Canadian Labour and Employment Law Journal* 249.

Kiefer, Nicholas M. "Economic Duration Data and Hazard Functions" (1988) 26:2 *Journal of Economic Literature* 646.

Kim, Pauline T. *"Collective and Individual Approaches to Protecting Employee Privacy: The Experience with Workplace Drug Testing"* (2006) 66 *Louisiana Law Review* 1009.

Knopff, Rainer & Thomas Flanagan. *Human Rights & Social Technology: The New War on Discrimination* (Ottawa: Carleton University Press, 1989).

Lamoureux, François. "Commentaires" in Guylaine Vallée et al, eds. *Le droit à l'égalité: les tribunaux d'arbitrage et le Tribunal des droits de la personne* (Montréal: Les Éditions Thémis, 2004) 121.

Langille, Brian. "Equal Partnership in Canadian Labour Law" (1983) 21:3 *Osgoode Hall Law Journal* 496.

———. Speech delivered at the Bora Laskin Award Ceremony, 22 October 2013, online: www.queensu.ca/clcw/sites/webpublish.queensu.ca.clcwwww/files/files/Bernard%20Adell%20Tributes.pdf.

Laskin, Bora. "Collective Bargaining and Individual Rights" (1963) 6 *Canadian Bar Journal* 278.

———. "Problems of Procedure and Proof in Labour Arbitration" (1962) 5:1 *Canadian Public Administration* 76.

Lemieux, Valerie J Matthews. "The Ongoing Debate Over the Scope of *Weber — Who Has Jurisdiction*?" in *Annual Review of Civil Litigation*, Todd Archibald & Michael Cochrane, eds. (Toronto: Carswell, 2001) 141.

Levinson, Ariana R. "What the Awards Tell Us about Labor Arbitration of Employment Discrimination Claims" (2013) 46:3 *Michigan Journal of Law Reform* 790.

Lichtenstein, Nelson. "Great Expectations: The Promise of Industrial Jurisprudence and its Demise, 1930-1960," in Nelson Lichtenstein & Howell John Harris eds. *Industrial Democracy in America: The Ambiguous Promise* (Cambridge UK: Cambridge University Press, 1993) 113.

Lokan, Andrew & Maryth Yachnin. "From *Weber* to *Parry Sound*: The Expanded Scope of Arbitration" (2004) 11 *Canadian Labour and Employment Law Journal* 1.

Luciw, Sonia Regenbogen. "*Parry Sound* and Its Successors in the Supreme Court of Canada: Implications for the Scope of Arbitral Authority" (2004) 11 *Canadian Labour and Employment Law Journal* 365.

MacDonald, Roderick A. "Access to Justice in Canada Today: Scope, Scale, Ambitions" in Julia H Bass, WA Bogart & Frederick H Zemans, eds. *Access to Justice for a New Century: The Way Forward* (Toronto: Law Society of Upper Canada, 2005) 19.

MacDowell, Laurel Sefton. "The Formation of the Canadian Industrial Relations System During World War Two" (1978) 3 *Labour/Le Travail* 175.

MacDowell, Richard. "Labour Arbitration — The New Labour Court?" (2000) 8 *Canadian Labour and Employment Law Journal* 121.

MacFarlane, Julie. *The National Self-Represented Litigants Project: Identifying and Meeting the Needs of Self-Represented Litigants, Final Report* (May 2013), online: www.lsuc.on.ca/uploadedFiles/For_the_Public/About_the_Law_Society/Convocation_Decisions/2014/Self-represented_project.pdf.

Mactavish, Anne L & JF Lenz. "Civil Actions for Conduct Addressed by Human Rights Legislation — Some Recent Substantive and Procedural Developments" (1996) 4 *Canadian Labour and Employment Law Journal* 375.

Mancini, Marc. "Les droits et libertés de la personne en milieu syndical: l'arbitre de grief ou le Tribunal des droits de la personne, quel est le forum compétent?" (2009) 68 *Revue du Barreau* 327.

Martel, Nancy & Pierre E Moreau. *Le devoir de juste représentation* (Montréal: LexisNexis Canada, 2009).

McPhillips, David C, Peter R Sheen & Wayne Moore, "Expedited Arbitration: A New Experience for British Columbia" in William Kaplan et al, eds. (1996-1997) 1 *Labour Arbitration Year Book* (Toronto: Lancaster House, 1996) 29.

Ménard, Yves-Christian. *La discrimination en milieu de travail et le devoir juridique de représentation syndicale: une analyse socio-juridique* (LLM Thesis, Université de Montréal Faculté des études supérieures, 2011) [unpublished].

Morin, Fernand. "Être et ne pas être à la fois salarié! Ou les arrêts *Garon/Fillion* et *le Code civil du Québec* — Suites et poursuites," in Barreau du Québec, ed. *Développements récents en droit du travail 2006, volume 245* (Cowansville: Éditions Yvon Blais, 2006) 21.

———. "Fragilité des limites conventionnelles à l'arbitrage de grief: l'arrêt *Parry Sound*" (2003) 58:4 *Relations industrielles* 690.

———. "Pertinence, cohérence et conséquences de l'arrêt *Parry Sound*" in Barreau du Québec, *Développements récents en droit du travail* (Cowansville: Éditions Yvon Blais, 2004) 29.

———. "Effets combinatoires de deux codes: *Code du travail* et *Code civil du Québec*" (1994) 49:2 *Relations Industrielles* 227.

Mullan, David. "Tribunals and Courts — The Contemporary Terrain: Lessons from Human Rights Regimes" (1999) 24:2 *Queen's Law Journal* 643.

Murray, Gregor. "Tribute to Bernie Adell" in *Tributes: Professor Emeritus Bernard "Bernie" Adell*, online: www.queensu.ca/clcw/sites/webpublish.queensu.ca.clcwwww/files/files/Bernard%20Adell%20Tributes.pdf.

Nadeau, Denis. "L'arbitrage des griefs: vecteur d'intégration des droits de la personne dans les rapports collectifs du travail" in Le Tribunal des droits de la personne et le Barreau du Québec. *La Charte des droits et libertés de la personne: Pour qui et jusqu'où?* (Cowansville: Éditions Yvon Blais, 2005) 153.

———. "L'arrêt *Morin* et le monopole de representation des syndicats: assises d'une fragmentation" (2004) 64 *Revue du Barreau* 161.

———. "La perméabilité du droit au sein des rapports collectifs du travail et la compétence arbitrale: nouveau regard sur la valse-hésitation de la Cour suprême du Canada" (2010) 69 *Revue du Barreau* 219.

———. "Le tribunal des droits de la personne du Québec et le principe de l'exclusivité de l'arbitrage de grief ou l'histoire d'une usurpation progressive de compétence" (2000) 60 *Revue du Barreau* 387.

Nedelsky, Jennifer. *Law's Relations: A Relational Theory of Self, Autonomy, and Law* (Oxford: Oxford University Press, 2011).

Nerlove, Marc & S James Press. *Univariate and Multivariate Log-Linear and Logistic Models* (Santa Monica, CA: Rand Corporation, 1973).

Nolan, Dennis R & Roger I Abrams. "American Labor Arbitration: The Early Years" (1983) 35:3 *University of Florida Law Review* 373.

Nordlund, Willis J. *The Quest for a Living Wage: The History of the Federal Minimum Wage Program* (Westport CT: Greenwood Press, 1997).

Notebaert. Gérard. "Faut-il réformer le système l'arbitrage de grief au Québec ?" (2008) 53:1 *McGill Law Journal* 103.

O'Brien, Ruth. "A Sweat Shop of the Whole Nation: The *Fair Labor Standards Act* and the Failure of Regulatory Unionism" (2001) 15:1 *Studies in American Political Development* 33.

Ontario Human Rights Commission. *Guidelines on the Application of Section 34 of the Ontario Human Rights Code* (Ontario: OHRC, September 1996).

Ontario Human Rights Code Review Task Force. *Achieving Equality: A Report on Human Rights Reform* (Toronto: Government of Ontario, 1992).

Ontario Labour Relations Board. "Rules of Procedure" (Ottawa: OLRB, March 2016), online: www.olrb.gov.on.ca/english/Rules_of_Procedure.pdf.

Ontario Law Reform Commission. *Report on Avoiding Delay and Multiple Proceedings in the Adjudication of Workplace Disputes* (Toronto: Ontario Law Reform Commission, 1995).

———. *Study Paper on Prospects for Civil Justice*, by Roderick A Macdonald (Toronto: OLRC, 1995).

Ontario Ministry of Labour. "Collective Bargaining, Agreements and Negotiations: FAQ" (Ottawa: OML, 7 October 2015), online: www.labour.gov.on.ca/english/lr/faqs/lr_faq1.php.

———. *Looking Forward: A New Tribunal for Ontario's Workplaces, Consultation Paper* (Ontario: Ministry of Labour, 2001).

Ontario Ministry of the Attorney General. *Report of the Ontario Human Rights Review 2012*, by Andrew Pinto (Ottawa: MAG, November 2012).

Ontario. Human Rights Tribunal of Ontario. *Rules of Procedure*, 30 April 2014.

Park, Lori L. "Fair Representation and Conflict of Interest: Sexual Harassment Complaints Between Co-Workers" (1997) 6 *Dalhousie Journal of Legal Studies* 121.

Picher, Michel G. "Defining the Scope of Arbitration: The Impact of *Weber*: an Arbitrator's Perspective" in Kevin Whitaker et al, eds. (1999–2000) 1 *Labour Arbitration Year Book* (Toronto: Lancaster House, 2000) 99.

———. "*Gilmer* in the U.S. and *Weber* in Canada: Workplace Arbitration Exalted — And Assaulted" 1 *Labour Arbitration Year Book* (Toronto: Lancaster House, 1999) 1.

Pink, Ronald & DC Wallbridge. "The Future of Labour Arbitration" (Paper delivered at The 2010 Administrative, Labour and Employment and Privacy and Access Conference, Ottawa, 26–27 November 2010) (2010) *Canadian Bar Association.*

Pleasence, Pascoe & Nigel J Balmer. "Caught in the Middle: Justiciable Problems and the Use of Lawyers" in Michael Trebilcock, Anthony Duggan & Lorne Sossin, eds. *Middle Income Access to Justice* (Toronto: University of Toronto Press, 2012) 27.

Ponak, Allen & Corliss Olson. "Time Delays in Grievance Arbitation" (1992) 47:4 *Industrial Relations* 690.

Ponak, Allen, Daphne G Taras & Piers Steel. "Personality and Time Delay Among Arbitrators" in Paul D Staudohar & Mark I Lurie, eds. *Arbitration 2010: The Steelworkers Triology at 50: Proceedings of the Sixty-Third Annual Meeting, National Academy of Arbitrators, Philadelphia, Pennsylvania, May 26–29 2010* (Arlington, VA: BNA, 2011).

Ponak, Allen et al, "Using Event History Analysis to Model Delay in Grievance Arbitration" (1996) 50:1 *Industrial and Labor Relations Review* 105.

Pothier, Dianne. "Developments in Employment Law: The 1994–95 Term" (1996) 7 *Supreme Court Law Review, Second Series* 293.

Radin, Margaret Jane. *Boilerplate: The Fine Print, Vanishing Rights, and the Rule of Law* (Princeton NJ: Princeton University Press 2014).

Robert, Chantal & Guylaine Vallée. "Le traitement des plaintes concernant la discrimination en matière d'emploi par l'arbitre et par le Tribunal des droits de la personne du Québec: une étude comparative exploratoire" (2000) 41 *Les Cahiers de Droit* 95.

Rose, Joseph B. "Statutory Expedited Grievance Arbitration: The Case of Ontario" (1986) 41:4 *Arbitration Journal* 30.

Samuel, Howard D. "Troubled Passage: the Labor Movement and the Fair Labor Standards Act," (2000) 123:12 *Monthly Labor Review* 32.

Schenk, Christopher. "Unions and Democracy," online: (2014) *Canadian Centre for Policy Alternatives* www.policyalternatives.ca/sites/default/files/uploads/publications/2014/04/unions_and_democracy.pdf.

Schucher, Karen. *Coercing Justice? Exploring the "Aspirations and Practice" of Law as a Tool in Struggles Against Social Inequalities* (PhD Dissertation, Osgoode Hall Law School of York University, 2014) at 14–17, online: http://digitalcommons.osgoode.yorku.ca/cgi/viewcontent.cgi?article=1008&context=phd.

Selmi, Michael. "The Value of the EEOC: Reexamining the Agency's Role in Employment Discrimination Law" (1996) 57:1 *Ohio State Law Journal* 1.

Sénéchal, Carole. "Le contenu explicite de la convention collective, un leurre?" (2013) 43 *Revue Générale de Droit* 89.

Sheppard, Colleen. "Caring in Human Relations and Legal Approaches to Equality" (1992–1993) 2 *National Journal of Constitutional Law* 305.

———. "The Promise and Practice of Protecting Human Rights: Reflections on the Quebec *Charter of Human Rights and Freedoms*" in Faculté de droit de l'Université McGill, ed. *Mélanges Paul-André Crépeau*, (Cowansville, Québec: Éditions Yvon Blais, 1997) 641.

———. *Inclusive Equality: The Relational Dimensions of Systemic Discrimination in Canada* (Montreal & Kingston: McGill-Queen's University Press, 2010).

Shilton, Elizabeth. "Choice But No Choice: Adjudicating Human Rights Claims in Unionized Workplaces in Canada" (2013) 38:2 *Queen's Law Journal* 461.

———. "Enforcing Workplace Pension Rights for Unionized Employees: Is There a '*Weber* Gap'?" (2015) 19 *Canadian Labour and Employment Law Journal* 135.

———. "'Everybody's Business': Human Rights Enforcement and the Union's Duty to Accommodate" (2014) 18:1 *Canadian Labour and Employment Law Journal* 209.

———. "Labour Arbitration and Public Rights Claims: Forcing Square Pegs into Round Holes" (2016) 41:2 *Queen's Law Journal* 275.

Shulman, Harry. "Reason, Contract and Law in Labor Relations" (1955) 68:6 *Harvard Law Review* 999.

Simmons, Gordon. "Arbitral *Stare Decisis*: An Unheralded but Important Doctrine in Canadian Arbitral Jurisprudence" (1986) 11:2 *Queen's Law Journal* 347.

Social Justice Tribunals Ontario, "Human Rights Tribunal of Ontario: Rules of Procedure," Rule 19A: Summary Hearings (Ottawa: SJTO, 10 May 2016), online: www.sjto.gov.on.ca/documents/hrto/Practice%20Directions/HRTO%20Rules%20of%20Procedure.html.

Sovern, Michael I. *Legal Restraints on Racial Discrimination in Employment* (NY: Twentieth Century Fund, 1966).

Sran, Garry et al. "Why Unions Matter: Unions, Income Inequality and Regressive Labour Laws" in Matthew Behrens, ed. *Unions Matter: Advancing Democracy, Economic Equality, and Social Justice* (Toronto: Between the Lines, 2014) 13.

Statistics Canada. "Long Term Trends in Unionization" by Diane Galarneau & Thao Sohn, Catalogue no 75-006-X (Ottawa: Statistics Canada, 2013) at 2, online: www.statcan.gc.ca/pub/75-006-x/2013001/article/11878-eng.pdf.

Steinberg, Ronnie. *Wages and Hours: Labor and Reform in Twentieth-Century America* (New Brunswick NJ: Rutgers University Press, 1982).

Stone, Katherine VW. "The Steelworkers' Trilogy: The Evolution of Labor Arbitration" in Laura Cooper and Catherine Fisk, eds. *Labour Law Stories* (New York: Foundation Press, 2005).

Stone, Katherine Van Wezel. "The Post-War Paradigm in American Labor Law" (1981) 90:7 *Yale Law Review* 1509.

———. "Mandatory Arbitration of Individual Employment Rights: The Yellow Dog Contract of the 1990s" (1996) 73 *Denver University Law Review* 1017.

Summers, Clyde W. "Individual Rights in Collective Agreements and Arbitration" (1962) 37:3 *New York University Law Review* 362.

———. "Union Powers and Workers' Rights" (1951) 49:6 *Michigan Law Review* 805.

———. "Teamster Joint Grievance Committees: Grievance Disposal Without Adjudication" (1985) 7:3 *Berkeley Journal of Employment & Labour Law* 313.

Surdykowski, George T. "The Limits of Grievance Arbitration: *Weber* and *Pilon* in Perspective" in Kevin Whitaker et al, eds. (1999–2000) 1 *Labour Arbitration Year Book* (Toronto: Lancaster House, 2000) 67.

Swan, Kenneth P. "Ships Passing in the Night: Arbitrators and the Courts" in Kevin Whitaker et al, eds, (1999–2000) 1 *Labour Arbitration Year Book* (Toronto: Lancaster House, 2000) 1.

Swinton, Katherine E & Kenneth P Swan. "The Interaction Between Human Rights Legislation and Labour Law" in Kenneth P Swan & Katherine E Swinton, eds. *Studies in Labour Law* (Toronto: Butterworths, 1983) 111.

Szalai, Imre. *Outsourcing Justice: The Rise of Modern Arbitration Laws in America* (Durham NC: Carolina Academic Press 2013).

Thompson, Mark. "Expedited Arbitration: Promise and Performance" in William Kaplan, Jeffery Sack & Morley Gunderson, eds. (1992) 1 *Labour Arbitration Year Book* (Toronto: Lancaster House, 1992) 41.

Thornicroft, Kenneth W. "Accounting for Delay in Grievance Arbitration" (1993) 44:9 *Labor Law Journal* 543.

Thornicroft, Kenneth W. "Sources of Delay in Grievance Arbitration" (1995) 8:1 *Employee Responsbilities and Rights Journal* 57.

Trubek, David M. "Critical Moments in Access to Justice Theory: The Quest for the Empowered Self" in Allan C Hutchinson, ed. *Access to Civil Justice* (Toronto: Carswell, 1990) 107.

Trudeau, Gilles. "L'arbitrage des griefs au Canada: plaidoyer pour une réforme devenue nécessaire" (2005) 84:2 *Canadian Bar Review* 249.

———. "Synthèse des délibérations" in *Le Code civil et les relations de travail* (Québec: Département des relations industrielles de l'Université Laval, 1993) 79.

———. "The Internal Grievance Process and Grievance Arbitration in Quebec: An Illustration of the North American Methods of Resolving Disputes Arising from the Application of Collective Agreements" (2002) 44:3 *Managerial Law* 27.

Tucker, Eric. "Renorming Labour Law: Can We Escape Labour Law's Recurring Dilemmas?" (2010) 39:2 *Industrial Law Journal* 99.

———. "Shall Wagnerism Have No Dominion?," online: (2014) 21 *Just Labour: A Canadian Journal of Work and Society* 1, online: www.justlabour.yorku.ca/index.php?page=toc&volume=21.

Tunley, M Philip & Brian PLJ Smeenk. "Defamation in a Labour and Employment Context" (2006–007) 32 *Advocate's Quarterly* 83.

US Department of Labor: Bureau of Labor Statistics, News Release: "Union Members—2014" (USDL-15-0072) (January 23, 2015), online: www.bls.gov/news.release/archives/union2_01232015.pdf.

Vallée, Guylaine. "Les lois de l'emploi et la convention collective" in Dominic Roux & Anne-Marie Laflamme, eds. *Rapports hiérarchiques ou anarchiques des règles en droit du travail: Chartes, normes d'ordre public, convention collective, contrat de travail, etc.* (Montréal : Wilson & Lafleur Ltée, 2008) 81.

Vallée, Guylaine & Dalia Gesualdi-Fecteau. "La constitutionnalisation du droit du travail: une menace ou une opportunité pour les rapports collectifs de travail?" (2007) 48 *Cahiers de droit* 153.

Vallée, Guylaine et al. *Le droit à l'égalité: les tribunaux d'arbitrage et le Tribunal des droits de la personne* (Montréal, Les Éditions Thémis, 2004).

Veilleux, Diane. "Tribunal des droits de la personne du Québec, arbitre de griefs: quel doit être le forum compétent?" in Guylaine Vallée et al, eds, *Le droit à l'égalité: les tribunaux d'arbitrage et le Tribunal des droits de la personne* (Montréal, Les Éditions Thémis, 2004) 215.

Verge, Pierre. "L'affirmation constitutionnelle de la liberté d'association: une nouvelle vie pour l'autonomie collective?" (2010) 51 *Cahiers de droit* 353.

———. "Les lois du travail sous le prisme du nouveau code civil: Les premiers intervenants," in *Le Code civil et les relations de travail* (Québec: Département des relations industrielles de l'Université Laval, 1993).

Visser, Jelle & Daniele Checchi. "Inequality and the Labor Market: Unions" in Wiemer Salverda, Brian Noland & Tim M Smeeding, eds. *The Oxford Handbook of Economic Inequality* (Oxford: Oxford University Press, 2009) 230.

Vosko, Leah F. "'Rights without Remedies': Enforcing Employment Standards in Ontario by Maximizing Voice among Workers in Precarious Jobs" (2013) 50:4 *Osgoode Hall Law Journal* 845.

Walker, Charles R. "Life in the Automotive Factory" (1958:1) 36 *Harvard Business Review* 111.
Walsworth, Scott. "What do Unions do to Innovation? An Empirical Examination of the Canadian Private Sector" (2010) 65:4 *Relations industrielles/ Industrial Relations* 543.
Weil, David. "Regulating the Workplace: The Vexing Problem of Implementation" (1996) 7 *Advances in Industrial & Labor Relations* 247.
Weil, David. *The Fissured Workplace: Why Work Became So Bad for So Many and What Can Be Done to Improve It* (Cambridge MA: Harvard University Press, 2014).
Weiler, Paul C. "The Role of the Labour Arbitrator: Alternative Versions" (1969) 19:1 *University of Toronto Law Journal* 16.
———. *Reconcilable Differences: New Directions in Canadian Labour Law* (Toronto: Carswell, 1980).
White, Ahmed. *The Last Great Strike: Little Steel, the CIO, and the Struggle for Labor Rights in New Deal America* (Berkeley: University of California Press, 2016).
Winkler, Warren K. "Arbitration as a Cornerstone of Industrial Justice" (Kingston, ON: Queen's University School of Policy Studies, 2011).
Winkler, Warren. "Labour Arbitration and Conflict Resolution: Back to Our Roots" (2010 Don Wood Lecture delivered at the School of Policy Studies, Queen's University, 30 November 2010), (Kingston: Queen's Industrial Relations Centre, 2010), online: http://irc.queensu.ca/articles/labour-arbitration-and-conflict-resolution-back-our-roots.
Woodiwiss, Anthony. *Human Rights* (London and New York: Routledge, 2005).

# Table of Cases

# Index

VOLUMES 1 THROUGH 58 (OUT OF PRINT)

## VOLUME 59

Vice President, Global Medical Reference: Mary Gatsch
Editor: Yonah Korngold



Editorial Office:
Elsevier
1600 John F. Kennedy Blvd,
Suite 1800
Philadelphia, PA 19103-2899

International Standard Serial Number: 0065-3101
International Standard Book Number: 13: 978-1-4557-7271-1

Printed and bound by CPI Group (UK) Ltd, Croydon, CR0 4YY

Transferred to digital print 2013

# ADVANCES IN
## Pediatrics

## CONTRIBUTORS

SEAN J. BARNETT, MD, MS, FACS, FAAP, Assistant Professor of Surgery and Pediatrics, Division of Pediatric General & Thoracic Surgery, Cincinnati Children's Hospital Medical Center, Cincinnati, Ohio

RAM N. BISHNOI, MD, Department of Pediatric Cardiology, Johns Hopkins University School of Medicine, Bloomberg Children's Center M2309, Baltimore, Maryland

JENNIFER BRUNY, MD, Assistant Professor, Department of Surgery, Children's Hospital of Colorado, University of Colorado School of Medicine, Aurora, Colorado

SHANNON L. CASTLE, MD, Research Fellow, Department of Surgery, Children's Hospital Los Angeles, Keck School of Medicine, University of Southern California, Los Angeles, California

JOHN D. COULSON, MD, Department of Pediatric Cardiology, Johns Hopkins University School of Medicine, Bloomberg Children's Center M2309, Baltimore, Maryland

FRANK DIAMOND, MD, Division of Endocrinology and Diabetes, All Children's Specialty Physicians, All Children's Hospital/Johns Hopkins Medicine, St Petersburg, Florida

BURRIS "DUKE" DUNCAN, MD, Professor Emeritus, Family and Child Health, College of Public Health and Pediatrics, College of Medicine, University of Arizona, Tucson, Arizona

KACEY C. ERNST, PhD, MPH, Assistant Professor, Epidemiology, College of Public Health, University of Arizona, Tucson, Arizona

KRISTINA N. FEJA, MD, MPH, Attending Physician, Division of Allergy, Immunology and Infectious Diseases, The Children's Hospital at Saint Peter's University Hospital, New Brunswick; Adjunct Assistant Professor, School of Public Health, University of Medicine and Dentistry of New Jersey, Piscataway, New Jersey; Clinical Assistant Professor of Pediatrics, Drexel University College of Medicine, Philadelphia, Pennsylvania

HENRI R. FORD, MD, MHA, Professor of Surgery and Vice Dean for Medical Education, Vice President and Surgeon-in-Chief, Department of Surgery, Children's Hospital Los Angeles, Keck School of Medicine, University of Southern California, Los Angeles, California

CHRISTOPHER P. GAYER, MD, PhD, Assistant Professor of Surgery, Department of Surgery, Children's Hospital Los Angeles, Keck School of Medicine, University of Southern California, Los Angeles, California

PALLAVI IYER, MD, Medical Director, Division of Endocrinology & Diabetes, All Children's Specialty Physicians, All Children's Hospital/Johns Hopkins Medicine, St Petersburg, Florida

MICHAEL S. KAPPY, MD, PhD, Professor of Pediatrics, University of Colorado Denver School of Medicine; Children's Hospital Colorado, Aurora, Colorado

FREDERICK M. KARRER, MD, The David R. and Kiku Akers Chair in Pediatric Surgery; Professor of Surgery and Pediatrics, Division of Pediatric Surgery, Children's Hospital Colorado, University of Colorado School of Medicine, Aurora, Colorado

KENNY Y. KWONG, MD, Associate Clinical Professor of Pediatrics, Division of Allergy-Immunology, Department of Pediatrics, Harbor-UCLA Medical Center, Torrance, California

SYDNEY LEIBEL, MD, Allergist, Allergy-Immunology, Kindercare Pediatrics, Toronto, Ontario, Canada

AYESHA MIRZA, MD, FAAP, Department of Pediatrics, University of Florida, Jacksonville, Florida

MOHAMMED MORTAZAVI, MD, Department of Pediatrics; Pediatric Sports Medicine, UC Davis Medical Center, Sacramento, California

JOHN P. MOYER, MD, Professor of Pediatrics, University of Colorado School of Medicine; Department of Pediatrics, Children's Hospital of Colorado, Morrison, Colorado

ANNE M. MURPHY, MD, Professor, Pediatric Cardiology, Johns Hopkins University, Baltimore, Maryland

KATHRYN NEUBAUER, MD, Resident, Department of Pediatrics, Johns Hopkins Hospital, Baltimore, Maryland

MELANIE NIES, MD, Johns Hopkins Medical Institution, Bloomberg Children's Center, Department of Pediatric Cardiology/Taussig Heart Center, Baltimore, Maryland

STEPHANIE PAPILLON, MD, Research Fellow, Department of Surgery, Children's Hospital Los Angeles, Keck School of Medicine, University of Southern California, Los Angeles, California

BETH S. PHILLIPS, MPH, Carter Center Technical Assistant, Guinea Worm Eradication Program, South Sudan

MOBEEN H. RATHORE, MD, FAAP, CPE, Department of Pediatrics, University of Florida; Wolfson Children's Hospital, Jacksonville, Florida

RICHARD E. RINGEL, MD, Department of Pediatric Cardiology, Johns Hopkins University School of Medicine, Bloomberg Children's Center M2309, Baltimore, Maryland

JONATHAN P. ROACH, MD, Transplant Surgery Fellow, Division of Transplant Surgery, University of Colorado School of Medicine, Aurora, Colorado

PIERRE RUSSO, MD, Director, Anatomic Pathology and Professor, Department of Pathology and Laboratory Medicine, The Children's Hospital of Philadelphia, The University of Pennsylvania Perelman School of Medicine, Philadelphia, Pennsylvania

PRIYA SEKAR, MD, MPH, Johns Hopkins Medical Institution, Bloomberg Children's Center, Department of Pediatric Cardiology/Taussig Heart Center, Baltimore, Maryland

RASHMI SHETGIRI, MD, MSHS, Division of General Pediatrics, Department of Pediatrics, University of Texas Southwestern Medical Center and Children's Medical Center, Dallas, Texas

MORITZ M. ZIEGLER, MD, Former Surgeon-in-Chief and the Ponzio Family Chair, Children's Hospital of Colorado; Professor, Department of Surgery, University of Colorado School of Medicine, Aurora, Colorado

ROBERT W. TOLAN, Jr, MD, FAAP, FIDSA, Chief, Division of Allergy, Immunology and Infectious Diseases, The Children's Hospital at Saint Peter's University Hospital, New Brunswick, New Jersey; Clinical Associate Professor of Pediatrics, Drexel University College of Medicine, Philadelphia, Pennsylvania

## CONTENTS

VOLUME 60 • 2013

## Bullying and Victimization Among Children

By Rashmi Shetgiri



## Slums Are Not Places for Children to Live: Vulnerabilities, Health Outcomes, and Possible Interventions

By Kacey C. Ernst, Beth S. Phillips, and Burris "Duke" Duncan

**Update on Allergen Immunotherapy for Treatment of Allergic Diseases**
By Kenny Y. Kwong and Sydney Leibel

## Advances in Noninvasive Imaging in Pediatric Cardiology

By Melanie Nies and Priya Sekar



## Recent Advances in Interventional Pediatric Cardiology

By Ram N. Bishnoi, John D. Coulson, and Richard E. Ringel



## Sudden Cardiac Death in Young Athletes

By Mohammed Mortazavi

## Enteropathies of Infancy and Childhood

By Pierre Russo



## Necrotizing Enterocolitis: Contemporary Management and Outcomes

By Stephanie Papillon, Shannon L. Castle, Christopher P. Gayer, and Henri R. Ford

## Surgical Management of Adolescent Obesity

By Sean J. Barnett

Advances in Pediatrics 60 (2013) xix–xx

ADVANCES IN PEDIATRICS

# Introduction

Michael S. Kappy, MD, PhD

The editors are pleased to present volume 60 in our series of volumes addressing advances in pediatrics across many disciplines.

Our annual feature, "Foundations of Pediatrics," honors individuals who made significant contributions to our specialty during their lives. This year's honoree is Helen Taussig, a champion for children with congenital heart disease who helped establish the Blalock-Taussig procedure while at Johns Hopkins Hospital, thereby saving the lives of many. Her contributions to medicine and to women in academia were far-reaching and are described in the article by Neubauer and Murphy.

Another ongoing contribution is that of Drs Mirza and Rathore, who contribute their fourth biennial update on immunization practices.

Advances in a variety of disciplines are described in this volume, as follows:

## GENERAL PEDIATRICS

"Bullying and Victimization Among Children" (Shetgiri), "Slums Are Not Places for Children to Live: Vulnerabilities, Health Outcomes, and Possible Interventions" (Ernst et al), and "Detecting Disorders of Vitamin D Deficiency in Children" (Iyer and Diamond).

## INFECTIOUS DISEASES/IMMUNOLOGY

"Infections Related to International Travel and Adoption" (Feja and Tolan) and "Update on Allergen Immunotherapy for Treatment of Allergic Disease" (Kwong and Leibel).

## CARDIOLOGY

"Advances in Noninvasive Imaging in Pediatric Cardiology" (Nies and Sekar), "Advances in Interventional Pediatric Cardiology" (Bishnoi et al), and "Prevention of Sudden Cardiac Deaths in Young Athletes" (Mortavazi).

## GASTROENTEROLOGY

"Enteropathies of Infancy and Childhood" (Russo) and "Necrotizing Enterocolitis: Contemporary Management and Outcomes" (Papillon et al).

## SURGERY

"Historical Development of Pediatric Surgical Quality–The First 100 Years" (Bruny and Ziegler), "Abdominal Organ Transplantation in Children" (Roach

0065-3101/13/$ – see front matter
http://dx.doi.org/10.1016/j.yapd.2013.04.017 

and Karrer), with an Introduction by John Moyer, a parent whose son became an organ donor, and "Surgical Management of Adolescent Obesity" (Barnett).

As always, the editors welcome comments about each volume of *Advances in Pediatrics* and suggestions for future articles.

Michael S. Kappy, MD, PhD
Department of Pediatrics
University of Colorado Denver School of Medicine
Children's Hospital Colorado
13123 East 16th Avenue
B-265, Aurora, CO 80045, USA

*E-mail address:* michael.kappy@childrenscolorado.org

Advances in Pediatrics 60 (2013) 1–9

ADVANCES IN PEDIATRICS

# Helen Brooke Taussig

## Pediatric Cardiology Leader and Innovator

Kathryn Neubauer, MD, Anne M. Murphy, MD*

Pediatric Cardiology, Johns Hopkins University, Ross Building 1144, 720 Rutland Avenue, Baltimore, MD 21205, USA

**Keywords**

• Helen Taussig • Pediatric cardiology • Cyanotic heart defects • Johns Hopkins

**Key points**

- Dr Helen Taussig was a pioneer as a woman in academic medicine and as a leader in pediatric cardiology. She was the second woman promoted to Professor at The Johns Hopkins University School of Medicine, although her promotion and recognition occurred much later than her achievements warranted.
- The development of treatment of congenital heart defects was hastened by her careful observations as a clinician and her collaboration with Dr Alfred Blalock and other specialists.
- Dr Taussig received recognition not only for her pioneering work but also for her advocacy, which led to the Food and Drug Administration not permitting use of thalidomide in the United States and her leadership and election to president of the American Heart Association. She received the Presidential Medal of Freedom in 1964.

## EARLY LIFE AND EDUCATION

Helen Brooke Taussig was born on May 24th, 1898 in Cambridge, Massachusetts. Her parents were Frank William Taussig and Edith Guild Taussig (Fig. 1). Helen's father was a well-known professor at Harvard who authored many economics textbooks and served as head of the United States Tariff Commission from 1917 to 1919. Her mother studied biology and botany at Radcliffe College and had a love of knowledge that she passed on to her daughter. Her paternal grandfather studied chemistry in Prague before immigrating to the United States and served as a physician during the Civil War. The family engrained strong values in their children; in particular, scholarship and learning were valued above material wealth. The family partook in picnics

*Corresponding author. *E-mail address*: amurphy2@jhmi.edu

0065-3101/13/$ – see front matter
http://dx.doi.org/10.1016/j.yapd.2013.04.003 

**Fig. 1.** Photograph of Helen Taussig, MD, in 1940. (*Courtesy of* the Alan Mason Chesney Medical Archives of the Johns Hopkins Medical Institutions, Baltimore, MD, with permission.)

in the country on weekends, and spent summers enjoying the outdoors of their Cape Cod home. When Helen was 11 her mother died from tuberculosis, but she received ongoing strong support and affection from her father who encouraged her education [1–4].

Helen was highly curious as a child and young adult, focusing on many subjects with a lifelong favorite being botany. Although she had an immense love of learning, she struggled with dyslexia, and as a result had difficulty with reading comprehension throughout school [1]. In grade school, teachers would make the students stand and read aloud until they made a mistake, and Helen was embarrassed and frustrated that she made mistakes easily. She worked through her homework and reading with the help of her father who was positive and supportive. Her reading improved but continued to be a struggle [1]. Even into adulthood and her academic life as a pediatric cardiologist, writing remained a challenge, but she persisted, and published more than 100 articles, recognizing that publishing research was necessary to advance medicine and science [4].

Helen spent 2 years at Radcliffe College, her mother's alma mater. At Radcliffe, she was a strong student and played tennis and basketball. After a trip to California with her father, she transferred to the University of California at Berkeley for her remaining 2 years, graduating in 1921. She flourished in this environment. She continued to do well academically, was a senior advisor to the freshman students, and enjoyed hiking and exploring the outdoors on weekends with her friends.

After college, Helen returned to Cambridge. She set up an appointment with the Dean of the Harvard School of Public Health to discuss her career. During this appointment, she was told Harvard would allow women to attend medical classes but would not admit them as degree candidates. She questioned the logic of taking classes without credit and was told the point was that no woman would attend! At this point, Helen told the Dean she would not "disappoint" him by attending [1].

After this encounter, she thought more seriously about becoming a physician, an idea she had considered during college; however, she lacked the prerequisites. She attended a histology class at Harvard where she had to sit in the back of the classroom during lectures and do her laboratory work in a small room without the other students so as not to "contaminate the male students" [1]. Her professor, Dr John Lewis Bremer, recognized her intelligence and spoke to her frankly about not wasting her time at Harvard but going to Boston University where women were welcome to take premedical courses and earn credit for them. Helen Taussig followed this advice directly [1].

While at Boston University she took an anatomy course and once again was noticed for intelligence and perseverance, this time by Dr Alexander Begg, who involved her in research about mammalian cardiac muscle [1]. After much hard work in the laboratory, she was able to demonstrate the intrinsic contractile activity of mammalian cardiac muscle. Scientists had shown reptilian cardiac muscle beat intrinsically, but this had not been previously demonstrated in mammalian cardiac muscle. The paper was published in the *American Journal of Physiology*, which was a remarkable achievement for such a young student.

After she completed her premedical requirements Dr Begg encouraged her to apply to The Johns Hopkins University School of Medicine, which was founded in part because of the philanthropy of a group of women led by Mary Elizabeth Garrett and M. Carey Thomas, under the condition that men and women would be admitted on an equal basis [1]. She was accepted into the class of 1927. Although she studied extremely hard, when it came time to apply for a medical internship, there was only one slot for a woman per year and another woman achieved a slightly higher score. While awaiting the results of her application for internship, she worked in the adult heart clinic at Johns Hopkins run by one of her early mentors at Hopkins, Dr Edward Perkins Carter. After being turned down for the internship position, Dr Carter invited her to finish out the year in the heart clinic [5]. The next year, 1928, Dr Edwards Park, the new chief of pediatrics at Johns Hopkins recognized her talent and offered her a position as a pediatric resident.

## EARLY CAREER AT JOHNS HOPKINS

At the time Dr Taussig began her residency at Johns Hopkins, Dr Park was making changes in the hospital and clinics. He realized that children with chronic illness were well cared for in the hospital, but their long-term follow-up care was not adequate [2]. Dr Park organized clinics focusing on specific areas, including a cardiology clinic [2].

Dr Park appointed Dr Clifton Briggs Leech to be the first director of the children's heart station at Johns Hopkins. Dr Leech graduated from Boston University Medical School in 1919. He went on to study a new device, the electrocardiographic apparatus, with Dr Paul Dudley White [6], and he was recruited to Johns Hopkins to start a pediatric heart clinic. While at Johns Hopkins, Dr Leech made many contributions to the heart station and pediatric cardiology including extensive research on endocarditis and congenital heart block. Dr Leech was to leave in a year or two, and Dr Park started approaching Dr Taussig to ask her to be Dr Leech's successor. At the time, she was doing some additional work in Boston and New York. Initially through letters she said although honored, she did not believe she had the experience or breadth of knowledge to accept the position, but in 1930, Dr Taussig accepted Dr Park's offer and became the head of the new pediatric cardiology clinic at the Johns Hopkins Hospital [6].

Dr Park gave the clinic radiographic equipment; an electrocardiogram machine; and a new piece of equipment, the fluoroscope. He also served as an academic mentor and prompted Helen to use the equipment to study congenital heart disease. Initially she was reluctant to use the new diagnostic equipment and instead focused her studies and research on rheumatic heart disease, which was the major clinical cardiac problem in children at that time.

During the early years as the director of the pediatric cardiology clinic, Dr Taussig began to lose her hearing [1]. This caused problems using her stethoscope, communicating with patients and families, teaching, and attending lectures. She used many types of hearing aids, an amplifying stethoscope, and learned to lip read. None of these worked as well as when she learned to "listen" with her hands, a talent she perfected over the years by laying her hands extremely gently over a child's chest, feeling murmurs other physicians could not hear with a stethoscope. Thus, although the hearing problem was a disability, it actually may have sharpened her clinical acumen in other ways.

When antibiotics became available to treat streptococcal infections, the number of children affected with rheumatic heart disease decreased, giving her more time to study children with cyanotic heart defects. With additional prompting from Dr Park, she began using fluoroscopy to study congenital heart defects. These two things together perked her interest in congenital heart disease and the "blue babies" seen in the Harriet Lane Clinic.

Dr Taussig used chest radiographs, fluoroscopy, and the patient's history and physical examination to document their clinical presentation thoroughly. Her work was also enhanced by the studies of Dr Maude Abbott, a pathologist at McGill University in Canada, who studied the pathology of congenital heart disease after being inspired by Dr William Osler at the Johns Hopkins Hospital [1,7]. Dr Abbott had examined thousands of malformed hearts over her career as the curator of the McGill University medical museum. She went on to publish the *Atlas of Congenital Cardiac Disease* and had an exhibit with specimens and diagrams of anatomy, embryology, and physiology and clinical correlations. Dr Abbott traveled throughout the United States and Europe, and her exhibit gained worldwide recognition and spread interest in malformations worldwide [7]. Dr Abbott's work and interactions with Dr Taussig at conferences and through correspondence helped Dr Taussig link together the radiograph, fluoroscopy, and the anatomy of malformations.

She applied this knowledge to assess her patients, their clinical presentation, and physical examination, and she was able to bring these modalities to propose clinical diagnoses [7]. She concluded that it was possible to formulate an anatomic diagnosis while the patient was alive rather than at autopsy [2]. Through clinical experience, she realized that many children with the same malformations and had similarities in their history and physical examination and their radiographic and fluoroscopic studies. She was excited to discover that she could recognize babies with tricuspid atresia, with right ventricular hypoplasia, and pulmonary stenosis by the characteristic cardiac contour of the heart on radiograph in association with left axis deviation on electrocardiogram [2]. Recognition of clinical presentation as a result of underlying defects would soon be translated into therapy.

## THE BLALOCK-TAUSSIG OPERATION

One of Dr Taussig's key clinical observations was the decreased pulmonary vascular markings noted during fluoroscopy in many of her cyanotic patients. She realized that the anatomy in these children resulted in decreased pulmonary blood flow [4]. This further supported her observations that blue babies often worsened after closure of the ductus arteriosus, and that a continued systemic-to-pulmonary blood flow might reduce the cyanosis in these infants [1].

In 1939 when Dr Robert Gross, in Boston, ligated a patent ductus arteriosus in a child, Dr Taussig thought that making a patent ductus arteriosus–like anastomosis to supply more blood to the lungs might help her patients who were cyanotic because of reduced pulmonary blood flow. She traveled to Boston to propose this to Dr Gross, who said he was not interested in her idea [1,5]. On returning to Hopkins she awaited a surgeon who would be more receptive to this approach.

In 1941 Dr Alfred Blalock arrived at Hopkins from Vanderbilt University and brought with him his laboratory technician, Mr Vivien Thomas. Dr Taussig thought Dr Blalock would be open to her idea because of his prior research. Dr Blalock and Mr Thomas had performed an anastomosis between the subclavian artery and pulmonary artery in dogs as part of experiments designed to produce a model of pulmonary hypertension while at Vanderbilt. Although it did not produce the expected result, Thomas gained the technical skills to perform this anastomosis [8]. Dr Park had also suggested to Dr Blalock to use the subclavian artery to bypass the aortic obstruction in patients with coarctation of the aorta. Although Blalock and Thomas only performed this procedure on dogs, Helen Taussig discussed this surgery with them as an example to support her proposed anastomosis between the systemic and pulmonary arteries [5]. Blalock, Taussig, and Thomas discussed the idea of using such an approach to help her cyanotic patients, and Thomas set to work creating a dog experimental model with decreased blood flow to the lungs and then alleviating cyanosis by anastomosing the subclavian artery to the pulmonary artery. This historic meeting in 1943 is mentioned by several authors. Most credit Helen Taussig for the concept for the approach, including Vivien Thomas, who referred to Dr Taussig as a very passionate individual who advocated strongly for her patients who had no other options [5]. However, it should be noted that a dissenting view of the origin of the concept for this approach was put forth by Dr William Longmire, a senior surgical resident at the time of the first shunt surgeries, who gave Dr Blalock the credit for the concept. It is possible that Longmire was not aware of the early conversations between Drs. Taussig and Blalock and Mr Thomas a year previously [5].

Mr Thomas's experiments continued for more than a year; however, Dr Blalock only observed a few. Blalock performed one procedure in the laboratory with Vivien Thomas. However, before he had the opportunity to perform additional work in the laboratory, a critically ill 15-month-old infant was admitted to the hospital with profound cyanosis. On November 29th, 1944, Dr Blalock performed surgery on this young girl with Mr Thomas standing behind him offering advice through the course of the surgery. Dr Taussig accompanied her patient to the operating room, and watched the progress of the surgery that day [1]. The infant survived to go home from the hospital, but died at a second surgery only a few months later. However, two additional, more successful, surgeries were performed before Blalock and Taussig published their work "The Surgical Treatment of Malformations of the Heart" in May 1945 [9]. Three years after the first surgery Drs Taussig and Blalock toured Europe lecturing in London, Stockholm, and Paris. Unfortunately, as has been well documented, Vivien Thomas did not receive acknowledgment in the original manuscript and was unrecognized for his contributions for years, although ultimately in 1976, he received an honorary doctoral degree from Johns Hopkins in a gesture typically reserved for senior professors, deans, and department chairs. A portrait of Vivian Thomas was commissioned and remains on display in the building named for Blalock at the Johns Hopkins Hospital [5].

## LATER CAREER AND HONORS

By 1952, Dr Taussig alone made numerous referrals of her patients to Dr Blalock for the Blalock-Taussig shunt, as is it was ultimately called, and which had a mortality rate of only 15% [10]. Later in her career, she published a paper on the outcomes of the first 1000 children who underwent this operation. Subsequent advances in the field permitted full operative repair for tetralogy of Fallot and repair and palliation of many other cyanotic defects. Most of these patients continued to live happy and productive lives [10].

Dr Taussig continued to study congenital heart malformations and in 1947, published the first textbook solely about congenital heart defects, *Congenital Malformations of the Heart.* This textbook continued to be the "bible" of pediatric cardiology for decades. Her career was also marked by her stature as a mentor of students, residents, and fellows [3]. Many of her fellows went on to lead pediatric cardiology programs themselves in the United States and abroad [3]. Training others was essential to the growth of the field as newer surgical approaches evolved.

Dr Taussig also made innumerable additional contributions to general pediatrics, pediatric cardiology, and medical education. One specific contribution was investigating the possible causes of an increase in limb malformations (eg, phocomelia) seen in Europe. She initially learned of the increase in these malformations from Dr Alois Beuren of Germany, one of her former fellows [4]. After her own further investigation, Dr Taussig's concern about the role of the drug thalidomide in this malformation led her to alert others to the dangers of this drug including in testimony before Congress [4]. The Food and Drug Administration ultimately never approved thalidomide for use in the United States. She also brought to the public awareness the risk of taking any drug while pregnant, because of the lack of knowledge of their effect on the developing fetus.

Her patients, friends, and colleagues consistently describe Dr Taussig as warm, loving, compassionate, and gentle [3,4]. Yet there are anecdotes about her strong-willed temperament and abruptness. She was passionate, intense, and cared very deeply for her work and patients and may have displayed impatience with those who did not maintain her standards. Dr Catherine Neill, who was a fellow and later colleague and friend to Dr Taussig, wrote about her personality: "She did achieve a peace and serenity with age, as several tributes and photographs have attested. However, serenity alone does not win ball games; nor in the labyrinths of academic medicine does it ensure continuing protection of academic turf" [4]. This statement makes clear that quietly accepting the status quo does not always achieve success or progress in medicine.

Dr Taussig was well known for her profound devotion to her patients [1]. In the evenings after work, she read and replied to letters from patients, saved the photos they sent, and encouraged continued correspondence. There are many accounts about how gentle she was with her patients and their families. She once said that out of all the awards and honors she received it was hearing from her patients that was the most gratifying. She also had many patients name their daughters "Helen" in her honor, which she believed was the best award she ever received [1].

Helen very graciously and frequently hosted visitors at her Baltimore home. Every 2 to 3 years she would have a large event at her home on Lake Roland in Baltimore for all her current and former fellows and their families. She treasured the friendships she made and often regarded her fellows and their families as her own family [3,4,11].

In her free time, she continued with her love of botany. Her house had a massive garden. She was also very fond of dogs; many of her friends have said that she was never without a dog by her side or on her lap when she was at home [1]. She continued to spend her summers on Cape Cod and also continued her father's tradition of working in the mornings and relaxing in the afternoons and evenings. She had guests stay under the condition they fix their own breakfasts and not disturb her during her morning work period. It was during her visits to Cape Cod that she completed her textbook [1].

Dr Taussig was appointed professor of pediatrics at the Johns Hopkins University in 1959, a promotion that she had long awaited. Dr Taussig officially retired in 1963. She published more than 40 articles after her official retirement and continued to teach. Although her promotion to professor and many awards were delayed compared with those achieved by Blalock, ultimately she received more than 30 awards and many honorary degrees, including one from Harvard. In 1964 she received the Medal of Freedom, the highest civilian honor in the United States, from President Lyndon Johnson. She also became the first woman to be the President of the American Heart Association, and in 1965, was awarded the prestigious Albert Lasker Award [2,4]. Dr Taussig died suddenly in an automobile accident in 1986, and was deeply grieved by her friends and patients. At the time of her death she was continuing research on the embryology of heart defects in birds, and her last paper was published posthumously [3].

Dr Taussig began her life in a privileged and scholarly family that supported her education and innate curiosity from a young age. These advantages would open many doors for a young man in the early 1900s, but could not overcome the fact she was a woman. This did not deter her from pursuing a career that changed an entire field of medicine. She also faced personal obstacles including the early loss of her mother, her dyslexia, and hearing loss. Despite these obstacles, she persevered and flourished professionally and enjoyed the great affection of colleagues and patients. Helen Taussig was a leader with an innovative spirit and strong will who transformed the care of children with congenital heart disease.

## References

[1] Baldwin J. To heal the heart of a child: Helen Taussig, M.D. New York: Walker & Company; 1992.

[2] Engle MA. Biographies of great American pediatricians–Helen Brooke Taussig: the mother of pediatric cardiology. Pediatr Ann 1982;11(7):629–31.

[3] McNamara DG, Manning JA, Engle MA, et al. Helen Brooke Taussig: 1898 to 1986. J Am Coll Cardiol 1987;10(3):662–71.

[4] Neill CA. Helen Brooke Taussig. J Pediatr 1994;125(3):499–502.

[5] Evans WN. The Blalock-Taussig shunt: the social history of an eponym. Cardiol Young 2009;19(2):119–28.

[6] Evans WN. Clifton Briggs Leech: first director of the pediatric cardiac clinic at the Johns Hopkins Harriet Lane Home for Invalid Children. Cardiol Young 2009;19(1):2–9.

[7] Evans WN, Beland MJ. The paediatric cardiology Hall of Fame: Maude Elizabeth Abbott. Cardiol Young 2010;20(2):124–32.

[8] Brogan TV, Alfieris GM. Has the time come to rename the Blalock-Taussig shunt? Pediatr Crit Care Med 2003;4(4):450–3.

[9] Blalock A, Taussig HB. The surgical treatment of malformations of the heart in which there is pulmonary stenosis or pulmonary atresia. JAMA 1945;128:189–202.
[10] Ellis H. Notable women in healthcare. Helen Taussig: children's cardiologist. J Perioper Pract 2009;19(12):438–9.
[11] Dunn PM. Dr Helen Taussig (1898 1986): pioneering American paediatric cardiologist. Arch Dis Child Fetal Neonatal Ed 2008;93(1):F74–6.

Advances in Pediatrics 60 (2013) 11–31

ADVANCES IN PEDIATRICS

# Immunization Update IV

Ayesha Mirza, MD[a], Mobeen H. Rathore, MD, CPE[a,b,*]

[a]Department of Pediatrics, University of Florida, 653-1 West 8th Street, LRC 3rd Floor, L-13, Jacksonville, FL 32209, USA; [b]Wolfson Children's Hospital, 800 Prudential Drive, Jacksonville, FL 32207, USA

**Keywords**

• Immunizations • Pertussis • Seasonal influenza vaccines • Adolescent vaccines • Pediatric vaccines

**Key points**

- Several strategies have been suggested and several implemented to increase overall immunization rates with pertussis-containing vaccines, including cocooning of newborn infants too young to be vaccinated and vaccination of pregnant women.
- Other reasons for the increased numbers of ongoing cases of pertussis include waning immunity in vaccinated individuals over time, particularly those immunized with DTaP (diphtheria, tetanus and acellular pertussis) as opposed to the older whole-cell DTP (diphtheria, tetanus, pertussis) vaccine.
- The CDC recommends at least 1 dose of mumps, measles, and rubella (MMR) vaccine for children between the ages of 6 and 11 months who will be traveling outside the United States. Children 12 months and older, are considered immune as long as they have received 2 doses of MMR vaccine. If any child received the first dose before 12 months of age, that dose should not be counted and the child should receive 2 doses after 12 months of age with the second dose at least 28 days apart.
- Vaccines against all serogroups of *Neisseria meningitides* are likely to be licensed in the near future. However, some important questions remain: their effectiveness on pathogenic strains with different geographic distribution, their impact on carriers, and the timing of the appearance of escape mutants once herd immunity has been achieved.
- In February 2012, the US Food and Drug Administration approved a new seasonal quadrivalent live attenuated influenza vaccine, FluMist Quadrivalent (MedImmune). This vaccine is not anticipated to be available until the 2013/2014 influenza season, at which time it is expected to replace the currently available seasonal trivalent, live, intranasal influenza formulation (FluMist, MedImmune).

*Corresponding author. 653-1 West 8th Street, Jacksonville, FL 32209. *E-mail address:* mobeen.rathore@jax.ufl.edu

0065-3101/13/$ – see front matter
http://dx.doi.org/10.1016/j.yapd.2013.04.001 

In 2012, both pertussis (whooping cough) and measles remained in the news in the United States. Both are microorganisms that have no nonhuman hosts or environmental niche and both are therefore entirely preventable with immunization. Theoretically, the availability of highly effective vaccines with wide-scale immunization programs across the globe should make this feasible. Why then has it not been possible to eradicate these highly contagious infectious diseases? The United States is in the grip of perhaps one of the largest epidemics of reported pertussis in 50 years. On September 20, 2012 approximately 29,000 cases of pertussis and 14 pertussis-related deaths mostly in infants less than 3 months of age had been reported by the Centers for Disease Control and Prevention (CDC) [1].

In 2011, 17 outbreaks of measles and 222 cases of measles were reported in the United States according to the CDC [2]. In 2000, measles was declared eliminated in the United States as a result of high vaccination coverage and effective public health measures. Although measles no longer occurs year round in the United States, it still remains endemic in several countries making it essential that immunization continues within the United States. This fourth article in a series on immunizations begins by trying to understand the potential causes of the resurgence of these vaccine-preventable diseases, and updates on recently approved vaccines, current immunizations, and related recommendations are presented.

## OVERVIEW OF RECENT VACCINE-PREVENTABLE DISEASE OUTBREAKS

Pertussis remains endemic in the United States. Universal immunization against pertussis reduced the average incidence of reported cases from 157 per 100,000 population in the early 1940s to less than 1 per 100,000 in 1973 [3]. This was in contrast to the prevaccine era when reported cases of pertussis reached epidemic proportions every 2 to 5 years; more than 265,000 cases were reported in 1934 [4]. Despite this dramatic decrease, however, cycles of outbreaks continue to occur (Figs. 1 and 2). The most recent outbreaks that occurred in California in 2010 and in Washington State in 2012 give us reason to pause and consider the potential causes of ongoing cases despite recommendations for universal vaccination of all children, adolescents, and adults.

The seeming resurgence of this vaccine-preventable disease is multifactorial [5]. Increased public awareness of pertussis as a cause of a prolonged cough illness in an adult as well as a severe and protracted cough illness in children has led to earlier recognition and care. Improved methods of diagnosis using polymerase chain reaction (PCR) assays also contribute greatly to better diagnosis of cases.

Pertussis has a high basic reproduction number (Ro) close to 12 to 17, which is equivalent to the number of secondary cases resulting from 1 case introduced into a fully susceptible population [6]. Transmission extinguishes itself when Ro is less than 1. The goal of vaccination is to bring this number to less than 1, therefore 92% to 95% of the population must be protected to halt

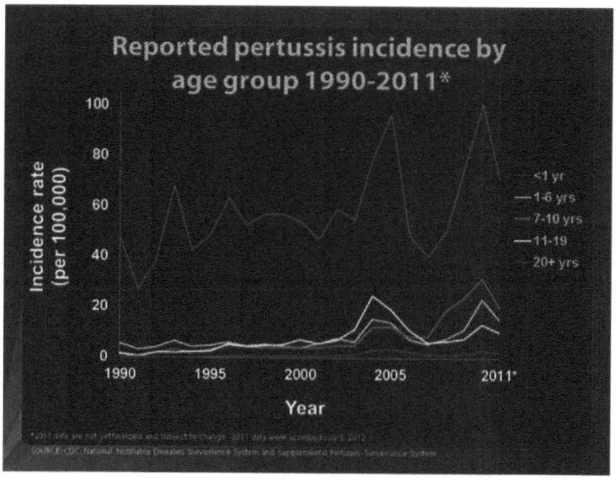


**Fig. 1.** Pertussis incidence (per 100,000 persons) by age group in the United States from 1990 to 2011. Infants aged <1 year, who are at greatest risk for severe disease and death, continue to have the highest reported rate of pertussis. Although adolescents (aged 11–19 years) and adults (aged >20 years) accounted for approximately 47% of reported cases in 2011, persons aged 7 to 10 years continued to contribute a significant proportion of cases (18%). (*Data from* CDC. Available at: http://www.cdc.gov/pertussis/surv-reporting.html. Accessed November 10, 2012.)

infection against pertussis. That point has not yet been reached, therefore until newer vaccines that afford greater longer-term and durable protection become available, the vaccines that are currently must be fully utilized. According to the CDC, whereas school vaccination coverage in 2011/2012 among grantees in

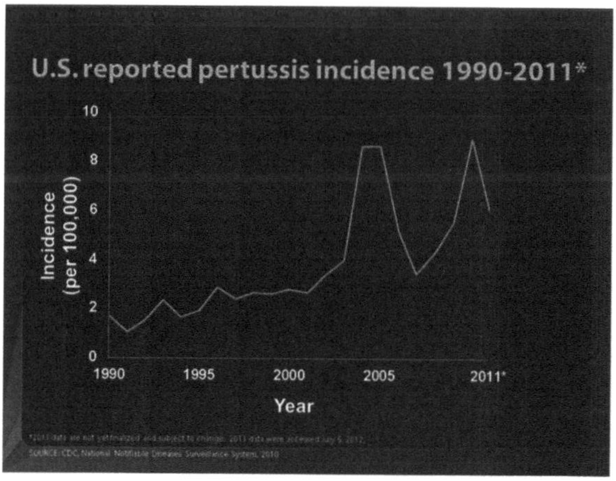


**Fig. 2.** Pertussis incidence per 100,000 persons in the United States from 1990 to 2011. The overall incidence of pertussis peaked most recently in 2010, and rates declined nationally during 2011. (*Data from* CDC. Available at: http://www.cdc.gov/pertussis/surv-reporting.html. Accessed November 10, 2012.)

the 47 states and DC for DTaP (diphtheria, tetanus, and acellular pertussis), poliovirus, and hepatitis B vaccines were all at or higher than the Healthy People 2020 target of 95% or more, rates in adolescents were less optimal. Vaccination coverage among US adolescents aged 13 to 17 years eligible for the Vaccines for Children (VFC) program in 2009, was 52.5% (±2.4%) for 1 or more dose of Tdap (tetanus, diphtheria, acellular pertussis). Vaccine coverage for non-VFC eligible adolescents was significantly higher (57.1% [±1.5%] for ≥1 dose of Tdap) [7]. Adult immunization against pertussis remains at less than 10% [8]. Disparities such as poverty and illiteracy may further increase these differences in immunization rates.

Other reasons for the increased numbers of ongoing cases include waning immunity in vaccinated individuals over time, particularly those immunized with DTaP as opposed to the older whole-cell DTP (diphtheria, tetanus, pertussis) vaccine [4]. Licensed vaccines currently in use are approximately 85% effective overall, and evidence is increasing that immunity may wane more rapidly than anticipated [9]. This was also observed in the 2010 California epidemic [10]. Seventy-nine percent of pertussis cases in children aged 7 to 10 years with vaccination histories had received the recommended 5 doses of DTaP vaccine, with the fifth dose most often administered around 4 years of age, suggesting that immunity from the fifth dose may wane before the administration of the Tdap booster at age 11 to 12 years. This was also supported by the fact that fewer cases were observed in adolescents, thus suggesting that disease incidence in this age group declines as the Tdap coverage increases. The more recent outbreak in Washington State in 2012 also supports the early waning of immunity from acellular vaccines [11].

The question of whether there have been any genetic changes in *Bordetella pertussis* itself also arises. Molecular typing of pertussis isolates in the United States suggests that *B pertussis* strains have evolved since vaccinations were introduced in the 1940s [12]. The commonly circulating strains of *B pertussis* in the United States encode different alleles (a gene that occupies a given locus on a specific chromosome) compared with the strains used for manufacture of the pertussis vaccines, but the relevance of these allele changes remains to be fully elucidated. Because *B pertussis* has no nonhuman host, the selective pressures it encounters are limited to the human immune system and the vaccine, but the influence of this selection pressure versus natural evolution on the modern US *B pertussis* population is unclear. For example, minor types are beginning to emerge, including the reemergence of vaccine-type alleles. In addition, it is possible that the vaccine policies of other nations may have contributed to the makeup of the US *B pertussis* population. This means that as vaccine coverage rates improve among adolescents and adults, changes in the *B pertussis* population should be monitored through molecular typing.

Several strategies have been suggested and several implemented to increase overall immunization rates with pertussis-containing vaccines, including cocooning of newborn infants too young to be vaccinated and vaccination of pregnant women [13]. On June 22, 2011, the Advisory Committee on

Immunization Practices (ACIP) made recommendations for the use of Tdap in unvaccinated pregnant women and updated recommendations on cocooning and special situations [14]. For infants, transplacentally transferred maternal antibodies might provide protection against pertussis in early life and before beginning the primary DTaP series. The half-life of transferred maternal pertussis antibodies is approximately 6 weeks. The effectiveness of maternal antipertussis antibodies in preventing infant pertussis is not yet known but they likely do confer protection and modify the severity of pertussis illness. In addition, the mother is protected and not likely to pass the infection to her baby. It is recommended that the mother be immunized preferably in the second or third trimester (after 20 weeks' gestation). One potential concern about immunizing mothers is interference with the infant's immune response to the primary DTaP immunization. The blunting of the infant's immune response is not entirely clear because the correlates of protection in the case of pertussis are not fully understood. Available evidence suggests that because maternal antibody declines rapidly, the effect of any blunting that may occur is short lived.

Other strategies that have been suggested include immunizing parents and other close family contacts in the pediatric office setting [13]. This strategy takes the concept of cocooning a step further and has been recommended by the ACIP since 2005. However, it has had only moderate success. Although maternal immunizations have increased, there has not been a parallel increase in vaccine uptake by other close family members.

Another bold recommendation released most recently on October 24, 2012 by the ACIP has been to recommend that a Tdap booster vaccine be given to pregnant women during each pregnancy, despite concern about the lack of data for the safety of multiple Tdap vaccinations [15]. According to the CDC, because the antibody response to Tdap vaccine peaks 1 month after immunization, and then decreases significantly after 1 year, women who received the vaccine during a previous pregnancy may not have the same protection during future pregnancies. If not administered during pregnancy, the vaccine should be administered in the immediate postpartum period. The lack of specific safety data in this particular population was a concern, however other available data suggest that there is no serious risk of adverse events. Pediatricians should be aware of these new recommendations for Tdap vaccination for adolescents who are pregnant regardless of their previous Tdap vaccination history, particularly in areas of the country where pertussis cases are on the increase.

Increased and continuing education is a first initial step when it comes to improving disease awareness and recognition among the general public and health care providers. Although there has been increased media attention and increasing public awareness over the last several years, there can never be enough emphasis on public education campaigns. The importance of maintaining a high index of suspicion for the disease in persons with a compatible illness also cannot be overemphasized. As pointed out in the CDC editorial [4], lack of adequate chemoprophylaxis for exposed persons to prevent development of disease was notable in the California outbreak. It is easy to understand why recognition of cases, outside of household contacts, with what is considered significant exposure, may be difficult in an ongoing epidemic. Further administration of chemoprophylaxis may not be adequate to interrupt ongoing transmission and stop a community outbreak. However, it is a disease control and prevention measure and in situations such as community outbreaks and epidemics, it should be implemented as diligently as possible.

A final word on pertussis; most recently a phase I, single-center, dose-escalating, placebo-controlled study on a genetically modified *B pertussis* strain given as a single intranasal dose to healthy adult male volunteers was completed [16,17]. This vaccine has been under study for several years in France. The aim is to develop an effective vaccine for infants aged 0 to 6 months that can provide protection in early infancy before other available vaccines can be given. The goal is not to replace the current vaccines but to provide extra protection to the most vulnerable by adding a first nasal vaccine to protect very early in life. More information on this will be forthcoming as the data continue to be analyzed.

Although it may seem to the reader that there is excessive emphasis being placed on pertussis immunizations, both maternal as well as infant, when the high mortality associated with this disease in early infancy is considered even too much is not enough. The 14 pertussis-related deaths in California are a stark reminder of this fact.

Now turning to the measles story; 90% of the reported cases in 2011 were associated with importation from other countries. Most patients (86%) were unvaccinated or had unknown vaccination status. Although measles vaccination coverage remains above the *Healthy People* 2010 target of greater than 90% for 1 or more dose of measles, mumps and rubella (MMR) vaccine at 91.6% in children 19 to 35 months of age [18], the numbers of cases reported should serve to increase our awareness that measles remains endemic in many parts of the world and there is no place for complacency about the current immunization rates. Travelers remain at the highest risk particularly those less than 12 months of age. The CDC recommends at least 1 dose of MMR vaccine for children between the ages of 6 and 11 months who will be traveling outside the United States [19]. Children 12 months and older are considered immune as long as they have received 2 doses of MMR vaccine. If any child received the first dose before 12 months of age, that dose should not be counted and the child should receive 2 doses after 12 months of age with the second dose at least 28 days apart.

## NEW VACCINE LICENSURES

### Meningococcal groups C and Y and *haemophilus* B tetanus toxoid conjugate vaccine (HiB Mening CY) (MenHibrix)

On June 14, 2012, the US Food and Drug administration (FDA) approved 4 doses of a combination *Haemophilus* B meningococcal groups C and Y conjugate vaccine [20]. This is intended for use at ages 2, 4, 6 and 12 months and is manufactured by GlaxoSmithKline Biologicals. The first dose may be given as early as 6 weeks of age and the last dose as late as 18 months of age. The vaccine has been shown to have a noninferior response to the current *Haemophilus* B tetanus toxoid vaccine (HiB-TT), and is also immunogenic against meningococcal serogroups C and Y. With the licensure of HiB Mening CY, there are now 2 vaccines that have been approved by the FDA in the United States for use in infants; the other one is Men ACWY-D (Menactra, Sanofi Pasteur).

Both the United Kingdom and Canada have had successful immunization programs against meningococcal serogroup C disease, which have decreased the incidence of the disease in young infants. Overall, the incidence in Europe has declined since the introduction of serogroup C meningococcal vaccines in 1999 from 1.67 cases/100,000 to 1.01 cases/100,000 in 2006 [21].

The epidemiology of meningococcal disease varies widely. Global disease incidence rates may be as high as 1000/100,000 population in the meningitis belt in sub-Saharan Africa. In the United States, the annual incidence has been 0.5 to 1.1/100,000 or about 1400 to 2800 cases annually. Although the highest disease incidence is among infants, a second peak occurs in adolescents and young adults between the ages of 14 and 25 years. The incidence and distribution of the different meningococcal serogroups A, B, C, Y and W 135 also varies widely from region to region, country to country, and changes from time to time. In recent years, there has been an increase in the incidence of meningococcal Y disease in the United States (Fig. 3) [22]. Although overall the incidence of meningococcal disease in North America and Europe is relatively low, the high morbidity and mortality caused by the disease warrant a public health policy inclusive of an immunization program to combat the disease.

In January 2011, the FDA approved Men ACWY-CRM (Novartis Vaccines and Diagnostics) for use in individuals aged from 2 to 55 years, Following this,

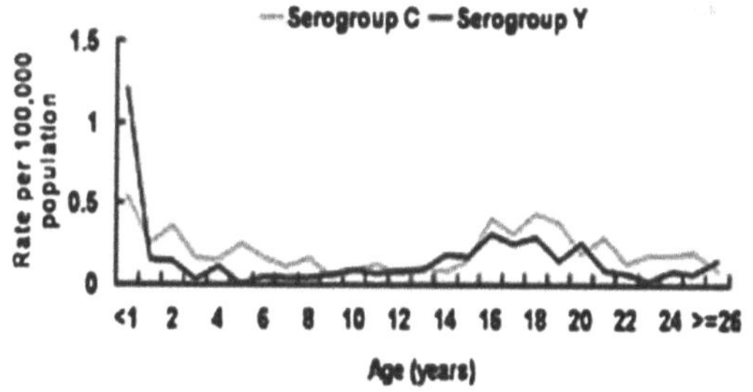


**Fig. 3.** Annual incidence of meningococcal disease (serogroup C and serogroup Y), by age. Active Bacterial Core surveillance (ABCs), United States 1999 to 2008. (*Data from* CDC. Updated recommendations for use of meningococcal conjugate vaccines — Advisory Committee on Immunization Practices (ACIP), 2010. MMWR Morb Mortal Wkly Rep 2011;60(3):73; and *From* CDC. Meningococcal disease. Epidemiology and prevention of vaccine-preventable diseases. The pink book: course textbook. 12th edition. 2012. Available at: http://www.cdc.gov/vaccines/pubs/pinkbook/mening.html. Accessed November 10, 2012.)

in April 2011 the FDA approved the first vaccine to prevent meningococcal disease in infants and toddlers (Men ACWY-D; Menactra, Sanofi Pasteur). This vaccine was approved for use in infants as a 2-dose series at 9 and 12 months of age [23].

Following FDA approval and based on a review of data from clinical studies, the ACIP recommended the use of Men ACWY-D as a 2-dose series given 3 months apart among children aged 9 to 23 months of age at increased risk of meningococcal disease [24]; this includes children with persistent complement deficiencies (C5-9, properdin, factor H or D), children who are traveling to or residents of countries where meningococcal disease is epidemic or hyperendemic, and children who are in a defined risk group during a community or institutional meningococcal outbreak. In addition, because of their high risk for invasive pneumococcal disease, children with functional or anatomic asplenia should be vaccinated with Men ACWY-D beginning at age 2 years to avoid interference with the immunologic response to the infant series of pneumococcal conjugate vaccine (PCV). If children aged 2 years or more with functional or anatomic asplenia have not yet received all recommended doses of PCV, they should receive all recommended doses separated from Men ACYW-D by at least 4 weeks.

The ACIP also approved updated recommendations for the use of Men ACWY-D and Men ACWY-CRM (Menveo, Novartis Vaccines and Diagnostics) in adolescents and adults at persistent high risk of meningococcal disease [25]. Men ACWY-CRM is the third meningococcal vaccine approved for use in adolescents and adults but is still awaiting FDA review for use in infants. The other vaccine approved for adolescent and adult use is the polysaccharide meningococcal vaccine (MPSV4-Menomune, Sanofi Pasteur) which has been available since the 1970s.

The ACIP January 2011 updates for the use of quadrivalent meningococcal vaccines (Men ACWY-D and Men ACWY-CRM) in adolescents and older adults at persistent high risk of meningococcal disease are as follows:

1. Adolescents should be routinely immunized at 11 to 12 years of age and given a booster dose at 16 years of age.
2. Adolescents who receive their first dose of meningococcal vaccine at or after 16 years of age do not need a booster dose.
3. Adolescents who received their first dose at 13 to 15 years of age should receive a booster dose at age 16 to 18 years of age or up to 5 years after their first dose.
4. A 2-dose primary series should be administered 2 months apart for those who are at increased risk of invasive meningococcal disease because of persistent complement component (eg, C5 to C9, properdin, factor H, or factor D) deficiency (9 months to 54 years of age) or functional or anatomic asplenia (2 to 54 years of age) and for adolescents with human immunodeficiency virus infection.
5. A booster dose should be given 3 years after the primary series if the primary 2-dose series was given between 2 and 6 years of age and every 5 years for persons whose 2-dose primary series or booster dose was given at 7 years of age or older who are at risk of invasive meningococcal disease because of persistent

component (e.g., C5 to C9, properdin, factor H, or factor D) deficiency or functional or anatomic asplenia.

### Meningococcal serogroup B vaccines

Meningococcal serogroup B causes endemic disease in much of the developed world including North America and Canada. However, efforts to develop a vaccine have been hampered by the poor immunogenicity of the capsule, which consists of polysialic acid and is present in many human glycoproteins. What makes this unique is that it is similar to many carbohydrates found in fetal brain tissue lending itself to some degree of immune tolerance. Researchers at Novartis Vaccines and Diagnostics have used a process called reverse vaccinology and genome sequencing technology on the serogroup B strain to overcome the difficulties of developing a vaccine based on capsular components [26]. Use of this technology allowed the identification of new protein antigens capable of eliciting antibody responses to bacterial antigens. A new vaccine 4CMenB (Novartis Vaccines and Diagnostics) based on a combination of 3 highly immunogenic antigens identified using reverse vaccinology along with the outer membrane vesicle (OMV) of the New Zealand vaccine strain was tested in initial clinical trials beginning in 2008 [27–29]. The addition of OMV further increases strain coverage due to the presence of immunogenic antigens. Currently, this vaccine is in phase III trials. Available data on its safety and immunogenicity are encouraging. Other vaccines under development include using other components of the bacterial outer membrane of the cell wall. Pfizer is also currently working on one such vaccine using factor H binding protein (fHbp) (also a component of the Novartis 4CMenB vaccine) and developing a vaccine containing fHbp variants [30].

Vaccines against all serogroups of *Neisseria meningitides* are likely to be licensed in the near future. However, some important questions remain: their effectiveness on pathogenic strains with different geographic distribution, their impact on carriers, and the timing of the appearance of escape mutants once herd immunity has been achieved.

### Influenza vaccines

Following the 2009/2010 pandemic influenza season, both the 2010/2011 and 2011/2012 influenza seasons were relatively mild. The 2011/2012 season had the lowest and shortest peak for influenzalike illness compared with recent years (Fig. 4) [31]. A total of 26 pediatric deaths were reported during the 2011/2012 influenza season (Fig. 5). Some of the reasons for the mild season included good vaccine and virus match over the last few years, improved vaccine coverage although still far from optimal: 27% (2009 H1N1 monovalent), 43% in 2010/2011%, and 46% by preliminary estimates in 2011/2012 with higher coverage in children. Immunity from natural infection was also a factor that contributed to the milder season.

For the 2012/2013 influenza virus season, the H1N1 virus used to make the 2012/2013 influenza vaccine is the same virus that was included in the

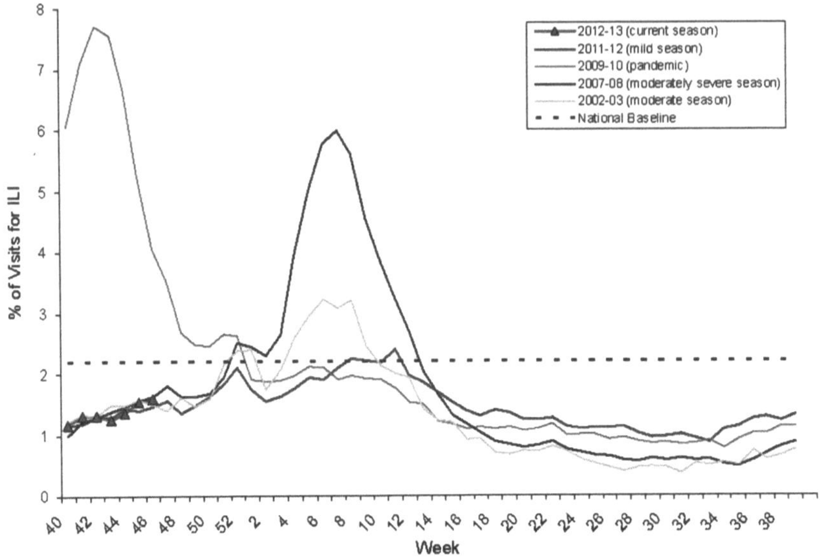


**Fig. 4.** Percentage of visits for influenzalike illness (ILI) reported by the US Outpatient Influenza-like Illness Surveillance network (ILINet), weekly national summary, 2012/2013 and selected previous seasons. (*From* CDC. FluView: A weekly surveillance report prepared by the influenza division. Available at: http://www.cdc.gov/flu/weekly/weeklyarchives2012-2013/picILI46.htm. Accessed November 22, 2012.)

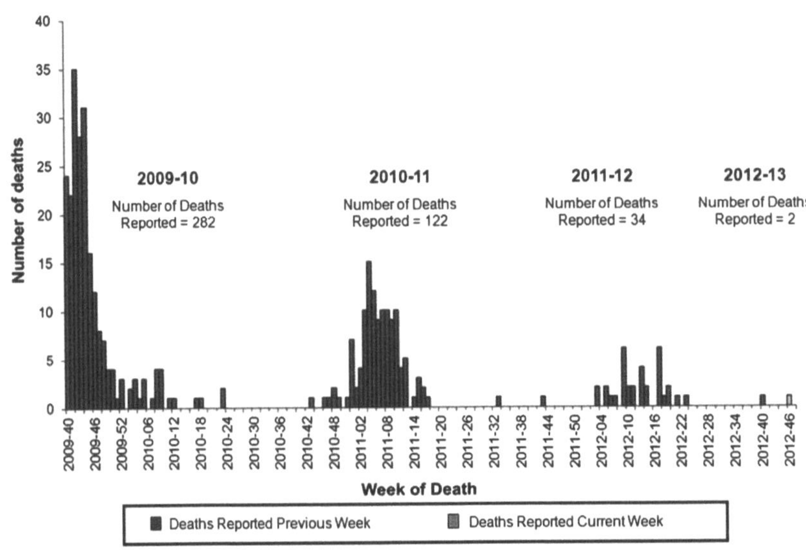


**Fig. 5.** Number of influenza-associated pediatric deaths by week of death: 2009/2010 season to present. (*From* CDC. FluView: A weekly surveillance report prepared by the influenza division. Available at: http://www.cdc.gov/flu/weekly/weeklyarchives2012-2013/IPD46.htm. Accessed November 22, 2012.)

2011/2012 vaccine. The recommended influenza H3N2 and B vaccine viruses are different from those in the 2011/2012 influenza vaccine for the Northern Hemisphere. There have been some changes in the number of dosages recommended for children (Fig. 6).

All currently available influenza vaccines are trivalent and contain A (H1N1), A (H3N2), and B viral antigens. There are 2 antigenically distinct lineages of influenza B viruses referred to as Victoria and Yamagata lineages. Immunization against B virus strains of one lineage provides limited cross-protection against strains in the other lineage. Because of this and the difficulty of predicting which B virus lineage will predominate during a given season, inclusion of a second influenza B vaccine virus strain in seasonal influenza vaccines has been proposed. A recent analysis indicates that the impact of such a quadrivalent vaccine could result in a modest reduction in influenza-associated outcomes, depending on adequate vaccine supply, coverage, effectiveness, and incidence of influenza associated with the 2 influenza B lineages [32].

In February 2012, the FDA approved a new seasonal quadrivalent live attenuated influenza vaccine (FluMist Quadrivalent; MedImmune) [33]. This vaccine is not anticipated to be available until the 2013/2014 influenza season, at which time it is expected to replace the currently available seasonal trivalent, live, intranasal influenza formulation (FluMist, MedImmune) [34]. Inactivated quadrivalent influenza vaccines are currently under development. The immunogenicity and safety of quadrivalent live attenuated influenza vaccine have been studied in children and the vaccine seems to be safe and the immunogenicity noninferior to that of trivalent live attenuated influenza vaccine [35].

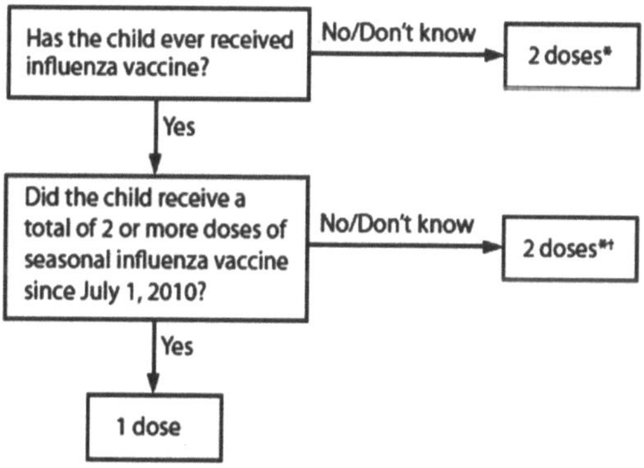


**Fig. 6.** Influenza vaccine dosing algorithm for children aged 6 months to 8 years. ACIP, United States, 2012/2013 influenza season. Children are recommended to receive 2 doses this season, even if 2 doses of seasonal influenza vaccine were received before the 2010/2011 season. This is illustrated in 2 approaches for determining the number of doses required for children aged 6 months to 8 years, both of which are acceptable. *Doses should be administered at least 4 weeks apart. †This algorithm takes into consideration only doses of seasonal influenza vaccine received since July 1, 2010. (*From* CDC. Prevention and control of influenza with vaccines: recommendations of the Advisory Committee on Immunization Practices (ACIP) – United States, 2012-2013 influenza season. MMWR Morb Mortal Wkly Rep 2012;61(32):613–61.)

As if the influenza saga were not complicated enough, there is a new influenza virus variant that has been in circulation since July 2011. Influenza viruses that normally circulate in pigs are called variant viruses when they are found in people. The influenza A H3N2 variant viruses, also known as H3N2v with the matrix gene from the 2009 H1N1 pandemic virus, were first detected in people in July 2011 [36]. From July to December 2011, 12 cases of H3N2v were detected in the United States. From January to September 2012, 307 cases of H3N2v infection were identified across 11 states. Most of these infections were identified in individuals with prolonged exposure to pigs at agricultural fairs and, so far, limited human to human spread has been reported. Children younger than age 10 years have little or no immunity against H3N2v virus. The CDC continues to monitor the situation and all new cases of H3N2v and other influenza variants will continue to be reported and followed closely.

In 2010, the ACIP recommended annual influenza vaccination for all persons aged 6 months or more. Given that vaccinating health care workers against influenza decreases the risk of transmission of influenza to vulnerable patients in the hospital setting, the ACIP further recommends influenza immunization for all health care personnel to protect themselves, their household contacts, and vulnerable patients with whom they may be in contact [37]. Overall rates of immunization in health care workers remain suboptimal although vaccination recommendations have been effective in increasing influenza immunization rates. Many institutions have resorted to mandating influenza vaccination for their staff [38].

### Rotavirus vaccines

Since the introduction of rotavirus vaccines in 2006/2007, wide-scale surveillance, which includes immunization registries and large case-control studies, showed vaccine effectiveness in the 80% to 90% range against acute gastroenteritis and 100% against hospitalization for those with the complete 3-dose series [39–41]. These reductions have been sustained more than time [42]. Health care providers seem to have jumped on board right away once rotavirus vaccines became available and were deemed safe with no concerns for intussusceptions. In our own hospital, we have seen a remarkable decline in the number of rotavirus-related hospitalizations since the introduction of the current vaccines. Most of our hospitalists no longer routinely order tests for rotavirus. According to the US 2011 vaccination coverage report among children aged 19 to 35 months, the coverage for rotavirus vaccines remained above the *Healthy People* 2020 target of 90% at 93.9% [18]. This enthusiasm for immunization against rotavirus is not surprising given the morbidity caused by this infection before the availability of the current vaccines.

Decrease in rotavirus infections has been seen worldwide when rotavirus vaccines have gradually been implemented. The field effectiveness of the vaccines has been around 80% in Latin America. Trials in Africa have yielded efficacy rates between 50% and 80% [43]. In addition to the currently available vaccines, there are some vaccine candidates being development for local use [44].

## Pneumococcal vaccines

After the introduction of the 13-valent pneumococcal conjugate vaccine (PCV13) in March 2010, the ACIP recommended that all children henceforth be immunized with PCV13, which would replace the 7-valent pneumococcal vaccine (PCV7) [45]. It was recommended that even those children between the ages of 14 and 59 months who had completed their pneumococcal vaccination receive a supplemental dose of PCV13. The rationale for the additional supplemental dose was as follows: the rate of invasive pneumococcal disease (IPD) in US children is highest among those less than 12 months old at approximately 40 cases/100,000 population but remains at approximately 10 cases/100,000 population for those between 3 and 5 years of age. Therefore, 13,000 cases of IPD could be prevented over the next 10 years by vaccinating children between the ages of 16 and 59 months with PCV13, assuming that all 13.2 million children in this age group were vaccinated [46,47]. Hence, IPD could be prevented in a substantial number of children by immunization against PCV13 even though they were already immunized with PCV7. One of the premises here was that children aged 16 to 59 months were still susceptible to infection from the 6 additional serotypes (1/3/5/6A/7F/19A) not present in PCV7 and therefore presented an important risk for the spread of IPD to the rest of the population.

An additional dose of PCV13 was also recommended for children with underlying medical conditions who have completed their PCV7 immunization series. For children aged 6 to 18 years with high-risk conditions such as sickle cell disease, human immunodeficiency virus (HIV) infection or other immunocompromising conditions, and cochlear implant and cerebrospinal fluid leaks, regardless of whether they had received PCV7 or the 23-valent polysaccharide vaccine, a single dose of PCV13 was recommended. If both PCV13 and PCV23 are used in these children, PCV13 should be administered first followed by the administration of PCV23 at least 8 weeks later, due to the greater opsonophagocytic antibody response following immunization when PCV13 was given before PCV23. Covalent linking of the capsular polysaccharide to a protein enhances immunogenicity and increases serum antibody levels. The coupling of a polysaccharide antigen to a protein converts the polysaccharide from a T-cell independent to a T-cell dependent antigen to which young children can respond immunologically. These protein carriers are T-cell dependent antigens that stimulate a T helper cell response that primes the vaccinated individual for an amnestic or booster response.

Immunization with PCV13 is expected significantly decrease the rates of nasopharyngeal carriage similar to that seen with PCV7, thereby reducing the burden of IPD not only in children but also in susceptible adults (Fig. 7). The need for PCV13 was evident because of the increasing prevalence of replacement serotypes such as 19A after PCV7 immunization. Replacement serotypes refer to the increase in non-PCV7 serotypes following decline in PCV7 serotypes after immunization. Apart from 19A, other serotypes that have been responsible for IPD after PCV7 immunization include 1/5/7F/33F and serotype

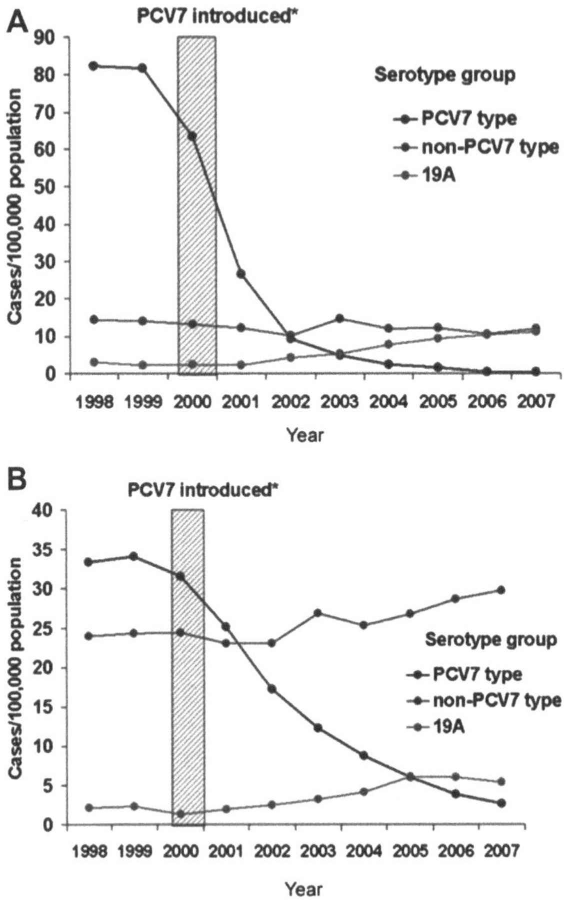


**Fig. 7.** Changes in IPD incidence by serotype group among children less than 5 years of age (*A*) and adults aged 65 years or more (*B*) 1998 to 2007. *Seven-valent pneumococcal conjugate vaccine (PCV7) was introduced in the United States for routine use among young children and infants in the second half of 2000. (*From* Pilishvili T, Lexau C, Farley M, et al. Sustained reductions in invasive pneumococcal disease in the era of conjugate vaccine. J Infect Dis 2010;201:32–41; with permission.)

15. The predominant replacement serotypes seen in children less than 5 years of age are also the replacement serotypes seen in adults 65 years of age and older [48].

## Human papillomavirus vaccines

Immunization rates for human papillomavirus (HPV) vaccines have shown some improvement but overall continue to remain far lower than other adolescent vaccines. According to the National Immunization survey of adolescents aged 13 to 17 years in the United States in 2011, rates for 1 or more dose of

HPV vaccine went from 48.7% to 53% and for 3 or more doses of HPV vaccine from 32% to 34.8% [49]. There are multiple reasons for these low rates and several studies have been done in different populations to look at the reasons for the low uptake of this vaccine. The causes remain multifactorial and range from lower vaccine uptake among adolescents in general to parental and adolescent attitudes toward the vaccine itself as well as different health beliefs toward the vaccine, knowledge about HPV infection, concerns about safety, and concerns for increased sexual activity among adolescents given the vaccine [50–52]. What is clear from all the data available so far is that a physicians' recommendation remains key to determining the uptake of the vaccine. This is also true for other vaccines; vaccination for influenza is a good example. In addition, understanding and addressing individual health beliefs in the right ethnic, cultural, and religious contexts are also extremely important factors if HPV immunization rates are to be improved [53–55]. Furthermore, dispelling erroneous beliefs is also critical. Because HPV is a sexually transmitted infection, many parents fear that giving the vaccine would give young teens a false sense of security and thus lead to increased sexual activity. However, that has not proved to be true so far [56–58].

Another factor in the debate about HPV vaccination rates that cannot be ignored is the issue of male vaccination. On October 25, 2011, the ACIP recommended that the quadrivalent HPV vaccine be used routinely in males [59]. Vaccine efficacy, vaccine coverage of females, the effect of HPV-associated diseases on the quality of life, and the preponderance of heterosexual transmission in the epidemiology of HPV were all factors that made male immunization cost effective for preventing disease caused by vaccine types of HPV in both genders. The ACIP also recommend that males aged 13 to 21 years who have not been vaccinated previously or who have not previously completed the 3-dose vaccine series as well as males aged 22 to 26 years be vaccinated.

However, the cost of this vaccine will make male immunization prohibitive for most developing countries where 80% of cervical cancers occur; these countries simply do not have the resources to make this a universal immunization recommendation for all adolescent females as well as males.

On the scientific front, currently licensed HPV vaccines are prophylactic in nature and not designed to control established HPV infections and associated premalignant and malignant lesions. HPV vaccines can be characterized into 2 categories: preventive and therapeutic vaccines. Preventive vaccines focus on humoral immunity. They focus on HPV viruslike particles (VLP) encoding L1 and/or L2 viral capsid proteins. B cells bind to the HPV VLPs and are activated by TH2 (differentiated CD4+ T helper cells) to become plasma cells, which secrete antibodies. These neutralizing antibodies block primary HPV infection, inducing protection against HPV. Therapeutic HPV vaccination focuses more on cell-mediated immunity [60]. Cell-mediated immunity involves the interaction between professional antigen-presenting cells, particularly dendritic cells and T cells. Dendritic cells present the major histocompatibility complex (MHC)/peptide complex to T cells and prime naive T cells to become effector CD4+ T cells if presented via MHC class II, or effector CD8+ T cells if presented via MHC class I. These effector T cells then mediate therapeutic effects; effector CD8+ T cells, also known as cytotoxic T lymphocytes (CTL) mediate antigen-specific killing of tumor cells and effector CD4+ T cells differentiate into T helper cells to either augment CTL immune response or activate B cells to make antibodies (Fig. 8) [60]. New second-generation HPV vaccines, both prophylactic and therapeutic, are currently under development to address other HPV types and to create vaccines that are more cost effective and thereby allow more individuals to be vaccinated [61,62].

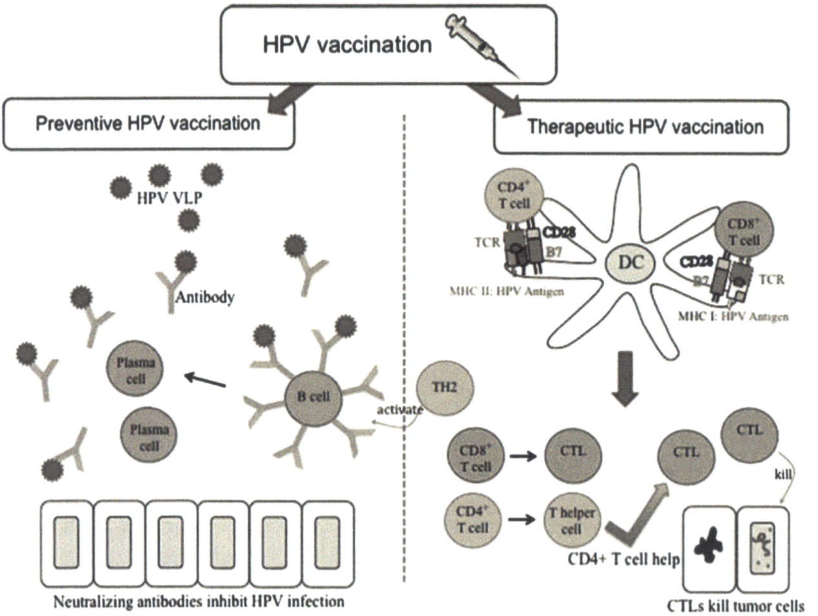


**Fig. 8.** Therapeutic and preventive HPV vaccines. (*From* Lin K, Roosinovich E, Ma B, et al. Therapeutic HPV DNA vaccines. Immunol Res 2010;47:86–112; with permission.)

## MMR vaccine

Immunizations in immunocompromised patients are not the focus of this review, but the changes to MMR vaccination for children with HIV infection must be mentioned. This recommendation is based on studies of children receiving measles vaccines as infants before the initiation of antiretroviral therapy (ART). These studies show that after 6 months or more after immunization, the percentage of children with detectable antibody levels varied from 6% to 83%. Antibody levels were also significantly lower in individuals infected with HIV compared with those exposed to HIV but not infected. The new recommendations include revaccinating with the MMR vaccine HIV-infected children who received their initial vaccination before receiving ART provided they remain on ART and are immunologically and virologically stable [63]. Providers who offer primary care to children with HIV infection should ensure that they are familiar with these new recommendations. In case there are any doubts, this should be discussed with the child's infectious disease provider who is specifically involved with managing the child's HIV infection.

## GLOBAL VACCINE NEWS

India has been taken off the list of polio endemic countries with no reported cases in the previous year ( 2011) [64]. This leaves only 3 polio endemic countries: Pakistan, Afghanistan, and Nigeria. It seems that finally the world is a step closer to polio eradication. If India with its population of more than 1 billion and all the other problems that face most developing countries (poverty, illiteracy, government bureaucracy) can achieve this goal, then the remaining countries have hope as well. Pakistan became the first country in south Asia to introduce the pneumococcal vaccine in 2012. Approximately 352,000 children die before they reach their fifth birthday in Pakistan and 1 in 5 of these deaths is caused by pneumonia [65]. In Africa, Ghana became the first country to introduce both the pneumococcal and rotavirus vaccines in early 2012. Currently, 9 GAVI-eligible countries have introduced rotavirus vaccines (Nicaragua, Bolivia, Honduras, Guyana, Sudan, Ghana, Rwanda, Moldova, and Yemen) [66].

All this is wonderful news not just for the countries involved but for the rest of the world as well. Not only will this reduce morbidity and mortality in the countries involved but it will also decrease the global spread of these infections.

## OTHER VACCINE-RELATED ISSUES

Since the article by Wakefield was published in *Lancet* in 1998, parental fears related to vaccines continue to surface despite the fact that the article was retracted, the author discredited, and hundreds of millions of dollars invested in research since then have shown no link between vaccines and autism. In a recent study from Portland, Oregon, it was reported that 9.5% of parents used alternative vaccination schedules [67]. Several other studies have also reported on alternate immunization schedules [68,69]. Although the reasons described are many, a common theme seems to be to not overwhelm the immune systems with too many vaccines. This seems rather ironic given that infants and children are exposed to hundreds of antigenic stimuli on a daily basis and they seem to tolerate this without any difficulty. This practice of staggering vaccines is also dangerous given that dangers of vaccine-preventable diseases are are still being faced in the United States as mentioned in the discussion at the beginning of this article. Pediatricians need to stand firm when faced with these arguments from parents and present the abundant evidence regarding the dangers of delaying age-appropriate immunizations.

On a completely different note, the ACIP have voted to recommend a joint immunization schedule for 2013 thus combining the 0 to 6 years and 7 to

18 years schedules to avoid confusion arising from 2 separate schedules with complicated footnotes for each schedule. Therefore, a single schedule covering children from 0 to 18 years is expected in the future.

## SUMMARY

Given the constantly changing scenarios in the immunization world with new vaccines and immunization updates for current vaccines, it does remain somewhat of a challenge for pediatricians to keep pace with current recommendations. Ongoing education of caregivers also remains challenging. However, we must keep ourselves well informed. Making sure our children stay healthy and free of vaccine-preventable diseases should be the goal of every pediatrician.

### References

[1] CDC. Pertussis: outbreaks. Available at: http://www.cdc.gov/pertussis/outbreaks.html. Accessed October 13, 2012.
[2] CDC. Outbreak notice - measles, United States, 2011. MMWR Morb Mortal Wkly Rep 2012;61:253–7. Available at: http://wwwnc.cdc.gov/travel/notices/outbreak-notice/measles.htm. Accessed August 30, 2012.
[3] Cherry JD. Epidemic pertussis in 2012 - the resurgence of a vaccine preventable disease. N Engl J Med 2012;367:785–7.
[4] Brooks GF, Buchanan TM. Pertussis in the United States. J Invest Dermatol 1970;122: 123–5.
[5] Cherry JD. Why do pertussis vaccines fail? Pediatrics 2012;129:968–70.
[6] Clark TA. Responding to pertussis. J Pediatr 2012;161(6):980–2.
[7] Lindley MC, Smith PJ, Rodewald LE. Vaccination coverage among US adolescents aged 13-17 years eligible for the Vaccines for Children program 2009. Public Health Rep 2011;126(Suppl 2):124–34.
[8] CDC. Adult vaccination coverage-United States 2010. MMWR Morb Mortal Wkly Rep 2012;61:66–72.
[9] Clark TA, Messonnier NE, Hadler SC. Pertussis vaccines: time for something new? Trends Microbiol 2012;20:211–3.
[10] Winter K, Harriman K, Zippric J, et al. California pertussis outbreak, 2010. J Pediatr 2012;161(6):1091–6.
[11] CDC. Pertussis epidemic - Washington, 2012. MMWR Morb Mortal Wkly Rep 2012;61: 517–22.
[12] Schmidtke AJ, Boney KO, Martin SW. Population diversity among *Bordetella pertussis* isolates, United States, 1935–2009. Emerg Infect Dis 2012;18:1248–55.
[13] CDC. Updated recommendations for use of tetanus toxoid, reduced diphtheria toxoid and acellular pertussis toxoid (Tdap) in pregnant women and persons who have or anticipate having close contact with an infant aged <12 months — Advisory Committee on Immunization Practices (ACIP) 2011. MMWR Morb Mortal Wkly Rep 2011;60:1424–6. Available at: http://www.cdc.gov/mmwr/preview/mmwrhtml/mm6041a4.htm. Accessed August 30, 2012.
[14] Lessin HR, Edwards KM. Committee on Practice and Ambulatory Medicine, Committee on Infectious Diseases. Immunizing parents and other close family contacts in the pediatric office setting. Pediatrics 2012;129:e247–53.
[15] CDC. Advisory Committee for Immunization Practices recommends Tdap immunization for pregnant women. Available at: http://www.cdc.gov/media/releases/2012/a1024_Tdap_immunization.html. Accessed December 1, 2012.

[16] First adult safety trial on nasal live attenuated *B. pertussis* vaccine. Available at: http://clinicaltrials.gov/ct2/show/NCT01188512. Accessed October 13, 2012.
[17] Skerry CM, Mahon BP. A live attenuated *Bordetella pertussis* vaccine provides long term protection against virulent challenge in a murine model. Clin Vaccine Immunol 2011;18:187–93.
[18] CDC. National, state and local area vaccination coverage among children aged 19-35 months- United States, 2011. MMWR Morb Mortal Wkly Rep 2012;61:689–96.
[19] CDC. Outbreak notice: measles update. Available at: http://wwwnc.cdc.gov/travel/notices/outbreak-notice/measles.htm. Accessed December 5, 2012.
[20] FDA. Vaccine approvals. Available at: http://www.fda.gov/BiologicsBloodVaccines/Vaccines/ApprovedProducts/ucm308573.htm. Accessed 13 October, 2012.
[21] EU-IBIS Network. Invasive meningococcal disease in Europe. London 2007. Health Protection Agency, 2006. Available at: http://www.hpa-bioinformatics.org.uk/euibis/neisseria.htm. Accessed October 13, 2012.
[22] Black SB, Plotkin SA. Meningococcal disease from the public health policy perspective. Vaccine 2012;30(Suppl 2):B37–9.
[23] FDA news release. FDA approves the first vaccine to prevent meningococcal disease in infants and toddlers. Available at: http://www.gavialliance.org/library/news/press-releases/2012/pakistan-is-first-south-asian-country-to-launch-vaccine-against-childhood-pneumonia/. Accessed May 17, 2013.
[24] CDC. Recommendation of the ACIP for use of quadrivalent meningococcal conjugate vaccine (Men ACWY-D) among children aged 9 through 23 months at increased risk for invasive meningococcal disease. MMWR Morb Mortal Wkly Rep 2011;60:1391–2.
[25] CDC. Licensure of a meningococcal conjugate vaccine for children aged 2 through 10 years and updated booster dose guidance for adolescents and other persons at increased risk for meningococcal disease-ACIP, 2011. MMWR Morb Mortal Wkly Rep 2011;60:1018–9.
[26] Dull PM, McIntosh ED. Meningococcal vaccine development–from glycoconjugates against MenACWY to proteins against MenB–potential for broad protection against meningococcal disease. Vaccine 2012;30(Suppl 2):B18–25.
[27] Serruto D, Bottomley MJ, Ram S, et al. The new multicomponent vaccine against meningococcal serogroup B, 4CMenB: immunological, functional and structural characterization of the antigens. Vaccine 2012;30(Suppl 2):B87–97.
[28] Ismaili S, Ypma E, Vienken K, et al. The first use of an investigational multicomponent meningococcal serogroup B vaccine (4CMenB) in humans. Hum Vaccin 2011;7(6):646–53.
[29] Sandbu S, Feiring B, Oster P, et al. Immunogenicity and safety of a combination of two serogroup B meningococcal outer membrane vesicle vaccines. Clin Vaccine Immunol 2007;14:1062–9.
[30] Harris SL, Zhu D, Murphy E, et al. Preclinical evidence for the potential of a bivalent fHbp vaccine to prevent *Neisseria meningitides* serogroup C disease. Hum Vaccin 2011;7:S68–74.
[31] CDC. Influenza virus activity. Available at: http://www.cdc.gov/vaccines/acip/meetings/downloads/slides-jun-2012/02-influenza-finelli.pdf. Accessed November 24, 2011.
[32] Reed C, Metlzer MI, Finelli A, et al. Public health impact of including two lineages of influenza B in a quadrivalent seasonal influenza vaccine. Vaccine 2012;30:1993–8.
[33] FDA approves first quadrivalent vaccine to prevent seasonal influenza. Available at: http://www.fda.gov/NewsEvents/Newsroom/PressAnnouncements/ucm294057.htm. Accessed December 1, 2012.
[34] CDC. Prevention and control of influenza with vaccines: recommendations of the Advisory Committee on Immunization Practices (ACIP) - United States, 2012-2013 influenza season. MMWR Morb Mortal Wkly Rep 2012;61:613–8.
[35] Block SL, Falloon J, Hirschfield JA, et al. Immunogenicity and safety of a quadrivalent live attenuated influenza vaccine in children. Pediatr Infect Dis J 2012;31:745–51.

[36] CDC. Influenza A (H3N2) variant virus. Available at: http://www.cdc.gov/flu/swineflu/h3n2v-cases.htm. Accessed December 1, 2012.
[37] CDC. Prevention and control of influenza with vaccines: recommendations of the advisory committee in immunization practices (ACIP). MMWR Recomm Rep 2010;59(RR-8):1–68.
[38] Johnson JG, Talbot TR. New approaches for influenza vaccination for health care workers. Curr Opin Infect Dis 2011;24:363–9.
[39] Dennehy PH. Effects of vaccine on rotavirus disease in the pediatric population. Curr Opin Pediatr 2012;24:76–84.
[40] Cortes JE, Curns AT, Tate JE, et al. Rotavirus vaccine and health care utilization for diarrhea in U.S. children. N Engl J Med 2012;365:1108–17.
[41] Sahni LC, Boom JA, Patel MM, et al. Use of an immunization information system to assess the effectiveness of pentavalent rotavirus in US children. Vaccine 2010;28:6314–7.
[42] Tate JE, Mutuc JD, Panozzo CA, et al. Sustained decline in rotavirus detections in the United States following the introduction of rotavirus vaccine in 2006. Pediatr Infect Dis J 2011;30: S30–4.
[43] Vesikari T. Rotavirus vaccination: a concise review. Clin Microbiol Infect 2012;18(Suppl 5):57–63; http://dx.doi.org/10.1111/j.1469-0691.2012.03981.x.
[44] Shaw AR. The rotavirus saga revisited. Annu Rev Med 2012;64:165–74.
[45] Paradiso PR. Advances in pneumococcal disease prevention: 13-valent penumococcal conjugate vaccine for infants and children. Clin Infect Dis 2011;52:1241–7.
[46] Rubin JL, McGarry LJ, Strutton DR, et al. Public health and economic impact of the 13-valent pneumococcal conjugate vaccine (PCV13) in the United States. Vaccine 2010;28: 7634–43.
[47] CDC. Licensure of a 13-valent pneumococcal conjugate vaccine (PCV13) and recommendations for use among children - ACIP, 2010. MMWR Morb Mortal Wkly Rep 2010;59: 258–61.
[48] Tan TQ. Pediatric invasive pneumococcal disease in the United States in the era of pneumococcal conjugate vaccines. Clin Microbiol Rev 2012;25:409–19.
[49] CDC. National and state vaccination coverage among adolescents aged 13-17 years-United States, 2011. MMWR 2012;61:671–7.
[50] Kessels SJ, Marshall HS, Watson M, et al. Factors associated with HPV vaccine uptake in teenage girls: a systematic review. Vaccine 2012;30:3546–56.
[51] Dorell CG, Yankey D, Santibanez TA, et al. Human papillomavirus vaccination series initiation and completion, 2008-2009. Pediatrics 2011;128:830–9.
[52] Baldwin AS, Bruce CM, Tiro JA. Understanding how mothers of adolescent girls obtain information about the HPV vaccine: association between mothers' health beliefs, information seeking, and vaccination intentions in an ethnically diverse sample. J Health Psychol 2012; http://dx.doi.org/10.1177/1359105312445078.
[53] Hamish T, Clarke L, Alexander KA. Barriers to HPV immunization for African American adolescent females. Vaccine 2012;30:6472–6.
[54] Kester LM, Zimet GD, Fortenberry JD, et al. A national study of HPV vaccination of adolescent girls: rates, predictors and reasons for non vaccination. Matern Child Health J 2012; http://dx.doi.org/10.1007/s10995-012-1066-z.
[55] Ylitalo KR, Lee H, Mehta MK. Health care provider recommendation, human papillomavirus vaccination and race/ethnicity in the US National Immunization Survey. Am J Public Health 2012;103(1):164–9.
[56] Bednarczky RA, Davis R, Ault K, et al. Sexual activity-related outcomes after human papillomavirus vaccination of 11-12 years olds. Pediatrics 2012;130:798–805.
[57] Mullins TL, Zimet GD, Rosenthal SL, et al. Adolescent perception of risk and need for safer sexual behaviors after first human papillomavirus vaccination. Arch Pediatr Adolesc Med 2012;166:82–8.
[58] Liddon NC, Leichliter JS, Markowitz LE. Human papillomavirus and vaccine and sexual behavior among adolescent and young women. Am J Prev Med 2012;42:44–52.

[59] CDC. Recommendations on the use of quadrivalent human papillomavirus vaccine in males-ACIP, 2011. MMWR Morb Mortal Wkly Rep 2011;60:1705–8.
[60] Lin K, Roosinovich E, Ma B, et al. Therapeutic HPV DNA vaccines. Immunol Res 2010;47: 86–112.
[61] Gersch ED, Gissmann L, Garcea RL. New approaches to prophylactic human papillomavirus vaccines for cervical cancer prevention. Antivir Ther 2012;17:425–34.
[62] MMR vaccine recommendations in HIV infected children. Available at: http://www.healio.com/infectious-disease/vaccine-preventable-diseases/news/print/infectious-disease-news/%7Bcd97bc12-9af6-4c62-a4fc-d071652cd47f%7D/acip-recommends-changes-to-mmr-vaccine-for-children-with-hiv. Accessed December 4, 2012.
[63] Ma B, Maraj B, Tran NP, et al. Emerging human papillomavirus vaccines. Expert Opin Emerg Drugs 2012;17:469–92.
[64] World Health Organization. Polio in India. Available at: http://www.who.int/mediacentre/factsheets/fs114/en/. Accessed December 3, 2012.
[65] GAVI Alliance. Pneumococcal vaccines. Available at: http://www.gavialliance.org/library/news/press-releases/2012/pakistan-is-first-south-asian-country-to-launch-vaccine-against-childhood-pneumonia/. Accessed May 17, 2013.
[66] GAVI Alliance. Rotavirus vaccines. Available at: http://www.gavialliance.org/support/nvs/rotavirus-vaccine-support-timeline/. Accessed November 20, 2012.
[67] Robison SG, Groom H, Young C. Frequency of alternative immunization schedule use in a metropolitan area. Pediatrics 2012;130:32–8.
[68] Dempsey AF, Schaffer S, Singer D, et al. Alternative vaccination schedule preferences among parents of young children. Pediatrics 2011;128:848–56.
[69] Smith PJ, Humiston SG, Parnell T, et al. The association between intentional delay of vaccine administration and timely childhood vaccine coverage. Public Health Rep 2010;125: 534–41.

Advances in Pediatrics 60 (2013) 33–51

ADVANCES IN PEDIATRICS

# Bullying and Victimization Among Children

Rashmi Shetgiri, MD, MSHS*

Division of General Pediatrics, Department of Pediatrics, University of Texas Southwestern Medical Center and Children's Medical Center, 5323 Harry Hines Boulevard, Dallas, TX 75390-9063, USA

**Keywords**

• Bullying • Aggression • Prevention • Intervention • Risk factors

**Key points**

- Bullying affects a large proportion of children in the United States and internationally.
- Bullies, victims, and bully-victims are at high risk for negative short-term and long-term consequences.
- Slight decreases in US trends in bullying and victimization may be caused by increased awareness and response to bullying and bullying-related incidents.
- School-based bullying interventions seem to be promising; implementing programs with fidelity and enlisting adequate parental involvement and school personnel effort increase the likelihood of success.
- Parents, providers, and schools can work together to prevent and intervene in childhood bullying.

## INTRODUCTION

### Definition of bullying

Bullying is an important public health problem, affecting 1 in 3 US children. The most commonly used definition of bullying was developed by Daniel Olweus in the 1970s and 1980s [1,2]. Olweus describes bullying as "intentional, repeated,

Funding source: supported in part by grant K23HD068401 to Dr Shetgiri from the Eunice Kennedy Shriver National Institute of Child Health & Human Development. The content is solely the responsibility of the authors, and does not necessarily represent the official views of the Eunice Kennedy Shriver National Institute of Child Health & Human Development or the National Institutes of Health.

Conflict of interest: the author has no conflicts of interest to disclose.

*Division of General Pediatrics, Department of Pediatrics, UT Southwestern Medical Center, 5323 Harry Hines Boulevard, Dallas, TX 75390-9063. *E-mail address:* rashmi.shetgiri@utsouthwestern.edu

0065-3101/13/$ – see front matter
http://dx.doi.org/10.1016/j.yapd.2013.04.004 

negative (unpleasant or hurtful) behavior by 1 or more persons directed against a person who has difficulty defending himself or herself" [1]. This definition applies to such aggressive behavior inflicted by a person or group with seemingly more power on a person or group with less power [1,3,4]. The power differential may be because of physical size, psychological/social power, or other factors [5]. The key elements are listed in Box 1 [3,5,6].

## Types of bullying

Bullying includes direct and indirect forms of aggression (Table 1) [2,6,7].

Physical and verbal aggression are direct forms of bullying, consisting of an overt expression of power. Physical bullying includes any type of physical assault, such as hitting, pushing, kicking, choking, and forcefully taking something from the victim [4,7–9]. Verbal bullying includes verbal harassment or intimidation in the form of name-calling, threatening, taunting, malicious teasing, and psychological intimidation using words to harm victims [4,5,7–9]. Stealing, vandalizing, and making faces or obscene gestures also are ways in which children are bullied [4,8].

Indirect bullying primarily consists of relational aggression, which includes social exclusion of victims through the manipulation of social relationships by bullies or injuring the reputation of the victims [5,8,9]. Gossiping, slandering, sabotage, and convincing peers to exclude victims are forms of relational bullying [7–9]. Bullying most often occurs in areas with little adult supervision, such as playgrounds and school hallways [8]. Verbal and relational bullying can be more difficult to identify than physical bullying [8]. Relational bullying is more common among girls and can lead to feelings of rejection at a critical time in social development [8].

Cyber bullying is an emerging form of bullying and is defined as harm inflicted through threatening, harassing, taunting, or intimidating a peer using an electronic medium, such as computers, cell phones, and other electronic devices (see Table 1) [6,7,10]. Similar to definitions of traditional bullying, cyber bullying definitions include that the behavior is aggressive, with the intent to harm [6]. However, unlike traditional bullying, cyber bullying definitions do not include a power differential between the bully and victim, and not all cyber bullying definitions include that the behavior is repetitive [6]. This is a particularly insidious form of bullying because it can occur at school and at home, is difficult to detect and verify, quickly reaches a wide audience, and is easily

**Box 1: Key elements of bullying**

1. A physical, verbal, or psychological attack or intimidation
2. An actual or perceived power imbalance between the perpetrator(s) or victim(s)
3. Intent to cause fear, or harm to the victim
4. It is repeated and produces the desired effect

**Table 1**
Types of bullying

| Type of bullying | Method/behavior |
|---|---|
| Traditional forms of bullying | |
| Physical bullying (direct) | Hitting, pushing, kicking, choking, forcefully taking something from victim |
| Verbal bullying (direct) | Name-calling, threatening, taunting, malicious teasing, psychological intimidation using words |
| Relational bullying (indirect) | Gossiping, slandering, sabotage, convincing peers to exclude victims |
| Cyber bullying | Threatening, harassing, taunting, intimidating using electronic medium |

accessible for more than 80% of adolescents who have access to media technology [6,7,11]. The most commonly used electronic media for cyber bullying are listed in Box 2 [6].

Cyber bullies use these media by sending cruel or threatening messages, taking over the victim's email account and sending embarrassing or vicious messages to others, which appear as if they have come from the victim, creating Web sites with pictures or jokes about the victim and inviting other classmates to participate in ridiculing the victim online, and tricking the victim to reveal sensitive information through email or instant messaging and then forwarding it to others [6].

Physical and cyber bullying peak in middle school, then decrease, whereas verbal bullying may continue to be increased throughout high school [6,10,12]. More than half of cyber bullying victims are not bullied offline [6]. However, involvement in cyber bullying can signal involvement in other types of bullying perpetration and victimization [12,13]. Those who are physically or cyber bullied are more likely to be verbally or relationally bullied as well [13].

*Characteristics of bullies*

Bullying consists of 3 main types of participants: bullies, victims, and bully-victims (Table 2).

Bullies are not a homogeneous group. Some bullies have well-developed social skills and use bullying to gain or maintain dominance in their peer group [8,14]. Bullies may have a positive attitude toward violence and lack empathy for their victims [8]. Approximately 10% of bullies show consistently high rates

**Box 2: Electronic media used for cyber bullying**

- Text messaging/cell phones
- Internet Web sites or chat rooms
- Email
- Computer instant messaging

**Table 2**
Characteristics of bullies, bully-victims, and victims

| Bullies | Bully-victims | Victims |
|---|---|---|
| Dominant | Impulsive | Physically smaller than peers |
| Boys more than girls | Low self-esteem | Low self-esteem |
| Defiant behaviors | Poor social skills | Difficulty making friends |
| Drug use | Poor problem-solving skills | Less assertive than peers |
| Comorbid conditions (attention-deficit/ hyperactivity disorder, depression, oppositional/ conduct disorder) | Comorbid conditions (anxiety, attention-deficit/ hyperactivity disorder, depression, oppositional/ conduct disorder) | Comorbid conditions (anxiety, loneliness, depression) |

of bullying over time [15]. Thirteen percent of students bully in early adolescence but are no longer bullying by the end of high school [15]. Boys are more likely to be classified as bullies than girls [16]. Bullies are more likely to manifest defiant behavior and negative attitudes toward school, and to use drugs [16]. Bullies also may show comorbid conditions, such as attention-deficit disorder, depression, and oppositional-conduct disorder [8].

### Characteristics of bully-victims

Bully-victims are those who bully others and are bullied themselves; they also are known as reactive bullies or provocative/aggressive victims [8]. These may be impulsively aggressive children who respond with aggression to being bullied, or victims who transition from victimization to bullying behavior over a period of time [14,17]. There is less information about bully-victims compared with the other groups, although this group seems to have the most severe and broadest range of adjustment problems [16,18,19]. Children in this group may have attention problems, low self-esteem, and especially high rates of depression and oppositional-conduct disorder [8,14]. They are more anxious and less popular than bullies, have poor social skills and problem-solving, tend to annoy peers, and may, therefore, not be well liked by peers or teachers [8,14]. They are more likely to come from families with inconsistent or poor parenting, low warmth, and may learn aggressive behavior from home [8].

### Characteristics of victims

Most bullying victims are passive or submissive victims (vs provocative/aggressive). They may be physically smaller, less assertive, more anxious, insecure, or sensitive than bullies [8,17]. Victims of bullying also may have difficulty making friends and may relate better with adults than peers [8]. They also may have lower self-esteem, which may result in their being less likely to report victimization from bullying [8]. Compared with bullies and bully-victims, victims report the highest levels of loneliness and anxiety, whereas bullies report the lowest [16]. Victims have the lowest social status among peers and bullies have the highest; however, bully-victims are most avoided by classmates [16].

## Characteristics of cyber bullies and victims

Cyber bullies and victims show some unique behaviors. Bullies are not necessarily stronger than their victims, they are usually anonymous, and are not able to see the distress caused by their bullying [6]. Cyber bullying occurs at school and at home and may be more difficult to identify and intervene with than other forms of bullying [6]. Cyber bullying also is more difficult to trace, and therefore, bullies have less fear of being identified [6]. Most cyber bullying incidents occur outside the school day [20]. Cyber bullying at school is most commonly via texting, and victims are unlikely to report these incidents because of rules prohibiting cell phone use during school [20]. Although students report that they know how to circumvent school Web site filters to access social networking sites at school, they do not use these sites often during the school day [20].

Cyber bullies are more likely to be aggressive, to display delinquent behavior, have delinquent peers, and be involved in substance use [6]. They also report poor parental monitoring, worse relationships with parents, and poor emotional bonding with their parents, compared with children uninvolved in cyber bullying [6]. More than one-third of cyber bullies report cyber bullying for fun, one-fourth state that they bully in retaliation, and a few state that they bully because they felt bad about themselves [6]. Cyber bullies may be victims or perpetrators of traditional offline bullying. Most cyber bullies know their victims; however, less than one-third of victims know their bullies in person [6].

Victims of cyber bullying often do not know who is cyber bullying them and are hesitant to report bullying to parents for fear of losing electronic media privileges [6,20]. Victims are even less likely to report cyber bullying to school officials than to parents [20]. Children who cyber bully others, who are victims of traditional forms of bullying, and have social problems are more likely to be victims of cyber bullying [6].

## Risk and protective factors for bullying perpetration

Child, parental, peer, and community risk factors that increase the risk of bullying perpetration are listed in Box 3.

Maternal and paternal depression also may influence child bullying perpetration. Maternal depression is associated with bullying [36]. This relationship may be mediated by poorer quality of interactions between depressed mothers and their children, or decreased maternal attachment to the child, which are associated with bullying [30,37]. Interactions between depressed mothers and their children are more likely to be irritable, critical, and hostile [38,39]. Chronic depression also is associated with poor parenting behaviors [40] and negative child outcomes [36,39]. The relationship between paternal depression and child bullying perpetration is less clear. Some studies suggest that depression in fathers is associated with worse socioemotional development in the child [38] and more internalizing and externalizing behaviors [41]. One study found that fathers who bullied when they were in school were more likely to have children who bullied [42].

**Box 3: Risk factors for bullying perpetration**

- Younger age of the child [10,21,22]
- Male gender [23,24]
- Presence of depression [22,25,26], mental health problems [25], or emotional/developmental/behavioral problems [27,28]
- Low academic achievement [29]
- Substance use [22]
- Exposure to child abuse and domestic violence [26,30]
- African American or Latino race/ethnicity [10,25,30–32]
- High levels of anger in the child [33,34]
- Parental use of corporal punishment [24]
- Poor parent-child communication [29]
- Suboptimal maternal mental health [27,28]
- Parental anger with their child [27,28]
- Parents' reporting that their child bothers them a lot [27,28]
- Lack of parental monitoring [24]
- High family conflict [35]
- Poor relationships with classmates [29]
- Negative influences from peers [24]
- Living in an unsafe neighborhood [24]

Living in a 2-parent family [43], maternal warmth [23,30], parental involvement with their child [23,27,28,30,44], positive adult role models [24], and high parental support [10,37] are protective against bullying perpetration.

### Risk and protective factors for victimization

Factors that increase the risk of victimization are listed in Box 4.

Children who have few friends, no reciprocal best friend [2], or friendships that are low in supportiveness and protection are more likely to experience rejection and isolation by peers and be victimized by bullies [2,45]. Children with these types of peer relationships are more likely to be marginalized, making it easier and more socially acceptable for bullies to target them [2]. On the contrary, among those children who have personal characteristics that increase the risk for victimization, such as internalizing problems, but have more friends and protective peer relationships, these relationships can be protective against victimization [2]. This finding is especially true when these peer relationships are with prosocial or physically stronger peers [2]. Teachers' warm and caring behavior toward all students in the class also is protective against child victimization [2].

### Risk factors for bully-victimization

Several factors, listed in Box 5, are associated with higher risk of being a bully-victim.

**Box 4: Risk factors for victimization from bullying**

- Being physically weaker
- Low self-worth
- Negative self-perceptions
- Low social competence
- Poor social skills and problem-solving abilities
- Internalizing behaviors (depression, anxiety)
- Insecure mother-child attachment
- Maternal overprotectiveness
- Intrusive or coercive parenting
- Child abuse

*Data from* Espelage DL, Swearer SM. Research on school bullying and victimization: what have we learned and where do we go from here? School Psychol Rev 2003;32(3):365–83; and Cook CR, Williams KR, Guerra NG, et al. Predictors of bullying and victimization in childhood and adolescence: a meta-analytic investigation. Sch Psychol Q 2010;25(2):65–83.

## PREVALENCE AND TRENDS IN BULLYING AND VICTIMIZATION

### Worldwide trends in bullying and victimization

Studies show variability in the prevalence of bullying and victimization across countries, ranging from 15% to more than 50% [46]. Early estimates of bullying prevalence in Norway in the 1980s found that 15% of Norwegian students in elementary or middle school were involved in bullying; 9% as victims, 6% to

**Box 5: Risk factors for being a bully-victim**

- Emotional dysregulation
- Hyperactivity
- Low social competence
- Poor problem-solving skills
- Poor self-esteem
- Negative perceptions about others
- Poor academic performance
- Peer rejection and isolation
- Negative influences from those peers with whom the child interacts
- Disconnectedness from school

*Data from* Espelage DL, Swearer SM. Research on school bullying and victimization: what have we learned and where do we go from here? School Psychol Rev 2003;32(3):365–83; and Cook CR, Williams KR, Guerra NG, et al. Predictors of bullying and victimization in childhood and adolescence: a meta-analytic investigation. Sch Psychol Q 2010;25(2):65–83.

7% as bullies, and 1.5% as both bullies and victims [1]. In a study comparing trends in bullying and victimization from 1994 to 2006 in 27 European and North American countries, most showed significant decreases, with the United Kingdom and North America showing no change or slight increases [46]. In a 2005 to 2006 study of 40 countries, 26% of children in sixth to 10th grade were involved in bullying, 10.7% as bullies, 12.6% as victims, and 3.6% as bully-victims [47].

### Bullying and victimization trends in the United States

The prevalence of bullying in the United States changed throughout the 1990s and early 2000, with slight decreases in occasional and chronic bullying and victimization from 1994 to 2006 [46]. Nearly 30% of US children in sixth to 10th grades surveyed in 1998 to 1999 reported being involved in moderate or frequent bullying [3,8]; 13% as bullies, 10.6% as victims, and 6.3% as bully-victims (Fig. 1) [3]. This finding means that almost 6 million students were directly involved in bullying at the time of the survey [3,8]. A 1996 study showed that 1 of 2 middle and high school students reported knowing that bullying has occurred at their school, and more than 40% had personally witnessed bullying [48]. In 2001, bullying involvement among US children in sixth to 10th grades had decreased to 21%, with 9% as bullies, 9% as victims, and 3% as both bullies and victims (see Fig. 1) [29]. A 2005 to 2006 study that examined different types of bullying showed that 21% of sixth-grade to 12th-grade students were involved in occasional physical bullying, 53% in verbal bullying, 51% in relational bullying, and 14% in cyber bullying (Fig. 2) [10]. Victimization from physical bullying has decreased from 2003 to 2008; however, victimization from emotional bullying is not significantly changed [49]. Variations in the prevalence of bullying among studies may be, in some part, attributable to variability in how bullying is measured and the types of bullying examined.

A wide range of involvement in cyber bullying has been reported. Almost half of children have witnessed cyber bullying, 4% to 20% identify themselves

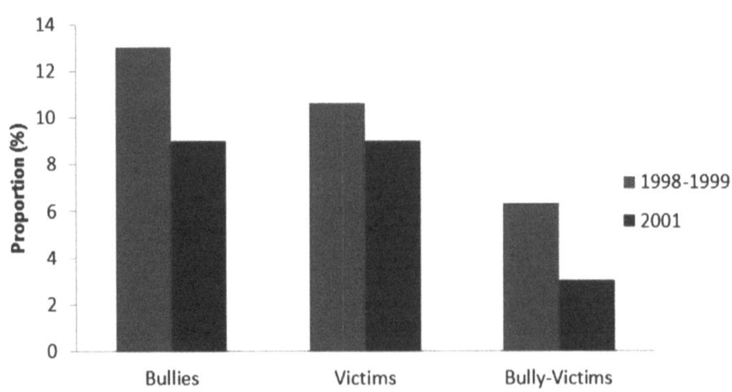


**Fig. 1.** Prevalence of moderate or frequent bullying in the United States from 1998 to 2001.

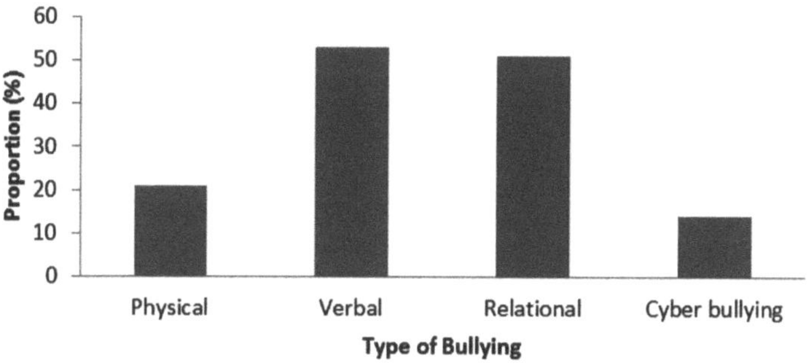


**Fig. 2.** Prevalence of occasional bullying in the United States in 2005–2006.

as cyber bullies, 9% to 35% as victims of cyber bullying, and 7% as cyber bully-victims [6,7,10]. Eight percent of children report being cyber bullied monthly or more often. Of those children who were bullied, half were victimized more than once, and almost 1 in 3 were victimized more than 3 times in the previous year [6]. Children report cyber bullying via various methods: 60% have been ignored by others online, 50% were disrespected by others, 30% have been called names, 21.4% have been threatened by others, 19.8% were annoyed by others, 19.3% were made fun of by others, and 18.8% had rumors spread about them by others [6].

## CLINICAL CORRELATION

### Consequences of bullying and victimization

There are significant short-term and long-term psychosocial consequences of bullying. Bullies may experience poor school adjustment and academic performance, higher rates of alcohol and substance use, and increased externalizing behavior, such as fighting and weapon-carrying [3,8,18,25,31,50,51]. Long-term consequences include antisocial development, intimate partner violence perpetration, unemployment, delinquency, and criminality in adulthood [8,15,19]. One study found that 60% of boys who bullied in sixth to ninth grades had at least 1 criminal conviction by age 24 years and 35 years; 40% of these boys had 3 or more convictions by this time [8]. Perpetrators of bullying also are more likely to have children who bully [8].

Victimization is associated with negative consequences. Bullying victims experience anxiety, depression, poor academic performance, and psychosomatic complaints, such as headaches and abdominal pain, especially in the morning [8,52–55]. This situation may lead to chronic absenteeism from school, with 1 study showing that 7% of US students in eighth grade stayed home from school at least 1 day a month because of bullying [8]. Victims also may experience difficulty sleeping and have nightmares [8]. Long-term consequences include lower self-esteem, poor academic achievement, and poor psychosocial adjustment as adults [52–55]. Victims are more likely than nonvictims to carry weapons to school for safety or retaliation, and have a greater likelihood of perpetrating school shootings [52–55]. A study of school-associated homicides in the 1990s found that almost 20% of perpetrators had been bullied, and perpetrators of school shootings were more than twice as likely their victims to have been bullied [52].

Bully-victims may be at highest risk for serious consequences, including perpetrating school shootings [8]. Bully-victims are at higher risk of weapon-carrying, fighting, alcohol and substance use, depression, anxiety, psychosomatic complaints, and psychiatric illnesses as adults, compared with bullies, victims, and children uninvolved in bullying [8]. Compared with bullies and victims, bully-victims have more conduct problems and school disengagement, and are socially ostracized by peers [16].

## Bullying and suicide

Bullying is significantly associated with suicidal ideation and suicide attempts. Studies in Europe, Asia, and the United States have found higher risk of suicidal ideation in victims and perpetrators of bullying [7,56]. More frequent involvement in bullying is associated with higher risk, and these risks seem to be higher for girls than for boys [7,56]. Boys who are bullied are 2.5 times more likely to have suicidal ideation than nonbullied boys, and bullied girls are more than 4 times as likely as nonbullied girls to have suicidal ideation. Similar relationships exist for bullies, with bullying boys and girls at higher risk for suicidal ideation than nonbullying children, and girls at higher risk than boys [7]. Lesbian/gay/bisexual youth and children with learning disabilities, who are victimized by bullying, are at particularly high risk of suicidal ideation and suicide attempts [56]. Bully-victims are at highest risk [56]. Although bullying and victimization are associated with higher risk of suicidal ideation, bullying involvement explains only a small proportion of the variability in suicidal ideation [7]. The relationships between bullying involvement and suicidal ideation for boys are mediated by childhood depression and externalizing problems, such as conduct disorder [57]. This finding suggests that bullying involvement is more likely to be a contributor than the sole cause of suicidal ideation [7]. However, among girls who are frequently victimized, the association with suicide attempts and completed suicides persists even after accounting for depression and conduct problems [57]. The difference between boys and girls may be because girls are more likely to be victimized by relational bullying, whereas boys are more likely to be victimized by physical bullying [57].

## Antibullying interventions

There are no rigorously evaluated, effective primary care–based bullying interventions. School-based interventions to reduce bullying have been studied in Asia, Europe, and North America (Table 3) [58].

### *School-based interventions*

Bullying interventions are primarily school based and consist of whole-school multidisciplinary interventions, curriculum interventions, social and behavioral skills group training interventions, and other single-component

**Table 3**
Antibullying interventions

| Type of intervention | Results |
|---|---|
| Whole-school, multidisciplinary, school-based (Olweus Bullying Prevention Program, Bergen) | Reduced school bullying, effective at 5-year follow-up |
| Whole-school, multidisciplinary, school-based (Olweus program adaptations in United States) | Effective in suburban elementary school students and white students, ineffective in rural elementary and middle school students |
| Whole-school (Sheffield Anti-Bullying Project) | Reduced bullying and victimization in intervention schools compared with some, but not all, control schools |
| Whole-school (Sevilla Anti-Violencia Escolar) | Reduced bullying and victimization in intervention schools using pre-post evaluation |
| Classroom-based (Second Step Violence Prevention Program) | Some reduction of antisocial behavior and aggression, improvement in social competence |
| Social skills group training | Reduced aggression and bullying in elementary school students, ineffective for older students |
| Zero-tolerance policies in schools | Increase drop-out, suspension, and future incidents of misbehavior |

interventions [59]. Evaluations of these interventions show variable results in the United States and internationally.

The whole-school approach directs interventions to the entire school context, rather than only bullies or victims [60]. It is based on the theory that bullying is a systemic problem, which involves multiple contexts, such as individual students, peers, teachers, and parents [60]; bullying interventions, therefore, need to be directed at changing all of these contexts. The Olweus Bullying Prevention Program was the first evaluated, whole-school, multidisciplinary school-based intervention [59,60]. It consists of a videotaped classroom curriculum, school personnel training, and materials for parents [59]. It includes intervention components at the individual student, classroom, school, and community levels [1]. Initial evaluations of this program in Bergen, Norway reported significant reductions in school bullying [59]. Victimization from bullying decreased from 10% to 3.6%, and bullying perpetration decreased from 7.6% to 3.6% [1]. A 5-year follow-up study of this intervention in Norway, from 2001 to 2006, showed continued effectiveness in bullying and victimization [1]. However, evaluations of the program in other locations in Norway and the United States have shown variable results [59]. In the United States, for example, the program showed decreased self-reported bullying and victimization in suburban California elementary schools, reductions in relational and physical victimization in white students only in Washington, and no effects on victimization in rural South Carolina elementary and middle schools [1,61]. This variability in effectiveness may be caused by modifications to the original curriculum, decreased staff involvement, or lack of fidelity in replication of the Bergen model [59].

Other whole-school interventions include the Sheffield Anti-Bullying Project, which includes a school antibullying policy, antibullying curriculum, individual and peer-level intervention, and playground intervention [61]. This intervention has shown decreases in bullying and victimization compared with some schools. The Sevilla Anti-Violencia Escolar program showed reductions in bullying and victimization in intervention schools using a pre-post design for the evaluation [61]. Whole-school programs in Germany, Belgium, and Switzerland show variable outcomes depending on age, type of bullying, and reporter of bullying [61]. A few interventions in Canada and Switzerland have been shown to be ineffective or to increase bullying [61].

A 2008 meta-analysis of school bullying intervention programs concluded that these types of interventions were effective in improving social competence, self-esteem, and peer acceptance among students, and in enhancing teacher knowledge and efficacy about intervention [5]. However, this study also stated that the small effects produced by these programs on bullying were unlikely to be practically meaningful [5]. Another review concurred with this finding that school-based antibullying programs do not seem to have a practically significant reduction in bullying [4] but found that they may be effective in reducing bullying for at-risk youth.

A 2009 meta-analysis of 44 school-based bullying intervention programs identified elements that are associated with reductions in bullying and victimization [58]. Programs with the characteristics listed in Box 6 are most likely to be effective. Box 7 lists specific program components that are important. Parent trainings/meetings, firm disciplinary methods, and the use of videos were found to be the most effective components.

The investigators concluded that results of the effectiveness of school-based antibullying programs were encouraging [58]. It seems that increased time and effort invested in program implementation may result in better outcomes [61]. Parent training and education also seem to be essential components for effective interventions [58]. However, school-based interventions have minimal parental involvement, and primarily target children or school personnel [62]. Interventions with a substantial component focused on parenting and parent-child interactions may be useful to consider in future program implementation.

**Box 6: Bullying intervention program characteristics most likely to be effective**

- Programs inspired by the Olweus Bullying Prevention Program
- Include parental involvement
- Longer duration of the program
- Inclusion of multiple important components

**Box 7: Important program components for reducing bullying and victimization**

- Parent trainings and meetings (most effective for victimization and bullying)
- Firm disciplinary methods (most effective for victimization and bullying)
- Use of videos (most effective for victimization)
- Information for parents
- Teacher training
- Classroom management
- Classroom rules
- School conferences
- Whole-school antibullying policy
- Spending more time working with peers increased victimization

Interventions of classroom-based curricula in isolation and social and behavioral skills training group interventions had variable results [59]. The Second Step Violence Prevention program, a classroom-based intervention, had some success in reducing antisocial behaviors and aggression and improving social competence [4]. Social skills training interventions may be effective for some children [8]. One study of elementary school students who had difficulties with peers found that a social skills group training intervention reduced aggression and bullying; such interventions with older children were ineffective [59]. A mentoring program for at-risk children was effective in decreasing bullying, fighting, and depression [59].

*Zero-tolerance policies in schools*

Zero-tolerance policies in isolation are ineffective in reducing bullying [63]. These policies result in higher suspension and expulsion rates, but do not increase consistency of school discipline, and worsen school climate. Student suspension is associated with higher likelihood of future suspension and drop-out and an increase, rather than a decrease, in misbehavior. Students view suspension and expulsion as ineffective, and studies of parents and communities regarding zero tolerance are inconclusive. There is no evidence that zero-tolerance policies, as currently practiced, improve school safety or student behavior [63]. Interventions that include zero-tolerance policies as well as other components have not been evaluated [8].

*Cyber bullying interventions*

There are no evidence-based cyber bullying interventions, and, therefore, children are left to handle cyber bullying in various ways. Victims respond to cyber bullying by blocking the sender, ignoring the message, telling the bully to stop, and staying offline; almost 25% of victims do nothing [6,20]. More than half of victims tell a friend, and some tell a parent, sibling, or other adult. Almost 25% of victims tell no one, and a few respond to cyber bullying by bullying others [6]. Students report that they do not know how to respond when they are bystanders to cyber bullying and are unsure of how to request the removal of negative material from Web sites [20].

## Antibullying policies

In response to recent incidents of school bullying and bullying-related suicides, there has been a push for antibullying initiatives at the federal, state, and local levels. The US Department of Health and Human Services, Health Resources and Services Administration, launched its antibullying campaign in 2001 [64]. The campaign has partnered with several agencies and community organizations to raise awareness about bullying and its prevention. The first White House Conference on Bullying Prevention was held in March 2011.

No federal antibullying laws exist. However, federal civil rights laws do address discriminatory harassment based on race, color, national origin, sex, and disability [64]. Fifty states have antibullying laws in their state education or criminal codes, and 42 states also have model policies that provide guidance to school districts in these states [64]. Many of these state laws include a definition of bullying, although all do not include cyber bullying. These laws also may state the scope of environments in which the law is applicable, and direct local school districts to enact antibullying policies [64]. Local antibullying policies may vary by region and school district.

## Clinical management of bullying

Organizations for clinical professionals have recognized the need for clinicians to have a role in bullying prevention and intervention [65,66]. The American Academy of Pediatrics and the American Medical Association have issued policy statements about bullying and provide educational resources for providers and patients [65,67]. Providers are encouraged to identify children at risk for bullying, provide counseling for children and families, screen for comorbidities, and advocate for bullying prevention at the local, state, and national level [65,66].

### *Identification*

Providers can identify bullies and victims using several methods. All school-age children can be screened for bullying involvement during health maintenance visits using tools such as the American Academy of Pediatrics Bright Futures materials. Providers also can use questions such as those listed in Box 8 to probe about bullying.

Some children are at especially high risk of bullying and victimization (Box 9). These children should be screened for bullying at all provider visits and should be asked directly about any involvement in bullying.

### *Screening and counseling*

Children involved in bullying should be screened for anxiety, depression, and other mental health problems. Providers can screen bullies for attention-deficit/hyperactivity disorder or other emotional, developmental, or behavioral problems using validated measures such as the Pediatric Symptom Checklist or Children's Behavior Checklist [68] and refer them to mental health

**Box 8: Questions to identify children involved in bullying**

- How are things going at school?
- Do you enjoy school?
- Do you have friends at school? Outside school? Tell me the name of 1 of your friends.
- Has anyone picked on you or been mean to you at school? Outside school? On the Internet/your computer or your cell phone?
- Have you picked on anyone or been mean to anyone at school? Outside school? Using the Internet/your computer or your cell phone?
- Have you ever been in any pushing or shoving fights?

professionals for further evaluation and counseling. Bullies, victims, bully-victims, and their parents should be provided with resources and strategies for dealing with bullying and victimization. These strategies include referring children and families to mental health providers for screening and counseling, promoting parent-child involvement and communication, directing parents to informational resources such as the US Department of Health and Human Services Web site (http://www.stopbullying.gov), and encouraging parents to work with teachers, counselors, and school district leadership to address the bullying. Additional recommendations for victims could include enrollment in activities

**Box 9: Identifying children at high risk of bullying involvement**

- Present with signs of victimization
  - Physical bruises
  - Torn clothes
  - Constantly requesting or stealing money from family members to pay bullies
- Present with nonspecific and psychosomatic complaints
  - Headaches
  - Abdominal pain
  - Enuresis
  - Difficulty sleeping or nightmares
  - Feeling sad
- Refusal to go to school or worsening academic performance
- Children with chronic medical problems
- Children with emotional, developmental, or behavioral problems (eg, attention-deficit/hyperactivity disorder, learning disabilities)

*Data from* Smokowski PR, Kopasz KH. Bullying in school: an overview of types, effects, family characteristics, and intervention strategies. Child Sch 2005;37(2):101–10; and Williams K, Chambers M, Logan S, et al. Association of common health symptoms with bullying in primary school children. Br Med J 1996;313:17–9.

to build confidence and self-esteem, practicing scenarios on how to respond in assertive, nonviolent ways to bullying, and promoting friendships with protective peers. Increased supervision and monitoring of children's cell phone and Internet use by parents may be beneficial for preventing cyber bullying [6]. Parents should be aware of their child's school's policy on technology use, and schools can provide information to parents about cyber bullying [20].

*Advocacy*

Clinicians can educate themselves about state and local antibullying policies and inform parents about them. Parents and providers could advocate with schools to consider limiting or prohibiting cell phone use at school, and enforcing consequences for policy violations [20]. Providers also can work with schools to advocate for the use of effective antibullying programs.

## SUMMARY

Bullying affects many children in the United States and internationally. Bullies, victims, and bully-victims are at high risk for negative short-term and long-term consequences. Slight decreases in trends in bullying and victimization may be the result of increased awareness and response to bullying and bullying-related incidents. Despite this situation, many children are still affected by bullying. School-based bullying interventions seem to be promising; however, it is important to choose an evidence-based program, to administer the program with fidelity, and to enlist adequate parental involvement and school personnel effort to make the program effective. Additional research on effective intervention strategies is needed. Clinicians can play a role in identifying bullies and victims, evaluating them for comorbid conditions, and providing resources and referrals as necessary. Parents, providers, and schools can work together to prevent and intervene in childhood bullying.

## References

[1] Olweus D, Limber SP. Bullying in school: evaluation and dissemination of the Olweus bullying prevention program. Am J Orthopsychiatry 2010;80(1):124–34.

[2] Espelage DL, Swearer SM. Research on school bullying and victimization: what have we learned and where do we go from here? School Psych Rev 2003;32(3):365–83.

[3] Nansel TR, Overpeck M, Pilla RS, et al. Bullying behaviors among US youth: prevalence and association with psychosocial adjustment. JAMA 2001;285(16):2094–100.

[4] Ferguson CJ, San Miguel C, Kilburn JC, et al. The effectiveness of school-based anti-bullying programs: a meta-analytic review. Crim Justice Rev 2007;32(4):401–14.

[5] Merrell KW, Gueldner BA, Ross SW. How effective are school bullying intervention programs? A meta-analysis of intervention research. Sch Psychol Q 2008;23(1):26–42.

[6] Kiriakidis SP, Kavoura A. Cyberbullying: a review of the literature on harassment through the Internet and other electronic means. Fam Community Health 2010;33(2):82–93.

[7] Hinduja S, Patchin JW. Bullying, cyberbullying, and suicide. Arch Suicide Res 2010;14: 206–21.

[8] Smokowski PR, Kopasz KH. Bullying in school: an overview of types, effects, family characteristics, and intervention strategies. Child Sch 2005;37(2):101–10.

[9] Lamb J, Pepler DJ, Craig W. Approach to bullying and victimization. Can Fam Physician 2009;55:356–60.

[10] Wang J, Iannotti RJ, Nansel TR. School bullying among adolescents in the United States: physical, verbal, relational, and cyber. J Adolesc Health 2009;45:368–75.
[11] David-Ferdon C, Hertz MF. Electronic media, violence, and adolescents: an emerging public health problem. J Adolesc Health 2007;41:S1–5.
[12] Wang J, Iannotti RJ, Luk JW. Patterns of adolescent bullying behaviors: physical, verbal, exclusion, rumor, and cyber. J Sch Psychol 2012;50(4):521–34.
[13] Wang J, Iannotti RJ, Luk JW, et al. Co-occurrence of victimization from five subtypes of bullying: physical, verbal, social exclusion, spreading rumors, and cyber. J Pediatr Psychol 2010;35(10):1103–12.
[14] Barker ED, Arsenault L, Brendgen M, et al. Joint development of bullying and victimization in adolescence: relations to delinquency and self-harm. J Am Acad Child Adolesc Psychiatry 2008;47(9):1030–8.
[15] Pepler D, Jiang D, Craig W, et al. Developmental trajectories of bullying and associated factors. Child Dev 2008;79(2):325–38.
[16] Juvonen J, Graham S, Schuster MA. Bullying among young adolescents: the strong, the weak, and the troubled. Pediatrics 2003;112(6):1231–7.
[17] Pellegrini AD, Bartini M, Brooks F. School bullies, victims, and aggressive victims: factors relating to group affiliation and victimization in early adolescence. J Educ Psychol 1999;91(2):216–24.
[18] Olweus D. Bullying at school: what we know and what we can do. Cambridge (MA): Blackwell; 1993.
[19] Farrington DP, Ttofi MM. Bullying as a predictor of offending, violence and later life outcomes. Crim Behav Ment Health 2011;21(2):90–8.
[20] Agatston PW, Kowalski R, Limber S. Students' perspectives on cyber bullying. J Adolesc Health 2007;41:S59–60.
[21] Kumpulainen K, Rasanen E, Henttonen I. Children involved in bullying: psychological disturbance and the persistence of the involvement. Child Abuse Negl 1999;23(12):1253–62.
[22] Carlyle KE, Steinman KJ. Demographic differences in the prevalence, co-occurrence, and correlates of adolescent bullying at school. J Sch Health 2007;77(9):623–9.
[23] Flouri E, Buchanan A. The role of mother involvement and father involvement in adolescent bullying behavior. J Interpers Violence 2003;18(6):634–44.
[24] Espelage DL, Bosworth K, Simon TR. Examining the social context of bullying behaviors in early adolescence. J Couns Dev 2000;78(3):326–33.
[25] Sourander A, Helstela L. Persistence of bullying from childhood to adolescence–a longitudinal 8-year follow-up study. Child Abuse Negl 2000;24(7):873–81.
[26] Yang S, Kim J, Kim S, et al. Bullying and victimization behaviors in boys and girls at South Korean primary schools. J Am Acad Child Adolesc Psychiatry 2006;45:69–77.
[27] Shetgiri R, Lin H, Avila RM, et al. Parental characteristics associated with bullying perpetration in US children aged 10-17 years. Am J Public Health 2012;102(12):2280–6.
[28] Shetgiri R, Lin H, Flores G. Trends in risk and protective factors for child bullying perpetration in the United States. Child Psychiatry Hum Dev 2013;44(1):89–104.
[29] Spriggs AL, Iannotti RJ, Nansel TR, et al. Adolescent bullying involvement and perceived family, peer, and school relations: commonalities and differences across race/ethnicity. J Adolesc Health 2001;41:283–93.
[30] Bowes L, Arseneault L, Maughan B, et al. School, neighborhood, and family factors are associated with children's bullying involvement: a nationally representative longitudinal study. J Am Acad Child Adolesc Psychiatry 2009;48(5):545–53.
[31] Nansel TR, Craig W, Overpeck MD, et al. Cross-national consistency in the relationship between bullying behaviors and psychosocial adjustment. Arch Pediatr Adolesc Med 2004;158(8):730–6.
[32] Kumpulainen K, Rasanen E, Henttonen I, et al. Bullying and psychiatric symptoms among elementary school-age children. Child Abuse Negl 1998;22(7):705–17.

[33] Bosworth K, Espelage D, Simon T. Factors associated with bullying behavior in middle school students. J Early Adolesc 1999;19(3):341–62.
[34] Espelage DL, Bosworth K, Simon TR. Short-term stability and prospective correlates of bullying in middle-school students: an examination of potential demographic, psychosocial, and environmental influences. Violence Vict 2001;16:411–26.
[35] Stevens V, De Bourdeaudhuij I, Van Oost P. Relationship of the family environment to children's involvement in bully/victim problems at school. J Youth Adolesc 2002;31(6): 419–28.
[36] Georgiou SN. Bullying and victimization at school: the role of mothers. Br J Educ Psychol 2008;78:109–25.
[37] Zimmerman FJ, Glew GM, Christakis DA, et al. Early cognitive stimulation, emotional support, and television watching as predictors of subsequent bullying among grade-school children. Arch Pediatr Adolesc Med 2005;159:384–8.
[38] Kane P, Garber J. The relations among depression in fathers, children's psychopathology, and father-child conflict: a meta-analysis. Clin Psychol Rev 2004;24:339–60.
[39] Fihrer I, McMahon CA, Taylor AJ. The impact of postnatal and concurrent maternal depression on child behaviour during the early school years. J Affect Disord 2009;119:116–23.
[40] McLearn KT, Minkovitz CS, Strobino DM, et al. The timing of maternal depressive symptoms and mothers' parenting practices with young children: implications for pediatric practice. Pediatrics 2006;118:e174–82.
[41] Ramchandani P, Stein A, Evans J, et al. Paternal depression in the postnatal period and child development: a prospective population study. Lancet 2005;365:2201–5.
[42] Farrington DP. Understanding and preventing bullying. In: Tonry M, editor. Crime and justice: a review of research. Chicago: University of Chicago Press; 1993. p. 381–458.
[43] Kim YS, Koh Y, Leventhal BL. Prevalence of school bullying in Korean middle school students. Arch Pediatr Adolesc Med 2004;158(8):737–41.
[44] Lee C. An ecological systems approach to bullying behaviors among middle school students in the United States. J Interpers Violence 2011;26:1664–93.
[45] Cook CR, Williams KR, Guerra NG, et al. Predictors of bullying and victimization in childhood and adolescence: a meta-analytic investigation. Sch Psychol Q 2010;25(2): 65–83.
[46] Molcho M, Craig W, Due P, et al. Cross-national time trends in bullying behaviour 1994–2006: findings from Europe and North America. Int J Public Health 2009;54:S225–34.
[47] Craig W, Harel-Fisch Y, Fogel-Grinvald H, et al. A cross-national profile of bullying and victimization among adolescents in 40 countries. Int J Public Health 2009;54:S216–24.
[48] Nolin MJ, Davies E, Chandler K. Student victimization at school. J Sch Health 1996;66(6): 216–21.
[49] Finkelhor D, Turner H, Ormrod R, et al. Trends in childhood violence and abuse exposure: evidence from 2 national surveys. Arch Pediatr Adolesc Med 2010;164:238–42.
[50] Olweus D. Bullying among schoolchildren: intervention and prevention. In: Peters RD, McMahon RJ, Quinsey VL, editors. Aggression and violence throughout the life span. London: Sage; 1992. p. 100–25.
[51] Solberg ME, Olweus D. Prevalence estimation of school bullying with the Olweus bully/victim questionnaire. Aggress Behav 2003;29:239–68.
[52] Anderson M, Kaufman J, Simon TR, et al. School-associated violent deaths in the United States, 1994-1999. JAMA 2001;286(21):2695–702.
[53] Rigby K. Consequences of bullying in schools. Can J Psychiatry 2003;48(9):583–90.
[54] Salmon G, West A. Physical and mental health issues related to bullying in schools. Curr Opin Psychiatry 2000;13(4):375–80.
[55] Spector ND, Kelly SF. Pediatrician's role in screening and treatment: bullying, prediabetes, oral health. Curr Opin Pediatr 2006;18(6):661–70.
[56] Kim YS, Leventhal B. Bullying and suicide. A review. Int J Adolesc Med Health 2008;20(2): 133–54.

[57] Klomek AB, Sourander A, Niemela S, et al. Childhood bullying behaviors as a risk for suicide attempts and completed suicides: a population-based birth cohort study. J Am Acad Child Adolesc Psychiatry 2009;48(3):254–61.
[58] Farrington DP, Ttofi MM. School-based programs to reduce bullying and victimization. Campbell Systematic Reviews 2009;6:1–148.
[59] Vreeman RC, Carroll AE. A systematic review of school-based interventions to prevent bullying. Arch Pediatr Adolesc Med 2007;161(1):78–88.
[60] Smith JD, Schneider BH, Smith PK, et al. The effectiveness of whole-school anti-bullying programs: a synthesis of evaluation research. School Psych Rev 2004;33(4):547–60.
[61] Smith PK, Ananiadou K, Cowie H. Interventions to reduce school bullying. Can J Psychiatry 2003;48:591–9.
[62] Stevens V, De Bourdeaudhuij I, Van Oost P. Anti-bullying interventions at school: aspects of programme adaptation and critical issues for further programme development. Health Promot Int 2001;16(2):155–67.
[63] American Psychological Association Zero Tolerance Task Force. Are zero tolerance policies effective in the schools? An evidentiary review and recommendations. Am Psychol 2008;63(9):852–62.
[64] US Department of Health and Human Services, Health Resources and Services Administration. Stop Bullying.gov Website. Available at: http://www.stopbullying.gov. Accessed December 5, 2012.
[65] Sege RD, Wright JL, Smith GA, et al. Policy statement: role of the pediatrician in youth violence prevention. Pediatrics 2009;124:393–402.
[66] Lyznicki JM, McCaffree MA, Robinowitz CB. Childhood bullying: implications for physicians. Am Fam Physician 2004;70:1723–30.
[67] Fleming M, Towey KJ, Limber SP, et al. Educational forum on adolescent health: youth bullying. Chicago: American Medical Association; 2002.
[68] Jellinek MS, Murphy JM, Little M, et al. Use of the Pediatric Symptom Checklist to screen for psychosocial problems in pediatric primary care: a national feasibility study. Arch Pediatr Adolesc Med 1999;153(3):254–60.

Advances in Pediatrics 60 (2013) 53–87

ADVANCES IN PEDIATRICS

# Slums Are Not Places for Children to Live

## Vulnerabilities, Health Outcomes, and Possible Interventions

Kacey C. Ernst, PhD, MPH[a,*], Beth S. Phillips, MPH[b], Burris "Duke" Duncan, MD[c]

[a]Epidemiology, College of Public Health, University of Arizona, Tucson, AZ 85724, USA; [b]Guinea Worm Eradication Program, South Sudan; [c]Family and Child Health, College of Public Health and Pediatrics, College of Medicine, University of Arizona, Tucson, AZ 85724, USA

**Keywords**

• Children • Slums/informal settlements • Poverty • Health • Education • Social • Interventions

**Key points**

- Describe the geographic distribution of slum areas and assess the conditions of informal settlements or slums.
- Illustrate how and to what magnitude these conditions are associated with poor child health outcomes.
- Demonstrate health, economic, and social disparities between children living in slums and nonslum portions of the city and in rural areas.
- Summarize successful interventions that have either directly improved child health outcomes or improved conditions associated with residing in slum areas.

## INTRODUCTION

> "... I would describe people living here as those who are surviving purely by luck. They live from day to day. When it comes to living conditions it is quite hard, here I am living with my son and my grandchildren. There is no freedom at all. God did not create a human to live like the way we are living here" (Never-married woman, 63 years old, Korogocho) [1].

Slums. Little to no infrastructure, filthy conditions, staggering poverty; adults living in these conditions, such as the woman cited above, will undoubtedly

*Corresponding author. *E-mail address:* kernst@email.arizona.edu

0065-3101/13/$ – see front matter
http://dx.doi.org/10.1016/j.yapd.2013.04.005 

experience poor health outcomes. But children who grow up under these conditions suffer a dual burden, as they have yet to fully develop physically and mentally. What are the primary factors that drive poor health outcomes of children residing in slum conditions and what can be done to reduce these disparities? Fairly recently, global attention has turned toward the conditions in slum areas with the inclusion of Millennium Development Goal (MDG) 7 Target 7D: "By 2020, to have achieved a significant improvement in the lives of at least 100 million slum dwellers" [2]. That seemingly lofty goal is followed by "slum improvements, though considerable, are failing to keep pace with the growing ranks of the urban poor." That is a gross understatement. Even the MDG target falls far short of the need. The number of slum dwellers is growing at an alarming rate: a tripling of slum dwellers in less than 3 decades [3]. In 1976, 1.5 billion people lived in urban areas, and one-third were slum dwellers. In 2002, 3 billion or 47% of the world's population lived in cities and 1 billion or 16% lived in slums. It is expected that this number will double by 2030 [4]. Most of the urbanization is occurring in the least developed countries and many municipalities do not have the infrastructure to deal with the rapid expansion and lack the financial and human resources to provide basic utilities. In all regions of the developing world, the growth of slums, also known as informal settlements, is appallingly apparent. In Africa alone, close to 70 million live in slums; 6 of every 10 urban dwellers [5]. This will likely continue to expand, as currently, 38% of the 297 million Africans live in urban areas [6], with an additional 60 million migrating into urban areas every year [5]. In India, as of 2007, approximately 170 million people lived in slums and one-third of them were children.

The rapid pace of urbanization is global. Families and individuals move from rural to urban areas for several key perceptions, many are misperceptions: (1) employment opportunities and higher incomes, (2) availability of more and better social services and health care, (3) improved water supply and infrastructure, (4) a greater variety of educational opportunities, and (5) the reality of increasingly fractionated family lands yet more mouths to feed, declining crop production, and/or decreasing income from sale of crops. Many rural-urban migrants are poorer and less educated than their nonmigrant neighbors. As an example, in Nigeria, 62% of rural to urban migrants met the poor index compared with 13% of rural nonmigrants, and with 19% of those living in the city [7]. Sixty-five percent of the mothers leaving the rural areas had no education, as compared with 28% of those who did not migrate and 44% of those living in the city. Seeking a new and better life in the urban areas, these poorest of the poor and less educated from rural communities immigrate to the city. Yet on arrival, work is often scarce and individuals and families find themselves joining the urban poor. Residing in slum areas, they may find less access to the resources and services they were seeking when they left the rural areas (Table 1).

The plight of children living in slums or informal settlements is the theme of this article; it is a call to arms. Although the task is daunting, there are

**Table 1**
Trade-offs for migration from rural to urban areas

| Urban-poor advantage | Urban-poor penalty |
|---|---|
| Perceived improved opportunities for employment | Less food security |
| Considered a transient location | Crowded living conditions |
| Closer to services and perceived to be more accessible | Increased exposure to contagious diseases |
| Higher immunization coverage | Indoor air pollution |
| More family planning programs | Decreased social, family, and financial support (at least initially) |
| Averages of health indicators exceed rural averages (may be misleading as averages mask wide socioeconomic disparities) | Less child care advice from elders |
| Home ownership relates to greater independence and satisfaction to overcoming living conditions | Lack of social capital, trust, or personal security |
| Others could include: | Mental health issues |
| Freedom/independence from strict family/gender expectations? | Lack of clean water |
| Better educational opportunities? | Insufficient sanitary facilities |
| Desire to be modern/Western/developed? | Fee-for-services predominate with government services, although usually free, being crowded |
| | Quality of closer services is low and costly |
| | Lack access to emergency transport services |
| | Schools a distance from living area |
| | Insecurity and violence |
| | No security of tenure |
| | Many have been forced to leave rural areas (husband's choice or financial reasons) |
| | **Expectations not met** |

successful model programs that have been implemented to improve health outcomes for children in slums. Pediatricians are in a unique position to raise awareness of what happens to this vulnerable population and advocate for just and successful policies. As advocates of the young, we have an obligation to accept the challenge to speak out and enlist the ministries and politicians to enact policies that will improve the lives of all children.

## AIM

The objective of this article was to describe the geographic distribution of slum areas and then progressively assess the conditions of informal settlements or slums, demonstrate how and to what magnitude these conditions are associated with poor child health outcomes compared with rural and nonslum urban areas, and, finally, to optimistically describe successful interventions that have either directly improved health outcomes or improved conditions associated with residing in slum areas.

## METHODS

### Data collection

The primary variable proportion of urban populations residing in slums was downloaded from the United Nations (UN) publically available Web site for all countries, with data available from 2005 to present [8]. Condition variables and child health and development variables were downloaded from the Henry J. Kaiser Family Foundation (HJKFF) for US Global Health Policy Web site [9]. Data presented on the HJKFF Web site originate from multiple sources, including the World Bank (WB), the World Health Organization, and the UN. National-level slum population indicators included proportions of the population dwelling in urban areas, urban population residing in slums, and total national population in slums. Confounding factors included gross domestic product (GDP) per capita, proportion of population earning less than $1.25 per day, access to clean water and sanitation, and the unemployment rate. Childhood health outcomes included coverage with measles-containing vaccine (MCV), child malnutrition, low birth weight babies, total birth rate, neonatal mortality, infant mortality, under-5 mortality, and maternal mortality ratio. Of the immunizations available, MCV was chosen because of the relevance of MCV vaccine in slum settings with the very crowded conditions and the range in coverage that was seen across countries (Table 2).

## Analyses

*Worldwide geographic distribution of slum areas*

Mapping software, ArcMap version 10.0 (Environmental Systems Resource Institute, Redlands, CA), was used to create a map of slum populations as a percentage of urban populations (Fig. 1). Table 1 lists the countries singly with data on urban slums and health outcomes that were outlined previously.

*Relative disparities in pediatric health outcomes among rural, urban, and urban-slum populations*

Searches were made to identify reports that analyzed key pediatric health outcomes by region: rural, urban slum, urban nonslum. Relative percent difference was calculated between urban-slum and rural to determine if residing in slums is associated with better or worse health outcomes.

*Associations between proportion of slum dwellers and pediatric health outcomes*

Associations between percentage of national populations residing in slums and key pediatric health outcomes were taken from the UN-STATS for MDG 7 Target 7D. Unadjusted Pearson correlations were calculated using SAS 9.2 (SAS, Inc., Cary, NC) and presented with the correlation coefficient and $P$ value.

Multivariate analyses were further conducted to determine if the associations between child health outcomes and proportion of the urban population residing in slum areas persisted after adjustment for percentage of country's population that resided in urban areas, GDP per capita, percentage of population living on less than $1.25 per day, and region of the world (Asia, North Africa, sub-Saharan Africa, Latin America, Caribbean). Selected child health indicators included low birth weight, malnutrition, proportion of population receiving MCV vaccination, infant mortality, under-5 mortality, and maternal mortality.

*Literature review*
A critical review of the peer-reviewed and gray literature was conducted to identify proximal and distal characteristics of the slums that may be associated with child health outcomes, the extent to which these factors influence child health, and to identify and present model interventions that have either directly or indirectly influenced the health of the child residing in slums.

## RESULTS

### Geographic distribution of slums worldwide

Slums in the developing world constitute a significant portion of the population (see Table 2). Although most urban dwellers in sub-Saharan Africa reside in slum areas, the total proportion of the population residing in slums in sub-Saharan Africa has not surpassed a third of the national population except in Angola (39%), Guinea-Bissau (36%), Sierra Leone (39%), and Central African Republic (36%). In Latin America, urban dwellers constitute a much higher proportion of the population but the highest proportion of a national population residing in slum areas is in Bolivia (31%), followed by Peru (27%) and Nicaragua (26%). In Asia, Iraq (35%), Lebanon (46%), and Mongolia (36%) top the list for proportion of national population residing in slum areas. As seen in Fig. 1, the proportion of urban dwellers residing in slums is not necessarily in the same countries in which the highest proportion of a national population resides in slums.

### Relative disparities in pediatric health outcomes among rural, urban-nonslum, and urban-slum populations

Most country-level reports do not separate out urban-slum from other urban areas. We identified 2 reports, one from Kenya and one from Bangladesh, that highlight the disparity among urban nonslum, urban slum, and rural. For most indicators, both reports indicated rural dwellers had overall better health outcomes than urban-slum dwellers (Table 3) [10,11].

### Associations between proportion of slum dwellers and pediatric health outcomes

Unadjusted correlations are high between both exposure variables and child health indicators (Table 4). Only unemployment is not correlated significantly with the proportion of the population residing in a slum area. After adjustment for other factors, multinomial linear regression indicates that the proportion of the urban population residing in slums is highly correlated with MCV immunization coverage, infant mortality, under-5 mortality, and the maternal mortality ratio. It is not however, independently associated with childhood malnutrition or proportion of low birth weight infants after adjustment for the other factors (Table 5).

### Literature review

*Overview of slum regions*
Factors detrimental to child health and development cluster in slum areas despite their sometimes startlingly close geographic proximity to where some of the best resources in a nation are located (Fig. 2). Settlements are generally

**Table 2**
Country-level indicators of slum populations and related exposures and health outcomes

| Indicators of slum populations | | Health outcomes | | | | | | | | | | |
|---|---|---|---|---|---|---|---|---|---|---|---|---|
| Region | Country | Year slum data collected | Percent urbanites, % | Percent urbanites in slums | Percent citizens in slums, % | MCV coverage rate, % | Low birth weight, % | Child malnutrition, % | Birth rate (newborns/ pop) | Infant mortality rate | Under-5 mortality rate | Maternal mortality ratio |
| Asia | Bangladesh | 2009 | 25 | 61.6 | 15 | 96 | 22 | 40 | 23 | 49 | 46 | 240 |
| | Cambodia | 2005 | 21 | 78.9 | 17 | 93 | 9 | 29 | 25 | 54 | 43 | 250 |
| | China | 2009 | 51 | 29.1 | 15 | 99 | 3 | 3 | 12 | 16 | 15 | 37 |
| | India | 2009 | 31 | 29.4 | 9 | 74 | 28 | 43 | 21 | 46 | 61 | 200 |
| | Indonesia | 2009 | 43 | 23 | 10 | 89 | 9 | 19 | 18 | 27 | 32 | 220 |
| | Iraq | 2009 | 67 | 52.8 | 35 | 76 | 15 | 7 | 28 | 40 | 38 | 63 |
| | Jordan | 2009 | 83 | 19.6 | 16 | 98 | 13 | 2 | 27 | 16 | 21 | 63 |
| | Laos | 2005 | 27 | 79.3 | 21 | 69 | 11 | 31 | 26 | 58 | 42 | 470 |
| | Lebanon | 2005 | 87 | 53.1 | 46 | 79 | N/A | N/A | 15 | 15 | 9 | 25 |
| | Mongolia | 2007 | 63 | 57.9 | 36 | 98 | 5 | 5 | 21 | 36 | 31 | 63 |
| | Myanmar (Burma) | 2005 | 31 | 45.6 | 14 | 99 | 9 | N/A | 19 | 48 | 62 | 200 |
| | Nepal | 2009 | 17 | 58.1 | 10 | 88 | 21 | 38 | 22 | 43 | 48 | 170 |
| | Pakistan | 2009 | 35 | 46.6 | 16 | 80 | 32 | N/A | 24 | 61 | 72 | 260 |
| | Philippines | 2009 | 63 | 40.9 | 26 | 79 | 21 | 21 | 25 | 19 | 25 | 99 |
| | Saudi Arabia | 2005 | 81 | 18 | 15 | 98 | N/A | 5 | 19 | 16 | 9 | 24 |
| | Syria | 2007 | 54 | 22.5 | 12 | 80 | 10 | 10 | 24 | 15 | 15 | 70 |
| | Thailand | 2009 | 34 | 27 | 9 | 98 | 7 | 7 | 13 | 16 | 12 | 48 |
| | Turkey | 2009 | 77 | 13 | 10 | 97 | 11 | N/A | 18 | 23 | 15 | 20 |
| | Vietnam | 2009 | 31 | 35.2 | 11 | 96 | 5 | 20 | 17 | 20 | 22 | 59 |
| | Yemen | 2007 | 34 | 76.8 | 26 | 71 | 10 | 26 | 37 | 77 | 168 | 540 |

| | | | | | | | | | | | | |
|---|---|---|---|---|---|---|---|---|---|---|---|---|
| Caribbean | Dominican Republic | 2009 | 66 | 14.8 | 10 | 79 | 11 | 3 | 19 | 21 | 25 | 150 |
| | Haiti | 2009 | 47 | 70.1 | 33 | 59 | 25 | 17 | 24 | 52 | 70 | 350 |
| | Jamaica | 2005 | 52 | 60.5 | 31 | 88 | 12 | 2 | 19 | 14 | 18 | 110 |
| | St. Lucia | 2005 | 28 | 11.9 | 3 | 95 | 11 | N/A | 14 | 12 | 16 | 35 |
| | Trinidad and Tobago | 2005 | 13 | 24.7 | 3 | 92 | 19 | N/A | 14 | 27 | 28 | 46 |
| Latin America | Argentina | 2009 | 91 | 20.8 | 19 | 93 | 7 | 2 | 17 | 11 | 14 | 77 |
| | Belize | 2007 | 44 | 18.7 | 8 | 98 | 14 | 4 | 26 | 21 | 17 | 53 |
| | Bolivia | 2009 | 66 | 47.3 | 31 | 84 | 6 | 4 | 24 | 41 | 51 | 190 |
| | Brazil | 2009 | 84 | 26.9 | 23 | 97 | 8 | 2 | 17 | 21 | 16 | 56 |
| | Chile | 2005 | 87 | 9 | 8 | 91 | 6 | 1 | 14 | 7 | 9 | 25 |
| | Colombia | 2009 | 76 | 14.3 | 11 | 88 | 6 | 3 | 17 | 16 | 18 | 92 |
| | Costa Rica | 2005 | 62 | 10.9 | 7 | 83 | 7 | 1 | 16 | 9 | 10 | 40 |
| | Ecuador | 2005 | 66 | 21.5 | 14 | 98 | 10 | N/A | 20 | 19 | 23 | 110 |
| | El Salvador | 2005 | 63 | 28.9 | 18 | 89 | N/A | 7 | 17 | 20 | 15 | 81 |
| | French Guiana | 2005 | 81 | 10.5 | 9 | N/A | N/A | N/A | N/A | N/A | N/A | N/A |
| | Guatemala | 2009 | 50 | 38.7 | 19 | 87 | 11 | 12 | 26 | 25 | 30 | 120 |
| | Guyana | 2009 | 29 | 33.2 | 10 | 98 | 19 | 10 | 17 | 36 | 36 | 280 |
| | Honduras | 2005 | 50 | 34.9 | 17 | 99 | 10 | 8 | 25 | 20 | 21 | 100 |
| | Mexico | 2007 | 77 | 14.4 | 11 | 98 | 7 | 3 | 19 | 17 | 16 | 50 |
| | Nicaragua | 2007 | 57 | 45.5 | 26 | 99 | 9 | 6 | 19 | 22 | 26 | 95 |
| | Panama | 2005 | 65 | 23 | 15 | 97 | N/A | N/A | 19 | 11 | 20 | 92 |
| | Paraguay | 2005 | 59 | 17.6 | 10 | 93 | 6 | 3 | 17 | 22 | 22 | 99 |
| | Peru | 2007 | 74 | 36.1 | 27 | 96 | 8 | 5 | 19 | 22 | 18 | 67 |
| | Suriname | 2005 | 67 | 3.9 | 3 | 85 | 11 | 7 | 17 | 29 | 30 | 130 |
| North Africa | Egypt | 2009 | 43 | 13.1 | 6 | 96 | 13 | 5 | 24 | 24 | 21 | 66 |
| | Morocco | 2009 | 58 | 13.1 | 8 | 95 | N/A | N/A | 19 | 26 | 33 | 100 |

*(continued on next page)*

**Table 2**
***(continued)***

| Indicators of slum populations | | | | | | Health outcomes | | | | | | |
|---|---|---|---|---|---|---|---|---|---|---|---|---|
| Region | Country | Year slum data collected | Percent urbanites, % | Percent urbanites in slums | Percent citizens in slums, % | MCV coverage rate, % | Low birth weight, % | Child malnutrition, % | Birth rate (newborns/pop) | Infant mortality rate | Under-5 mortality rate | Maternal mortality ratio |
| Sub-Saharan Africa | Angola | 2009 | 59 | 65.8 | 39 | 88 | N/A | 15 | 39 | 84 | 158 | 450 |
| | Benin | 2009 | 44 | 69.8 | 31 | 72 | 15 | 18 | 38 | 60 | 106 | 350 |
| | Burkina Faso | 2007 | 24 | 59.5 | 14 | 63 | 16 | 25 | 43 | 80 | 146 | 300 |
| | Burundi | 2005 | 10 | 64.3 | 6 | 92 | 11 | 35 | 41 | 60 | 139 | 800 |
| | Cameroon | 2009 | 49 | 46.1 | 23 | 76 | 11 | 14 | 32 | 60 | 127 | 690 |
| | Central African Republic | 2009 | 38 | 95.9 | 36 | 62 | 13 | N/A | 36 | 97 | 164 | 890 |
| | Chad | 2009 | 28 | 89.3 | 25 | 28 | N/A | N/A | 39 | 94 | 169 | 1100 |
| | Comoros | 2007 | 28 | 68.9 | 19 | 72 | N/A | N/A | 31 | 69 | 79 | 280 |
| | Congo | 2009 | 63 | 49.9 | 31 | 90 | 13 | 11 | 40 | 74 | 99 | 560 |
| | Equatorial Guinea | 2005 | 40 | 66.3 | 27 | 51 | N/A | N/A | 35 | 75 | 118 | 240 |
| | Ethiopia | 2009 | 17 | 76.4 | 13 | 57 | 20 | 33 | 43 | 75 | 77 | 350 |
| | Gabon | 2005 | 73 | 38.7 | 28 | 55 | N/A | N/A | 35 | 49 | 66 | 230 |
| | Gambia, The | 2007 | 59 | 34.8 | 21 | 91 | 11 | 15 | 33 | 70 | 101 | 360 |
| | Ghana | 2009 | 44 | 40.1 | 18 | 91 | 13 | 13 | 27 | 47 | 78 | 350 |
| | Guinea | 2007 | 28 | 45.7 | 13 | 58 | 12 | 20 | 37 | 59 | 126 | 610 |
| | Guinea-Bissau | 2005 | 43 | 83.1 | 36 | 61 | 11 | 17 | 35 | 94 | 161 | 790 |
| | Ivory Coast | 2009 | 50 | 57 | 29 | 49 | 17 | 28 | 30 | 63 | 115 | 400 |

| | | | | | | | | | | | |
|---|---|---|---|---|---|---|---|---|---|---|---|
| Kenya | 2009 | 32 | 54.7 | 18 | 87 | 8 | 16 | 32 | 44 | 73 | 360 |
| Lesotho | 2009 | 23 | 53.7 | 12 | 85 | N/A | 16 | 27 | 53 | 86 | 620 |
| Liberia | 2009 | 47 | 68.3 | 32 | 40 | 14 | 19 | 36 | 73 | 78 | 770 |
| Madagascar | 2009 | 31 | 76.2 | 24 | 70 | 16 | N/A | 37 | 50 | 62 | 240 |
| Malawi | 2009 | 15 | 68.9 | 10 | 96 | 14 | 13 | 40 | 79 | 83 | 460 |
| Mali | 2009 | 33 | 65.9 | 22 | 56 | 19 | 26 | 45 | 109 | 176 | 540 |
| Mozambique | 2009 | 31 | 80.5 | 25 | 82 | 15 | 16 | 39 | 77 | 103 | 490 |
| Namibia | 2009 | 39 | 33.5 | 13 | 74 | 16 | 17 | 21 | 46 | 42 | 200 |
| Niger | 2009 | 20 | 81.7 | 16 | 76 | 27 | 38 | 50 | 110 | 125 | 590 |
| Nigeria | 2009 | 51 | 62.7 | 32 | 71 | 12 | 25 | 39 | 74 | 124 | 630 |
| Rwanda | 2009 | 17 | 65.1 | 11 | 95 | 6 | 17 | 36 | 63 | 54 | 340 |
| Senegal | 2009 | 42 | 38.8 | 16 | 82 | 19 | 14 | 36 | 55 | 65 | 370 |
| Sierra Leone | 2005 | 40 | 97 | 39 | 80 | 14 | 19 | 38 | 77 | 185 | 890 |
| Somalia | 2009 | 34 | 73.6 | 25 | 46 | N/A | 31 | 42 | 104 | 180 | 1000 |
| South Africa | 2009 | 62 | 23 | 14 | 78 | N/A | 9 | 19 | 43 | 47 | 300 |
| Tanzania | 2009 | 26 | 63.5 | 17 | 93 | 10 | 15 | 32 | 66 | 68 | 460 |
| Togo | 2005 | 37 | 62.1 | 23 | 67 | 11 | 21 | 35 | 50 | 110 | 300 |
| Uganda | 2009 | 15 | 60.1 | 9 | 75 | 14 | 15 | 47 | 61 | 90 | 310 |
| Zaire | 2007 | 29 | 51.7 | 15 | 71 | N/A | N/A | 33 | 54 | 77 | 200 |
| Zambia | 2009 | 39 | 57.3 | 22 | 83 | 11 | 13 | 44 | 65 | 83 | 440 |
| Zimbabwe | 2009 | 29 | 24.1 | 7 | 92 | 11 | 13 | 32 | 28 | 67 | 570 |

*Abbreviation:* N/A, not available.

*Data from* Kaiser Family Foundation. Country Data: Customized dcta sheets, 2012. Available at: http://kff.org/globaldata/. Accessed May 16, 2013.

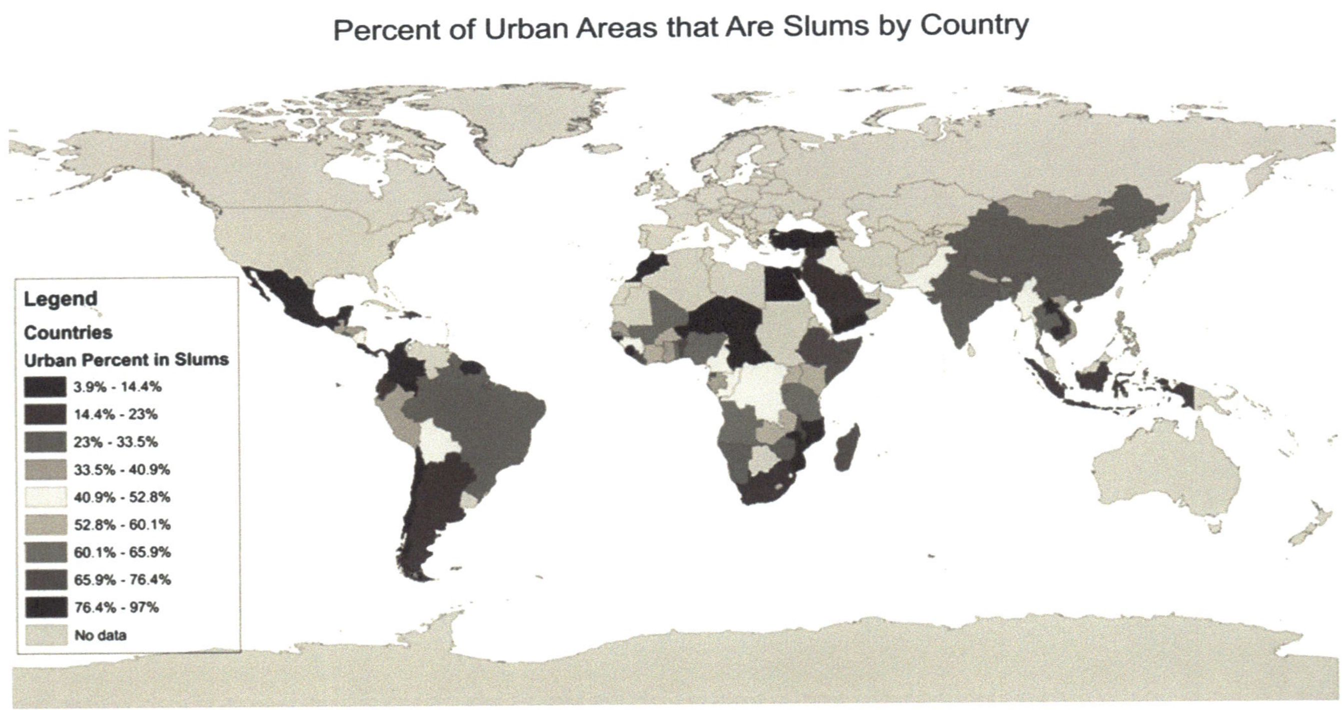


**Fig. 1.** Distribution of urban slums worldwide. (*Data from* Kaiser Family Foundation. Country Data: Customized data sheets, 2012. Available at: http://kff.org/globaldata/. Accessed May 16, 2013.)

**Table 3**
Health outcomes in urban-nonslum, urban-slum, and rural areas in Kenya and Bangladesh

| Country | Health indicator | Urban nonslum | Urban slum | Rural | Slums worse than rural |
|---|---|---|---|---|---|
| Kenya | Infant mortality | 39 | 91 | 76 | 15 per 1000 |
| | Under-5 mortality (per 1000) | 62 | 150 | 114 | 36 per 1000 |
| | Stunting | 24% | 47% | 32% | 15% |
| | Primary school attendance ages 6–13 | 97% | 91% | 90% | 1% |
| | Secondary attendance ages 14–17 | 66% | 65% | 80% | 15% |
| Bangladesh | Under-5 mortality (per 1000) | 53 | 95 | 66 | 29% |
| | Skilled birth attendant | 45 | 15 | 19 | 4% |
| | Improved sanitation | 54 | 9 | 54 | 43% |
| | Secondary school attendance | 53 | 18 | 48 | 30% |
| | Gender parity in school attendance | 1.08 | 1.26 | 1.18 | |

*Data from* African Population, Health Research Center. Population and health dynamics in Nairobi's informal settlements. Nairobi (Kenya): African Population and Health Research Center; 2002; and UNICEF Bangladesh. Understanding urban inequalities in Bangladesh: a prerequisite for achieving vision 2021. A study based on the 2009 multiple indicator cluster survey. Bangladesh: UNICEF; 2010.

informal, springing up around areas of higher economic growth without approval or planning and often on land deemed undesirable (hillsides subject to flood and erosion, toxic landfills, or waste dumps). As a result, water and sanitation facilities are not planned and dwellings are often temporary and unstable. In these areas, there is little government investment in the construction

**Table 4**
Pearson's coefficients (*r*) between proportion of urban populations residing in slums and health outcomes and exposure variables for countries in the developing world: an ecological analysis

| | Correlation coefficient and *P* value | |
|---|---|---|
| | *r* | *P* |
| Exposure variables | | |
| Access to clean water (n = 66)[a] | −0.765 | <.0001 |
| Access to sanitation (n = 66) | −0.756 | <.0001 |
| Proportion of population <$1.25 per day (n = 63) | 0.777 | <.0001 |
| Percentage of population that resides in urban areas (n = 69) | −0.529 | <.0001 |
| GDP of country (n = 66) | −0.469 | <.0001 |
| Birth rate (n = 83) | 0.718 | <.0001 |
| Unemployment rate (n = 51) | 0.238 | .09 |
| Health outcome variables | | |
| Low birth weight (n = 58) | 0.303 | .02 |
| Child malnutrition (n = 54) | 0.591 | <.0001 |
| MCV immunization coverage rate (n = 68) | −0.573 | <.0001 |
| Infant mortality rate (n = 83) | 0.816 | <.0001 |
| Under-5 mortality rate (n = 83) | 0.741 | <.0001 |
| Maternal mortality ratio (n = 82) | 0.711 | <.0001 |

*Abbreviations:* GDP, gross domestic product; MCV, measles-containing vaccine.
[a]Number of countries (n) varies by availability of data.

**Table 5**
Multiple linear regression of health indicators with percentage of urban population residing in a slum area as the primary predictor for developing countries

| Health outcome | β | *P* |
|---|---|---|
| Low birth weight (n = 58) | 0.009 | .848 |
| Child malnutrition (n = 54) | 0.070 | .401 |
| MCV immunization coverage rate (n = 68) | −0.379 | .005 |
| Infant mortality rate (n = 83) | 0.556 | <.0001 |
| Under-5 mortality rate (n = 83) | 0.724 | .013 |
| Maternal mortality ratio (n = 82) | 3.73 | .015 |

All models adjusted for percentage of country residing in urban areas, gross domestic product per capita, percentage of population living on less than $1.25 per day and world region.
*Abbreviation:* MCV, measles-containing vaccine.

of roads, schools, and health facilities. In the most extreme cases, the governments may demolish slum areas as a way of forcing these large populations to move elsewhere. This cycle leads to less investment of the slum dwellers in improving their own conditions, as all could be eliminated by someone else at any time without notice. All of these factors work synergistically to affect multiple facets of child health and development. This is described in detail from both short-term and long-term perspectives.

**Fig. 2.** A startling contrast: slums adjacent to high-income apartment complexes. Favela de Paraisópolis. The favela (shanti town) on the left is ironically called Paraisópolis (Paradise City). Paraisópolis is situated in the center of metropolitan São Paulo, bordering on middle-income and upper-income residential areas. It lies in a large steep-sided ravine and has a physically challenging geography. It is an extremely densely populated area, with an estimated population of 80,000 to 100,000 people. Photo: Tuca Vieira.

*Slum development and land tenure*

Typically etched into outskirts or inner parts of cities, slums usually begin unplanned and often are located in areas with a high risk for landslides, floods, and other natural disasters [12]. Hazardous and toxic waste and fumes are commonplace in these informal settlements. Land ownership is the exception rather than the rule [12–15]. WB evidence suggests that in developing countries, as many as half of urban residents do not possess any type of legal document demonstrating that they have tenure security or own the land or property [16]. The socio-political context of slum areas limits the residents' ability to secure tenure or land ownership [13–15]. In Nigeria, for example, an urban land-seeker waits an average of 274 days and pays more than 27% of the property value in "official fees" before securing a land registration title [17]. To obtain governmental services, documentation, such as utility bills, identification cards, voter registration forms, and municipal tax receipts, is often required and whereas private services often do not require such documentation, these fee-based services are unaffordable for most slum residents [12].

Most developing countries do not formally count slum dwellers in their census; therefore effectively concealing the existence of slums and increasing slum residents' vulnerability to unlawful evictions. Indeed, available data indicate that forcible evictions are increasing. Between 2000 and 2002, 6.7 million residents were evicted; 2.5 million more than the 4.2 million evicted during the preceding 2 years, 1998 to 2000 [18]. Evictions and demolition of slum areas are commonplace and have been reported in every region [13,19–21]. Evictions and demolitions may precede redevelopment efforts and can greatly disturb the livelihoods of both communities and individual residents, place huge psychological and economic stress on individuals and families, and expose these groups to increased risk of violence and exploitation [22,23].

## Slum infrastructure

*Water and sanitation*

Access to clean water and adequate sanitation are often quite limited in slum areas. Without any planning for the informal settlements, laying of pipes for water and sewage are rarely put in place. Our analysis demonstrates that in countries with higher urban-slum populations, water and sanitation access is lower (see Table 4). Regionally, sub-Saharan Africa has the least number of household connections to water, with rates as high as 99% in Liberia, followed by Asia, with a high of 85% in Afghanistan, and Latin America, with a high of 19% in El Salvador [24]. Rates of access are highly variable, even within country. In Kenya, for example, although 52% of urban households have access to residential water [24], a survey in a Nairobi slum indicated only 19% of the population has household connections [25]. Water access in these slum communities may be from a combination of public standpipes, unprotected wells, and water from vendors. Although boreholes and protected wells may be developed in the informal settlements, it does not guarantee the availability of safe water, because of a lack of sanitation and the resulting groundwater contamination [24].

Lack of infrastructure for disposing of waste is readily apparent in slum areas. Not only is waste generated within the slum itself, but often slums are located adjacent to larger community dumpsites. Human waste disposal is of particular concern. Community-shared toilets are the norm. However, community toilets may not be maintained, may be far too few in number, or may not exist at all. In Kibera, a large slum in Nairobi, 40,000 people shared 10 latrines (1998) and in a slum in India 120,000 people shared 19 latrines [26]. The result is open defecation or "flying toilet" (disposal of excrement in a plastic bag that is thrown into the environment) [27]. National-level statistics do not distinguish between urban areas and urban-slum areas, and conditions in slum areas are often far worse than that reported on a country level. Improved sanitation, as defined by MDG, includes household-owned flush toilets, piped sewer systems, ventilated improved pit latrines, pit latrines with slab, or composting toilets. In Uganda, improved sanitation in urban areas is 34% overall with 50% of the population using shared toilets [28]. However, in a focused survey undertaken in a large Ugandan slum, only 20% of individuals had access to their own toilet facility, but many do not qualify as improved facilities; 79% of residents used shared or public toilet facilities [29].

*Roads*

Despite being close to large urban areas with many resources, the infrastructure to travel relatively short distances from the slums to the inner city is generally nonexistent. Most residents of slum areas restrict travel outside the slum area to obtain only those things deemed to be absolutely necessary [30,31]. In some of the older, more-established slum areas, transport is more readily available; major roadways have been paved, making access easier [12]. Most slums, however, consist of a haphazard mix of paved and dirt roads, with narrow side roads and paths zigzagging throughout. Moreover, public transportation is rarely available and/or exorbitantly expensive in urban low-income areas throughout the world [30,31].

*Electrification*

Electrification of slums is a contentious and complex issue, although increasingly gaining attention and support by governments of developing countries because of an ever-growing number of slum dwellers and to discourage illegal service providers [32]. Many slum residents and communities are either unable to afford the service fees or lack the necessary documents (such as legality of tenure) to set up electrification. Therefore, many private electricity companies have historically avoided servicing these areas. This situation does not mean, however, that slum households do not have electricity. Rather, many slum dwellers obtain electricity for their homes through illegal channels, as these service providers are easier to find and engage than are the legal services [33]. Evidence from the World Research Institute (WRI) suggests that as much as 7% of slum household expenditures go toward energy; this percentage grows as incomes lessen. Specifically, for slum households in Asia, energy expenditures are second only to food costs, whereas energy ranks third after housing and food for households with a low socioeconomic status in Latin American, Africa, and Eastern Europe [32]. Many of the slum dwellers with electricity use outdated appliances and/or the illegal service providers connect them in ways that make their consumption of electricity unnecessarily high, resulting in their payment to the illegal electricians very high [34]. This electrification context also exposes occupants to increased risk of electrical injuries and multiple-house fires [35]. Given the inability or difficulty to access electricity, many urban-slum dwellers rely on cook stoves and open fires to prepare food. In 8 major cities in India, the use of solid fuels that require ventilation are twofold to fivefold higher in slum areas than in nonslum areas [36].

*Housing conditions*

Slums are inextricably linked to inadequate, flimsy, and insecure housing. The very definition of a slum includes components related to housing, durability, tenure security, and the number of occupants [5,12]. Definitions for "durability of housing," "security of tenure," and "overcrowding" vary by country and agencies but data suggest that globally, 18% of urban homes are nonpermanent structures and more than 25% do not meet urban building regulations or codes [37]. Most of these are likely located in slum areas of the city. The vast majority of slum residents do not hold secure tenure, and as many as 20% of the world's urban population lives in overcrowded conditions [12]. This section briefly describes the general housing situation in slums through focus on housing durability and occupancy and, where available, provides short regional examples (tenure has been discussed previously).

*Housing durability.* Commonly understood as "permanent and adequate structure in a nonhazardous location, protecting its inhabitants from the extremes of climatic conditions, such as rain, heat, cold, or humidity," durability is sorely lacking in most slum dwellings the world over [12]. In a slum, it is rare that the home the occupants first erect has wall, roof, and floor that are made of permanent materials. A house might begin as a shelter of cardboard and other scraps that slowly are replaced by less temporary materials, such as a corrugated iron roof or a cement floor. Although the permanency and durability of the structure varies generally, housing in slums is marked by their hazardous, temporary materials located on the outskirts of cities. In Addis Ababa, Ethiopia, nearly three-quarters of slum dwellers used temporary materials to erect their walls, as opposed to 58% of nonslum residents [38]. Regional variations suggest the housing durability, as measured by floor material, is most flimsy in Asia and relatively strong in Latin America. More than 73% of urban dwellers reside in nonpermanent dwellings in Asia and more than half of these are in Southern Asia [39]. In Bangladesh, Nepal, and Pakistan almost a third of urban residents lack durable housing [12]. One in 10 urban residents in sub-Saharan Africa lives in nonpermanent structures versus fewer than 1 in 100 of urban North Africans.

*Occupancy.* Crowded conditions are commonplace in the slum areas. The standardized indicator for overcrowding developed by UN-HABITAT is more than 3 people sharing the same room [12]. Millions of the individuals who live in slums inhabit 1 room that is shared with 5, 6, or 7 others, all occupying a small space that may serve as kitchen, bedroom, and sitting room. Living in congested spaces not only limits privacy and safety, but it also exposes occupants to increased disease transmission and infection via the poor ventilation of small, overcrowded dwellings. The risk of eviction is heightened, as the overcrowding often violates rental agreements and/or damages property. Overcrowding varies by region. In Nairobi, Kenya, an example from sub-Saharan Africa, more than half of urban residents reside in slum communities that occupy only 5% of the land area of the city. Density in the slum area is 75,758 people per square mile versus 3.987 people per square mile in the non-slum areas, an almost 19-fold difference [10]. As many as two-thirds of the urban population in Asia is considered overcrowded, whereas in Latin America and the Caribbean, it ranges from 10% to 30% of the urban population [12,39].

## Access to social services

### *The social-political context*

The limitation on delivery of social services to urban-slum dwellers does not occur in a vacuum. Global and national-level policies have highly influenced access to health care and education in many developing nations. Following independence, many newly emerging nations began to accumulate a large amount of debt and experienced a growing financial imbalance. Loans were sought from the WB and the International Monetary Fund (IMF). Large loans were given with the stipulation that the country would restructure its economy by improving the management of payments, increase economic efficiency, and encourage private sector investments: Structured Adjustment Programs (SAP). The emphasis was on economic development, not social services. Education and health services were viewed as nonproductive, and to "save the country's economy" many service programs were sold to private firms where unfortunately, profits took priority over services. Governmental social safety nets were lost as user fees for health care and education were another stipulation for WB and IMF loans. Local governments received an immediate cash flow and shed the responsibilities and expense of providing services to the citizens. Local officials were happy but the people suffered. Relegating social services to the private sector meant limiting access to health care and education. User fees for these services, including the purchase of clean water, deepened the level of poverty and of health as the poor could not afford even modest fees and did without. Some SAPs demanded an increase in exports of goods and food, which limited domestic consumption. To their credit, members of the WB saw the deterioration of health care and educational opportunities, and recently have tried to reverse these trends. But it is too little too late, certainly too late to meet the MDGs. Skosireva and Holaday state that: "SAPs have either created or worsened poverty levels or, at the very least, have ignored the adverse effects of the program on the poor [40]."

*Health care*

Access to health care in urban slums varies not only by country but also by region within countries. Matthews and colleagues [41] analyzed Demographic and Health Survey (DHS) data from 30 developing countries in Africa, Asia, and Latin America to determine indicators of maternal health care among the urban poor, as compared with the rural population. Their purpose was to see if there was an "urban advantage" or "urban penalty" for women. The investigators recognized a gap between different urban populations and speculated that the urban poor in many countries were at a disadvantage from their previous rural neighbors who did not migrate to the city. They found massive inequality in both urban and rural areas but greater inequality between slum urbanites or nonslum urbanites. The inequalities arose from exclusion; the urban poor did not have access to health care services and in some cities the slum dwellers were treated as if they did not even exist. However, there was a vast difference in the service gap among different countries. In some, the exclusion was not limited to the poor; services were insufficient for all strata of wealth. In others, it was primarily the poor who were excluded. And in some countries the urban population was well served without wealth or class distinction; a goal to strive for!

Even when governmental programs to provide public clinics are established in a country, few of these are constructed in slum areas because of their tenuous nature [42]. Health care access is minimal at best in urban slums and is often predominated by private for-profit clinics [43]. Government investment in health care infrastructure in slums is limited. A study in Nairobi slums indicated that of 503 clinics serving what is reportedly the largest slum community in all of sub-Saharan Africa, only 6 (1%) were public and 79 (16%) were private not-for-profit clinics. Nearly all of the private for-profit clinics 418 (83%) in Nairobi slums are of dubious quality [44,45]. The more qualified practices are expensive, forcing the use of cheaper private facilities that are often not licensed and operate out of small shacks and maternity homes without complying with any standards of care. Despite the poor quality, it is the less expensive private facilities that are the ones most often used by the residents. Women residing in slum areas, as elsewhere, prefer to deliver their babies in health care facilities where access is easy and quality is perceived to be high [46]. Given the difficulties already illustrated in transportation, access to public and nonprofit clinics of higher quality outside the slum areas is problematic; however, a lack of health care facilities is not apparent in all slum areas. In Chennai, India, slum residents were satisfied with their access to health care facilities with a mix of both government and private clinics within close proximity to residents; however, government clinics here were also somewhat limited, and individuals preferred the private clinics, considering them to provide better services [47].

*Education*

Being an unrecognized population affects not only the health sector but the education sector as well. National-level standards for school access are not being met in urban-slum areas. For example, in an Indian slum in Mumbai, the distance to elementary schools exceeds 2 km, despite a 1993 mandate that all children reside within 1 km of elementary schools. Investment in this infrastructure in these "hidden" populations is scanty. Again this acts synergistically with the inaccessibility of public transportation. Schools are not within walking distance but cannot be accessed by public transportation in a timely and economically feasible manner [48]. This has resulted in great disparities in access to education for the children living in urban slums. For example, in Guatemala (1999) only 54% of children living in slums were enrolled in primary education, as compared with 61% in rural areas and 73% in nonslum urban areas [12]. In Nairobi slums, educational achievement was far below that of their nonslum urban counterparts. Maternal education is strongly correlated with the educational achievement of a child. Women with no education in the slums constituted 5.1% of the population compared with 1.2% in the rest of the city. And in the nonslum areas, 54% of women had achieved at least some secondary school as compared with only 32% in slum areas [10]. This slum/nonslum education gap is persistent across generations and world region. In Delhi, India, 10% of the slum children never attended school compared with 31% of nonslum children [49]. In Bangladesh, evidence suggests that children in urban slums have less achievement in education than do their rural counterparts. Literacy rates are 52% in children from urban slums as compared with 70% in rural areas [49]. Even if children do begin school in a slum region, their education may be summarily disrupted. Many parents face the pragmatic pull between needs for basic sustenance and education for their children. Parents living in informal settlements have little if any savings and loss of livelihood, whether from natural disaster, illnesses, or loss of their or their children's employment directly affects their ability to buy food and pay bills, including fees for their children's education [50]. And those children who are able to remain in school face issues of school quality. Classrooms are often overcrowded and lack instructional materials and enough desks and/or chairs. Many students do not even have shoes, pens, or paper.

## CHILD HEALTH IMPACTS

The preceding describes the abhorrent conditions found in slum areas. These exposures exert a detrimental and often lifelong impact on nearly all aspects of the health and development of children. Our review of the literature indicated that there are 6 primary domains in which these conditions influence health and survival through childhood; (1) the maternal and neonatal period, (2) nutritional status, (3) mental health and development, (4) frequency of infectious diseases, (5) exposure to and perpetration of violence, and (6) unintended accidents and injury.

Overall, the likelihood of a child surviving life in slum areas is less than counterparts living in other urban areas and less than those in rural areas. Even within slums, children have differing health outcomes (see Table 3). The literature is contradictory as to whether children born into slums are at greater or lesser risk of death than those who migrate in as older children [51,52]. However, the most vulnerable periods were immediately following migration [51,52]. With the rapid influx of new migrants into the city, this observation will have a large negative impact on MDG 4: reduce child mortality.

## Maternal and neonatal vulnerabilities

Influences on child health and development begin at conception. Maternal surroundings and care received during the prenatal period can greatly influence both immediate and longer-term outcomes. In urban-slum areas, a large problem is inaccessible health care. Antenatal monitoring, delivery care, and newborn care are all extremely important to maternal and neonatal and infant survival. Maternal mortality is often overlooked as a pediatric health issue; yet, if a mother dies, the chances of survival of her newborn child are dramatically reduced and the impact on older surviving children can be devastating [53–55]. The primary causes of maternal death are hemorrhage, sepsis, hypertensive disorders, prolonged or obstructed labor, and unsafe abortion; conditions generally addressable through the availability of quality care before, during, and after delivery. In Bangladesh, only 15% of women in urban slums had a skilled attendant at birth compared with 19% in rural areas and 45% in urban-nonslum areas [11]. In neighboring India, only 41% of births of the urban very poor were attended by a medical doctor or nurse midwife compared with 87.2% of the nonpoor. Maternal mortality is disproportionately higher in slum areas than nationally [56]. In the slums of Nairobi, neonatal mortality was 50% higher (30.4 per 1000 live births) as compared with the rest of the city (20.8 per 1000 live births) and postneonatal mortality in the slums was 60.9 per 1000 live births as compared with 16.9 per 1000 live births in the rest of the city. The high rate of neonatal deaths in the first few days of life is largely the result of asphyxia or sepsis. To address those 2 problems, it is essential that the attending person is trained in the skills needed to recognize and address them and has the resources necessary to respond quickly to asphyxia and to take the appropriate action to manage sepsis.

It is not just that services are inadequate in the slums, maternal factors and environmental exposures also play a role: age, nutritional status before and during the pregnancy, child spacing, parity, and exposure to toxins put slum families at a disadvantage. Of adolescent girls aged 15 to 17 living in Nairobi slums, 19% have given birth compared with 2.5% in the other parts of Nairobi and 9.3% of those living in rural communities. By age 18 to 20, the percentage in the slums has increased to 52%, in the nonslum area of Nairobi to 24%, and in rural Kenya to 44% [10]. Highest risks for the under-5 mortality rates were seen in children born to women younger than 20 (150.0), women 40 to 49 years old (281.7), and in multiparous ($\geq$7) women (255.5) [10].

## Mental health and development

Just as the home environment affects child physical health, it also affects children's mental health. Children in single-family detached dwellings enjoy better mental health then children living with multiple families living within the same building [57]. Additional evidence suggests that children living in urban poor conditions where violence and eviction are real possibilities experience more behavioral and emotional problems compared with children living in rural areas or nonslum locales [58,59]. Uncertainty is an everyday reality in slums, where many residents are unsure of their employment, their next meal, or shelter tenure. This insecurity is a constant purveyor of anxiety and stress [60]. Numerous studies document that the tenuous conditions so typical of informal settlements negatively affect children's relationships with their family and peers, slows their growth and development and cognitive abilities, and worsens self-esteem and educational attainment [5,61–63]. In developing nations and especially in informal settlements, community resources to address mental health disparities and support those children with mental and behavioral health issues are severely limited [58].

### Infectious disease

Slum conditions are an ideal incubator for infectious diseases and their transmission. Rural to urban migration and peri-urban slums are cited as one of the leading social factors related to emerging and reemerging infectious disease [64]. The chances of infectious disease introduction are higher with poor sanitation and a constant influx of in-migrating individuals. Once introduced, the extremely crowded conditions in the slums ensures close contact with infected individuals and creates a haven for the rapid spread of contagion from the infected to the unexpecting. Outbreaks spread quickly. The severe acute respiratory syndrome (SARs) epidemic in Hong Kong in 2002 and 2003 exemplifies how a disease originating in a somewhat isolated rural area can explode in an urban setting [64]. But it is not just new infections, but age-old infections that disproportionately burden slum dwellers. Tuberculosis transmission dramatically increases with overcrowding and is a magnitude higher in slum regions, exposing the young and the very young [65–71]. Lack of access to clean water in the slums has led to multiple cholera outbreaks [72–75]. Poor infrastructure to keep out flood waters has led to outbreaks of leptospirosis [76,77]. High levels of infection in the slums set up a vicious cycle of poverty. Some infections, such as HIV/AIDS, meningitis, and malaria, have a direct impact on mental development. Other common illnesses, such as diarrhea and respiratory infections, reduce school enrollment and attendance [78–83]. Even if preventive measures, such as vaccinations, are available for a disease, children residing in slums are less likely to be vaccinated [84–86], and lack of access to screening and treatment for all infectious diseases perpetuates the disease transmission cycle, as carriers of infectious agents pass them to others over longer periods of time. The very nature of slums has an indirect influence on disease transmission. Sexual debut in urban-slum areas is earlier and abject poverty and homelessness in the slums can force adolescents into the commercial sex trade at a very young age [87–92]; factors highly correlated with sexually transmitted infections.

### Food security and malnutrition

Undernutrition is a major underlying factor in one-third to one-half of all childhood deaths. Both short-term and long-term lack of food leads to malnutrition. In urban slums, food is almost exclusively obtained from the market [93]. Household food security and thus nutritional status is determined by the in-hand cash the family has to purchase food. With ever-increasing housing prices and the need to pay exorbitant fees for utilities, purchasing of food is often sacrificed and the food that is purchased may be of low nutritional value; particularly detrimental for the urban poor who, if working, are most often engaged in hard manual labor [94,95]. These factors paired with high levels of diarrheal disease and frequent respiratory infections lead to poor childhood nutrition [96]. Overall, malnutrition has been shown to be lower in urban areas in developing countries; however, this masks the great disparity between urban-nonslum areas and urban slums. A regional analysis indicated that when stratified by socioeconomic status, intraurban inequities were more pronounced that urban-rural inequities [97]. This greater disparity in urban areas was also supported by our findings in Kenya and Bangladesh (see Table 2).

Malnutrition manifests itself in different ways, but stunting, a sign of chronic malnutrition, is an often-used measure to determine the nutritional status of a population. Across multiple regions, analyses have demonstrated that stunting in children residing in urban slums is high and higher than in nonslum urban areas and even higher than in rural areas [98–101]. In Niger, stunted development affects twice as many children in rural and poor urban areas as in children from nonslum areas of the cities: 4 to 5 of 10 as compared with 1 of 4. Children living in rural areas and in city slums were 4 times more likely to be malnourished than children from nonslum urban areas. In the Democratic Republic of Congo, malnutrition affected 41% of children from poor urban areas and only 16% from nonslum urban areas. Likewise in Bolivia, India, and Bangladesh, malnutrition is twice as prevalent in the city slums and rural areas as in the nonslum areas of the cities. In children older than 15 months, the prevalence of stunting in Nairobi is close to 27%, whereas in the slums of Nairobi, stunting was more than twice that at 57% [102]. The impact of climate change and flooding has also been associated with food insecurity and malnutrition [95], and the threats of environmental disaster are a constant presence in many urban slum communities. The situation is dire in urban slums and some argue that there is a need to rethink Food Program strategies that in the past have focused primarily on rural areas and refugee resettlements [98].

### Accidents and injuries

The World Health Organization report of 2008 estimates that nearly 1,000,000 children die each year from unintentional injuries [103]. Such injuries are much higher in low-income and middle-income countries, higher in urban than rural areas, and highest in city slums, and include burns, poisoning, falls, and traffic accidents.

In 2004, the global death toll for children from fire was nearly 96,000, with low-income and middle-income countries baring the greatest burden: 11 times the rate of high-income countries (4.3 vs 0.4/100,000) [103]. Fire is a major hazard in slum areas. Crowded and highly flammable tinderbox dwellings with often illegal and unsafe electrification and open fires for cooking that use solid fuel or kerosene invite fires that are often uncontrollable. In such an environment, fires spread quickly. Once one shack is ignited, adjacent structures quickly incinerate. Because many cities do not recognize these informal settlements, fire departments are not responsible for responding and even if they do, there is no infrastructure for piped water to extinguish the flames. As a result, whole communities are lost and families are forced to fend for themselves once again [103]. Less dramatic but extremely common are household burns from scalding. Research has consistently shown that pediatric burns are much greater in slum areas and are the result of disorganized homes, lower maternal education, and/or lack of parental supervision [104–106].

Kerosene, also known as paraffin oil, is used for cooking and not only presents a fire hazard but is often kept in soft drink bottles, inviting unintended poisonings. In dilapidated homes with no locked cabinets, the bottles are easily accessed by young ones. Although not isolated to informal settlement housing, Ahmed and colleagues [107] report that low socioeconomic status increases the odds ratio of unintentional poisonings 9.2 times that of a control group. In families in which the mother had no formal education, the odds of an unintentional poisoning were 4.2. Socioeconomic status is a strong risk factor for poisonings because of limited or no storage space at all to guard dangerous substances and keep them out of reach of children, and the risk is even greater as many parents in slums are less aware of the dangers these items present.

Traffic deaths are high and in most resource-limited settings; infant seats, seat belts, and helmets are virtually nonexistent. In low-income and middle-income countries, most people walk, roads are not well maintained, traffic is chaotic, and often motorists with little regard for those on the side of the road simply speed along with horn blaring as those on foot scamper to get out of the way. Children are vulnerable and injuries are common. The proportion of childhood pedestrian accidents from road traffic crashes in high-income countries is between 5% and 10%, whereas in low-income and middle-income countries it ranges between 30% and 40% [103].

## Violence

Not unlike other places where a lack of employment options and limited safe recreational options intersects with increased access to illegal substances, children living in slums are more likely than their nonslum peers to abuse illegal substances and participate in street gangs and violence [108]. In its 2011 World Development Report, the WB outlines the major contributors to violence and conflict, several of which mirror the characteristics of slums (low income, youth unemployment, and rapid urbanization). In other words, slums and the conditions that lead to their existence perpetuate and encourage violence. Based on surveys conducted among children and adolescents in urban areas of Colombia, the Democratic Republic of Congo, Côte d'Ivoire, Gaza, Mali, Sierra Leone, and the West Bank, the WB finds that "the main motivations young people cited for becoming rebels or gang members are very similar–unemployment, idleness, [seeking] self-respect, and self-protection, all well ahead of revenge, injustice, or belief in the cause" [109]. Even if children do not join gangs or militias, or are victims of violence, the chronic experience of living in an insecure, violent atmosphere can have a severe adverse effect on the development of children. Child exposure to crime and violence, both in developing and developed countries, has been associated with poor academic performance and higher school dropout rates, aggression, anxiety, depression, and other behavior problems [110].

Violence is not solely relegated to the external slum environment, but also to within households. Impoverished areas are known to have higher rates of spousal and child abuse [111,112]. Witnessing and being victims to this type of abuse are highly correlated with negative physical and mental health outcomes in children [113].

Most recently available data suggest that of the children who engage in labor (215 million), most are in urban areas and at least half (115 million) are working under hazardous conditions [114]. From domestic labor and factory work to armed conflict and gang membership to food preparation and shoe shining, children in informal settlements are often forced to participate in dangerous, illegal work to help support their families and to survive [5]. Young girls, in particular, are often forced to work in the sex trade, and as domestic workers are at risk for sexual abuse. Evidence from Kenya suggests that domestic workers experience increased psychological problems, such as bedwetting and insomnia, compared with other children [115].

## INTERVENTIONS

Working to reduce pediatric health disparities in slums can seem an overwhelming task, given the multitude of adverse conditions and all the health outcomes that are in jeopardy. Approaches can be arranged into 2 major strategies: top-down or bottom-up. Top-down approaches usually involve governmental or nongovernmental agencies undertaking broad-scale programs. Bottom-up approaches generally are community-based initiatives that use community resources internal to the slums to bring about change from within. Both of these strategies may involve more fundamental infrastructure changes and include improving housing structure, developing roadways, and access to water and sanitation that have a distal impact on health. Interventions that work to effect more immediate change in health outcomes include improved access to quality health care and respectable local schools and the training of community health workers. There are success stories in both of these strategies. This section highlights several examples of programs that have reduced health disparities in the urban poor.

The concept of slum upgrading is to improve the well-being of individuals residing in slum areas by providing infrastructure improvements coupled with social interventions are generally performed by a governmental entity or a well-funded large nongovernmental organization (NGO). Common infrastructure improvements include water, sanitation, waste collection, housing, access roads, footpaths, storm drainage, lighting, public telephones, schools, health posts, and community centers. Social improvements can include better provision of health and education services, regularization of areas with insecure tenure, day care, training, and social protection programs (Fig. 3) [116].

City Alliance for Cities without Slums is a global coalition of cities and their development partners that was initiated in 1999 and provides funding for projects to reduce urban poverty in developing nations. It was created by the WB and the UN Centre for Human Settlements (Habitat) in response to MDG 11. The focus is to fund city development projects and slum upgrading projects that address issues from a physical, social, economic, organizational, and environmental perspective. It seeks to integrate a top-down approach but also enlists community involvement from local citizens, community groups, and business partners. All aspects of slum upgrading were allowed to be addressed by proposals including development of infrastructure, removal of environmental hazards, construction of community facilities, improved access to social development, and development of a land tenure system. To date, nearly 400 projects in developing nations have been funded through Cities Alliance addressing multiple aspects of slum improvement [117].

Despite the pervasive nature of slum upgrading programs, rigorous evaluation of their efficacy is lacking [118]. A recent analysis was made of the effects of upgrading in Ahmedabad, India, a city with more than 3.9 million people, 40% of whom reside in slums. The strategy was solely infrastructure improvement and included connections to a water supply for individual households, toilets and underground sewage for individual households, storm water drainage, stone paving of internal and approach roads, solid waste management, and street lighting. Participating individuals paid the equivalent of $40 USD to participate. An assessment of insurance claims data from the local micro-insurance cooperative demonstrated a highly significant reduction in diarrheal disease from 32.0% to 13.5%.

**Fig. 3.** Slum renovations in Brazil. A typical slum (*left*) ... transformed in Brazil (*right*). Upgrading of unserviced settlements is justified as the centerpiece of a global strategy for improving the living conditions of the urban poor. (*Reprinted* with permission from WHO.)

To get at the core of slum rejuvenation, one must address urban poverty. This requires a long-lasting commitment to make improvements that take a long and sustained concerted effort. Communities in Bahia (Salvador), Brazil, and their partners have demonstrated this commitment through a near decade-long endeavor to improve the lives of people living in the Alagados district of Salvador. Alagados long stood as one of the worst areas in Brazil. Despite multiple governmental interventions from the 1960s to 1990s, permanent change was never achieved. In the 1990s,the existing *Novos Alagados* scheme joined with the *Ribiera Azul* initiative, a cooperative of Cities Alliance that provided technical support from the Bahia state government and the Italian government. The area was divided into 2 regions: one slated for infrastructure and social improvements and one restricted to only social improvements. The infrastructure improvements included access to main roads, storm water drainage, water supply, basic sanitation, and solid waste collection, whereas the social improvements in both sectors included health, education, provision of day care centers, food and nutritional aid, support for young people and children at risk, professional skills training, and income generation through providing support to local cooperatives. Although no health outcome changes were assessed, there were significant improvements in factors associated with improved health outcomes. From 2000 to 2006, garbage collection improved from 50% to 80%, water network connection increased from 37% to 71%, electricity 72% to 88%, sewage 21% to 84%, and homes without sanitary facilities decreased from 31% to 3%. In addition, social programs trained 1339 social agents, 306 individuals trained in job skills, and 68 young people found jobs [119].

Infrastructure spending can elevate the slums to the standards of the rest of the urban areas. It is estimated that a 1% increase in health expenditure as a share of GDP is associated with a 5.1% to 5.7% reduction in slum areas. This finding is consistent with that of Edelman and Mitra [120], who showed an inverse association between public spending on health and slum regions at the state level in India. Increased infrastructure spending can also encourage families to make self-improvements to their housing [121,122]. Furthermore, investment in shared infrastructure, including access to clean water, sanitation, and power supply, can serve as a means for preventing the formation of new slums, reducing the health burden faced by slum dwellers and delivering major benefits in economic growth, poverty alleviation, and environmental sustainability.

Yet, large-scale infrastructure interventions are not always required to make improvements in the health and well-being of slum dwellers and in some cases a highly top-down redevelopment program can be devastating to communities [22]. Empowerment programs are an alternative way to create change from within the slum [122]. They are designed to develop the capacity of individuals and communities negotiating and coordinating with existing institutions and government to improve their own health. Several models of successful empowerment programs are illustrated [123]. BRAC (Bangladesh Rural Action Committee) started as a relief organization in 1972 in a remote rural village in Bangladesh. It has expanded to 11 countries in Asia, Africa, the Caribbean, and, most recently, the Philippines. BRAC is reportedly the largest development organization in the world, touching the lives of 126 million people. The basis of its operation is organizing poor communities using their own human and material resources "creating an ecosystem in which the poor have the chance to seize control of their own lives." BRAC works with the marginalized and the disadvantaged who have been excluded from the mainstream. The focus is on women (women make up 95% of the membership) and on organizing the poor through Village Organizations (VOs). Each VO has 30 to 40 women with access to a variety of services, such as microfinance, education, health care, agriculture, handicrafts, environmental sustainability, and disaster preparedness, as well as social and legal issues. A central goal is to empower women who in their homes have had little decision making, but as a group can come together to voice their concerns and offer advice and solutions for community problems. They influence change. BRAC works under the premise that people are not poor because they have no potential but because they lack opportunities. The goal of BRAC is to provide individuals with opportunities and unleash the potential.

Focused small-scale interventions have also had impacts in urban slum communities. A hand-washing intervention in Nepal delivered hand hygiene messaging through community health workers on a daily basis for 2 weeks in the homes of mothers of 3-month-old to 12-month-old infants followed with biweekly meetings over a 6-month period with a community motivator. Diarrheal morbidity in the intervention group was 41% less than the control group [123]. Low-cost interventions to improve behavior have also improved exclusive breastfeeding rates in Kenyan slums. Peer training was conducted and home-based intensive counseling sessions were performed 7 times following delivery. At 6 months, exclusive breastfeeding was 2.5 times higher in the home-based intervention group [124]. Both studies indicate that even with very limited resources, small improvements to the health and well-being of children in urban slums can be achieved.

## DISCUSSION

Our investigations into the effects of residing in slum areas have demonstrated consistent relationships between the appalling environmental conditions and impacts on infant and childhood development, morbidity, and mortality. The problem is global. Even after controlling for region and other explanatory factors, there were strong relationships between infant mortality and under-5 mortality and the proportion of populations in a country residing in slums. In Africa, most of the urban population resides in slums and in Asia a large and growing population resides in urban slums. Interestingly, we did not find an association between urban-slum population and low birth weight or childhood malnutrition. These correlations are at a national level and certainly other studies have indicated that stunting is higher in urban-slum areas. It is possible that our aggregate analysis masked individual associations that would have been identified at the household levels.

The findings in Kenya and Bangladesh were striking. When urban-slum and urban-nonslum areas are disaggregate, health outcomes were consistently poorer in urban slums than in rural areas. This implies that the urban penalties may exceed the urban advantages for many slum dwellers. Certainly these analyses need to be replicated across multiple countries and regions to determine if this is isolated to these 2 countries or if it is consistent across the globe. Yet, it is unlikely that this will impact the steady stream of migrants from rural to urban areas. Although the chances of success may be slim in the immigration process, the ceiling for opportunities in rural areas is much lower.

Although cross-cutting measures, such as slum upgrading projects and small focused interventions, can have an impact, the real roots of the problem lie not just in the infrastructure and access to social programs in these areas, but in the lack of real and perceived opportunities for these marginalized populations. Individuals residing in slums rank low on the social gradient and political agendas. The lower the socioeconomic position a person occupies, the worse the health and the lower the life expectancy. Some of the specific social determinates that affect health include the wealth index of the household, the employment of the head of the household, the presence of the mother to care for the children, the level of social support, the degree of crowding within the home, the educational attainment of the mother, food security, access to clean potable water, sufficient sanitary facilities, and available close-by quality health services and schools. Slum dwellers score low on these determinates. These social determinates of health are largely responsible for the great differences in the types of morbidities, the severity of illnesses, and the level of access to treatment for them. Although country-level disparities are readily apparent, many statistics internal to a nation merely dichotomize by urban versus rural. This hides the slum outcomes in the urban figures, thereby worsening the urban figures and making rural dwellers a bit better off than all those who live in the city. Yet in reality, rural dwellers fair better than those who live in slums, but far worse than those urbanites that do not live in slums [81]. Household-level factors, combined with an overarching lack of recognition from local and national governments, manifested through lack of land rights, exclusion from census, and lack of investment in schools and health care centers delivers the message of "no worth"; the ultimate in exclusion. Many slum communities border on the edge of the wealthy urbanite communities, accentuating the divide between the populations. This added stress enhances morbidities and shortens lives.

But children can be successfully brought out of the slums and out of poverty. Programs must provide opportunities for the mental development of children and need to be paired with programs to keep their bodies healthy if the cycle is going to be broken. If either component is lacking, the struggle to rise from their existing circumstances will be increased. Mental development must be achieved through both formal education and programs that instill confidence in a child's ability to make a difference in his or her surroundings.

What does all this mean for the clinicians practicing in areas with slum residents or pediatricians who want to make a difference? Other than through often long-range advocacy efforts, it is difficult for pediatricians to see what effect they can have. However, we should not despair, for the intermediate and the proximate determinants (immunization rate, knowledge of oral rehydration therapy, and access to sanitation) had a stronger influence on child mortality than did gross national income per capita [125]. In addition, pediatricians can facilitate those from marginalized populations accessing health care by removing the barriers of misperceptions of families and judgmental attitudes of providers. Many marginalized groups are hesitant to access even existing health care facilities when the staff and clinicians are seen as nonresponsive to their needs or lack understanding of their cultural beliefs [126]. Learning more about the communities and getting involved can go a long way in making in-roads in the receptivity of parents to simple behavior modifications that will improve child health. All of these areas are within the realm of the pediatrician (Table 6).

## SUMMARY AND RECOMMENDATIONS

The abhorrent conditions found in slum areas are neither right nor just for children. Their health is jeopardized. Their education is hampered. Their potential is thwarted. They are devoid of opportunities. Slum living is disastrous for children and ensures a waste of the world's "most precious resource." The conditions found in slums break almost every article in the UN Convention on the Rights of the Child; a convention that all but 2 sovereign nations have ratified [127]. To allow children to grow up in slums even violates the convention's preamble: "Recalling that, in the Universal Declaration of Human Rights, the United Nations has proclaimed that childhood is entitled to special care and assistance, Convinced that the family, as the fundamental group of society and the natural environment for the growth and well-being of all its members and particularly children, should be afforded the necessary protection and assistance so that it can fully assume its responsibilities within the community, Recognizing that the child, for the full and harmonious development of his or her personality, should grow up in a family environment, in an atmosphere of happiness, love and understanding." And Article 27: "1. States Parties recognize the right of every child to a standard of living adequate for the child's physical, mental, spiritual, moral and social development. 2. The parent(s) or others responsible for the child have the primary responsibility to secure, within their abilities and financial capacities, the conditions of living necessary for the child's development. 3. States Parties, in accordance with national conditions and within their means, shall take appropriate measures to assist parents and others responsible for the child to implement this right and shall in case of need provide material assistance and support programs, particularly with regard to nutrition, clothing and housing."

The cycle of family poverty reaching its zenith in slum dwellers predetermines that the children will be malnourished, have repeated bouts of illness, and lack even basic education, all of which ensnares the young adult in low-paying jobs or no job at all, perpetuating the cycle of poverty. Families stuck

**Table 6**
Taking action: recommendations for pediatricians to improve health equity in urban slums

| Realm of action | What you can do |
|---|---|
| Visit the depressed areas of cities in the countries you visit | If you have a close open relationship with your colleagues in countries you visit, discuss the situation with them. |
| Listen and observe | Apply the strategies of "positive deviants" and learn from the families who are doing well and invite them to teach those who are not. |
| Educate local community health workers | Discuss with these influential women and encourage them to empower the mothers in slum areas. It is they who will make a difference and your interest and encouragement will help. (Pediatricians know how to educate mothers and spend their lives empowering mothers to take charge of their lives and the lives of their children.) [125] |
| Study the pertinent international conventions (Convention on the Rights of the Child) and the policies of the government | Add the appropriate articles of the conventions to your discussions with your colleagues and those in power. |
| Advocate while there | Encourage your local colleagues to discuss the inequalities with those in political position to improve the lives of children and their families. |
| Advocate while at home | Bring the plight of these children to the attention of your representatives and your friends: expose the injustices. |
| Investigate and learn the problems | Go beyond the direct medical problem at hand and inquire about health behaviors at home to address underlying issues if possible. |
| Connect with others | Maintain lists of local community programs and social services that patients in need can be connected to. |

in the morass of slum living cannot emerge without some assistance. A just and fair society demands that governments recognize this growing population and accept the responsibility of providing the basic services and the opportunities to extract families from this vicious cycle; some governments have done so and more are attempting to do so. NGOs usually accept 1 or 2 pieces of the puzzle and often do a good job. Pediatricians are in a unique position to assist families at a household level to break the cycle. These providers are thrown into the arena in caring for children who are affected by this dynamic. They may act as a bridge for mother and child to see opportunities outside of the slums. It is our challenge to take a holistic view and see the children as the pivotal point and do everything possible to intercept the cycle and prevent its recurrence.

## References


[1] Mudege NN, Zulu EM. In their own words: assessment of satisfaction with residential location among migrants in Nairobi slums. J Urban Health 2011;88:219–34.

[2] United Nations. Millenium Development Goal 7: Ensure environmental sustainability, 2012. Available at: http://www.un.org/millenniumgoals/environ.shtml. Accessed May 16, 2013.

[3] Moreno EL. Global Urban Observatory. Slums of the world: the face of urban poverty in the new millennium? Monitoring the millennium development goal, target 11–world-wide slum dweller estimation. Nairobi (Kenya): UN-HABITAT; 2003.

[4] Khan MM, Kraemer A. Socio-economic factors explain differences in public health-related variables among women in Bangladesh: a cross-sectional study. BMC Public Health 2008;8:254.

[5] United Nations Children's Fund. State of the World's Children: Children in an Urban World. In: State of the World's Children Reports: UN. New York: UNICEF; 2012.

[6] United Nations Environment Programme, AMCEN Secretariat. Africa environment outlook: past, present, and future perspectives. Stevenage, Hertfordshire: Earthprint for and on behalf of the United Nations Environment Programme, 2002. Available at: http://www.unep.org/dewa/Africa/publications/aeo-1/. Accessed May 16, 2013.

[7] Antai D, Wedren S, Bellocco R, et al. Migration and child health inequities in Nigeria: a multilevel analysis of contextual- and individual-level factors. Trop Med Int Health 2010;15:1464–74.

[8] United Nations. Slum population as percentage of urban, percentage. 2012. Available at: http://data.un.org/Data.aspx?d=MDG&f=seriesRowID%3A710. Accessed October 27, 2012.

[9] Kaiser Family Foundation. Country Data: Customized data sheets. 2012. Available at: http://kff.org/globaldata/. Accessed October 15, 2012.

[10] African Population, Health Research Center. Population and health dynamics in Nairobi's informal settlements. Nairobi (Kenya): African Population and Health Research Center; 2002.

[11] Understanding urban inequalities in Bangladesh: a prerequisite for achieving vision 2021. A study based on the 2009 multiple indicator cluster survey, 2010. Available at: http://www.unicef.org/bangladesh/Urban_paper_lowres.pdf. Accessed May 16, 2013.

[12] UN-HABITAT. State of the World's Cities 2006/07: the millennium development goals and urban sustainability: 30 years of shaping the habitat agenda. London: Earthscan; 2006.

[13] Baten A, Ahemd M, Azad A. Eviction and the challenges of protecting the gains: a case study of slum dwellers in a Dhaka city. Dushtha Shasthya Kendra. Extreme Poverty Research Group. 2011. Available at: http://www.dfid.gov.uk/r4d/PDF/Outputs/EEP/Shiree-WP3.pdf. Accessed November 12, 2012.

[14] Kironde JM. The regulatory framework, unplanned development and urban poverty: findings from Dar es Salaam, Tanzania. Land Use Pol 2006;23:460–72.

[15] Payne G. Getting ahead of the game: a twin-track approach to improving existing slums and reducing the need for future slums. Environ Urban 2005;17:135–45.

[16] World Bank. Land policies for growth and poverty reduction. Washington, DC: World Bank; 2003.

[17] Arnot B, Meadows J. Reforming the land registration process in Nigeria. 5th FIG Regional Conference. Accra (Ghana): March 8–11, 2006.

[18] Center on Housing Rights and Evictions. Seven million left homeless as forced evictions double in two years. COHRE Media Release. 2003. Available at: http://www.cohre.org. Accessed November 15, 2012.

[19] Kapp C. Operation "Restore Order" wreaks havoc in Zimbabwe. Lancet 2005;366:1151–2.

[20] Klopp JM. Remembering the destruction of Muoroto: slum demolitions, land and democratisation in Kenya. Afr Stud 2008;67:295–314.

[21] Mukhija V. Squatters as developers? : slum redevelopment in Mumbai. Aldershot, Hampshire, England; Burlington, VT: Ashgate; 2003.
[22] Hao P, Sliuzas R, Geertman S. The development and redevelopment of urban villages in Shenzhen. Habitat Int 2011;35:214–24.
[23] Hooper M, Ortolano L. Confronting urban displacement: social movement participation and post-eviction resettlement success in Dar es Salaam, Tanzania. J Plan Educ Res 2012;32:278–88.
[24] Dagdeviren H, Robertson RA. Access to water in the slums of the developing world. Brasilia-DF (Brazil): International Policy Centre for Inclusive Development; 2009.
[25] Gulyani S, Bassett EM. Retrieving the baby from the bathwater: slum upgrading in Sub-Saharan Africa. Environ Plann C Gov Policy 2007;25:486–515.
[26] Davis M. Planet of the slums. London: Verso; 2007.
[27] World Health Organization. Meeting the MDG drinking water and sanitation target: the urban and rural challenge of the decade. Geneva (Switzerland): 2006. Available at: http://www.who.int/water_sanitation_health/monitoring/jmpfinal.pdf. Accessed December 15, 2012.
[28] World Health Organization. Estimates for the use of improved sanitation facilities: Uganda. Geneva (Switzerland): 2012. Available at: http://www.childinfo.org/files/SAN_Uganda.pdf. Accessed May 16, 2013.
[29] Tumwebaze IK, Orach CG, Niwagaba C, et al. Sanitation facilities in Kampala slums, Uganda: users' satisfaction and determinant factors. Int J Environ Health Res 2013; 23(3):191–204.
[30] Faiz A. Transportation and the urban poor. ITE J 2011;81:40–3.
[31] Gakenheimer R. Urban mobility in the developing world. Transp Res Pt A-Policy Pract 1999;33:671–89.
[32] Smyser C. Slum electrification programmes: an overview of global versus African experience. Promoting energy access for the urban poor in Africa: approaches and challenges in slum electrification. Available at: http://www.unhabitat.org/downloads/docs/7803_91408_Overview%20of%20Slum%20Electrification%20in%20Africa.Final%20report.pdf: UN-HABITAT & GENSUS, 2009. Accessed October 27, 2012.
[33] U.S. Agency for International Development. Innovative Approaches to Slum Electrification. Available at: http://pdf.usaid.gov/pdf_docs/PNADB219.pdf: Bureau for Economic Growth, Agriculture and Trade, USAID, 2004. Accessed October 27, 2012.
[34] Energy Sector Management Assistant Program. Summaries of best practices from case studies in four countries: Bangladesh, Brazil, Colombia, and India. 2012. Available at: http://www.esmap.org/sites/esmap.org/files/FINAL_EA-Case%20Studies.pdf. Accessed October 27, 2012.
[35] Keyes N. Innovative approaches urgently needed to deliver energy to urban poor. World Bank Blogs: Sustainable Cities. World Bank; 2012. Available at: http://blogs.worldbank.org/sustainablecities/innovative-approaches-urgently-needed-to-deliver-energy-to-urban-poor. Accessed October 27, 2012.
[36] Gupta K, Arnold F, Lhungdim H. Health and living conditions in eight Indian cities. Deonar (Mumbai): International Institute for Population Sciences; 2009.
[37] UNHABITAT. The State of the World's Cities Report 2001. Nairobi (Kenya): UN-HABITAT; 2001.
[38] Martínez-Martín J. Monitoring intra-urban inequalities with GIS-based indicators: with a case study in Rosario, Argentina. ITC Dissertation Series, Utrecht University and ITC. Utrecht (Netherlands): Utrecht University; 2005.
[39] UN-HABITAT. The challenge of slums: global report on human settlements 2003. Nairobi (Kenya): UN-HABITAT; 2003.
[40] Skosireva AK, Holaday B. Revisiting structural adjustment programs in sub-Saharan Africa: a long-lasting impact on child health. World Med Health Pol 2010;2:73–88.

[41] Matthews Z, Channon A, Neal S, et al. Examining the "urban advantage" in maternal health care in developing countries. PLoS Med 2010;7:pii:e1000327.
[42] Baker JL. Dhaka: improving living conditions for the urban poor. Washington, DC: World Bank; 2007.
[43] Shetty P. Health care for urban poor falls through the gap. Lancet 2011;377:627–8.
[44] African Population and Health Research Center. Strengthening information systems, knowledge sharing, and partnerships for addressing urban health vulnerabilities in the slums of Nairobi, Kenya. Nairobi (Kenya): African Population and Health Research Center; 2009.
[45] Zulu E, Beguy D, Ezeh A, et al. Overview of migration, poverty and health dynamics in Nairobi City's slum settlements. J Urban Health 2011;88:185–99.
[46] Fotso JC, Mukiira C. Perceived quality of and access to care among poor urban women in Kenya and their utilization of delivery care: harnessing the potential of private clinics? Health Policy Plan 2012;27:505–15.
[47] Ergler CR, Sakdapolrak P, Bohle H-G, et al. Entitlements to health care: why is there a preference for private facilities among poorer residents of Chennai, India? Soc Sci Med 2011;72:327–37.
[48] Subbaraman R, O'brien J, Shitole T, et al. Off the map: the health and social implications of being a non-notified slum in India. Environment and Urbanization 2012;24:643–63.
[49] Tsujita Y. Deprivation of education: a study of slum children in Delhi, India. EFA Global Monitoring Report 2010. EFA, 2010. Available at: http://unesdoc.unesco.org/images/0018/001865/186592e.pdf. Accessed November 12, 2012.
[50] United Nations Centre for Human Settlements, United Nations Human Settlements Programme. The state of the world's cities 2010/2011 - Cities for All: Bridging the Urban Divide. Nairobi (Kenya): UNCHS (Habitat); 2010. p. v. Available at: http://www.unhabitat.org/pmss/listItemDetails.aspx?publicationID=2917. Accessed May 16, 2013.
[51] Islam MM, Azad KM. Rural-urban migration and child survival in urban Bangladesh: are the urban migrants and poor disadvantaged? J Biosoc Sci 2008;40:83–96.
[52] Bocquier P, Beguy D, Zulu EM, et al. Do migrant children face greater health hazards in slum settlements? Evidence from Nairobi, Kenya. J Urban Health 2011;88:266–81.
[53] Anderson FW, Morton SU, Naik S, et al. Maternal mortality and the consequences on infant and child survival in rural Haiti. Matern Child Health J 2007;11:395–401.
[54] Reed HE, Koblinsky MA, Mosely WH. Consequences of maternal morbidity & maternal mortality: report of a workshop. Washington, DC: National Academy Press; 2000.
[55] Razzaque A, Hossain A, DaVanzo J, et al. Effect of maternal mortality on under-five survival: evidence from Matlab, Bangladesh. Population Association of America. San Francisco (CA): 2012.
[56] Ziraba AK, Madise NJ, Mills SL, et al. Maternal mortality in Kenya: what is the situation in the Nairobi informal settlements? New Orleans (LA): Population Association of America; April 17–19, 2008.
[57] Evans GW, Wells NM, Chan HY, et al. Housing quality and mental health. J Consult Clin Psychol 2000;68:526–30.
[58] Bhatia SK, Bhatia SC. Childhood and adolescent depression. Am Fam Physician 2007;75:73–80. Available at: http://www.aafp.org/afp/2007/0101/p73.html. Accessed October 29, 2012.
[59] Patel V, Flisher AJ, Nikapota A, et al. Promoting child and adolescent mental health in low and middle income countries. Journal of Child Psychology and Psychiatry. 2008:313–34. Available at: www.sangath.com/images/file/Promoting%20child%20and%20adolescent%20mental%20health%20.pdf. Accessed October 29, 2012.
[60] Flournoy R, Yen IH. The influence of community factors on health: an annotated bibliography. PolicyLink. 2004. Available at: www.policylink.org/atf/cf/%7B97c6d565-bb43-406d-a6d5-eca3bbf35af0%7D/ANNOTATEDBIBLIOGRAPHY_FINAL.PDF. Accessed October 30, 2012.

[61] Liang H, Flisher AJ, Chalton DO. Mental and physical health of out of school children in a South African township. Eur Child Adolesc Psychiatry 2002;11:257–60.
[62] Nair MK, Radhakrishnan SR. Early childhood development in deprived urban settlements. Indian Pediatr 2004;41:227–37.
[63] Richter LM. Poverty, underdevelopment and infant mental health. J Paediatr Child Health 2003;39:243–8.
[64] Weiss RA, McMichael AJ. Social and environmental risk factors in the emergence of infectious diseases. Nat Med 2004;10:S70–6.
[65] Kyobutungi C, Ziraba AK, Ezeh A, et al. The burden of disease profile of residents of Nairobi's slums: results from a demographic surveillance system. Popul Health Metr 2008;6:1.
[66] David AM, Mercado SP, Becker D, et al. The prevention and control of HIV/AIDS, TB and vector-borne diseases in informal settlements: challenges, opportunities and insights. J Urban Health 2007;84:i65–74.
[67] Bhagyalaxmi A, Kadri AM, Lala MK, et al. Prevalence of tuberculosis infection among children in slums of Ahmedabad. Indian Pediatr 2003;40:239–43.
[68] Marsh DR, Kadir MM, Husein K, et al. Adult mortality in slums of Karachi, Pakistan. J Pak Med Assoc 2000;50:300–6.
[69] Wallerstein C. Tuberculosis ravages Philippine slums. BMJ 1999;319:402.
[70] Sanghavi DM, Gilman RH, Lescano-Guevara AG, et al. Hyperendemic pulmonary tuberculosis in a Peruvian shantytown. Am J Epidemiol 1998;148:384–9.
[71] Burger H, Kaiser HE. Crowding. Vivo 1996;10:249–53.
[72] Nair GB, Ramamurthy T, Sur D, et al. *Vibrio cholerae/mimicus* in fecal microbiota of healthy children in a cholera endemic urban slum setting in Kolkata, India. Microbiol Immunol 2012;56:789–91.
[73] Sur D, Sarkar BL, Manna B, et al. Epidemiological, microbiological & electron microscopic study of a cholera outbreak in a Kolkata slum community. Indian J Med Res 2006;123: 31–6.
[74] Thakur JS, Swami HM, Dutt R, et al. Epidemiological investigation of cholera outbreak in a periurban slum colony in Chandigarh. Indian J Med Sci 2001;55:429–33.
[75] Legros D, McCormick M, Mugero C, et al. Epidemiology of cholera outbreak in Kampala, Uganda. East Afr Med J 2000;77:347–9.
[76] Lim VK. Leptospirosis: a re-emerging infection. Malays J Pathol 2011;33:1–5.
[77] Reis RB, Ribeiro GS, Felzemburgh RD, et al. Impact of environment and social gradient on *Leptospira* infection in urban slums. PLoS Negl Trop Dis 2008;2:e228.
[78] Brown LK, Lourie KJ, Pao M. Children and adolescents living with HIV and AIDS: a review. J Child Psychol Psychiatry 2000;41:81–96.
[79] Fernando SD, Rodrigo C, Rajapakse S. The 'hidden' burden of malaria: cognitive impairment following infection. Malar J 2010;9:366.
[80] Guo Y, Li X, Sherr L. The impact of HIV/AIDS on children's educational outcome: a critical review of global literature. AIDS Care 2012;24:993–1012.
[81] Kihara M, de Haan M, Were EO, et al. Cognitive deficits following exposure to pneumococcal meningitis: an event-related potential study. BMC Infect Dis 2012;12:79.
[82] Puthanakit T, Aurpibul L, Louthrenoo O, et al. Poor cognitive functioning of school-aged children in Thailand with perinatally acquired HIV infection taking antiretroviral therapy. AIDS Patient Care STDS 2010;24:141–6.
[83] Zimmerman GA, Castro-Faria-Neto H. Persistent cognitive impairment after cerebral malaria: models, mechanisms and adjunctive therapies. Expert Rev Anti Infect Ther 2010;8:1209–12.
[84] Mathew JL. Inequity in childhood immunization in India: a systematic review. Indian Pediatr 2012;49:203–23.
[85] Mutua MK, Kimani-Murage E, Ettarh RR. Childhood vaccination in informal urban settlements in Nairobi, Kenya: who gets vaccinated? BMC Public Health 2011;11:6.

[86] Sharma R, Desai VK, Kavishvar A. Assessment of immunization status in the slums of Surat by 15 clusters multi indicators cluster survey technique. Indian J Community Med 2009;34:152–5.
[87] Potdar R, Mmari K. Factors influencing sexual initiation, multiple partners and condom use among male slum youth in Pune, India. Glob Public Health 2011;6:843–58.
[88] Dodoo FN, Zulu EM, Ezeh AC. Urban-rural differences in the socioeconomic deprivation—sexual behavior link in Kenya. Soc Sci Med 2007;64:1019–31.
[89] Senaratna BC, Wijewardana BV. Risk behaviour of street children in Colombo. Ceylon Med J 2012;57:106–11.
[90] Karmacharya D, Yu D, Dixit S, et al. A study of the prevalence and risk factors leading to HIV infection among a sample of street children and youth of Kathmandu. AIDS Res Ther 2012;9:25.
[91] Dhawan J, Gupta S, Kumar B. Sexually transmitted diseases in children in India. Indian J Dermatol Venereol Leprol 2010;76:489–93.
[92] Marshall BD, Wood E. Sex work and sex exchange among street children: an urgent need for a global response. J Adolesc Health 2009;44:201–2.
[93] Ruel M, Garrett J, Morris SS. Urban challenges to food and nutrition security: a review of food security, health, and caregiving in the cities. Washington, DC: Food Consumption and Nutrition Division, International Food Policy Research Institute; 1998.
[94] Sala MA. The quality of food, clothing and shelter provided to orphaned children under foster care in Kibera slums in Kenya. East Afr J Public Health 2009;6:312–6.
[95] Goudet SM, Faiz S, Bogin BA, et al. Pregnant women's and community health workers' perceptions of root causes of malnutrition among infants and young children in the slums of Dhaka, Bangladesh. Am J Public Health 2011;101:1225–33.
[96] Rodriguez L, Cervantes E, Ortiz R. Malnutrition and gastrointestinal and respiratory infections in children: a public health problem. Int J Environ Res Public Health 2011;8:1174–205.
[97] Fotso JC. Child health inequities in developing countries: differences across urban and rural areas. Int J Equity Health 2006;5:9.
[98] Olack B, Burke H, Cosmas L, et al. Nutritional status of under-five children living in an informal urban settlement in Nairobi, Kenya. J Health Popul Nutr 2011;29:357–63.
[99] Thuita FM, Mwadime RK, Wang'ombe JK. Child nutritional status and maternal factors in an urban slum in Nairobi, Kenya. East Afr Med J 2005;82:209–15.
[100] Chesire EJ, Orago AS, Oteba LP, et al. Determinants of under nutrition among school age children in a Nairobi peri-urban slum. East Afr Med J 2008;85:471–9.
[101] Das S, Bapat U, Shah More N, et al. Nutritional status of young children in Mumbai slums: a follow-up anthropometric study. Nutr J 2012;11:100.
[102] UN-Habitat. Cities for all: bridging the urban divide: 2010/2011 State of the World's Cities. Nairobi (Kenya): UN-Habitat; 2010.
[103] Peden M, Oyegbite K, Ozanne-Smith J, et al. World report on child injury prevention. In: Press W, editor. Geneva (Switzerland): World Health Organization; 2008. Available at: http://whqlibdoc.who.int/publications/2008/9789241563574_eng.pdf; 2008. Accessed May 16, 2013.
[104] Daisy S, Mostaque AK, Bari TS, et al. Socioeconomic and cultural influence in the causation of burns in the urban children of Bangladesh. J Burn Care Rehabil 2001;22:269–73.
[105] Delgado J, Ramirez-Cardich ME, Gilman RH, et al. Risk factors for burns in children: crowding, poverty, and poor maternal education. Inj Prev 2002;8:38–41.
[106] Parbhoo A, Louw QA, Grimmer-Somers K. A profile of hospital-admitted paediatric burns patients in South Africa. BMC Res Notes 2010;3:165.
[107] Ahmed B, Fatmi Z, Siddiqui AR. Population attributable risk of unintentional childhood poisoning in Karachi Pakistan. PLos One 2011;6:e26881.
[108] Thomas de Benitez S. State of the world's street children: violence consortium for street children. Consortium for Street Children, 2007. Available at: http://www.streetchildren.

org.uk/_uploads/publications/state_of_the_world_-_violence.pdf. Accessed December 10, 2012.

[109] World Bank. World development report 2011: conflict, security and development. Washington, DC: World Bank; 2012.

[110] Baker-Henningham H, Meeks-Gardner J, Chang S, et al. Experiences of violence and deficits in academic achievement among urban primary school children in Jamaica. Child Abuse Negl 2009;33:96–306.

[111] Rogosch FA, Dackis MN, Cicchetti D. Child maltreatment and allostatic load: consequences for physical and mental health in children from low-income families. Dev Psychopathol 2011;23:1107–24.

[112] Sambisa W, Angeles G, Lance PM, et al. Prevalence and correlates of physical spousal violence against women in slum and nonslum areas of urban Bangladesh. J Interpers Violence 2011;26:2592–618.

[113] Jonson-Reid M, Kohl PL, Drake B. Child and adult outcomes of chronic child maltreatment. Pediatrics 2012;129:839–45.

[114] International Labor Office. Accelerating action against child labour: global report under the follow-up to the ILO Declaration on Fundamental Principles and Rights at Work. Geneva (Switzerland): ILO; 2010. Available at: http://www.ilo.org/global/publications/books/WCMS_127688/lang–en/index.htm. Accessed October 20, 2012.

[115] Bourdillon M. Children as domestic employees: problems and promises. J Child Poverty 2009;15(1):1–18.

[116] Field E, Kremer M. Impact evaluation for slum upgrading interventions, 2008. Available at: http://scholar.harvard.edu/field/publications/impact-evaluation-slum-upgrading-interventions. Accessed May 16, 2013.

[117] Cities Alliance: Cities without slums. Our Projects, 2012: Overview of projects funded through Cities Alliance. Available at: http://www.citiesalliance.org/. Accessed May 15, 2013.

[118] Butala NM, VanRooyen MJ, Patel RB. Improved health outcomes in urban slums through infrastructure upgrading. Soc Sci Med 2010;71:935–40.

[119] Alliance C. Alagados—the story of the integrated slum upgrading in Salvador (Bahia), Brazil. Washington, DC: Cities Alliance; 2008.

[120] Edelman B, Mitra A. Slum dweller's access to basic amenities: the role of political contact, its determinants and adverse effects. RURDS 2006;18(1):25–40.

[121] Mayo SK, Malpezzi S, Gross DJ. Shelter strategies for the urban poor in developing countries. World Bank Res Obs 1986;1:183–204.

[122] Sheuya SA. Improving the health and lives of people living in slums. Ann N Y Acad Sci 2008;1136:298–306.

[123] Langford R, Lunn P, Panter-Brick C. Hand-washing, subclinical infections, and growth: a longitudinal evaluation of an intervention in Nepali slums. Am J Hum Biol 2011;23:621–9.

[124] Ochola SA, Labadarios D, Nduati RW. Impact of counselling on exclusive breast-feeding practices in a poor urban setting in Kenya: a randomized controlled trial. Public Health Nutr 2012;1–9.

[125] Schell CO, Reilly M, Rosling H, et al. Socioeconomic determinants of infant mortality: a worldwide study of 152 low-, middle-, and high-income countries. Scand J Public Health 2007;35:288–97.

[126] Scheppers E, van Dongen E, Dekker J, et al. Potential barriers to the use of health services among ethnic minorities: a review. Fam Pract 2006;23:325–48.

[127] United Nations. Convention on the Rights of the Child. 1990. Available at: http://www2.ohchr.org/english/law/crc.htm. Accessed September 15, 2012.

Advances in Pediatrics 60 (2013) 89–106

ADVANCES IN PEDIATRICS

# Detecting Disorders of Vitamin D Deficiency in Children: An Update

Pallavi Iyer, MD*, Frank Diamond, MD

Division of Endocrinology & Diabetes, All Children's Specialty Physicians, All Children's Hospital/ Johns Hopkins Medicine, 601 5th Street South, Dept 7854, St Petersburg, FL 33701, USA

**Keywords**

• Vitamin D • Children • Extraskeletal • Rickets

**Key points**

- Rickets caused by vitamin D deficiency is still of clinical importance, especially in certain high-risk children.
- Although the definition of vitamin D deficiency is debated, most studies define it as a vitamin D concentration of less than 20 ng/mL.
- Newer research points toward extraskeletal effects of vitamin D, although continued studies are needed.
- Children with chronic illnesses have a higher prevalence of vitamin D deficiency and may benefit from higher doses of vitamin D supplementation.

## INTRODUCTION

Vitamin D–deficient rickets was once thought to have become a rare entity in children [1], especially since the realization of the role of sunlight in preventing rickets and the introduction of cod liver oil as a dietary supplement and public health efforts to fortify milk became commonplace. However, we continue to see an increase in the prevalence of vitamin D deficiency and now are beginning to understand the role of vitamin D in a wide variety of metabolic processes including not only calcium homeostasis and bone metabolism but also in skin, cancer, immunity, and energy metabolism. Vitamin $D_3$, cholecalciferol, is synthesized in the skin by the action of ultraviolet light and hydroxylated in

Disclosures: None.
Funding Sources: None.

*Corresponding author. *E-mail address*: iyerp@allkids.org

0065-3101/13/$ – see front matter
http://dx.doi.org/10.1016/j.yapd.2013.04.006 

the liver and kidney to the active hormone, $1,25(OH)_2D_3$, calcitriol. Vitamin $D_2$, ergocalciferol, is derived from plant sterols. Both orally ingested vitamin $D_2$ and $D_3$ are absorbed in chylomicrons through lymphatic channels then converted to calcitriol. A lack of vitamin D or resistance to its actions causes clinical rickets in growing children and osteomalacia in adults. Despite a growing awareness of the importance of vitamin D in health, even in sunny environments, rickets remains a prevalent medical problem whose prevention needs to be more actively addressed by primary care providers.

### Synthesis and actions of vitamin D

In the epidermis, 7-dehydrocholesterol (provitamin D) is converted to previtamin D by the action of the sun's ultraviolet B waves (UV-B 290–315) and its generated local heat (37°C). Previtamin D isomerizes to cholecalciferol and passes to dermal capillaries where it binds to vitamin D–binding protein (DBP). Vitamin $D_3$ is also ingested in fatty fish (salmon, herring, cod, mackerel, sardines), shitake mushrooms, organ meats (liver), egg yolks, and cod liver oil. Ergocalciferol is consumed in plants and yeast, wherein it derives from ergosterol. A double bond between carbons 22 and 23 and a methyl group at carbon 24 distinguishes vitamin $D_2$ from $D_3$. Both forms of vitamin D are used in supplemented foods and drinks, such as bread, cereal, milk, and orange juice. Vitamin $D_2$ is the form present in most prescribed vitamin D supplements. Vitamin $D_2$ and $D_3$ ingested from food incorporate into micelles in gut enterocytes and then are processed into chylomicrons that pass through the intestinal lymphatics into the circulation. Both forms of vitamin D are 25-hydroxylated in the liver and then similarly metabolized to $1,25(OH)_2D_3$, the active metabolite in the kidney. Vitamin $D_3$, however, is more potent than vitamin $D_2$ because of a greater affinity for DBP [2]; when taken in equivalent doses, it causes a greater increase in serum calcidiol (25[OH]D) [3,4]. Less than 10% of circulating vitamin D originates from dietary intake, emphasizing the importance of cutaneous synthesis of cholecalciferol to adequate body vitamin D stores [5]. Physiologic metabolism of previtamin $D_3$ to lumisterol, tachysterol, and various inactivated photoproducts during excessive sun exposure protects against the development of hypervitaminosis D.

Vitamin $D_2$ and $D_3$ are transported to the liver by the DBP where they are converted to 25(OH)D, whose concentrations are expressed as nanograms per milliliter. Because calcidiol has little feedback effect on its own synthesis, its serum levels approximate total body stores of vitamin D. The half-life of circulating calcidiol is 2 to 3 weeks [6]. Rare patients have been described with rickets caused by a mutation in *CYP2R1*, the 25-hydroxylase cytochrome P450 enzyme [7]. However, most clinically significant calcidiol deficiencies result from inadequate dietary intake (including vegetarian or food-allergy limited diets), limited sun exposure, disease states causing malabsorption of fat-soluble vitamins (eg, celiac disease, gastric and small bowel resection, pancreatic insufficiency including cystic fibrosis, Crohn disease), or severe liver disease that may effect 25-hydroxylation.

The hormone 25(OH)D is filtered by the glomerulus and reabsorbed in the proximal tubule, entering tubular mitochondria where it is 1-hydroxylated to the biologically active hormone 1,25$(OH)_2$D, whose concentrations are expressed in picograms per milliliter. Cytochrome P450 mono-oxygenase 25-hydroxyvitamin D 1-alpha-hydroxylase, encoded by *CYP27B1*, regulates 1,25$(OH)_2$D synthesis. It is stimulated by parathyroid hormone (PTH), PTH-related protein (PTHrP), calcitonin (in the straight renal tubules), hypocalcemia, hypophosphatemia, growth hormone, prolactin, 24,25-dihydroxy-vitamin D, and insulin like growth factor-1. It is suppressed by elevated concentrations of calcium and phosphorus, by inhibitory auto feedback, by the actions of osteocyte-derived fibroblast growth factor (FGF23), and indirectly by suppression of synthesis of PTH [8]. The half-life of calcitriol is 4 hours [9]. Unlike calcidiol, calcitriol does not cross the placenta [10]. Calcitriol is metabolized in bone, intestine, liver, and kidney by glucuronidation, sulfation, and hydroxylation to water-soluble products, such as calcitrolic acid, that are excreted in urine and bile [11].

The 1-alpha hydroxylation is also performed in macrophages, lymph nodes, bowel, breast, placenta, osteoblasts, and keratinocytes, suggesting important paracrine and autocrine functions of calcitriol. Nuclear receptors for calcidiol are present in more than 30 tissues [9]. Calcitriol binding to its nuclear vitamin D receptor regulates the expression of more than 900 genes important for bone metabolism, cell growth, heart, skin, pancreatic islet, and immune function as well as energy metabolism [12]. Within seconds to minutes of binding to its nuclear receptor, calcitriol promotes intestinal absorption of calcium, opening of voltage-gated calcium channels in osteoblasts, endothelial cell migration, and pancreatic beta cell release of insulin [12]. Calcitriol promotes bone elongation by directly stimulating growth plate chondrocytes, increasing the generation of osteoblasts and type 1 collagen formation, and suppressing bone resorption by osteoclasts. Calcitriol inhibits transcription of *PTH* in the parathyroid glands [12].

Calcidiol that is passed through the placenta may last beyond the expected 8 weeks based on the half-life because of its storage in fat [6]. In postpartum lactating mothers, calcitriol and PTH levels are low to low normal; calcium levels exceed those of nonpregnant patients because PTHrP stimulates calcium resorption from the mother's bones for transfer into her breast milk. Maternal bone mineral density declines 3% to 10% in breastfeeding women by 6 months after delivery and then increases after weaning [13].

## Environmental effects on concentrations of vitamin D

Latitude, season, time of day, cloud cover, and air pollution alter the path of solar light through the ozone layer and influence the rate of cutaneous vitamin D synthesis. Gestational exposure to air pollution results in lower cord blood serum levels of 25(OH)D [14]. Chronically ill children who remain indoors are at increased risk for vitamin D deficiency as are individuals who remain covered for cultural or religious reasons. In northern areas at more than

40° latitude in winter, there is little vitamin D synthesis in skin because only minimal UV-B radiation reaches earth. Vitamin D deficiency is, therefore, most likely to present at the end of winter and less likely to be encountered at the end of summer. Melanin in dark-skinned individuals acts as a natural sunblock, substantially reducing UV-B–initiated vitamin D synthesis in skin. Exposure of the skin to ultraviolet radiation is quantified as a minimum erythema dose (MED), the quantity of UV radiation exposure that results in minimal redness. Sun exposure in the southern part of the United States of 4 to 10 minutes for pale individuals and 60 to 80 minutes for dark-skinned individuals produces one MED at noon in the summertime [15]. Data from the National Health and Nutrition Examination Survey (NHANES) III demonstrated that non-Hispanic black adolescents have a 20-fold greater risk of calcidiol levels less than 20 ng/mL compared with non-Hispanic whites [16]. The prevalence of vitamin D concentrations less than 20 ng/mL in American children aged 1 to 11 years is about 15%, whereas 1% to 2% have levels less than 10 ng/mL [16,17]. Children taking various medications may require higher preventative doses of vitamin D. Anticonvulsants and antiretrovirals increase the metabolism of calcidiol and calcitriol. Glucocorticoids raise vitamin D requirements because they block calcitriol-mediated intestinal absorption of calcium. Ketoconazole and other antifungal agents limit vitamin D synthesis through the inhibition of 1-alpha-hydroxylation [18].

## Clinical, biochemical, and roentgenographic findings in rickets

Rickets is a clinical state characterized by abnormal formation of the cartilaginous growth plate with impaired cartilage mineralization. There is failure of apoptosis of hypertrophied chondrocytes resulting in disorganization of the epiphysis. Osteomalacia results from impaired mineralization of the bone matrix. Rickets and osteomalacia are often present simultaneously while the growth plates remain open and the child is continuing to grow; only osteomalacia results following epiphyseal closure [19]. Rickets may be caused by deficiency or resistance to vitamin D, primary calcium deficiency (calciopenic rickets), or depleted concentrations of serum phosphorus (phosphopenic rickets). The current review focuses on pathologic changes related to disorders and deficiency of vitamin D. In infancy, rickets may present with irritability; tremors; failure to thrive; large anterior fontanelle; frontal bossing; craniotabes (soft skull); Harrison groove; increased infections, including pneumonia; reversible cardiomyopathy (related to hypocalcemia); and rib or extremity fractures sometimes found unexpectedly on chest radiographs. Apnea, stridor, and wheezing may also occur. Congenital rickets may result from vitamin D deficiency of the pregnant mother, especially in the dark-skinned, exclusively breast-fed infants born in winter. In older infants starting to lift up their head and upper torso, bowing of the forearms may occur. The diagnosis of rickets should be considered in older infants and toddlers with delayed walking and developmental delay. Hyperreflexia may be present. Delayed and decayed dentition, musculoskeletal pain caused by periosteal swelling, widened wrists and ankles, knock knee or bow legs (genu valgum or varum), windswept deformity (valgus of one leg and varus of the other), and widened costochondral junctions (rachitic rosary) are all manifestations of expanded and uncalcified cartilage characteristic of the disease (Fig. 1A). Short stature and anorexia may occur in older children with vitamin D deficiency [11]. The contribution of vitamin D sufficiency to normal bone mineral density is supported by evidence of an association of reduced stress fracture risk in active young girls who receive vitamin D supplementation [20]. Vitamin D deficiency presenting with hypocalcemic seizures or tetany occurs more frequently during rapid growth in infancy or adolescence when the calcium demand may outstrip circulating calcium available through PTH-stimulated bone resorption.

Biochemically, in advanced vitamin D–deficiency rickets, calcium and phosphorus levels are low, with a secondary increase of PTH and an elevated alkaline phosphatase. Among other functions, alkaline phosphatase hydrolyzes organic phosphates to augment the local concentration of phosphate in the skeletal matrix to values that promote deposition of hydroxyapatite onto type 1 collagen fibers. Early in the development of rickets, elevated PTH may transiently correct hypocalcemia, which recurs with progression of the disease. Calcidiol levels are generally low; calcitriol concentrations may be low, normal, or high. Elevated PTH may initially stimulate calcitriol synthesis and increase levels; but later in the illness, calcitriol concentrations decrease because of the reduced concentrations of precursor. Radiographic features include early osteopenia followed by metaphyseal widening, loss of definition of the

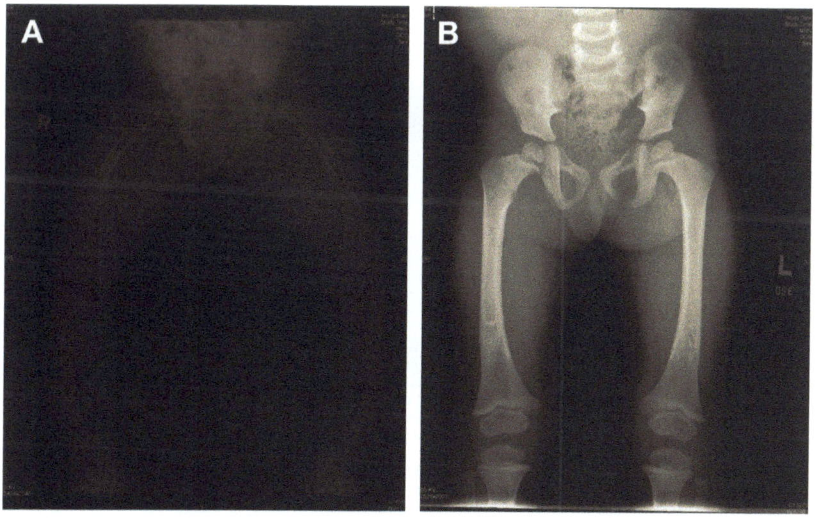


**Fig. 1.** (*A*) A 20-month-old girl with vitamin D–deficiency rickets and genu varum and metaphyseal widening. (*B*) At 10 months after treatment with 4000 units of $D_2$ daily. (*Courtesy of* Michael S. Kappy, MD, Aurora, CO.)

epiphyseal/metaphyseal interface, and with progression, fraying, cupping, and further widening of the growth plate from proliferation of unmineralized cartilage. Coarse trabeculation forms in the metaphysis. Occasional areas of osteitis fibrosa cystic may also occur. Looser zones, pseudofractures with sclerotic borders, form perpendicular to the cortices, especially in the femur in severe rickets and osteomalacia [21]. Radiographic changes of rickets are best sought in rapidly growing bones, such as the distal ulna and the metaphyses at the knees.

## Defining vitamin D deficiency

Efforts to define serum levels of vitamin D deficiency have been based on physiologic parameters, including optimal bone mineralization, measurement of PTH, changes in alkaline phosphatase and bone markers, calcium balance studies, and skeletal development. There continues to be an active scientific debate as to what constitutes the limits of healthy concentrations of vitamin D in children. Multisite pooled data from adults, children, and adolescents suggest that the interaction between serum levels of calcidiol and PTH is linear, with no clearly discernible inflection point at which increasing calcidiol suppresses PTH [22]. Elevated alkaline phosphatase concentrations have been reported in children at calcidiol levels less than 20 ng/mL, and radiologic changes of rickets and low bone density have been described at 25(OH)D concentrations of less than 16 to 18 ng/mL [12,23]. An Institute of Medicine's review of the medical literature found "little or no additional benefit with serum levels above 20 ng/mL, and a clear plateau of the effect between 12 and 16 ng/mL" (Fig. 2) [24]. The committee did not find that "a higher level of 25(OH)D, ie, 30 ng/mL, would be beneficial for bone health," [24] and their report states that a level of 20 ng/mL is adequate for more than 97% of the population. The American Academy of Pediatrics and the Institute of Medicine both define the lower

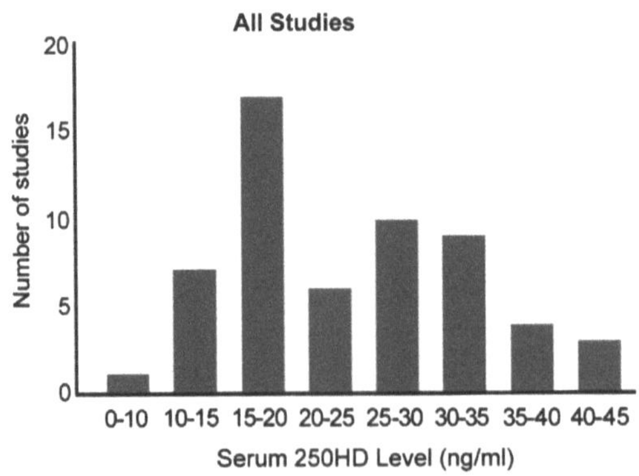


**Fig. 2.** Levels of serum 25(OH)D at which serum PTH plateaus and/or is suppressed, as demonstrated by 59 studies reviewed by Sai AJ, et al. (*From* Sai AJ. Relationship between vitamin D, parathyroid hormone, and bone health. J Clin Endocrinol Metab 2011;96:E436–46. Copyright 2011, The Endocrine Society.)

normal concentration of serum calcidiol at 20 ng/mL [25,26]. The Drug and Therapeutics Committee of the Pediatric Endocrine Society defines the significance of vitamin D levels as follows: 20 to 100 ng/mL, sufficiency; 15 to 20 ng/mL, insufficiency; and less than 15 ng/mL, deficiency [9]. The Endocrine Society defines calcidiol values as the following: vitamin D deficiency, less than 20 ng/mL; insufficiency, 21 to 29 ng/mL; and sufficiency, 30 ng/mL or more (Table 1) [27]. Significant variability in commercial 25(OH)D assays further complicates an accurate definition [9,28]. An expert consensus statement reports that high-performance liquid chromatography and liquid chromatography, tandem mass spectrometry (LC/MS/MS) are preferable measurement methods over immunoassays [29].

## Preventing nutritional vitamin D deficiency

If taken reliably, 400 IU of vitamin D ingested daily provides a protective oral dose of vitamin D to both breast- and formula-fed infants; all infant formulas contain at least this dosage [30]. The vitamin D content of breast milk averages approximately 22 IU/L, ranging from 15 to 50 IU/L. Thus, ingestion of 30 oz of breast milk a day provides well less than the daily requirement in an exclusively breast-fed baby, especially if he or she is kept indoors without sun exposure [31]. Infant formulas are supplemented with 40 to 100 IU of vitamin D per 100 kcal of formula to provide 400 IU/L (33 oz). However, some bottle-fed infants are given a combination of formula and breast milk and may fail to ingest a volume of formula that would provide adequate vitamin D. For this reason, formula-fed infants may also require supplementation with vitamin D. The Endocrine Society's Clinical Practice Guidelines recommend that infants and children aged 0 to 1 year receive at least 400 IU/d and children aged 1 year and older be given 600 IU/d to maximize bone health [27]. Children with a high risk for vitamin D deficiency may necessitate even higher doses [32]. Premature babies may require greater than 400 IU of daily vitamin D supplementation from birth because of the insufficient duration of placental

**Table 1**
Definitions of vitamin D deficiency, insufficiency, and sufficiency

| | 25(OH)D concentrations (ng/mL) |
|---|---|
| PES (2008) | Deficiency: <15<br>Insufficiency: 15–20<br>Sufficiency: 21–100 |
| IOM (2011) | Deficiency: <20<br>Sufficiency: >20 |
| Endocrine Society (2011) | Deficiency: <20<br>Insufficiency: 20–29<br>Sufficiency: 30–100 |

Definitions are as defined by the Pediatric Endocrine Society [9], Institute of Medicine [25], and the Endocrine Society [27] statements.
*Abbreviations:* IOM, Institute of Medicine; PES, Pediatric Endocrine Society.

vitamin transfer, feeding problems, and liver and kidney issues related to prematurity. High doses of vitamin D (4000–6400 IU) administered to breastfeeding mothers have been shown to increase calcidiol levels in their infants to concentrations achieved with direct infant supplementation, without creating vitamin D toxicity in the mother [33]. Less than 15% of breast- and breast/formula-fed infants and 20% to 35% of exclusively formula-fed infants receive adequate protective intake of vitamin D because many parents mistakenly think that breast milk contains adequate vitamin D. Less than one-third of clinicians routinely prescribe vitamin D supplements to breast-feeding babies [34].

The duration of sun exposure needed to maintain satisfactory vitamin D levels in older infants varies with latitude, skin pigmentation, and the amount of skin exposed to sunlight. In Cincinnati, at 38° north latitude, 20 minutes per day of exposure of the hands and face generated adequate concentrations of circulating vitamin D; however, in Beijing, at 40° north, 2 hours of exposure was needed from September to October [35]. Air pollution may have also been a factor in the subjects reported from China. To maintain an infant's calcidiol concentration of more than 11 ng/mL, an exclusively breast-fed baby less than 6 months of age requires about 30 minutes per week of sun exposure wearing only a diaper or 2 hours a week of sunshine fully dressed without a hat [36]. A baby wearing only a diaper requires only a quarter of the sun exposure as a fully dressed baby wearing a hat to generate similar synthesis of vitamin D in the skin. Thus, at least a fifth of the baby's skin should be exposed to sunlight for serum vitamin D levels to increase [36]. Sunscreens as low as a sun protection factor of 8 can lower vitamin D synthesis in skin by 95% [15]. It is important to recall that the American Academy of Pediatrics continues to recommend that children less than 6 months of age avoid direct sunlight so as to reduce the risk of skin cancer [37].

Calcidiol levels in obese individuals are lower than those in nonobese individuals, and concentrations increase with weight loss, despite constant intake of vitamin D [25]. Adipocytes are reservoirs of vitamin D and also contain both vitamin D 25-hydroxylase and L-alpha-hydroxylase activity, suggesting that adipose tissue may be a site of vitamin D synthesis as well as storage [7].

### Medical therapy for vitamin D–deficiency rickets

Rickets may be treated with daily doses of vitamin D for a 2- to 3-month period (see Fig. 1B), larger weekly doses for 8 weeks, or a single large dose (so-called stoss or push therapy). The Drug and Therapeutics Committee of the Pediatric Endocrine Society recommends treatment dosages of 1000 IU/d for infants in the first month of life, 1 to 5000 IU/d for babies aged 1 month to 1 year, and 5 to 10,000 IU/d for children older than 12 months [9]. Commonly prescribed vitamin D products include vitamin D3 (D-Visol), 400 IU/mL; ergocalciferol (Drisdol) 8000 IU/mL; and cholecalciferol (Replesta), 50,000-IU wafers and gel caps. Some studies report the administration of 100,000 to 600,000 IU of vitamin D orally over 1 to 5 days for infants and children older than 1 month in whom compliance or follow-up care is of concern. Daily maintenance therapy is then prescribed [38]. Injectable high-dose vitamin D is no longer marketed in the United States. Ergocalciferol (Drisdol) should be used with caution at very high doses because it contains propylene glycol that may be toxic in excessive amounts. In adolescents and young adults, 50,000 IU of vitamin D prescribed orally once weekly for 8 weeks has successfully treated rickets. Calcium supplementation should accompany the initiation of vitamin D therapy, even in the absence of low serum calcium, to prevent the development of hypocalcemia as PTH normalizes and bone remineralizes (hungry bone syndrome). This supplementation is particularly required if stoss therapy is prescribed. Approximately 75 mg/kg/d of elemental calcium in divided doses should be prescribed. As radiographic healing begins (2–4 weeks) and alkaline phosphatase levels normalize, the dosage of vitamin D can be lowered to 400 IU/d. Rarely, the administration of vitamin D to infants, even at prophylactic doses, may result in a severe hypercalcemic crises caused by the mutation of *CYP24A1* encoding 25-hydroxyvitamin D3 24-hydroxylase, a key enzyme required for calcitriol degradation. In one reported case, hypercalcemia in a 4-month-old infant was so severe and intractable as to require acute hemodialysis [39].

## Other forms of vitamin D–related rickets

### *Vitamin D–dependent rickets I (pseudovitamin D–deficiency rickets)*

Inactivating mutations of both alleles of *CP27B1* results in type 1 vitamin D–dependent rickets (pseudovitamin D–deficiency rickets [PDDR]) characterized by low levels of calcitriol, calcium, and phosphorus, with secondary hyperparathyroidism. Very high calcitriol levels (300–1000 pg/mL) indicate vitamin D resistance caused by a mutated vitamin D nuclear receptor.

PDDR is a rare recessive disorder, usually presenting with active rickets after 6 months of age, that occurs in many populations but more commonly in French Canadians from Quebec (g958del G in exon 2), suggesting a founder effect. Delay in walking is a common presentation; other findings include hypotonia, seizures, growth retardation, and dyspnea caused by rib fractures. Deletions, splice-site mutations, and insertions in *CYP27B1* alter the 1-alpha hydroxylase enzyme's heme-binding domain, completely inactivating enzyme action in in vitro studies [40]. Edouard and colleagues [41] assessed the short- and long-term effects of calcitriol therapy in a cohort of affected children ranging from 1 month to 2.6 years of age treated for 2 to 26 years. Treatment with $1,25(OH)_2D$ corrected both biochemical abnormalities and bone mineral density Z-score deficits within 3 months, whereas height Z-scores improved gradually. Adult patients who had received calcitriol therapy before their pubertal growth spurt achieved normal heights, whereas patients treated after puberty were stunted (−2.2 SD). Because the long-term follow-up of treated patients revealed normal areal bone mineral density and a lack of skeletal fragility, the investigators speculated that local synthesis of calcitriol in chondrocytes and osteoblast does not seem necessary for adult skeletal development [41]. Female patients had healthy pregnancies and gave birth to eucalcemic newborns.

*Vitamin D-dependent rickets II (hereditary vitamin D-resistant rickets)*
Children with hereditary vitamin D-resistant rickets (HVDRR) have partial or total resistance to 1,25(OH)$_2$D. They present with hypocalcemia and severe rickets in the first few months of life. In these patients, calcidiol concentrations are normal, but calcitriol levels are markedly increased. Sparse body hair and alopecia, sometimes including eyebrows and eyelashes, is common. The autosomal recessive disorder results from multiple heterozygous mutations of the vitamin D receptor (VDR) gene. Mutations in the VDR DNA-binding domain (DBD) cause complete vitamin D resistance despite normal vitamin D binding to its receptor. Mutations in the ligand-binding domain interrupt ligand binding or heterodimerization with retinoid x receptor (RXR) or interfere with coactivator binding to the VDR [42]. Patients affected with a DBD, RXR heterodimerization, or compound heterozygous defects have associated alopecia. Those individuals with mutations affecting VDR ligand-mediated transactivation and coactivation recruitment have normal body hair [42].

Alterations in the vitamin D receptors may affect calcitriol binding, reduced binding site number, lowered binding affinity, disordered receptor translocation to the nucleus, or altered hormone-receptor complex DNA binding because of the changes in receptor zinc binding fingers [43].

Some patients respond to treatment with high dosages of calcitriol (20–200 ug/d). In nonresponders, high-dose calcium administration is prescribed. If oral calcium absorption by passive diffusion cannot correct the hypocalcemia, intravenous calcium administration has been used, sometimes as pulse therapy with oral administration between infusions [44]. Oral calcium administration alone may be sufficient in older children, and spontaneous healing of rickets off all therapy has been reported in some patients with HVDRR as they age [45]. Independent of vitamin D action or therapy with phosphate, sustained normalization of serum calcium may correct hypophosphatemia and elevations of alkaline phosphatase by normalizing PTH levels. Rachitic bone fully remineralizes despite a lack of vitamin D action [46].

## Vitamin D metabolism and actions outside the classic pathway

Defining vitamin D deficiency in pediatric patients with chronic illnesses is even more challenging. In this population, vitamin D deficiency and insufficiency are often characterized similarly to healthy cohorts. However, the newer research into the possible extraskeletal effects of vitamin D makes aiming for vitamin D sufficiency even more attractive for children with underlying inflammatory processes.

VDR and the *CYP27B1* enzyme are present in various tissues, including skeletal muscle, skin, colon, breast, prostate, pancreas, heart, brain, lymphocytes, and monocytes. However, production and catabolism of 1,25(OH)$_2$D differs in nonrenal tissues.

Innate immunity is the body's inborn ability to recognize and attack foreign materials. In monocytes, macrophages, and mucosal cells, the activation of toll-like receptors (TLRs) upregulates the expression of *CYP27B1* [47]. Binding of

$1,25(OH)_2D$ to VDR stimulates the production of the protein cathelicidin, which has antimicrobial activity. The production of $1,25(OH)_2D$ in these cells is regulated by the availability of 25(OH)D rather than by PTH and FGF23 [48]. However, these cells do not express *CYP24A1*; thus, $1,25(OH)_2D$ is not processed to its inactive form $24,25(OH)_2D$, causing an overproduction of $1,25(OH)_2D$ in inflammatory diseases [49]. Adaptive immunity refers to learned mechanisms for fighting invaders. This branch of immunity is mediated by T cells producing cytokines and B cells producing immunoglobulins. Specific T cells ($Th_1$ and $Th_{17}$) and B cells encourage the destruction of offenders, whereas other T cells (T regulatory [$T_{reg}$] and $Th_2$) suppress immune responses that might be detrimental to the host and promote tolerance. Overall, vitamin D suppresses the adaptive immune response by inhibiting proliferation and differentiation of B cells, production of immunoglobulins, and proliferation of $Th_1$ and $Th_{17}$ cells. In contrast, interleukins beneficial for $Th_2$ and $T_{reg}$ cells are increased by $1,25(OH)_2D$, protecting against self-damage (ie, preventing autoimmunity) (Fig. 3).

There are several TLRs with specific functions for innate immunity, such as TLR2/TLR4 for cancer, TLR2/1 and TLR4 for mycobacterial infections, TLR4 and TLR6 for bacterial, and TLR7 for viral illnesses and autoimmunity [50]. Thus, TLR-mediated production of $1,25(OH)_2D$ may have autocrine roles in the immune response to bacterial, viral, cancerous, proinflammatory, and autoimmune diseases.

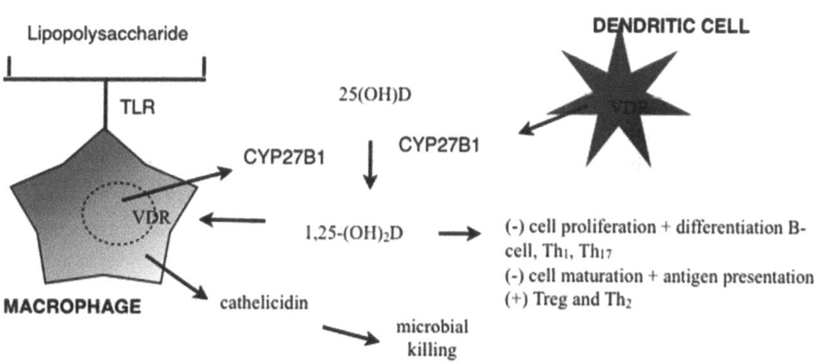


**Fig. 3.** Vitamin D on the innate and adaptive immune system. Bacterial products, such as lipopolysaccharide binding to TLR on the macrophage (part of the innate immune system), induce CYP27B1 to metabolize 25(OH)D to $1,25(OH)_2D$. In turn, $1,25(OH)_2D$ binds to VDR and promotes production of cathelicidin to aid with microbial killing. As part of the adaptive immune system, the dendritic cell acts as the antigen-presenting cell. Conversion of 25(OH)D to $1,25(OH)_2D$ via *CYP27B1* promotes suppressor T-cell action of $T_{reg}$ and $Th_2$ cells important in building tolerance. In contrast, $1,25(OH)_2D$ inhibits cell proliferation and differentiation of inflammatory T cells, like $Th_1$ and $Th_{17}$, and inhibits production of immunoglobulins from B cells. (*Data from* Sai AJ. Relationship between vitamin D, parathyroid hormone, and bone health. J Clin Endocrinol Metab 2011;96:E436–46.)

As previously discussed, pancreatic insulin-producing beta cells also express $1,25(OH)_2D$ and VDR [51]. In beta cells, $1,25(OH)_2D$ induces insulin secretion through exocytosis and degranulation of insulin. In pathologic conditions, treatment with $1,25(OH)_2D$ leads to the expression of genes involved in intracellular trafficking, intercellular junction formation, and cytoskeletal organization [52]. $1,25(OH)_2D$ also mediates intracellular calcium signaling in adipocytes, promoting lipogenesis and inhibiting lipolysis, putatively through inhibition of uncoupling protein-2 [50].

Keratinocytes express *CYP27B1,* VDR, and *CYP24* and, thus, are able to regulate $1,25(OH)_2D$ production and catabolism to $24,25(OH)_2D$. The epidermis is part of the innate immune system. However, the $1,25(OH)_2D$ in keratinocytes also promotes differentiation of keratinocytes and inhibits proliferation [48]. In VDR mutated individuals with HVDRR, but not in patients with PDDR, alopecia is a clinical finding suggesting that VDR acts independently of $1,25(OH)_2D$ in proliferation and differentiation of cells required in hair follicle cycling. Other actions of $1,25(OH)_2D$ in the keratinocyte are to protect against UV-B damage of DNA by promoting repair, reducing cell death, and increasing expression of p53 [53].

Metastatic cells also express VDR and *CYP27B1*, and *in vitro* and animal studies suggest mechanisms for reduction in cancerous cell growth. $1,25(OH)_2D$ limits cancer cell proliferation via the regulation of genes, such as cyclin-dependent kinase inhibitors, and the inhibition of the expression of insulin-like growth factor 1 and prosurvival proteins like telomerase reverse transcriptase. $1,25(OH)_2D$ also has antiangiogenic and antimetastatic effects on tumor cells. Calcitriol's antiinflammatory effects repress the prostaglandin pathway [50].

## Vitamin D in children with chronic illness

With growing evidence of the importance of vitamin D sufficiency for nonskeletal effects, vitamin D status has been examined in chronic medical conditions. Patients with certain disorders have risk factors for suboptimal vitamin D stores because of reduced sunlight exposure, decreased absorption of fat-soluble vitamins, suboptimal nutritional states, and medication interference with vitamin D or calcium absorption. Further, the proinflammatory states could potentially benefit from higher levels of 25(OH)D for functional innate immunity. The effects of $1,25(OH)_2D$ may also be beneficial in the prevention of autoimmune diseases and cardiovascular health. The possible role of vitamin D in some chronic diseases of childhood is reviewed later.

### *Sickle cell disease*

Sickle cell disease (SCD-SS) is marked by chronic pain caused by ischemia and vasoocclusive bone infarction. Children with SCD-SS are at an increased risk for developing vitamin D deficiency because of the increased melanin concentration in the skin, decreased outdoor activities, and poor intake of vitamin D. In a study by Rovner and colleagues [54], the prevalence of vitamin D deficiency (defined as $<$11 ng/mL) in this population was 33%, with a median concentration of 15 ng/mL. Even when compared with a healthy African American cohort from the same geographic area, the risk of vitamin D deficiency was 5-fold greater in children with SCD-SS. A case report described complete resolution of chronic bone pain in a 16-year-old girl with SCD-SS with repletion of vitamin D levels [55]. A pilot study of 39 patients with SCD-SS randomized to placebo or weekly high-dose cholecalciferol administration for 6 weeks suggested improvement in pain-free days in the vitamin D group, although the results did not reach statistical significance [56].

*Type 1 diabetes mellitus*

Given the role of $1,25(OH)_2D$ in immune modulation, specifically in building tolerance, the prevalence of hypovitaminosis D and its role in the development of autoimmune diseases is being studied. Vitamin D is thought to be important in preventing the development of type 1 diabetes based on an animal study showing that nonobese diabetic mice who received calcitriol supplementation reduced their chances of developing type 1 diabetes by 80% [57]. In human patients, a large longitudinal birth-cohort study showed that children who received 2000 IU of vitamin D daily reduced their risk of developing type 1 diabetes by 80% [58]. Similarly, a case-control study found supplementation with cod liver oil (which contains both vitamin D and omega-3 fatty acids) lowered the risk of developing type 1 diabetes [59]. Other investigators have reported a higher prevalence of hypovitaminosis D in children with type 1 diabetes mellitus compared with healthy controls [60–63]. In contrast, a recent large prospective study of children at risk of developing diabetes (first-degree relative of someone with type 1 diabetes or the presence of high-risk HLA class II typing) found that intake of vitamin D or vitamin D levels did not correlate with the presence of islet autoimmunity or the development of type 1 diabetes [64]. Intervention trials with calcidiol and calcitriol in newly diagnosed patients with type 1 diabetes show variable results in the protection of beta cell function over time [65].

*Inflammatory bowel disease*

In children with inflammatory bowel disease (IBD), the prevalence of vitamin D deficiency is high because of decreased oral intake, decreased absorption, reduced sun exposure (caused by decreased activity), interaction with immunosuppressive agents, and the use of glucocorticoid therapy [66]. In an Australian study, 19% of children with IBD were vitamin D deficient (25[OH]D: <20 ng/mL) and 38% were insufficient (25[OH]D: 20–30 ng/mL) [67]. Although these patients are at risk for decreased bone mineral density and fractures, their 25(OH)D levels did not correlate with their bone mineral density Z scores [68]. A recent expert opinion guideline for pediatric patients with IBD recommends the following: (1) screening with dual energy x-ray absorptiometry scan in high-risk patients, (2) use of steroid-sparing therapies for reducing inflammation, (3) nutritional support in those with delay of growth and development, (4) optimization of vitamin D levels with a goal of at least 32 ng/mL of 25(OH)D, and (5) weight-bearing exercises [69].

*Cystic fibrosis*

Another common pediatric chronic illness with poor gastrointestinal absorption of vitamin D is cystic fibrosis (CF). Numerous studies from large CF centers have shown that 90% of these patients have 25(OH)D levels less than 30 ng/mL. Several factors contribute to poor vitamin D stores in this population, including poor intestinal absorption caused by pancreatic insufficiency, chronic glucocorticoid therapy, reduced sunlight exposure, decreased DBP, and reduced fat in which to store vitamin D [70]. Although the vitamin D stores are poor in patients with CF, the resultant clinical significance is less well defined. Fracture rates in patients with CF are comparable with rates in healthy controls [71]. Despite the paucity of data, the CF foundation released consensus recommendations of yearly screening for 25(OH)D in late winter with a therapeutic goal of 30 ng/mL. A stepwise treatment plan based on age and 25(OH)D status (graded by <20 ng/mL, 20–30 ng/mL, >30 ng/mL) was outlined [72]. In patients with CF with poor adherence to chronic medication regimen, stoss therapy has also shown benefit in maintaining 25(OH)D concentrations more than 30 ng/mL, even after 12 months [73].

*Cancer*

There have been several reports in the adult literature regarding the benefits of vitamin D for decreasing the risk of developing cancer or decreasing morbidity and mortality with cancer, specifically colorectal, breast, and prostate cancer [74]. Treatment with vitamin D metabolites in these patients has been limited by toxicities caused by hypervitaminosis D. In pediatric patients with a history of malignancy, prevalence of vitamin D deficiency (<15 ng/mL) was 25% and insufficiency (15–20 ng/mL) was 30% [74]. Even after acute treatment, long-term survivors of childhood cancer are at risk of developing vitamin D deficiency over time [75]. Currently, no guidelines are published discussing pediatric malignancy–specific target vitamin D concentrations or treatment strategies.

## SUMMARY

Vitamin D deficiency and vitamin D–deficient rickets continue to be of clinical importance globally. Recognizing the clinical, radiographic, and biochemical manifestations of rickets is important in distinguishing different types of rickets. Recent guidelines in defining, preventing, and treating vitamin D deficiency in infants, children, and adolescents can direct clinicians appropriately. In children with chronic illnesses, defining vitamin D deficiency is fraught with similar concerns as it is in the general public. However, making these patients vitamin D replete may aid skeletal development as well as the overall health of chronically ill children.

### References

[1] Harrison HE. A tribute to the first lady of public health (Martha M. Eliot). V. The disappearance of rickets. Am J Public Health Nations Health 1966;56(5):734–7.

[2] Armas LA, Hollis BW, Heaney RP. Vitamin D2 is much less effective than vitamin D3 in humans. J Clin Endocrinol Metab 2004;89(11):5387–91.
[3] Holick MF. Vitamin D: evolutionary, physiological and health perspectives. Curr Drug Targets 2011;12(1):4–18.
[4] Autier P, Gandini S, Mullie P. A systematic review: influence of vitamin D supplementation on serum 25-hydroxyvitamin D concentration. J Clin Endocrinol Metab 2012;97(8): 2606–13.
[5] Norris JM. Can the sunshine vitamin shed light on type 1 diabetes? Lancet 2001;358(9292):1476–8.
[6] Fraser DR. Vitamin D. Lancet 1995;345(8942):104–7.
[7] Schuster I. Cytochromes P450 are essential players in the vitamin D signaling system. Biochim Biophys Acta 2011;1814(1):186–99.
[8] Oliveira RB, Moyses RM. FGF-23: state of the art. J Bras Nefrol 2010;32(3):323–31.
[9] Misra M, Pacaud D, Petryk A, et al. Vitamin D deficiency in children and its management: review of current knowledge and recommendations. Pediatrics 2008;122(2): 398–417.
[10] Kovacs CS. Vitamin D in pregnancy and lactation: maternal, fetal, and neonatal outcomes from human and animal studies. Am J Clin Nutr 2008;88(2):520S–8S.
[11] Holick MF. Resurrection of vitamin D deficiency and rickets. J Clin Invest 2006;116(8): 2062–72.
[12] Root AW. Disorders of mineral metabolism. In: Sperling MA, editor. Pediatric endocrinology. 4th edition. Philadelphia: Elsevier; 2013. [In press].
[13] Weisman Y. Maternal, fetal and neonatal vitamin D and calcium metabolism during pregnancy and lactation. Endocr Dev 2003;6:34–49.
[14] Baiz N, Dargent-Molina P, Wark JD, et al. Gestational exposure to urban air pollution related to a decrease in cord blood vitamin d levels. J Clin Endocrinol Metab 2012;97(11):4087–95.
[15] Holick MF. Sunlight and vitamin D for bone health and prevention of autoimmune diseases, cancers, and cardiovascular disease. Am J Clin Nutr 2004;80(Suppl 6):1678S–88S.
[16] Saintonge S, Bang H, Gerber LM. Implications of a new definition of vitamin D deficiency in a multiracial us adolescent population: the National Health and Nutrition Examination Survey III. Pediatrics 2009;123(3):797–803.
[17] Mansbach JM, Ginde AA, Camargo CA Jr. Serum 25-hydroxyvitamin D levels among US children aged 1 to 11 years: do children need more vitamin D? Pediatrics 2009;124(5): 1404–10.
[18] Holick MF, Krane SM, Potts JT. Calcium, phosphorus and bone metabolism: calcium-regulation hormones. In: Fauci AS, Baunwald E, Isselbacher KJ, editors. Harrison's principles of internal medicine. New York: McGraw-Hill; 1995. p. 2214.
[19] Pitt MJ. Rickets and osteomalacia are still around. Radiol Clin North Am 1991;29(1): 97–118.
[20] Sonneville KR, Gordon CM, Kocher MS, et al. Vitamin D, calcium, and dairy intakes and stress fractures among female adolescents. Arch Pediatr Adolesc Med 2012;166(7): 595–600.
[21] Chapman T, Sugar N, Done S, et al. Fractures in infants and toddlers with rickets. Pediatr Radiol 2010;40(7):1184–9.
[22] Hill KM, McCabe GP, McCabe LD, et al. An inflection point of serum 25-hydroxyvitamin D for maximal suppression of parathyroid hormone is not evident from multi-site pooled data in children and adolescents. J Nutr 2010;140(11):1983–8.
[23] Spence JT, Serwint JR. Secondary prevention of vitamin D-deficiency rickets. Pediatrics 2004;113(1 Pt 1):e70–2.
[24] Rosen CJ, Abrams SA, Aloia JF, et al. IOM committee members respond to Endocrine Society vitamin D guideline. J Clin Endocrinol Metab 2012;97(4):1146–52.

[25] Ross AC, Manson JE, Abrams SA, et al. The 2011 report on dietary reference intakes for calcium and vitamin D from the Institute of Medicine: what clinicians need to know. J Clin Endocrinol Metab 2011;96(1):53–8.
[26] Hollis BW. Circulating 25-hydroxyvitamin D levels indicative of vitamin D sufficiency: implications for establishing a new effective dietary intake recommendation for vitamin D. J Nutr 2005;135(2):317–22.
[27] Holick MF, Binkley NC, Bischoff-Ferrari HA, et al. Evaluation, treatment, and prevention of vitamin D deficiency: an Endocrine Society clinical practice guideline. J Clin Endocrinol Metab 2011;96(7):1911–30.
[28] Barake M, Daher RT, Salti I, et al. 25-hydroxyvitamin D assay variations and impact on clinical decision making. J Clin Endocrinol Metab 2012;97(3):835–43.
[29] de la Hunty A, Wallace AM, Gibson S, et al. UK Food Standards Agency Workshop Consensus Report: the choice of method for measuring 25-hydroxyvitamin D to estimate vitamin D status for the UK National Diet and Nutrition Survey. Br J Nutr 2010;104(4):612–9.
[30] Tsang RC, Zlotkin SH, Nichols BL, et al. Nutrition during infancy: principles and practice. 2nd edition. Cincinnati (OH): Digital Education Publishing; 1997.
[31] Henderson A. Vitamin D and the breastfed infant. J Obstet Gynecol Neonatal Nurs 2005;34(3):367–72.
[32] Sowers M, Eyre D, Hollis BW, et al. Biochemical markers of bone turnover in lactating and nonlactating postpartum women. J Clin Endocrinol Metab 1995;80(7):2210–6.
[33] Basile LA, Taylor SN, Wagner CL, et al. The effect of high-dose vitamin D supplementation on serum vitamin D levels and milk calcium concentration in lactating women and their infants. Breastfeed Med 2006;1(1):27–35.
[34] Williamson S, Greene S. Rickets: prevention message is not getting through. BMJ 2007;334(7607):1288.
[35] Wharton B, Bishop N. Rickets. Lancet 2003;362(9393):1389–400.
[36] Specker BL, Valanis B, Hertzberg V, et al. Sunshine exposure and serum 25-hydroxyvitamin D concentrations in exclusively breast-fed infants. J Pediatr 1985;107(3):372–6.
[37] Ultraviolet light: a hazard to children. American Academy of Pediatrics. Committee on Environmental Health. Pediatrics 1999;104(2 Pt 1):328–33.
[38] Shah BR, Finberg L. Single-day therapy for nutritional vitamin D-deficiency rickets: a preferred method. J Pediatr 1994;125(3):487–90.
[39] Schlingmann KP, Kaufmann M, Weber S, et al. Mutations in CYP24A1 and idiopathic infantile hypercalcemia. N Engl J Med 2011;365(5):410–21.
[40] Wang JT, Lin CJ, Burridge SM, et al. Genetics of vitamin D 1alpha-hydroxylase deficiency in 17 families. Am J Hum Genet 1998;63(6):1694–702.
[41] Edouard T, Alos N, Chabot G, et al. Short- and long-term outcome of patients with pseudo-vitamin D deficiency rickets treated with calcitriol. J Clin Endocrinol Metab 2011;96(1):82–9.
[42] Malloy PJ, Feldman D. Genetic disorders and defects in vitamin d action. Endocrinol Metab Clin North Am 2010;39(2):333–46, Table of contents.
[43] Brooks MH, Bell NH, Love L, et al. Vitamin-D-dependent rickets type II. Resistance of target organs to 1,25-dihydroxyvitamin D. N Engl J Med 1978;298(18):996–9.
[44] Ma NS, Malloy PJ, Pitukcheewanont P, et al. Hereditary vitamin D resistant rickets: identification of a novel splice site mutation in the vitamin D receptor gene and successful treatment with oral calcium therapy. Bone 2009;45(4):743–6.
[45] Hirst MA, Hochman HI, Feldman D. Vitamin D resistance and alopecia: a kindred with normal 1,25-dihydroxyvitamin D binding, but decreased receptor affinity for deoxyribonucleic acid. J Clin Endocrinol Metab 1985;60(3):490–5.
[46] Panda DK, Miao D, Bolivar I, et al. Inactivation of the 25-hydroxyvitamin D 1alpha-hydroxylase and vitamin D receptor demonstrates independent and interdependent effects of calcium and vitamin D on skeletal and mineral homeostasis. J Biol Chem 2004;279(16):16754–66.

[47] Liu PT, Stenger S, Li H, et al. Toll-like receptor triggering of a vitamin D-mediated human antimicrobial response. Science 2006;311(5768):1770–3.
[48] Bikle D. Nonclassic actions of vitamin D. J Clin Endocrinol Metab 2009;94(1):26–34.
[49] Bikle DD. Vitamin D and immune function: understanding common pathways. Curr Osteoporos Rep 2009;7(2):58–63.
[50] Rosen CJ, Adams JS, Bikle DD, et al. The nonskeletal effects of vitamin D: an Endocrine Society scientific statement. Endocr Rev 2012;33(3):456–92.
[51] Bland R, Markovic D, Hills CE, et al. Expression of 25-hydroxyvitamin D3-1alpha-hydroxylase in pancreatic islets. J Steroid Biochem Mol Biol 2004;89–90(1–5): 121–5.
[52] Wolden-Kirk H, Overbergh L, Gysemans C, et al. Unraveling the effects of 1,25(OH)(2) D(3) on global gene expression in pancreatic islets. J Steroid Biochem Mol Biol 2012. [Epub ahead of print].
[53] Gupta R, Dixon KM, Deo SS, et al. Photoprotection by 1,25 dihydroxyvitamin D3 is associated with an increase in p53 and a decrease in nitric oxide products. J Invest Dermatol 2007;127(3):707–15.
[54] Rovner AJ, Stallings VA, Kawchak DA, et al. High risk of vitamin D deficiency in children with sickle cell disease. J Am Diet Assoc 2008;108(9):1512–6.
[55] Osunkwo I. Complete resolution of sickle cell chronic pain with high dose vitamin D therapy: a case report and review of the literature. J Pediatr Hematol Oncol 2011;33(7): 549–51.
[56] Osunkwo I, Ziegler TR, Alvarez J, et al. High dose vitamin D therapy for chronic pain in children and adolescents with sickle cell disease: results of a randomized double blind pilot study. Br J Haematol 2012;159(2):211–5.
[57] Mathieu C, Waer M, Laureys J, et al. Prevention of autoimmune diabetes in NOD mice by 1,25 dihydroxyvitamin D3. Diabetologia 1994;37(6):552–8.
[58] Hypponen E, Laara E, Reunanen A, et al. Intake of vitamin D and risk of type 1 diabetes: a birth-cohort study. Lancet 2001;358(9292):1500–3.
[59] Stene LC, Joner G. Use of cod liver oil during the first year of life is associated with lower risk of childhood-onset type 1 diabetes: a large, population-based, case-control study. Am J Clin Nutr 2003;78(6):1128–34.
[60] Bener A, Alsaied A, Al-Ali M, et al. High prevalence of vitamin D deficiency in type 1 diabetes mellitus and healthy children. Acta Diabetol 2009;46(3):183–9.
[61] Bin-Abbas BS, Jabari MA, Issa SD, et al. Vitamin D levels in Saudi children with type 1 diabetes. Saudi Med J 2011;32(6):589–92.
[62] Greer RM, Portelli SL, Hung BS, et al. Serum vitamin D levels are lower in Australian children and adolescents with type 1 diabetes than in children without diabetes. Pediatr Diabetes 2013;14(1):31–41.
[63] Mutlu A, Mutlu GY, Ozsu E, et al. Vitamin D deficiency in children and adolescents with type 1 diabetes. J Clin Res Pediatr Endocrinol 2011;3(4):179–83.
[64] Simpson M, Brady H, Yin X, et al. No association of vitamin D intake or 25-hydroxyvitamin D levels in childhood with risk of islet autoimmunity and type 1 diabetes: the Diabetes Autoimmunity Study in the Young (DAISY). Diabetologia 2011;54(11):2779–88.
[65] Gabbay MA, Sato MN, Finazzo C, et al. Effect of cholecalciferol as adjunctive therapy with insulin on protective immunologic profile and decline of residual beta-cell function in new-onset type 1 diabetes mellitus. Arch Pediatr Adolesc Med 2012;166(7):601–7.
[66] Pappa HM, Gordon CM, Saslowsky TM, et al. Vitamin D status in children and young adults with inflammatory bowel disease. Pediatrics 2006;118(5):1950–61.
[67] Levin AD, Wadhera V, Leach ST, et al. Vitamin D deficiency in children with inflammatory bowel disease. Dig Dis Sci 2011;56(3):830–6.
[68] El-Matary W, Sikora S, Spady D. Bone mineral density, vitamin D, and disease activity in children newly diagnosed with inflammatory bowel disease. Dig Dis Sci 2011;56(3): 825–9.

[69] Pappa H, Thayu M, Sylvester F, et al. Skeletal health of children and adolescents with inflammatory bowel disease. J Pediatr Gastroenterol Nutr 2011;53(1):11–25.
[70] Hall WB, Sparks AA, Aris RM. Vitamin d deficiency in cystic fibrosis. Int J Endocrinol 2010;2010:218691.
[71] Rovner AJ, Zemel BS, Leonard MB, et al. Mild to moderate cystic fibrosis is not associated with increased fracture risk in children and adolescents. J Pediatr 2005;147(3):327–31.
[72] Tangpricha V, Kelly A, Stephenson A, et al. An update on the screening, diagnosis, management, and treatment of vitamin D deficiency in individuals with cystic fibrosis: evidence-based recommendations from the Cystic Fibrosis Foundation. J Clin Endocrinol Metab 2012;97(4):1082–93.
[73] Shepherd D, Belessis Y, Katz T, et al. Single high-dose oral vitamin D(3) (stoss) therapy - a solution to vitamin D deficiency in children with cystic fibrosis? J Cyst Fibros 2012;12(2):177–82.
[74] Modan-Moses D, Pinhas-Hamiel O, Munitz-Shenkar D, et al. Vitamin D status in pediatric patients with a history of malignancy. Pediatr Res 2012;72(6):620–4.
[75] Rosen GP, Beebe KL, Shaibi GQ. Vitamin D levels differ by cancer diagnosis and decline over time in survivors of childhood cancer. Pediatr Blood Cancer 2013;60(6):949–52.

Advances in Pediatrics 60 (2013) 107–139

ADVANCES IN PEDIATRICS

# Infections Related to International Travel and Adoption

Kristina N. Feja, MD, MPH[a,b,c], Robert W. Tolan, Jr, MD[a,b,*]

[a]Division of Allergy, Immunology and Infectious Diseases, The Children's Hospital at Saint Peter's University Hospital, 254 Easton Avenue, New Brunswick, NJ 08901, USA; [b]Drexel University College of Medicine, 2900 West Queen Lane, Philadelphia, PA 19129, USA; [c]School of Public Health, University of Medicine and Dentistry of New Jersey, 683 Hoes Lane West, Piscataway, NJ 08854, USA

**Keywords**

• Travel medicine • International adoptees • Evaluating ill pediatric traveler • Malaria

**Key points**

- Health care providers must be proactive in screening patients with travel plans to optimize pretravel preventive efforts.
- Children visiting friends and relatives are at increased risk for travel-related morbidity.
- Illness in a returning pediatric traveler must be assumed to be travel-related until such diagnoses are excluded.
- The details of a travel history (when? why? where?) are key to formulating a differential diagnosis.
- International adoptees must be thoroughly evaluated for infectious diseases.
- Vaccinations need to be updated for every child who is planning to travel and for all internationally adopted children.

## INTRODUCTION

In an increasingly accessible world in which children frequently travel with their parents, it is important to remember that infectious diseases know no boundaries. International tourism is on the rise, with international tourist arrivals worldwide increasing from 528 million in 1995 to 990 million in 2011; forecasts predict more than 1 billion arrivals in 2012 [1,2]. According to the

Disclosures: None.

*Corresponding author. MOB 3110, 254 Easton Avenue, New Brunswick, NJ 08901. *E-mail address:* RTolan@saintpetersuh.com

0065-3101/13/$ – see front matter
http://dx.doi.org/10.1016/j.yapd.2013.04.007 

Office of Travel and Tourism Industries monthly surveys of outbound United States residents at major international gateway airports, more than 58 million traveled outside the United States (including Mexico and Canada) in 2011 [3]. Of those traveling overseas (to countries other than Canada or Mexico), 66% (17,800,000) were going to the Caribbean, Asia, Central America, South America, the Middle East, and Africa. Top destinations included the United Kingdom, France, Italy, the Dominican Republic, Germany, Jamaica, China, Spain, and India. Seven percent of adults travel with children; this translates into approximately 1.9 million children traveling internationally each year [4]. Approximately 15% of returning travelers from the developing world self-report health symptoms, and 8% require medical evaluation [5]. Therefore, pediatric health care providers should be familiar with the differential diagnoses of diseases in returning child travelers, their evaluation, and their management.

## PRETRAVEL ASSESSMENT AND ADVICE

Every international trip ideally should start with a pretravel consultation. However, data show that children are less likely than adults to receive pretravel advice [6]. Parents often do not volunteer their travel plans. Therefore, pediatric health care providers need to actively screen families for upcoming travel plans. To best determine the travel risks facing a child, it is important to determine where, when, for how long, and why the child is traveling. Providers should obtain details about itinerary, accommodations, high-risk activities, and the intended use of local health care facilities, so that advice can be tailored to the child's specific situation [7]. A pretravel consultation, including recommendations for vaccines (both routine and travel-related), prophylactic medications, avoidance of insect bites, and food and water safety can greatly increase the safety of children traveling abroad. Parents of children with chronic illnesses should be advised to carry a summary of medical records and enough medications to last the entire trip.

The reason for travel is an important factor in determining the risk for acquiring disease. In 2011, 39% of United States residents traveling overseas (not including Canada or Mexico) stated leisure/recreation/holidays as the main purpose for travel, whereas 35% were visiting friends and relatives (VFR). However, when all purposes of travel were taken into account the proportion listing VFR increased to 46% [4]. Those VFR have increased risk of acquiring travel-related illnesses such as malaria, typhoid fever, intestinal parasites, hepatitis A, hepatitis B, and tuberculosis because they:

- Are less likely to receive pretravel advice
- Are less likely to follow any such advice they receive
- Are more likely to go to underdeveloped destinations with poor public health infrastructures
- Are likely to stay longer
- Are more likely to consume local food and water
- Are more likely to have more close contact with local populations [7–9]

Immigrants VFR are 8 times more likely to contract malaria (especially falciparum malaria) and 7 times more likely to fall victim to typhoid fever, compared with tourist travelers [9]. In today's increasingly global world, varying characteristics within this population have prompted new terms, such as travelers VFR and immigrant VFR, leading some experts to propose better-defined criteria so that studies can more accurately assess specific risks [10].

Children are more likely than adults to be VFR (17% vs 10%) and VFR travel increases the younger the child [6]. In the Boston area travel clinics, 35% of children younger than 18 years were VFR and, of these, 46% were younger than 5 years, compared with less than 5% in the non-VFR group [8]. These children are at increased risk because of the lack of preexisting immunity to diseases that their parents may have been exposed to as children while growing up in the destination country [7]. Special attention should be paid to these children, with emphasis on educating the parents, who often are unaware of the level of risk or have a different level of perceived risk, especially when they are traveling to their country of origin.

## ROUTINE IMMUNIZATIONS

Developed countries have greatly reduced the incidence of vaccine-preventable infections with comprehensive vaccination programs. However, these diseases remain endemic in many regions of the world. Therefore, parents should be informed of these risks, and pediatric health care providers should make sure that the child has had all age-appropriate routine vaccines. Often, vaccines can be given early or on an accelerated schedule to provide optimal protection to the traveling child. Diphtheria, tetanus, pertussis, and *Haemophilus influenzae* type b (Hib) vaccination should be up to date, as these diseases are endemic worldwide.

### Measles

Measles is still common in some parts of Europe, Asia, the Pacific, and Africa, with thousands of cases detected in 2012 in Ukraine, Romania, France, Spain, Italy, and the United Kingdom [11]. These outbreaks have resulted in an increased number of reported cases (222) in 2011 in the United States [12,13], 90% of which were imported from abroad [13]. Measles is an extremely contagious disease, so it is recommended that all travelers 6 months or older be vaccinated. Children 6 to 11 months of age should be given 1 dose of measles-mumps-rubella (MMR) vaccine. Because of decreased immunogenicity in this age group owing to the presence of maternal measles antibodies, they will require 2 more doses starting at 12 to 15 months of age. Nonimmune travelers 12 months or older should receive 2 doses of MMR separated by at least 28 days [14].

### Hepatitis A

Hepatitis A virus (HAV) infection, related to a region's level of sanitation, is intermediately to highly endemic in parts of Africa, Central and South America, Southern and Eastern Europe, the Middle East, and Asia [15]. According to the

World Health Organization (WHO), there are approximately 1.4 million cases of HAV infection each year [16]. Transmission occurs after ingestion of contaminated food or water or direct contact with an infectious person. Asymptomatic, infected children may shed HAV for months, becoming a source of infection for their community. Nonimmune children 12 months or older traveling to these regions should receive at least 1 dose of HAV vaccine, preferably at least 2 weeks before travel, to allow protective antibody production to occur. Infants younger than 12 months should be given 0.02 mL/kg of immunoglobulin (intramuscular) before travel, which will provide protection for up to 3 months; for longer trips a dose of 0.06 mL/kg is recommended at departure and every 5 months thereafter [17].

### Hepatitis B

It is estimated that 350 million people worldwide have chronic hepatitis B (HB) infection. Much of the world, except Western Europe, the United States, parts of Canada and South America, Australia, and New Zealand, has high (>8%) or intermediate (2%–8%) prevalence of chronic HB infection (by HB surface antigen [HBsAg] status) [18]. Because the risk of development of chronic infection is inversely related to the age of primary infection, all children should be immunized with 3 doses of the recombinant vaccine. If the optimal 3 doses cannot be completed before travel, 1 or 2 doses will still provide some protection.

### Polio

Although polio was eliminated from the Americas in 1991 by the Global Polio Eradication Initiative, as of December 4, 2012 there were still 205 cases reported in Pakistan, Nigeria, Afghanistan, and Chad [19]. Children traveling to high-risk areas should receive a 4-dose series of inactivated polio vaccine (IPV) at 2, 4, 6 to 18 months, and 4 to 6 years of age. An accelerated schedule (first dose at ≥6 weeks of age, second dose in ≥4 weeks, third dose in ≥4 weeks, and fourth dose in 6 months) is available if needed to obtain protection for travel to an endemic region. A single, lifetime booster dose is recommended for adults 18 years and older who travel to areas with polio cases, even if they received the full series as a child [20].

### Meningococcus

Meningococcal disease outbreaks (mostly serogroup W-135) secondary to overcrowding have occurred during pilgrimages to Mecca. Therefore, Saudi Arabia requires proof of vaccination with quadrivalent vaccine within 3 years for those traveling during the annual Hajj and Umrah pilgrimages. The "African Meningitis Belt" is an area with a population of 400 million inhabitants extending from Senegal to Ethiopia in sub-Saharan Africa in which large, yearly epidemics of meningococcal disease (predominantly serogroup A) occur during the dry season (December to June). There were more than 22,000 recorded cases in 2010, with a case fatality rate of greater than 10%, and 800,000 cases in the prior 15 years [21]. Furthermore, scattered outbreaks can occur anywhere worldwide. Routine vaccination with quadrivalent conjugated vaccine

(MCV4) is recommended at 11 to 12 years of age with a booster dose at 16 years. Vaccination is also recommended for children traveling to the meningitis belt or other epidemic areas, with 2 doses of MCV4 given 8 weeks apart for 9- to 23-month-olds and 1 dose for 2- to 10-year-olds. Booster doses are recommended 3 years later if the initial dose was given at younger than 7 years of age, then every 5 years if still at high risk. If the first dose was given at 7 years of age or older, a booster dose should be given every 5 years if still at high risk [22]. Protective antibody levels ensue in approximately 7 to 10 days.

### Influenza

Annual influenza vaccination should be provided for children from the age of 6 months, and should be given 2 weeks or more before departure for those traveling to the southern hemisphere between April and September. Travel to the northern hemisphere in winter months, travel lasting longer than 30 days, and VFR are also risk factors for infection [23].

### Pneumococcus

In 2005, the WHO estimated that 1.6 million deaths were due to pneumococcal infection [24]. Although travel in itself does not increase a child's risk for pneumococcal infection, lack of access to appropriate health care can lead to poor outcome if pneumococcal disease occurs. Therefore, all children younger than 5 years old should receive the 13-valent pneumococcal conjugate vaccine (PCV-13), given in 3 doses (2, 4, and 6 months), plus 1 booster (12–15 months). Older children at high risk for invasive disease should also receive 23-valent polysaccharide vaccine. A more detailed immunization schedule, based on age and risk group, is available in the American Academy of Pediatrics (AAP) Red Book 2012. Although the distribution of serotypes causing invasive pneumococcal disease varies among North America, Europe, Australia, Africa, Latin America, and Asia [25], PCV-13 should cover more than 80% of serogroups in each region [26].

## TRAVEL VACCINATIONS

### Yellow fever

Yellow fever virus, transmitted by mosquitoes of the *Aedes* or *Haemagogus* spp, belongs to the genus Flavivirus and causes acute hemorrhagic disease with a high case fatality rate in Africa and South America. An estimated 200,000 cases occur yearly worldwide, leading to 30,000 deaths [27]. However, only 3199 cases were reported to the WHO from 8 countries in Africa (n = 2570) and 5 countries in South America (n = 629) between 2000 and 2004 [28]. The case fatality rate varied from 11% in Africa to 47% in South America in 2004 [29].

Some countries require proof of vaccination at entry because the mosquito vector and potential host is present, so that introduction of the virus by an infected person can lead to ongoing transmission in that country. Other countries require proof of vaccination owing to the risk of transmission of yellow fever. Areas at risk for transmission of yellow fever (currently 31 countries in Africa and 13 countries in Central and South America) are determined by the WHO through case counts, yellow fever sero-surveys, and presence of vectors and animal reservoirs. A current country list for yellow fever vaccine requirements is available at the WHO International Travel and Health Web site: http://www.who.int/ith/chapters/ith2012en_chap6.pdf. (Appendix 1 lists important Internet links to various travel-related sources.) Because of the lack of specific treatment and high case fatality rate, yellow fever vaccination is recommended for all travelers 9 months or older who are visiting an area with evidence of persistent or periodic virus transmission, or visiting countries that require proof of vaccination. Owing to adverse events from the vaccine, only patients traveling to high-risk areas or those traveling to countries with requirements should be vaccinated. The live, attenuated virus vaccine is administered as a single injection with repeat doses required every 10 years. Although most adverse events are mild (low-grade fever, headache, or myalgias in 10%–30% of recipients), some patients contract yellow fever vaccine–associated neurologic disease, which includes meningoencephalitis, Guillain-Barré syndrome, acute disseminated encephalomyelitis, bulbar palsy, and Bell palsy. This disease spectrum occurs more frequently in young infants and those older than 60 years. Another adverse event, yellow fever vaccine–associated viscerotropic disease (which can result in multiorgan failure and death), is also seen more in older (>60 years) vaccinees. Yellow fever vaccine is contraindicated in:

- Infants younger than 6 months
- Those with a history of hypersensitivity reaction to vaccine components (eggs, chicken, or gelatin)
- Those with thymus disorders
- Immunosuppressed patients

Precautions should be used in infants aged 6 to 8 months and, whenever possible, travel to yellow fever–endemic areas should be postponed or avoided. Precautions should also be taken in older (>60 years) travelers, especially if they are receiving their first dose of vaccine, those with asymptomatic human immunodeficiency virus (HIV) infection, pregnant or breastfeeding women, and those with certain chronic medical conditions. Inactivated vaccines and oral Ty21a vaccine may be given at any time relative to yellow fever vaccination. However, live virus vaccines should be administered simultaneously or 30 days apart [30]. The most current vaccination requirements should be checked at the Centers for Disease Control and Prevention (CDC) travel Web site (www.cdc.gov/travel/) or the WHO Travel and Health Web site (http://www.who.int/topics/travel/en/), or with the embassy or consulate of the destination country.

### Typhoid fever

*Salmonella* Typhi, the cause of typhoid fever, is endemic in developing countries; travel to South Central Asia (the Indian subcontinent) poses the highest risk of disease [31,32]. There are approximately 22 million cases a year, resulting in 200,000 deaths worldwide [33]. Children account for a 38% to 42% of cases [32,34], therefore any child traveling to an area with recognized risk for typhoid fever should be vaccinated. There are 2 vaccines available, intramuscular Vi capsular polysaccharide vaccine (ViCPS) and an oral live vaccine, which contains an attenuated *Salmonella* Typhi strain (Ty21a). Both vaccines have an efficacy ranging from 50% to 80% [22]. Parents should be educated that the vaccine is not completely effective, so food and water safety measures should still be carefully observed. Children 2 years or older should receive 1 dose of ViCPS 2 weeks or more before travel. A booster dose is recommended every 2 years if there is ongoing risk. The Ty21a vaccine is for children 6 years and older, as it comes in the form of a capsule that should be swallowed whole. A total of 4 capsules should be taken 1 hour before meals 48 hours apart, with completion of the series 1 week before travel for maximum efficacy. A booster dose is needed every 5 years. The capsules should be refrigerated but not frozen, and should not be taken with liquids warmer than 37°C. Doses should be delayed for longer than 72 hours after receipt of any antibiotic. This vaccine is contraindicated in immunocompromised patients [33]. *Salmonella* Paratyphi may cause a similar illness, but there is no vaccine currently available.

### Japanese encephalitis

Japanese encephalitis virus (JEV) is the most common vaccine-preventable cause of encephalitis. The mosquito-borne disease is endemic in parts of Asia and the western Pacific, and affects mostly children. Although most cases are asymptomatic, of the symptomatic cases 25% end in death and 50% result in severe neurologic sequelae [35]. There is no specific treatment. Transmission predominantly occurs in rural, agricultural areas where there is rice cultivation and flooding irrigation. Therefore, short-term travelers who visit only major urban centers are at low risk. The CDC recommends vaccination for those traveling for 1 month or more to endemic areas during the JEV transmission season. Vaccine should also be considered for:

- Those traveling to endemic areas for less than 1 month, but who plan to participate in outdoor activities
- Those traveling to an area with an ongoing JEV outbreak
- Those who are going to an endemic area, but are unsure of their plans regarding destinations, activities, or duration of stay [36]

The inactivated, mouse brain–derived JEV vaccine (JE-MB) that was available since 1992 for children upward of 1 year old is no longer manufactured, and the remaining doses expired in 2011. A new, inactivated, Vero cell culture–derived JEV vaccine (JE-VC, trade name IXIARO), given in 2 doses 28 days apart, was licensed in the United States in 2009 for persons 17 years and older. At present, there is no Food and Drug Administration (FDA)-licensed JEV vaccine for children younger than 17 years. Pediatric safety and immunogenicity trials are currently under way in children 2 months to 17 years of age in the Philippines and the United States, but FDA licensure for use in children is not expected for several years [37]. Options to consider for children traveling to rural areas with ongoing transmission and prolonged stay are:

- Enroll the patient in one of the ongoing vaccine trials in the United States (sites located in New York, Maryland, Massachusetts, North Carolina, and Florida)
- Use the vaccine off-label
- Have the child receive vaccination at an international traveler's health clinic in Asia (sites available at: http://www.cdc.gov/japaneseencephalitis/vaccine/vaccineChildren.html)

More country-specific details to assess risk are available at the CDC travel Web site.

### Rabies

Rabies is a fatal viral encephalitis transmitted via saliva from a rabid mammal, usually through a bite wound. Only a few places worldwide have no risk of rabies. Bats, foxes, raccoons, and other wild animals can transmit the virus. However, in Central and South America, Asia, and Africa, more than 90% of human cases are transmitted by dogs [38]. Rabies is most common in children younger than 15 years [39], most likely owing to children's curiosity and attraction to animals. Therefore, children traveling to rabies-enzootic countries should avoid contact with stray animals, wild animals, and bats, and should be vaccinated if immediate access to appropriate medical care (including biologics) is limited. The primary vaccination schedule includes 3 1.0-mL intramuscular injections of human diploid cell rabies vaccine or purified chick embryo cell vaccine on days 0, 7, and 21 or 28. If a fully vaccinated child is exposed to rabies, 2 booster doses of vaccine should be given on days 0 and 3 after exposure, but no rabies immunoglobulin is needed.

### Bacille Calmette-Guérin

Bacille Calmette-Guérin (BCG) has variable efficacy in preventing tuberculosis (TB), but it is most useful in preventing serious disease (meningitis and miliary TB) in young children. Children who have traveled in the prior 12 months are more likely to have positive tuberculin skin tests (TST) than are those who have not traveled [40]. Vaccination may be considered in young children who will have a long-term stay in a highly TB-endemic area. A more common and practical approach than vaccination is to test children before travel with a TST or an interferon-$\gamma$ release assay (IGRA) if older than 4 years, and then again 12 weeks after returning from travel to assess for TB infection.

## MALARIA PREVENTION

Malaria is a parasitic disease caused by protozoan *Plasmodium* and is transmitted by *Anopheles* mosquitoes. Although global malaria incidence has decreased by 17% since 2000, according to WHO estimates there were approximately 216 million cases of malaria leading to 655,000 deaths in 2010. Eighty-one percent of cases and 91% of deaths occurred in Africa, where *Plasmodium falciparum* is common (Fig. 1) [41]. Young children often lack immunity and are most

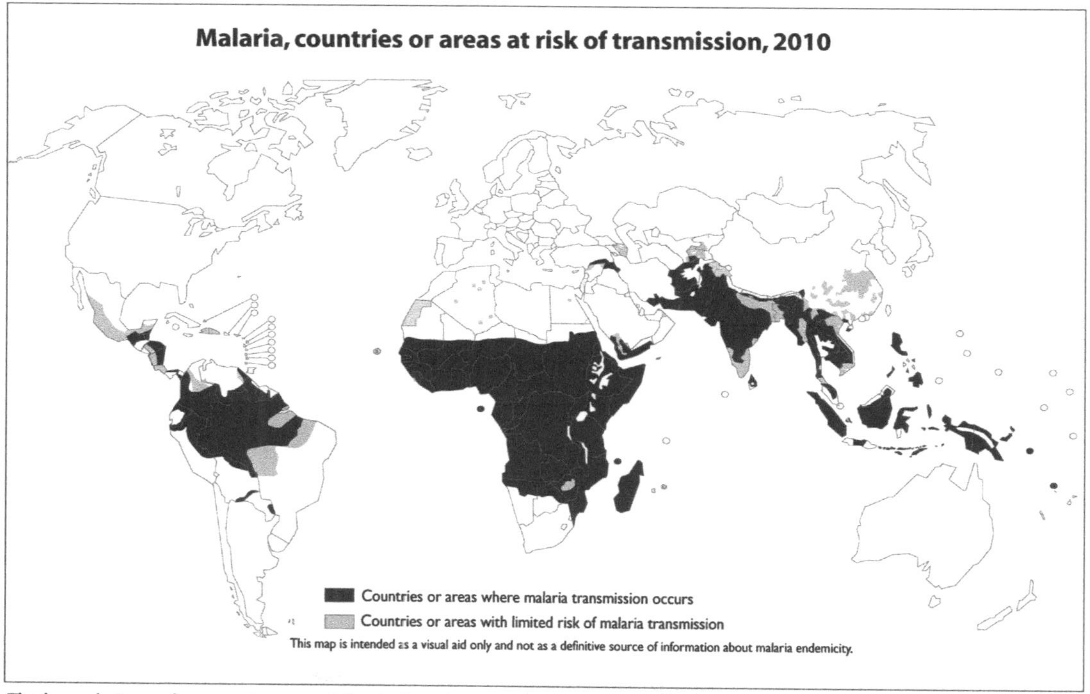


The boundaries and names shown and the designations used on this map do not imply the expression of any opinion whatsoever on the part of the World Health Organization concerning the legal status of any country, territory, city or area or of its authorities, or concerning the delimitation of its frontiers or boundaries. Dotted lines on maps represent approximate border lines for which there may not yet be full agreement.

World Health Organization

**Fig. 1.** Countries or areas at risk of transmission of malaria, 2010. (*From* World Health Organization. World malaria report. 2011. Available at: http://www.who.int/malaria/publications/atoz/9789241564403/en/index.html. Accessed December 1, 2012.)

likely to acquire severe malaria, including cerebral malaria, as evidenced by the fact that approximately 86% of deaths globally occur in children younger than 5 years [41]. WHO travel guidelines recommend that "parents should be advised not to take infants or young children to areas where there is a risk of falciparum malaria" [42]. It is therefore extremely important to prescribe the appropriate prophylactic medication for children traveling to regions where malaria transmission occurs.

Factors to be evaluated before prescribing malaria prophylaxis include:

- The presence of malaria transmission at the destination
- The amount of time until departure
- The antimalarial drug resistance patterns at the destination
- The length of travel
- The weight of child
- The ability of the child to swallow tablets or capsules

Chemoprophylaxis always needs to be started before travel (from 1–2 days to >2 weeks) and taken 7 days to 4 weeks after leaving the malaria-endemic area. There are daily and weekly dosing schedules, depending on the agent. If a weekly regimen is used, phrases such as "Malaria Monday" can help with adherence. The CDC has an interactive Web site called CDC Malaria Map Application with detailed, country-specific maps, information about drug resistance, and recommendations for prophylaxis (http://cdc-malaria.ncsa.uiuc.edu/).

Medications are somewhat limited in children by age, weight, and medication form. Doxycycline should not be given to children younger than 8 years, because of permanent staining of the teeth. Atovaquone-proguanil and mefloquine (according to the WHO) should not be given to infants weighing 5 kg or less. Primaquine should not be given to children deficient in glucose-6-phosphate dehydrogenase (G6PD). Doxycycline and chloroquine phosphate come in suspension form. However, mefloquine, primaquine, and atovaquone-proguanil come only in tablet form, which sometimes needs to be divided. Pharmacists can pulverize tablets and put them in a gelatin capsule or, if children are unable to swallow caplets or tablets, then pulverized drug can be mixed with a small amount of sweet food (eg, apple sauce, chocolate syrup, jelly) and the mixture fed to the child. Table 1 contains detailed dosing information.

Although there are few studies, most antimalarials are safe for long-term prophylaxis (>6 months), except for chloroquine, during the use of which retinal toxicity can occur after a cumulative dose of 100 g [42]. In the case of long-term travel, parents should be reminded to increase the chemoprophylaxis dose based on the growing child's weight gain.

## Prevention of insect bites

Malaria prophylaxis should always be accompanied by personal protective measures that prevent mosquito and insect bites. There are multiple mosquito-borne illnesses in the tropics, such as malaria, dengue fever, yellow fever, Japanese encephalitis, and chikungunya. For some of these illnesses

**Table 1**
Malaria prophylaxis

| Drug (form) | Where | Pediatric dose | Schedule | Comments |
|---|---|---|---|---|
| Atovaquone-proguanil (pediatric tablet, adult tablet) | All areas | 5–8 kg: 1/2 ped tab QD<br>>8–10 kg: 3/4 ped tab QD<br>>10–20 kg: 1 ped tab QD<br>>20–30 kg: 2 ped tab QD<br>>30–40 kg: 3 ped tab QD<br>>40 kg: 1 adult tab QD | 1–2 d before travel → 7 d after leaving<br>Take with food, milky drink | Good for last-minute and short travel<br>Side effects uncommon: abdominal pain, nausea, vomiting, headache<br>Expensive |
| Doxycycline (tablet, suspension) | All areas | 2.2 mg/kg QD<br>Maximum 100 mg/d | 1–2 d before travel → 4 wk after leaving | CI: <8 y, pregnancy<br>Side effect: sun sensitivity, GI<br>Cheapest<br>Good for last minute |
| Chloroquine phosphate (tablet, suspension) | Areas with chloroquine-sensitive malaria | 5 mg/kg base (8.3 mg/kg salt) Q week<br>Maximum 300 mg base | 1–2 wk before travel → 4 wk after leaving<br>Same day of week | Good for long travel<br>May exacerbate psoriasis |
| Mefloquine (tablet) | Areas with mefloquine-sensitive malaria | ≤9 kg (WHO limit >5 kg): 4.6 mg/kg base (5 mg/kg salt) Q week<br>>9–19 kg: 1/4 tab Q week<br>>19–30 kg: 1/2 tab Q week<br>>30–45 kg: 3/4 tab Q week<br>>45 kg: 1 tab Q week | ≥2 wk before travel → 4 wk after leaving<br>Same day of week | Good for long trips<br>CI: psychiatric disorders, seizures<br>Not recommended for patients with cardiac conduction abnormalities |
| Primaquine (tablet) | Short travel to areas with principally *P. vivax* | 0.5 mg/kg base (0.8 mg/kg salt) QD<br>Maximum 30 mg base QD | 1–2 d before travel → 7 d after leaving | CI: G6PD deficiency, pregnancy, lactation (unless infant has normal G6PD level)<br>Good for short travel |

All drugs are taken orally.

*Abbreviations:* CI, contraindication; G6PD, glucose-6-phosphate dehydrogenase; GI, gastrointestinal; ped, pediatric; QD, once daily; Q week, once weekly; tab, tablet.

*Adapted from* Arguin PM, Mali S. Malaria. In: Brunette GW, Kozarsky PE, Magill AJ, et al, editors. CDC health information for international travel 2012. New York: Oxford University Press; 2012. p. 236–7.

the only preventive measure is avoiding mosquito bites. Travelers should avoid peak hours of biting (*Anopheles* mosquitoes tend to bite from dusk to dawn, whereas *Aedes* mosquitoes, the transmitters of dengue virus and chikungunya, bite during the daytime).

Protective measures include the use of insect repellents, mosquito nets, mosquito coils, aerosol sprays, and protective clothing. Conventional insect repellents include DEET (*N,N*-diethyl-*meta*-toluamide; ≤30% strength for children) and picaridin; biopesticide repellents include oil of lemon eucalyptus, PMD (para-menthane-3,8-diol), and IR3535 [43]. These agents should be applied to exposed skin, avoiding contact with mucous membranes and damaged skin, and with strict adherence to the manufacturer's instructions. DEET has the longest-lasting protective effect when compared with IR3535 and other repellents, such as soybean oil and citronella [44]. The repellent effect lasts longer when applied to the clothing and when higher-concentration products are used (except DEET >50%) [43,45]. Permethrin-treated clothing not only repels but also kills ticks, mosquitoes, and other insects. When using sunscreen, the sunscreen should be applied first and the insect repellent second. Most repellents can be used on infants older than 2 months [43].

Insecticide-treated nets are highly effective in protecting against mosquitoes during sleep, although some resistance to the insecticide has been noted to arise [45]. Indoor sleeping quarters should be sprayed with aerosol sprays before bedtime to kill insects. Furthermore, protective clothing, such as long-sleeved shirts, long pants, hats, and closed shoes, offer protection. Securing screens on windows and doors and air conditioning is also effective in keeping out insects [45]. Any one of these measures has a protective effect, and more than one measure in combination has an additive effect [46].

## WATER AND FOOD SAFETY

Multiple infections can be transmitted by contaminated food and water, including typhoid fever, hepatitis A, salmonellosis, campylobacteriosis, shigellosis, cholera, norovirus infection, helminths, and traveler's diarrhea. Contamination by human or animal feces can occur because of a lack of proper hygiene and sanitation. Food and water aboard commercial airlines can also be contaminated in the departure country. Therefore, it is imperative to educate parents on how to avoid contaminated food and water both for their children and themselves.

### Water

Contamination of tap water in many developing countries makes it unsafe for drinking, preparing food or drinks, cooking, making ice, and brushing teeth [47]. When traveling to regions with an unsafe water supply, children should only drink bottled water from an unopened, sealed container or water that has been brought to a visible rolling boil for at least 1 minute. It is not uncommon to find bottled water with a broken seal that has been refilled with tap water. Beverages made with boiling water, such as coffee and tea, are generally safe. Bottled carbonated water is safer than noncarbonated water, but the outer surface of beverage containers should be cleaned before drinking from the container directly. For further advice on disinfecting and filtering water, the reader is referred to the CDC Yellow Book Section on Water Disinfection for Travelers: http://wwwnc.cdc.gov/travel/yellowbook/2012/chapter-2-the-pre-travel-consultation/water-disinfection-for-travelers.htm.

Exposure to contaminated water can also occur through recreational water use, such as in swimming pools, spas, rivers, freshwater ponds, lakes, or ocean beaches. These activities can lead to a variety of illnesses, including diarrheal diseases, skin infections from contaminated wounds, leptospirosis, schistosomiasis (transmitted by snails), legionellosis, and pseudomonal infections. Travelers should avoid swimming in contaminated bodies of water, wading barefoot in shallow waters, having warm freshwater enter the nose, and swimming with open wounds in ocean water [47,48].

### Food

Hands should be washed properly before preparing or consuming food. Children should eat thoroughly cooked food that is still hot and steaming, because cooked food left standing for hours can allow bacterial growth and may be recontaminated from food handling. Breastfeeding infants younger than 6 months is a good way to ensure food safety. Boiled water should be used to prepare formulas. Raw fruits and vegetables should be washed with clean water then peeled. Fruits and vegetables that cannot be peeled and properly washed, such as raspberries and lettuce, are common causes of food-borne diseases. The CDC's slogan "boil it, cook it, peel it, or forget it," can easily be remembered by families (Box 1).

## EPIDEMIOLOGY OF INFECTIOUS DISEASES IN TRAVELERS

Years ago, data for rates of illness in returning travelers were usually limited to institutions or travel clinics serving a single geographic area, focusing on a single disease or a particular high-risk destination. In 1995, the International Society of Travel Medicine and CDC established the GeoSentinel Surveillance Network, consisting of 54 travel clinics in 24 countries on 6 continents, which have seen more than 43,000 travelers from 237 destination countries. The goal was to have clinician-based sentinel surveillance of travel-related morbidity and to collect data on demographics, travel history, clinical symptoms, reason for travel, pretravel advice, and diagnoses using standardized lists of individual diagnoses. These diagnoses were grouped into broad-spectrum categories.

A study by Freedman and colleagues [31] analyzed disease in more than 17,000 ill travelers from 1996 to 2005 categorized by the place of exposure. Overall morbidity in travelers, listed in order of decreasing rate (cases per 1000 patients) was found to be:

- Systemic febrile illness (226)
- Acute diarrhea (222)
- Skin disorders (170)

**Box 1: Food and water safety preventive measures**

- Drink bottled water (with intact seal) or boil for 1 minute. If boiling is not possible, a combination of methods should be used, such as filtration followed by chemical disinfection
- Avoid ice, including popsicles and flavored ices
- Avoid brushing teeth with unsafe water
- Avoid swallowing water during showering or bathing
- Always wash hands thoroughly with soap and water before preparing or consuming food
- Eat thoroughly cooked food that is still hot and steaming
- Avoid raw vegetables and fruits that cannot be peeled or shelled, and those with damaged skin
- Peel fruits/vegetables yourself after washing hands
- Avoid foods (including ice cream) and drinks from street and beach vendors
- Boil unpasteurized (raw) milk before consumption and avoid other unpasteurized dairy products
- Avoid dishes containing raw or undercooked eggs, seafood, and meats

*Adapted from* Watson JC, Hlavsa MC, Griffin PM. Food & water precautions. In: Brunette GW, Kozarsky PE, Magill AJ, et al, editors. CDC health information for international travel 2012. New York: Oxford University Press; 2012. p. 74–6; and World Health Organization. Common sense precautions for avoiding unsafe food and drink. In: World Health Organization. International travel and health: situation as on 1 January 2012. Geneva: WHO Press; 2012. p. 48.

- Chronic diarrhea (113)
- Nondiarrheal gastrointestinal disorders (82)
- Respiratory illnesses (77)
- Nonspecific symptoms (70)

There are significant differences in proportionate morbidity noted among different regions. Systemic febrile illnesses are diagnosed disproportionately more in patients who travel to sub-Saharan Africa (371 cases/1000 patients) and Southeast Asia (248 cases/1000 patients), whereas acute diarrhea is found disproportionately more frequently in those who travel to South Central Asia (including the Indian subcontinent; 327 cases/1000 patients) and Central America (234 cases/1000 patients). Skin disorders are seen more frequently in patients traveling to South America and the Caribbean. This study also confirms that illnesses thought to occur rarely, such as Ebola, Japanese encephalitis, rabies, tetanus, diphtheria, plague, tularemia, murine typhus, Rift Valley fever, polio, anthrax, yellow fever, primary amoebic meningoencephalitis ($n = 0$), Hantavirus, cholera, Ross River virus, African trypanosomiasis, legionellosis, and meningococcal meningitis ($n = 1$), are truly rare in travelers [31].

Hagmann and colleagues [6] performed an analysis on GeoSentinel Surveillance Network data from 1997 to 2007 for 1591 pediatric and 32,668 adult travelers with laboratory-confirmed or probable diagnoses, and compared the two groups. Asia, sub-Saharan Africa, and Latin America are the most frequently visited regions by both groups, accounting for 75% of children's travel. When compared with adults, children are more likely to stay longer than 30 days, present in the first week after returning (45%–46% of 0–11-year-olds vs 34% of adults), and be hospitalized for their illness (16% of 0–5-year-olds vs 10% of adults). Diagnoses fall into 4 major categories, diarrhea (28%) being the most common, followed by skin disorders (25%), systemic febrile illnesses (23%), and respiratory illnesses (11%). Vaccine-preventable diseases accounted for 2% of cases [6].

## EVALUATING THE ILL CHILD TRAVELER

First, all ill children should be asked if they have traveled outside the United States or their country of residence at any time, as this information is often not volunteered by the parents and often not obtained by providers. A history of travel, especially in the last 6 months, to a developing country will result in a different evaluation with a different set of differential diagnoses. The most important component of the evaluation of an ill returning child traveler is a comprehensive, very detailed history that incorporates the questions listed in Box 2.

The detailed history will establish risk factors for different diseases.

Once the place of travel is obtained, the diseases specific to that country/region should be determined. The CDC's Traveler's Health Web site has a destination section (http://wwwnc.cdc.gov/travel/destinations/list.htm), which provides specific information on a particular country's latest outbreaks,

**Box 2: Important components of a travel history**

Where did the child travel to? (country with exact area/city, urban vs rural)

When did the child travel and for how long?

What was the reason for travel (tourism, VFR)?

Did the child receive pretravel advice? (routine and travel vaccinations, malaria prophylaxis)

Review water sources used (tap vs bottled or boiled water, ice, brushing teeth, unpasteurized milk)

Review food sources used (restaurants, street vendors, raw foods, unpasteurized dairy products)

Any ill contacts encountered during the trip? (diarrhea, fevers, chronic cough, tuberculosis)

Did the child have any contact with animals or insects? (bed nets)

What type of activities did the child participate in? (swimming, camping, hiking)

Did the child receive any medical care in the destination country? (names of medications)

Symptoms (exact start time, chronology, fever characteristics)

transmission risks for yellow fever and malaria, and other specific health information. The exact timing of the travel and onset of symptoms will help determine the incubation period of the disease (Table 2).

If the child required medical care in the destination country, the parents may not know what medication the child received. The parents should then be asked to bring in medication bottles, any paperwork received, or have information faxed from the foreign provider, regardless of the language used. Often children will receive a course of fluoroquinolones for presumed typhoid fever during a febrile episode, and diagnostic evaluation may not be performed. The importance of receiving culture results or medication names should be stressed, so the parents have the incentive to perform the necessary legwork. In the era of Internet access, a little investigative work can yield considerable useful information.

The diagnostic approach to the ill returned traveler depends on the history. A general approach, which should be modified as appropriate, is shown in Box 3.

## Systemic febrile illness

Fever in a returning traveler, especially a child, requires prompt and thorough evaluation. Although posttravel systemic febrile illness results in a smaller proportionate morbidity among children than in adults [6,31], these illnesses, such as malaria, typhoid fever, and dengue, tend to be the most serious. Whereas only 14% of children with all diagnoses required hospitalization, this number increased to 36% of children with systemic febrile illnesses [6]. This percentage of hospitalized children increased to 39% with a specific diagnosis of dengue fever, 60% with typhoid fever, and 69% with malaria. Older pediatric age, male gender, and prolonged travel (>30 days) were all associated with systemic febrile illness [6]. In 24% to 40% of travelers, no specific cause for the fever was identified [31,49].

**Table 2**
Incubation period for travel-related illnesses

| Disease | Average incubation period | Range in days |
|---|---|---|
| Dengue | 4–7 d | 3–14 |
| Chikungunya | 3–7 d | 2–12 |
| Malaria | 7 d to 3 mo to y | |
| Typhoid fever | 7–14 d | 3–60 |
| *Salmonella* gastroenteritis | 6–72 h | |
| Hepatitis A | 28 d | 15–50 |
| Hepatitis B | 90 d | 14–160 |
| Yellow fever | 3–6 d | |
| Schistosomiasis | 1–3 mo | |
|   *S japonicum* | 4–6 wk | |
|   *S mansoni* | 6–8 wk | |
|   *S haematobium* | 10–12 wk | |

**Box 3: Evaluation of the ill child after international travel**

Thorough physical examination
Complete blood count and differential
Electrolytes and liver function tests
Malaria smears with fever spikes × 3
Blood cultures with fever spikes × 3
Stool: cultures, ova and parasites × 3
Epstein-Barr virus and cytomegalovirus titers
Dengue titers (if appropriate)
Influenza testing (if appropriate)
Hepatitis serologies (A, B, C)
TST or IGRA
HIV testing, Rapid plasma reagin test
Chest radiograph

*Malaria*

Malaria is the most common specific cause of systemic febrile illness in both adults (28%) and children (35%) who have traveled abroad [6,31,49] and is 1 of the 3 most common causes in all regions of the developing world [31]. Malaria is also the single most frequent cause of mortality in travelers among all diagnoses, accounting for 33% to 55% of deaths [31,49]. In 2010, 1691 cases of malaria were reported in the United States, 99.8% of which were imported. Two hundred thirty-two (15%) occurred in children younger than 18 years, of whom only 5 were known to have taken appropriate chemoprophylaxis [50,51].

Of the *Plasmodium* species, *P falciparum* is the most drug resistant, causes the most severe disease, presents soonest, and accounts for a majority of infections acquired in Africa and the Americas. Both *Plasmodium vivax,* which accounts for most infections acquired in Asia, and *Plasmodium ovale* can cause relapses from hypnozoites that remain dormant in the liver for extended periods, sometimes leading to presentation months or years after returning from travel. *Plasmodium malariae* causes milder disease, whereas *Plasmodium knowlesi* usually infects monkeys, but sporadic cases have occurred in humans staying in forested areas in Southeast Asia [42]. For 40% of travelers with nonfalciparum malaria, the interval between onset of symptoms and return from travel was longer than 3 months; for 13% it was 7 to 12 months [52].

The majority (78%) of malaria cases in children seen at the GeoSentinel Network sites are infections with *P falciparum* [6]. Children, especially young ones who lack immunity, and immunocompromised individuals are at increased risk for severe malaria, defined as:

- Severe anemia (<7 g/dL)
- Jaundice

- Neurologic symptoms
- Renal failure
- Acute respiratory distress syndrome
- Parasitemia of 5% or greater

A particular form of severe malaria is cerebral malaria, which can lead to cerebral edema, coma, and death. Falciparum malaria may lead to death if not treated within 24 hours of developing symptoms [42]. Therefore, any child with fever returning from a malaria-endemic area (especially sub-Saharan Africa) within 3 months has a medical emergency and should be evaluated immediately [42].

Symptoms are nonspecific and include fever preceded by chills, headache, myalgias, anorexia, vomiting, diarrhea, and abdominal pain. Sometimes patients only experience fever and chills, with a sense of well-being maintained between fevers. Fevers rarely follow patterns described in textbooks. Anemia, hepatosplenomegaly, and slight jaundice may be present. The mainstay of diagnosis remains Giemsa-stained thick and thin blood smears, which should ideally be obtained during a fever. Thick smears identify the presence of parasites, whereas thin smears allow determination of the species and percentage of parasitemia. Accuracy of the diagnosis depends on the experience of the examiner, which can be a problem in areas where malaria is rarely seen. Polymerase chain reaction (PCR) testing and rapid diagnostic tests are not readily available. Because treatment is determined by species and level of parasitemia, an accurate diagnosis is essential.

Severe malaria should be treated aggressively with parenteral antimalarial drugs, usually in combination with or followed by oral drugs, as well as supportive care. Intravenous quinidine gluconate, the first-line drug, is often difficult to find owing to its cardiac side effects. Its use requires careful monitoring for prolonged QT syndrome. Intravenous artesunate is available as an investigational new drug through the CDC, and is stockpiled regionally for access, sometimes within hours, in many parts of the United States. Uncomplicated malaria may be treated with oral medications. Detailed malaria treatment guidelines with pediatric doses for clinicians are available at http://www.cdc.gov/malaria/diagnosis_treatment/treatment.html. In addition, the CDC Malaria Hotline at 770-488-7788 is available 24 hours a day to help with diagnosis and treatment. A 14-day course of primaquine phosphate should be administered to those without G6PD deficiency who have *P ovale* or *P vivax* infection to eradicate the hypnozoites and prevent relapses.

*Dengue*

Dengue is caused by 4 serotypes of dengue virus, a flavivirus transmitted by the *Aedes aegypti* mosquito. The WHO estimates that 50 million cases occur each year, resulting in 500,000 hospitalizations [53]. Dengue accounts for the second most common specific diagnosis among travelers with systemic febrile illness [31,54], but was more frequent than malaria in all regions of the developing world except sub-Saharan Africa and Central America [31]. In children it accounted for 6% of all systemic febrile illnesses [6]. Dengue occurs in more than 100 countries in tropical and subtropical regions, with epidemics in 2012 being reported from Somalia, Kenya, Madeira, Saudi Arabia, Pakistan, Yemen, and large parts of Latin America, Southeast Asia, and the Western Pacific regions. Dengue is a reportable disease in the United States (since 2009) and recent cases have been identified in Key West, Florida. The CDC maintains an interactive map of global dengue activity at http://www.healthmap.org/dengue/index.php.

Dengue infection presents as a spectrum of disease from asymptomatic (about half), a nonspecific febrile illnesses (often with first infection), classic dengue fever (DF), to the more severe forms of dengue hemorrhagic fever (DHF) and dengue shock syndrome (DSS). The last 2 require multiple exposures to the virus. The case definition of DF includes sudden onset of fever and 2 or more of the following:

- Headache
- Retroorbital pain
- Arthralgias (often severe)
- Myalgias
- Rash (diffuse erythematous maculopapular rash that usually appears as the fever subsides)
- Hemorrhagic manifestations (petechiae, easy bruising)
- Leukopenia

DHF occurs in approximately 1% of DF, usually as the fever is subsiding, and is defined by all the following: fever or history of fever for 2 to 7 days; hemorrhagic manifestations or a positive tourniquet test; thrombocytopenia ($\leq$100,000 cells/mm$^3$); and evidence of plasma leakage (hemoconcentration, pleural effusion, ascites, or hypoproteinemia). If, in addition, severe hypotension, tachycardia, weak pulse, narrow pulse pressure, and signs of hypoperfusion develop, it is categorized as DSS, which may have a case fatality rate of 40% to 50% without hospital care [55,56].

The diagnosis is based on serologic testing, PCR, or antigen tests. Serologic titers for antidengue virus immunoglobulin (Ig)M and IgG usually become positive after 5 days of symptoms, so acute and convalescent titers are useful. There is cross-reaction with other flaviviruses, such as West Nile virus, yellow fever, and JEV. CDC laboratories perform this test in Puerto Rico. PCR testing on the serum, plasma, or cerebrospinal fluid (CSF), and NS-1 virus antigen testing are useful in the first 5 days of symptoms, during viremia. The CDC has a testing algorithm for dengue diagnosis, with further details at http://www.cdc.gov/dengue/clinicalLab/laboratory.html. Treatment is based on early recognition and supportive care, usually necessitating hospitalization in more severe forms.

*Typhoid fever*

Typhoid fever is a bacterial infection caused by *Salmonella* Typhi and is transmitted via the ingestion of contaminated food or water. Infection caused by

*Salmonella* Paratyphi is termed paratyphoid fever, whereas infection caused by other *Salmonella* species is called enteric fever. Clinical findings do not differentiate these infections. The rate of typhoid fever (141 cases/1000 patients) in travelers returning from South Central Asia is much higher than from any other region in the developing world, but comparable to that of dengue for the region (142 cases/1000 patients) [31]. In children, enteric fever accounts for 6% of all systemic febrile illnesses with 67% caused by *Salmonella* Typhi and 24% by *Salmonella* Paratyphi (9% unspecified). Eighty-three percent of children with salmonellosis traveled to Asia [6].

Children usually present with gradually increasing fevers, headache, malaise, anorexia, constipation (more frequently than diarrhea in older children), occasional hepatosplenomegaly, and (rarely) rose spots. Focal disease such as meningitis, hepatosplenic abscesses, and osteoarticular infection can occur. Diagnosis is confirmed by isolating the organism in blood, stool, urine, or bone marrow. Because it causes a very low-grade bacteremia, a single blood culture is positive in only half of cases, thereby necessitating multiple, preferably large-volume, blood cultures to be drawn for evaluation. The Widal test is unreliable and is not used in the United States.

Antibacterial treatment is often intravenous, or intravenous then oral therapy based on sensitivities. Effective agents include ceftriaxone, ciprofloxacin, and azithromycin. However, there is increasing fluoroquinolone resistance on the Indian subcontinent. A CDC active laboratory surveillance effort found resistance to 5 or more agents in 17% of *S* Typhi isolates with a strong association to travel to the Indian subcontinent [34]. Furthermore, fluoroquinolones should be used with caution in nalidixic acid–resistant strains, as this pattern predicts decreased clinical response to fluoroquinolones [57]. Parents and patients should be reassured that fevers usually last 3 to 5 days or more, even on effective therapy.

*Chikungunya fever*

Chikungunya is an alphavirus transmitted by the mosquitoes *Aedes aegypti* and *Aedes albopictus*, which bite aggressively during the day. Initially identified in East Africa in 1953, a new epidemic in Kenya in 2004 spread to the Indian Ocean Islands and then to India 2 years later, leading to approximately 2 million cases globally in 2006 [54]. Cases have been reported throughout the tropics in Asia, Africa, Australia, Spain, and Italy [58]. Because the vector is found worldwide and humans have high levels of viremia, this disease has definite potential to be spread to new areas by infected travelers. Thirty-seven cases were reported in international travelers in the United States in 2006 [59].

Symptoms, which occur in at least 75% of cases, are similar to those of dengue, with sudden onset of fever and joint symptoms (arthralgia, stiffness, and arthritis, usually affecting the distal joints), which are more pronounced than in dengue. Other symptoms include maculopapular rash in 50% of patients, headache, fatigue, myalgias, nausea, and vomiting. The fatigue may last for weeks, whereas joint symptoms may last for months. Diagnostic tests include serum or CSF IgM and neutralizing antibody; more specialized testing, such as PCR, is available at most state health departments or the CDC Arbovirus Diagnostic Laboratory [60]. Commercial laboratory testing is limited. Treatment is supportive.

*Yellow fever*

Most cases of yellow fever are asymptomatic. However, for symptomatic disease the incubation is short (3–6 days). It begins with a nonspecific flu-like illness (fever, chills, headache, myalgia, arthralgia, nausea, and vomiting). Following a period of remission, approximately 15% of patients will develop severe hemorrhagic disease with fulminant hepatitis and renal failure [30]. The diagnosis is based on RNA PCR testing if early in disease. In overt disease, serologic tests for virus-specific IgM and IgG should be used; however, they can cross-react with other flaviviruses. The local or state health departments or CDC (800-CDC-INFO) should be contacted for assistance with diagnosis. Treatment is supportive.

*Viral syndromes*

Viral syndromes, including Epstein-Barr virus (EBV) and cytomegalovirus (CMV), can also occur in travelers. In one study, 13% of systemic febrile illness in returning travelers from malaria-endemic areas to Finland was due to acute viral illness (EBV, CMV, or human herpesvirus-6 infection) [61]. Viral syndromes account for 28% (the second most common cause), and mononucleosis syndromes (mostly viral, but including toxoplasmosis as well) account for approximately 4% of systemic febrile illnesses among children in the GeoSentinel Surveillance Network [6]. Therefore, EBV and CMV titers, as well as other available viral studies, should be included in the evaluation of a febrile child returning from international travel.

### Gastrointestinal

Traveler's diarrhea is transmitted by consumption of contaminated food and water or exposure to contaminated recreational water, and has bacterial (predominant), parasitic, and viral causes. Multiple organisms are identified in up to 10% of cases [62]. Symptoms are usually defined as 3 or more loose stools in a 24-hour period with at least 1 of the following: nausea, vomiting, cramps, fever, fecal urgency, tenesmus, or bloody, mucus-containing stools [63].

According to the CDC and WHO, traveler's diarrhea can affect up to 70% to 80% of travelers to high-risk destinations [64,65]. In travelers returning from a developing region, the broader category of acute diarrhea is the second most common, following systemic febrile illness; chronic diarrhea (lasting >2 weeks) for which the cause is generally not determined, is fourth [31]. Young children are especially vulnerable to traveler's diarrhea. In pediatric travelers, the most common syndrome diagnosed is diarrhea (80% acute, 20% chronic), accounting for 28% of all morbidity. The proportionate morbidity is highest in travelers to the Middle East and North Africa [6].

Bacterial causes of diarrhea include enterotoxigenic *Escherichia coli* (ETEC), *Campylobacter*, *Salmonella*, *Shigella*, enteropathogenic *E coli* (EPEC), other *E coli*,

*Aeromonas*, and *Plesiomonas* species. Acute diarrhea in returning travelers is caused by bacteria in 29% to 39% of cases [6,62]. The most common bacteria reported are *Campylobacter* spp (25%–37%), followed by *Salmonella* spp (24%–32%), and EPEC (24%) [6,62]. Travel to Southeast Asia is associated with bacterial diarrhea, predominantly caused by *Campylobacter* [31]. Blood and mucus in the stools is associated with bacterial causes of diarrhea.

Parasites are identified as a cause in 25% to 34% of cases, with *Giardia* causing the majority [6,62]. Other causes, such as *Entamoeba histolytica* and *Cryptosporidium* spp, are relatively uncommon. The highest risk for returning with giardiasis is in travelers to the Indian subcontinent, East Africa, and Central America, and in children younger than 7 years [66]. Prolonged stay was more common among travelers with parasitic than with bacterial diarrhea [62].

Viruses accounted for 27% of traveler's diarrhea in one study of Austrian travelers [62]. Causes include rotavirus, adenovirus, norovirus, and astrovirus [62,64]. Norovirus was found to be an important cause of traveler's diarrhea in persons traveling to Guatemala, India, and Mexico [67]. It is especially prevalent (21%) in travelers whose symptoms present within 4 days of returning from travel [68].

Stool cultures (often as many as 3) and 3 sets of stool for ova and parasite examination should be part of the evaluation of the pediatric traveler with diarrhea. The sooner the specimens are sent after the onset of symptoms, the more likely a pathogen will be recovered [62]. Traveler's diarrhea is mostly a self-limited disease, with recovery expected within a few days. However, (especially) young children are at risk for developing dehydration. When symptoms occur, children should continue drinking safe water, and breastfeeding should be continued for infants. If there is moderate to large stool output, oral rehydration solution should be started in the amounts of 1/4 to 1/2 cup (50–100 mL) after each loose stool (up to ~0.5 L/day) for children younger than 2 years; 1/2 to 1 cup (100–200 mL) after each loose stool (up to ~1 L/day) for children 2 to 9 years; and as much as wanted (up to ~2 L/day) for patients 10 years and older. Whenever possible, treatment should be pathogen specific. If empiric therapy is required, azithromycin is recommended as first-line empiric therapy for children, owing to increasing fluoroquinolone resistance. Of note, antimotility drugs, such as loperamide, should not be used in children younger than 12 years [65].

Hepatitis A infection can present with fever, nausea, vomiting, malaise, anorexia, and jaundice. Most children younger than 6 years are asymptomatic, with increasing symptoms and jaundice seen in older children. The diagnosis is made with a positive anti-HAV IgM. Treatment is supportive.

## Skin disorders

Among all patients seen in the GeoSentinel Surveillance Network, skin infections accounted for 18% of diagnoses. The 10 most common cutaneous diagnoses are cutaneous larva migrans (CLM), insect bite, skin abscess, superinfected insect bite, allergic reaction, rash of unknown etiology, dog bite, superficial fungal infection, dengue, and leishmaniasis [69]. In children seen in the same network, skin disorders account for 25% of all diagnoses. Both animal bites and CLM caused a higher percentage of skin conditions in children than in adults [6,69].

Animal bites account for 24% of skin disorders in children. Dog bites are the most frequent (52%) animal bites, followed by cat bites (20%), and monkey bites (19%). Ninety-seven percent of children sustaining animal bites receive rabies postexposure prophylaxis [6]. The proportionate morbidity for sustaining an animal bite is highest in Southeast Asia [69,70]. Pediatricians should make sure that children with animal bites receive the necessary rabies postexposure prophylaxis and that wound infections are treated with antibiotics.

The rates of CLM are highest in the Caribbean [31,69,71], where dog feces on the beach are the source of infection. The larvae of the dog hookworm (*Ancylostoma brasiliense*) enter the skin (usually on the feet), causing an intensely pruritic serpiginous track or bullae at the site of migration of the larvae. The diagnosis is clinical and symptoms are self-limited, lasting weeks to months. Rarely, pneumonitis may complicate CLM. Oral albendazole or mebendazole is used for treatment. Leishmaniasis, amebiasis, African trypanosomiasis, and Chagas disease may also present with cutaneous manifestations.

### Eosinophilia

Eosinophilia, defined as 450 or more blood eosinophils per microliter in peripheral blood, may be caused by several conditions such as allergies, asthma, drug hypersensitivity, neoplasms, or infections. However, new-onset eosinophilia in a returning traveler from the tropics is likely the result of a helminth infection, even if the person is otherwise completely asymptomatic at the time. An estimated 10% to 73% of returning travelers and immigrants from the tropics with eosinophilia could have a potentially serious infection [72]. It is also important to remember that not all patients with helminth infections have eosinophilia. The majority of these infections are caused by schistosomiasis, filariasis, strongyloidiasis, and intestinal nematode infection. Helminth infections account for 2% of diagnoses in children in the GeoSentinel Network, 14% of whom were hospitalized [6].

Schistosomiasis (infection with *Schistosoma haematobium, mansoni,*or *japonicum*) is acquired after contact with contaminated fresh water, where the infective larvae develop in snails and then penetrate the skin. It is endemic in Africa, Asia, and Central and South America, with most cases in travelers occurring after visiting sub-Saharan Africa [31]. The life cycle leads to Katayama fever, characterized by fever, headache, myalgias, rash, pain in the right upper quadrant, bloody diarrhea, and pulmonary symptoms. Depending on the species and target organ, liver, renal, and intestinal damage may occur. The diagnosis is made by detecting the parasite egg in stool or urine or by serologic tests, but the latter do not differentiate between recent and past infection. Praziquantel is used for treatment [73–75].

Filarial infections include *Loa loa*, onchocerciasis, and lymphatic filariasis. The diagnosis is made by detecting microfilaria on blood smears obtained at night. Treatment is combination therapy with albendazole and ivermectin or diethylcarbamazine.

Strongyloidiasis is caused by *Strongyloides stercoralis.* Infective larvae found in the soil penetrate the skin causing skin, pulmonary, and gastrointestinal symptoms during their migration, which can occasionally lead to gram-negative sepsis and/or meningitis. However, most infections are asymptomatic. Immunosuppression can lead to hyperinfection or disseminated disease with a high mortality rate. The diagnosis is made by identifying larvae in the stool. Treatment consists of ivermectin. Wearing shoes can prevent infection [76].

Intestinal nematode infections, such as hookworm infection, can also cause eosinophilia. Many infections are asymptomatic. However, children may develop vague abdominal pain, nausea, anemia, protein malnutrition, long-term fatigue, and impaired cognition. The diagnosis is made by identifying eggs in stool samples. Treatment is albendazole or mebendazole [77].

### Respiratory

Respiratory illnesses, such as acute respiratory infection, bronchitis, bacterial pneumonia, tonsillitis, influenza, and acute sinusitis, account for 14% of diagnoses in returning travelers with fever, and lead to hospitalization in 24% [78]. In returning ill pediatric travelers, respiratory illnesses account for 11% of diagnoses [6]. Upper respiratory infections (38%), hyperactive airways disease (20%), and acute otitis media (17%) are the most common diagnoses [6]. Ill travelers with fever and respiratory symptoms traveling from a region with ongoing influenza transmission (such as the southern hemisphere from April to September) should be evaluated for influenza and other respiratory viruses.

Healthy children returning from TB-endemic countries (eg, China, India, South Africa, Indonesia, Pakistan) with substantial contact with the local population should be evaluated for TB infection after each trip [79]. An example of substantial contact is a cumulative stay of longer than 7 days with friends or relatives. Testing with a TST or IGRA in the case of BCG-vaccinated children 4 years and older should be performed ideally 10 weeks or more after returning [79]. If either of these tests is positive, a chest radiograph should be performed to identify disease, which often consists solely of hilar or mediastinal lymphadenopathy in an otherwise well-appearing child.

### Sexually transmitted infections

A survey of sub-Saharan African communities revealed that 40% of males and 21% of females acquired a new sexual partner while visiting their countries of origin [80]. A recent review of GeoSentinel data reveals that nongonococcal or nonspecific urethritis (30%), acute HIV infection (28%), and syphilis (22%) are the 3 most common diagnoses of sexually transmitted infection (STI) made in returning travelers. Male gender, VFR status, lack of pretravel consultation, and travel for less than 30 days are significantly associated with a diagnosis of STI [81]. Acute HIV infection can present with fever, flu-like symptoms, and lymphadenopathy. Ill adolescent travelers should also be evaluated for

HIV, syphilis, hepatitis C virus, and HB (if not fully immunized), and other STIs as clinically indicated.

## INTERNATIONAL ADOPTEES

There were a total of 233,934 intercountry adoptions in the United States from 1999 to 2011. Sixty percent of adoptees were females and 39% were children younger than 1 year old. The principal source countries for adoptions in 2011 were China, Ethiopia, Russia, South Korea, and Ukraine, and the number of adoptions (n = 9319) was lower in 2011 than in any previous year since 1999 [82]. The care of international adoptees should begin with a review of their vaccination status and evaluation for infectious diseases within 30 days of arrival, but ideally within 2 weeks of entering the country [83].

### Vaccines

Internationally adopted children should be protected against vaccine-preventable diseases similarly to United States–born children, yet on their arrival to the United States they may not be up to date according to the CDC/Advisory Committee on Immunization Practices (ACIP) immunization guidelines. This situation may be secondary to inefficient performance of a country's immunization program or the fact that several vaccinations have not been introduced into routine childhood immunization schedules of certain countries. Vaccination coverage among 19- to 35-month-old foreign-born children in 1999 to 2000 was found to be lower when compared with United States–born children, especially for Hib and HB [84]. According to 2011 WHO estimates, 83% of children worldwide received 3 doses of diphtheria-pertussis-tetanus (DPT) vaccine in infancy, leaving 22 million children unprotected. About half of these incompletely immunized children live in India, Indonesia, and Nigeria. As of the end of 2011, the following vaccines have been introduced into routine childhood immunization schedules in these percentages of countries:

- 3 doses of HB vaccine (93%)
- 3 doses of Hib (91%)
- PCV (37%)
- Rotavirus vaccine (16%)

Despite the introduction of Hib in 91% of countries, global coverage remains only 43% [85]. For these reasons, the vaccination status of all international adoptees should be carefully reviewed.

Children who have not received any vaccines or for whom reliable documentation reveals inadequate vaccination history should be started on a catch-up schedule according to current AAP Red Book guidelines. Most vaccines currently available worldwide are produced with adequate quality control measures and should be considered reliable. Only written documentation should be accepted as proof of receipt of a vaccine. Documentation can be accepted if the vaccine, dose, age at receipt, and interval between doses is comparable with WHO or CDC schedules. Caregivers should make sure that vaccines were not given before the minimum age and sooner than the minimum time interval between doses [86].

If records are unavailable or deemed unreliable, serologic testing may be performed to determine the presence of protective antibody titers. Serologic tests on 495 children adopted in the Netherlands revealed adequate protection only in 48% to diphtheria, 56% to tetanus, and 71% to polio [87]. Infants 6 to 12 months of age can have antibody testing to poliovirus, diphtheria, and tetanus toxoids. The latter 2 can serve as a marker for receipt of DPT, because pertussis serologies are not a reliable marker for immunity. Children older than 12 months can have hepatitis A, measles, mumps, rubella, and varicella antibodies measured (before that age maternal antibodies may cause false-positive results). MMR should be used for vaccination of mumps (2 doses needed) and rubella (1 dose sufficient) in nonimmune children, even if measles antibodies are present. No further HB vaccine is needed if the child is: HBsAg positive or HB surface antibody (HBsAb) and HB core antibody (HBcAb) positive, or HBsAb positive and HB vaccine was given appropriately. If testing is unavailable and vaccine receipt cannot be confirmed, the pediatric health care provider should proceed with reimmunization [83]. Other vaccines not part of the United States vaccine schedule may have been administered to international adoptees, such as BCG, meningococcal polysaccharide vaccine (termed epidemic cerebrospinal meningitis vaccine in China), or JEV vaccine [86].

## Evaluation for infectious diseases

International adoptees are at increased risk for acquiring infectious diseases arising from their previous social situation, variable access and quality of health care, and increased prevalence of infectious diseases in their country of origin. Some countries do not have consistent prenatal screening for HB, HIV, or syphilis, and the prevalence of TB, intestinal parasites, and other diseases may be higher than in the United States. Screening these children is not only important for their own health but also for the health of their adoptive families.

Multiple studies have shown that approximately 22% to 26% of international adoptees have gastrointestinal parasites, and 15% to 19% have *Giardia intestinalis* [87–89]. Other pathogens found include *Blastocystis hominis*, *Dientamoeba fragilis*, *Entamoeba coli*, *Hymenolepis nana*, *Ascaris lumbricoides*, and *S stercoralis*. Bacterial pathogens include *Campylobacter*, *Salmonella*, and *Shigella* [87–89]. Therefore, all children, regardless of presence or absence of symptoms, should have 3 stools collected 2 to 3 days apart for examination for ova and parasites. Sending 3 specimens is important to optimize pathogen recovery [89]. Antigen testing for *Giardia* and *Cryptosporidium* should also be included. Children with diarrhea should also have stool cultures performed [90]. Parasitic and bacterial pathogens should be treated in most cases with repeat testing several weeks later to verify clearance.

The AAP also recommends *Trypanosoma cruzi* serologic testing of all children from endemic countries and lymphatic filariasis serologic testing of children older than 2 years from endemic countries. Lastly, children with eosinophilia and stools negative for ova and parasites should have *Strongyloides* serologies. *Schistosoma* serologies should also be sent (according to some experts, even in the absence of eosinophilia) if they are from sub-Saharan Africa, Southeast Asia, or parts of Latin America [83].

Much of the world outside of Australia, parts of South America, North America, and Europe is considered to have intermediate or high prevalence of chronic HB infection. Testing of mothers and immunoprophylaxis of exposed infants to prevent perinatal transmission often does not occur. In the United States and the Netherlands, 1% to 3% of internationally adopted children were found to have positive HBsAg on initial screening [87,88,91]. Therefore, this population should be tested for HBsAg, HBsAb, and HBcAb to determine if the child has past, acute, or chronic infection or was successfully immunized [90]. Experts recommend repeat testing in 6 months to identify any children who were infected just before the initial testing [91,92]. Some experts recommend repeat testing after 12 months of age if initial evaluation was done before 12 months (at which time maternal HBsAb may still be present) [91]. If acute or chronic infection is diagnosed in a child, family and household members should be educated about modes of transmission, tested, and vaccinated if not immune. Ideally the parents should have received the vaccination before traveling internationally for the purposes of adoption. In these children, further testing (HB extracellular [HBe]Ag, HBeAb, α-fetoprotein, liver function tests, and quantitative PCR testing for viral load) is needed.

The AAP also recommends screening for hepatitis C virus infection with antibody testing for all adoptees [83]. Routine testing for hepatitis A is not recommended for adoptees. However, because of multiple HAV outbreaks among persons exposed to asymptomatic, newly arrived adoptees, the ACIP updated its policy on HAV vaccine recommendations in 2009 to state that all previously unvaccinated people anticipating close contact with an international adoptee coming from an HAV-endemic country should be vaccinated [93].

Although the diagnosis of HIV or syphilis in internationally adopted children is rarely made, prenatal screening for syphilis and HIV is uncommon in developing countries. Furthermore, congenital syphilis is endemic in Russia and other nearby countries [92], and may be underdiagnosed or undertreated. Therefore, all internationally adopted children should have testing for syphilis with nontreponemal and treponemal tests. Infected children should undergo serial testing as well as ophthalmologic, audiology, neurologic, and developmental evaluations, and be treated appropriately [92]. HIV-1 and HIV-2 serologies should be sent, with repeat testing considered 6 months later to detect seroconversion, in case infection occurred just before adoption [90].

As many international adoptions derive from countries with a high prevalence of TB and children are often exposed to institutionalized settings, latent TB infection is found in 14% to 21% of adopted children on initial screening [88,94,95]. Some studies have shown that repeat TST more than 2 months following the initial TST revealed an additional 13% to 20% positives, which were explained by *Mycobacterium tuberculosis* infection just before adoption, false-negative results on initial TST from transient immunosuppression owing to malnutrition, or possibly a boosting phenomenon [94,95]. According to AAP Red Book recommendations, an immediate TST or IGRA is indicated for children immigrating from TB-endemic countries (eg, Asia, the Middle East, Africa, Latin America, the former Soviet Union), including international adoptees. IGRA is preferred to TST for children older than 4 years who received BCG vaccination or who are unlikely to return for TST reading [79]. Furthermore, the CDC Yellow Book recommends repeat TST 3 to 6 months after arrival if the first TST is negative. Children found to have a positive TST, but no evidence of active TB disease, should be treated with isoniazid for 9 months to prevent active disease in the future.

## References

[1] United Nations World Tourism Organization. World Tourism Barometer January 2012;10:1–6. Available at: http://mkt.unwto.org/en/barometer/january-2012-advance-release. Accessed November 30, 2012.

[2] United Nations World Tourism Organization. World Tourism Barometer November 2012;10:1–8. Available at: http://mkt.unwto.org/en/barometer/november-2012-volume-10. Accessed November 30, 2012.

[3] Office of Travel and Tourism Industries, International Trade Administration, U.S. Department of Commerce. 2011 United States Resident Travel Abroad. Available at: http://www.tinet.ita.doc.gov/outreachpages/download_data_table/2011_US_Travel_Abroad.pdf. Accessed November 18, 2012.

[4] Office of Travel and Tourism Industries, International Trade Administration, U.S. Department of Commerce. Profile of U.S. resident travelers visiting overseas destinations: 2011 outbound. Available at: http://tinet.ita.doc.gov/outreachpages/download_data_table/2011_Outbound_Profile.pdf. Accessed November 18, 2012.

[5] Steffen R, Rickenbach M, Wilhelm U, et al. Health problems after travel to developing countries. J Infect Dis 1987;156(1):84–91.

[6] Hagmann S, Neugebauer R, Schwartz E, et al. Illness in children after international travel: analysis from the GeoSentinel Surveillance Network. Pediatrics 2010;125(5):e1072–80.

[7] Angell SY, Behrens RH. Risk assessment and disease prevention in travelers visiting friends and relatives. Infect Dis Clin North Am 2005;19(1):49–65.

[8] Han P, Yanni E, Jentes ES, et al. Health challenges of young travelers visiting friends and relatives compared with those traveling for other purposes. Pediatr Infect Dis J 2012;31(9):915–9.

[9] Leder K, Tong S, Weld L, et al. Illness in travelers visiting friends and relatives: a review of the GeoSentinel Surveillance Network. Clin Infect Dis 2006;43(9):1185–93.

[10] Barnett ED, MacPherson DW, Stauffer WM, et al. The visiting friends or relatives traveler in the 21st century: time for a new definition. J Travel Med 2010;17(3):163–70.

[11] Centers for Disease Control and Prevention. Traveler's health, outbreak notice measles update. Available at: http://wwwnc.cdc.gov/travel/notices/outbreak-notice/measles.htm. Accessed November 19, 2012.

[12] High number of reported measles cases in the U.S. in 2011—linked to outbreaks abroad, June 22, 2011. Available at: http://emergency.cdc.gov/HAN/han00323.asp. Accessed November 19, 2012.

[13] Centers for Disease Control and Prevention (CDC). Measles–United States, 2011. MMWR Morb Mortal Wkly Rep 2012;61(15):253–7.

[14] Fielbelkorn AP, Uzicanin A. Measles (rubeola). In: Brunette GW, Kozarsky PE, Magill AJ, et al, editors. CDC health information for international travel 2012. New York: Oxford University Press; 2012. p. 244–7.
[15] World Health Organization. Hepatitis A. Available at: http://www.who.int/csr/disease/hepatitis/whocdscsredc2007/en/index.html. Accessed October 29, 2012.
[16] World Health Organization. Hepatitis A fact sheet no. 328, July 2012. Available at: http://www.who.int/mediacentre/factsheets/fs328/en/index.html. Accessed October 29, 2012.
[17] American Academy of Pediatrics. Hepatitis A. In: Pickering LK, Baker CJ, Kimberlin DW, et al, editors. Red Book: 2012 report of the Committee on Infectious Diseases. Elk Grove Village (IL): American Academy of Pediatrics; 2012. p. 361–9.
[18] World Health Organization. Hepatitis B. In: World Health Organization, International travel and health: situation as on 1 January 2012. Geneva (Switzerland): WHO Press; 2012. p. 94–7.
[19] Global polio eradication initiative. Polio This Week. Available at: http://www.polioeradication.org/Dataandmonitoring/Poliothisweek.aspx. Accessed December 12, 2012.
[20] Alexander JP, Wallace GS, Wassilak SG. Poliomyelitis. In: Brunette GW, Kozarsky PE, Magill AJ, et al, editors. CDC health information for international travel 2012. New York: Oxford University Press; 2012. p. 266–9.
[21] World Health Organization. Global health observatory, meningococcal meningitis. Available at: http://www.who.int/gho/epidemic_diseases/meningitis/en/index.html. Accessed November 19, 2012.
[22] Mackell SM. Vaccine recommendations for infants & children. In: Brunette GW, Kozarsky PE, Magill AJ, et al, editors. CDC health information for international travel 2012. New York: Oxford University Press; 2012. p. 497–512.
[23] Leder K, Sundararajan V, Weld L, et al. Respiratory tract infections in travelers: a review of the GeoSentinel surveillance network. Clin Infect Dis 2003;36(4):399–406.
[24] World Health Organization. Pneumococcal disease. International travel and health: situation as on 1 January 2012. Geneva (Switzerland): WHO Press; 2012. p. 109–11.
[25] Hausdorff WP, Bryant J, Paradiso PR, et al. Which pneumococcal serogroups cause the most invasive disease: implications for conjugate vaccine formulation and use, part I. Clin Infect Dis 2000;30(1):100–21.
[26] Hausdorff WP, Feikin DR, Klugman KP. Epidemiological differences among pneumococcal serotypes. Lancet Infect Dis 2005;5(2):83–93.
[27] World Health Organization Yellow fever fact sheet. No. 100. Jan 2011. Available at: http://www.who.int/mediacentre/factsheets/fs100/en/. Accessed November 22, 2012.
[28] World Health Organization Global Alert and Response (GAR). Epidemiological trends and current situation of yellow fever. Available at: http://www.who.int/csr/disease/yellowfev/surveillance/en/index.html. Accessed November 22, 2012.
[29] World Health Organization. The yellow fever situation in Africa and South America in 2004. Wkly Epidemiol Rec 2005;80(29):250–6.
[30] Gershman M, Staples JE. Yellow fever. In: Brunette GW, Kozarsky PE, Magill AJ, et al, editors. CDC health information for international travel 2012. New York: Oxford University Press; 2012. p. 332–46.
[31] Freedman DO, Weld LH, Kozarsky PE, et al. Spectrum of disease and relation to place of exposure among ill returned travelers. N Engl J Med 2006;354(2):119–30 [Erratum in: N Engl J Med 2006;355(9):967].
[32] Ekdahl K, de Jong B, Andersson Y. Risk of travel-associated typhoid and paratyphoid fevers in various regions. J Travel Med 2005;12(4):197–204.
[33] Bhattarai A, Mintz E. Typhoid & paratyphoid fever. In: Brunette GW, Kozarsky PE, Magill AJ, et al, editors. CDC health information for international travel 2012. New York: Oxford University Press; 2012. p. 323–5.

[34] Ackers ML, Puhr ND, Tauxe RV, et al. Laboratory-based surveillance of Salmonella serotype Typhi infections in the United States: antimicrobial resistance on the rise. JAMA 2000;283(20):2668–73.
[35] Kaltenböck A, Dubischar-Kastner K, Schuller E, et al. Immunogenicity and safety of IXIARO (IC51) in a phase II study in healthy Indian children between 1 and 3 years of age. Vaccine 2010;28(3):834–9.
[36] Hills SL, Nett RJ, Fischer M. Japanese encephalitis. In: Brunette GW, Kozarsky PE, Magill AJ, et al, editors. CDC health information for international travel 2012. New York: Oxford University Press; 2012. p. 205–14.
[37] Centers for Disease Control and Prevention. JE vaccines for U.S. children. Available at: http://www.cdc.gov/japaneseencephalitis/vaccine/vaccineChildren.html. Accessed November 30, 2012.
[38] World Health Organization. Rabies epidemiology. Available at: http://www.who.int/rabies/epidemiology/en/. Accessed November 30, 2012.
[39] World Health Organization. Rabies. Available at: http://www.who.int/rabies/en/. Accessed November 30, 2012.
[40] Lobato MN, Hopewell PC. *Mycobacterium tuberculosis* infection after travel to or contact with visitors from countries with a high prevalence of tuberculosis. Am J Respir Crit Care Med 1998;158(6):1871–5.
[41] World Health Organization. World malaria report 2011. Available at: http://www.who.int/malaria/publications/atoz/9789241564403/en/index.html. Accessed December 1, 2012.
[42] World Health Organization. Malaria. International travel and health: situation as on 1 January 2012. Geneva (Switzerland): WHO Press; 2012. p. 144–67.
[43] Zielinski-Gutierrez E, Wirtz RA, Nasci RS, et al. Protection against mosquitoes, ticks, other insects & arthropods. In: Brunette GW, Kozarsky PE, Magill AJ, et al, editors. CDC health information for international travel 2012. New York: Oxford University Press; 2012. p. 86–9.
[44] Fradin MS, Day JF. Comparative efficacy of insect repellents against mosquito bites. N Engl J Med 2002;347(1):13–8.
[45] World Health Organization. Insects and other vectors of disease. International travel and health: situation as on 1 January 2012. p. 43–6.
[46] Blair DC. A week in the life of a travel clinic. Clin Microbiol Rev 1997;10(4):650–73.
[47] Watson JC, Hlavsa MC, Griffin PM. Food & water precautions. In: Brunette GW, Kozarsky PE, Magill AJ, et al, editors. CDC health information for international travel 2012. New York: Oxford University Press; 2012. p. 74–6.
[48] World Health Organization. Common sense precautions for avoiding unsafe food and drink. International travel and health: situation as on 1 January 2012. Geneva (Switzerland): WHO Press; 2012. p. 48.
[49] Bottieau E, Clerinx J, Schrooten W, et al. Etiology and outcome of fever after a stay in the tropics. Arch Intern Med 2006;166(15):1642–8.
[50] Mali S, Kachur SP, Arguin PM, et al. Malaria surveillance—United States, 2010. MMWR Surveill Summ 2012;61(2):1–17.
[51] Ladhani S, El Bashir H, Patel VS, et al. Childhood malaria in East London. Pediatr Infect Dis J 2003;22(9):814–9.
[52] Bottieau E, Clerinx J, Van Den Enden E, et al. Imported non-*Plasmodium falciparum* malaria: a five-year prospective study in a European referral center. Am J Trop Med Hyg 2006;75(1):133–8.
[53] Tomashek KM. Dengue fever & dengue hemorrhagic fever. In: Brunette GW, Kozarsky PE, Magill AJ, et al, editors. CDC health information for international travel 2012. New York: Oxford University Press; 2012. p. 156–62.
[54] Wilson ME, Freedman DO. Etiology of travel-related fever. Curr Opin Infect Dis 2007;20(5):449–53.

[55] Centers for Disease Control and Prevention. Dengue homepage. Clinical guidance. Available at: http://www.cdc.gov/dengue/clinicalLab/clinical.html. Accessed December 5, 2012.
[56] World Health Organization. Dengue. International travel and health: situation as on 1 January 2012. Geneva (Switzerland): WHO Press; 2012. p. 62.
[57] Crump JA, Barrett TJ, Nelson JT, et al. Reevaluating fluoroquinolone breakpoints for *Salmonella enterica* serotype Typhi and for non-Typhi salmonellae. Clin Infect Dis 2003;37(1): 75–81.
[58] Staples JE, Hills SL, Powers AM. Chikungunya. In: Brunette GW, Kozarsky PE, Magill AJ, et al, editors. CDC health information for international travel 2012. New York: Oxford University Press; 2012. p. 144–6.
[59] Centers for Disease Control and Prevention (CDC). Update: Chikungunya fever diagnosed among international travelers—United States, 2006. MMWR Morb Mortal Wkly Rep 2007;56(12):276–7.
[60] Centers for Disease Control and Prevention. Chikungunya diagnosis. Available at: http://www.cdc.gov/chikungunya/diagnosis/index.html. Accessed December 7, 2012.
[61] Siikamäki HM, Kivelä PS, Sipilä PN, et al. Fever in travelers returning from malaria-endemic areas: don't look for malaria only. J Travel Med 2011;18(4):239–44.
[62] Reinthaler FF, Feierl G, Stünzner D, et al. Diarrhea in returning Austrian tourists: epidemiology, etiology, and cost-analyses. J Travel Med 1998;5(2):65–72.
[63] Löscher T. Clinical presentation and management of travelers' diarrhea. In: Keystone JS, Kozarsky PE, Freedman DO, et al, editors. Travel medicine. 2nd edition. Philadelphia: Elsevier; 2008. p. 197–203.
[64] Connor BA. Travelers' diarrhea. In: Brunette GW, Kozarsky PE, Magill AJ, et al, editors. CDC health information for international travel 2012. New York: Oxford University Press; 2012. p. 56–60.
[65] World Health Organization. Traveler's diarrhoea. International travel and health: situation as on 1 January 2012. Geneva (Switzerland): WHO Press; 2012. p. 36–7.
[66] Ekdahl K, Andersson Y. Imported giardiasis: impact of international travel, immigration, and adoption. Am J Trop Med Hyg 2005;72(6):825–30.
[67] Koo HL, Ajami NJ, Jiang ZD, et al. Noroviruses as a cause of diarrhea in travelers to Guatemala, India, and Mexico. J Clin Microbiol 2010;48(5):1673–6.
[68] Apelt N, Hartberger C, Campe H, et al. The prevalence of norovirus in returning international travelers with diarrhea. BMC Infect Dis 2010;10:131.
[69] Lederman ER, Weld LH, Elyazar IR, et al. Dermatologic conditions of the ill returned traveler: an analysis from the GeoSentinel Surveillance Network. Int J Infect Dis 2008;12(6):593–602.
[70] Gautret P, Schwartz E, Shaw M, et al. Animal-associated injuries and related diseases among returned travellers: a review of the GeoSentinel Surveillance Network. Vaccine 2007;25(14):2656–63.
[71] Jackett G. Infections, dermatologic conditions in the returned pediatric traveler. Pediatr Ann 2011;40(7):362–7.
[72] Ustianowski A, Zumla A. Eosinophilia in the returning traveler. Infect Dis Clin North Am 2012;26(3):781–9.
[73] American Academy of Pediatrics. Schistosomiasis. In: Pickering LK, Baker CJ, Kimberlin DW, et al, editors. Red Book: 2012 report of the Committee on infectious diseases. Elk Grove Village (IL): American Academy of Pediatrics; 2012. p. 643–5.
[74] Montgomery S. Schistosomiasis. In: Brunette GW, Kozarsky PE, Magill AJ, et al, editors. CDC health information for international travel 2012. New York: Oxford University Press; 2012. p. 287–91.
[75] Klion AD. Eosinophilia. In: Keystone JS, Kozarsky PE, Freedman DO, et al, editors. Travel medicine. 2nd edition. Philadelphia: Elsevier; 2008. p. 551–9.

[76] Fox LM. Strongyloides. In: Brunette GW, Kozarsky PE, Magill AJ, et al, editors. CDC health information for international travel 2012. New York: Oxford University Press; 2012. p. 299–300.
[77] American Academy of Pediatrics. Hookworm infections. In: Pickering LK, Baker CJ, Kimberlin DW, et al, editors. Red Book: 2012 report of the Committee on infectious diseases. Elk Grove Village (IL): American Academy of Pediatrics; 2012. p. 411–3.
[78] Wilson ME, Weld LH, Boggild A, et al. Fever in returned travelers: results from the GeoSentinel Surveillance Network. Clin Infect Dis 2007;44(12):1560–8.
[79] American Academy of Pediatrics. Tuberculosis. In: Pickering LK, Baker CJ, Kimberlin DW, et al, editors. Red Book: 2012 report of the Committee on infectious diseases. Elk Grove Village (IL): American Academy of Pediatrics; 2012. p. 736–59.
[80] Fenton KA, Chinouya M, Davidson O, et al. HIV transmission risk among sub-Saharan Africans in London travelling to their countries of origin. AIDS 2001;15(11):1442–5.
[81] Matteelli A, Schlagenhauf P, Carvalho AC, et al. Travel-associated sexually transmitted infections: an observational cross-sectional study of the GeoSentinel surveillance database. Lancet Infect Dis 2012; http://dx.doi.org/10.1016/S1473-3099(12)70291-8. pii:S1473–3099(12)70291-8.
[82] U.S. Department of State, Bureau of Consular Affairs. Intercountry adoption statistics. Available at: http://adoption.state.gov/about_us/statistics.php. Accessed December 9, 2012.
[83] American Academy of Pediatrics. Medical evaluation of internationally adopted children for infectious diseases. In: Pickering LK, Baker CJ, Kimberlin DW, et al, editors. Red Book: 2012 report of the Committee on infectious diseases. Elk Grove Village (IL): American Academy of Pediatrics; 2012. p. 191–9.
[84] Strine TW, Barker LE, Mokdad AH, et al. Vaccination coverage of foreign-born children 19 to 35 months of age: findings from the National Immunization Survey, 1999-2000. Pediatrics 2002;110(2 Pt 1):e15.
[85] World Health Organization. Global routine vaccination coverage, 2011. Wkly Epidemiol Rec 2012;87(44):432–5.
[86] Lee PJ. Vaccines for travel and international adoption. Pediatr Infect Dis J 2008;27(4): 351–4.
[87] van Schaik R, Wolfs TF, Geelen SP. Improved general health of international adoptees, but immunization status still insufficient. Eur J Pediatr 2009;168(9):1101–6.
[88] Saiman L, Aronson J, Zhou J, et al. Prevalence of infectious diseases among internationally adopted children. Pediatrics 2001;108(3):608–12.
[89] Staat MA, Rice M, Donauer S, et al. Intestinal parasite screening in internationally adopted children: importance of multiple stool specimens. Pediatrics 2011;128(3):e613–22.
[90] Staat MA. Infectious disease issues in internationally adopted children. Pediatr Infect Dis J 2002;21(3):257–8.
[91] Stadler LP, Mezoff AG, Staat MA. Hepatitis B virus screening for internationally adopted children. Pediatrics 2008;122(6):1223–8.
[92] Miller LC. International adoption: infectious diseases issues. Clin Infect Dis 2005;40(2): 286–93.
[93] American Academy of Pediatrics Committee on Infectious Diseases. Recommendations for administering hepatitis A vaccine to contacts of international adoptees. Pediatrics 2011;128(4):803–4.
[94] Trehan I, Meinzen-Derr JK, Jamison L, et al. Tuberculosis screening in internationally adopted children: the need for initial and repeat testing. Pediatrics 2008;122(1):e7–14.
[95] Mandalakas AM, Kirchner HL, Zhu X, et al. Interpretation of repeat tuberculin skin testing in international adoptees: conversions or boosting. Pediatr Infect Dis J 2008;27(10):913–9.

## APPENDIX 1: INTERNET RESOURCES

| | |
|---|---|
| WHO international travel and health Web site: reference, updates, maps | http://who.int/ith/en/index.html |
| WHO International Travel and Health: Vaccine preventable diseases and vaccines; yellow fever vaccine requirements | http://www.who.int/ith/chapters/ith2012en_chap6.pdf |
| CDC Travel Health | www.cdc.gov/travel |
| CDC Yellow Book 2012 online: travel health reference with updates online | http://wwwnc.cdc.gov/travel/page/yellowbook-2012-home.htm |
| CDC Travel Health Destination Section | http://wwwnc.cdc.gov/travel/destinations/list.htm |
| Japanese encephalitis vaccine information for children | http://www.cdc.gov/japaneseencephalitis/vaccine/vaccineChildren.html |
| CDC water disinfection for travelers | http://wwwnc.cdc.gov/travel/yellowbook/2012/chapter-2-the-pre-travel-consultation/water-disinfection-for-travelers.htm |
| CDC Measles Outbreak Update | http://wwwnc.cdc.gov/travel/notices/outbreak-notice/measles.htm |
| CDC malaria application map | http://cdc-malaria.ncsa.uiuc.edu/ |
| CDC malaria treatment guidelines | http://www.cdc.gov/malaria/diagnosis_treatment/treatment.html |
| CDC Chikungunya diagnostic testing | http://www.cdc.gov/chikungunya/diagnosis/index.html |
| CDC Dengue testing algorithm | http://www.cdc.gov/dengue/clinicalLab/laboratory.html |
| Dengue Map: interactive map showing global activity | http://www.healthmap.org/dengue/index.php |

Advances in Pediatrics 60 (2013) 141–165

ADVANCES IN PEDIATRICS

# Update on Allergen Immunotherapy for Treatment of Allergic Diseases

Kenny Y. Kwong, MD[a,*], Sydney Leibel, MD[b]

[a]Division of Allergy-Immunology, Department of Pediatrics, Harbor-UCLA Medical Center, 1000 West Carson Street, N-25, Torrance, CA 90509, USA; [b]Allergy-Immunology, Kindercare Pediatrics, 301-491 Eglinton Avenue, Toronto, Ontario M5N 1A8, Canada

**Keywords**

• Immunotherapy • Allergy • Allergic rhinitis • Asthma • Allergic march

**Key points**

- Allergen immunotherapy is effective in treatment of allergic rhinitis, allergic conjunctivitis, and asthma.
- Allergen immunotherapy significantly reduces risk of developing asthma in allergic children.
- Allergen immunotherapy significantly reduces risk of sensitization to additional allergens in children already sensitized.
- Effective allergen immunotherapy requires identification of clinically relevant allergens and in the administration of correct doses.

## INTRODUCTION

Allergen immunotherapy (or simply immunotherapy) was the first and only effective therapy used to treat allergic diseases more than a century ago before the development of modern allergic medications [1]. Through the twentieth century, the advent of each new class of antiallergy agent brought forth predictions of the demise of immunotherapy. The end for immunotherapy, whether because of H1 antagonists, topical steroids, monoclonal antiimmunoglobulin (Ig) E antibodies, or biologics, never materialized. These potent and selective agents have reduced morbidity and mortality in a large number of patients with allergies and asthma. However, significant numbers of patients have

Funding Sources: KY Kwong, Thermo-Fisher Scientific; S Leibel, none.

Conflict of Interest: KY Kwong, consultant and Speaker's Bureau for Thermo-Fisher Scientific; S Leibel, none.

*Corresponding author. *E-mail address:* kkwong@labiomed.org

0065-3101/13/$ – see front matter
http://dx.doi.org/10.1016/j.yapd.2013.04.008 

suboptimal or no response to these therapies. Many other patients are responsive but suffer unacceptable side effects from these agents. Others may prefer immunotherapy as an effective alternative to pharmacologic agents. Immunotherapy also remains the only antiallergy therapy that induces immune tolerance to allergens resulting in a cure in up to 50% of patients who are compliant with treatment over time [2]. In young patients with allergic rhinitis who are predisposed to development of asthma, immune modulation from immunotherapy often results in prevention of asthma development [3]. Moreover, immunotherapy is protective against development of sensitization to multiple allergens (polysensitization) in patients who have already developed allergic sensitization to a single allergen (monosensitized) [4,5]. Taken together, immunotherapy remains a potent therapeutic agent in the treatment of allergic diseases. This article discusses the current understanding of the mechanisms involved in immunotherapy, which diseases are effectively treated with immunotherapy, and future directions of this important form of treatment.

## ALLERGIC DISEASES EFFECTIVELY TREATED WITH IMMUNOTHERAPY

### Case study

A 13-year-old boy presents to his pediatrician's office for continued evaluation and treatment of seasonal and perennial allergic rhinitis. The patient's symptoms began at approximately 5 to 6 years of age and consist of watery nasal discharge, pruritus, sneezing and congestion. Over the last 2 years these have worsened in severity and frequency, with progression to almost daily and nightly symptoms. Intranasal steroids were initiated on a routine basis 1 year ago with moderate improvement of some symptoms. Despite addition of as-needed nonsedating oral antihistamines, decongestants, and leukotriene receptor antagonist, the patient still experienced persistent symptoms. In vitro IgE testing performed and corroborated by history showed that he was allergic to dust mite, cat, grasses, and trees endemic to his area. Environmental controls were instituted with covering of bedding in dust mite–proof covers, removal of the carpet from the patient's bedroom, and use of a high-efficiency particulate air (HEPA) filter during the evening. These controls resulted in some further improvements in symptoms. Because of partial improvement of symptoms despite use of multiple pharmacologic agents and allergen avoidance the patient was started on subcutaneous immunotherapy to dust mites, grasses, and trees once a week. The patient did not own a cat. After 8 months the patient achieved the maintenance dose of immunotherapy and was switched to once-a-month injections. Over the next few months his symptoms improved gradually and he was able to discontinue most of his allergic medications 4 months after first reaching his maintenance immunotherapy dose.

Given the effectiveness of immunotherapy to treat allergic rhinitis it was tempting for early allergy providers to use this treatment modality to target other allergic diseases such as atopic dermatitis and food allergies. However, studies have shown that immunotherapy is most effective for allergic rhinitis, allergic conjunctivitis, allergic asthma, and stinging insect hypersensitivity. As such, the American College of Asthma Allergy and Immunology (ACAAI) and the American Academy of Asthma Allergy and Immunology (AAAAI) recommend immunotherapy only for the treatment of these conditions [6].

### Allergic rhinitis

Rigorous double-blind placebo-controlled studies have repeatedly shown high efficacy of immunotherapy in the treatment of seasonal and perennial allergic rhinitis [7–10]. A large meta-analysis involving 759 patients in 16 studies compared immunotherapy with placebo. Fifteen studies (94%) showed that immunotherapy was effective, as shown by reduction in symptoms, medication use, and allergen-specific IgE. Allergens used in these studies included dust mites, ragweed, grass and tree pollen, and mold [11]. Immunotherapy had a 1.81 odds risk of clinical improvement.

### Allergic conjunctivitis and rhinoconjunctivitis

Some patients have allergic conjunctivitis alone but many have allergic rhinoconjunctivitis. Ocular symptoms often mirror nasal symptoms, particularly with forms of conjunctivitis such as vernal keratoconjunctivitis [12]. Although there are fewer rigorous studies showing the efficacy of immunotherapy in allergic conjunctivitis alone because of coexistence with nasal disease, there is ample clinical evidence and experience that shows immunotherapy to be effective in ocular allergic disease [13,14].

### Allergic asthma

Immunotherapy is a well-accepted treatment modality for bronchial asthma in the United States. However, there are well-controlled studies that raise questions regarding immunotherapy's efficacy in these patients, particularly when there is sensitization to multiple allergens. In carefully selected asthmatic patients who are sensitized to grass pollen, cats, and dust mites, immunotherapy clearly shows clinical effectiveness. In 75 randomized control trials, 3188 subjects were analyzed in a meta-analysis. Allergens studied included dust mites, animal dander, pollen, and mold. Multiple allergens were included in 6 studies. Although results were not as dramatic as those for allergic rhinitis, they clearly favored immunotherapy rather than placebo in asthmatic patients. Symptom scores and bronchial hyper-reactivity improved, whereas medication requirements diminished with immunotherapy compared with placebo [15]. However, a few large-scale, double-blind, placebo-controlled studies recently failed to show significant advantage of immunotherapy both in adults and children with persistent asthma compared with specialist-driven standard of care treatment [16,17]. In the pediatric study, patients had moderate persistent asthma and were multiallergen sensitive [16]. Although immunotherapy is likely an effective treatment of bronchial asthma, careful selection of patient phenotypes and allergen sensitization may be required for optimal efficacy.

### Stinging insect hypersensitivity

Immunotherapy is a mainstay in prevention of anaphylaxis and reduction of risk of progression to anaphylaxis in patients in response to various stinging insects. These insects include Hymenoptera (bees, wasps, hornets, and yellow jackets), fire ants, and bed bugs [18,19]. Well-controlled studies have shown that patients who achieve maintenance immunotherapy with insect venom have greatly diminished risk of anaphylaxis on re-sting or bite [20,21]. In general, immunotherapy is indicated when patients have experienced anaphylaxis to stinging insects, and in patients more than 16 years of age who experienced systemic cutaneous nonanaphylactic reactions to insect stings. Children younger than 16 years who have systemic cutaneous anaphylactic reactions and children and adults with large local reactions to insect stings have low risk of disease progression and do not need to receive venom immunotherapy. This article does not include stinging insect immunotherapy but there are multiple reviews on this subject [18,22,23].

### Case study

A 5-year-old boy presents for consultation for risk of development of asthma. At 3 years of age he developed allergic rhinitis with symptoms of frequent rhinorrhea, clear nasal discharge, and nasal pruritus. These symptoms are currently fairly well controlled with a routine intranasal corticosteroid and as-needed nonsedating antihistamine. His parents both have persistent asthma. Furthermore, the patient's 2 older siblings have severe persistent asthma requiring high-dose corticosteroids for control and have frequent urgent-care visits. The parents wonder whether anything can be done to prevent, or at least attenuate, development of asthma in their youngest son. The patient was skin tested and found to be sensitized to dust mites and grass pollen. He was given environmental controls and started on dust mite and grass pollen immunotherapy once weekly. Within a few months of reaching maintenance injections the patient's nasal symptoms improved and intranasal corticosteroids could be discontinued. He received monthly maintenance immunotherapy for the next 5 years and never developed asthma symptoms.

### Prevention of development of asthma and further allergen sensitization

Apart from observations by a century of immunotherapy administering providers, large-scale prospective studies have also shown the protective effects of immunotherapy against development of asthma and further allergen sensitization in allergic patients. In the Preventive Allergy Treatment (PAT) study, children with rhinoconjunctivitis associated with birch and/or grass pollen allergy were randomized to receive immunotherapy to these allergens or placebo for 3 years. Children who received active immunotherapy had a 2.5-fold reduced risk ($P<.001$) of development of asthma compared with the placebo group [3]. Longer term studies include a 14-year follow-up of children given immunotherapy versus placebo. At the date of the children's 16th birthday, 22% of patients given placebo, compared with 72% who received immunotherapy, were asthma free [24]. In an open but large-scale study, 7182 patients with single-allergen sensitization were given immunotherapy. At the end of 3 years, 27% of these patients developed additional allergen sensitization compared with 68% of open controls consisting of 1214 patients [25]. In a similar study, 45% of monosensitized children receiving immunotherapy developed additional allergen sensitivity compared with 100% of similar patients who were given placebo [26].

Compared with conventional modalities of treatment of allergies and asthma, immunotherapy to date remains the only therapy that can significantly reduce risk of disease progression.

### Atopic dermatitis and urticaria/angioedema

Recent evidence supports the role of aeroallergens in the pathogenesis of atopic dermatitis [27–31]. Aeroallergen immunotherapy logically should be effective in the treatment of atopic dermatitis. A small number of studies have shown that immunotherapy, especially with dust mite, improves atopic dermatitis scores [32,33]. Patients with more severe disease seem to have less improvement with immunotherapy [34]. Thus, immunotherapy may have a potential role in the treatment of patients with atopic dermatitis who are sensitized to inhalant allergens, particularly for those with concomitant respiratory allergy. In contrast with atopic dermatitis, there is no evidence that immunotherapy has any effect on either acute or chronic urticaria/angioedema.

## MECHANISMS OF IMMUNOTHERAPY: TARGETING MULTIPLE POINTS OF THE ALLERGIC CASCADE

Immunologic changes resulting from immunotherapy are complex and the precise pathways involved are being continuously elucidated. At present, a rigorous body of evidence supports that multiple areas of the allergic cascade are involved (Fig. 1), including modulation of T-lymphocyte response, induction of regulatory T lymphocytes, and IgE and IgG responses [35].

Patients genetically and environmentally predisposed to atopy exhibit a preferential TH2 lymphocyte response to various allergenic antigens. On exposure to previously sensitized allergens, TH2 lymphocyte responses elaborate cytokines such as interleukin (IL)-4 and IL-13, which facilitate development of IgE (IgE switching) against the associated antigen [36]. Furthermore, TH2 lymphocytes may also secrete cytokines such as IL-5 that recruit and activate inflammatory cells such as eosinophils and basophils, which express inflammatory peptides into the local milieu. Persistence of these signals from chronic allergen exposure results in chronic inflammation in most patients with allergic rhinitis and asthma [37,38]. Data have shown that successful immunotherapy with previously sensitized allergens results in a change from a TH2 to TH1 lymphocyte response, which results in reduction of IgE switching in preference for more IgG responses [39].

Immunotherapy with allergens such as grass pollen, house dust mite, and insect venom has been shown to generate T-regulatory cells that elaborate regulatory cytokines, namely IL-10 and TGF-b [40]. T-regulatory cells may in part

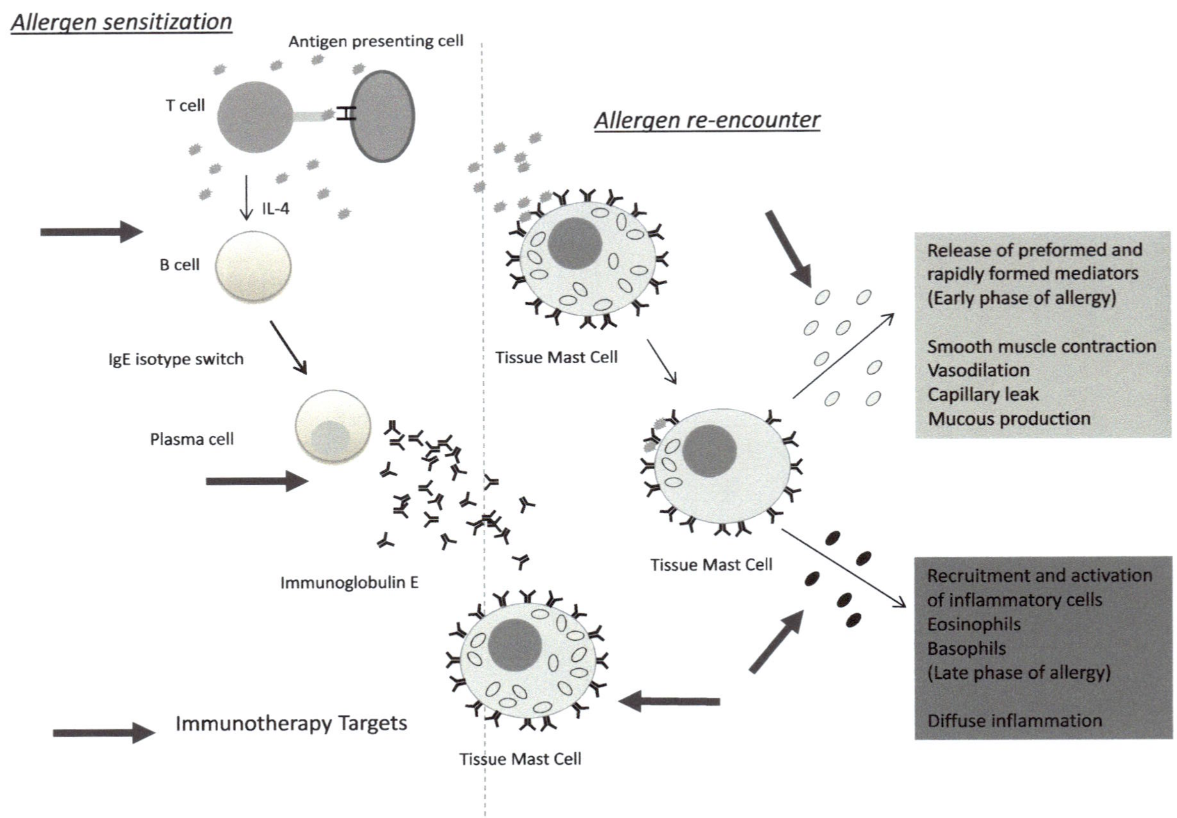


**Fig. 1.** Targets of immunotherapy along the allergic cascade.

serve as dampeners of lymphocyte activation, reducing the skewed TH2 lymphocyte responses in allergic patients [41]. B-cell–specific IgE production has been shown to be inhibited, whereas IgG4 expression is conversely stimulated by IL-10 from T-regulatory cells [42]. Proinflammatory cytokine release from mast cells and eosinophils can be inhibited by IL-10. In addition, elective inhibition of the CD28 costimulatory pathway by IL-10 elicits T-cell tolerance during immunotherapy [43,44].

## CAVEATS ON CLINICAL RESPONSE TO IMMUNOTHERAPY

### Case study

A 14-year old girl with perennial and seasonal allergic rhinitis tested positive for dust mite, grass, and tree pollen. She was started on immunotherapy, initially twice weekly for 4 months until she achieved maintenance dose, and thereafter she received once-monthly injections. Three months later she began experiencing fewer symptoms, and by 14 months did not require intranasal steroids or antihistamines. She continued immunotherapy until she was 19 years of age, when she was no longer covered by her parents' health insurance. Her allergic rhinitis symptoms seem to have resolved.

In general, several levels of clinical response can be observed with immunotherapy treatment. These levels include early, progressive, persistent, and preventative effects.

Within a year of attaining maintenance doses of immunotherapy, most patients experience improvement in allergy symptoms and reduction in rescue medication use. This early effect has been documented in multiple large-scale randomized studies. For instance, symptom scores for rhinoconjunctivitis improved and medication requirements were reduced in hundreds of recruited subjects after immunotherapy with grass pollen antigen in several well-controlled studies [45–47]. These results have been duplicated for other allergens [8,10].

Continued treatment with immunotherapy beyond the first year results in further reduction in symptoms and medication needs. Robust studies have shown this effect with grass pollen, dust mite, dog, and cat antigens, although smaller and similar studies have shown efficacy with many other allergens such as tree and weed pollens [48,49]. In addition, studies have shown that immunotherapy during the second year may produce decreased symptoms and medication requirements of a larger magnitude compared with the first year of treatment [50]. During this progressive effect, many studies show improvement in objective measures in addition to subjective symptom improvement. For instance, asthmatic patients allergic to dust mite and grass pollen and receiving immunotherapy had reduced airway hyper-reactivity in response to methacholine by the 18th and 24th month of allergen injections respectively [51,52]. In addition, studies have shown that, in asthmatic children and adults, immunotherapy significantly attenuates allergen-induced late-phase airway responses [53]. It is also likely that changes in the immune response to allergen exposure (as described previously) occur during this phase of immunotherapy. Increased expression of interferon-gamma representing a TH1 lymphocyte pattern was found in peripheral blood of patients receiving grass pollen immunotherapy after 12 months of treatment, but not after 3 months [54]. Pollen-specific IgG levels similarly increased minimally after 1 year of grass pollen immunotherapy, but significantly during the second year of treatment in another study [55].

One of the most convincing arguments for immunotherapy as a mainstay for treatment of allergic diseases despite relative inconvenience is the persistence effect even after cessation of treatment. Although this occurs only in approximately half of patients, this is the only treatment that can afford a cure for allergic disorders. In a large randomized trial, patients with allergic rhinitis who previously received grass pollen immunotherapy were given either placebo or continued grass pollen antigen. Patients who were discontinued from active immunotherapy (placebo group) had sustained symptom improvement and medication scores that were not significantly different from those in the active (continued treatment) group. This effect was persistent for 3 years after discontinuation of therapy [2]. In the aforementioned PAT study, children who received immunotherapy had sustained eye and nasal symptom improvements for up to 10 years after discontinuation of therapy compared with similar children who never received treatment [3].

As previously discussed, immunotherapy significantly reduces the progression of allergic disease and sensitization to new allergens in atopic patients (interruption of the atopic march).

## CLINICAL EFFECTIVENESS OF IMMUNOTHERAPY VERSUS PHARMACOLOGIC TREATMENT OF ALLERGIC DISEASES AND HOW IMMUNOTHERAPY FITS IN WITH REGULAR THERAPY

The AAAAI/ACAAI joint task force's third practice parameter on allergen immunotherapy recommends specific indications for immunotherapy (Box 1) [6]. However, these indications are broad, and considerable discretion is left to both the provider and patient with regard to initiating immunotherapy. Scenarios range from one extreme, wherein immunotherapy is begun because of patient demand without any trials of medications and environmental controls, to the opposite extreme, in which immunotherapy is withheld by providers and insurance payers until every modality of treatment is exhausted. It is likely that, in many instances, which patient receives immunotherapy is dictated by insurance coverage, provider's knowledge or passion to start treatment, and the insistence of patients themselves. However, given the broad indications for immunotherapy, knowledge of efficacy of immunotherapy compared with regular treatment helps providers and patients decide whether to begin immunotherapy in a rational manner.

The most straightforward decision to initiate immunotherapy is when patients do not respond optimally to standard medical therapy, which is especially evident with allergic rhinitis. At present, first-line treatments of allergic rhinitis with frequent symptoms are intranasal corticosteroids with nonsedating antihistamines and oral decongestants added on an as-needed basis [56]. Despite

**Box 1: General indications for allergen immunotherapy**

For allergic rhinitis, allergic conjunctivitis, and asthma: in patients in whom there is (1) evidence of specific IgE antibodies to allergens, and (2) clinical history and symptoms that are consistent with exposure to these allergens, immunotherapy may be indicated based on (but not limited to) the following factors:

- Patient's preference/acceptability
- Poor adherence
- Multiple and or high-dose medication requirements
- Incomplete response to allergen avoidance
- Medication side/adverse effects
- Therapy for coexisting allergic rhinitis and asthma
- Potential prevention of allergic march and development of asthma in patients with allergic rhinitis

Potential indication: atopic dermatitis, in which inhalant allergen is associated with disease.

Indications for allergen immunotherapy in patients with Hymenoptera stings:

- Anaphylactic reaction to Hymenoptera sting in both children and adults with demonstrable clinical significant specific IgE to Hymenoptera venom
- Cutaneous nonanaphylactic systemic reaction to hymenoptera sting in adults and children older than 16 years with demonstrable IgE antibodies to hymenoptera venom
- Children and adults with systemic reactions to fire ants with demonstrable IgE antibodies

Potential indication: patients with large local reactions to Hymenoptera stings that are deliberating and frequent.

*Adapted from* Cox L, Nelson H, Lockey R, et al. Allergen immunotherapy: a practice parameter third update. J Allergy Clin Immunol 2011;127(1):S1–55; with permission.

commercial advertisements suggesting that these agents are effective for a most patients with rhinitis, large bodies of evidence show that a significant number of patients achieve incomplete relief of symptoms. The National Allergy Survey Assessing Limitations showed that, despite current treatments, significant numbers of patients with allergic rhinitis had difficulty with sleep, decreased quality of life, and reduced work productivity. Twenty-eight percent of patients were dissatisfied with intranasal steroids because of bothersome side effects [57]. In one study using budesonide irrigation, only 60% of patients achieved significant symptom resolution [58].

Response to inhaled corticosteroids in patients with asthma follows a bell-shaped response curve. In a study with the primary outcome set as number of symptom-free days, a large number of patients placed on either fluticasone or montelukast experienced increased number of symptom-free days; however, up to 16% of patients had no change in asthma-free days [59]. A similar study with change in forced expiratory volume in 1 second ($FEV_1$) as primary outcome showed that 20% to 30% of patients with asthma given inhaled beclomethasone or oral montelukast experienced no improvement in $FEV_1$ [60]. In a large study involving pediatric patients with asthma, there was a differential response to combination therapy involving either corticosteroids plus long-acting bronchodilator or montelukast. Neither combination strategies were able to produce complete asthma control in 100% of the patients [61]. In the Gaining Control of Asthma (GOAL) study, up to 70% of patients never achieved asthma control despite being given high-dose inhaled corticosteroid/long-acting bronchodilator agents [62]. A similar percentage of pediatric patients in a real-world inner-city disease management program also failed to achieve asthma control despite guideline-based care [63]. Although there are less rigorous studies examining differential response to medications in patients with allergic rhinitis, international consensus groups have found that a significant number of patients experience chronic unacceptable symptoms despite guideline-based treatment [64].

Despite the availability of multiple preparations of intranasal corticosteroids, a significant number of patients experience bothersome side effects such as nasal irritation and postnasal drip. For instance, in the NASL (National Survey Assessing Limitations) survey up to 66% of patients surveyed indicated that they experienced discomfort at least some of the time from these agents, and 28% of patients in the survey who requested changing intranasal corticosteroids cited side effects of the current preparation as the reason for switching [57]. Studies have shown that inhaled corticosteroids also produce troublesome side effects in a significant number of asthmatics. In one survey, up to 40%, 30%, and 14% of patients experienced cough during inhalation, thirsty feeling, or dysphonia respectively while taking either inhaled budesonide or beclomethasone [65]. Furthermore, side effects were more frequent and severe with increased daily doses of medication.

Although most agents used in the treatment of asthma and allergies have excellent safety profiles, there are some side effects associated with their use. In particular, inhaled corticosteroids used at high doses result in small but tangible adverse side effects. Less severe and reversible effects include dysphonia, oral irritation, and oral thrush [66]. More lasting effects include growth velocity reduction in children [67,68]. This growth rate reduction is thought to be transient and ultimate adult height was found to be unaffected because of catch-up growth in earlier studies. However, recent evidence suggests that this catch up does not occur. The reduction in ultimate height in these children compared with their predicted midparental height is small, in the magnitude of 0.3 to 0.5 cm [69].

In addition, despite favorable outcomes associated with multiple pharmacologic agents, compliance plays a major role in achieving disease control in many patients with asthma and allergies. Multiple studies have shown that noncompliance with medication plays a role in most patients who do not achieve control of their symptoms [70,71].

Taken together, these data show that immunotherapy may be beneficial in a spectrum of clinical scenarios. These scenarios include when medications do not adequately control symptoms, when medications control symptoms but have bothersome side effects, when medications control symptoms but result in adverse side effects, when compliance with medications are poor, and when patients prefer receiving once-weekly to once-monthly allergy injections compared with daily inhaled, intranasal, and oral medications. The provider should work in concert with patients in deciding whether immunotherapy is a good clinical choice in each scenario.

## SAFETY AND ADVERSE EVENTS ASSOCIATED WITH ALLERGEN IMMUNOTHERAPY

Injection of allergens into previously sensitized patients incurs the risk of allergic reactions that range from local urticaria to anaphylactic shock and death. Emergency equipment should be available during immunotherapy administration for potential systemic reactions (Box 2). However, the risk of serious anaphylactic reactions is rare when immunotherapy is administered appropriately. In an AAAAI longitudinal survey of physician AAAAI members from 1990 to 2001, the incidence of reported near-fatal reactions (NFR) was 23 per year, culminating in 5.4 events per 1 million injections. The total number of fatal reactions during this survey period was 41, culminating in 1 fatal reaction per 2.5 million injections [72]. However, large local reactions associated with immunotherapy are common, ranging from 26% to 86%. Most studies have shown that large local reactions, although a discomfort to the patient, are benign. Patients who experience large local reactions are usually not at any higher risk of systemic reactions with the next injection [73,74]. Only 1 study found that patients with large local reactions of 25 mm or larger have a higher

**Box 2: Examples of emergency equipment recommended for treatment of immunotherapy systemic reactions**

Aqueous adrenaline 1:1000

Oxygen delivery equipment

Airway patency equipment

Intravenous fluid equipment

H1 antagonist

H2 antagonist

Corticosteroids

Glucagon (for patients receiving β-blockers)

Equipment for intravenous access, intramuscular medication delivery, blood pressure monitoring

*Adapted from* Cox L, Nelson H, Lockey R, et al. Allergen immunotherapy: a practice parameter third update. J Allergy Clin Immunol 2011;127(1):S1–55; with permission.

likelihood of subsequent systemic reactions [75]. In addition, almost all patients receiving immunotherapy have transient local pain and discomfort at the injection site.

Risks of severe allergic reactions are associated with several factors and these can be minimized when immunotherapy is administered in an appropriate fashion. Because morbidity is associated with asthma, immunotherapy should not be given to patients with unstable or poor asthma control [6]. Up to 70% of systemic reactions occur within 30 minutes of injection [76]. In the AAAAI fatal and NFR survey, 96% of patients experiencing NFR and 77% who died after immunotherapy had onset of symptoms within 30 minutes of the initial injection [77]. Therefore, patients should receive immunotherapy in a medical setting that is equipped to handle anaphylactic emergencies and wait at least 30 minutes before leaving. A longer observation period is necessary for more sensitive patients who may also be given self-injectable adrenaline for late reactions, although these are rare [6].

### High-risk patients

Although immunotherapy is generally safe for patients with various underlying diseases such as immune deficiency, caution must be taken with patients who are at higher risk of morbidity and mortality from anaphylaxis. Death from anaphylaxis is often caused by respiratory failure and therefore patients with uncontrolled asthma are poor candidates for immunotherapy until their disease is controlled [77–79]. Likewise, patients previously well but experiencing asthma exacerbations should not receive their injections until clinically improved [6]. Relative contraindications to immunotherapy include certain medications that may antagonize agents used for the treatment of anaphylaxis and may themselves increase the risk of anaphylaxis. These agents include β-blockers and angiotensin-converting enzyme inhibitors [80–82]. These patients should be switched to other agents whenever possible if immunotherapy is to be initiated. Immunotherapy is generally safe for pregnant patients but risk to the fetus occurs if there are systemic reactions resulting in placental-utero insufficiency. In general, patients who become pregnant while on immunotherapy can continue but not have any dose escalation to reduce risk of systemic reactions [83,84]. Patients with unstable cardiovascular disease similarly have reduced survivability during systemic reactions and the benefits of immunotherapy must be carefully weighed against the risks. For instance, a patient with anaphylaxis to bee stings and who has unavoidable exposure to bees may elect to receive venom immunotherapy despite having unstable angina [6,85].

## PRACTICAL ASPECTS OF IMMUNOTHERAPY

### Case study

The mother of a 14-year-old boy with seasonal and perennial allergic rhinitis hears that allergy shots may better control her son's allergy symptoms. She brings him to a provider who performs an allergy blood test, which is positive for everything, including dust mites, dog, cat, several species of mold, multiple species of grass, trees, and weeds. A history of environmental associations with allergy symptoms is not taken. The provider starts the patient on immunotherapy consisting of 4 shots twice a week. Each shot is drawn from a vial consisting of mixtures of several different antigens. After 18 months of shots the patient's allergy symptoms have not significantly improved.

Careful selection of antigens administered in correct doses is necessary for effective immunologic and clinical changes to occur in response to subcutaneous injection therapy. Improper selection and mixing of allergens, subtherapeutic doses, and use of allergens with no clinical association to symptoms often results in minimal clinical response.

## Allergen selection

Skin testing is often the preferred method for identification of antigens for immunotherapy, although modern specific IgE serum tests are acceptable alternatives. Patients may have positive skin or serum IgE tests to certain allergens but have no clinical consequence when exposed to them (sensitized but with no clinical reactivity). Therefore, it is imperative that the provider takes a detailed history to determine which allergens correlate with clinical symptoms before using the particular allergen for immunotherapy. For instance, a patient may have a positive skin test to dogs but show no symptoms when exposed to dogs. Use of canine antigen for immunotherapy therefore would not result in any therapeutic benefit. Inclusion of clinically irrelevant allergens may also result in dilution of other relevant allergens, reducing overall effectiveness.

There is diverse flora in the United States, with local geographic areas having a predominance of certain species. Given the large numbers of pollen species in the United States, it is impossible to test for every single one. Moreover, there is extensive cross reactivity between grass allergens, thus only a few species are required even if patients are clinically reactive to more. Cross reactivity between trees and between weeds is much less. Thus the immunotherapy provider must have knowledge of the local aerobiology to choose a practical but relevant series of allergens for testing. Omitting clinically relevant allergens results in decreased effectiveness of immunotherapy.

Pollens such as grass and ragweed have been shown in multiple studies to be effective and safe in immunotherapy [86–88]. However, there are many other clinically relevant pollens that have not undergone similar study. Extrapolation of known data to these is reasonable and likely effective. At present there are no commercially available allergens to some clinically relevant molds such as ascospores and others may be antigenically suboptimal, including *Aspergillus* and *Cladosporium* [89–91]. Certain molds are found predominantly indoors, whereas others are found outdoors. Thus the provider must ascertain the clinical relevance of each. For patients clinically reactive to dander from animals such as dogs and cats, the first line of treatment should be avoidance. However, avoidance is not possible in some patients, such as veterinarian staff, or because of personal choice. In such cases, cat and dog antigen immunotherapy is effective. Multiple studies have shown that dust mite immunotherapy is effective and useful in conjunction with dust mite avoidance strategies. In addition, patients clinically reactive to cockroach benefit from cockroach immunotherapy, particularly together with aggressive pest elimination strategies [92].

## Antigen standardization

The minimum amount of antigen needed to achieve clinical improvement is called the maintenance dose. At present, this dose has been determined for a range of allergens (Table 1). In the past, allergists prepared their own extracts by compounding various allergens from local fauna using weight-per-volume formulas, which often resulted in wide ranges of allergen concentrations being given to patients. Current commercial extracts have more consistent antigen content and many allergens are standardized in terms of equivalent biologic units. In the United States, these are calculated based on the amount of antigen required to elicit a certain erythema size in subjects highly sensitized to that particular allergen. Standardized antigens are available for dust mite, cat, and grasses. Other antigens, such as dog and trees, are still prepared by the weight-to-volume method. Providers should use standardized antigens for immunotherapy when possible to ensure that maintenance doses are achieved.

Most studies showing effectiveness of immunotherapy have used only single allergens. In reality, patients are usually allergic to multiple antigens (polysensitized) and may need multiple allergens administered for immunotherapy. Most patients are able to tolerate up to 4 subcutaneous injections per session.

**Table 1**
Examples of effective dosing ranges for standardized and nonstandardized licensed antigens in the United States

| Allergen extract | Labeled potency/ concentration | Probable effective dose range |
|---|---|---|
| Dust mites: *Dermatophagoides farinae/ Dermatophagoides pteronyssinus* | 3000, 5000, 10,000, and 30,000 AU/mL | 500–2000 AU |
| Cat hair/pelt | 5000 and 10,000 BAU/mL | 1000–4000 BAU |
| Bermuda grass | 10,000 BAU/mL | 300–1500 BAU |
| Standardizes miscellaneous grass | 100,000 BAU/mL | 1000–4000 BAU |
| Short ragweed | 1:10, 1:20 wt/vol, 100,000 AU/mL | 6–12 μg or 1000–4000 AU |
| Nonstandardized AP dog | 1:100 wt/vol | 15 μg |
| Nonstandardized pollen extracts | 1:10 to 1:40 wt/vol, 10,000–40,000 PNU/mL | 0.5 mL of 1:100 or 1:200 wt/vol |
| Nonstandardized mold/fungi | 1:10 to 1:40 wt/vol, 10,000–40,000 PNU/mL | Highest dose tolerated |

*Abbreviations:* AP, acetone precipitated; AU, Allergy units; BAU, Bioequivalent allergy units; PNU, Protein nitrogen unit, wt/vol, weight/volume.

*Adapted from* Cox L, Nelson H, Lockey R, et al. Allergen immunotherapy: a practice parameter third update. J Allergy Clin Immunol 2011;127(1):S1–55; with permission.

Thus several antigens are often combined in a single injection stock vial. Subcutaneous injection of more than 0.4 to 0.5 mL is usually difficult to tolerate long term. Although there are a limited number of studies that have examined efficacy of multiantigen immunotherapy, it is likely that this mode of immunotherapy is effective. Care must be taken not to combine too many antigens in a single stock vial and dilute the effective maintenance concentrations of each antigen. Thus the provider must be skilled in including clinically relevant antigens and excluding those that are irrelevant [6].

### Immunotherapy schedule

There are 2 phases involved in immunotherapy: buildup and maintenance. The former involves gradually increasing concentrations of antigen over weeks and the latter is when therapeutic doses are achieved and maintained over time. If the starting allergen doses are too dilute, then the time needed to achieve maintenance is prolonged and unnecessarily large numbers of injections are given. In contrast, if the starting doses contain too much antigen, then the risk of reactions is increased. Current guidelines recommend starting at 1:10,000 to 1:1000 dilution of the maintenance concentration. Doses are usually increased 1 to 3 times a week depending on patients' convenience, and their ability to tolerate the number of injections. Table 2 shows a typical schedule. Maintenance is usually achieved in 3 to 6 months. Very sensitive patients may have to begin at more dilute concentrations and dose escalation frequency needs to be slowed when there are systemic reactions. Large local reactions without systemic symptoms usually do not necessitate dose escalation reduction [6]. Once maintenance dosing is achieved, dosing intervals may be spaced to once monthly [93].

### Cluster and rush immunotherapy

Because conventional immunotherapy requires months of injections before maintenance is achieved, efforts have been made to adjust dosing and reduce time to the maintenance phase. Cluster immunotherapy involves giving 2 or more injections of allergens per session, which results in achieving maintenance doses in as early as 4 weeks compared with 3 to 6 months. Rush immunotherapy involves giving multiple injections over the course of hours, resulting in maintenance doses in as little as 6 days. Risk of reactions associated with both cluster and rush immunotherapy are increased, although most are not severe. Premedication also reduced the risk of these reactions. Patients usually require to be hospitalized for rush schedules.

### Duration of immunotherapy

Patients usually experience improvement of symptoms within 1 year of achieving maintenance doses. Vigorous studies in venom immunotherapy show that 5 years of therapy is sufficient for most subjects to be protected against future stings. Although there are fewer similar studies involving inhalant allergens, it is accepted that 3 to 5 years of inhalant immunotherapy provides the best chance of a cure for patients with allergic rhinitis. Approximately half of patients who have no to minimal symptoms after 3 to 5 years of immunotherapy

**Table 2**
Sample immunotherapy injection record

Patient Name

Medical Record Number

Date of Birth

***Vial A Extract Name:***______________

| Dilution<br>Color<br>Vial Number | 1:10,000 (w/v)<br>Silver<br>5 | 1:1000 (w/v)<br>Green<br>4 | 1:100 (w/v)<br>Blue<br>3 | 1:10 (w/v)<br>Yellow<br>2 | 1:1 (w/v)<br>Red<br>1 |
|---|---|---|---|---|---|
| Expiration Date | / / | / / | / / | / / | / / |

**Vial A**

| | Date | Time | Peak flow | Health screen | Vial Dilution / Vial Number<br>Arm | Volume injected | Local reaction (mm) | Injector sign. |
|---|---|---|---|---|---|---|---|---|
| 1 | / / | | | Normal/Abnorm | R L | | | |
| 2 | / / | | | Normal/Abnorm | R L | | | |
| 3 | / / | | | Normal/Abnorm | R L | | | |
| 4 | / / | | | Normal/Abnorm | R L | | | |
| 5 | / / | | | Normal/Abnorm | R L | | | |
| 6 | / / | | | Normal/Abnorm | R L | | | |
| 7 | / / | | | Normal/Abnorm | R L | | | |
| 8 | / / | | | Normal/Abnorm | R L | | | |
| 9 | / / | | | Normal/Abnorm | R L | | | |
| 10 | / / | | | Normal/Abnorm | R L | | | |
| 11 | / / | | | Normal/Abnorm | R L | | | |
| 12 | / / | | | Normal/Abnorm | R L | | | |
| 13 | / / | | | Normal/Abnorm | R L | | | |
| 14 | / / | | | Normal/Abnorm | R L | | | |
| 15 | / / | | | Normal/Abnorm | R L | | | |
| 16 | / / | | | Normal/Abnorm | R L | | | |
| 17 | / / | | | Normal/Abnorm | R L | | | |
| 18 | / / | | | Normal/Abnorm | R L | | | |
| 19 | / / | | | Normal/Abnorm | R L | | | |
| 20 | / / | | | Normal/Abnorm | R L | | | |
| 21 | / / | | | Normal/Abnorm | R L | | | |
| 22 | / / | | | Normal/Abnorm | R L | | | |
| 23 | / / | | | Normal/Abnorm | R L | | | |
| 24 | / / | | | Normal/Abnorm | R L | | | |
| 25 | / / | | | Normal/Abnorm | R L | | | |
| 26 | / / | | | Normal/Abnorm | R L | | | |
| 27 | / / | | | Normal/Abnorm | R L | | | |
| 28 | / / | | | Normal/Abnorm | R L | | | |

relapse. Therefore, some patients elect to continue treatment for longer periods of time [2].

Taken together, it is highly recommended that immunotherapy be prescribed and administered by trained providers such as allergist-immunologists and performed in appropriate medical settings.

## FUTURE DEVELOPMENTS

### Sublingual allergen immunotherapy

The inconvenience, pain, and risk of rare but severe systemic reactions associated with injection immunotherapy have caused clinicians to develop other modalities of allergen delivery. Bronchial, intranasal, and oral routes have proved to be ineffective [94–96]. Direct oral absorption of antigen was first introduced in the United States in the 1940s but did not gain acceptance. Dust mite antigen delivered via this route was first described in 1986 and intense interest and studies remerged in sublingual immunotherapy (SLIT), particularly in Europe [97,98]. The World health Organization (WHO) and the European Academy of Allergy and Immunology currently support the use of SLIT in allergen desensitization of pediatric and adult patients with allergic diseases. In the United States, clinicians offering this modality of treatment do so in an off-label fashion because there are no US Food and Drug Administration (FDA)–approved formulations of SLIT allergens.

Studies have shown similar efficacy between SLIT and subcutaneous immunotherapy (SCIT), although studies involving the latter are more extensive and comprehensive. SLIT has been shown to be effective in treatment of allergic rhinitis and asthma in pediatric patients [99,100]. Both symptom improvement and reduction of medication requirements have been shown with SLIT [101]. Similar to SCIT, studies have shown that improvements in asthma symptoms caused by SLIT, although statistically significant, were small [102,103]. In addition, SLIT has been shown to interrupt the allergic march in atopic children. Marogna and colleagues [104] randomized 216 children to receive either medication alone or in combination with SLIT. After 3 years, 34.8% of control patients developed new allergen sensitizations compared with 3.1% of patients receiving SLIT. Patients given SLIT also had reduced bronchial reactivity and fewer developed mild persistent asthma compared with control patients. In a similar study, patients given SLIT for 4 to 5 years were statistically less likely to develop asthma compared with control patients. This effect was maintained for 4 to 5 years after discontinuation of therapy [105].

Immunologic changes following SLIT mirror those achieved with SCIT. These changes include reduction in skin reactivity to antigen, decreases in antigen-specific IgE, increase in antigen-specific IgG4, changes in T-regulatory cells, and tolerance to allergen [106,107].

A key advantage of SLIT compared with SCIT is safety. In one large review, local oral reactions were most common with SLIT, with prevalence of 0.68 per 1000 doses in some studies. There were 14 serious systemic reactions in 1,019,826 SLIT administrations resulting in the rate of severe reactions of 0.056% compared with 0.6% in patients who received SCIT [108]. Rare immunologic disorders such as eosinophilic esophagitis have been associated with SLIT; however, it is unclear whether there was a causal relationship or coincidental development of the diseases in the patients receiving SLIT [109]. The safety profile of SLIT has allowed SLIT dosing in Europe to be performed at the patient's home.

Although SLIT is not currently standard of care in the United States owing to lack of FDA-approved antigens, a rapidly growing number of American providers are offering it on an off-label basis. Given the similar efficacy, convenience of at-home dosing, no need for injection, and better safety profile, it is likely that SLIT will play a major role in the near future in the United States for treatment of allergic diseases.

## OTHER ROUTES OF ADMINISTRATION

Intranasal, epicutaneous (transdermal), and intralymphatic injection routes have been used to deliver allergen immunotherapy in a limited numbers of studies. The intranasal route has been found to be effective, but many patients experienced bothersome side effects. Patients receiving transdermal delivery of antigen via a patch did not have significantly better symptom scores compared with patients receiving placebo via the same method. Intralymphatic injection of cat antigen resulted in improvement in symptoms after only 3 single injections over a 4-week period [110]. This improvement was similar to that achieved with conventional SCIT over a 3-year period. The effectiveness and safety of sublingual immunotherapy has reduced interest in intranasal and epicutaneous routes. More studies are needed to determine the efficacy and safety of this more invasive form of immunotherapy.

## COMBINATION WITH ANTI-IGE THERAPY (OMALIZUMAB)

Many patients with unstable asthma are unable to tolerate reactions associated with immunotherapy despite optimal treatment with controller medication. Monoclonal antibody against soluble IgE (omalizumab) is highly effective in the treatment of difficult-to-control asthma [111]. Concurrent immunotherapy treatment with omalizumab has been shown to significantly decrease rates of systemic reactions, particularly with cluster and rush schedules [112,113]. Addition of omalizumab to conventional immunotherapy with birch and grass immunotherapy improved asthma control and reduced medication use compared with immunotherapy or omalizumab alone [114].

## ADDITION OF IMMUNOREGULATORY ADJUVANTS

Immunotherapy results in changes in lymphocyte polarization from TH2 toward TH1, resulting in reduction and increase of allergen-specific IgE and IgG4 respectively [115]. Immunostimulatory oligonucleotide DNA sequences such as CpG motifs are found on bacteria cell walls and facilitate this TH2 to TH1 shift via toll-like receptors (TLRs). Addition of TLR9 agonist to ragweed antigen was shown to decrease allergic rhinitis symptoms after 6 doses in 25 adults [116]. However, a subsequent larger study did not yield similar results [6,117]. A TLR4 receptor agonist MPL (monophosphoryl lipid A) linked to grass pollen significantly reduced symptoms in a large multicenter study with patients who had grass-induced and tree-induced allergic rhinitis [118]. More studies are needed to assess efficacy and safety of these agents.

## IMMUNOTHERAPY FOR FOOD ALLERGY

There is an unmet need to develop treatment modalities for food allergy, given its increasing prevalence. At present, avoidance and early treatment of severe systemic reactions with intramuscular adrenaline are the only recommended treatments [119]. Omalizumab and other agents such as Chinese herbs have been shown to be effective but are non–FDA approved and off-label [120]. Immunotherapy for food allergies was previously considered too dangerous and not effective. However, recent studies have shown that sublingual immunotherapy results in tolerance to foods including milk, egg, peanut, and hazelnut [6]. Moreover, immunologic changes such as reduction in skin reactivity and basophil activation were associated with these treatments, suggesting that there was real tolerance and not merely temporary saturation of IgE receptors, as in penicillin desensitization [121]. Reactions were noted in up to half of patients given peanut immunotherapy, although most were mild and attenuated with antihistamines and sodium cromolyn [122]. More studies are needed before immunotherapy can be adopted for treatment of food allergies.

## IMMUNOTHERAPY FOR POLLEN FOOD ALLERGY SYNDROME

Pollen food allergy syndrome (PFAS) is a local-contact IgE-mediated reaction to fruits and vegetables localized to the mouth that rarely proceeds to systemic symptoms or anaphylaxis. PFAS rarely occurs in young children and develops in older children, teens, and adults. Sensitization does not occur in the gastrointestinal tract because fruit and vegetable antigen is easily broken down during digestion. Fruit and vegetable antigen has extensive cross reactivity with inhalant allergens such as between apples and birch pollen. Atopic patients who develop sensitization to inhalant allergens and develop respiratory disease, like allergic rhinitis, may cross sensitize to fruit and vegetable antigens. It is logical that immunotherapy for inhalant allergens would protect against PFAS. Small studies involving birch-sensitized patients with PFAS to apples showed reduced reactivity to the fruit after birch pollen immunotherapy [123,124]. PFAS is the most common type of food hypersensitivity in adults and older children; it currently has no treatment other than avoidance or cooking to denature the antigen. Thus immunotherapy may be a future modality to treat this more benign but troublesome disease.

## SUMMARY

Immunotherapy remains an effective treatment of allergic diseases both as monotherapy and in synergy with other modern antiallergic therapies. Immunotherapy remains the only therapy that can afford a cure in a significant number of patients with allergies. It has evolved from its primitive beginnings from crude extracts to biologically standardized antigens. Concurrent immunotherapy has become more effective and patient populations likely to benefit more narrowly identified. Ongoing research will likely result in improved effectiveness, faster time to efficacy, improved safety, greater ease of administration, and expansion of the number of allergic diseases treated by immunotherapy.

## References


[1] Noon L. Prophylactic inoculation for hay fever. Lancet 1911;1:1572.

[2] Durham SR, Walker SM, Varga EM, et al. Long-term clinical efficacy of grass pollen immunotherapy. N Engl J Med 1999;341:468–75.

[3] Möller C, Dreborg S, Ferdousi HA, et al. Pollen immunotherapy reduces the development of asthma in children with seasonal rhinoconjunctivitis (the PAT-study). J Allergy Clin Immunol 2002;109(2):251–6.

[4] Des Roches A, Paradis L, Menardo JL, et al. Immunotherapy with a standardized *Dermatophagoides pteronyssinus* extract. VI. Specific immunotherapy prevents the onset of new sensitizations in children. J Allergy Clin Immunol 1997;99(4):450–3.

[5] Pajno GB, Barberio G, De Luca F, et al. Prevention of new sensitizations in asthmatic children monosensitized to house dust mite by specific immunotherapy. A six-year follow-up study. Clin Exp Allergy 2001;31(9):1392–7.

[6] Cox L, Nelson H, Lockey R, et al. Allergen immunotherapy: a practice parameter third update. J Allergy Clin Immunol 2011;127(Suppl 1):S1–55.

[7] Varney VA, Gaga M, Frew AJ, et al. Usefulness of immunotherapy in patients with severe summer hay fever uncontrolled by antiallergic drugs. BMJ 1991;302(6771):265–9.

[8] Bødtger U, Poulsen LK, Jacobi HH, et al. The safety and efficacy of subcutaneous birch pollen immunotherapy – a one-year, randomized, double-blind, placebo-controlled study. Allergy 2002;57(4):297–305.

[9] Ferrer M, Burches E, Peláez A, et al. Double-blind, placebo-controlled study of immunotherapy with *Parietaria judaica*: clinical efficacy and tolerance. J Investig Allergol Clin Immunol 2005;15(4):283–92.

[10] Varney VA, Tabbah K, Mavroleon G, et al. Usefulness of specific immunotherapy in patients with severe perennial allergic rhinitis induced by house dust mite: a double-blind, randomized, placebo-controlled trial. Clin Exp Allergy 2003;33(8):1076–8.

[11] Ross RN, Nelson HS, Finegold I. Effectiveness of specific immunotherapy in the treatment of allergic rhinitis: an analysis of randomized, prospective, single- or double-blind, placebo-controlled studies. Clin Ther 2000;22(3):342–50.

[12] Bielory L. Allergic and immunologic disorders of the eye. Part II: ocular allergy. J Allergy Clin Immunol 2000;106(6):1019–32.

[13] Dreborg S, Agrell B, Foucard T, et al. A double-blind, multicenter immunotherapy trial in children, using a purified and standardized *Cladosporium herbarum* preparation. I. Clinical results. Allergy 1986;41(2):131–40.

[14] Alvarez-Cuesta E, Cuesta-Herranz J, Puyana-Ruiz J, et al. Monoclonal antibody-standardized cat extract immunotherapy: risk-benefit effects from a double-blind placebo study. J Allergy Clin Immunol 1994;93(3):556–66.

[15] Abramson MJ, Puy RM, Weiner JM. Allergen immunotherapy for asthma. Cochrane Database Syst Rev 2010;(8) CD001186.

[16] Adkinson NF Jr, Eggleston PA, Eney D, et al. A controlled trial of immunotherapy for asthma in allergic children. N Engl J Med 1997;336(5):324–31.

[17] Creticos PS, Reed CE, Norman PS, et al. Ragweed immunotherapy in adult asthma. N Engl J Med 1996;334(8):501–6.

[18] Golden DB, Moffitt J, Nicklas RA, et al. Stinging insect hypersensitivity: a practice parameter update 2011. Joint Task Force on Practice Parameters; American Academy of Allergy, Asthma & Immunology (AAAAI); American College of Allergy, Asthma & Immunology (ACAAI); Joint Council of Allergy, Asthma and Immunology. J Allergy Clin Immunol 2011;127(4):852–4.e1–23.

[19] Bonifazi F, Jutel M, Biló BM, et al. Prevention and treatment of Hymenoptera venom allergy: guidelines for clinical practice. EAACI Interest Group on Insect Venom Hypersensitivity. Allergy 2005;60(12):1459–70.

[20] Hunt KJ, Valentine MD, Sobotka AK, et al. A controlled trial of immunotherapy in insect hypersensitivity. N Engl J Med 1978;299(4):157–61.

[21] Reisman RE, Livingston A. Venom immunotherapy: 10 years of experience with administration of single venoms and 50 micrograms maintenance doses. J Allergy Clin Immunol 1992;89(6):1189–95.
[22] Tracy JM, Khan FS, Demain JG. Insect anaphylaxis: where are we? The stinging facts 2012. Curr Opin Allergy Clin Immunol 2012;12(4):400–5.
[23] Bilò MB. Anaphylaxis caused by Hymenoptera stings: from epidemiology to treatment. Allergy 2011;66(Suppl 95):35–7.
[24] Johnstone DE, Dutton A. The value of hyposensitization therapy for bronchial asthma in children–a 14-year study. Pediatrics 1968;42(5):793–802.
[25] Purello-D'Ambrosio F, Gangemi S, Merendino RA, et al. Prevention of new sensitizations in monosensitized subjects submitted to specific immunotherapy or not. A retrospective study. Clin Exp Allergy 2001;31(8):1295–302.
[26] Des Roches A, Paradis L, Paradis J. Immunotherapy for asthma. N Engl J Med 1997;336(26):1912.
[27] Novak N, Bieber T, Leung DY. Immune mechanisms leading to atopic dermatitis. J Allergy Clin Immunol 2003;112(Suppl 6):S128–39.
[28] Schäfer T, Heinrich J, Wjst M, et al. Association between severity of atopic eczema and degree of sensitization to aeroallergens in schoolchildren. J Allergy Clin Immunol 1999;104(6):1280–4.
[29] Scalabrin DM, Bavbek S, Perzanowski MS, et al. Use of specific IgE in assessing the relevance of fungal and dust mite allergens to atopic dermatitis: a comparison with asthmatic and nonasthmatic control subjects. J Allergy Clin Immunol 1999;104(6):1273–9.
[30] Takai T, Ikeda S. Barrier dysfunction caused by environmental proteases in the pathogenesis of allergic diseases. Allergol Int 2011;60(1):25–35.
[31] Kato T, Takai T, Fujimura T, et al. Mite serine protease activates protease-activated receptor-2 and induces cytokine release in human keratinocytes. Allergy 2009;64(9):1366–74.
[32] Bussmann C, Maintz L, Hart J, et al. Clinical improvement and immunological changes in atopic dermatitis patients undergoing subcutaneous immunotherapy with a house dust mite allergoid: a pilot study. Clin Exp Allergy 2007;37:1277–85.
[33] Werfel T, Breuer K, Rueff F, et al. Usefulness of specific immunotherapy in patients with atopic dermatitis and allergic sensitization to house dust mites: a multi-centre, randomized, dose-response study. Allergy 2006;61:202–5.
[34] Pajno GB, Caminiti L, Vita D, et al. Sublingual immunotherapy in mite-sensitized children with atopic dermatitis: a randomized, double-blind, placebo-controlled study. J Allergy Clin Immunol 2007;120:164–70.
[35] Akdis CA, Akdis M. Mechanisms of allergen-specific immunotherapy. J Allergy Clin Immunol 2011;127(1):18–27.
[36] Bacharier LB, Geha RS. Molecular mechanisms of IgE regulation. J Allergy Clin Immunol 2000;105(2 Pt 2):S547–58.
[37] Sanderson CJ. Interleukin-5, eosinophils, and disease. Blood 1992;79(12):3101–9.
[38] Gelfand EW. Inflammatory mediators in allergic rhinitis. J Allergy Clin Immunol 2004;114(Suppl 5):S135–8.
[39] Creticos PS, Van Metre TE, Mardiney MR, et al. Dose response of IgE and IgG antibodies during ragweed immunotherapy. J Allergy Clin Immunol 1984;73(1 Pt 1):94–104.
[40] Jutel M, Akdis M, Budak F, et al. IL-10 and TGF-beta cooperate in the regulatory T cell response to mucosal allergens in normal immunity and specific immunotherapy. Eur J Immunol 2003;33(5):1205–14.
[41] Larché M. Regulatory T cells in allergy and asthma. Chest 2007;132(3):1007–14.
[42] Meiler F, Klunker S, Zimmermann M, et al. Distinct regulation of IgE, IgG4 and IgA by T regulatory cells and toll-like receptors. Allergy 2008;63(11):1455–63.
[43] Joss A, Akdis M, Faith A, et al. IL-10 directly acts on T cells by specifically altering the CD28 co-stimulation pathway. Eur J Immunol 2000;30(6):1683–90.

[44] Akdis CA, Blesken T, Akdis M, et al. Role of interleukin 10 in specific immunotherapy. J Clin Invest 1998;102(1):98–106.
[45] Frew AJ, Powell RJ, Corrigan CJ, et al, UK Immunotherapy Study Group. Efficacy and safety of specific immunotherapy with SQ allergen extract in treatment-resistant seasonal allergic rhinoconjunctivitis. J Allergy Clin Immunol 2006;117(2):319–25.
[46] Dahl R, Kapp A, Colombo G, et al. Efficacy and safety of sublingual immunotherapy with grass allergen tablets for seasonal allergic rhinoconjunctivitis. J Allergy Clin Immunol 2006;118(2):434–40.
[47] Didier A, Malling HJ, Worm M, et al. Optimal dose, efficacy, and safety of once-daily sublingual immunotherapy with a 5-grass pollen tablet for seasonal allergic rhinitis. J Allergy Clin Immunol 2007;120(6):1338–45.
[48] Hedlin G, Graff-Lonnevig V, Heilborn H, et al. Immunotherapy with cat- and dog-dander extracts. V. Effects of 3 years of treatment. J Allergy Clin Immunol 1991;87(5):955–64.
[49] Walker SM, Varney VA, Gaga M, et al. Grass pollen immunotherapy: efficacy and safety during a 4-year follow-up study. Allergy 1995;50(5):405–13.
[50] Winther L, Malling HJ, Moseholm L, et al. Allergen-specific immunotherapy in birch- and grass-pollen-allergic rhinitis. I. Efficacy estimated by a model reducing the bias of annual differences in pollen counts. Allergy 2000;55(9):818–26.
[51] Pichler CE, Helbling A, Pichler WJ. Three years of specific immunotherapy with house-dust-mite extracts in patients with rhinitis and asthma: significant improvement of allergen-specific parameters and of nonspecific bronchial hyperreactivity. Allergy 2001;56(4):301–6.
[52] Walker SM, Pajno GB, Lima MT, et al. Grass pollen immunotherapy for seasonal rhinitis and asthma: a randomized, controlled trial. J Allergy Clin Immunol 2001;107(1):87–93.
[53] Arvidsson MB, Löwhagen O, Rak S. Allergen specific immunotherapy attenuates early and late phase reactions in lower airways of birch pollen asthmatic patients: a double blind placebo-controlled study. Allergy 2004;59(1):74–80.
[54] Durham SR, Ying S, Varney VA, et al. Grass pollen immunotherapy inhibits allergen-induced infiltration of CD4+ T lymphocytes and eosinophils in the nasal mucosa and increases the number of cells expressing messenger RNA for interferon-gamma. J Allergy Clin Immunol 1996;97(6):1356–65.
[55] Osterballe O, Løwenstein H, Norn S, et al. Immunotherapy with grass pollen major allergens. Immunological results from a prospective 3-year double blind study. Allergy 1982;37(7):491–501.
[56] Bousquet J, Van Cauwenberge P, Khaltaev N, et al. Allergic rhinitis and its impact on asthma. Aria Workshop Group; World Health Organization. J Allergy Clin Immunol 2001;108(Suppl 5):S147–334.
[57] Stoloff SW. The National Allergy Survey Assessing Limitations (NASAL): patient and health care professional perspectives in allergic rhinitis. J Fam Pract 2012;61(Suppl 2):S1–33.
[58] Nader ME, Abou-Jaoude P, Cabaluna M, et al. Using response to a standardized treatment to identify phenotypes for genetic studies of chronic rhinosinusitis. J Otolaryngol Head Neck Surg 2010;39(1):69–75.
[59] Zeiger RS, Bird SR, Kaplan MS, et al. Short-term and long-term asthma control in patients with mild persistent asthma receiving montelukast or fluticasone: a randomized controlled trial. Am J Med 2005;118(6):649–57.
[60] Malmstrom K, Rodriguez-Gomez G, Guerra J, et al. Oral montelukast, inhaled beclomethasone, and placebo for chronic asthma. A randomized, controlled trial. Montelukast/Beclomethasone Study Group. Ann Intern Med 1999;130(6):487–95.
[61] Lemanske RF Jr, Mauger DT, Sorkness CA, et al. Step-up therapy for children with uncontrolled asthma receiving inhaled corticosteroids. N Engl J Med 2010;362(11):975–85.
[62] Bateman ED, Boushey HA, Bousquet J, et al. Can guideline-defined asthma control be achieved? The Gaining Optimal Asthma ControL study. Am J Respir Crit Care Med 2004;170(8):836–44.

[63] Jones CA, Clement LT, Morphew T, et al. Achieving and maintaining asthma control in an urban pediatric disease management program: the Breathmobile Program. J Allergy Clin Immunol 2007;119(6):1445–53.
[64] Bousquet J, Bachert C, Canonica GW, et al. Unmet needs in severe chronic upper airway disease (SCUAD). J Allergy Clin Immunol 2009;124(3):428–33.
[65] Irwin RS, Richardson ND. Side effects with inhaled corticosteroids: the physician's perception. Chest 2006;130(Suppl 1):41S–53S.
[66] National Asthma Education and Prevention Program. Expert Panel Report 3 (EPR-3): guidelines for the diagnosis and management of asthma-summary report 2007. J Allergy Clin Immunol 2007;120(Suppl 5):S94–138.
[67] The Childhood Asthma Management Program Research Group. Long-term effects of budesonide or nedocromil in children with asthma. N Engl J Med 2000;343(15):1054–6.
[68] Guilbert TW, Morgan WJ, Zeiger RS, et al. Long-term inhaled corticosteroids in preschool children at high risk for asthma. N Engl J Med 2006;354(19):1985–9.
[69] Kelly HW, Sternberg AL, Lescher R, et al. Effect of inhaled glucocorticoids in childhood on adult height. N Engl J Med 2012;367(10):904–12.
[70] Harold S. Nelson Immunotherapy for inhalant allergens Middleton's Allergy Principles and Practice. 7th edition. St Louis(MO): Mosby, Elsevier; 2009. Chapter 95. p. 1657–77.
[71] Desai M, Oppenheimer JJ. Medication adherence in the asthmatic child and adolescent. Curr Allergy Asthma Rep 2011;11(6):454–64.
[72] Amin HS, Liss GM, Bernstein DI. Evaluation of near-fatal reactions to allergen immunotherapy injections. J Allergy Clin Immunol 2006;117:169–75.
[73] Tankersley MS, Butler KK, Butler WK, et al. Local reactions during allergen immunotherapy do not require dose adjustment. J Allergy Clin Immunol 2000;106(5):840–3.
[74] Kelso JM. The rate of systemic reactions to immunotherapy injections is the same whether or not the dose is reduced after a local reaction. Ann Allergy Asthma Immunol 2004;92(2): 225–7.
[75] Roy SR, Sigmon JR, Olivier J, et al. Increased frequency of large local reactions among systemic reactors during subcutaneous allergen immunotherapy. Ann Allergy Asthma Immunol 2007;99(1):82–6.
[76] Greineder DK. Risk management in allergen immunotherapy. J Allergy Clin Immunol 1996;98(6 Pt 3):S330–4.
[77] Bernstein DI, Wanner M, Borish L, et al. Twelve-year survey of fatal reactions to allergen injections and skin testing: 1990-2001. J Allergy Clin Immunol 2004;113:1129–36.
[78] Bousquet J, Hejjaoui A, Dhivert H, et al. Immunotherapy with a standardized *Dermatophagoides pteronyssinus* extract. Systemic reactions during the rush protocol in patients suffering from asthma. J Allergy Clin Immunol 1989;83:797–802.
[79] Lockey RF, Nicoara-Kasti GL, Theodoropoulos DS, et al. Systemic reactions and fatalities associated with allergen immunotherapy. Ann Allergy Asthma Immunol 2001;87: 47–55.
[80] Toogood JH. Risk of anaphylaxis in patients receiving beta-blocker drugs. J Allergy Clin Immunol 1988;81:1–5.
[81] Kaplan AP, Joseph K, Silverberg M. Pathways for bradykinin formation and inflammatory disease. J Allergy Clin Immunol 2002;109:195–209.
[82] Ober AI, MacLean JA, Hannaway PJ. Life-threatening anaphylaxis to venom immunotherapy in a patient taking an angiotensin-converting enzyme inhibitor. J Allergy Clin Immunol 2003;112:1008–9.
[83] Metzger WJ, Turner E, Patterson R. The safety of immunotherapy during pregnancy. J Allergy Clin Immunol 1978;61(4):268–72.
[84] Shaikh WA. A retrospective study on the safety of immunotherapy in pregnancy. Clin Exp Allergy 1993;23(10):857–60.
[85] Alvarez-Cuesta E, Bousquet J, Canonica GW, et al. Standards for practical allergen-specific immunotherapy. Allergy 2006;61:1–20.

[86] Franklin W, Lowell FC. Comparison of two dosages of ragweed extract in the treatment of pollinosis. JAMA 1967;201:915–7.
[87] Dolz I, Martinez-Cocera C, Bartolome JM, et al. A double-blind, placebo controlled study of immunotherapy with grass-pollen extract Alutard SQ during a 3-year period with initial rush immunotherapy. Allergy 1996;51:489–500.
[88] Creticos PS, Marsh DG, Proud D, et al. Responses to ragweed-pollen nasal challenge before and after immunotherapy. J Allergy Clin Immunol 1989;84:197–205.
[89] Malling HJ, Djurup R. Diagnosis and immunotherapy of mould allergy. VII. IgG subclass response and relation to the clinical efficacy of immunotherapy with *Cladosporium*. Allergy 1988;43:60–70.
[90] Malling HJ. Diagnosis and immunotherapy of mould allergy. IV. Relation between asthma symptoms, spore counts and diagnostic tests. Allergy 1986;41:342–50.
[91] Salvaggio JE, Burge HA, Chapman JA. Emerging concepts in mold allergy: what is the role of immunotherapy? J Allergy Clin Immunol 1993;92:217–22.
[92] Kang BC, Johnson J, Morgan C, et al. The role of immunotherapy in cockroach asthma. J Asthma 1988;25:205–18.
[93] Brown A. The perennial treatment of seasonal hayfever. J Allergy 1932;3:113–9.
[94] Tari MG, Mancino M, Monti G. Immunotherapy by inhalation of allergen in powder in house dust allergic asthma–a double-blind study. J Investig Allergol Clin Immunol 1992;2:59–67.
[95] Passalacqua G, Albano M, Pronzato C, et al. Long-term follow-up of nasal immunotherapy to *Parietaria*: clinical and local immunological effects. Clin Exp Allergy 1997;27:904–8.
[96] Pajno GB, Vita D, Caminiti L, et al. Children's compliance with allergen immunotherapy according to administration routes. J Allergy Clin Immunol 2005;116:1380–1.
[97] Warner JO. Low dose sublingual therapy in patients with allergic rhinitis due to house dust mite. Clin Allergy 1986;16(5):387–8.
[98] Penagos M, Compalati E, Tarantini F, et al. Efficacy of sublingual immunotherapy in the treatment of allergic rhinitis in pediatric patients 3 to 18 years of age: a meta-analysis of randomized, placebo-controlled, double-blind trials. Ann Allergy Asthma Immunol 2006;97:141–8.
[99] Penagos M, Passalacqua G, Compalati E, et al. Metaanalysis of the efficacy of sublingual immunotherapy in the treatment of allergic asthma in pediatric patients, 3 to 18 years of age. Chest 2008;133:599–609.
[100] La Rosa M, Ranno C, André C, et al. Double-blind placebo-controlled evaluation of sublingual-swallow immunotherapy with standardized *Parietaria judaica* extract in children with allergic rhinoconjunctivitis. J Allergy Clin Immunol 1999;104(2 Pt 1):425–32.
[101] Wilson DR, Lima MT, Durham SR. Sublingual immunotherapy for allergic rhinitis: systematic review and meta-analysis. Allergy 2005;60:4–12.
[102] Calamita Z, Saconato H, Pela AB, et al. Efficacy of sublingual immunotherapy in asthma: systematic review of randomized-clinical trials using the Cochrane Collaboration method. Allergy 2006;61:1162–72.
[103] Nieto A, Mazon A, Pamies R, et al. Sublingual immunotherapy for allergic respiratory diseases: an evaluation of meta-analyses. J Allergy Clin Immunol 2009;124:157–61.
[104] Marogna M, Tomassetti D, Bernasconi A, et al. Preventive effects of sublingual immunotherapy in childhood: an open randomized controlled study. Ann Allergy Asthma Immunol 2008;101(2):206–11.
[105] Di Rienzo V, Marcucci F, Puccinelli P, et al. Long-lasting effect of sublingual immunotherapy in children with asthma due to house dust mite: a 10-year prospective study. Clin Exp Allergy 2003;33(2):206–10.
[106] Cosmi L, Santarlasci V, Angeli R, et al. Sublingual immunotherapy with *Dermatophagoides* monomeric allergoid down-regulates allergen-specific immunoglobulin E and increases both interferon-gamma- and interleukin-10-production. Clin Exp Allergy 2006;36(3): 261–72.

[107] Bohle B, Kinaciyan T, Gerstmayr M, et al. Sublingual immunotherapy induces IL-10-producing T regulatory cells, allergen-specific T-cell tolerance, and immune deviation. J Allergy Clin Immunol 2007;120(3):707–13.
[108] Cox LS, Larenas Linnemann D, Nolte H, et al. Sublingual immunotherapy: a comprehensive review. J Allergy Clin Immunol 2006;117(5):1021–35.
[109] Ridolo E, De Angelis GL, Dall'aglio P. Eosinophilic esophagitis after specific oral tolerance induction for egg protein. Ann Allergy Asthma Immunol 2011;106(1):73–4.
[110] Senti G, Crameri R, Kuster D, et al. Intralymphatic immunotherapy for cat allergy induces tolerance after only 3 injections. J Allergy Clin Immunol 2012;129(5):1290–6.
[111] Milgrom H, Berger W, Nayak A, et al. Treatment of childhood asthma with anti-immunoglobulin E antibody (omalizumab). Pediatrics 2001;108(2):E36.
[112] Casale TB, Busse WW, Kline JN, et al. Omalizumab pretreatment decreases acute reactions after rush immunotherapy for ragweed-induced seasonal allergic rhinitis. J Allergy Clin Immunol 2006;117:134–40.
[113] Massanari M, Nelson H, Casale T, et al. Effect of pretreatment with omalizumab on the tolerability of specific immunotherapy in allergic asthma. J Allergy Clin Immunol 2010;125(2):383–9.
[114] Kuehr J, Brauburger J, Zielen S, et al. Efficacy of combination treatment with anti-IgE plus specific immunotherapy in polysensitized children and adolescents with seasonal allergic rhinitis. J Allergy Clin Immunol 2002;109(2):274–8.
[115] Till SJ, Francis JN, Nouri-Aria K, et al. Mechanisms of immunotherapy. J Allergy Clin Immunol 2004;113(6):1025–34.
[116] Creticos PS, Schroeder JT, Hamilton RG, et al. Immunotherapy with a ragweed toll-like receptor 9 agonist vaccine for allergic rhinitis. N Engl J Med 2006;355:1445–55.
[117] Dynavax reports interim TOLAMBA TM ragweed allergy results from DARTT Trial 01/08/2007 press release. 2007. Available at: http://investors.dynavax.com/ releasedetail.cfm?ReleaseID=231013. Accessed October 9, 2012.
[118] Drachenberg KJ, Wheeler AW, Stuebner P, et al. A well-tolerated grass pollen specific allergy vaccine containing a novel adjuvant, monophosphoryl lipid A, reduces allergic symptoms after only four preseasonal injections. Allergy 2001;56:498–505.
[119] Burks AW, Jones SM, Boyce JA, et al. NIAID-sponsored 2010 guidelines for managing food allergy: applications in the pediatric population. Pediatrics 2011;128(5):955–65.
[120] Kim EH, Burks W. Managing food allergy in childhood. Curr Opin Pediatr 2012;24(5): 615–20.
[121] Kim EH, Bird JA, Kulis M, et al. Sublingual immunotherapy for peanut allergy: clinical and immunologic evidence of desensitization. J Allergy Clin Immunol 2011;127(3):640–6.
[122] Patriarca G, Nucera E, Roncallo C, et al. Oral desensitizing treatment in food allergy: clinical and immunological results. Aliment Pharmacol Ther 2003;17:459–65.
[123] Bucher X, Pichler WJ, Dahinden CA, et al. Effect of tree pollen specific, subcutaneous immunotherapy on the oral allergy syndrome to apple and hazelnut. Allergy 2004;59: 1272–6.
[124] Hansen KS, Khinchi MS, Skov PS, et al. Food allergy to apple and specific immunotherapy with birch pollen. Mol Nutr Food Res 2004;48:441–8.

Advances in Pediatrics 60 (2013) 167–185

ADVANCES IN PEDIATRICS

# Advances in Noninvasive Imaging in Pediatric Cardiology

Melanie Nies, MD*, Priya Sekar, MD, MPH

Johns Hopkins Medical Institution, Bloomberg Children's Center, Department of Pediatric Cardiology/Taussig Heart Center, 1800 Orleans Street, M2303, Baltimore, MD 21230, USA

**Keywords**

• Pediatric cardiology • Congenital heart disease • Noninvasive imaging • Echocardiography • Cardiac MRI • Review

**Key points**

- Transthoracic echocardiography is the first-line noninvasive diagnostic imaging modality in pediatric congenital and acquired heart disease, with cardiac MRI and CT representing important adjuncts.
- Noninvasive imaging is increasingly supplanting the need for invasive diagnostic cardiac catheterization.
- Major congenital heart disease can be identified prenatally by fetal echocardiography, allowing for appropriate pregnancy and perinatal planning.
- Cardiac MRI/MRA is excellent for noninvasive assessment of anatomy and hemodynamics; it should be obtained only by those with expertise in CHD.
- Recent advances in noninvasive imaging include three-dimensional echocardiography, myocardial strain imaging, exercise stress echocardiography, ICE, cardiac MRI, and CT.
- Evidence-based indications for echocardiography exist from fetal life through adulthood and should be familiar to practitioners ordering echocardiographic studies.

## INTRODUCTION

An important trend over the past two decades has been toward noninvasive diagnosis of pediatric acquired and congenital heart disease. Extraordinary advances in the field have elevated echocardiography to the gold standard of noninvasive imaging [1]. This article begins with a brief background of echocardiographic history, followed by applications of echocardiography from fetal life through adolescence to provide a framework for describing advances in

*Corresponding author. *E-mail address*: mnies1@jhmi.edu

0065-3101/13/$ – see front matter
http://dx.doi.org/10.1016/j.yapd.2013.04.002 

noninvasive imaging. Also described are the important complementary roles of cardiac magnetic resonance imaging (cMRI) and cardiac computed tomography (CCT).

Although echocardiography can be obtained as a well-tolerated procedure that avoids the need for radiation, it should not be obtained indiscriminately; this point is eloquently made by Cheitlin and colleagues [2,3]. Through each section of this article the indications for obtaining an echocardiogram are summarized. Levels of evidence for echocardiographic indications are as follows:

Class I: Conditions for which there is evidence or general agreement that a given procedure or treatment is useful and effective.

Class II: Conditions for which there is conflicting evidence or a divergence of opinion about the usefulness and efficacy of a procedure or treatment. IIa: Weight of evidence or opinion is in favor of usefulness or efficacy. IIb: Usefulness or efficacy is less well established by evidence or opinion.

Class III: Conditions for which there is evidence or general agreement that the procedure or treatment is not useful or effective and in some cases may be harmful.

## ECHOCARDIOGRAPHY: DIAGNOSIS OF PEDIATRIC HEART DISEASE FROM FETAL LIFE THROUGH ADULTHOOD

The first generation of echocardiography, one-dimensional m-mode, was developed in the 1970s, with the transformative addition of two-dimensional echocardiography in the 1980s. Doppler ultrasound, for investigation of blood flow, was introduced over the ensuing several years. By the 1990s, three-dimensional echocardiography and cMRI were being applied to congenital heart disease, followed by CCT.

## FETAL ECHOCARDIOGRAPHY

Fetal echocardiography is integral in prenatal diagnosis of congenital heart disease, family counseling, prognostication, planning for surgical and nonsurgical intervention, prenatal arrhythmia diagnosis, and management and future genetic counseling. Many class I indications for fetal echocardiography exist, and include maternal indications (family history of a first-degree relative with congenital heart disease; maternal diabetes or systemic lupus erythematosus; metabolic disorders; teratogenic exposure; prostaglandin synthetase inhibitor exposure, such as ibuprofen; rubella infection; autoimmune disease; familial inherited disorders; and in vitro fertilization) and fetal indications (abnormal obstetric ultrasound screen, extracardiac or chromosomal anomaly, arrhythmia, hydrops, increased first-trimester nuchal translucency, multiple gestation, and suspicion of twin-twin transfusion syndrome). However, fetal echocardiography has the highest yield after referral for suspected cardiac abnormality on level 1 sonogram and thus relies heavily on the expertise of obstetric sonographers [4].

Fetal echocardiography is currently recommended between 18 and 22 weeks gestational age, when the fetal heart is large enough to accurately diagnose major congenital heart disease, but early enough in pregnancy such that options exist for pregnancy termination and potential fetal intervention. Surprisingly, a diagnosis of congenital heart disease by fetal echocardiography has not been shown to reduce mortality, but fetal echocardiography has been shown to improve morbidity, such as physiologic state and surgical outcome [4–10]. In addition, fetal dysrhythmias can be managed, potentially preventing fetal hydrops.

After a diagnosis of congenital heart disease has been made, it is important to consider the site of delivery; ductal-dependent lesions require postnatal care at tertiary care facilities. Some lesions, such as hypoplastic left heart syndrome with intact atrial septum, represent true postnatal emergencies requiring advanced planning among multidisciplinary teams (Fig. 1).

Fetal echocardiography has limitations; therefore, careful postnatal physical examination and clinical assessment, especially for patients at high risk for congenital heart disease, remains vital, even if fetal echocardiography did not reveal any abnormalities. Because of the differences between fetal and postnatal circulation, certain lesions cannot be diagnosed with certainty by fetal echocardiography including small ventral ventricular septal defects, mild valve abnormalities, coronary artery anomalies, persistent patency of the ductus arteriosus, and some atrial septal defects. Furthermore, aortic coarctation cannot be definitively ruled out, although specific factors seen on fetal echocardiography can help to qualify the risk of postnatal aortic coarctation.

## NEONATAL PERIOD: NEONATAL INTENSIVE CARE UNIT AND NURSERY

Confirmatory postnatal echocardiogram is one indication for obtaining an echocardiogram in the neonatal intensive care unit (NICU) or newborn nursery. Other class I indications include anatomic evaluation in the setting of

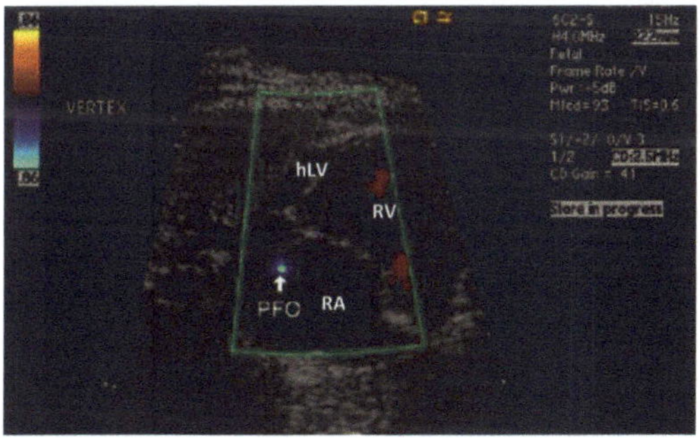


**Fig. 1.** Fetal echocardiogram from a patient with double outlet right ventricle, hypoplastic left ventricle, and nearly intact atrial septum, with an inadequate amount of flow through a patent foramen ovale (PFO) for systemic blood flow. Advanced planning involving pediatric cardiology, pediatric cardiothoracic surgery, neonatal intensive care, pediatric intensive care, and obstetrics and gynecology was necessary for the immediate postnatal atrial septal stenting procedure required for survival. hLV, hypoplastic left ventricle; RA, right atrium; RV, right ventricle.

extracorporeal membrane oxygenation (ECMO); signs or symptoms of congenital heart disease (cyanosis, respiratory distress, congestive heart failure, abnormal arterial pulses); cardiomegaly; dextrocardia or abnormal visceral situs on chest radiograph; pathologic murmur; chromosomal or extracardiac abnormalities associated with congenital heart disease (CHD); lack of expected improvement in cardiopulmonary status in a premature infant with a clinical diagnosis of pulmonary disease; systemic maternal disease associated with neonatal comorbidity; presence of a syndrome associated with cardiovascular disease and dominant inheritance or multiple affected family members; arrhythmia or electrocardiogram abnormality suggesting structural heart disease; and nonimmune fetal hydrops. Notably, echocardiography is not recommended for a history of nonsustained fetal ectopy in the absence of postpartum arrhythmia, or acrocyanosis with normal upper- and lower-extremity pulse oximetry saturations (class III).

Increasingly, neonatologists are becoming interested in the use of echocardiography not only for comprehensive diagnosis of congenital heart disease, but also for assessment of hemodynamic status, resulting in requests for "targeted" neonatal echocardiograms. Given that neonates in the NICU are at higher risk of underlying congenital heart disease and are transitioning from fetal to postnatal circulation, this concept poses a challenge [11]. To address this challenge, the American Society of Echocardiography recommends comprehensive echocardiography for infants with a strong clinical suspicion of congenital heart disease or arrhythmia, and for hemodynamically unstable infants, even without suspicion for CHD. Thus, the role of targeted neonatal echocardiography should be restricted to hemodynamically stable infants who have undergone comprehensive echocardiogram to exclude congenital heart disease, or have no clinical suspicion of congenital heart disease. When a targeted neonatal echocardiogram is appropriate, indications for standard targeted neonatal echocardiograms include clinically suspected patent ductus arteriosus (PDA), perinatal asphyxia, concern for low systemic blood flow state, persistent pulmonary hypertension of the newborn (PPHN), and CDH. Indications for focused targeted neonatal echocardiograms include suspected pericardial or pleural effusion, central line, and ECMO cannulation [11].

A burgeoning population of premature infants in the NICU are diagnosed with pulmonary hypertension related to bronchopulmonary dysplasia [12], resulting in frequent echocardiographic evaluation. No guidelines exist for screening selection or follow-up intervals in pediatric pulmonary hypertension [13–15]. Currently, echocardiographic evaluation of pulmonary hypertension uses tricuspid regurgitant jet velocity to calculate right ventricular systolic pressure and pulmonary artery pressure, in the absence of pulmonary stenosis (Figs. 2 and 3), which has been shown to be a sensitive marker of the presence or absence of pulmonary hypertension [15]. However, directly measured right ventricular systolic pressure correlated poorly to tricuspid regurgitant jet velocity in the cardiac catheterization laboratory [15,16], and when tricuspid regurgitant jet is inadequate, right ventricular systolic pressure can only be qualitatively

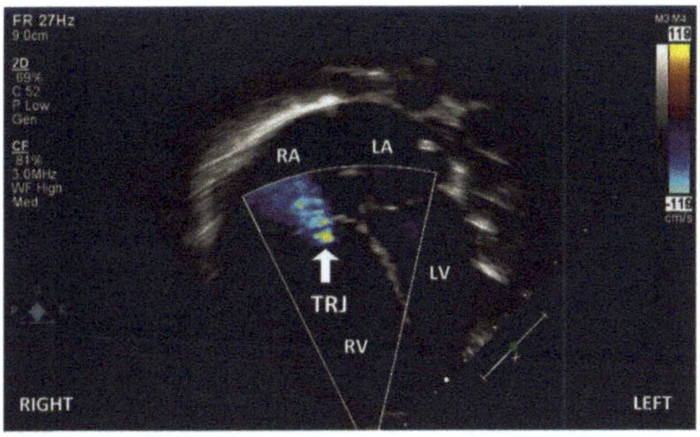


**Fig. 2.** Transthoracic echocardiogram (apical four-chamber view) showing moderate tricuspid regurgitation in the setting of severe pulmonary hypertension. LA, left atrium; LV, left ventricle; TRJ, tricuspid regurgitant jet.

assessed by interventricular septal position. In the future, tricuspid annular plane systolic excursion (Fig. 4), speckle tracking of the right ventricle (RV), and three-dimensional echocardiography will likely improve quantitative diagnosis after further pediatric normative data are obtained [12].

The role of echocardiography is also expanding before discharge from the hospital after birth, because of the advent of mandatory pulse oximetry screening in many states. Recently, the Secretary of Health and Human Services recommended that screening for complex congenital heart disease be added to the uniform screening panel, and the American Academy of Pediatrics endorsed this recommendation [17]. Briefly, there are several lesions, described as "critical congenital heart disease," which can result in postnatal emergencies as the ductus arteriosus closes. Seven of these lesions have been identified as amenable to detection by screening pulse oximetry, including dextrotransposition of the great arteries, hypoplastic left heart syndrome, pulmonary atresia with intact atrial septum, tetralogy of Fallot, total anomalous pulmonary

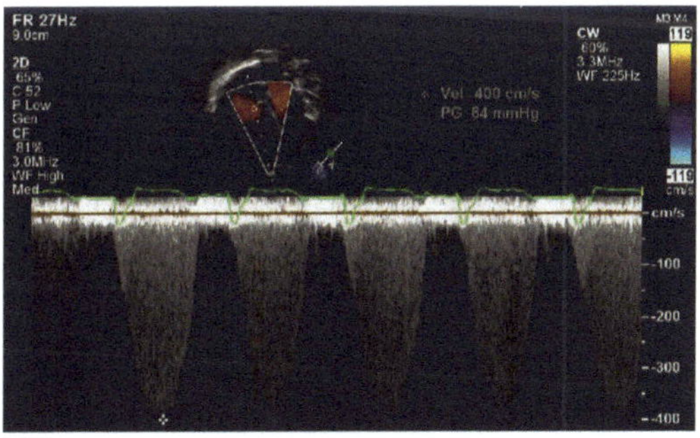

**Fig. 3.** Continuous-wave Doppler of the tricuspid regurgitant jet estimates an RV systolic pressure of 64 mm Hg plus the right atrial pressure, consistent with the clinical scenario of pulmonary hypertension.

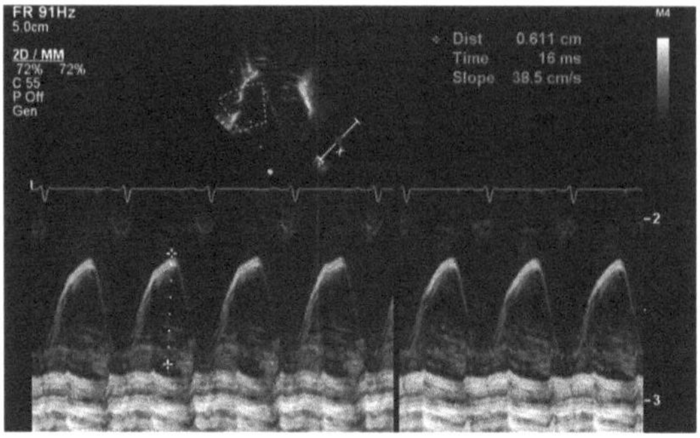


**Fig. 4.** The method of tricuspid annular plane excursion can be used to evaluate RV systolic function using transthoracic echocardiography.

venous return, tricuspid atresia, and truncus arteriosus, which collectively represent 17% to 31% of congenital heart disease [18]. After review of the evidence, including a scientific statement from the American Heart Association and American Academy of Pediatrics on the role of pulse oximetry in examination of newborns for congenital heart disease [19], the Centers for Disease Control and Prevention endorsed an algorithm for pulse oximetry screening and subsequent screening echocardiogram [20]. Other lesions, some of which represent critical congenital heart disease, can be difficult to detect by screening pulse oximetry and echocardiogram. Thus, similar to fetal echocardiography, postnatal physical examination and clinical assessment are vitally important.

After discharge as a neonate, echocardiography can play a critical role in diagnosing cardiogenic shock in infants with ductal-dependent lesions presenting to the emergency room with rapid decompensation in the first 1 to 2 weeks of life because of delayed closure of the ductus arteriosus.

## CHILDHOOD: THE ROLE OF NONINVASIVE IMAGING IN THE INPATIENT SETTING

In the setting of pediatric hospital admission, the role of echocardiography in acquired heart disease, including myocarditis, Kawasaki disease (KD), and infective endocarditis, merits further discussion. Current class I indications for obtaining an echocardiogram for acquired heart disease include baseline echocardiograms in KD, myopericarditis, HIV, and rheumatic fever; additional indications include severe renal disease and systemic hypertension, assessment of potential cardiac or cardiopulmonary transplant donors and recipients, and initiation of vasodilator therapy for pulmonary artery hypertension. Class IIa indications include suspected bacterial sepsis or rickettsial disease in an acutely ill child; noncardiac disease states that affect the heart (eg, pulmonary hypertension); thromboembolic disease states, such as thromboembolic event; family history of tuberous sclerosis complex; and patients with indwelling catheters plus sepsis, cyanosis, right heart failure, embolism, or superior vena cava syndrome. Echocardiogram is not recommended for routine surveillance of indwelling catheters (class III).

MRI is increasingly used in confirming the diagnosis of myocarditis, but echocardiography remains the first-line study for diagnosis, demonstrating changes in systolic and diastolic function in a nonvascular distribution in the fulminant phase (0–2 weeks) and subclinical systolic and diastolic dysfunction that requires future evaluation. Echocardiography can also identify structural and anatomic reasons for left ventricle (LV) dysfunction, such as volume- and pressure-loading lesions (eg, aortic stenosis); anomalous left coronary artery from the pulmonary artery; and congenital coronary ostial stenosis [21]. In the chronic phase, stress echocardiography can be obtained before return to normal activities. Although there are no specific protocols for stress echocardiography in the pediatric population, studies exist with normative values for healthy children, cancer survivors, and heart transplant recipients [22–25]. In our institution, after resolution of myocarditis with acute change in LV function, we typically recommend a follow-up exercise stress echocardiogram (ESE) 6 months after the acute phase, before lifting sports restrictions.

Echocardiography also remains first-line for evaluation of KD. Although KD does not require echocardiography for diagnosis if classic criteria are met [26], all patients with KD require an echocardiogram for evaluation of systolic function, coronary arteries, and pericardial effusion, especially because coronary artery aneurysms rarely form before Day 10 of illness. When classic criteria are not met but clinical suspicion is high, echocardiography can definitively diagnose KD. Echocardiography is recommended at baseline, at 2 weeks, and then 6 to 8 weeks after diagnosis in the absence of coronary artery aneurysm; in the case of aneurysm formation, a pediatric cardiologist is typically involved and recommends treatment, activity restriction, and echo periodicity, with at least annual echocardiograms. Notably, echocardiography is not indicated for long-term follow-up of KD in patients with no coronary abnormalities during the acute phase of the disease.

Transthoracic echocardiography remains the first-line screening test for suspected infective endocarditis (or subacute bacterial endocarditis) in pediatrics. When transthoracic echocardiography is nondiagnostic, transesophageal echocardiography (TEE) should be obtained. The diagnostic algorithm for infective endocarditis was updated by the American Heart Association in 2007 [27]. Patients at the highest risk include those with congenital heart disease, especially repaired or palliated cyanotic disease (because of abnormal, high-velocity jets of blood resulting in endothelial damage), and prosthetic material, such as mechanical valves. Among patients with structurally normal hearts, the highest risk groups are intravenous drug users and newborns with central lines (endothelial damage during placement provides a nidus for infection) [28].

Finally, among the acquired heart diseases that can be evaluated by echocardiography, rheumatic heart disease in the United States is rare, but represents the leading worldwide cause of acquired heart disease, which most frequently presents as valvular dysfunction.

One of the main uses of echocardiography in the inpatient setting is preoperative and postoperative assessment by TEE in cardiac patients [29] to assess operative success. Postoperative TEE results have been shown to result in important interventions [30].

In the intensive care unit, echocardiography also has an important role in ECMO [31] and ventricular-assist device (VAD) therapy. Although venoarterial (VA) ECMO provides gas exchange and circulatory support, venovenous (VV) ECMO provides gas exchange only and requires adequate cardiac function to support systemic output. Thus, pre-ECMO echocardiographic assessment is vital to ensure adequate cardiac function for VV ECMO. In addition, pre-ECMO echocardiography identifies potentially reversible causes of cardiovascular compromise (eg, pericardial tamponade) and rules out progressive, irreversible causes of dysfunction that would make ECMO futile. Contraindications that can be identified by echocardiography include aortic dissection, severe aortic regurgitation, and total anomalous pulmonary venous return. Pre-ECMO assessment clarifies cardiac and extracardiac cervical arterial anatomy for cannulation and is important for cannula placement and troubleshooting [32,33]. There are no evidence-based guidelines for weaning ECMO, and echocardiography during ECMO clamp trials has an important role in determining the adequacy of cardiac function. Echocardiography has an important role in guiding left VAD therapy. Pre-VAD echocardiography can identify patent foramen ovale, significant aortic regurgitation, cardiac thrombi, and evaluate right heart function, which can guide the decision to pursue left VAD alone versus BiVAD to support the RV and LV.

## THE ROLE OF NONINVASIVE IMAGING IN THE PEDIATRIC OUTPATIENT SETTING

In the outpatient setting, echocardiograms are obtained for children with known congenital heart disease and for the indications described previously; echocardiography also has a role in preoperative evaluation for noncardiac procedures and continued evaluation of patients with connective tissue disease, chronic illnesses including hypertension, sickle cell disease (who are at risk for development of pulmonary hypertension), and primary or secondary cardiomyopathies. Baseline and serial echocardiography is indicated for patients exposed to cardiotoxic therapeutic medications [3] to monitor function in the short and long term.

Echocardiography often guides percutaneous catheter-based interventions, such as endomyocardial biopsies in heart transplant patients and device closure of atrial and ventricular septal defects and PDAs. Intracardiac echocardiography (ICE) is also available for catheter-based interventions.

## INTRACARDIAC ECHOCARDIOGRAPHY

ICE is a specialized echo modality that allows imaging in two planes; the ability to introduce the probe through an 8F catheter femoral venous sheath [34] has implications for use during cardiac catheterization. In our experience, ICE has been used mainly for guiding percutaneous atrial septal defect and patent foramen ovale closure. Reports also describe using ICE for percutaneous pulmonary valve placement and PDA closure [35–39].

## EXERCISE AND DOBUTAMINE STRESS ECHOCARDIOGRAPHY

ESE and dobutamine stress echocardiography (DSE) are important adjuncts for children with acquired and congenital heart disease to evaluate ventricular response and regional wall motion abnormality (indicating adequacy of coronary perfusion) under physiologic stress; however, future risk and prognostic implications are lacking. Limited pediatric ESE and DSE data exist for acquired heart disease [22–25] and select subsets of patients with congenital heart disease [40] but there is no standardized protocol [21]. For ESE at our institution, the Bruce protocol (treadmill protocol typically used in exercise stress test) is used with echocardiographic imaging at baseline, immediately after peak exercise, and 20 minutes after cessation of exercise. Common indications include recovered myocarditis before lifting sports restrictions, coronary involvement, or left ventricular outflow tract obstruction. DSE, which is performed with increasing infusion rate of dobutamine, has been studied in the adolescent and adult population with prognostic significance [22,23,41], and in adults for prognosis after myocardial infarction, to assess recovery of left ventricular function and survival [41–43]. The analysis of regional wall motion abnormality in DSE and ESE requires advanced training among pediatric cardiologists.

The diagnostic accuracy of a stress echocardiogram can be improved by contrast echocardiography. A commercially available transpulmonary contrast agent is injected into a systemic vein, crosses the pulmonary bed, and opacifies the left heart, clearly defining the endomyocardial border and improving quantification of systolic function. Agitated saline "bubble" studies can identify right-to-left shunts (either intracardiac or intrapulmonary shunts, such as patent foramen ovale or pulmonary arteriovenous malformations). After administration of agitated saline into a systemic vein, microbubbles enter the right side of the heart, causing immediate opacification. In the absence of right-to-left shunts, most bubbles are filtered out by the pulmonary bed, with very few bubbles returning to the left heart. Immediate return of bubbles to the left side of the heart indicates an intracardiac shunt, whereas bubble return after three to four cardiac cycles indicates an intrapulmonary shunt.

## NEW ECHO TECHNOLOGY: THREE-DIMENSIONAL ECHOCARDIOGRAPHY AND STRAIN

Three-dimensional echocardiography (Fig. 5) is increasingly incorporated in routine echo assessment. When correlated with MRI, three-dimensional echocardiography has superior volume measurements and less intraobserver and interobserver variation than one-dimensional (or m-mode) and two-dimensional imaging for the LV, and can be obtained with ease using semiautomated border detection [44,45]. Although three-dimensional echocardiography is especially helpful for quantitation of left ventricular volume, function, and

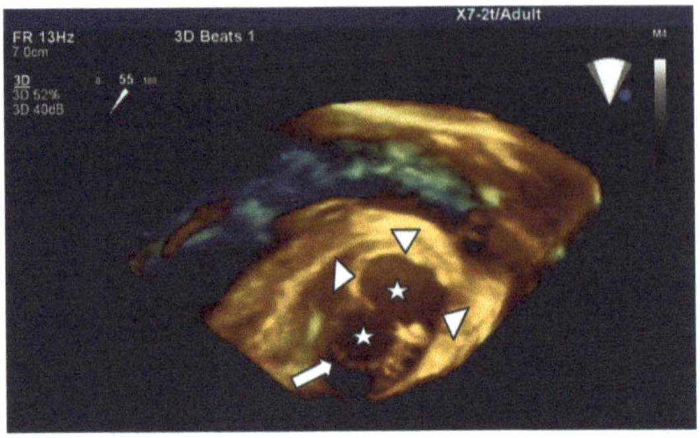


**Fig. 5.** Three-dimensional transthoracic echocardiogram from the parasternal short axis view of a bicommissural aortic valve with severe prolapse of the aortic valve leaflets. The aortic valve is seen en face; a prolapsing leaflet is marked with an *arrow*, the aortic annulus by *arrowheads*, and the orifice of the valve by *asterisks*.

mass, right ventricular volume by three-dimensional echocardiography has been shown in small studies to have superior correlation to MRI and angiography than two-dimensional echocardiography [45,46], but is not yet ready for clinical application [21]. The superior correlation to MRI using three-dimensional echocardiography versus two-dimensional echocardiography is also seen in single ventricular physiology and various cardiomyopathies [47,48]. Pediatric morphometric values are still lacking, but will expand as three-dimensional echocardiography is increasingly used on a routine basis [47].

Myocardial strain evaluates the rate of myocardial tissue deformation over time (Fig. 6), and is a surrogate to assess myocardial contractility. Myocardial deformation is measured by tracking highly reproducible, ultrasound reflectors (speckles). This technique of speckle tracking allows for translational movement during the cardiac cycle and assessment of diastolic function [49–53]. The *Journal of the American Society of Echocardiography* recently published pediatric reference values in healthy children [54]. In pediatric oncology patients who have received cardiotoxic chemotherapeutic agents, abnormal strain is more sensitive for preclinical left ventricular dysfunction than ejection fraction and fractional shortening [55]. Other diseases in which ventricular strain abnormalities have been observed, allowing for early identification of myocardial dysfunction, which may influence treatment, include congenital aortic stenosis [56–59], Duchenne muscular dystrophy, hypertrophic cardiomyopathy [60], and prediction of cardiac transplantation rejection [61].

## OTHER IMAGING MODALITIES: CCT AND CMRI

When echocardiography is inadequate, CCT and cMRI are important adjuncts. CT has specific advantages in pediatric cardiac patients, including accessibility; excellent three-dimensional reconstruction; rapidity of acquisition; superior

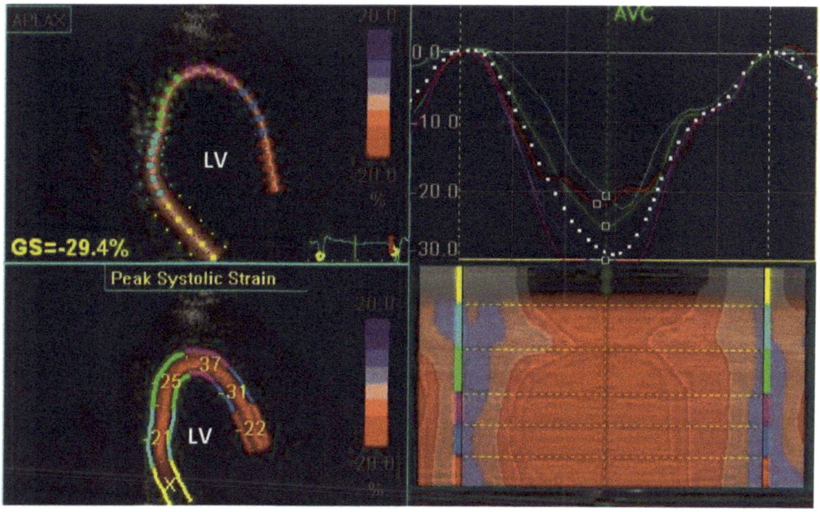


**Fig. 6.** Evaluation of regional myocardial segmental strain using speckle tracking.

evaluation of pulmonary arteries, pulmonary veins, stents, and in-stent stenosis; and evaluation of extracardiac structures. The foremost disadvantage is radiation exposure, but when chosen for specific applications, CCT has advantages over echocardiography and MRI. In comparison with echocardiography, it is not limited by transthoracic windows and body habitus, and can be used to obtain imaging of the pulmonary arteries and veins not possible using echocardiography alone. This superior ability of CCT to provide a roadmap of the pulmonary arteries with extent and location of pulmonary artery can shorten or even preclude diagnostic cardiac catheterization (which also involves radiation because of the need for fluoroscopy).

Advantages of CT over MRI include the ability to assess stents (typically in the pulmonary arteries or aorta) and in-stent stenosis (highly sensitive and specific for stenosis more than 20%) [62,63]. CT can also be used when metallic implants would either be a contraindication to MRI or cause unacceptable artifact. Further, CCT can generate excellent three-dimensional reconstructions and provide important information about the airways, which are often involved in patients with congenital heart disease [64].

Cardiac magnetic resonance angiography (MRA; a subtype of MRI that generates images of the arteries; Figs. 7 and 8) and CT are useful in coronary artery evaluation, provided image acquisition is timed to the cardiac cycle to prevent significant motion artifact (electrocardiogram gating) [65]. Congenital coronary artery malformations that are difficult to characterize using echocardiography can be seen well on cMRI and CCT [66], as can assessment of coronary artery aneurysm in KD.

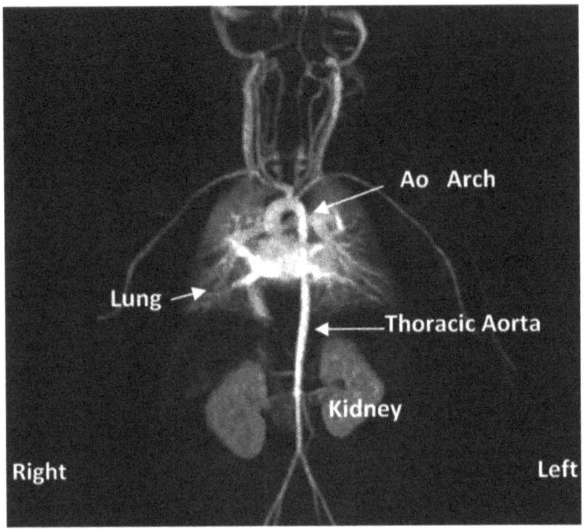


**Fig. 7.** An example of a cardiac MRA in the same patient as Fig. 9. This is an anterior view, but because of intravenous contrast (gadolinium) administration, posterior structures can be seen, including nearly the entire descending and thoracic aorta, and vascular supply to the lungs and pulmonary venous return. Ao arch, aortic arch.

## CMRI

cMRI (Figs. 9 and 10) is garnering an increasingly important role in noninvasive functional, hemodynamic, and anatomic assessment of pediatric patients, in the role of an adjunctive diagnostic modality and an alternative to invasive imaging by angiography obtained by cardiac catheterization. cMRI has an important role in noninvasive hemodynamic assessment and when transthoracic echocardiography is inadequate. cMRI is invaluable for assessment of

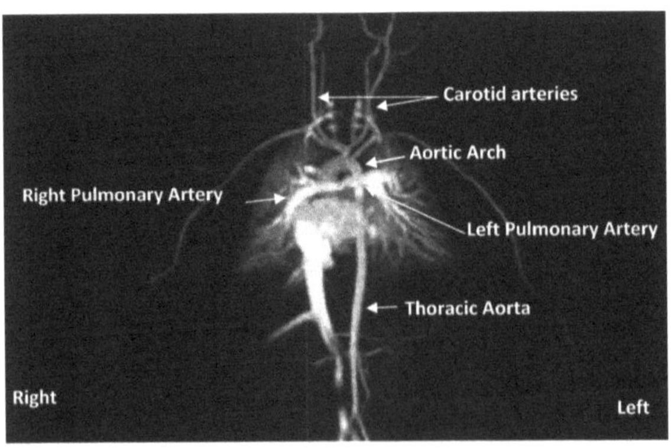


**Fig. 8.** An example of a cardiac MRA in the same patient as Figs. 7 and 9. Again, this view is from the anterior, but in this slice, the pulmonary arteries can be seen (which was the indication for the cardiac MRI/MRA).

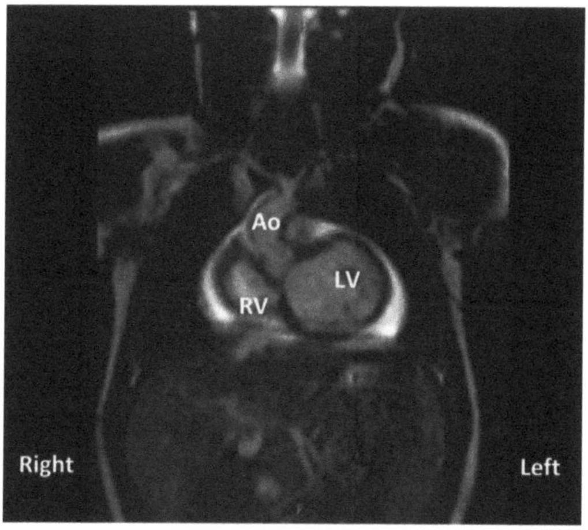


**Fig. 9.** Example of a cMRI of an infant with a hypoplastic right ventricle and multiple ventricular septal defects not amenable to closure (not seen in this image) culminating in the decision to pursue single ventricle palliation. A cardiac MRI/MRA was obtained to evaluate the branch pulmonary arteries before upcoming stage II single ventricle repair, bidirectional Glenn cavopulmonary anastomosis.

right ventricular function and volume, given that RV analysis by two-dimensional echocardiography is unreliable because of the complex geometric configuration of the RV. Tsai-Goodman and colleagues [67] found the most common indications of cMRI in 99 infants younger than 1 year of age to be delineation of thoracic vasculature (55%) followed by airway compression (25%) and evaluation of cardiac tumors (6%). They speculated further that cMRI was likely to be used even more in congenital heart disease as an

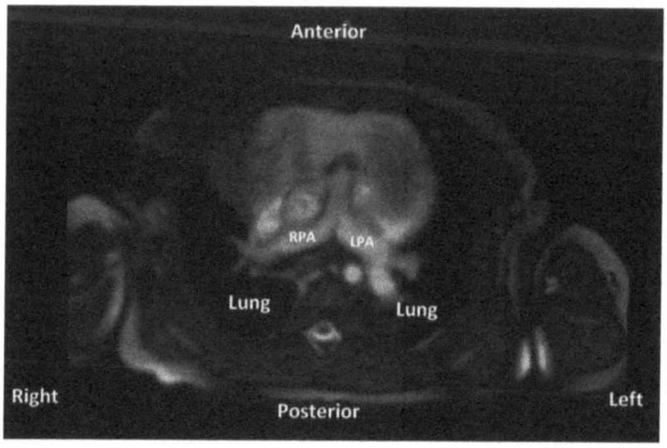


**Fig. 10.** In this axial slice of a cMRI from the same patient in Figs. 7–9, the pulmonary arteries are visualized branching from the main pulmonary artery and traveling posterior to the heart to supply the lungs. LPA, left pulmonary artery; RPA, right pulmonary artery.

alternative to cardiac catheterization [67]. Thus, cMRI is becoming an attractive alternative to invasive angiographic evaluation by cardiac catheterization, which had previously been standard of care in single ventricle anatomy before bidirectional Glenn and Fontan completion.

MRI provides excellent imaging of extracardiac vascular anatomy and quantification of regurgitant fraction, right ventricular volume and function, and pulmonary and systemic blood flow (Qp and Qs, respectively) [68]. The three-dimensional information and high resolution of MRI allows for accurate chamber measurement even with complex geometry and anatomy. This is particularly important for quantification of right ventricular volume and function (by ejection fraction), both of which are unreliably measured by echocardiography. Thus, it is the gold standard for noninvasive RV and LV volume, stroke volume, and functional assessment.

cMRI has unique advantages, including lower intraobserver and interobserver variability than two-dimensional echocardiography for LV and RV volume and ejection fraction [69], and existing age- and gender-specific percentiles for ventricular size and mass as reference values for children [70–72]. Although not widely used, stress cMRI is possible, using either dobutamine or supine exercise methods [73–75].

An important application of cMRI is in the determination of myocardial viability using delayed contrast enhancement. In necrotic myocardium or areas of fibrosis (myocardial scar), washout of the contrast agent is delayed. Distinctive patterns of enhancement correspond to various disease states, such as adult coronary artery disease, acute and chronic myocardial infarction, and myocardial fibrosis in hypertrophic cardiomyopathy [76]. An important use of delayed contrast enhancement in pediatrics is in myocarditis: delayed enhancement localized to the subepicardial region of the myocardium is highly suggestive of myocarditis (in contrast to the subendocardial, transmural delayed enhancement of ischemic disease, such as myocardial infarction, which also occurs in a vascular distribution according to the coronary artery involved) [77,78].

## SUMMARY

Echocardiography remains first-line for most congenital and acquired heart disease, with new technologies allowing for increasingly sophisticated and sensitive detection of abnormalities, often presaging overt clinical disease. The collection of normative values also continues to grow, allowing for greater generalizability to multiple subgroups of congenital and acquired heart disease. Meanwhile, the indications for CCT and CT angiography, and MRI and MRA, continue to expand. In the future, the accessibility and safety of these noninvasive imaging modalities will decrease the need for invasive diagnostic procedures, improve diagnostic ability, and allow for more accurate prognostication. Pediatric practitioners caring for patients from fetal life through adolescence represent a vital link in identifying undiagnosed patients likely to benefit from noninvasive imaging, and providing comprehensive care for patients with acquired and congenital heart disease.

## References

[1] Mertens L, Friedberg MK. The gold standard for noninvasive imaging in congenital heart disease: echocardiography. Curr Opin Cardiol 2009;24(2):119–24; http://dx.doi.org/10.1097/HCO.0b013e328323d86f.

[2] Cheitlin MD, Alpert JS, Armstrong WF, et al. ACC/AHA guidelines for the clinical application of echocardiography. A report of the American College of Cardiology/American Heart Association task force on practice guidelines (committee on clinical application of echocardiography). Developed in collaboration with the American Society of Echocardiography. Circulation 1997;95(6):1686–744.

[3] Cheitlin MD, Armstrong WF, Aurigemma GP, et al. ACC/AHA/ASE 2003 guideline update for the clinical application of echocardiography: summary article: a report of the American College of Cardiology/American Heart Association task force on practice guidelines (ACC/AHA/ASE committee to update the 1997 guidelines for the clinical application of echocardiography). Circulation 2003;108(9):1146–62; http://dx.doi.org/10.1161/01.CIR.0000073597.57414.A9.

[4] Rychik J, Ayres N, Cuneo B, et al. American Society of Echocardiography guidelines and standards for performance of the fetal echocardiogram. J Am Soc Echocardiogr 2004;17(7):803–10; http://dx.doi.org/10.1016/j.echo.2004.04.011.

[5] Verheijen PM, Lisowski LA, Stoutenbeek P, et al. Prenatal diagnosis of congenital heart disease affects preoperative acidosis in the newborn patient. J Thorac Cardiovasc Surg 2001;121(4):798–803; http://dx.doi.org/10.1067/mtc.2001.112825.

[6] Tworetzky W, McElhinney DB, Reddy VM, et al. Improved surgical outcome after fetal diagnosis of hypoplastic left heart syndrome. Circulation 2001;103(9):1269–73.

[7] Copel JA, Tan AS, Kleinman CS. Does a prenatal diagnosis of congenital heart disease alter short-term outcome? Ultrasound Obstet Gynecol 1997;10(4):237–41; http://dx.doi.org/10.1046/j.1469-0705.1997.10040237.x.

[8] Kumar RK, Newburger JW, Gauvreau K, et al. Comparison of outcome when hypoplastic left heart syndrome and transposition of the great arteries are diagnosed prenatally versus when diagnosis of these two conditions is made only postnatally. Am J Cardiol 1999;83(12):1649–53.

[9] Bonnet D, Coltri A, Butera G, et al. Detection of transposition of the great arteries in fetuses reduces neonatal morbidity and mortality. Circulation 1999;99(7):916–8.

[10] Allan LD, Cook A, Sullivan I, et al. Hypoplastic left heart syndrome: effects of fetal echocardiography on birth prevalence. Lancet 1991;337(8747):959–61.

[11] Mertens L, Seri I, Marek J, et al. Targeted neonatal echocardiography in the neonatal intensive care unit: practice guidelines and recommendations for training. Writing group of the American Society of Echocardiography (ASE) in collaboration with the European Association of Echocardiography (EAE) and the Association for European Pediatric Cardiologists (AEPC). J Am Soc Echocardiogr 2011;24(10):1057–78; http://dx.doi.org/10.1016/j.echo.2011.07.014.

[12] Collaco JM, Romer LH, Stuart BD, et al. Frontiers in pulmonary hypertension in infants and children with bronchopulmonary dysplasia. Pediatr Pulmonol 2012;47(11):1042–53; http://dx.doi.org/10.1002/ppul.22609.

[13] Khemani E, McElhinney DB, Rhein L, et al. Pulmonary artery hypertension in formerly premature infants with bronchopulmonary dysplasia: clinical features and outcomes in the surfactant era. Pediatrics 2007;120(6):1260–9; http://dx.doi.org/10.1542/peds.2007-0971.

[14] Kim GB. Pulmonary hypertension in infants with bronchopulmonary dysplasia. Korean J Pediatr 2010;53(6):688–93; http://dx.doi.org/10.3345/kjp.2010.53.6.688.

[15] Mourani PM, Sontag MK, Younoszai A, et al. Clinical utility of echocardiography for the diagnosis and management of pulmonary vascular disease in young children with chronic lung disease. Pediatrics 2008;121(2):317–25; http://dx.doi.org/10.1542/peds.2007-1583.

[16] Hill KD, Lim DS, Everett AD, et al. Assessment of pulmonary hypertension in the pediatric catheterization laboratory: current insights from the magic registry. Catheter Cardiovasc Interv 2010;76(6):865–73; http://dx.doi.org/10.1002/ccd.22693.
[17] Mahle WT, Martin GR, Beekman RH III, et al. Section on Cardiology and Cardiac Surgery Executive Committee. Endorsement of health and human services recommendation for pulse oximetry screening for critical congenital heart disease. Pediatrics 2012;129(1): 190–2; http://dx.doi.org/10.1542/peds.2011-3211.
[18] Knapp AA, Metterville DR, Kemper AR, et al. Evidence review: critical congenital cyanotic heart disease, Final Draft, September 3, 2010. Prepared for the Maternal and Child Health Bureau, Health Resources and Services Administration. Available at: http://www.hrsa.gov/advisorycommittees/mchbadvisory/heritabledisorders/nominate condition/reviews/cyanoticheart.pdf. Accessed May 17, 2013.
[19] Mahle WT, Newburger JW, Matherne GP, et al. Role of pulse oximetry in examining newborns for congenital heart disease: a scientific statement from the American Heart Association and American Academy of Pediatrics. Circulation 2009;120(5):447–58; http://dx.doi.org/10.1161/CIRCULATIONAHA.109.192576.
[20] Kemper AR, Mahle WT, Martin GR, et al. Strategies for implementing screening for critical congenital heart disease. Pediatrics 2011;128(5):e1259–67; http://dx.doi.org/10.1542/peds.2011-1317.
[21] Lai W, Mertens L, Cohen M, et al. Echocardiography in pediatric and congenital heart disease: from fetus to adult. Oxford (UK): Wiley; 2009.
[22] De Wolf D, Suys B, Verhaaren H, et al. Low-dose dobutamine stress echocardiography in children and young adults. Am J Cardiol 1998;81(7):895–901.
[23] Michelfelder EC, Witt SA, Khoury P, et al. Moderate-dose dobutamine maximizes left ventricular contractile response during dobutamine stress echocardiography in children. J Am Soc Echocardiogr 2003;16(2):140–6; http://dx.doi.org/10.1067/mje.2003.3.
[24] Zilberman MV, Goya G, Witt SA, et al. Dobutamine stress echocardiography in the evaluation of young patients with Kawasaki disease. Pediatr Cardiol 2003;24(4):338–43; http://dx.doi.org/10.1007/s00246-002-0327-9.
[25] Pahl E, Crawford SE, Swenson JM, et al. Dobutamine stress echocardiography: experience in pediatric heart transplant recipients. J Heart Lung Transplant 1999;18(7):725–32.
[26] Newburger JW, Takahashi M, Gerber MA, et al. Diagnosis, treatment, and long-term management of Kawasaki disease: a statement for health professionals from the committee on rheumatic fever, endocarditis and Kawasaki disease, council on cardiovascular disease in the young, American Heart Association. Circulation 2004;110(17):2747–71; http://dx.doi.org/10.1161/01.CIR.0000145143.19711.78.
[27] Wilson W, Taubert KA, Gewitz M, et al. Prevention of infective endocarditis: guidelines from the American Heart Association: a guideline from the American Heart Association rheumatic fever, endocarditis, and Kawasaki disease committee, council on cardiovascular disease in the young, and the council on clinical cardiology, council on cardiovascular surgery and anesthesia, and the quality of care and outcomes research interdisciplinary working group. Circulation 2007;116(15):1736–54; http://dx.doi.org/10.1161/CIRCULATIONAHA.106.183095.
[28] Noel GJ, O'Loughlin JE, Edelson PJ. Neonatal *Staphylococcus epidermidis* right-sided endocarditis: description of five catheterized infants. Pediatrics 1988;82(2):234–9.
[29] Younoszai AK, Mossad E, Motta P, et al. Transesophageal echocardiography in pediatric cardiology. 2007;12(3).
[30] Randolph GR, Hagler DJ, Connolly HM, et al. Intraoperative transesophageal echocardiography during surgery for congenital heart defects. J Thorac Cardiovasc Surg 2002;124(6):1176–82; http://dx.doi.org/10.1067/mtc.2002.125816.
[31] Platts DG, Sedgwick JF, Burstow DJ, et al. The role of echocardiography in the management of patients supported by extracorporeal membrane oxygenation. J Am Soc Echocardiogr 2012;25(2):131–41; http://dx.doi.org/10.1016/j.echo.2011.11.009.

[32] Kuenzler KA, Arthur LG, Burchard AE, et al. Intraoperative ultrasound reduces ECMO catheter malposition requiring surgical correction. J Pediatr Surg 2002;37(5):691–4.
[33] Thomas TH, Price R, Ramaciotti C, et al. Echocardiography, not chest radiography, for evaluation of cannula placement during pediatric extracorporeal membrane oxygenation. Pediatr Crit Care Med 2009;10(1):56–9; http://dx.doi.org/10.1097/PCC.0b013e3181937409.
[34] Luxenberg DM, Silvestry FE, Herrmann HC, et al. Use of a new 8 French intracardiac echocardiographic catheter to guide device closure of atrial septal defects and patent foramen ovale in small children and adults: initial clinical experience. J Invasive Cardiol 2005;17(10):540–5.
[35] Bartel T, Konorza T, Arjumand J, et al. Intracardiac echocardiography is superior to conventional monitoring for guiding device closure of interatrial communications. Circulation 2003;107(6):795–7.
[36] Bartel T, Konorza T, Neudorf U, et al. Intracardiac echocardiography: an ideal guiding tool for device closure of interatrial communications. Eur J Echocardiogr 2005;6(2):92–6; http://dx.doi.org/10.1016/j.euje.2004.07.007.
[37] Cao QL, Zabal C, Koenig P, et al. Initial clinical experience with intracardiac echocardiography in guiding transcatheter closure of perimembranous ventricular septal defects: feasibility and comparison with transesophageal echocardiography. Catheter Cardiovasc Interv 2005;66(2):258–67; http://dx.doi.org/10.1002/ccd.20463.
[38] Mullen MJ, Dias BF, Walker F, et al. Intracardiac echocardiography guided device closure of atrial septal defects. J Am Coll Cardiol 2003;41(2):285–92.
[39] O'Leary PW. Intracardiac echocardiography in congenital heart disease: are we ready to begin the fantastic voyage? Pediatr Cardiol 2002;23(3):286–91; http://dx.doi.org/10.1007/s00246-001-0194-9.
[40] Kimball TR. Pediatric stress echocardiography. Pediatr Cardiol 2002;23(3):347–57; http://dx.doi.org/10.1007/s00246-001-0198-5.
[41] Otasevic P, Popovic ZB, Vasiljevic JD, et al. Head-to-head comparison of indices of left ventricular contractile reserve assessed by high-dose dobutamine stress echocardiography in idiopathic dilated cardiomyopathy: five-year follow up. Heart 2006;92(9):1253–8; http://dx.doi.org/10.1136/hrt.2005.073999.
[42] Paraskevaidis IA, Adamopoulos S, Tsiapras D, et al. Prognostic usefulness of echocardiographic dobutamine in younger (14 to 25 years) and older (40 to 55 years) patients with idiopathic dilated cardiomyopathy. Am J Cardiol 2004;93(2):251–5.
[43] Marmor A, Schneeweiss A. Prognostic value of noninvasively obtained left ventricular contractile reserve in patients with severe heart failure. J Am Coll Cardiol 1997;29(2):422–8.
[44] Caiani EG, Corsi C, Zamorano J, et al. Improved semiautomated quantification of left ventricular volumes and ejection fraction using 3-dimensional echocardiography with a full matrix-array transducer: comparison with magnetic resonance imaging. J Am Soc Echocardiogr 2005;18(8):779–88; http://dx.doi.org/10.1016/j.echo.2004.12.015.
[45] Jenkins C, Chan J, Hanekom L, et al. Accuracy and feasibility of online 3-dimensional echocardiography for measurement of left ventricular parameters. J Am Soc Echocardiogr 2006;19(9):1119–28; http://dx.doi.org/10.1016/j.echo.2006.04.002.
[46] Papavassiliou DP, Parks WJ, Hopkins KL, et al. Three-dimensional echocardiographic measurement of right ventricular volume in children with congenital heart disease validated by magnetic resonance imaging. J Am Soc Echocardiogr 1998;11(8):770–7.
[47] Heusch A, Rubo J, Krogmann ON, et al. Volume measurement of the left ventricle in children with congenital heart defects: 3-dimensional echocardiography versus angiocardiography. Cardiology 1999;92(1):45–52; http://dx.doi.org/10.1159/000006945.
[48] Altmann K, Shen Z, Boxt LM, et al. Comparison of three-dimensional echocardiographic assessment of volume, mass, and function in children with functionally single left ventricles

with two-dimensional echocardiography and magnetic resonance imaging. Am J Cardiol 1997;80(8):1060–5.
[49] Marwick TH. Measurement of strain and strain rate by echocardiography: ready for prime time? J Am Coll Cardiol 2006;47(7):1313–27; http://dx.doi.org/10.1016/j.jacc.2005.11.063.
[50] Stoylen A, Slordahl S, Skjelvan GK, et al. Strain rate imaging in normal and reduced diastolic function: comparison with pulsed Doppler tissue imaging of the mitral annulus. J Am Soc Echocardiogr 2001;14(4):264–74.
[51] Weidemann F, Eyskens B, Sutherland GR. New ultrasound methods to quantify regional myocardial function in children with heart disease. Pediatr Cardiol 2002;23(3):292–306; http://dx.doi.org/10.1007/s00246-001-0195-8.
[52] Cho GY, Chan J, Leano R, et al. Comparison of two-dimensional speckle and tissue velocity based strain and validation with harmonic phase magnetic resonance imaging. Am J Cardiol 2006;97(11):1661–6; http://dx.doi.org/10.1016/j.amjcard.2005.12.063.
[53] Boettler P, Hartmann M, Watzl K, et al. Heart rate effects on strain and strain rate in healthy children. J Am Soc Echocardiogr 2005;18(11):1121–30; http://dx.doi.org/10.1016/j.echo.2005.08.014.
[54] Marcus KA, Mavinkurve-Groothuis AM, Barends M, et al. Reference values for myocardial two-dimensional strain echocardiography in a healthy pediatric and young adult cohort. J Am Soc Echocardiogr 2011;24(6):625–36; http://dx.doi.org/10.1016/j.echo.2011.01.021.
[55] Eidem BW. Identification of anthracycline cardiotoxicity: left ventricular ejection fraction is not enough. J Am Soc Echocardiogr 2008;21(12):1290–2; http://dx.doi.org/10.1016/j.echo.2008.10.008.
[56] Dogan V, Ocal B, Orun UA, et al. Strain and strain rate echocardiography findings in children with asymptomatic congenital aortic stenosis. Pediatr Cardiol 2013; http://dx.doi.org/10.1007/s00246-012-0619-7.
[57] Friedberg MK, Wu S, Slorach C. Left-right ventricular interactions in pediatric aortic stenosis: right ventricular myocardial strain before and after aortic valvuloplasty. J Am Soc Echocardiogr 2013; http://dx.doi.org/10.1016/j.echo.2012.12.014.
[58] Marcus KA, de Korte CL, Feuth T, et al. Persistent reduction in left ventricular strain using two-dimensional speckle-tracking echocardiography after balloon valvuloplasty in children with congenital valvular aortic stenosis. J Am Soc Echocardiogr 2012;25(5):473–85; http://dx.doi.org/10.1016/j.echo.2012.01.009.
[59] Mi Y, Radle-Hurst T, Rentzsch A, et al. The novel two-dimensional strain reflects improvement and remodeling of left-ventricular function better than conventional echocardiographic parameters after aortic valve repair in pediatric patients. Pediatr Cardiol 2013;34(1):30–8; http://dx.doi.org/10.1007/s00246-012-0376-7.
[60] Ganame J, Pignatelli RH, Eidem BW, et al. Myocardial deformation abnormalities in pediatric hypertrophic cardiomyopathy: are all etiologies identical? Eur J Echocardiogr 2008;9(6):784–90; http://dx.doi.org/10.1093/ejechocard/jen150.
[61] Kailin JA, Miyamoto SD, Younoszai AK, et al. Longitudinal myocardial deformation is selectively decreased after pediatric cardiac transplantation: a comparison of children 1 year after transplantation with normal subjects using velocity vector imaging. Pediatr Cardiol 2012;33(5):749–56; http://dx.doi.org/10.1007/s00246-012-0205-z.
[62] Eichhorn JG, Long FR, Hill SL, et al. Assessment of in-stent stenosis in small children with congenital heart disease using multi-detector computed tomography: a validation study. Catheter Cardiovasc Interv 2006;68(1):11–20; http://dx.doi.org/10.1002/ccd.20760.
[63] Hoffmann R, Mintz GS, Dussaillant GR, et al. Patterns and mechanisms of in-stent restenosis. A serial intravascular ultrasound study. Circulation 1996;94(6):1247–54.
[64] Chen SJ, Lee WJ, Wang JK, et al. Usefulness of three-dimensional electron beam computed tomography for evaluating tracheobronchial anomalies in children with congenital heart disease. Am J Cardiol 2003;92(4):483–6.

[65] Spuentrup E, Buecker A, Stuber M, et al. Navigator-gated coronary magnetic resonance angiography using steady-state-free-precession: comparison to standard T2-prepared gradient-echo and spiral imaging. Invest Radiol 2003;38(5):263–8; http://dx.doi.org/10.1097/01.RLI.0000064341.68310.c0.
[66] Datta J, White CS, Gilkeson RC, et al. Anomalous coronary arteries in adults: depiction at multi-detector row CT angiography. Radiology 2005;235(3):812–8; http://dx.doi.org/10.1148/radiol.2353040314.
[67] Tsai-Goodman B, Geva T, Odegard KC, et al. Clinical role, accuracy, and technical aspects of cardiovascular magnetic resonance imaging in infants. Am J Cardiol 2004;94(1):69–74; http://dx.doi.org/10.1016/j.amjcard.2004.03.033.
[68] Allen D, Shaddy F. Moss and Adams' heart disease in infants, children and adolescents. 7th edition. Philadelphia: Lippincott Williams and Wilkins; 2008.
[69] Sorensen TS, Korperich H, Greil GF, et al. Operator-independent isotropic three-dimensional magnetic resonance imaging for morphology in congenital heart disease: a validation study. Circulation 2004;110(2):163–9; http://dx.doi.org/10.1161/01.CIR.0000134282.35183.AD.
[70] Beerbaum P, Korperich H, Barth P, et al. Noninvasive quantification of left-to-right shunt in pediatric patients: phase-contrast cine magnetic resonance imaging compared with invasive oximetry. Circulation 2001;103(20):2476–82.
[71] Semelka RC, Tomei E, Wagner S, et al. Interstudy reproducibility of dimensional and functional measurements between cine magnetic resonance studies in the morphologically abnormal left ventricle. Am Heart J 1990;119(6):1367–73.
[72] Sarikouch S, Peters B, Gutberlet M, et al. Sex-specific pediatric percentiles for ventricular size and mass as reference values for cardiac MRI: assessment by steady-state free-precession and phase-contrast MRI flow. Circ Cardiovasc Imaging 2010;3(1):65–76; http://dx.doi.org/10.1161/CIRCIMAGING.109.859074.
[73] Tulevski II, Lee PL, Groenink M, et al. Dobutamine-induced increase of right ventricular contractility without increased stroke volume in adolescent patients with transposition of the great arteries: evaluation with magnetic resonance imaging. Int J Cardiovasc Imaging 2000;16(6):471–8.
[74] Tulevski II, van der Wall EE, Groenink M, et al. Usefulness of magnetic resonance imaging dobutamine stress in asymptomatic and minimally symptomatic patients with decreased cardiac reserve from congenital heart disease (complete and corrected transposition of the great arteries and subpulmonic obstruction). Am J Cardiol 2002;89(9):1077–81.
[75] Roest AA, Kunz P, Lamb HJ, et al. Biventricular response to supine physical exercise in young adults assessed with ultrafast magnetic resonance imaging. Am J Cardiol 2001;87(5):601–5.
[76] Wilson JM, Villareal RP, Hariharan R, et al. Magnetic resonance imaging of myocardial fibrosis in hypertrophic cardiomyopathy. Tex Heart Inst J 2002;29(3):176–80.
[77] Cummings KW, Bhalla S, Javidan-Nejad C, et al. A pattern-based approach to assessment of delayed enhancement in nonischemic cardiomyopathy at MR imaging. Radiographics 2009;29(1):89–103; http://dx.doi.org/10.1148/rg.291085052.
[78] Laissy JP, Messin B, Varenne O, et al. MRI of acute myocarditis: a comprehensive approach based on various imaging sequences. Chest 2002;122(5):1638–48.

Advances in Pediatrics 60 (2013) 187–200

ADVANCES IN PEDIATRICS

# Recent Advances in Interventional Pediatric Cardiology

Ram N. Bishnoi, MD*, John D. Coulson, MD, Richard E. Ringel, MD

Department of Pediatric Cardiology, Johns Hopkins University School of Medicine, 1800 Orleans Street, Bloomberg Children's Center M2309, Baltimore, MD 21287, USA

**Keywords**

• Interventional cardiology • Pediatric cardiology • Percutaneous closure devices • Fetal cardiac interventions

**Key points**

- Interventional pediatric cardiology is rapidly evolving. Techniques are improving thanks to the use of smaller introducers and sheaths, low-profile balloons, and novel devices.
- Surgical procedures are being partially replaced by percutaneous interventions or hybrid approaches.
- Based on a better understanding of cardiac development, fetal cardiac interventions are being attempted to alter the history of severe obstructive lesions.

## ATRIAL SEPTAL DEFECT DEVICE CLOSURE

Percutaneous closure of secundum atrial septal defect (ASD) has become the preferred treatment, except for very large or eccentrically positioned defects, for which surgery may still be preferred. Procedural technique and available devices have rapidly advanced since King and colleagues [1] reported on the first transcatheter closure of an ASD in humans in 1976. Several devices have been investigated in the United States, but only 2 are currently approved by the U.S. Food and Drug Administration (FDA): the Amplatzer Septal Occluder (ASO) and the Helex Septal Occluder. The ASO has become the most widely used device since its introduction in 1997 because of its high closure rates, overall safety, ease of deployment, retrievability, and ability to close large defects. Most studies demonstrate very low procedural risk of ASD closure using the Amplatzer septal occluder. Du and colleagues [2] published their experience in closing

*Corresponding author. *E-mail address*: rbishno1@jhmi.edu

0065-3101/13/$ – see front matter
http://dx.doi.org/10.1016/j.yapd.2013.04.009 

ASDs with deficient septal rims and showed no significant difference in the rate of complete closure at 24 hours and 6 months' follow-up when compared with ASDs with sufficient rims (>5 mm). However, concerns have been raised regarding use of the ASO in the presence of a deficient retroaortic septal rim, with reports of cardiac erosion [3,4]. This complication is rare, with an estimated occurrence of 2 per thousand implants. A published review of all reported erosions suggested that device oversizing and deficient anterosuperior (retroaortic) rim are risk factors for cardiac perforation [4]. This finding has led many implanters to modify their implant guidelines and techniques. Erosions have not been reported with the Helex device, although a case of Helex wire frame fracture leading to mitral valve perforation has been reported. For most patients these devices are safe and highly effective, but further technological advancement is still needed to develop the ideal device.

Nonsurgical closure of a large secundum ASD can be technically challenging, even when using the ASO. Different deployment strategies have been described, including the use of specially shaped sheaths, deployment of ASO in the left or right pulmonary vein, and use of the balloon-assist technique [5] (deployment of the device using the support of a balloon-tipped catheter inflated across the defect). For urgent ASD closure in infants, other approaches are sometimes needed, such as accessing the right atrium from a transhepatic approach or even via hybrid procedures to close secundum ASDs through a per-atrial approach [6].

Modifications of the Amplatzer septal occluder have been reported. Amin and colleagues [7] described fenestration of an Amplatzer septal occluder to only partially occlude ASDs in patients for whom a small "pop-off" is indicated to allow shunting across the atrial septum at times of stress. The ASO can also be used to completely close Fontan fenestrations, when indicated. The Cribriform Amplatzer Septal Occluder (St. Jude Medical, Inc, St. Paul, MN, USA) is used to close multiple, closely spaced ASDs or those lying within an atrial septal aneurysm [8].

New devices have been introduced in Europe, such as the Intrasept (Cardia Inc., Eagan, MN, USA), Occlutech Figulla device (Occlutech GmbH, Jena, Germany), and, more recently, the totally bioabsorbable Immediate Release Patch device (Custom Medical Devices, Athens, Greece). Closure of 12 ASDs and 1 fenestration was attempted using the Immediate Release Patch. Of the 13 devices used, 12 were implanted successfully, whereas 1 moved from the original position and was retrieved percutaneously. After a median follow-up of 11 months, a trivial residual shunt remained in 2 patients and a significant residual shunt remained in 1. The major conceptual advantages of this device include absence of a metallic frame, bioabsorbability, and potential application for defects up to 30 mm using only 3 device sizes. The device is also reported to be easily retrieved and able to occlude defects with a deficient rim, and even some ostium primum- and sinus venosus-type defects [9].

Finally, using intracardiac echocardiography in patients as small as 15 kg to help guide the implantation can eliminate the need for tracheal and esophageal intubation and, for older children, the need for general anesthesia.

## PATENT FORAMEN OVALE CLOSURE

Patent foramen ovale (PFO) closure in patients with previous cerebral embolic events remains controversial. The first randomized trial of a PFO device closure concluded in 2010 without showing a benefit in reducing stroke recurrence using the STARFlex device in patients with a prior cryptogenic stroke. More recently the randomized RESPECT study was more supportive of a role for closure of a PFO in patients who experienced cryptogenic stroke. Even though the trial did not technically meet its primary end point, many experts believe the results support the hypothesis that PFO closure with the Amplatzer PFO Occluder reduces the risk of stroke recurrence. When the study data are analyzed for patients who actually received the Amplatzer device and excluded the intent-to-treat patients who had not yet received a device, the device closure showed a clear benefit in reducing stroke recurrence. At 2 years, the recurrence rate for patients treated medically was 3.0% versus 1.6% in patients receiving the device. By 5 years of follow-up, the difference was 6.4% versus 2.2% (results presented at the 24th annual Transcatheter Cardiovascular Therapeutics scientific symposium) [10].

Using PFO closure devices to treat migraine headaches is even more controversial. Although multiple single-center case series have been reported, only one small randomized trial was conducted. This study again used the STARFlex device and was not found to reduce the occurrence or severity of migraine headache recurrences [11]. However, both the device and the trial were widely criticized and the results of the Amplatzer PREMIUM trial are awaited to show whether closure of the PFO can reduce morbidity related to migraine headaches.

## PATENT DUCTUS ARTERIOSUS OCCLUSION

Surgical closure of patent ductus arteriosus (PDA) has been performed for more than 60 years. PDA transcatheter closure was introduced in 1967 and has become the preferred treatment for most PDAs after the neonatal period. Cook embolization coils are commonly used to occlude small PDAs. Past device designs to occlude large PDAs were associated with major drawbacks, including an unacceptable incidence of residual shunt and/or embolization and partial aortic or pulmonary artery luminal obstruction. Other problems included complex delivery systems and the need for a large delivery sheath. The Amplatzer Duct Occluder (ADO) (AGA Medical Corporation, Plymouth, MN, USA) was introduced in 1998 and adopted quickly by most interventionists for the occlusion of small to moderate and some large PDAs.

In 2004, Pass and colleagues [12] reported the immediate and short-term results of the multicenter USA Amplatzer PDA occlusion device trial. A total of 439 patients with moderate to large PDAs were treated at a median age of 1.8 years (range, 0.2–70.7 years) and weight of 11 kg (4.5–164.5 kg). ADO implantation was successful in 435 of 439 patients. The overall morbidity was 9.4% and no deaths occurred. The median follow-up was 12 months and the 1-year occlusion rate was 99.7%. Concern has been raised regarding PDA closure using the ADO in infants less than 6 kg with large symptomatic ducts, because of the risk of aortic and/or pulmonary obstruction [13–15]. However, the softer and more flexible Amplatzer Vascular Plug II is being used effectively for some infants with a PDA. The range of ductal anatomy and patient size manageable safely in the catheter laboratory will expand even further when the Amplatzer Duct Occluder II becomes available in the United States.

## VASCULAR OCCLUSION: COLLATERALS AND FISTULAS

Transcatheter embolization has become the preferred treatment for aortopulmonary collaterals, pulmonary arteriovenous fistulas, venous collaterals, and coronary artery fistulas, replacing surgical intervention in most cases. Intravascular coils have been used for decades and have proved to be successful for interventional occlusions of small- or medium-sized vessels. However, they have several drawbacks, sometimes being time-consuming to deploy and subject to recanalization, and they are not ideal in larger fistulas because of the risk of embolization to the systemic circulation. In 2001, Qureshi and Tynan [16] reported their experience using mainly controlled-release coils.

The Amplatzer Vascular Plugs are designed to obviate most of the difficulties associated with coil embolization. These woven nitinol, fabric-free devices, are available in sizes that range from 3 to 22 mm, and can be delivered through low-profile sheaths or guiding catheters (4–8 French). The second-generation plug has a multisegmented and multilayered design of nitinol to allow more efficient occlusion, and extended rims to improve wall apposition and reduce the risk of device embolization. The newest version of the vascular plug, the AVP IV, is a bilobed device with low profile, capable of delivery through 4- or 5-French catheters, the same size catheters used to deliver most embolization coils.

## MUSCULAR VENTRICULAR SEPTAL DEFECT DEVICE CLOSURE

Surgical closure of muscular ventricular septal defects (VSDs) can be challenging for surgeons. It also involves a significant risk of morbidity, including residual shunting reoperation and ventricular dysfunction caused by right or left ventriculotomy [17]. Lock and colleagues [18] reported an early experience of transcatheter closure of muscular VSDs in 1988, using the Rashkind double umbrella device (USCI Angiographics, Billerica, MA, USA). AGA Medical Corporation (St. Jude Medical, Inc., Plymouth, MN, USA) has introduced a new family of lesion-specific Amplatzer devices to close muscular VSDs (mVSDs). The self-expanding nitinol mVSD device consists of 2 retention disks linked via a central connecting waist, which is 7 mm wide. Both retention disks are 5 mm larger than the connecting waist. Device size (4–18 mm) is usually chosen equal to or 1 to 2 mm greater than the largest measured diameter of the VSD. Various approaches can be used, according to the anatomy of the mVSD: femoral vein for anterior defects and jugular vein for midmuscular and apical defects. Especially for infants, a hybrid, perventricular approach is often required. Via median sternotomy, the heart is exposed and a pursestring suture is formed to allow access through the right ventricular free wall. Under continuous echocardiographic guidance a guidewire is manipulated across the VSD, after which the vascular sheath is advanced, followed by device deployment. As discussed later, hybrid procedures have the advantage of avoiding cardiopulmonary bypass while overcoming vascular access limitations and hemodynamic instability in small patients [19,20].

Immediate and midterm results of mVSD closure using the Amplatzer mVSD occluder have been reported by Holzer and colleagues [21]. In this US registry, the preliminary results included 83 procedures in 75 patients with a median age of 1.4 years who underwent percutaneous or perventricular closure of hemodynamically significant muscular VSDs. The device was implanted successfully in 72 of 83 (86.7%) procedures. Major procedure- or device-related complications occurred in 10.7% patients. Closure rates were excellent and increased from 47.2% at 24 hours postprocedure to 92.3% at 12-month follow-up. Results of the European registry concerning transcatheter closure of congenital VSDs were reported by Carminati and colleagues [22]. Of the 430 patients, 119 had mVSDs. The Amplatzer mVSD occluder was the device used most frequently.

## PERIMEMBRANOUS VSD DEVICE CLOSURE

Percutaneous attempts to close perimembranous VSDs (pmVSDs) with Rashkind and buttoned devices were reported in the late 1990s, but with a high incidence of residual shunt and complications. The Amplatzer pmVSD occluder was introduced in 2002 as the first device designed specifically for pmVSD occlusion. This self-expandable device is also made of nitinol wire with Dacron fabric incorporated. It consists of 2 flat disks linked via a central connecting waist that is 0.5 mm long. The left disk is asymmetric with almost no superior (aortic) rim and a longer 5 mm inferior rim. Holzer and colleagues [23] reported encouraging initial and midterm results of an international registry involving 100 patients. Successful implantation of the pmVSD occluder was achieved in 93% patients. No procedure-related deaths occurred. However, complications were reported in 29 of 100 patients, including the development of complete atrioventricular block in 2 patients, requiring permanent pacemaker implantation, and 9 patients with new or increased aortic insufficiency (none experiencing progression or requiring surgery). At 6-month follow-up, complete closure rate was 83.6%, but the major concern has been the development of complete atrioventricular block during the procedure, shortly after or even several months later, requiring pacemaker implantation at rates ranging from 2% to 5.7% in multicenter studies [23–26]. This device was not approved for use in the United States. Newer, softer devices are in development and testing, with the hope that they will allow for safer, equally effective, nonsurgical membranous VSD closure.

## BALLOON VALVULOPLASTY FOR AORTIC STENOSIS

Aortic valvuloplasty is an established procedure that is regarded as a valid alternative to the surgical management of congenital aortic valve stenosis in pediatric patients. A consensus seems to favor percutaneous dilatation in patients younger than 18 years with no valvular calcifications and favorable valvular anatomy.

In a neonatal series of 110 patients younger than 1 month, McCrindle and colleagues [27] reported the results of surgical versus transcatheter balloon valvuloplasty in neonatal critical aortic stenosis. Early mortality was 11% and 18%, respectively, with no significant difference, even after adjustment for differences in patient characteristics. Likewise, major complication rates were not significantly different. Freedom from aortic reintervention was similar for both groups (91%, 68%, 58%, and 48% at 1 month, 6 months, 1 year, and 5 years, respectively). The rate of significant aortic regurgitation was higher after balloon valvuloplasty than after surgery, although not significantly. The same team reported in another study that the only independent predictor of time-related mortality was the presence of moderate or severe left ventricular endocardial fibroelastosis [28]. In a series of 188 patients including neonates and older children, Fratz and colleagues [29] reported 10-year rates of freedom from aortic valve surgery after balloon aortic valvuloplasty of 59% in patients younger than 1 month and 70% in those aged at least 1 month.

Use of right ventricular pacing during balloon inflation has become a widely accepted technique for decreasing left ventricular stroke volume and pressure, thus increasing balloon stability during inflation and reducing trauma to the aortic valve [30].

## BALLOON VALVULOPLASTY FOR PULMONARY STENOSIS

Pulmonary valvuloplasty is an effective and safe treatment for pulmonary valve stenosis, and is considered the preferred treatment for nondysplastic valves. Classic balloon dilatation may be ineffective for dysplastic valves, but can be helpful in reducing right ventricular hypertension and postponing and sometimes eliminating the need for surgical valvectomy. Palliative balloon dilation and intraoperative balloon pulmonary annuloplasty of the right ventricular outflow tract (RVOT) in patients with tetralogy of Fallot is advocated by many teams to help avoid a transannular patch and contribute to annulus growth, but its implementation remains controversial [31–33]. Implantation of stents in the RVOT in symptomatic newborns with tetralogy of Fallot is a new concept and the results are encouraging, but this approach is controversial [34].

## MITRAL BALLOON VALVULOPLASTY

Percutaneous mitral commissurotomy (using the Inoue technique) is the preferred treatment for postrheumatic mitral stenosis, wherein fusion of commissure is a predominant mechanism, but the procedure remains controversial in patients with congenital mitral stenosis. McElhinney and colleagues [35] from Boston reported their experience with transcatheter and surgical (valvuloplasty and replacement) therapy for severe congenital mitral stenosis in 108 infants and children with a median age of 18 months. Balloon mitral valvuloplasty was the preferred mode of treatment in most cases, especially in those with typical congenital mitral stenosis (thickened leaflets, short or absent chordae tendineae, and 2 separate, but often closely spaced, papillary muscles) and double-orifice mitral valve. Surgery was favored when mitral stenosis was caused by a supravalvular ring or when significant mitral regurgitation or important associated anomalies requiring cardiotomy were present. Overall survival was 77% at 5 years. After percutaneous treatment, significant mitral regurgitation occurred in 28% of cases, and freedom from failure of biventricular repair or mitral valve reintervention was 55% at 1 year compared with 69% after surgical valvuloplasty. However, these results reflect the experience of only one large referral center, and surgery is the usual approach in most other institutions.

## BALLOON DILATATION AND STENTING OF PULMONARY ARTERIES

Percutaneous intervention has become the preferred treatment for stenotic pulmonary arteries, most frequently after surgery. The inclusion of high-pressure balloons and stents in the interventionist's armamentarium at the beginning of the 1990s has improved results considerably. McMahon and colleagues [36] reported their series of 664 Palmaz stent implantations in 338 patients with a mean age of 12.2 years. The ratio of right ventricular to aortic pressure decreased from 0.66 before stenting to 0.45 immediately after stenting, and was 0.50 at a mean follow-up of 5.6 years. Five deaths were reported, including 1 fulminant pulmonary edema and 1 massive hemoptysis. The rate of restenosis was 2%. Patients with a diagnosis of isolated congenital pulmonary artery stenosis had a less-optimal outcome and a higher complication rate. Cutting balloons have been used successfully in the setting of small-vessel pulmonary artery stenoses resistant to high-pressure balloon angioplasty [37]. Further technological advances, such as biodegradable stents, may further expand the indications for pulmonary artery stent implantation to all age groups [38].

## BALLOON DILATATION AND STENTING OF COARCTATION OF THE AORTA

The best therapeutic approach for patients with aortic coarctation remains controversial, though recent evidence suggests that catheter-based intervention is an excellent approach as the primary treatment modality for many patients with coarctation. The technique remains highly controversial in neonates and infants because of a very high incidence (>50% in most series) of recoarctation. It is a possible alternative to surgery for children (aged 1–7 years), but is associated with a 10% to 15% late aneurysm rate. For patients near adult size (>7 years or >35 kg), primary stenting is used increasingly. However, younger patients will usually need planned elective redilatation after complete growth.

A multi-institutional registry reported an immediate success rate of 97.9% (563 of 565 procedures) after stenting native and recurrent aortic coarctation in patients aged older than 4 years, and an acute complication rate of 14.3% (81 of 565), including 2 deaths, 6 aneurysms, and 9 aortic dissections [39].

The risk of aortic dissection after implantation of bare stent is higher in cases of nearly atretic coarctation or if coarctation is associated with a hypoplastic aortic arch.

Several series report the growing use of covered stents, with an almost 100% immediate success rate and good midterm results [40–42]. The Covered Cheatham Platinum Stent (NuMED, Inc., Hopkinton, NY, USA), made of platinum–iridium alloy and covered with expandable polytetrafluoroethylene, is used most widely.

## BALLOON DILATATION AND STENTING OF PULMONARY VEINS

Congenital pulmonary vein stenosis is a rare condition, usually with a guarded prognosis. Neither surgery nor percutaneous intervention (balloon dilatation or stenting) achieves freedom from reintervention or death at midterm follow-up. Further catheter-based interventions have been attempted, such as dilatation using high-pressure balloons and cutting balloons to treat native lesions or in-stent stenosis. Again, immediate improvement is usually seen angiographically, but recurrent stenosis occurs in most patients.

## PERCUTANEOUS PULMONARY VALVE IMPLANTATION

Many patients with congenital heart disease (eg, tetralogy of Fallot, pulmonary atresia, transposition of great arteries, truncus arteriosus, aortic valve disease requiring the Ross procedure) require placement of a right ventricle-to-pulmonary artery conduit. The lifespan of a bioprosthetic right ventricular-to-pulmonary artery conduit is limited because of progressive obstruction and/or regurgitation. Endovascular treatment using balloon dilatation and bare stent implantation were increasingly accepted to extend conduit lifespan and reduce the number of open heart surgeries.

The team from Boston Children's Hospital reported its experience with endovascular stenting of obstructed right ventricular-to-pulmonary artery conduits [43]. Over a 15-year period, deployment of bare stents was attempted in 242 obstructed conduits in 221 patients. No deaths occurred and only one failure of attempted stent placement was reported. Acute complications requiring surgical stent removal occurred in 5 patients. Median freedom from conduit replacement after stent placement was 2.7 years.

Although it resolves the problem of conduit obstruction, bare stent placement inescapably leads to creation or worsening of pulmonary regurgitation. To overcome this problem, Bonhoeffer and colleagues [44] were the first to report on their experience with transcatheter pulmonary valve replacement (Fig. 1) in 2000 using a biologic valve harvested from a bovine jugular vein (Melody TPV, Medtronic, Inc., Minneapolis, MN, USA) and mounted in a balloon-expandable Cheatham Platinum Stent (NuMED). Owing to valve availability and size, and the need for a stiff structure to anchor the stent, indications for this valved stent are limited to patients with right ventricular-to-pulmonary artery conduits or bioprosthetic pulmonary valves with an internal

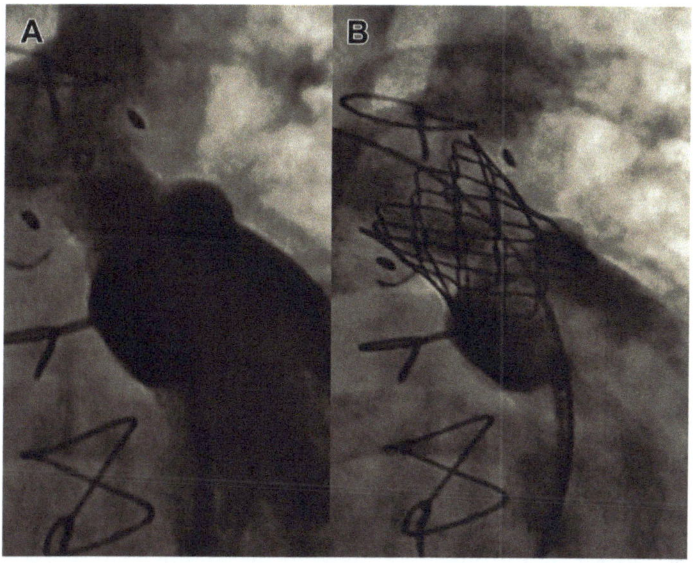


**Fig. 1.** (*A*) Right ventricular angiogram showing severely stenotic right ventricular-to-pulmonary artery conduit before transcatheter pulmonary valve implantation. (*B*) Right ventricular angiogram immediately after transcatheter pulmonary valve implantation.

diameter of at least 16 mm and not more than 22 mm at the time of Melody Transcatheter Pulmonary Valve implantation. In a recent study, Lurz and colleagues [45] reported on the immediate and long-term results of percutaneous pulmonary valve replacement performed by a single operator in 155 patients since the introduction of the Melody valved stent in 2000. Successful implantation was achieved in 150 of 155 patients (5 immediate explantations). Major complications included device dislodgement and instability ($\mathcal{N} = 2$), homograft rupture ($\mathcal{N} = 3$), compression of the left main coronary artery ($\mathcal{N} = 1$), and compression of the origin of the right pulmonary artery ($\mathcal{N} = 1$). Freedom from reoperation was 86% and 70% at 30 and 70 months, respectively. Beginning in January 2007, the Melody TPV was implanted in 150 patients with excellent results at 5 US centers under an Investigational Device Exemption protocol [46]. In January 2010, the Melody valve was approved for placement in dysfunctional RVOT conduits.

## HYBRID APPROACH

The use of complex transcatheter techniques in the management of congenital heart disease can be limited in small patients because of the use of large sheaths and their manipulation within the heart. Open heart surgery can also lead to significant morbidity and mortality in this population, specifically for interventions such as mVSD closure or stage I Norwood palliation. To overcome these limitations, interventional cardiologists and surgeons have worked hand-in-hand to develop hybrid procedures. These procedures have been attempted in different fields, mainly VSD closure, hypoplastic left heart syndrome (HLHS) management, and perventricular valve implantation. Hybrid interventions for HLHS require surgical, anesthetic, and interventional cardiology collaboration. The surgeon bands both pulmonary arteries through a median sternotomy, while the interventional cardiologist implants a stent in the arterial duct through a purse string in the main pulmonary artery. In cases of restrictive atrial septal communication, an atrioseptostomy is performed and/or a stent is placed across the septum.

Although the hybrid approach reduces the initial mortality of the first procedure, it leads predictably to increased interstage mortality and a more complex second stage palliation (arch reconstruction, stent excision, and bidirectional Glenn procedure) [47]. Over a 2-year period, Caldarone and colleagues [48] compared the results of 18 hybrid procedures with those of 25 classic Norwood stage I interventions in the treatment of mainly HLHS. Although not assigned randomly, no difference was found between the groups in terms of age and weight at the time of the procedure. Survival rate at 1 year was approximately 70%, with no significant difference between the groups. Similar conclusions were drawn by Pizarro and colleagues [49], who compared both approaches in 33 high-risk neonates with HLHS. Therefore, one can argue that this procedure still must be refined to match the surgical results in high-volume centers. However, it already represents an interesting alternative in centers with suboptimal surgical outcomes.

## FETAL INTERVENTIONS

Fetal cardiac interventions [50–53] generate a great deal of interest but are still controversial. They are based on the hypothesis that early relief of intracardiac obstacles might improve the development of the affected cardiac chambers. The first fetal dilatation of the aortic valve was accomplished in 1991. Early attempts resulted in limited success with high mortality, but more recent advancements in patient selection and techniques offer the prospect that fetal intervention may one day have a role in the management of critical congenital aortic stenosis and possible prevention of hypoplastic left heart syndrome. Fetal pulmonary valvuloplasty has seldom been reported. Atrial septostomy has been attempted in fetuses with HLHS and an intact or restrictive atrial septum.

## MISCELLANEOUS INTERVENTIONS

Transcatheter radiofrequency perforation of the right ventricular outflow tract is being performed with excellent results as initial therapy in patients with pulmonary valve atresia with or without intact ventricular septum [54–56]. Radiofrequency perforation is also used for atrial septal stenting in newborns with hypoplastic left heart syndrome with a restrictive atrial septal defect to create an alternative pathway for left atrial decompression.

The balloon-expandable Covered Cheatham Platinum Stents (NuMed, Inc., Hopkinton, NY, USA) are used to treat aortic coarctation and RVOT conduit tear during transcatheter pulmonary valve implantation. Recently, it has also been used successfully to treat traumatic aortic injury after blunt chest trauma [57]. These stents are widely available outside the United States, but not yet available to operators in the United States, except on a compassionate use basis or to investigators involved in the clinical trials of this device.

Animal studies have shown that the Glenn shunt, aorticopulmonary connections, and mitral valve implantation can be accomplished using transcatheter techniques. However, long-term animal studies and proper equipment will be required before these techniques can be attempted in humans. These novel techniques could someday allow for successful palliation of certain forms of congenital heart disease without surgical interventions such as Blalock-Taussig shunt, Glenn shunt, or mitral valve replacement [58,59].

## References

[1] Mills NL, King TD. Nonoperative closure of left-to-right shunts. J Thorac Cardiovasc Surg 1976;72(3):371–8.

[2] Du DZ, Koening P, Cao QL, et al. Comparison of transcatheter closure secundum atrial septal defect using the Amplatzer septal occlude associated with deficient-vs-sufficient rims. Am J Cardiol 2002;90:865–9.

[3] Divekar A, Gaamangwe T, Shaikh N, et al. Cardiac perforation after device closure of atrial septal defects with the Amplatzer septal occluder. J Am Coll Cardiol 2005;45: 1213–8.

[4] Amin Z, Hijazi ZM, Bass JL, et al. PFO closure complications from the AGA registry. Catheter Cardiovasc Interv 2008;72:74–9.

[5] Dalvi BV, Pinto RJ, Gupta A. New technique for device closure of large atrial septal defects. Catheter Cardiovasc Interv 2005;64:102–7.

[6] Diab KA, Cao QL, Bacha EA, et al. Device closure of atrial septal defects with the Amplatzer septal occluder: safety and outcome in infants. J Thorac Cardiovasc Surg 2007;134:960–6.

[7] Amin Z, Danford DA, Pedra CA. A new Amplatzer device to maintain patency of Fontan fenestrations and atrial septal defects. Catheter Cardiovasc Interv 2002;57:246–51.

[8] Cheatham JP, Hill SL, Chisolm JL. Initial results using the new cribriform Amplatzer septal occluder for transcatheter closure of multifenestrated atrial septal defects with septal aneurysm [abstract]. Catheter Cardiovasc Interv 2003;60:126.

[9] Zeinaloo A, Zanjani KS, Rastkar B, et al. Closure of interatrial defects by immediate-release patch. Pediatr Cardiol 2012;33:1253–8.

[10] Carroll JD. RESPECT trial for PFO closure for prevention of recurrent cryptogenic stroke. Presented at the 24th Annual Transcatheter Cardiovascular Therapeutics (TCT) scientific symposium. Miami (FL), October 25, 2012.

[11] Dowson A, Mullen MJ, Peatfield R, et al. Migraine Intervention with STARFlex Technology (MIST) trial: a prospective, multicenter, double-blind, sham-controlled trial to evaluate the effectiveness of patent foramen ovale closure with STARFlex septal repair implant to resolve refractory migraine headache. Circulation 2008;117:1397–404.

[12] Pass RH, Hijazi Z, Hsu DT, et al. Multicenter USA Amplatzer patent ductus arteriosus occlusion device trial: initial and 1-year results. J Am Coll Cardiol 2004;44:513–9.

[13] Al-Ata J, Arfi AM, Hussain A, et al. The efficacy and safety of the Amplatzer ductal occluder in young children and infants. Cardiol Young 2005;15:279–85.

[14] Butera G, De Rosa G, Chessa M, et al. Transcatheter closure of persistent ductus arteriosus with the Amplatzer duct occluder in very young symptomatic children. Heart 2004;90: 1467–70.

[15] Fischer G, Stieh J, Uebing A, et al. Transcatheter closure of persistent ductus arteriosus in infants using the Amplatzer duct occluder. Heart 2001;86:444–7.

[16] Qureshi SA, Tynan M. Catheter closure of coronary artery fistulas. J Interv Cardiol 2001;14:299–307.
[17] Griffiths SP, Turi GK, Ellis K, et al. Muscular ventricular septal defects repaired with left ventriculotomy. Am J Cardiol 1981;48:877–86.
[18] Lock JE, Block PC, McKay RG, et al. Transcatheter closure of ventricular septal defects. Circulation 1988;78:361–8.
[19] Amin Z, Berry JM, Foker JE, et al. Intraoperative closure of muscular ventricular septal defect in a canine model and application of the technique in a baby. J Thorac Cardiovasc Surg 1998;115:1374–6.
[20] Bacha EA, Cao QL, Galantowicz ME, et al. Multicenter experience with perventricular device closure of muscular ventricular septal defects. Pediatr Cardiol 2005;26: 169–75.
[21] Holzer R, Balzer D, Cao QL, et al. Device closure of muscular ventricular septal defects using the Amplatzer muscular ventricular septal defect occluder: immediate and midterm results of a US registry. J Am Coll Cardiol 2004;43:1257–63.
[22] Carminati M, Butera G, Chessa M, et al. Transcatheter closure of congenital ventricular septal defects: results of the European registry. Eur Heart J 2007;28:2361–8.
[23] Holzer R, de Giovanni J, Walsh KP, et al. Transcatheter closure of perimembranous ventricular septal defects using the Amplatzer membranous VSD occluder: immediate and midterm results of an international registry. Catheter Cardiovasc Interv 2006;68: 620–8.
[24] Butera G, Carminati M, Chessa M, et al. Transcatheter closure of perimembranous ventricular septal defects: early and longterm results. J Am Coll Cardiol 2007;50:1189–95.
[25] Thanopoulos BV, Rigby ML, Karanasios E, et al. Transcatheter closure of perimembranous ventricular septal defects in infants and children using the Amplatzer perimembranous ventricular septal defect occluder. Am J Cardiol 2007;99:984–9.
[26] Yip WC, Zimmerman F, Hijazi ZM. Heart block and empirical therapy after transcatheter closure of perimembranous ventricular septal defect. Catheter Cardiovasc Interv 2005;66: 436–41.
[27] McCrindle BW, Blackstone EH, Williams WG, et al. Are outcomes of surgical versus transcatheter balloon valvotomy equivalent in neonatal critical aortic stenosis? Circulation 2001;104:I152–8.
[28] Han RK, Gurofsky RC, Lee KJ, et al. Outcome and growth potential of left heart structures after neonatal intervention for aortic valve stenosis. J Am Coll Cardiol 2007;50: 2406–14.
[29] Fratz S, Gildein HP, Balling G, et al. Aortic valvuloplasty in pediatric patients substantially postpones the need for aortic valve surgery: a single-center experience of 188 patients after up to 17.5 years of follow-up. Circulation 2008;117:1201–6.
[30] Ing FF, Boramanand NK, Mathewson J, et al. Transcatheter aortic valvuloplasty assisted by right ventricular pacing. J Am Coll Cardiol 2002;39:412A.
[31] Godart F, Rey C, Prat A, et al. Early and late results and the effects on pulmonary arteries of balloon dilatation of the right ventricular outflow tract in tetralogy of Fallot. Eur Heart J 1998;19:595–600.
[32] Kreutzer J, Perry SB, Jonas RA, et al. Tetralogy of Fallot with diminutive pulmonary arteries: preoperative pulmonary valve dilation and transcatheter rehabilitation of pulmonary arteries. J Am Coll Cardiol 1996;27:1741–7.
[33] Sluysmans T, Neven B, Rubay J, et al. Early balloon dilatation of the pulmonary valve in infants with tetralogy of Fallot. Risks and benefits. Circulation 1995;91:1506–11.
[34] Dohlen G, Chaturvedi RR, Benson LN, et al. Stenting of the right ventricular outflow tract in the symptomatic infant with tetralogy of Fallot. Heart 2009;95:142–7.
[35] McElhinney DB, Sherwood MC, Keane JF, et al. Current management of severe congenital mitral stenosis: outcomes of transcatheter and surgical therapy in 108 infants and children. Circulation 2005;112:707–14.

[36] McMahon CJ, El Said HG, Vincent JA, et al. Refinements in the implantation of pulmonary arterial stents: impact on morbidity and mortality of the procedure over the last two decades. Cardiol Young 2002;12:445–52.
[37] Bergersen LJ, Perry SB, Lock JE. Effect of cutting balloon angioplasty on resistant pulmonary artery stenosis. Am J Cardiol 2003;91:185–9.
[38] Zartner P, Cesnjevar R, Singer H, et al. First successful implantation of a biodegradable metal stent into the left pulmonary artery of a preterm baby. Catheter Cardiovasc Interv 2005;66:590–4.
[39] Forbes TJ, Garekar S, Amin Z, et al. Procedural results and acute complications in stenting native and recurrent coarctation of the aorta in patients over 4 years of age: a multi-institutional study. Catheter Cardiovasc Interv 2007;70:276–85.
[40] Ewert P, Schubert S, Peters B, et al. The CP stent—short, long, covered—for the treatment of aortic coarctation, stenosis of pulmonary arteries and caval veins, and Fontan anastomosis in children and adults: an evaluation of 60 stents in 53 patients. Heart 2005;91:948–53.
[41] Tzifa A, Ewert P, Brzezinska-Rajszys G, et al. Covered Cheatham platinum stents for aortic coarctation: early- and intermediate-term results. J Am Coll Cardiol 2006;47:1457–63.
[42] Kenny D, Margey R, Turner MS, et al. Self-expanding and balloon expandable covered stents in the treatment of aortic coarctation with or without aneurysm formation. Catheter Cardiovasc Interv 2008;72:65–71.
[43] Peng LF, McElhinney DB, Nugent AW, et al. Endovascular stenting of obstructed right ventricle-to-pulmonary artery conduits: a 15-year experience. Circulation 2006;113: 2598–605.
[44] Bonhoeffer P, Boudjemline Y, Saliba Z, et al. Transcatheter implantation of a bovine valve in pulmonary position: a lamb study. Circulation 2000;102:813–6.
[45] Lurz P, Coats L, Khambadkone S, et al. Percutaneous pulmonary valve implantation: impact of evolving technology and learning curve on clinical outcome. Circulation 2008;117: 1964–72.
[46] McElhinney DB, Cheatham JP, Jones TK, et al. Stent fracture, valve dysfunction, and right ventricular outflow tract reintervention after transcatheter pulmonary valve implantation. Circ Cardiovasc Interv 2011;4:1–13.
[47] Galantowicz M, Cheatham JP. Lessons learned from the development of a new hybrid strategy for the management of hypoplastic left heart syndrome. Pediatr Cardiol 2005;26: 190–9.
[48] Caldarone CA, Benson L, Holtby H, et al. Initial experience with hybrid palliation for neonates with single-ventricle physiology. Ann Thorac Surg 2007;84:1294–300.
[49] Pizarro C, Derby CD, Baffa JM, et al. Improving the outcome of high-risk neonates with hypoplastic left heart syndrome: hybrid procedure or conventional surgical palliation? Eur J Cardiothorac Surg 2008;33:613–8.
[50] Kohl T, Sharland G, Allan LD, et al. World experience of percutaneous ultrasound-guided balloon valvuloplasty in human fetuses with severe aortic valve obstruction. Am J Cardiol 2000;85:1230–3.
[51] Tworetzky W, Wilkins-Haug L, Jennings RW, et al. Balloon dilation of severe aortic stenosis in the fetus: potential for prevention of hypoplastic left heart syndrome: candidate selection, technique, and results of successful intervention. Circulation 2004;110: 2125–31.
[52] Tulzer G, Arzt W, Franklin RC, et al. Fetal pulmonary valvuloplasty for critical pulmonary stenosis or atresia with intact septum. Lancet 2002;360:1567–8.
[53] Marshall AC, van der Velde ME, Tworetzky W, et al. Creation of an atrial septal defect in utero for fetuses with hypoplastic left heart syndrome and intact or highly restrictive atrial septum. Circulation 2004;110:253–8.
[54] Justo RN, Nykanen DG, Williams WG, et al. Transcatheter perforation of the right ventricular outflow tract as initial therapy for pulmonary valve atresia and intact ventricular septum in the newborn. Cathet Cardiovasc Diagn 1997;40:414–5.

[55] Walsh MA, Lee KJ, Chaturvedi R, et al. Radiofrequency perforation of the right ventricular outflow tract as a palliative strategy for pulmonary atresia with ventricular septal defect. Catheter Cardiovasc Interv 2007;69:1015–20.
[56] Lamers L, Garn B, Ellsworth E, et al. Decreased incidence of right-ventricular outflow tract complications using a retrograde snare technique for radiofrequency pulmonary valve perforation. Pediatr Cardiol 2012;33(8):1275–80.
[57] Goldstein BH, Hirsch R, Zussman ME, et al. Percutaneous Balloon-expandable covered stent implantation for treatment of traumatic aortic injury in children and adolescents. Am J Cardiol 2012;110:1541–5.
[58] Levi DS, Danon S, Gordon B, et al. Creation of transcatheter aorticopulmonary and cavopulmonary shunts using magnetic catheters: feasibility study in swine. Pediatr Cardiol 2009;30:397–403.
[59] Kondo N, Shuto T, McGarvey JR, et al. Melody valve-in-ring procedure for mitral valve replacement: feasibility in four annuloplasty types. Ann Thorac Surg 2012;93(3):783–8.

Advances in Pediatrics 60 (2013) 201–215

ADVANCES IN PEDIATRICS

# Sudden Cardiac Death in Young Athletes

Mohammed Mortazavi, MD[a,b,*]

[a]Department of Pediatrics, UC Davis Medical Center, 2521 Stockton Boulevard, Sacramento, CA 95817, USA; [b]Pediatric Sports Medicine, UC Davis Medical Center, 2805 J Street, Suite 300, Sacramento, CA 95817, USA

**Keywords**

• Sudden cardiac death • Hypertrophic cardiomyopathy
• Automated external defibrillator • Sports medicine • ECG • Incidence • Prevention

**Key points**

- Incidence of sudden cardiac death (SCD) is now recognized to be several times higher than once believed based on recent epidemiologic data such as the 2012 study of National Collegiate Athletic Association athletes across the country, which suggests an incidence of 1 per 44,000 athlete deaths per year.
- There are multiple causes of SCD in young athletes, with most attributed to hypertrophic cardiomyopathy.
- Improving ECG and echocardiography (echo) technology, along with the advent of the cardiac MRI and genetic studies, provide physicians with multiple screening and diagnostic options to identify lethal cardiac disease.
- Today, multiple treatment options exist for potentially lethal structural and arrhythmogenic cardiac disorders. With the medical therapy, surgical therapy, and genetic testing available, there can be many life years saved by identifying even one previously unidentified young athlete.
- For the purposes of the general pediatrician, it is critical to identify at-risk patients in the office who may require an ECG or further work up. Identification of these patients is emphasized at the preparticipation examination, but should not be excluded to athletes participating in organized sports who require clearance.

## INTRODUCTION

The death of a young healthy athlete has always been an unimaginable shock to the communities that endure them. These young athletes are often considered the models of health and the pillars of our society. Thus, it is difficult

*Department of Pediatrics, UC Davis Medical Center, Sacramento, CA. *E-mail address:* mohammed.mortazavi@ucdmc.ucdavis.edu

0065-3101/13/$ – see front matter
http://dx.doi.org/10.1016/j.yapd.2013.04.015 

to accept how suddenly and tragically they can fall victim to underlying deadly heart conditions. With the increase in the recognition of these tragedies, many questions have arisen regarding the best prevention strategies of sudden cardiac death (SCD) in our young population. SCD in young athletes has drawn significant attention over the last three decades, in particular with the deaths of several high-profile athletes due to various underlying cardiac conditions. Research of SCD in the young athlete has blossomed recently. As a result, many questions regarding the approach to primary and secondary prevention of SCD have manifested. As recently as 30 years ago, SCD in young athletes under the age of 35 was thought to be an extremely rare phenomenon, one that was compared with the chance of being struck by lightning. However, with improving reporting methods, screening technology, and autopsy identification of such conditions, the recent literature suggests otherwise [1–3].

There are multiple causes of SCD in young athletes with the most attributed to hypertrophic cardiomyopathy (HCM) [1,4–9]. Other common causes of SCD include anomalous coronary arteries, arrhythmogenic right ventricular dysplasia (ARVD), commotio cordis, and channelopathies [4,9]. Although myocardial infarction is the number one cause of SCD across all ages, it is a relatively rare cause in the young athlete under the age of 35, accounting for less than 3% [2,4,9].

Improving ECG and echocardiography (echo) technology, along with the advent of the cardiac MRI and genetic studies, provide physicians with multiple screening options to identify lethal cardiac disease. Today, multiple treatment options also exist for potentially lethal structural and arrhythmogenic cardiac disorders. With the medical therapy, surgical therapy, and genetic testing available today there can be many life years saved by identifying even one previously unidentified young athlete.

Recent studies in Italy and the United States suggest a higher incidence of silent, potentially lethal cardiac conditions than was previously believed [1–3,10]. As a result, demand for local ECG screening campaigns and even national screening programs has grown recently. As more screening programs continue to manifest, research continues to follow the efficacy and cost-effectiveness of ECG screening. For the purposes of the general pediatrician, it is critical to identify at-risk patients in the office who may require an ECG or even further work up. Identification of these patients is emphasized at the preparticipation examination, but it should not be excluded to athletes participating in organized sports who require clearance. To identify anyone at risk for SCD, questions regarding types of activity and any symptoms during activity should be asked of all pediatric patients during regular physicals. Ultimately, identification of a single, silent diagnosis that can be treated is the reason we screen thousands.

## EPIDEMIOLOGY AND INCIDENCE

Prevention of SCD first begins with understanding the real incidence of this phenomena, which has been quite a quandary when comparing epidemiologic data [1,2,4,9]. Although reporting of this phenomenon in the United States has improved with increasing media and Internet coverage, there is still a significant margin for underestimation when the general US population is considered. In contrast to our Italian counterparts, the United States does not have systemic mandatory reporting registry for SCD events. In Veneto Italy, Corrado and colleagues [2,3] have been following the trends of SCD in athletes under the age of 35 since the 1970s with an established mandatory reporting system. With the advantage of a socialized health care system that serves 95% of the population requiring mandatory reporting of all SCDs, the Italian incidence data has received much recognition [2,3].

The contrast between the Italian data and US incidence data was the source for much controversy and, ultimately, one of the key reasons for dismissing considerations of ECG screening programs in the United States through much of the 1980s and 1990s. Most SCD incidence data in the United States were produced by Maron and colleagues [9]. They reported incidence rates of SCD from 1980 to 2006 in all US athletes ages 12 to 39 in 38 different sports. They analyzed 1866 sudden deaths using media reporting registries. Their initial reports of SCD in the 1980s were exceedingly rare at less that 1 per 5000,000 deaths per athlete per year. However, this data showed a rise of about 6% per year to approximately 1 per 160,000 athlete deaths per year from 2000 to 2006 [9]. The question remained, was this a true dramatic increase in occurrence of this phenomena? Or was this a result of improved reporting with the advent of the Internet and improved media surveying. During this same period, the Italians were reporting the incidence of SCD in all persons 12 to 35 in Italy in a prospective observational study [3]. They followed trends of SCD using a mandatory socialized medicine registry along with media surveying data. This data showed several interesting trends:

1. Incidence of SCD was found to be 1 per 28,000 athlete deaths per year in 1980 before the advent of a national screening program using ECGs in Veneto, Italy.
2. Most of these deaths were due to HCM, ARVD, and anomalous coronaries.
3. This incidence was 1 per 100,000 deaths per year in nonathletes at that time, suggesting that athletic activity increases the risk for SCD by about threefold.
4. This incidence of SCD and, in particular, HCM was greatly reduced over time with the advent of ECG screening in 1980.

The discrepancy in incidence between the Italian and US data raises several questions. In particular, is there a significant lower incidence in the United States? Or is the US population not as well defined and thus SCD is underreported. One explanation has been that the primarily white Italian population cannot compared with the diverse US population, which includes many African American athletes. However, studies have shown that the incidence of SCD due to HCM is two to three times as high in African Americans when compared with whites [4–6,9]. HCM is also the leading cause of death in all young athletes in the United States [4–6,9]. So the question remained, if a study was done in the United States that looked at a defined population with a mandatory registry data, what would the results be? A more recent study done at the University of Washington by Harmon and colleagues [1] looking at incidence of SCD in the National Collegiate Athletic Association (NCAA) among all sports and across all divisions has provided insight on this question. Results showed that there was an overall incidence of 1 per 44,000 deaths per year in NCAA athletes between 2004 to 2008. This was a substantial difference with a threefold to sixfold higher incidence from previous large US studies. When this incidence is applied to the young athlete population in the United States, about 150 to 225 deaths per year can be approximated. Subgroup analysis showed that incidence was as high as 1 per 7,000 deaths per year in male African American athletes and as high as 1 per 3000 deaths per year in male African American division I basketball players [1]. Although the absolute number of deaths studied is still limited, ongoing data collection since 2008 in this well-defined NCAA population will provide much more insight on the most accurate incidence of this phenomenon in young American athletes [1]. The data from this study has certainly highlighted the potential benefit of ECG screening in these higher risk groups as primary prevention of SCD [1]. ECG screening programs for NCAA athletes are currently being investigated in a multi-institution study.

## CAUSES

Sudden cardiac death in young athletes has multiple causes. By far the most common cause of death is HCM, which accounts for 33% to 50% of cases of SCD [4,9]. The second most common cause of SCD in the United States is coronary anomalies of heart, accounting for 17%. This is followed by myocarditis, accounting for 6%, and several other causes such as ARVD, aortic stenosis, dilated cardiomyopathy (DCM), long QT syndrome, and other channelopathies, each accounting for 2% to 5% of cases of SCD [4,9]. Congenital heart diseases, which have a rising incidence of surviving into adolescents and adulthood also only accounted for less than 3% of causes of SCD [4–6,9].

HCM deserves special attention given its drastically higher prevalence and often silent presentation before SCD. HCM is a heterogeneous autosomal dominant genetic condition with more than 12 known genotypes and various phenotypes [4,11,12]. It results in abnormal structure and architecture of the left ventricle. HCM can lead to lethal left ventricular outlet obstruction or arrhythmia, in particular with activity. Abnormal architecture of thickened disorganized myocytes can lead to areas that undergo chronic infarction and subsequent fibrosis. These areas then become ectopic foci for deadly arrhythmias such as ventricular fibrillation. There are multiple subtypes of HCM described based on area of hypertrophy including septal, basal, apical, and concentric [4,9,12–14]. It is estimated that the prevalence of HCM is 1 per 500 in the general population and that it is more common in males and African Americans [9,12,13]. Phenotypically it is usually a silent disease without any symptoms. However, it can become suddenly lethal in certain cases, with exercise as a known trigger. When there is suspicion on history or physical, the diagnosis is then confirmed by ECG, echo, and specialized cardiac imaging if necessary.

Traumatic causes are typically not considered when discussing common causes of silent heart diseases causing SCD. Commotio cordis is a traumatic cause for SCD that deserves attention. Several studies have quoted up to 20% of all SCD in young athletes are due to this phenomenon [15]. Commotio cordis, meaning "agitation of the heart," occurs after a timely blunt force to the chest, during the T wave ascent, which causes the heart to go into lethal ventricular fibrillation [15]. Although commotio cordis can occur at any age, the mean age is 13 with a propensity for younger athletes with less developed chest walls. Studies have found modest forces such as a baseball at 40 miles per hour from 40 feet away creating enough force to set a child's heart into commotio cordis when hit in the precordial region during the ominous 40 m T wave ascent [15]. The sensitive zone of the precordium for induction of rhythm disturbances lies between the second and fourth rib to the left of the sternum. Commotio cordis is 90% lethal unless treated with an automated external defibrillator (AED) to defibrillate out of lethal rhythms back into sinus rhythm. AEDs can increase survival rates to 35% to 50% if administered in time, with some studies quoting survival rates of 90% to 100% when AED is administered within first minute [15].

## RISK FACTORS

Epidemiologic studies do show some general trends of risk factors for SCD among sport, sex, and race [1,4,9]. The highest risk sports for SCD are basketball, track, cross country, football, soccer, and swimming in descending order [9]. Lower intensity aerobic sports such as Bethesda class IA and IB sports are lowest risk for SCD, thus patients with many known potentially lethal heart diseases are restricted to these sports. Males have been shown to have an overall higher incidence of SCD than females and, in particular, a higher incidence of HCM. Traditionally, males were believed to have an 8 to 12 times higher incidence of SCD than females. However, recent studies that involve higher profile elite female athletes have suggested that males only have a 2 to 3 times higher risk for SCD [1]. In particular, SCD in female swimmers was noted to be of higher incidence than males [1]. This was postulated as perhaps a result of the higher incidence of long QT in females triggered by the dive reflex in swimmers [1,4,9]. ARVD has also been noted as more common in white athletes [2,3,9]. Based on studies in the United States, ARVD was found to be a relatively rare cause of SCD when compared with HCM, and almost exclusive to whites [9]. In current Italian studies, ARVD is the most common cause of SCD in their predominately white population [2,3]. This is in part because deaths due to HCM have been greatly reduced by their ECG screening program. Overall, the incidence of SCD in African American athletes has been noted to be about two to three times that of white athletes [1,9]. There is a considerable higher incidence of HCM in African Americans, which is likely the reason for their overall higher incidence of SCD [9].

## DIAGNOSIS AND PREVENTION

Diagnosis of cardiac conditions that predispose one to SCD is often very challenging. However, with a good history and physical (H&P) one can determine those in need of further testing or workup. Although these are relatively rare diseases, they can have catastrophic consequences if undiagnosed. In general, screening is best when it is most sensitive to avoid missing any diagnoses. Trying to increase sensitivity can decrease the specificity of screening, resulting in the need to rule out more initial false positives with further testing. Further testing usually involves an echo, but may require stress testing, more advanced imaging, or genetic testing.

The initial H&P will be the most critical place for general practitioners to identify any red flags that indicate need for further testing. In 2007, the American Heart Association (AHA) released their most recent statement on use of a 12-point H&P with the most critical questions for prevention of SCD (Table 1) [4]. Any positive findings on H&P should warrant an ECG and possible further workup depending on ECG results. Critical questions in the medical history include any personal history of cardiac symptoms (eg, chest pain, presyncope, syncope, excessive dyspnea on exertion) during exercise. If any of these symptoms are noted, it is critical to ask follow-up questions regarding quality, severity, and timing of symptoms. In particular, the specific timing of symptoms with respect to exercise is critical to discern. If they are reported during exercise, it is important to determine if symptoms were during exercise versus before or after exercise when one would be more likely to have normal physiologic symptoms. Any history of true syncopal episodes during exercise should be discerned and referred to a cardiologist. Additional history of a previously recognized murmur or hypertension should also trigger further questioning and an ECG to rule out the possibility of underlying heart disease. Family history of SCD or disability from heart disease in a close relative under the age of 50 should also initiate an ECG. Any relative with a known, potentially lethal genetic cardiac disorder such as HCM, DCM, long QT, or Marfan disease should also trigger further workup with an ECG. Physical examination findings of a pathologic heart murmur, decreased femoral pulses, stigmata of Marfan syndrome, hypertension, or asymmetric blood pressures should also trigger further workup with ECG and cardiology referral.

## ECG

In 2007, the AHA stance on the use of systematic ECG screening in the prevention of SCD was that this endeavor is currently too costly and not feasible as a national program [4]. They also noted potential medical legal and ethical concerns with disqualification and clearance of athletes as major barriers to having such a program [4]. Despite the Italian experience and International Olympic Committee's stance, which recommends an H&P and ECG for every athlete, the AHA comments that the international community cannot be generalized to the US population. In the United States, there are over 10 million athletes and no infrastructure to support screening initiatives such as those that have

**Table 1**
12-Point recommended participation H&P by the American Heart Association for prevention and screening of SCD in young athletes

| History and examination | Findings | Actions |
|---|---|---|
| Personal History | Chest pain or discomfort, presyncope during activity | ECG |
| | Syncope during activity | ECG, cardiology referral |
| | Excessive and unexplained dyspnea or fatigue during | ECG, rule out exercise induced asthma (pulmonary function test, exercise challenge) |
| | History of heart murmur | ECG |
| | High blood pressure | ECG, repeat blood pressure |
| Family History | Any relatives who died of SCD before age 50 | ECG, cardiology referral |
| | Close relative under age 50 with disability from heart disease | ECG |
| | Specific knowledge of certain cardiac conditions in family members: hypertrophic or DCM, long QT syndrome, Marfan syndrome, or clinically important arrhythmias | ECG, cardiology referral |
| Physical Examination | Heart murmur | ECG, cardiology referral for concerning pathologic murmurs |
| | Diminished or asymmetric femoral pulses | ECG, cardiology referral for further imaging |
| | Physical stigmata of Marfan syndrome | ECG, cardiology referral for further imaging |
| | Asymmetric of elevated (>140/90 mm Hg) blood pressure | ECG, cardiology referral for further imaging |

*Data from* Maron BJ, Thompson PD, Ackerman MJ, et al. Recommendations and considerations related to preparticipation screening for cardiovascular abnormalities in competitive athletes: 2007 update: a scientific statement from the American Heart Association Council on Nutrition, Physical Activity, and Metabolism: endorsed by the American College of Cardiology Foundation. Circulation 2007;115:1643–455.

grown successful in Italy and Europe [4]. Despite this, many leagues, community programs, and volunteer organizations in the United States have began to offer screening ECGs to athletes. Several studies of ECG screening in college athletes have suggested it to be a feasible and cost-effective life-saving screening tool [1,16]. The original model for ECG screening in Italy has been shown to reduce SCD by 89% over the last 30 years [2,3]. Their initiative was spearheaded by primary care sports medicine physicians who are the work force for reading all screening ECGs. They work in conjunction with cardiologists to evaluate all athletes deemed high risk by an abnormal ECG screen. Starting with very sensitive criteria in the 1980s, they have developed more specific criteria over time and have significantly reduced the false positive rate to less than 20% [2,3]. The University of Washington has been screening NCAA athletes with only a reported 10% to 12% false positive rate, using sports medicine physicians to lead the initiative to screen all athletes with ECGs [17]. A 2010 study at Harvard using echo confirmation found three athletes with potentially lethal heart disease out of 500 screened, two of which (HCM, myocarditis) required the ECG to make the diagnosis [16]. This study reported a false positive rate of 17% with screening ECGs [16]. A recent study done in Colorado that performed H&P along with screening ECG for 1000 high school athletes ages 13 to 18 found two potentially lethal diagnoses (long QT and Wolff-Parkinson-White [WPW] syndrome) based solely on the ECG screens. ECGs were read by a pediatric sports medicine primary care physician (PCP) before a pediatric cardiologist and a false positive rate of about 11% was noted from the initial PCP reads.

Many ECG screening programs are now using PCPs or primary care sports physicians in primary prevention of SCD. These programs all follow different models but, in general, PCPs are used for first-line screening of ECGs using very sensitive guidelines [2,3,17,18] Any positive findings are sent to cardiologists for review and determination if a cardiology consult is warranted based on the ECG findings. This approach may lead to a large number of false positives that require cardiology read or consults with further testing required. However, the literature shows the false positive rates have dramatically decreased over the last 20 years with the use of more specific ECG interpretation guidelines [18]. With continuing research, the first-line screening criteria initially established by Corrado and colleagues in Italy over three decades ago has grown more specific while maintaining an expected high sensitivity [2,3,11,18].

## ECG INTERPRETATION

The ECG criteria can be systematically reviewed by any PCP who is comfortable reading basic ECGs. Beginning with rate, rhythm, and axis, the PCP should evaluate for tachycardia, bradycardia, arrhythmia, and axis deviations. Heart rate (HR) in a young athlete is expected to be 60 to 100, but can be as low as 30 in the conditioned athlete [11,19,20]. True bradycardia with HR less than 30 should be assessed for heart block or sick sinus syndrome. Tachycardia is less common in athletes and thus the age of athlete must be considered as well as any recent activity or cause for anxiety during pulse examination. If true tachycardia is repeatedly noted, superventricular tachycardia (SVT) should be considered. With SVT, HR is typically greater than 220 and there is no beat-to-beat variability. Arrhythmias to screen for include atrial fibrillation, atrial flutter, and any other ventricular arrhythmias. Greater than two premature ventricular contractions (PVCs) per ECG strip should also warrant further investigation with repeat ECG or cardiology consult. True axis deviation may suggest several pathologic findings such as right ventricular hypertrophy (RVH) or HCM. Using the more refined criteria, evaluation for any right axis deviation greater than 115 and left axis deviation greater than −30 would be cause for concern and cardiologist consult [18]. Assessment of axis deviation in the pediatric athlete must also consider the age of the athlete. Rightward axis deviation, which is normal at birth, transitions to leftward axis in adolescence and adulthood depending on age. Thus, some younger athletes may still have normal transitioning right axis deviation. Other factors that can cause pathologic axis deviation include chronic pulmonary disease or systemic hypertension, in which case further cardiology workup is warranted [18].

Next, a review of ECG for any abnormal atrial abnormalities should be done. This involves an evaluation of the P waves, which represent atrial contraction. Any P wave greater than 2.5 mV in amplitude in any lead is concerning for right atrial enlargement. Left atrial enlargement manifests with prolonged total duration of the P wave greater than 120 ms, or a negative deflection of the P wave in V1, V2 that is both greater than 1 mV in amplitude and greater than 40 ms in duration. Atrial abnormalities are often found to be nonpathologic, but can be related to RVH, HCM, and increased pulmonary resistance, and should warrant a cardiology consult. After reviewing the morphology of the P wave, the PR interval should be calculated to rule out any findings of heart block. First-degree heart block or a PR interval of 200 to 300 ms is considered to be a normal physiologic manifestation of increased vagal tone seen in athlete's heart (AH) [11,12,19]. PR intervals greater than 300, progression of the PR interval, dropped P waves, or P-QRS dissociation are concerning for second and third degree heart block that should be further evaluated.

A thorough evaluation of the QRS complex should be done starting with the depth and width of Q waves. Abnormally wide or deep Q waves should rise concern and trigger further workup. Any Q waves deeper than 3 mV or longer than 40 ms in any leads other than leads III, AVR, AVL, and V1 should initiate a cardiology consult. Evaluation of QRS complex starts by ruling out any up-slanting QRS complex with short PR interval, usually less than 120 ms, that would be consistent with delta waves seen in WPW syndrome. Evaluation of the QRS complex should also involve assessment for any bundle branch blocks, or interventricular conduction delays (IVCDs), defined by a QRS interval greater than 120 ms. Right and left bundle branch blocks can be identified based on their specific morphology in V1 (RSR′, QS) and increased QRS interval greater than 120 ms. Most IVCDs in asymptomatic patients will lead to normal imaging and workups. However, associations with HCM, atrial septal defects, and Chagas disease in endemic countries exist [18]. Thus, IVCD should be taken seriously and cardiology consulted for possible further workup. Most computer interpretations will be more accurate than standard measurements for QRS duration and should be reviewed carefully along with visual inspection for any specific bundle branch block morphologies.

The R and S wave amplitudes should be measured to determine if there are any abnormally large amplitude concerning for RVH or left ventricular hypertrophy (LVH). In general, large R wave amplitudes in anterior leads such as V1 can be a sign of RVH. Specific recommendations include assessing for any R wave greater than 7 mm in V1, R/S ratio greater than 1, or the sum of the R wave in V1 and S in V5 or V6 that is greater than 10.5 mV [18]. These findings may warrant further workup for RVH, especially in athletes older than 30 years of age [18]. Any of the above findings for RVH plus right atrial enlargement, right axis deviation greater than 115, or T wave inversion in V2 or V3 are specifically concerning for pathologic RVH in the young athlete under the age of 30 and warrant further workup [18].

LVH typically presents with prominent R waves now in the lateral leads V4 to V6 or deep S waves in the anterior leads. There are several different methods of assessing for LVH including the Sokolow-Lyon Index (SLI) and Cornell voltage criteria. No one method is perfectly sensitive or specific, but use of combined criteria can improve sensitivity and specificity. Using the SLI, the sum of S in V1 and R in V5 or V6 greater than 35 mV is considered isolated LVH. This correlates with echo measurements of greater than 10 to 12 mm of concentric left ventricular myocardial wall thickness [11]. Isolated LVH is a very common finding in conditioned athletes secondary to physiologic hypertrophy and remodeling of the heart muscle in response to exercise. When findings of LVH are isolated without any other associated abnormalities, such as Q wave abnormalities, lateral lead T wave inversions, or ST changes, no further workup is necessary [18]. There have been several postulations that perhaps LVH can be a precursor to HCM; however, there is no evidence in the literature to suggest this. There is no study done to date that has followed a group of young adolescents with LVH to determine if any develop pathologic heart disease such as HCM.

## ST CHANGES OR T WAVES

ST segment changes may be associated with HCM and ARVD due to areas of infarction secondary to abnormal myocyte and vessel architecture. Any ST segment depression greater than 0.5 mV below the isoelectric line in the lateral leads, AVL, or lead I are concerning and should warrant further workup. ST segment depression greater than 1 mV in any lead should also warrant further workup. ST changes secondary to coronary artery disease and myocardial infarction are rare in the young athlete. However, other silent lethal cardiac diseases such as HCM and ARVD can present with ST depression without associated hypertrophy patterns on ECG [3,5,9,18]. ST segment elevation in lateral leads V3 to V6 that is less than 0.5 mV is commonly seen due to early repolarization in conditioned athletes and is a very common finding in AH [11,12]. Early repolarization may or may not be associated with LVH also commonly seen conditioned athletes. Recent epidemiologic studies have shown prevalence of greater than 50% in conditioned adult athletes [11,12,19]. Physiologic early repolarization can be confused with the abnormal J wave seen Brugada type 1 pattern, which resembles ST elevation from the isoelectric point. However, Brugada pattern is seen in V1 to V3, and the characteristic J wave usually has ST elevation significantly greater than 0.5 mV. Any ST segment elevation in V1 to V3 should be evaluated closely for Brugada syndrome and warrant cardiac consultation. Postexcitation potentials or epsilon waves are also seen in leads V1 to V3 with a post-QRS hump pattern seen before the T wave. Epsilon waves are usually associated with a T wave inversion. This pattern has been associated with ARVD and other cardiac pathologic conditions and deserves further workup [18].

## T WAVE INVERSIONS OR QT CHANGES

T wave inversion in certain leads can be concerning ECG findings. T wave inversions have been noted in 2% to 4% of the adult athlete population without any cardiac disease [18]. It is important to recognize that T wave inversions in anterior leads V1, AVR, and III can be normal. In females and children, T wave inversion in V1 to V3 is typically normal. T wave inversions in athletes under 18 were noted in the anterior leads in up to 20% of athletes [18]. Studies looking at T wave inversions in African Americans have noted an incidence of 14% and normal T wave inversion patterns in V2 to V4 [18]. However, if significant T wave inversions greater than 1 mV are noted in any of the lateral or inferior leads further workup is warranted. The European Consensus Statement has suggested any T wave inversions greater than 2 mV in two or more contiguous leads should be considered as a very significant abnormality requiring definite workup [18].

## QT INTERVALS

QT interval changes should be closely measured and reviewed for any prolonged or short QT syndromes. Criteria suggest QTc measurements in lead 2 or V5 using standard measurement of QT interval divided by square root of preceding RR interval. Any QTc measure less than 340 ms is considered short QT and requires referral. More commonly, long QT syndrome is seen defined by QTc greater than 470 in males and greater than 480 in females [18]. A QTc of 440 to 470 is considered borderline and should be followed with a repeat ECG or a stress ECG. Long QT syndrome is well defined with several different genotypes isolated and strongly associated with SCD risk. Long QT type 1 is the most common genotype, with exercise as the main known trigger for SCD. Genetic testing for the QT genotype can help determine appropriate therapy and prevention strategies as well as confirm diagnosis. These include treatments with beta blockers, activity restriction, and implantable cardioverter-defibrillators (ICDs). Family genetic testing can also help determine if other high-risk family members have the syndrome and may require treatment.

## ECG CRITERIA FOR AH

AH is a phenomenon that must be well understood in the interpretation of screening ECGs and prevention of SCD. The recognition of this phenomenon is not to identify uniquely conditioned hearts, but instead to prevent mistaking them for abnormal hearts. ECG criteria for AH include any one or combination of the following:

1. Bradycardia
2. First-degree atrioventricular block
3. Incomplete right bundle branch block
4. LVH
5. Early repolarization.

These findings in a young athlete should be expected and considered as normal. Identification of ECG findings of AH is critical to recognize to prevent many false positives. ECG criteria for AH is seen in up to 80% of elite adult athletes and 60% of pediatric athletes [4,12,19]. Comfort with routine recognition of these findings is important for the PCP to prevent a large influx of unnecessary referrals and workups.

## FURTHER WORKUP

Patients with concerning findings on H&P or ECG often will need to be referred for further cardiac workup. In general, any of the concerning ECG findings on (Table 2) should be reviewed with a cardiologist to determined whether a referral is needed [18]. Findings consistent with AH (Table 3) are normal and require no further workup if indeed ECG is limited to these isolated normal physiologic training changes. Despite ECG findings, any concerning symptoms such as true syncope, palpitations, or chest pain during exercise should be referred.

The additional workup by a cardiologist will depend on the diagnosis of suspicion. In general, this will involve an ECG, echo, and other possible workup. Stress ECGs may be required to make certain diagnoses such as catecholaminergic polymorphic ventricular tachycardia (CPVT), which is a lethal arrhythmia that is solely exercise induced. Cardiac MRI provides very detailed imaging of cardiac anatomy, which can be very helpful in multiple diagnoses including HCM, ARVD, and anomalous coronaries. Cardiac MRI can be performed dynamically to assess function, or with gadolinium to highlight abnormal cardiac tissue and fibrosis. Genetic studies available for disorders such as HCM and long QT are very helpful in characterizing the disease for optimum treatment when phenotypes are gene positive. Family genetic testing is important in all gene positive patients to help identify others that may have been affected by the disease.

**Table 2**
Abnormal ECG findings

| Assessment | Abnormality | ECG criteria |
|---|---|---|
| Rate | Sick sinus syndrome | HR <30 |
| | SVT | HR >220, no beat-to-beat variability |
| Rhythm | PVCs | 2 or more per ECG |
| | Ventricular arrhythmias | — |
| | Atrial fibrillation | — |
| | Atrial flutter | — |
| Axis | Left axis deviation | More leftward than −30 |
| | Right axis deviation | More rightward than 115 |
| P waves | Left atrial enlargement | P wave >120 ms OR P wave with negative deflection in V1, V2 with >1 mV, >40 ms |
| | Right atrial enlargement | P wave >2.5 mm in any lead |
| PR intervals | Second-degree heart block | PR >300 ms<br>Prolonged PR intervals,<br>Dropped P waves |
| | Third-degree heart block | P-QRS wave dissociation |
| Q waves | Abnormal Q waves | (>3 mV) OR (>40 ms) in any lead except III, aVR, aVL, or V1 |
| QRS | Delta wave | Up-slanting QRS (delta waves) and PR <120 ms |
| | Left bundle branch block | QRS >120 ms in V1 with QS wave pattern |
| | Right bundle branch block | QRS >120 ms in V1 with RSR′ pattern |
| | IVCD | QRS duration >120 ms in any lead |
| | RVH | R wave >7 mm in V1 or R/S ratio >1 |
| ST changes | ST segment depression | >0.5 mm below isoelectric line before T wave in leads V4, V5, V6, I, aVL or >1 mV in any lead |
| | Postexcitation potentials | Epsilon waves with T wave inversion V1 to V3 |
| | Brugada type 1 pattern | J-wave pattern in any of V1, V2, or V3 |
| T waves | T wave inversion | >1 mV in any lead other than V1, III, aVR (except V2, V3 in females) |
| QT abnormalities | Long QT | >470 ms males, >480 ms females |
| | Short QT | <340 ms |

## MEDICAL PREVENTION

Diagnosis of potentially lethal cardiac disease is critical to initiating medical management to prevent a sudden cardiac event or death. Depending on the cause, multitude medical options exist that are usually initiated and managed by a cardiologist. With the diagnosis of HCM, medications such as beta blockers may be started. Activity restriction to class IA sports per the Bethesda classification is recommended. ICDs are placed in some higher risk patients or patients with a history of near death events. A recent high-profile professional soccer player in Europe with the diagnosis of HCM did not comply with activity restriction recommendations and returned to soccer after treatment with beta blockers and an ICD. He had a subsequent event that would have likely resulted in death; however, while lying pulseless, his ICD shocked and revived him.

**Table 3**
Normal ECG findings of AH

| Finding | ECG criteria |
|---|---|
| Sinus bradycardia | HR 30–60 beats per minute |
| First-degree heart block | PR 200–300 ms |
| Incomplete RBBB | V1 RSR′ morphology with QRS 100–120 ms |
| Early repolarization | ST elevation <0.5 mV in V3–6 |
| Isolated LVH | S in V1 and R in V5 or V6 ≥35 mV |

Depending on area and severity of cardiac hypertrophy, a surgical myomectomy can be performed to prevent outlet obstructions. When known ectopic foci of arrhythmias exist, such as in WPW or certain cases of HCM or ARVD, ablation therapy can be used to ablate these foci. Channelopathies, such as Brugada syndrome, CPVT, and long QT syndrome, can be treated with beta blockage and anti-arrhythmic agents depending on specific type diagnosed with genetic testing.

Primary prevention of SCD begins with a thorough, well-informed H&P following the AHA 12-point questionnaire, followed by ECG screening for any high-risk athletes. Primary prevention also involves awareness and education of both the athletic and medical communities. The cost and effort spent on primary prevention to save a single life must be understood by all parties involved to have a successful screening program.

Secondary prevention involves being prepared to prevent a death when an event occurs. Too often, silent lethal cardiac conditions manifest for the first time as lethal arrhythmias or outlet obstructions leading to asystole. Cardiopulmonary resuscitation is the most helpful and applicable skill that can help directly save lives in these situations. The availability of AED devices can be critical in situations with shockable rhythms. Most deaths caused by HCM and commotio cordis are due to lethal ventricular fibrillation that can be shocked back to sinus rhythm by an AED. Most modern AEDs are very easy to use with simple three-step directions. Education about the function, use, and potential life-saving capabilities of AEDs are critical for community providers and officials. Funding and availability for AEDs has greatly increased in recent years and, today, many facilities such as schools and gyms will have an AED available. Healthcare professionals covering any sporting event should check with officials on the location of the AED and be prepared for its use, if necessary.

## References

[1] Harmon KG, Asif IM, Klossner D, et al. Incidence of sudden cardiac death in National Collegiate Athletic Association athletes. Circulation 2011;123:1594–600.

[2] Corrado D, Pelliccia A, Heidbuchel H, et al. Recommendations for interpretation of 12-lead electrocardiogram in the athlete. Eur Heart J 2010;31:243–59.

[3] Corrado D, Michieli P, Basso C, et al. How to screen athletes for cardiovascular diseases. Cardiol Clin 2007;25:391–7, v–vi.

[4] Maron BJ, Thompson PD, Ackerman MJ, et al. Recommendations and considerations related to preparticipation screening for cardiovascular abnormalities in competitive athletes: 2007 update: a scientific statement from the American Heart Association Council on Nutrition, Physical Activity, and Metabolism: endorsed by the American College of Cardiology Foundation. Circulation 2007;115:1643–55.
[5] Maron BJ. Sudden death in young athletes. N Engl J Med 2003;349:1064–75.
[6] Maron BJ, Shirani J, Poliac LC, et al. Sudden death in young competitive athletes. Clinical, demographic, and pathological profiles. JAMA 1996;276:199–204.
[7] Van Camp SP, Bloor CM, Mueller FO, et al. Nontraumatic sports death in high school and college athletes. Med Sci Sports Exerc 1995;27:641–7.
[8] Maron BJ, Roberts WC, McAllister HA, et al. Sudden death in young athletes. Circulation 1980;62:218–29.
[9] Maron BJ, Doerer JJ, Haas TS, et al. Sudden deaths in young competitive athletes: analysis of 1866 deaths in the United States, 1980–2006. Circulation 2009;119:1085–92.
[10] Drezner JA, Asif IM, Owens DS, et al. Accuracy of ECG interpretation in competitive athletes: the impact of using standised ECG criteria. Br J Sports Med 2012;46:335–40.
[11] Pelliccia A, Maron BJ, Culasso F, et al. Clinical significance of abnormal electrocardiographic patterns in trained athletes. Circulation 2000;102:278–84.
[12] Maron BJ. Structural features of the athlete heart as defined by echocardiography. J Am Coll Cardiol 1986;7:190–203.
[13] Maron BJ. Hypertrophic cardiomyopathy: a systematic review. JAMA 2002;287: 1308–20.
[14] Corrado P, Basso C, Schiavon M, et al. Pre-participation screening of young competitive athletes for prevention of sudden cardiac death. J Am Coll Cardiol 2008;52:1981–9.
[15] Maron BJ, Link MS, Wang PJ, et al. Clinical profile of commotio cordis: an underappreciated cause of sudden death in the young during sports and other activities. J Cardiovasc Electrophysiol 1999;10:114–20.
[16] Baggish AL, Hutter AM Jr, Wang F, et al. Cardiovascular screening in college athletes with and without electrocardiography: a cross-sectional study. Ann Intern Med 2010;152: 269–75.
[17] Drezner J, Corrado D. Is there evidence for recommending electrocardiogram as part of the pre-participation examination? Clin J Sport Med 2011;21(1):18–24.
[18] Uberoi A, Stein R, Perez MV, et al. Interpretation of the electrocardiogram of young athletes. Circulation 2011;124:746–57.
[19] Huston TP, Puffer JC, Rodney WM. The athletic heart syndrome. N Engl J Med 1985;313: 24–32.
[20] Fagard RH. Athlete's heart: a meta-analysis of the echocardiographic experience. Int J Sports Med 1996;17(Suppl 3):S140–4.

Advances in Pediatrics 60 (2013) 217–261

ADVANCES IN PEDIATRICS

# Enteropathies of Infancy and Childhood

Pierre Russo, MD

Department of Pathology and Laboratory Medicine, The Children's Hospital of Philadelphia, The University of Pennsylvania Perelman School of Medicine, 324 South 34th Street, Main Building, Room 5NW16, Philadelphia, PA 19104, USA

**Keywords**

• Intestinal biopsy • Esophagogastroduodenoscopy • Intestinal disorders • Children

**Key points**

- Esophagogastroduodenoscopy and intestinal biopsy have become routine in the investigation of pediatric gastrointestinal disorders.
- Intestinal biopsy remains the gold standard for the diagnosis of most disorders that cause chronic diarrhea and malabsorption in children.
- Many disorders that cause intractable diarrhea of infancy have been described in the past few decades.
- Understanding the biology and molecular mechanisms of some of these disorders has provided important insights into intestinal function.

## INTRODUCTION AND GENERAL REMARKS

The aims of this article are to review some of the entities that cause chronic intractable diarrhea and malabsorption of infancy and childhood, illustrating their characteristic features on small intestinal biopsies and specimens. These are listed in Box 1.

Chronic diarrhea, usually defined as lasting more than 2 weeks, can present particularly difficult diagnostic and therapeutic challenges, especially when it occurs in the neonate. Intractable diarrhea of infancy is a term coined by Avery and colleagues [1] to refer to these cases that at the time remained mainly undiagnosed and were associated with a high mortality. Better recognition and understanding of many of the disorders that cause intractable diarrhea of infancy, combined with advances in parenteral nutrition, immunosuppression, and the availability of bowel transplantation has improved the survival of many of these children, thus prompting the need for timely and accurate

*E-mail address:* russo@email.chop.edu

0065-3101/13/$ – see front matter
http://dx.doi.org/10.1016/j.yapd.2013.04.010 

**Box 1: Enteropathies of infancy and childhood**

Congenital transport and enzymatic deficiencies
- Glucose-galactose malabsorption
- Disaccharidase deficiency
- Lysinuric protein intolerance
- Abetalipoproteinemia
- Chylomicron retention disease
- Sodium chloride diarrhea
- Primary bile acid malabsorption

Inherited epithelial defects
- Microvillus inclusion disease
- Tufting enteropathy
- Enteroendocrine cell dysgenesis

Autoimmune enteropathy
Gluten-sensitive enteropathy (celiac disease)
Eosinophilic enteritis
Lymphangiectasia
Metabolic diseases and tumors

diagnosis. Furthermore, investigation of some of these disorders has led to significant advances in related fields of disease pathogenesis, transcending their relative clinical rarity. For example, the discovery that mutations in *FOXP3* underlie IPEX syndrome, resulting in the absence of naturally occurring T regulatory lymphocytes (Tregs), has opened new avenues in our understanding of the control of the immune response, autoimmunity, and immune tolerance.

## INTESTINAL BIOPSY IN CHILDREN

As pediatric esophagogastroduodenoscopy (EGD) has evolved into a routine outpatient procedure, the indications for its use have changed over the last few decades. At The Children's Hospital of Philadelphia, the first-time EGD rate increased 12-fold in a 20-year interval between 1985 and 2005, with isolated abdominal pain replacing gastrointestinal (GI) bleeding as the most frequent indication [2]. Much of this increase seems to have been driven by the dramatic increase in food allergy–related disorders such as eosinophilic esophagitis, by the increased prevalence of celiac disease and its clinically atypical forms, and by the routine use of EGD in addition to colonoscopy in the evaluation of children with suspected inflammatory bowel disease. According to a recent study from a tertiary pediatric center in the United Kingdom, the most frequent indications for endoscopy in children less than 1 year old were diarrhea, failure to thrive, reflux, and rectal bleeding [3]. Histologic abnormalities were detected in two-thirds of cases, whereas only 2% of mucosal biopsies were insufficient.

In current pediatric gastrointestinal practice, intestinal biopsies are most frequently obtained from the duodenum via forceps during EGD. Biopsies from both proximal and distal duodenum are recommended, including biopsies of endoscopically normal mucosa, as many disorders affecting the duodenum have a focal distribution. In children, for example, the lesions in gluten-sensitive enteropathy (GSE) may be patchy, and villous atrophy may coexist with normal mucosa [4]. Furthermore, villous atrophy may be limited to or most severe in the duodenal bulb at the time of diagnosis [4,5]. In general, the sampling of even endoscopically normal-appearing mucosa is recommended, because it may help to assess the background features of the mucosa, and histologic examination may also reveal clinically relevant findings unsuspected by the endoscopist (ie, granulomas) [6,7]. A recent pediatric study found that a routine duodenal biopsy performed for indications such as gastroesophageal reflux, vomiting, abdominal pain, anemia, and during the evaluation of Crohn disease yielded pathologic findings in about 17% of cases; conversely, a normal-appearing mucosa by endoscopy did not rule out abnormal histology [7].

Intestinal biopsy findings in some entities, such as congenital transport disorders, are associated with a normal biopsy, whereas others, such as autoimmune enteropathy or celiac disease, have variable degrees of villous atrophy with or without inflammation. Some diseases, such as abetalipoproteinemia or microvillous inclusion disease, present characteristic findings on an intestinal biopsy (Table 1). Histologic evaluation of the small bowel biopsy should proceed systematically, to include (1) adequacy of the sampling, as determined by the number and site of the biopsy specimens, (2) assessment of the villous architecture with evaluation of the villus-to-crypt (V:C) ratio, (3) evaluation of the length of the crypts (hyperplasia, hypoplasia), (4) the appearance of the surface enterocytes and their brush border, (5) an estimation of the number of intraepithelial lymphocytes, (6) the cellularity of the lamina propria (plasma cells may be absent or decreased in some primary immunodeficiencies), and (7) the presence of microorganisms (*Giardia, Cryptosporidium*). An adequate biopsy should have 4 to 5 well-oriented villi in a row, and observation of 4 normal villi in a row is generally an indication that the specimen is normal (Fig. 1) [8]. Accurate evaluation of villous morphology requires careful attention to proper orientation of the specimen. Some laboratories have found that orientation of the specimen on filter paper before fixation is helpful [9]. We have found that rapid immersion of the specimen in fixative is preferable to having the endoscopist place the biopsy on filter paper, which may result in excessive stretching or drying of the specimen. Poor quality of the specimen, procedural artifacts, and tangentional sectioning may lead to misinterpretations. In addition to obtaining biopsies for routine histology, samples may also be snap-frozen (for disaccharidase analysis) or submitted for electron microscopy (for confirmation of microvillous inclusion disease).

**Table 1**
Diagnostic findings on small intestinal biopsies

| Intestinal biopsy | Differential diagnosis |
|---|---|
| Normal | Sucrase-isomaltase deficiency |
| | Congenital lactase deficiency |
| | Fructose malabsorption |
| | Glucose-galactose malabsorption |
| | Congenital $Na^+/Cl^-$ diarrhea |
| Nonspecific Inflammatory Lesions | |
| Villous atrophy | Celiac disease |
| | Autoimmune enteropathy |
| Variable villous atrophy | Protracted infectious diarrhea |
| | Immunodeficiency states (most) |
| | Bacterial overgrowth |
| | Cow's milk or soy protein intolerance |
| | Chronic inflammatory bowel diseases |
| Specific Lesions | |
| Fat-filled enterocytes | Abetalipoproteinemia |
| | Anderson disease |
| Ectatic lymphatics | Lymphangiectasia |
| Dense inspissated mucus | Cystic fibrosis |
| Epithelial abnormalities | Microvillus inclusion disease |
| | Tufting enteropathy |
| | Enterocolitis cystica |
| Eosinophils | Eosinophilic gastroenteritides |
| Absence or paucity of inflammatory cells | Severe combined immunodeficiency |
| | Agammaglobulinemia |
| Infectious agent | *Giardia lamblia* infection |
| | Cryptosporidiosis |

## CONGENITAL DISORDERS OF INTESTINAL DIGESTION, ABSORPTION, AND TRANSPORT

Specific gene defects associated with various disorders of substrate transport have been recently characterized (Table 2), and provide a picture of enterocyte

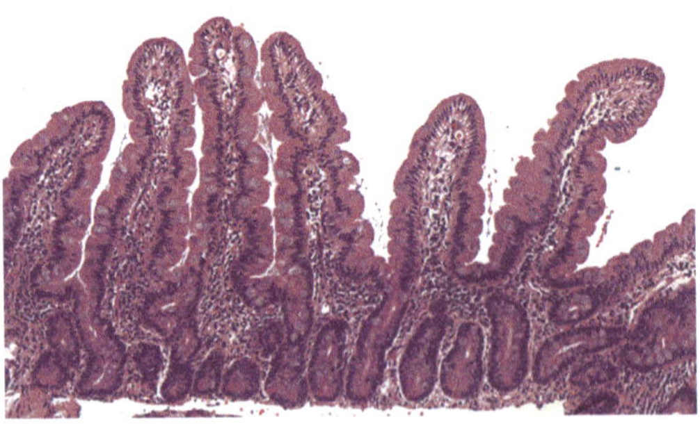

**Fig. 1.** Normal well-oriented duodenal biopsy in a 3-month-old child with at least 4 normal villi in a row and a villus/crypt ratio of (3 to 4):1 (hematoxylin and eosin [H&E], ×100).

**Table 2**
Molecular basis of disorders of digestion, absorption, and transport

| Disease | Gene | Location | Function |
|---|---|---|---|
| Disaccharidase Deficiency | | | |
| Congenital lactase deficiency | LCT | 2q21 | Lactase-phlorizin hydrolase activity |
| Sucrase-isomaltase deficiency | EC 3.2.1.48 | 3q25-q26 | Isomaltase-sucrase |
| Maltase-glucoamylase deficiency | MGAM | 7q34 | Maltase-glucoamylase activity |
| Ion and Nutrient Transport Defects | | | |
| Glucose-galactose malabsorption | SGLT1 | 22q13.1 | $Na^+$/glucose contransporter |
| Fructose malabsorption | GLUT5 | 1p36 | Fructose transporter |
| Fanconi-Bickel syndrome | GLUT2 | 3q26 | Basolateral glucose transporter |
| Cystic fibrosis | CFTR | 7q31.2 | cAMP-dependent $Cl^-$ channel |
| Acrodermatitis enteropathica | SLC39A4 | 8q24.3 | $Zn^{2+}$ transporter |
| Congenital chloride diarrhea | DRA | 7q22-q31.1 | $Cl^-$/base exchanger |
| Congenital sodium diarrhea | SPINT2* | 19q13.1 | Serine-protease inhibitor |
| Lysinuric protein intolerance | SLC7A7 | 14q11 | Hydrolyzes endo-/exopeptidases Amino acid basolateral transport |
| Congenital bile acid diarrhea | ABAT | 13q3 | Ileal $Na^+$/bile salt transporter |
| Pancreatic Insufficiency | | | |
| Enterokinase deficiency | PRSS7 | 21q21 | Proenterokinase |
| Trypsinogen deficiency | PRSS1 | 7q35 | Trypsinogen synthesis |
| Pancreatic lipase deficiency | PNLIP | 10q26.1 | Hydrolyzes triglycerides to fatty acids |
| Lipid Trafficking | | | |
| Abetalipoproteinemia | MTP | 4q22 | Transfer lipids to apolipoprotein |
| Hypobetalipoproteinema | APOB | 2p24 | Apolipoprotein that forms chylomicrons |
| Chylomicron retention disease | SAR1B | 5q31.1 | Intracellular chylomicron trafficking |

*This mutation has been associated with the syndromic form of congenital sodium diarrhea.

*Adapted from* Canani RB, Terrin G, Cardillo G, et al. Congenital diarrheal disorders: improved understanding of gene defects is leading to advances in intestinal physiology and clinical management. J Pediatr Gastroenterol Nutr 2010;50(4):362.

function at the molecular level. Except for the disorders associated with lipid trafficking, small intestinal biopsies in these cases are generally normal or only slightly abnormal. A normal-appearing small bowel mucosa from a patient with prolonged diarrhea, especially a young infant, should alert the clinician to a consideration of these entities.

### Carbohydrate malabsorption and disaccharidase deficiencies

Carbohydrate absorption begins with the breakdown of complex carbohydrates by salivary and gastric enzymes into oligosaccharides, which are then hydrolyzed to monosaccharides by specific disaccharidases located at the enterocyte brush border. There are 4 major disaccharidase enzymes: sucrase-isomaltase, glucoamylase-maltase, trehalose, and lactase-phlorizin hydrolase (or lactase-glycosyl ceramidase) [10]. Sucrase-isomaltase is responsible for the degradation of dietary sucrose. Glucoamylase-maltase hydrolyzes starch into small polymers. Lactase-phlorizin hydrolase degrades lactose, the main carbohydrate in milk. Trehalose occurs mainly in mushrooms. Trehalase deficiency is extremely rare, encountered mainly in Greenland natives and in Finns [11]. The expression of these enzymes on the intestinal brush border seems to follow a time-dependent sequence. Lactase-phlorizin hydrolase, highly expressed at birth, declines in early life in most people (although it persists to adult life in whites) [12]. Sucrase-isomaltase, undetectable at birth, reaches adult levels in the first few months of life. These changes coincide with the switch from milk to a solid diet. Internalization of the hexose molecule is then mediated by active glucose absorption across the brush-border membrane by the $Na^+$-dependent sodium/glucose cotransporter (SGLT1). Absence of SGLT1 results in glucose-galactose malabsorption [13,14]. The clinical picture of congenital disaccharidase deficiency and carbohydrate malabsorption is an osmotic diarrhea caused by the unabsorbed solute in the ileum. The more rapid transit through the GI tract in a child results in a more severe diarrhea than in an adult. The appearance of the small intestine in these cases is usually unremarkable, and the diagnosis is arrived at by the determination of disaccharidase activities in homogenates of small bowel biopsies or by breath testing.

### Lipid trafficking disorders

Most clinical disorders of fat malabsorption result either from severe liver disease, pancreatic disease (such as cystic fibrosis), or extensive ileal resection (as in Crohn disease) with loss of the enterohepatic circulation of bile acids. Intestinal biopsies play a limited role in the diagnosis of these disorders. However, primary abnormalities involving abnormalities of fat transport within the enterocyte, although much less frequent, can result in a characteristic vacuolization of the enterocyte in intestinal biopsies. The 3 main disorders of lipid trafficking are abetalipoproteinemia, hypobetalipoproteinemia, and chylomicron retention disorder (Anderson disease).

#### *Clinical features and pathogenesis*

The clinical and pathologic features of these entities are similar although their pathogenesis is different. Abetalipoproteinemia is an autosomal recessive disorder characterized by the absence of apolipoprotein (apo) B–containing lipoproteins. The molecular basis for the defect is a mutation of the gene coding for microsomal triglyceride transfer protein (MTP), located on chromosome 4q22 (see Table 2) [15]. MTP is responsible for assembly of lipoprotein particles, and for the proper folding of apo B, preventing its premature degradation [16].

Fatty acids within intestinal cells thus cannot be exported as chylomicrons. Patients have diarrhea and fat malabsorption, usually appearing within the first few months of life, with acanthocytosis and deficiencies in fat-soluble vitamins resulting in retinitis pigmentosa and neurologic symptoms. There is clinical heterogeneity, however, with signs and symptoms presenting in older patients in a significant proportion of cases. Serum levels of cholesterol and triglycerides are typically low, and do not increase after a fatty meal. Hypobetalipoproteinemia is an autosomal dominant disorder as a result of a mutation in the *apo B* gene located on chromosome 2, leading to a truncated apo B protein [17]. Homozygous patients have a clinical and histologic phenotype essentially indistinguishable from abetalipoproteinemia, whereas heterozygous patients have only a mild phenotype. Chylomicron retention (Anderson) disease is similar to abetalipoproteinemia in its GI manifestations and impact on growth, although acanthocytosis is usually absent and neurologic and ocular abnormalities are much less severe. Also, in contrast to abetalipoproteinemia, fasting serum triglyceride levels are normal and hypocholesterolemia is less marked. The causative gene, *SAR1B*, codes for a GTPase associated with coat protein carriers involved in endoplasmic reticulum to Golgi transport, particularly in chylomicron and low density lipoprotein transport [18].

*Pathologic features.* These disorders have overlapping pathologic features. The duodenal mucosa has a white appearance on endoscopy with normal esophageal and gastric mucosa. Villous morphology is preserved although some patients may demonstrate mild villous atrophy. The characteristic feature is diffuse vacuolization of the enterocytes resulting from fat accumulation, the vacuolar appearance resulting from leaching of the fat by routine histologic processing (Fig. 2A). Fat can be demonstrated by special stains on snap-frozen sections or on ultrastructural examination (see Fig. 2B). The extent of vacuolization may vary along different villi in the same patient [17]. Lipid vacuoles fill the enterocytes on electron microscopy (see Fig. 2C), and because the enterocyte cannot export lipids, no lipids are noted in the extracellular space or in the lacteals. Hepatic biopsies in abetalipoproteinemia typically reveal steatosis, with numerous non–membrane-bound lipid droplets noted in the hepatic cytoplasm [19]. Fibrosis evolving to cirrhosis has been reported in occasional patients [20].

## Other transport disorders

### *Amino acids*

Disorders of amino acid transport rarely feature prominent gastrointestinal manifestations, except for lysinuric protein intolerance, which results from mutations in the *SLCA7* gene; the *SLCA7* gene codes for the light chain subunit of the heterodimer amino acid transporter at the basolateral membrane of intestinal and renal epithelial cells [21]. Initially described in Finland, but now recognized worldwide, lysinuric protein intolerance clinically manifests as failure to thrive with vomiting and diarrhea. Hepatosplenomegaly, hematologic anomalies, neurologic involvement, including hyperammonemic coma are recurrent clinical features. Ornithine and arginine, urea cycle intermediates that fail to

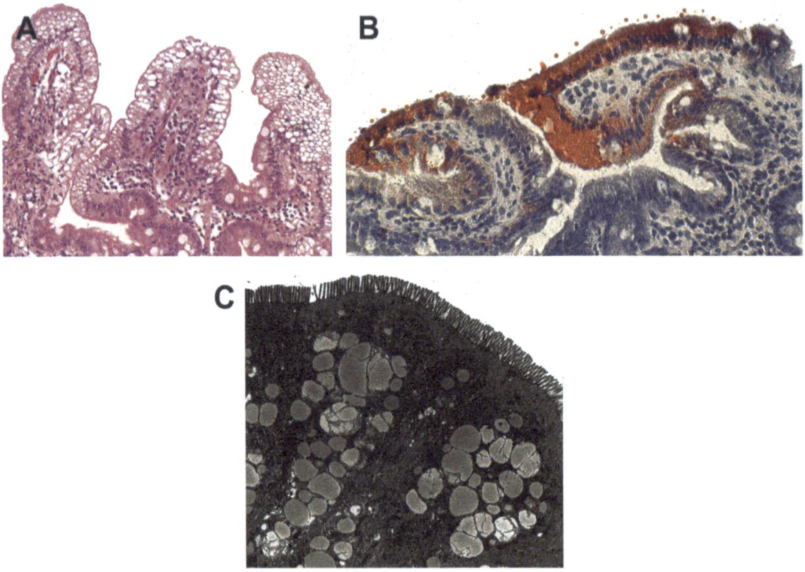


**Fig. 2.** Abetalipoproteinemia. (*A*) Duodenal biopsy from a 9-month-old boy with severe failure to thrive and increased liver enzymes. Villous structure is well preserved. There is diffuse vacuolization of the enterocytes (H&E, ×200). (*B*) Fat can be demonstrated on frozen sections (Oil-Red O stain, ×200). (*C*) Lipid filled supranuclear vacuoles of varying sizes are noted on ultrastructural examination. (*Courtesy of* Pierre Brochu, MD, Hôpital Ste-Justine, Montreal, Quebec.)

exit from intestinal epithelium in lysinuric protein intolerance, result in a urea cycle dysfunction with hyperammonemia and alteration in mental status. Two major complications, pulmonary alveolar proteinosis and renal disease are increasingly observed in patients with lysinuric protein intolerance [22,23]. The condition is recognized by the markedly increased urinary levels of lysine and other dibasic amino acids; DNA testing may be required for confirmation of the diagnosis. One 5-year-old boy was reported with chronic diarrhea and a flat gut on small intestinal biopsy, and unsuccessful treatment with a gluten-free diet [24]. Other complications associated with this disorder include lupus, hemophagocytic lymphohistiocytosis [25], and sudden infant death [26].

*Electrolytes and trace elements*

The biology of intestinal ion transport is a complex field with disorders ranging from rare selective deficiencies to multisystem disease such as cystic fibrosis. The understanding of solute transport is rapidly expanding as the individual transporter molecules that form part of the solute carrier family (SLC) class of proteins are cloned and functionally characterized [27]. Those defects presenting primarily with severe diarrhea include congenital chloride diarrhea and congenital sodium diarrhea. Intestinal biopsy in these cases has been reported as normal or showing only mild partial villus atrophy [28]. Congenital chloride diarrhea is caused by mutations in the solute-linked carrier family 26-member A3 (*SLC26A3*) gene. It manifests as a life-threatening congenital diarrhea. Long-term manifestations include renal disease, spematoceles, and male subfertility [29]. Congenital sodium diarrhea results in hyponatremia and metabolic acidosis. The syndromic form of this disorder has been linked to mutations in *SPINT2*, also characterized by choanal and anal atresia, hypertelorism, double kidney, cleft palate, and digital anomalies [30]. Intestinal biopsies in these cases are usually normal.

Acrodermatitis enteropathica is an autosomal recessive disorder resulting from a defect in the intestinal absorption of zinc. Mutations in a candidate gene, *ZIP4*, result in defective epithelial transport in the intestine and kidney [30]. There is a characteristic clinical picture of diarrhea and acral and orificial skin lesions. Rodin and Goldman [31] found pancreatic islet hyperplasia, absence of the thymus, and germinal centers, with plasmacytosis of the spleen and lymph nodes in autopsies. Inclusion bodies in Paneth cells have been reported in patients with this disorder [32,33]. A decrease in villus height is noted in animal models of zinc deficiency, which is corrected by zinc supplementation [34]. Interference with chylomicron development and function has been noted [35]. The disease is correctable by oral zinc supplementation. Severe zinc deficiency is also seen in other disorders such as the Cronkhite-Canada syndrome [36].

Menkes disease is an X-linked disorder that results from a defect in intestinal absorption of copper. Affected patients present characteristic hair shaft anomalies (pili torti), cerebral degeneration, hypopigmentation, abnormal bones, vomiting and diarrhea, and occasional protein-losing enteropathy. The disorder maps to Xq12-q13, and is caused by mutations in the *ATP7A* gene, which maps to Xq12-13, and encodes a copper-transporting P1B-type ATPase, part of a family of membrane proteins responsible for cation transport across membranes [37,38].

*Vitamins*

Congenital vitamin $B_{12}$ transport disorders include congenital intrinsic factor deficiency, a selective absence of intrinsic factor without any gastric anomaly, congenital pancreatic insufficiency of various causes, and congenital selective vitamin $B_{12}$ malabsorption, an autosomal recessive disorder characterized by megaloblastic anemia, hepatosplenomegaly, vomiting, diarrhea, and proteinuria, as a result of mutations in the gene *CUBN*, which codes for an ileal cell surface receptor protein, cubilin [39]. None of these disorders results in any significant histologic changes in intestinal biopsies.

A rare congenital disorder of intracellular vitamin $B_{12}$ metabolism due to cobalamin C deficiency has also been described in which patients presented with diarrhea, renal failure, and systemic thromboemboli in association with a striking gastric atrophy [40]. Protein-losing enteropathy responsive to hydroxycobalamin treatment has been reported in 1 patient with this disorder [41], presumably because the gastric anomaly.

*Bile acids*

Heubi and colleagues [42] described a severe refractory diarrhea caused by a primary disorder of bile acid absorption; intestinal biopsies were normal. A defect in the gene coding for an ileal $Na^+$-dependent bile acid transporter, SLC10A2, has been found in this disorder [43]. Bile acid-related diarrheas are much more commonly secondary to chronic pancreatic insufficiency [44], or to loss of ileal surface, as in short gut syndrome caused by necrotizing enterocolitis [45], or extensive ileal resection in Crohn disease [46,47].

## CONGENITAL DEFECTS OF INTESTINAL EPITHELIAL DIFFERENTIATION

### Microvillus inclusion disease

*Clinical features*

Microvillus inclusion disease (MVID) is an autosomal recessive disease characterized by refractory secretory diarrhea usually occurring within the first week of life, although a late-onset form may manifest in the first few months of life [48]. Investigation of clusters of cases within the Navajo population identified mutations in the gene *MYO5B* [49]. Homozygosity mapping of an extended Turkish kindred allowed Muller and colleagues [50] to locate the gene locus to chromosome 18q21. *MYO5B* codes for myosin Vb, part of a family of proteins responsible for actin-dependent organelle transport and regulation of endosome recycling [50]. Mutations in a related gene, *MYO5A*, cause Griscelli syndrome, an immunodeficiency disorder also characterized by abnormal transfer of melanin granules to keratinocytes [50]. Patients with MVID are dependent on total parenteral nutrition (TPN), although improved survival may require small bowel transplantation [51].

*Pathology*

Small bowel biopsies are usually characterized by severe villus atrophy, mild or moderate crypt hyperplasia, and a variable degree of inflammation in the lamina propria but without crypt destruction (Fig. 3A). The diagnosis may be strongly suspected on paraffin-embedded sections by the absence of a distinct brush border using the periodic acid–Schiff (PAS) stain, and by the presence of a diffuse PAS-positive staining of the apical portion of the enterocytes (see Fig. 3B, C). Similar observations are noted using immunohistochemical staining for alkaline phosphatase and anti-CD 10. More recent findings using antibodies against Rab 11a, a small guanosine triphosphatase (GTPase) protein on the surface of recycling endosomes, has provided further evidence that MVID is a disorder of apical plasma membrane recycling [52]. The pathognomonic ultrastructural features include absent or small stubby microvilli, and vesicular structures located toward the apex of the enterocytes containing microvilli and granules containing dense amorphous material (see Fig. 3E). Microvillus inclusions have also been reported in the colon, gallbladder, and renal tubular epithelium in these patients [53]. A variety of different inclusions has also been noted in patients with this disorder and finding the typical inclusions

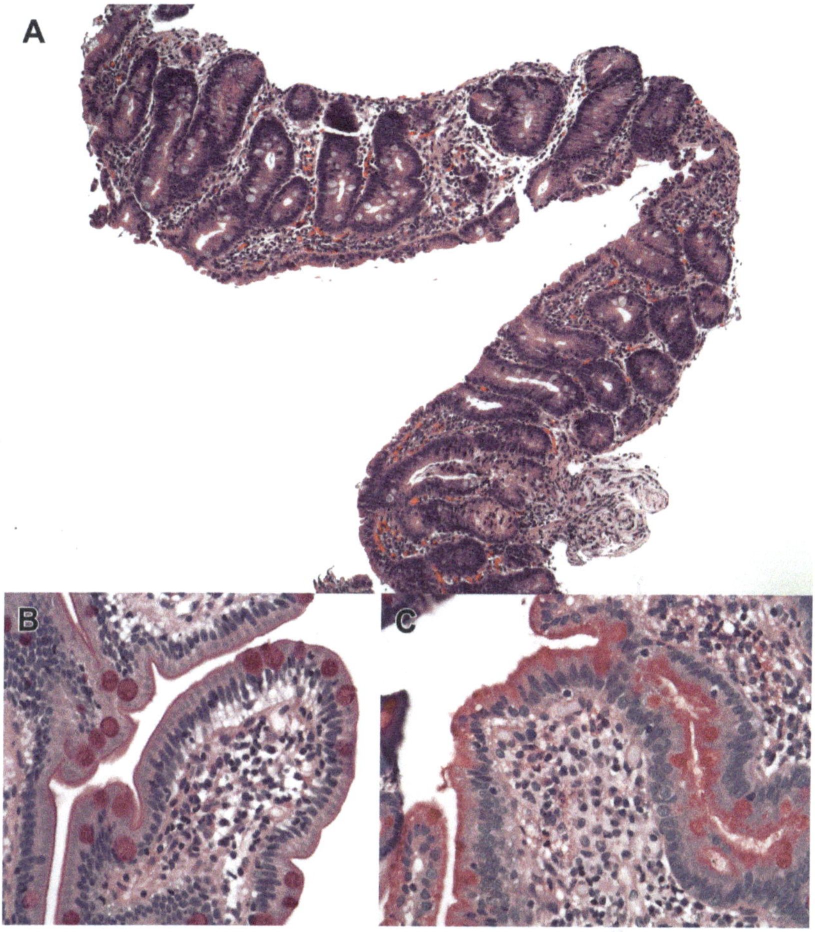


**Fig. 3.** MVID. (*A*) Biopsy from an 18-day-old boy shows total villus atrophy with normoplastic crypts and no significant inflammation (H&E, ×100). (*B, C*) PAS stain. The panel on the left (*B*) shows a normal brush border appearing as a thin distinct magenta line along the apical border of the enterocytes. Note the normal goblet cell staining. Contrast with (*C*), on the right, from a case of MVID, showing a lack of a distinct brush border and a diffuse positivity in the apical portion of the enterocyte cytoplasm. Goblet cells are also present (×400). (*D, E*) Ultrastructural features. (*D*) Normal duodenum with well-preserved microvilli. (*E*) Same case as (*A*). Enterocytes denuded of a brush border with a typical inclusion containing profiles of microvilli. Note also the presence of numerous surrounding vesicles containing dense amorphous material. (uranyl-lead, *A, B*, ×7000; *C, D*, ×14,000).

may require a prolonged search [54]. Atypical inclusions include the presence of numerous small electron-lucent vesicles, and accumulation of osmiophilic vermiform structures [55]. Cases with these features have been previously reported as MVID with atypical features or as microvillous dystrophy [56,57]. Genetic analysis will surely help in defining whether the ultrastructural, and

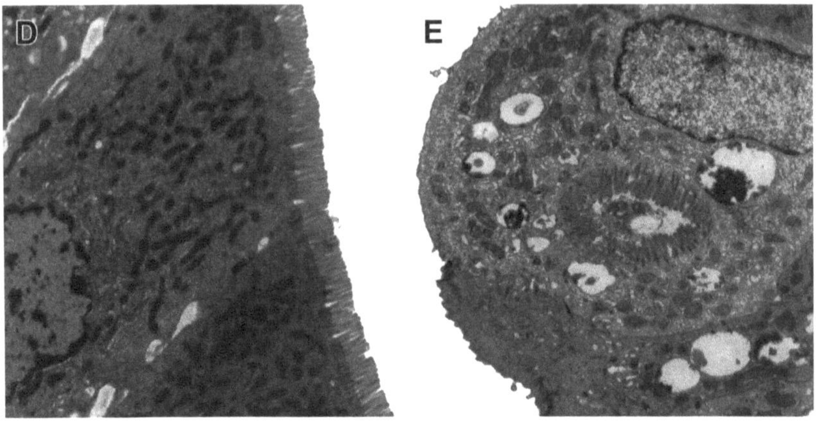


**Fig. 3.** Continued

sometimes clinical, variability represents different entities or variations in the spectrum of manifestations of a single disorder, especially given the enormous prognostic and therapeutic implications.

## Congenital tufting enteropathy (epithelial dysplasia)

*Clinical features*

First described by Reifen and colleagues [58], patients with tufting enteropathy present in the neonatal period with watery diarrhea. Prenatal history is uneventful and the disease seems to be inherited in an autosomal recessive fashion, as suggested by the finding of other affected siblings and frequent parental consanguinity. The incidence is estimated at 1/50,000 to 100,000 live births in Europe, and seems to be more frequent in patients of Arabic origin [59]. Cases of tufting enteropathy have been described in association with other malformations, including facial dysmorphism, micrognathia and anal imperforation [60], and choanal atresia and hair abnormalities [61]. Superficial punctate keratitis and conjunctival erosions have been observed in about 50% of patients [62]. In addition, an association has been reported between tufting enteropathy and autoimmune phenomena, including autoimmune anemia and thrombocytopenia [63], and chronic arthritis [64]. Using single nucleotide polymorphism (SNP) analysis in an affected kindred, Sivagnanam and colleagues [65] identified the epithelial cell adhesion molecule gene (*EpCAM*), located on chromosome 2p21, as the causative gene. EpCAM belongs to a family of cell adhesion receptors, associates with tight junction proteins, and is responsible for cell-cell interaction by recruiting actin filaments to sites of contact [66].

*Pathology*

The histologic hallmarks are severe villus atrophy with the formation of tufts of rounded, teardrop-shaped enterocytes that appear to shed into the lumen. There may be a mild increase in the lamina propria inflammatory cells, but intraepithelial leukocytes (IELs) do not seem to be significantly increased. The brush border is normal by PAS staining, and electron microscopic findings are nonspecific. Dilated crypts have also been described. Epithelial abnormalities typically vary over time and may be subtle or absent in the first biopsy (Fig. 4A).

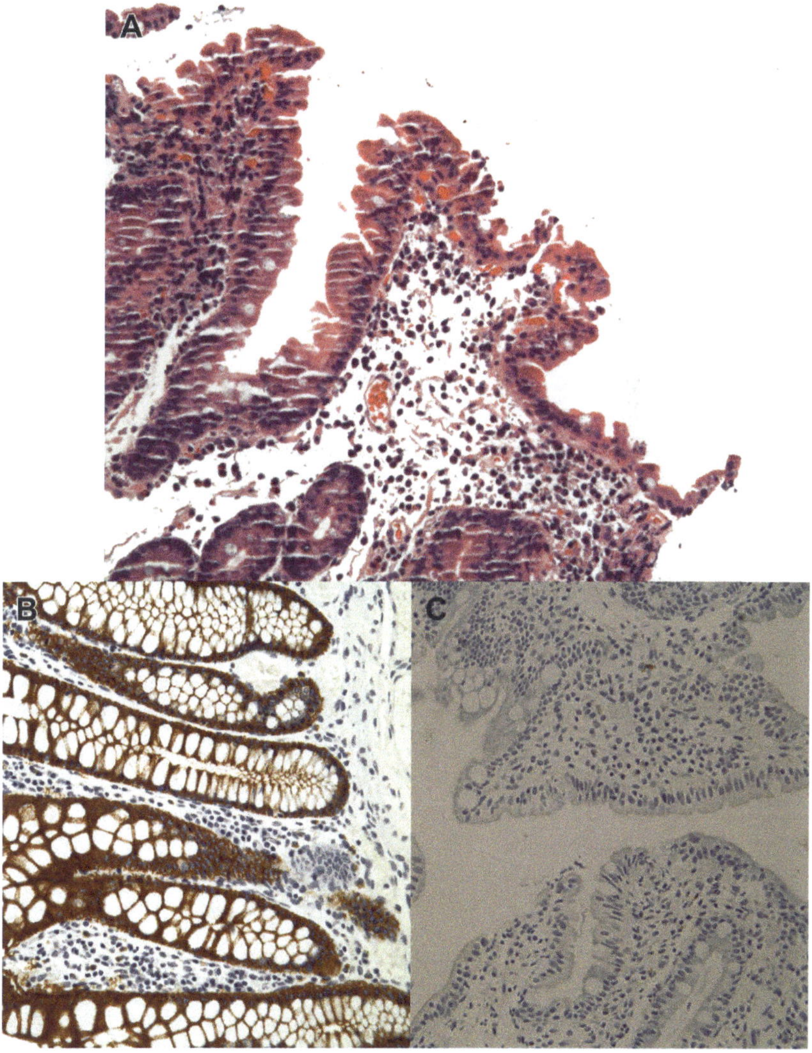


**Fig. 4.** Tufting enteropathy. (*A*) Duodenal biopsy from a 2-month-old child shows coalescence of surface epithelial cells into tufts with rounding up and shedding of the epithelial cells into the lumen (H&E, ×200). Immunostaining for MOC 31, an antibody against EpCAM. (*B*) Normal staining of colonic surface and crypt epithelium with a membranous accentuation. (*C*) Absence of staining in a case of tufting enteropathy (immunoperoxidase with hematoxylin counterstain, ×200).

Abnormalities in immunohistochemical staining for basement membrane laminin and heparan sulfate proteoglycan [53], ultrastructural irregularities of desmosomes, and abnormal distribution of α2β1 integrin [67] have been observed in patients with this disorder. Intestinal features resembling congenital tufting enteropathy have been noted in a knockout mouse model for transcription factor Elf3 [68]. A helpful feature is the finding that immunohistochemistry of the patient's intestinal tissue reveals decreased expression of EpCAM (see Fig. 4C) [69].

The disease seems to have a variable clinical course with some patients reported to have been weaned off TPN [70]. The report of a patient with similar clinical and biopsy features who was found to harbor a mutation in *SPINT2*, associated with congenital sodium diarrhea, suggests there may be phenotypic overlap between congenital tufting enteropathy and other congenital diarrheas [71].

A disorder that is probably related resulting from the absence of intestinal epithelial α6β4 integrin has been described. The salient features are severe watery diarrhea in the first 2 weeks of life in association with pyloric atresia, with extensive sloughing of the epithelium observed on biopsies [72]. Diarrhea has also been observed in cases of pyloric atresia–junctional epidermolysis bullosa, in which mutations in the genes coding for laminin-5 and α6β4 integrin have been described [73].

## Enteroendocrine cell dysgenesis (enteric anendocrinosis)

### *Clinical features*

Enteroendocrine cell dysgenesis (ECD) is a recently described autosomal recessive disorder associated with a congenital absence of enteroendocrine cells in the small and large bowel secondary to mutations in the *NEUROG3* gene, located on chromosome 10q21.3, required for differentiation of epithelial cells to the endocrine phenotype [74]. Affected patients are characterized by a congenital diarrheal syndrome with profound malabsortion of all nutrients from birth. Patients also typically develop insulin-dependent diabetes, some during infancy and others later in childhood [74,75]. Pancreatic exocrine function is normal. Neurogenin-3 null mice lack enteroendocrine cells [76], and are severely diabetic because neurogenin-3 is also required for pancreatic endocrine development in the rodent [77].

### *Pathology*

The intestinal biopsies may be normal or reveal villous atrophy; the severity of the changes is perhaps related to different mutations in the *NEUROG 3* gene (Fig. 5A) [75]. The brush border is normal, and goblet and Paneth cells are present. Inflammatory cells in the lamina propria do not appear significantly increased, and there is no crypt-destructive process. Electron microscopy confirms the presence of microvilli and the absence of microvillus inclusions [78]. The characteristic absence of enteroendocrine cells in the small bowel and colon is confirmed by immunohistochemistry for chromogranin A (see Fig. 5C). Patients with autoimmune polyglandular syndrome I may have absent or

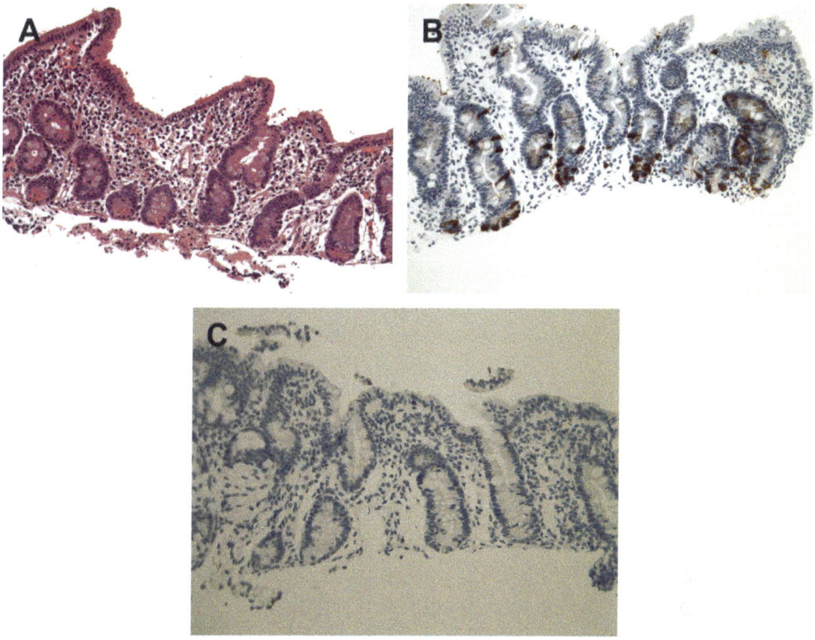


**Fig. 5.** Enteroendocrine cell dysgenesis. (*A*) Duodenal biopsy from a 10-month-old girl who presented with diarrhea shortly after birth and insulin-dependent diabetes at 10 months. There is partial villus atrophy, mild crypt hyperplasia, and no significant inflammation (H&E, ×200). (*B*) Normal distribution of enteroendocrine cells in the duodenum as revealed by immunostaining for chromogranin (avidin-biotin peroxidase, ×200). (*C*) Same case as (*A*), with complete absence of immunoreactivity for chromogranin (avidin-biotin peroxidase, ×200).

markedly reduced enteroendocrine cells, which may be transient [79,80]. Loss of enteroendocrine cells may be observed in patients with autoimmune enteropathy, along with loss of goblet and Paneth cells.

## Syndromatic diarrhea (tricho-hepato-enteric syndrome)

*Clinical features*

Although not known to be a disorder of intestinal epithelial differentiation, syndromic diarrhea and the tricho-hepato-enteric syndrome are discussed here because they enter into the differential diagnosis of early-onset diarrhea. Girault and colleagues [81] described a group of patients with dysmorphic features, consisting of a prominent forehead, broad nose, hypertelorism and wooly, easily removable abnormal hair (trichorrhexis nodosa), in association with intractable diarrhea and immunodeficiency, which they termed syndromatic intractable diarrhea, because of the constellation of extraintestinal manifestations. Most of the patients reported were of Middle Eastern origin, and there was parental consanguinity and a history of similarly affected siblings. The immunodeficiency was characterized by impaired T-cell and antibody responses despite normal immunoglobulin levels. Infants with similar clinical features had also been reported separately as the tricho-hepato-enteric syndrome (THE) [82,83], in which thin sparse hair (trichomalacia) was seen in association with hypertelorism and chronic diarrhea, and a history of premature delivery with intrauterine growth retardation. In addition, the cases described by Verloes [83] also presented with neonatal hemochromatosis, characterized by liver failure, cirrhosis, and multivisceral iron deposition. The phenotypic similarity between THE and the cases described by Girault led Fabre and colleagues [84] to suggest that these manifestations represented a spectrum of the same disorder. This seemed to be confirmed when mutations in *TTC37,* described in cases of THE [85], were also observed in patients with the features of syndromic diarrhea [86]. *TTC37* maps to chromosome 5q14.3-5q21.2 and codes for a tetratricopeptide repeat protein, thespin, whose function is as yet uncharacterized [85].

*Pathology*

Intestinal biopsies have revealed variable villous atrophy without a conspicuous increase in inflammatory cells and without specific features. Serially obtained biopsies suggest that villous atrophy can improve with time and that the inflammatory infiltrate is not consistent. The hair is described as wooly with microscopic features of trichorrhexis nodosa. Hepatic involvement is inconsistent. Hartley and colleagues [85] also observed ultrastructural platelet abnormalities consisting of reduced α-granules, and abnormal lipid inclusions and canalicular system.

We have observed trichorrhexis nodosa in a 3-month-old girl presenting with severe diarrhea and an immunodeficiency best characterized as common variable immunodeficiency. Hair abnormalities can be seen in association with chronic diarrhea in other disorders, typically in Menkes disease, zinc deficiency, and lysinuric protein intolerance.

### Autoimune enteropathy

*Clinical features*

Autoimmune enteropathy (AIE) is probably the most frequent disorder leading to infantile intractable diarrhea [87]. Most cases occur in infancy or the first year of life. There is a strong male preponderance, family history of other affected siblings, frequent extraintestinal involvement, and various circulating autoantibodies [88]. The clinical picture in infants is usually dominated by a secretory diarrhea, dermatitis, and various endocrine disorders, of which diabetes mellitus is the most frequent. Moreover, these patients also have numerous complications, mainly infectious, related to loss of the functional gut barrier, central lines, underlying immunodeficiency, and immunosuppressive therapy. However, this entity has also been reported in older children, in girls, and even in adults, in whom it may be responsible for a proportion of cases referred to as refractory sprue. In adults, the clinical picture seems to be that of celiac disease unresponsive to gluten withdrawal [89–96]. Corazza and colleagues [91] reported 4 adult women with refractory celiac disease, none of whom had had malabsorptive symptoms in childhood, thus confirming an adult onset. Akram and colleagues reported on a series of 15 (7 women) patients, aged 42 to 67 years, in whom celiac disease was excluded by lack of response to a gluten-free diet or absence of the celiac disease susceptibility HLA genotypes. All patients had protracted diarrhea, weight loss, and malnutrition.

*Pathogenesis*

The strongest and most consistently recognized association is with the X-linked syndrome of immunodysregulation, polyendocrinopathy, and enteropathy (IPEX syndrome) initially described by Powell and colleagues [97]. Extraintestinal disease in these patients includes insulin-dependent diabetes, thyroiditis, membranous glomerulopathy, and interstitial nephritis [98]. This syndrome has been related to mutations in the *FOXP3* gene (Xp11.23) [99], and humans bearing this mutation share a similar phenotype to that of the *scurfy* mouse, with absence of naturally occurring CD4+ CD25+ Tregs. Mutations in the *FOXP3* gene or in its promoter region result in impaired suppression of lymphocyte proliferation by Tregs after an initial inflammatory trigger, eventuating in an extensive autoimmune disorder [100,101]. However, about 50% of patients, including girls, with otherwise typical clinical manifestations of IPEX have no detectable mutations of FOXP3 [102]. The term "IPEX-like has been suggested to designate those cases [103].

*Pathology*

The entire GI tract is often involved in AIE, although the histopathologic findings are most severe in the duodenum and small bowel where biopsies are usually characterized by marked villous atrophy, crypt hyperplasia, and a mixed inflammatory infiltrate of the lamina propria. Inflammatory destruction of intestinal crypts with extensive apoptosis is a feature noted in many of the cases, similar to those noted in intestinal graft-versus-host disease, and confirm an immune-mediated attack against intestinal epithelium (Fig. 6A) [98]. A characteristic feature not routinely observed in other inflammatory intestinal diseases is depletion of goblet and Paneth cells. However, there can be marked variation in the histologic features, with some cases, especially in older children or adults, showing milder degrees of intestinal damage (see Fig. 6B). In contrast to cases of GSE with flat villi, intraepithelial lymphocytes tend to be relatively few in number. A concomitant crypt-destructive colitis and gastritis are present in most cases.

One of the hallmarks of this entity, noted since the first reports of AIE, is the presence of antienterocyte antibodies, detected by indirect immunofluorescence using the patient's serum on frozen sections of normal bowel. Positive fluorescent staining results in a linear pattern along the apex and basolateral border of the enterocyte (see Fig. 6C) [53,104–107]. The antibodies are predominantly immunoglobulin (Ig) G, and have been described as complement fixing [104], although IgM and IgA have also been described [106,108]. Antibodies reacting against mucus or goblet cells have also been described, and intestinal biopsies in these cases have shown a marked depletion of goblet cells (see Fig. 6D) [109,110].

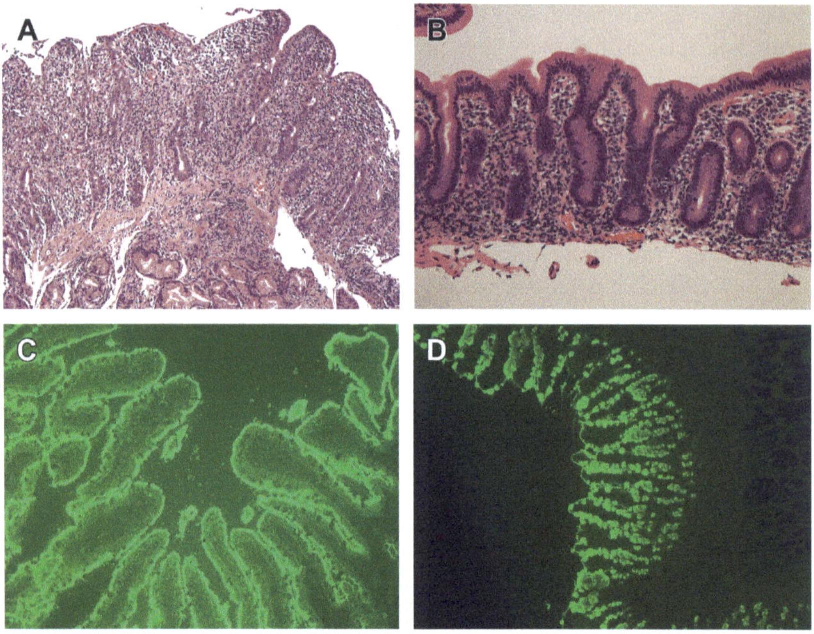


**Fig. 6.** Autoimmune enteropathy, IPEX. (*A*) Duodenal biopsy from a 3-month-old boy shows villous atrophy and a severe crypt-destructive inflammatory process (H&E, ×100). (*B*) A 25-year-old woman with Kabuki syndrome and long-standing diarrhea refractory to a gluten-free diet. The duodenal biopsy shows villous atrophy, crypt hyperplasia, but no significantly increased intraepithelial lymphocytes in the surface epithelium. Note the absence of Paneth and goblet cells (H&E, ×100). (*C*) Indirect immunofluorescence using the patient's serum reveals linear staining along the periapical portion of the enterocytes, consistent with the presence of circulating antienterocyte antibodies. (*D*) In another case, positive staining was noted in goblet cells.

The target of the antienterocyte antibodies is still a matter of investigation, although a 75-kDa antigen reactive with autoantibody in the sera of patients with the IPEX syndrome has been reported [111]. This protein is expressed in the epithelial cells of the small bowel, colon, and kidney, and may play a role in protein-protein interactions in the enterocyte. More than 1 antigen is likely to be involved. More recently, a 95-kDa antigen identified as villin has been reported in patients with IPEX [112].

However, the role of these antibodies in the pathogenesis and diagnosis of AIE is debatable. These antibodies have been reported to occur after the onset of the disease and to disappear before restoration of mucosal integrity [107], and may thus represent an epiphenomenon without playing a causative role in mucosal damage. Similar antienterocyte antibodies have also been described in adult patients with AIDS without digestive symptoms [113]. The specificity of antigoblet cell antibodies has also been questioned. Antigoblet cell antibodies have been detected in patients with chronic inflammatory bowel disease (Crohn disease and ulcerative colitis) and their first-degree relatives [114], and in a series of treated and untreated patients with celiac disease and controls [115]. The usefulness of these antibodies in the diagnosis of AIE in young infants is also probably limited, given that there is little IgG production in the first 3 months of life and that IgG detected in the infant is likely maternal in origin [116].

The differential diagnosis of AIE includes, in addition to celiac disease and graft-versus-host disease, Crohn disease and enterocolitis associated with various immunodeficiency states. A high index of suspicion for AIE should be present when there is a severe inflammatory crypt-destructive process with villous atrophy and increased apoptosis in the base of the crypts, loss of goblet and Paneth cells, or an intestinal inflammatory process in a patient with autoimmune phenomena. Testing for circulating antienterocyte antibodies is useful in the older child and adult, but may be of more limited use in the young infant. Immunostaining for the *FOXP3* gene product applied to formalin-fixed paraffin-embedded GI biopsies may be useful to screen for the IPEX syndrome in young patients with severe diarrhea [117]. Mortality in cases of AIE has been high, occurring in up to one-third of reported cases, but more frequent in the older descriptions. Diet changes and steroids alone have been largely ineffective, and the use of immunosuppressants seems to be necessary in most cases. Bone marrow transplantation may be curative. Immunosuppression is required in older children and adults [89]. A good response to sirolimus has been reported in IPEX-like cases [103]. Bone marrow transplantation seems to offer the only cure for IPEX [118].

Major differentiating features between various causes of severe diarrhea of early infancy are presented in Table 3.

### Autoimmune polyendocrine syndrome

Also known as autoimmune polyendocrinopathy, candidiasis, ectodermal dystrophy (APECED), autoimmune polyendocrine syndrome is an autosomal recessive disorder with heterogeneous clinical manifestations. It is caused by mutations in the *AIRE* gene, which codes for a transcription factor primarily expressed in medullary thymic epithelial cells where negative selection is believed to occur [119]. The type I form is characterized by various endocrinopathies of an autoimmune nature, often beginning in childhood or the early teenage years, by chronic mucocutaneous candidiasis as a result of a T-cell defect, starting soon after birth, and by dystrophy of ectodermal tissues [120]. Malabsorption can occur in up to 25% of patients, and seems to result from destruction of intestinal endocrine cells [79]. A specific deficiency of cholecystokinin-producing enteroendocrine cells has been reported in 1 patient, with seeming reappearance of the cells when the diarrhea abated [80]. Small bowel biopsies show mild changes or can even be normal, in contrast with the crypt-destructive inflammation usually seen in AIE.

### Celiac disease (GSE)

#### *Clinical manifestations and diagnosis*

Celiac disease is a life-long immune-mediated systemic disorder elicited by gluten, the major protein found in wheat, barley, and rye, in genetically

**Table 3**
Differentiating features of severe diarrhea of early infancy

| | Microvillous inclusion disease | Tufting enteropathy | Enteroendocrine cell dysgenesis | Autoimmune enteropathy |
|---|---|---|---|---|
| Presentation | First 2 wk | First 2 wk | First 2 wk | After 1 mo |
| Gene defect | MYO5b (18q21) | EpCAM (2p21) | NEUROG 3 (10q21.3) | FOXP3 (Xp11.23) in IPEX syndrome |
| Extraintestinal disease | Low γ-glutamyl transferase cholestasis after bowel transplantation | Dysmorphism; autoimmune diseases (arthritis) | Insulin-dependent diabetes | Polyendocrinopathies |
| Antienterocyte antibodies | No | No | No | Yes |
| Villous atrophy | Yes | Variable | Variable | Variable |
| Surface epithelium | Absent brush border | Tufting and desquamation | Normal | Normal or atrophic |
| Lamina propria inflammation | Minimal | Variable | Minimal | Usually increased |

predisposed individuals, resulting in damage to the intestinal mucosa and a variety of clinical manifestations and antibodies. The disease is most prevalent in western Europe and North America, with reported incidence rates of up to 1:100, but occurs worldwide [121]. The higher incidence rates observed more recently result from the more widespread use of serologic tests in detection and screening, from greater awareness of atypical and silent forms of the disease, and from recognition of an increased incidence of GSE in patients with Down syndrome, IgA deficiency, and diabetes [122]. Gluten is digested to the 33–amino acid alcohol-soluble gliadin, which is resistant to further enzymatic degradation. Gliadin seems to induce intestinal epithelial cells to express interleukin (IL)-15, which in turn leads to activation and proliferation of the characteristic intraepithelial CD8+ T lymphocytes. These become cytotoxic and kill enterocytes with surface MIC-A, an HLA class I-like protein expressed during stress. This results in increased intestinal permeability to gliadin, followed by its deamidation by tissue transglutaminase (tTG), an enzyme normally present in the gut, where it acts to stabilize granulation tissue during repair processes. Subsequent binding of deamidated gliadin to HLA molecules located on antigen-presenting cells results in secretion of inflammatory cytokines, and recruitment and activation of lamina propria T lymphocytes, with production of interferon-$\gamma$ and further tissue damage. The principal determinants of genetic susceptibility for celiac disease are major histocompatibility class II genes located on the short arm of chromosome 6. The HLA-DQ2 heterodimer is present in 95% of patients with celiac disease, and most of the remainder have the HLA-DQ8 heterodimer. HLA-DQ2 homozygous individuals have a 5-fold higher risk of disease development than HLA-DQ2 heterozygous individuals [123]. Expression of these HLA molecules is necessary but not sufficient to cause disease as the HLA-DQ2 haplotype is present in 30% to 40% of the Caucasian population. Outside the HLA region, several genes controlling the immune response have also been related to celiac disease [123].

*Clinical features*

The classic presentation occurs in a child aged 6 to 24 months after gluten ingestion, and consists of abdominal distension, diarrhea, and failure to thrive. The age at presentation of GSE seems to vary according to the age at introduction of gluten in the diet, and to the quantity consumed [124]. A variety of nongastrointestinal symptoms have also been associated with celiac disease, including dermatitis herpetiformis, short stature, delayed puberty, dental enamel hypoplasia, osteopenia, hepatitis, and iron deficiency anemia unresponsive to iron therapy [125]. Presenting symptoms in younger children may also include vomiting, abdominal distension, and failure to thrive, whereas growth retardation and delayed puberty may be major manifestations in older children. Serologic testing of children with short stature identified a prevalence rate of 8% to 10% of celiac disease [126]. The lack of classic symptomatology in older children and adults frequently results in delay of diagnosis [122]. Increased transaminase levels associated with a nonspecific hepatitis that normalize on a gluten-free diet have been reported in adults, although that association is unclear in children, as is iron deficiency anemia unresponsive to iron therapy [127].

*Diagnosis*

According to guidelines published in 2005 by the North American Society for Pediatric Gastroenterology, Hepatology, and Nutrition (NASPGHAN), the gold standard for diagnosis remains intestinal biopsy [125]. However, a stepwise approach is recommended with serologic testing as the initial step in symptomatic patients. Testing is also recommended for their first-degree relatives and in asymptomatic patients with conditions known to be associated with celiac disease, such as Down syndrome, Turner syndrome, Williams syndrome, autoimmune thyroiditis, and selective IgA deficiency [125]. In particular, routine screening of all patients with type 1 diabetes mellitus is recommended, in whom a prevalence rate of celiac disease up to 8% has been reported [128]. Measurements of serum IgA-tTG and IgA-endomyseal antibodies (EMA) have ranges of sensitivity and specificity of 90% to 100%, provided the patients are not IgA deficient, and are considered superior to antigliadin antibodies for the diagnosis of celiac disease [121,129]. For patients with low serum IgA levels, testing with IgG-tTG and IgG-EMA is recommended. Antibodies to tTG and EMA are more frequently falsely negative in children less than 2 years of age, in whom additional testing for antigliadin antibodies, or for deamidated gliadin peptides, is recommended [128,130]. Detecting celiac disease in individuals who are on a self-prescribed or parent-prescribed gluten-free diet is challenging as both celiac disease-specific antibodies and histology may normalize following a gluten-free diet. In those cases, testing for HLA-DQ2 and HLA-DQ8 may be useful as celiac disease is most unlikely in those who lack these markers [128].

*Pathology*

The histologic features of celiac disease have classically rested on a combination of a flat mucosa with villus atrophy, increased intraepithelial lymphocytes, crypt hyperplasia, enterocyte damage, and an increase in mononuclear cells (Fig. 7A, B). The damage is most severe proximally, but the entire length of the small bowel is sensitive to gluten. Accurate assessment depends on well-oriented multiple biopsies from both the proximal and distal duodenum, as the disease may be patchy, especially in newly diagnosed children [131,132]. Although recommendations are that biopsies be preferentially obtained from the more distal portion of the duodenum, where villi are somewhat longer and which is less subject to nonspecific changes, the bulb may be the more severe site or in some cases, the only site of involvement [4,5]. In a study of 102 pediatric patients by Bonamico and colleagues [4], histologic involvement of the duodenum was patchy in 16%, and the bulb was the only site of involvement in 25% of the patients. Intestinal biopsies in patients with celiac disease show a range of morphologic alterations, from preserved villous morphology with increased IELs to a flat mucosa with crypt hyperplasia and increased IELs

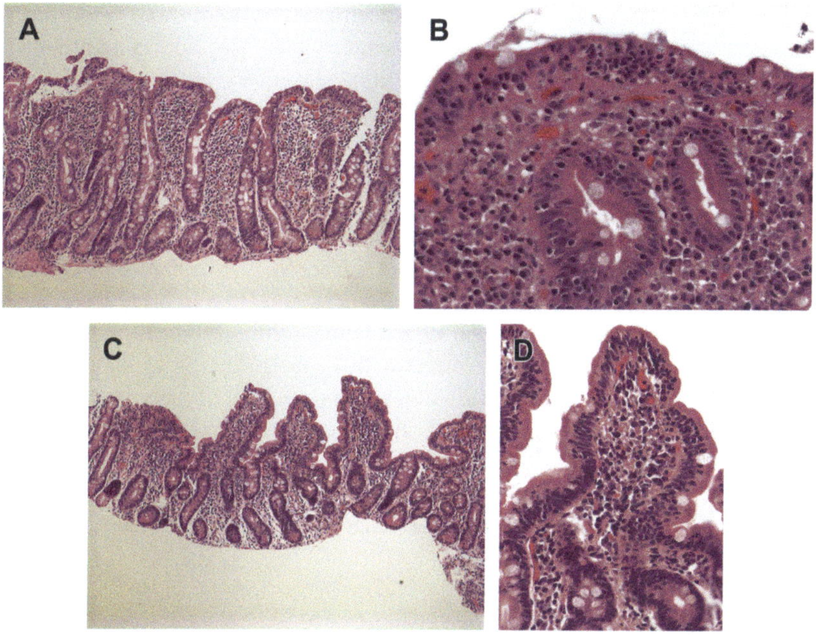


**Fig. 7.** Celiac disease. (*A*) Duodenal biopsy from a 4-year-old girl with 2 months' history of diarrhea and abdominal pain. There is total villous atrophy with hyperplasia of the crypts resulting in a reversal of the normal villus-to-crypt ratio (H&E, ×100). (*B*) Higher power view illustrates the increased intraepithelial lymphocytes (H&E, ×400). (*C*) Duodenal biopsy from a relatively asymptomatic 2-year-old girl with a positive EMA investigated at the mother's insistence because she has celiac disease. There is mild to moderate villous atrophy and crypt hyperplasia (H&E, ×100). (*D*) Higher power view confirms the increased intraepithelial lymphocytes (H&E, ×400).

(see Fig. 7C, D). There seems to be little association between symptomatology and degree of mucosal damage or with the extent of laboratory abnormalities, although it has been suggested that the length of injured bowel may correlate more closely with symptoms than the severity of villus flattening [133]. The Marsh-Oberhuber classification [134] describes the major histologic lesions associated with GSE, but is somewhat cumbersome in routine practice and has poor interobserver variability because of the number of diagnostic categories. More recent classifications, such as that proposed by Corazza and Villanaci [135] and by Ensari [136], limit the number of categories to 3: normal villi with increased IELs, mild to markedly shortened villi with increased IELs and crypt hyperplasia, and a flat mucosa with increased IELs. Increased IELs (>30 lymphocytes per 100 epithelial cells) are a cardinal feature of intestinal biopsies in patients with celiac disease, and in most cases rarely require enumeration. The dominant IELs in celiac disease are CD3+/CD4−/CD8+ $\gamma\delta$ T-cell receptor T lymphocytes, which are only 5% of the total in the normal mucosa [133,137]. Loss of the decrescendo pattern, in which IELs normally decrease from the base to the tip of the villus, is a useful feature to observe when assessing biopsies for celiac disease especially when villus morphology is preserved [133]. Patients with celiac disease have a persistent or increased density of IELs along the sides and especially the tips of the villi. Counting IELs per 100 enterocytes is impractical in routine practice, but when increased IELs are suspected but not definitive, counting IELs at the tips of 5 well-oriented villi (20 enterocytes at the tip of each) has been proposed as an alternative, equally precise method [138,139]. One study reported that counts of 6 to 12 IELs per 20 epithelial cells at the villus tip correlate with serologic evidence of GSE [139]. Celiac disease is frequently associated with increased IELs in other parts of the gastrointestinal tract, especially the stomach and colon, indicating a panenteric sensitivity to gluten, which can reverse with a gluten-free diet [140–143]. In 1 pediatric study, lymphocytic gastritis was found in 13% of patients with celiac disease, and seemed to be associated with greater mucosal damage and more profound laboratory abnormalities [143]. The fact that IELs are increased throughout the gut in celiac disease has led some to propose rectal biopsy after gluten challenge as a way to diagnose celiac disease, but this has not gained widespread acceptance [136,144].

*Differential diagnosis*

The differential diagnosis of celiac disease in a small bowel biopsy in children includes autoimmune enteropathy, nongluten food allergy, severe protein-caloric malnutrition (kwashiorkor), immunodeficiency disorders, viral and parasitic infections, and *Helicobacter pylori* gastritis (Table 4). Careful attention

**Table 4**
Distinguishing features of conditions that can mimic celiac disease in a small bowel biopsy

| Entity | Differentiating features |
|---|---|
| Autoimmune enteropathy (IPEX and IPEX-like) | Crypt-destructive inflammatory process with loss of goblet and Paneth cells<br>Crypt apoptosis<br>No significantly increased intraepithelial lymphocytes<br>Circulating antienterocyte antibodies |
| Nongluten food protein intolerance | Often associated with increased eosinophils<br>Variable villous atrophy<br>Positive allergy testing |
| Kwashiokor | History of severe protein malnutrition<br>No increased intraepithelial leukocytes |
| Primary immunodeficiency | Absence or paucity of plasma cells in the biopsy<br>Nodular lymphoid hyperplasia |
| Graft vs host disease | Crypt apoptosis with minimal inflammatory infiltrate |
| *Helicobacter pylori* infection | Usually in association with active gastritis caused by *Helicobacter pylori* rather than lymphocytic gastritis<br>Changes rarely extend beyond the duodenal bulb |
| Viral enteritis | Surface epithelial degenerative and regenerative changes<br>Some infections may have increased intraepithelial leukocytes<br>Histologic changes rapidly revert as symptoms abate |

to such morphologic features as crypt destruction and increased apoptosis in autoimmune enteropathy, and paucity of mononuclear cells in immunodeficiency diseases, in addition to clinical and serologic correlation, are essential for proper diagnosis. Refractory sprue is a term used to describe patients with severe villus atrophy, without evidence of lymphoma, that fails to improve on a gluten-free diet. In children, major diagnostic considerations include other non–gluten-related food intolerance and autoimmune enteropathy.

*Treatment and follow-up*

Treatment with a life-long gluten-free diet is recommended for all symptomatic children as well as for asymptomatic children belonging to high-risk groups with characteristic intestinal histologic abnormalities [125]. The availability of accurate serologic tests for both diagnosis and compliance measurement has greatly reduced the need for second biopsies or for gluten challenges. However, second biopsies may occasionally be necessary for those who have an unsatisfactory response to treatment [145]. Gluten restriction from the diet results in clinical and histologic improvement: enterocytes assume a more columnar appearance, and intraepithelial lymphocytes and lamina propria inflammation decrease. Full restoration of villus architecture may take up to several years in adults, and may be quicker in children [146]. After a gluten-free diet of 2 years, complete normalization of the intestinal mucosa was observed in two-thirds of pediatric patients but less than one-third of adults despite normalization of laboratory values [147].

## ALLERGIC ENTEROPATHY AND EOSINOPHILIC GASTROENTERITIS

### Introduction

Food allergy/hypersensitivity disorders can be defined as adverse immune-mediated reactions to food, in contrast to other nonimmune adverse food reactions. They include life-threatening allergic reactions as well as more chronic diseases such as eosinophilic gastroenteritis and celiac disease. Food allergies seem to affect between 6% and 8% of children in the United States and the United Kingdom, and studies in both countries seem to have confirmed that the prevalence of food allergy has increased in the last 10 to 15 years [148,149]. Immune mechanisms responsible for food allergy can be categorized into 3 general types: IgE-mediated disorders, cell-mediated disorders (without detectable IgE antibodies), and mixed IgE and cell-mediated responses.

IgE-mediated food allergies, such as gastrointestinal anaphylaxis or oral allergy syndrome are usually diagnosed clinically, and rarely (if ever) biopsied. On the other hand, mixed IgE and cell-mediated disorders are frequently encountered by the pathologist. A recent survey of eosinophilic gastrointestinal disease in the United States reported an overall prevalence rate of 52 and 28/100,000 for eosinophilic esophagitis and eosinophilic gastroenteritis (EG)/colitis, respectively, higher in urban versus rural settings and with a greater prevalence in the northeastern United States [150]. By comparison, the prevalence rate of celiac disease in the United States is about 625/100,000 (or 1/160). Cell-mediated and mixed IgE and cell-mediated disorders can be divided into the following categories:

- Eosinophilic esophagitis and gastroenteritis
- Food protein–induced enterocolitis
- Allergic (dietary protein) colitis and/or proctitis
- Gluten-induced enteropathy (celiac disease)

A discussion of eosinophilic esophagitis is beyond the scope of this article, and celiac disease is discussed in the previous section.

## EG

*Clinical presentation and diagnosis*

EG can be broadly defined by the presence of gastrointestinal symptoms with a pathologic eosinophilic infiltrate of 1 or more segments of the GI tract (typically the stomach and small bowel) without evidence of parasitic infection or other causes of secondary eosinophilic infiltration [151]. It seems to be most common in adults during the third and fourth decades, but has also been observed in pediatric patients of all ages. The foreign antigenic substances are mainly cow's milk in the infant, and egg and soy protein in the older child. Many of these allergic reactions are temporary, and seem to wane with age. Cross-reactivity between substances causing GI and respiratory allergic reactions has been demonstrated. Predisposing factors in the child include a family history of atopy, IgA deficiency, early exposure to the antigen, and preceding gastrointestinal infection possibly even including infection by *Helicobacter pylori* [152]. Symptoms depend on the location of the infiltrate, but most frequently include GI hemorrhage, nausea, vomiting, and diarrhea, although pancreatitis [153], abdominal mass [154], intestinal perforation [155], and duodenal ulcers [156] have also been reported. Some patients may develop a protein-losing enteropathy [157,158]. Peripheral eosinophilia is usually, but not always, increased [151]. Confirmation may include supervised food challenges and radioallergosorbent testing [159].

*Pathology*

Eosinophilic inflammation may involve 1 or more layers of the GI tract, and in 1970 Klein and colleagues [160] proposed a pathologic classification linked to the predominant level of eosinophilic infiltration: mucosal, mural, or serosal involvement. Mucosal involvement is by far the most common. In a recent survey of adult patients from the Mayo Clinic, 52/59 patients had mucosal involvement, 3 had mural involvement and in 4 the involvement was serosal [161]. As eosinophils are normal residents and part of the innate immune system of the GI tract, determining what constitutes a pathologic increase in the numbers of eosinophils can be problematic. Eosinophils (and other constituent inflammatory cells) in the bowel seem to follow a bell-shaped gradient with a zenith in the terminal ileum and cecum. Normal numbers of eosinophils may show geographic variation in the United States, with higher numbers of eosinophils observed in the southern United States compared with the north [162], and may also follow a seasonal distribution [163]. According to the few studies available on children, the mean numbers of eosinophils may reach up to 40 to 50 per high power field (HPF) in the cecum and ascending colon, decreasing to 10 to 20 eosinophils/HPF in the distal colon and rectum [164,165]. Given the absence of clear criteria on what constitutes pathologic eosinophilia, it is perhaps more prudent for the pathologist to suggest a diagnosis of EG when associated features indicating epithelial damage are also present [166,167]. Thus, small intestinal biopsies in EG usually reveal variable villus atrophy with some blunting, which can be focal (Fig. 8) [168]. Increased numbers of degranulated and intact eosinophils are present in the lamina propria, frequently with infiltration of the epithelium. There frequently is concomitant involvement of other portions of the GI tract, particularly the gastric antrum. Ulcers and eosinophilic microabscesses may be observed. Other diagnoses also need to be considered, such as immunodeficiency or chronic inflammatory bowel disease, and the pathologist should also look for features suggesting other diagnoses, ie, granulomas in Crohn disease. Increased numbers of eosinophils without epithelial damage, a situation not infrequently encountered in biopsy material, may nonetheless be evidence of a hypersensitivity-related disease, allowing for the segment of bowel involved and the possibility of normal geographic variation [169]. In that situation, the diagnosis of EG should be used with caution to avoid unwarranted therapy with steroids [166]. The mural form of eosinophilic enteropathy is more commonly seen in children, but can occur at any age. It results primarily in obstructive symptoms, and can involve any portion of the GI tract, although the antrum is the most frequent site. The diagnosis can be confirmed on specimens obtained at laparoscopy and laparotomy [170]. The serosal form is the

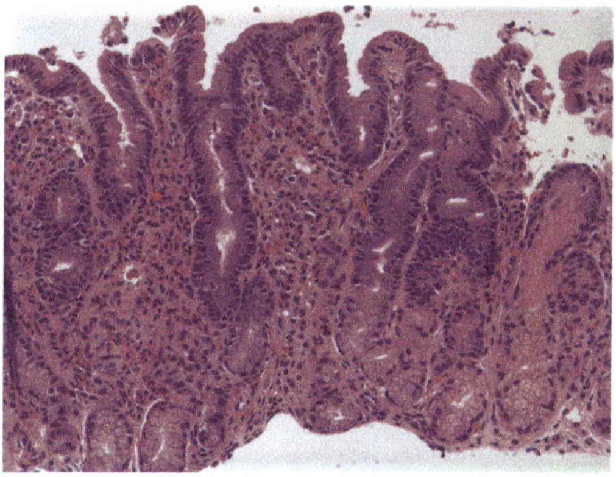

**Fig. 8.** Eosinophilic gastroenteritis. Duodenal biopsy from a 12-year-old boy with food allergy and increased eosinophils throughout the gastrointestinal tract. Note numerous eosinophils (and plasma cells) in association with villous atrophy and crypt distortion (all H&E, ×200).

rarest, typically causing ascites and abdominal pain, and can be diagnosed by paracentesis [171].

*Differential diagnosis*

Although eosinophilic infiltration of the GI tract is the defining feature of EG, not all food hypersensitivity reactions manifest with tissue eosinophilia, whereas eosinophilic infiltration of the GI tract includes numerous secondary causes that do not have an allergic basis. The differential diagnosis of EG includes parasitic infestation and other infections, drug reactions, Crohn disease, some primary immunodeficiencies, connective tissue disorders, inflammatory fibroid polyps, and the hypereosinophilic syndrome (Table 5). Posttransplant EG has been reported in patients on immunomodulator therapy who developed intestinal symptomatology with peripheral eosinophilia and an IgE-positive radioallergosorbent test for milk protein [172,173]. It is postulated that immunosuppressants such as cyclosporine and tacrolimus may play a role in initiating food allergy.

*Treatment and outcomes*

There is a paucity of controlled studies on the treatment and outcome of EG, but the mainstay of treatment seems to be dietary therapy and corticosteroids. According to a recent study, about 40% of adult patients had a spontaneous remission, and although most patients responded favorably to steroids, 50% had relapses and a chronic course [151]. Children seem to respond to an elemental diet, although food sensitivity persists in most cases [158]. Immunosuppression may be required in severe cases [174].

**Table 5**
Eosinophilic gastroenteropathies: differential diagnosis and helpful distinguishing features

| Entity | Distinguishing features |
|---|---|
| Infections, particularly parasitic | Stool for ova and parasites<br>Stool *Giardia* antigen, serology |
| *Helicobacter pylori* | |
| Medications | History of drug use: interferon, enalapril, cotrimoxazole, carbamazepine, aspirin, chlorpropamide, rifampicin |
| Crohn disease | May primarily show eosinophilic abscesses<br>Typically more of a focal lesion |
| Some primary immunodeficiencies: Omenn syndrome, hyper-IgE syndrome | History of frequent infections<br>Infectious agents in biopsy |
| Inflammatory fibroid polyp | Obstructive symptoms<br>Appearance of lesion on endoscopy |
| Posttransplant eosinophilic gastroenteritis | Use of immunomodulators such as tacrolimus |
| Connective tissue disorders (Churg-Strauss, polyarteritis nodosa) | Systemic disease with involvement of other organs<br>Fibrinoid changes in vessels |
| Hypereosinophilic syndrome | Other organ involvement, particularly soft tissue, heart, and central nervous system |

## Food protein-induced enterocolitis

*Clinical presentation and natural history*

Food protein-induced enterocolitis (FPIES) is a non–IgE-mediated GI food hypersensitivity disorder closely related to EG. Unlike EG, it usually presents acutely in infancy as profuse repetitive vomiting, diarrhea, dehydration, and lethargy, or more chronically as failure to thrive [175]. The cumulative incidence in 1 study was 0.34% of infants followed over a 2-year period [176]. The disease is most often triggered by cow's milk or soy, although a large variety of foods may also be allergens. Rice seems to be the most common solid food causing FPIES [175]. Management consists of removing the offending food from the diet. Feeding with an elemental diet is often necessary. FPIES resolves in most cases early in childhood.

*Pathology*

As the diagnosis of FPIES is mainly clinical, biopsies are not routinely performed, and description of pathologic features is scanty. Active colitis has been described, along with variable villous atrophy of the small bowel. Mucosal eosinophils may or may not be increased [177].

## Allergic (dietary protein) colitis and/or proctitis

*Clinical features and natural history*

Allergic proctitis/colitis is a disease of infants, presenting during the first 2 months of life with rectal bleeding shortly after the introduction of cow's milk or soy protein formulae. It also commonly occurs in breast-fed infants; cow's milk protein ingested by the mother is the triggering agent in breast milk [157]. There is evidence that minute amounts of substances in breast milk may act as allergens in the infant [178]. Growth is usually not affected, and peripheral eosinophilia is variable. Exclusion of other causes of rectal bleeding, such as infection, necrotizing enterocolitis, intussusception, and anal fissure is essential. Biopsies may be performed to rule out Hirschsprung disease in those infants presenting primarily with constipation. Endoscopic features include erythema, mucosal friability and focal erosions, and nodularity, the latter suggestive of nodular lymphoid hyperplasia. Disease is usually limited to the distal colon [179]. Eosinophils may be observed in stool smears, which should also be obtained to detect parasitic infection.

*Pathology*

The most characteristic biopsy findings are acute inflammation featuring increased numbers of eosinophils, usually with neutrophils, in all compartments of the mucosa, frequently infiltrating crypts (Fig. 9). The mucosal architecture is well preserved, and significant crypt architectural distortion is distinctly unusual and, if present, should suggest other disorders. Nodular lymphoid hyperplasia is a frequent concomitant finding. Increased eosinophil count to greater than 20/HPF, peripheral blood eosinophilia, and a low serum albumen level are the usual diagnostic features [180]. Eosinophil numbers may also vary as a result of dietary withdrawal therapies empirically attempted before obtaining the biopsies.

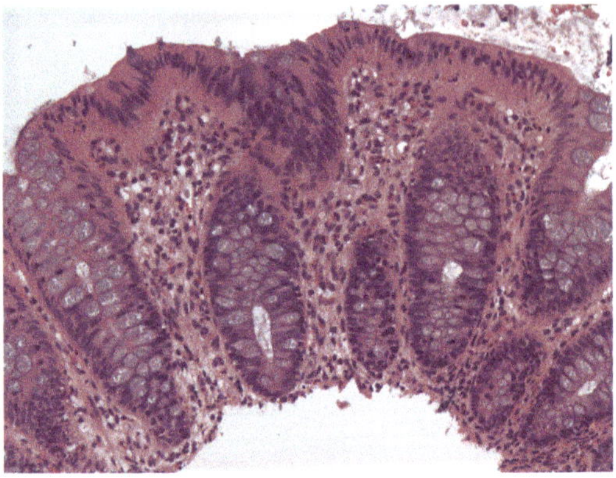

**Fig. 9.** An 18-day-old girl with bloody diarrhea caused by milk allergy. The biopsy features an increased number of eosinophils, frequently clustered, with infiltration of surface and crypt epithelium (H&E, ×200).

The differential diagnosis includes parasitic infections, such as *Dientamoeba fragilis*, which can be identified in stool smears [181]. Eosinophilic infiltrates can also be seen in cases of Hirschsprung disease [182] and, conversely, the clinical and radiologic features of allergic colitis can occasionally mimic aganglionosis [183,184]. The treatment is dietary change to a hypoallergenic formula. The condition is temporary, with most patients able to tolerate milk after 2 years of age.

## Lymphangiectasia

*Clinical manifestations and differential diagnosis*

Intestinal lymphangiectasia may be primary or secondary, and results in protein-losing enteropathy. Primary lymphangiectasia is a rare disorder usually diagnosed in children less than 3 years of age, who present with diarrhea, protein-losing enteropathy, hypoalbuminemia, hypogammaglobulinemia, and lymphopenia, resulting in secondary immunodeficiency. Malabsorption may cause deficiencies in fat-soluble vitamins. Primary disorders seem to result from congenital obstruction to lymph flow or abnormal lymphatic structure, and may be essentially limited to intestinal lymphatics, as in primary lymphangiectasia [185,186], or may involve multiple organs, as in hereditary lymphedema, also known as Milroy disease, associated with mutations in the gene encoding vascular endothelial growth receptor factor 3 [187–189]. Other disorders may be associated with characteristic congenital anomalies, such as the Turner, Noonan, and Hennekam syndromes [190,191]. Intestinal lymphangiectasia has also been reported in premature infants [192]. It has been postulated that congenital hypoplasia of lymphatics may also cause protein-losing enteropathy in neonates [193].

Secondary lymphangiectasia may be central, resulting from cardiac disease, or from local obstruction to lymphatics due to a variety of causes. In children, secondary immunodeficiency resulting from extensive protein losses in the stools has been reported with intestinal malrotation and cavernous hemangioma of the jejunum [194]. Cardiac causes of lymphangiectasia with protein-losing enteropathy usually result from obstruction to systemic venous return or from surgical procedures that cause increased systemic venous pressure [195,196]. Protein-losing enteropathy occurs in up to 10% of patients who have undergone the Fontan operation for correction of tricuspid atresia and other right-sided cardiac malformations, and carries a poor prognosis, with a 5-year survival rate of about 50% [197]. This procedure creates a direct communication between the systemic venous return and the pulmonary arterial system, resulting in chronically sustained increased systemic venous pressure. Associated factors that may contribute to protein-losing enteropathy in these patients include inflammatory mediators, decreased enterocyte heparin sulfate synthesis, and chronic mesenteric ischemia [198]. Localized forms of intestinal lymphangiectasia may be amenable to surgical resection [199].

*Pathologic features*

The endoscopic appearance is usually characteristic, with swollen opaque villi, white nodules, or submucosal elevations [200,201]. Histologic examination reveals blunted villi with dilated lacteals (Fig. 10). The finding of occasional dilated lymphatics in a biopsy of a patient without significant symptoms is not infrequent and of no diagnostic value. Conversely, mucosal biopsies may be nondiagnostic when the lesions are focal, and almost always miss lymphangiectasia of deeper layers of the bowel wall.

## METABOLIC DISORDERS AND TUMORS

### Metabolic diseases

Several congenital disorders of glycosylation (CDG) are associated with prominent GI manifestations. These are part of a large group of disorders related to

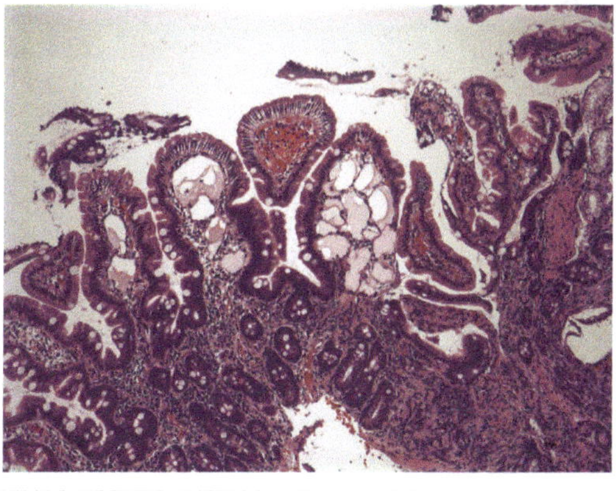

**Fig. 10.** Lymphangiectasia. The duodenal biopsy reveals distorted villi with dilated lymphatics (H&E, ×100).

defects in the synthesis and attachment of glycans to proteins and lipids, and currently comprise about 24 entities, most of which present with neurologic manifestations. Failure to thrive with diarrhea, protein-losing enteropathy, and hepatic abnormalities have been described mainly in phosphomannose isomerase deficiency (MPI-CDG, formerly CDG type Ib) and ALG6-CDG (formerly CDG type Ic) [202–204]. Small bowel biopsies are generally unremarkable or show mild nonspecific villous atrophy and inflammation unresponsive to gluten or cow's milk withdrawal; electron microscopic changes are characterized by distension of the smooth endoplasmic reticulum with lipid-containing inclusions [205] or insoluble precipitated protein [206]. Absence or marked reduction in the level of enterocyte heparan sulfate may explain the protein-losing enteropathy [207,208]. Reported hepatic abnormalities range from mild degrees of steatosis to congenital hepatic fibrosis; congenital hepatic fibrosis, without renal cysts, may be the only feature of MPI-CGD [203]. Dilatation of the crypts of the large intestine has also been observed in some cases (Fig. 11) [209]. A diagnosis of CDG can be confirmed by isoelectric focusing of serum transferrin; MPI-CDG can be treated with mannose. Murch [207] described 3 infant boys with massive diarrhea associated with abnormal intestinal glycosaminoglycans with a complete absence of heparan sulfate.

According to a report from a consortium of European centers [210], almost half of the patients with glycogen storage disease type Ib manifest protracted diarrhea and a clinical profile similar to chronic inflammatory bowel disease; defects in neutrophil function may underlie the enteritis in these patients. Several disorders resulting from deficient lysosomal degradation of glycoconjugates can present with severe diarrhea of infancy. Chronic diarrhea can be a feature of mucopolysaccharidoses (MPS), and has been reported with MPS III (Sanfilippo) (Fig. 12) [211]; nodular infiltration of the bowel wall may be noted endoscopically, although the diarrhea is likely most often caused by impairment of the autonomic nervous system. Infiltration of the mucosa and marked distortion

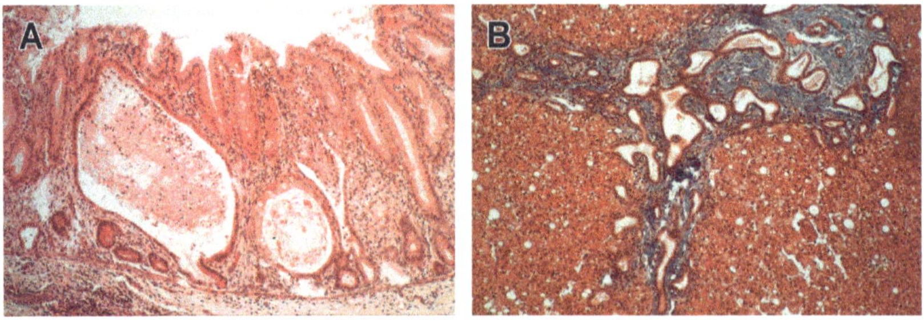


**Fig. 11.** Metabolic disease. Phosphomannose isomerase deficiency (MPI-CDG, CDG type Ib). (*A*) Cystically dilated crypts were noted in the colon of this 3-month-old boy. The duodenal biopsies were characterized by mildly dilated lymphatics (not shown). (*B*) The liver at autopsy had typical features of congenital hepatic fibrosis. The kidneys were normal, with no evidence of cystic disease (H&E, ×100).

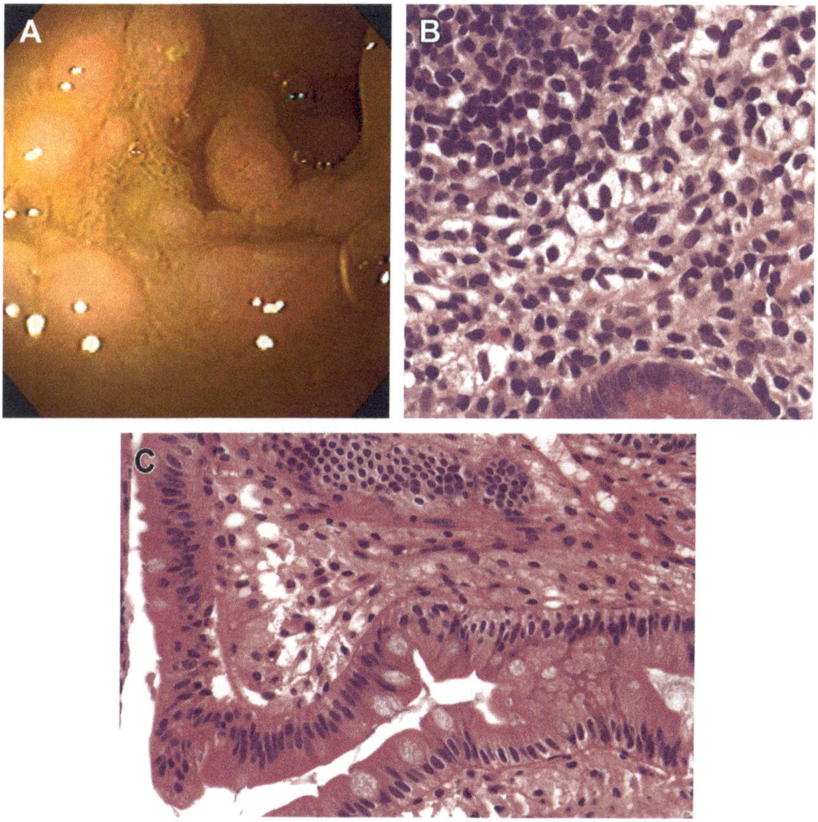


**Fig. 12.** Metabolic disease. (*A*) At endoscopy, multiple large erythematous friable nodules were seen in the bowel of this 1-year-old child with mucopolysaccharidosis type III. (*B*) The biopsy revealed small clusters of clear finely vacuolated macrophages. (*C*) Clusters of foamy macrophages are readily observed in this small bowel biopsy from a patient with Wolman disease (*B*, *C*, H&E, ×200). (*Courtesy of* Pierre Brochu, MD, Hôpital Ste-Justine, Montreal, Quebec.)

of the villi by foamy macrophages is characteristic of Wolman disease; shortening of the microvilli and impairment of disaccharidase activity are likely to underlie the diarrhea observed in these patients [212]. Tangier disease is a high-density lipoprotein deficiency syndrome characterized by accumulation of cholesterol in tissue macrophages throughout the body and prevalent atherosclerosis, resulting from mutations in the gene coding for ATP-binding cassette transporter 1 (*ABCA1*). Endoscopic examination reveals characteristic orange nodules in the mucosa, with accumulation of fat noted in the macrophages in the lamina propria and smooth muscle cells [213].

Glycolipid storage disorders are generally characterized in the GI tract by the presence of lipid deposits in Schwann cells, ganglia, muscle, and endothelial cells [214,215], usually without symptoms attributable to the deposits. However, more than half of the patients with Fabry disease, an X-linked disorder resulting in deficiency of α-galactosidase, experience gastrointestinal symptoms mimicking irritable bowel syndrome. There is accumulation of a lipid, globotriaosylceramide, in the enteric neurons interfering with normal gut motility and resulting in delayed gastric emptying, bacterial overgrowth, and subsequent diarrhea and steatorrhea [216]. Enzyme replacement therapy with agalsidase alfa has improved symptoms in these patients [217]. Severe protracted diarrhea in association with low cholesterol levels in the first month of life are important manifestations of some the more severe forms of peroxisomal disorders such as infantile Refsum disease [218]; this clinical presentation must be differentiated from lipid transport disorders such as abetalipoproteinemia. Cormier-Daire and colleagues [219] reported 2 infants with chronic diarrhea and villous atrophy due a respiratory chain complex III deficiency associated with mitochondrial DNA mutations; severe diarrhea has been described as a presenting manifestation in other disorders associated with mitochondrial DNA rearrangements [220]. Infantile systemic hyalinosis is a rare, apparently autosomal recessive disorder characterized by painful

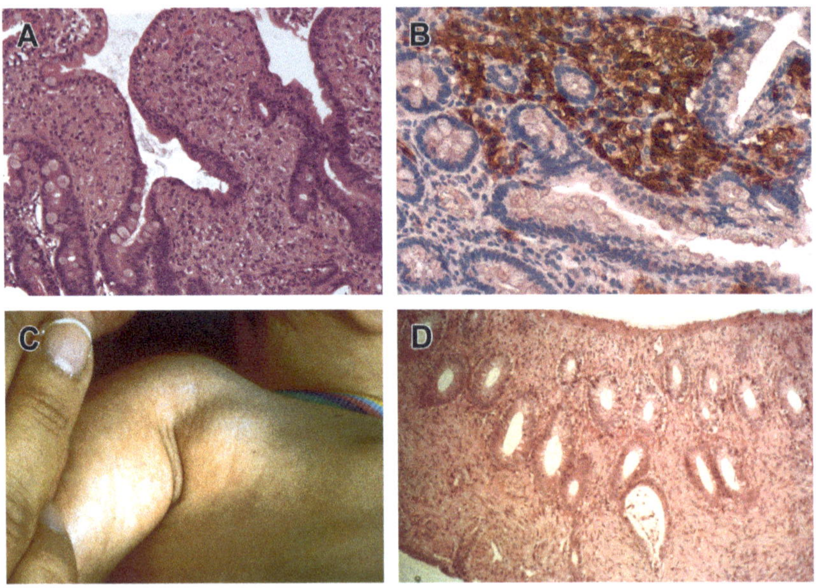


**Fig. 13.** Neoplastic infiltrates. (*A*) Langerhans cell histiocytosis of the bowel in this 1-month-old boy with a skin rash and diarrhea. The villi are distended and blunted by the infiltrate (H&E, ×200). (*B*) Immunohistochemistry for CD1a characteristically stains the infiltrating cells (H&E, ×400). (*C*) This 1-month-old boy presented with multiple subcutaneous nodules and diarrhea. Biopsy of 1 of the nodules was consistent with myofibromatosis. (*D*) Multiple colonic biopsies also revealed widespread involvement of the mucosa by myofibromatosis (H&E, ×200).

joint contractures and skin nodules resulting from widespread deposits of a hyaline substance in the skin, skeletal muscle, GI tract, and endocrine organs, well documented by Landing and Nadorra [221], although the first description of the disease was probably by Nezelof and colleagues [222]. Protein-losing enteropathy caused by intestinal lymphangiectasia has been described in many of these patients [223,224]. On electron microscopy, floccular amorphous material was observed around blood vessels in the dermis, and postulated to interfere with collagen formation [225]. The exact biochemical defect is unknown.

## Neoplastic disorders

Neoplasms rarely present as chronic diarrhea in children, especially infants and toddlers, although occasionally diarrhea may be a major or presenting manifestation. Some neoplasms cause symptoms by direct infiltration of the bowel wall, or by secretion of a hormone or substance that is active in the GI tract. Diffuse infiltration of the bowel resulting in severe diarrhea in neonates has been reported with Langerhans cell histiocytosis [226,227] and visceral myofibromatosis (Fig. 13) [228]. Neuroblastomas and ganglioneuroblastomas presenting with watery diarrhea, hypokalemia, and achlorhydria have been documented in numerous reports.

## References

[1] Avery GB, Villavicencio O, Lilly JR, et al. Intractable diarrhea in early infancy. Pediatrics 1968;41(4):712–22.
[2] Franciosi JP, Fiorino K, Ruchelli E, et al. Changing indications for upper endoscopy in children during a 20-year period. J Pediatr Gastroenterol Nutr 2010;51(4):443–7.
[3] Volonaki E, Sebire NJ, Borrelli O, et al. Gastrointestinal endoscopy and mucosal biopsy in the first year of life: indications and outcome. J Pediatr Gastroenterol Nutr 2012;55(1):62–5.
[4] Bonamico M, Mariani P, Thanasi E, et al. Patchy villous atrophy of the duodenum in childhood celiac disease. J Pediatr Gastroenterol Nutr 2004;38(2):204–7.
[5] Levinson-Castiel R, Hartman C, Morgenstern S, et al. The role of duodenal bulb biopsy in the diagnosis of celiac disease in children. J Clin Gastroenterol 2011;45(1):26–9.
[6] De Matos V, Russo PA, Cohen AB, et al. Frequency and clinical correlations of granulomas in children with Crohn disease. J Pediatr Gastroenterol Nutr 2008;46(4):392–8.
[7] Kori M, Gladish V, Ziv-Sokolovskaya N, et al. The significance of routine duodenal biopsies in pediatric patients undergoing upper intestinal endoscopy. J Clin Gastroenterol 2003;37(1):39–41.
[8] Gramlich T, Petras R. Small intestine. In: Mills SE, editor. Histology for pathologists. Philadelphia: Lippincott Williams & Wilkins; 2007. p. 603–26.
[9] Serra S, Jani PA. An approach to duodenal biopsies. J Clin Pathol 2006;59(11):1133–50.
[10] Naim HY, Zimmer KP. Geneticallt determined Disaccharidase Deficiency. In: Walker WA, Goulet O, Kleinman RE, et al, editors. Pediatric Gastrointestinal Disease. 4th Edition, Volume 1. Hamilton (Canada): BC Decker. p. 880–97.
[11] Gudmand-Hoyer E, Fenger HJ, Skovbjerg H, et al. Trehalase deficiency in Greenland. Scand J Gastroenterol 1988;23(7):775–8.
[12] Welsh JD, Poley JR, Bhatia M, et al. Intestinal disaccharidase activities in relation to age, race, and mucosal damage. Gastroenterology 1978;75(5):847–55.

[13] Hediger MA, Budarf ML, Emanuel BS, et al. Assignment of the human intestinal Na+/glucose cotransporter gene (SGLT1) to the q11.2—qter region of chromosome 22. Genomics 1989;4(3):297–300.
[14] Hediger MA, Kanai Y, You G, et al. Mammalian ion-coupled solute transporters. J Physiol 1995;482:7S–17S.
[15] Wetterau JR, Aggerbeck LP, Bouma ME, et al. Absence of microsomal triglyceride transfer protein in individuals with abetalipoproteinemia. Science 1992;258(5084):999–1001.
[16] Berriot-Varoqueaux N, Aggerbeck LP, Samson-Bouma M, et al. The role of the microsomal triglyceride transfer protein in abetalipoproteinemia. Annu Rev Nutr 2000;20:663–97.
[17] Peretti N, Sassolas A, Roy CC, et al. Guidelines for the diagnosis and management of chylomicron retention disease based on a review of the literature and the experience of two centers. Orphanet J Rare Dis 2010;5:24.
[18] Jones B, Jones EL, Bonney SA, et al. Mutations in a Sar1 GTPase of COPII vesicles are associated with lipid absorption disorders. Nat Genet 2003;34(1):29–31.
[19] Avigan MI, Ishak KG, Gregg RE, et al. Morphologic features of the liver in abetalipoproteinemia. Hepatology 1984;4(6):1223–6.
[20] Black DD, Hay RV, Rohwer-Nutter PL, et al. Intestinal and hepatic apolipoprotein B gene expression in abetalipoproteinemia. Gastroenterology 1991;101(2):520–8.
[21] Chillaron J, Roca R, Valencia A, et al. Heteromeric amino acid transporters: biochemistry, genetics, and physiology. Am J Physiol Renal Physiol 2001;281(6):F995–1018.
[22] Sebastio G, Sperandeo MP, Andria G. Lysinuric protein intolerance: reviewing concepts on a multisystem disease. Am J Med Genet C Semin Med Genet 2011;157(1):54–62.
[23] Sperandeo MP, Andria G, Sebastio G. Lysinuric protein intolerance: update and extended mutation analysis of the SLC7A7 gene. Hum Mutat 2008;29(1):14–21.
[24] Reinoso MA, Whitley C, Jessurun J, et al. Lysinuric protein intolerance masquerading as celiac disease: a case report. J Pediatr 1998;132(1):153–5.
[25] Bader-Meunier B, Parez N, Muller S. Treatment of hemophagocytic lymphohistiocytosis with cyclosporin A and steroids in a boy with lysinuric protein intolerance. J Pediatr 2000;136(1):134.
[26] de Klerk JB, Duran M, Huijmans JG, et al. Sudden infant death and lysinuric protein intolerance. Eur J Pediatr 1996;155(3):256–7.
[27] Kere J, Hoglund P. Inherited disorders of ion transport in the intestine. Curr Opin Genet Dev 2000;10(3):306–9.
[28] Keller KM, Wirth S, Baumann W, et al. Defective jejunal brush border membrane sodium/proton exchange in association with lethal familial protracted diarrhoea. Gut 1990;31(10):1156–8.
[29] Canani RB, Terrin G, Cardillo G, et al. Congenital diarrheal disorders: improved understanding of gene defects is leading to advances in intestinal physiology and clinical management. J Pediatr Gastroenterol Nutr 2010;50(4):360–6.
[30] Canani RB, Terrin G. Recent progress in congenital diarrheal disorders. Curr Gastroenterol Rep 2011;13(3):257–64.
[31] Rodin AE, Goldman AS. Autopsy findings in acrodermatitis enteropathica. Am J Clin Pathol 1969;51(3):315–22.
[32] Suzuki H, Igarashi Y, Konno T, et al. Inclusion bodies in Paneth cells in zinc deficiency. Lancet 1979;1(8118):734.
[33] Variend S, Phillips AD, Walker-Smith JA. The small intestinal mucosal biopsy in childhood. Perspect Pediatr Pathol 1984;8(1):57–78.
[34] Southon S, Gee JM, Bayliss CE, et al. Intestinal microflora, morphology and enzyme activity in zinc-deficient and Zn-supplemented rats. Br J Nutr 1986;55(3):603–11.
[35] Koo SI, Henderson DA, Algilani K, et al. Effect of marginal zinc deficiency on the morphological characteristics of intestinal nascent chylomicrons and distribution of soluble apoproteins of lymph chylomicrons. Am J Clin Nutr 1985;42(4):671–80.

[36] Bacher T, Schonekas H, Steurer KT, et al. The Cronkhite-Canada Syndrome. A rare differential diagnosis of generalized gastrointestinal polyposis. Dtsch Med Wochenschr 1997;122(21):676–81 [in German].
[37] Moller LB, Mogensen M, Horn N. Molecular diagnosis of Menkes disease: genotype-phenotype correlation. Biochimie 2009;91(10):1273–7.
[38] Vulpe C, Levinson B, Whitney S, et al. Isolation of a candidate gene for Menkes disease and evidence that it encodes a copper-transporting ATPase. Nat Genet 1993;3(1):7–13.
[39] Storm T, Emma F, Verroust PJ, et al. A patient with cubilin deficiency. N Engl J Med 2011;364(1):89–91.
[40] Russo P, Doyon J, Sonsino E, et al. A congenital anomaly of vitamin B12 metabolism: a study of three cases. Hum Pathol 1992;23(5):504–12.
[41] Ellaway C, Christodoulou J, Kamath R, et al. The association of protein-losing enteropathy with cobalamin C defect. J Inherit Metab Dis 1998;21(1):17–22.
[42] Heubi JE, Balistreri WF, Fondacaro JD, et al. Primary bile acid malabsorption: defective in vitro ileal active bile acid transport. Gastroenterology 1982;83(4):804–11.
[43] Oelkers P, Kirby LC, Heubi JE, et al. Primary bile acid malabsorption caused by mutations in the ileal sodium- dependent bile acid transporter gene (SLC10A2). J Clin Invest 1997;99(8):1880–7.
[44] Bruno MJ, Haverkort EB, Tytgat GN, et al. Maldigestion associated with exocrine pancreatic insufficiency: implications of gastrointestinal physiology and properties of enzyme preparations for a cause-related and patient-tailored treatment. Am J Gastroenterol 1995;90(9):1383–93.
[45] Ohkohchi N, Andoh T, Izumi U, et al. Disorder of bile acid metabolism in children with short bowel syndrome. J Gastroenterol 1997;32(4):472–9.
[46] Harewood GC, Murray JA. Approaching the patient with chronic malabsorption syndrome. Semin Gastrointest Dis 1999;10(4):138–44.
[47] Stelzner M, Somasundaram S, Khakberdiev T. Systemic effects of acute terminal ileitis on uninflamed gut aggravate bile acid malabsorption. J Surg Res 2001;99(2):359–64.
[48] Ruemmele FM, Schmitz J, Goulet O. Microvillous inclusion disease (microvillous atrophy). Orphanet J Rare Dis 2006;1:22.
[49] Erickson RP, Larson-Thome K, Valenzuela RK, et al. Navajo microvillous inclusion disease is due to a mutation in MYO5B. Am J Med Genet A 2008;146A(24):3117–9.
[50] Muller T, Hess MW, Schiefermeier N, et al. MYO5B mutations cause microvillus inclusion disease and disrupt epithelial cell polarity. Nat Genet 2008;40(10):1163–5.
[51] Halac U, Lacaille F, Joly F, et al. Microvillous inclusion disease: how to improve the prognosis of a severe congenital enterocyte disorder. J Pediatr Gastroenterol Nutr 2011;52(4): 460–5.
[52] Talmon G, Holzapfel M, Dimaio DJ, et al. Rab11 is a useful tool for the diagnosis of microvillous inclusion disease. Int J Surg Pathol 2012;20(3):252–6.
[53] Cutz E, Sherman PM, Davidson GP. Enteropathies associated with protracted diarrhea of infancy: clinicopathological features, cellular and molecular mechanisms. Pediatr Pathol Lab Med 1997;17(3):335–68.
[54] Iancu TC, Mahajnah M, Manov I, et al. The liver in congenital disorders of glycosylation: ultrastructural features. Ultrastruct Pathol 2007;31(3):189–97.
[55] Iancu TC, Mahajnah M, Manov I, et al. Microvillous inclusion disease: ultrastructural variability. Ultrastruct Pathol 2007;31(3):173–88.
[56] Mierau GW, Wills EJ, Wyatt-Ashmead J, et al. Microvillous inclusion disease: report of a case with atypical features. Ultrastruct Pathol 2001;25(3):275–9.
[57] Raafat F, Green NJ, Nathavitharana KA, et al. Intestinal microvillous dystrophy: a variant of microvillous inclusion disease or a new entity? Hum Pathol 1994;25(11):1243–8.
[58] Reifen RM, Cutz E, Griffiths AM, et al. Tufting enteropathy: a newly recognized clinicopathological entity associated with refractory diarrhea in infants. J Pediatr Gastroenterol Nutr 1994;18(3):379–85.

[59] Goulet O, Salomon J, Ruemmele F, et al. Intestinal epithelial dysplasia (tufting enteropathy). Orphanet J Rare Dis 2007;2:20.
[60] Abely M, Hankard GF, Hugot JP, et al. Intractable infant diarrhea with epithelial dysplasia associated with polymalformation. J Pediatr Gastroenterol Nutr 1998;27(3):348–52.
[61] Bird LM, Sivagnanam M, Taylor S, et al. A new syndrome of tufting enteropathy and choanal atresia, with ophthalmologic, hematologic and hair abnormalities. Clin Dysmorphol 2007;16(4):211–21.
[62] Roche O, Putterman M, Salomon J, et al. Superficial punctate keratitis and conjunctival erosions associated with congenital tufting enteropathy. Am J Ophthalmol 2010;150(1): 116–121.e1.
[63] El-Matary W, Dalzell AM, Kokai G, et al. Tufting enteropathy and skeletal dysplasia: is there a link? Eur J Pediatr 2007;166(3):265–8.
[64] Al-Mayouf SM, Alswaied N, Alkuraya FS, et al. Tufting enteropathy and chronic arthritis: a newly recognized association with a novel EpCAM gene mutation. J Pediatr Gastroenterol Nutr 2009;49(5):642–4.
[65] Sivagnanam M, Mueller JL, Lee H, et al. Identification of EpCAM as the gene for congenital tufting enteropathy. Gastroenterology 2008;135(2):429–37.
[66] Carpenter G, Red Brewer M. EpCAM: another surface-to-nucleus missile. Cancer Cell 2009;15(3):165–6.
[67] Kagitani K, Yamamoto T, Miki K, et al. Hypophosphatemic rickets accompanying congenital microvillous atrophy. J Bone Miner Res 1998;13(12):1946–52.
[68] Ng AY, Waring P, Ristevski S, et al. Inactivation of the transcription factor Elf3 in mice results in dysmorphogenesis and altered differentiation of intestinal epithelium. Gastroenterology 2002;122(5):1455–66.
[69] Salomon J, Espinosa-Parrilla Y, Goulet O, et al. A founder effect at the EPCAM locus in Congenital Tufting Enteropathy in the Arabic Gulf. Eur J Med Genet 2011;54(3): 319–22.
[70] Lemale J, Coulomb A, Dubern B, et al. Intractable diarrhea with tufting enteropathy: a favorable outcome is possible. J Pediatr Gastroenterol Nutr 2011;52(6):734–9.
[71] Sivagnanam M, Janecke AR, Muller T, et al. Case of syndromic tufting enteropathy harbors SPINT2 mutation seen in congenital sodium diarrhea. Clin Dysmorphol 2010;19(1):48.
[72] Lachaux A, Bouvier R, Loras-Duclaux I, et al. Isolated deficient alpha6beta4 integrin expression in the gut associated with intractable diarrhea. J Pediatr Gastroenterol Nutr 1999;29(4):395–401.
[73] Korber JS, Glasson MJ. Pyloric atresia associated with epidermolysis bullosa. J Pediatr 1977;90(4):600–1.
[74] Wang J, Cortina G, Wu SV, et al. Mutant neurogenin-3 in congenital malabsorptive diarrhea. N Engl J Med 2006;355(3):270–80.
[75] Pinney SE, Oliver-Krasinski J, Ernst L, et al. Neonatal diabetes and congenital malabsorptive diarrhea attributable to a novel mutation in the human neurogenin-3 gene coding sequence. J Clin Endocrinol Metab 2011;96(7):1960–5.
[76] Bjerknes M, Cheng H. Neurogenin 3 and the enteroendocrine cell lineage in the adult mouse small intestinal epithelium. Dev Biol 2006;300(2):722–35.
[77] Gradwohl G, Dierich A, LeMeur M, et al. neurogenin3 is required for the development of the four endocrine cell lineages of the pancreas. Proc Natl Acad Sci U S A 2000;97(4): 1607–11.
[78] Cortina G, Smart CN, Farmer DG, et al. Enteroendocrine cell dysgenesis and malabsorption, a histopathologic and immunohistochemical characterization. Hum Pathol 2007;26:26.
[79] Posovszky C, Lahr G, von Schnurbein J, et al. Loss of enteroendocrine cells in autoimmune-polyendocrine-candidiasis-ectodermal-dystrophy (APECED) syndrome with gastrointestinal dysfunction. J Clin Endocrinol Metab 2012;97(2):E292–300.

[80] Hogenauer C, Meyer RL, Netto GJ, et al. Malabsorption due to cholecystokinin deficiency in a patient with autoimmune polyglandular syndrome type I. N Engl J Med 2001;344(4): 270–4.
[81] Girault D, Goulet O, Le Deist F, et al. Intractable infant diarrhea associated with phenotypic abnormalities and immunodeficiency. J Pediatr 1994;125(1):36–42.
[82] Stankler L, Lloyd D, Pollitt RJ, et al. Unexplained diarrhoea and failure to thrive in 2 siblings with unusual facies and abnormal scalp hair shafts: a new syndrome. Arch Dis Child 1982;57(3):212–6.
[83] Verloes A, Lombet J, Lambert Y, et al. Tricho-hepato-enteric syndrome: further delineation of a distinct syndrome with neonatal hemochromatosis phenotype, intractable diarrhea, and hair anomalies. Am J Med Genet 1997;68(4):391–5.
[84] Fabre A, Andre N, Breton A, et al. Intractable diarrhea with "phenotypic anomalies" and tricho-hepato-enteric syndrome: two names for the same disorder. Am J Med Genet A 2007;143(6):584–8.
[85] Hartley JL, Zachos NC, Dawood B, et al. Mutations in TTC37 cause trichohepatoenteric syndrome (phenotypic diarrhea of infancy). Gastroenterology 2010;138(7):2388–98, 2398.e1–2.
[86] Fabre A, Martinez-Vinson C, Roquelaure B, et al. Novel mutations in TTC37 associated with tricho-hepato-enteric syndrome. Hum Mutat 2011;32(3):277–81.
[87] Montalto M, D'Onofrio F, Santoro L, et al. Autoimmune enteropathy in children and adults. Scand J Gastroenterol 2009;44(9):1029–36.
[88] Seidman EG, Lacaille F, Russo P, et al. Successful treatment of autoimmune enteropathy with cyclosporine. J Pediatr 1990;117(6):929–32.
[89] Akram S, Murray JA, Pardi DS, et al. Adult autoimmune enteropathy: Mayo Clinic Rochester experience. Clin Gastroenterol Hepatol 2007;5(11):1282–90 [quiz: 1245].
[90] Carroccio A, Volta U, Di Prima L, et al. Autoimmune enteropathy and colitis in an adult patient. Dig Dis Sci 2003;48(8):1600–6.
[91] Corazza GR, Biagi F, Volta U, et al. Autoimmune enteropathy and villous atrophy in adults. Lancet 1997;350(9071):106–9.
[92] Daum S, Sahin E, Jansen A, et al. Adult autoimmune enteropathy treated successfully with tacrolimus. Digestion 2003;68(2–3):86–90.
[93] Mais DD, Mulhall BP, Adolphson KR, et al. Thymoma-associated autoimmune enteropathy. A report of two cases. Am J Clin Pathol 1999;112(6):810–5.
[94] Marthinsen LM, Scott H, Ejderhamn J. Autoimmune enteropathy in Swedish children, 1985-2002: a call for strict diagnostic criteria. Scand J Gastroenterol 2008;43(9): 1102–7.
[95] Mirakian R, Collins P, Bottazzo GF. Autoimmune enteropathy in adults. Lancet 1997;350(9082):959–60.
[96] Mitomi H, Tanabe S, Igarashi M, et al. Autoimmune enteropathy with severe atrophic gastritis and colitis in an adult: proposal of a generalized autoimmune disorder of the alimentary tract. Scand J Gastroenterol 1998;33(7):716–20.
[97] Powell BR, Buist NR, Stenzel P. An X-linked syndrome of diarrhea, polyendocrinopathy, and fatal infection in infancy. J Pediatr 1982;100(5):731–7.
[98] Patey-Mariaud de Serre N, Canioni D, Ganousse S, et al. Digestive histopathological presentation of IPEX syndrome. Mod Pathol 2009;22(1):95–102.
[99] Bennett CL, Christie J, Ramsdell F, et al. The immune dysregulation, polyendocrinopathy, enteropathy, X-linked syndrome (IPEX) is caused by mutations of FOXP3. Nat Genet 2001;27(1):20–1.
[100] Ochs HD, Gambineri E, Torgerson TR. IPEX, FOXP3 and regulatory T-cells: a model for autoimmunity. Immunol Res 2007;38(1–3):112–21.
[101] Ochs HD, Torgerson TR. Immune dysregulation, polyendocrinopathy, enteropathy, X-linked inheritance: model for autoaggression. Adv Exp Med Biol 2007;601: 27–36.

[102] Torgerson TR, Ochs HD. Immune dysregulation, polyendocrinopathy, enteropathy, X-linked: forkhead box protein 3 mutations and lack of regulatory T cells. J Allergy Clin Immunol 2007;120(4):744–50 [quiz: 751–2].
[103] Yong PL, Russo P, Sullivan KE. Use of sirolimus in IPEX and IPEX-like children. J Clin Immunol 2008;28(5):581–7.
[104] Mirakian R, Richardson A, Milla PJ, et al. Protracted diarrhoea of infancy: evidence in support of an autoimmune variant. Br Med J (Clin Res Ed) 1986;293(6555):1132–6.
[105] Russo PA, Brochu P, Seidman EG, et al. Autoimmune enteropathy. Pediatr Dev Pathol 1999;2(1):65–71.
[106] Savage MO, Mirakian R, Wozniak ER, et al. Specific autoantibodies to gut epithelium in two infants with severe protracted diarrhoea. J Pediatr Gastroenterol Nutr 1985;4(2):187–95.
[107] Unsworth J, Hutchins P, Mitchell J, et al. Flat small intestinal mucosa and autoantibodies against the gut epithelium. J Pediatr Gastroenterol Nutr 1982;1(4):503–13.
[108] Charritat JL, Polonovski C. Pediatric autoimmune enteropathies with anti-cytoplasmic enterocytic auto-antibodies. Ann Pediatr (Paris) 1987;34(3):195–203 [in French].
[109] Moore L, Xu X, Davidson G, et al. Autoimmune enteropathy with anti-goblet cell antibodies. Hum Pathol 1995;26(10):1162–8.
[110] Rogahn D, Smith CP, Thomas A. Autoimmune enteropathy with goblet-cell antibodies. J R Soc Med 1999;92(6):311–2.
[111] Kobayashi I, Imamura K, Yamada M, et al. A 75-kD autoantigen recognized by sera from patients with X-linked autoimmune enteropathy associated with nephropathy. Clin Exp Immunol 1998;111(3):527–31.
[112] Kobayashi I, Kubota M, Yamada M, et al. Autoantibodies to villin occur frequently in IPEX, a severe immune dysregulation, syndrome caused by mutation of FOXP3. Clin Immunol 2011;141(1):83–9.
[113] Martin-Villa JM, Camblor S, Costa R, et al. Gut epithelial cell autoantibodies in AIDS pathogenesis. Lancet 1993;342(8867):380.
[114] Folwaczny C, Noehl N, Tschop K, et al. Goblet cell autoantibodies in patients with inflammatory bowel disease and their first-degree relatives. Gastroenterology 1997;113(1): 101–6.
[115] Biagi F, Bianchi PI, Trotta L, et al. Anti-goblet cell antibodies for the diagnosis of autoimmune enteropathy? Am J Gastroenterol 2009;104(12):3112.
[116] Morell A, Skvaril F, Hitzig WH, et al. IgG subclasses: development of the serum concentrations in "normal" infants and children. J Pediatr 1972;80(6):960–4.
[117] Heltzer ML, Choi JK, Ochs HD, et al. A potential screening tool for IPEX syndrome. Pediatr Dev Pathol 2007;10(2):98–105.
[118] Guerrerio AL, Frischmeyer-Guerrerio PA, Lederman HM, et al. Recognizing gastrointestinal and hepatic manifestations of primary immunodeficiency diseases. J Pediatr Gastroenterol Nutr 2010;51(5):548–55.
[119] Kampe O. Introduction: autoimmune polyendocrine syndrome type 1 (APS-1): a rare monogenic disorder as a model to improve understanding of tolerance and autoimmunity. J Intern Med 2009;265(5):511–3.
[120] Betterle C, Greggio NA, Volpato M. Clinical review 93: autoimmune polyglandular syndrome type 1. J Clin Endocrinol Metab 1998;83(4):1049–55.
[121] Rodrigues AF, Jenkins HR. Investigation and management of coeliac disease. Arch Dis Child 2008;93(3):251–4.
[122] Fasano A. Clinical presentation of celiac disease in the pediatric population. Gastroenterology 2005;128(4 Suppl 1):S68–73.
[123] Husby S, Koletzko S, Korponay-Szabo IR, et al. European Society for Pediatric Gastroenterology, Hepatology, and Nutrition guidelines for the diagnosis of coeliac disease. J Pediatr Gastroenterol Nutr 2012;54(1):136–60.
[124] Ascher H, Krantz I, Rydberg L, et al. Influence of infant feeding and gluten intake on coeliac disease. Arch Dis Child 1997;76(2):113–7.

[125] Hill ID, Dirks MH, Liptak GS, et al. Guideline for the diagnosis and treatment of celiac disease in children: recommendations of the North American Society for Pediatric Gastroenterology, Hepatology and Nutrition. J Pediatr Gastroenterol Nutr 2005;40(1):1–19.
[126] Tumer L, Hasanoglu A, Aybay C. Endomysium antibodies in the diagnosis of celiac disease in short-statured children with no gastrointestinal symptoms. Pediatr Int 2001;43(1):71–3.
[127] Bardella MT, Fraquelli M, Quatrini M, et al. Prevalence of hypertransaminasemia in adult celiac patients and effect of gluten-free diet. Hepatology 1995;22(3):833–6.
[128] Armstrong MJ, Hegade VS, Robins G. Advances in coeliac disease. Curr Opin Gastroenterol 2012;28(2):104–12.
[129] Giersiepen K, Lelgemann M, Stuhldreher N, et al. Accuracy of diagnostic antibody tests for coeliac disease in children: summary of an evidence report. J Pediatr Gastroenterol Nutr 2012;54(2):229–41.
[130] Maglio M, Tosco A, Paparo F, et al. Serum and intestinal celiac disease-associated antibodies in children with celiac disease younger than 2 years of age. J Pediatr Gastroenterol Nutr 2010;50(1):43–8.
[131] Magliocca FM, Bonamico M, Petrozza V, et al. Usefulness of endoscopic small intestinal biopsies in children with coeliac disease. Ital J Anat Embryol 2001;106(2 Suppl 1): 329–35.
[132] Scott BB, Losowsky MS. Patchiness and duodenal-jejunal variation of the mucosal abnormality in coeliac disease and dermatitis herpetiformis. Gut 1976;17(12):984–92.
[133] Goldstein NS. Proximal small-bowel mucosal villous intraepithelial lymphocytes. Histopathology 2004;44(3):199–205.
[134] Oberhuber G, Granditsch G, Vogelsang H. The histopathology of coeliac disease: time for a standardized report scheme for pathologists. Eur J Gastroenterol Hepatol 1999;11(10): 1185–94.
[135] Corazza GR, Villanacci V. Coeliac disease. J Clin Pathol 2005;58(6):573–4.
[136] Ensari A. Gluten-sensitive enteropathy (celiac disease): controversies in diagnosis and classification. Arch Pathol Lab Med 2010;134(6):826–36.
[137] Maki M, Holm K, Collin P, et al. Increase in gamma/delta T cell receptor bearing lymphocytes in normal small bowel mucosa in latent coeliac disease. Gut 1991;32(11):1412–4.
[138] Biagi F, Luinetti O, Campanella J, et al. Intraepithelial lymphocytes in the villous tip: do they indicate potential coeliac disease? J Clin Pathol 2004;57(8):835–9.
[139] Jarvinen TT, Collin P, Rasmussen M, et al. Villous tip intraepithelial lymphocytes as markers of early-stage coeliac disease. Scand J Gastroenterol 2004;39(5):428–33.
[140] Wolber R, Owen D, DelBuono L, et al. Lymphocytic gastritis in patients with celiac sprue or spruelike intestinal disease. Gastroenterology 1990;98(2):310–5.
[141] Wolber R, Owen D, Freeman H. Colonic lymphocytosis in patients with celiac sprue. Hum Pathol 1990;21(11):1092–6.
[142] Fine KD, Lee EL, Meyer RL. Colonic histopathology in untreated celiac sprue or refractory sprue: is it lymphocytic colitis or colonic lymphocytosis? Hum Pathol 1998;29(12): 1433–40.
[143] Bhatti TR, Jatla M, Verma R, et al. Lymphocytic gastritis in pediatric celiac disease. Pediatr Dev Pathol 2011;14(4):280–3.
[144] Loft DE, Marsh MN, Crowe PT. Rectal gluten challenge and diagnosis of coeliac disease. Lancet 1990;336(8720):953.
[145] Farrell RJ, Kelly CP. Celiac sprue. N Engl J Med 2002;346(3):180–8.
[146] Wahab PJ, Meijer JW, Mulder CJ. Histologic follow-up of people with celiac disease on a gluten-free diet. Am J Clin Pathol 2002;118:459–63.
[147] Bardella MT, Velio P, Cesana BM, et al. Coeliac disease: a histological follow-up study. Histopathology 2007;50(4):465–71.
[148] Lack G. Clinical practice. Food allergy. N Engl J Med 2008;359(12):1252–60.

[149] Sicherer SH, Sampson HA. Food allergy: recent advances in pathophysiology and treatment. Annu Rev Med 2009;60:261–77.
[150] Spergel JM, Book WM, Mays E, et al. Variation in prevalence, diagnostic criteria, and initial management options for eosinophilic gastrointestinal diseases in the United States. J Pediatr Gastroenterol Nutr 2011;52(3):300–6.
[151] de Chambrun GP, Gonzalez F, Canva JY, et al. Natural history of eosinophilic gastroenteritis. Clin Gastroenterol Hepatol 2011;9(11):950–956.e1.
[152] Matysiak-Budnik T, Heyman M. Food allergy and helicobacter pylori. J Pediatr Gastroenterol Nutr 2002;34(1):5–12.
[153] Euscher E, Vaswani K, Frankel W. Eosinophilic pancreatitis: a rare entity that can mimic a pancreatic neoplasm. Ann Diagn Pathol 2000;4(6):379–85.
[154] Sawaya SM, Misk RJ, Aftimos GP. Eosinophilic gastroenteritis: report of two cases and comment on the literature. Eur J Surg 1992;158(8):439–41.
[155] Agertoft A, Husby S, Host A. Intestinal perforation in a two-year-old child with eosinophilic gastroenteritis. Acta Paediatr Scand 1991;80(3):389–91.
[156] Deslandres C, Russo P, Gould P, et al. Perforated duodenal ulcer in a pediatric patient with eosinophilic gastroenteritis. Can J Gastroenterol 1997;11(3):208–12.
[157] Maloney J, Nowak-Wegrzyn A. Educational clinical case series for pediatric allergy and immunology: allergic proctocolitis, food protein-induced enterocolitis syndrome and allergic eosinophilic gastroenteritis with protein-losing gastroenteropathy as manifestations of non-IgE-mediated cow's milk allergy. Pediatr Allergy Immunol 2007;18(4): 360–7.
[158] Chehade M, Magid MS, Mofidi S, et al. Allergic eosinophilic gastroenteritis with protein-losing enteropathy: intestinal pathology, clinical course, and long-term follow-up. J Pediatr Gastroenterol Nutr 2006;42(5):516–21.
[159] Shaker M, Woodmansee D. An update on food allergy. Curr Opin Pediatr 2009;21(5): 667–74.
[160] Klein NC, Hargrove RL, Sleisenger MH, et al. Eosinophilic gastroenteritis. Medicine (Baltimore) 1970;49(4):299–319.
[161] Chang JY, Choung RS, Lee RM, et al. A shift in the clinical spectrum of eosinophilic gastroenteritis toward the mucosal disease type. Clin Gastroenterol Hepatol 2010;8(8):669–75 [quiz: e88].
[162] Pascal RR, Gramlich TL, Parker KM, et al. Geographic variations in eosinophil concentration in normal colonic mucosa. Mod Pathol 1997;10(4):363–5.
[163] Polydorides AD, Banner BF, Hannaway PJ, et al. Evaluation of site-specific and seasonal variation in colonic mucosal eosinophils. Hum Pathol 2008;39(6):832–6.
[164] Lowichik A, Weinberg AG. A quantitative evaluation of mucosal eosinophils in the pediatric gastrointestinal tract. Mod Pathol 1996;9:110–4.
[165] DeBrosse CW, Case JW, Putnam PE, et al. Quantity and distribution of eosinophils in the gastrointestinal tract of children. Pediatr Dev Pathol 2006;9(3):210–8.
[166] Collins MH. Histopathology associated with eosinophilic gastrointestinal diseases. Immunol Allergy Clin North Am 2009;29(1):109–17, x–xi.
[167] Hurrell JM, Genta RM, Melton SD. Histopathologic diagnosis of eosinophilic conditions in the gastrointestinal tract. Adv Anat Pathol 2011;18(5):335–48.
[168] Manuel PD, Walker-Smith JA, France NE. Patchy enteropathy in childhood. Gut 1979;20(3):211–5.
[169] Walker MM, Salehian SS, Murray CE, et al. Implications of eosinophilia in the normal duodenal biopsy - an association with allergy and functional dyspepsia. Aliment Pharmacol Ther 2010;31(11):1229–36.
[170] Khan S, Orenstein SR. Eosinophilic gastroenteritis. Gastroenterol Clin North Am 2008;37(2):333–48, v.
[171] Hyams JS, Treem WR, Schwartz AN. Recurrent abdominal pain and ascites in an adolescent. J Pediatr 1988;113(3):569–74.

[172] Dhawan A, Seemayer TA, Pinsinski C, et al. Posttransplant eosinophilic gastroenteritis in children. Liver Transpl Surg 1997;3(6):591–3.
[173] Saeed SA, Integlia MJ, Pleskow RG, et al. Tacrolimus-associated eosinophilic gastroenterocolitis in pediatric liver transplant recipients: role of potential food allergies in pathogenesis. Pediatr Transplant 2006;10(6):730–5.
[174] Trivedi A, Barr P, O'Loughlin EV, et al. Severe neonatal eosinophilic enterocolitis treated with immunosuppressive drugs. J Pediatr Gastroenterol Nutr 2010;51(3):362–3.
[175] Leonard SA, Nowak-Wegrzyn A. Food protein-induced enterocolitis syndrome: an update on natural history and review of management. Ann Allergy Asthma Immunol 2011;107(2):95–101 [quiz: 101, 162].
[176] Katz Y, Goldberg MR, Rajuan N, et al. The prevalence and natural course of food protein-induced enterocolitis syndrome to cow's milk: a large-scale, prospective population-based study. J Allergy Clin Immunol 2011;127(3):647–653.e1–3.
[177] Nowak-Wegrzyn A, Muraro A. Food protein-induced enterocolitis syndrome. Curr Opin Allergy Clin Immunol 2009;9(4):371–7.
[178] de Boissieu D, Matarazzo P, Rocchiccioli F, et al. Multiple food allergy: a possible diagnosis in breastfed infants. Acta Paediatr 1997;86(10):1042–6.
[179] Lake AM. Food-induced eosinophilic proctocolitis. J Pediatr Gastroenterol Nutr 2000;30(Suppl):S58–60.
[180] Machida HM, Catto Smith AG, Gall DG, et al. Allergic colitis in infancy: clinical and pathologic aspects. J Pediatr Gastroenterol Nutr 1994;19(1):22–6.
[181] Cuffari C, Oligny L, Seidman EG. Dientamoeba fragilis masquerading as allergic colitis. J Pediatr Gastroenterol Nutr 1998;26(1):16–20.
[182] Lowichik A, Weinberg AG. Eosinophilic infiltration of the enteric neural plexuses in Hirschsprung's disease. Pediatr Pathol Lab Med 1997;17(6):885–91.
[183] Andiran F, Dayi S. Hirschsprung's disease or allergic colitis or necrotising enterocolitis? Pediatr Radiol 2000;30(12):881.
[184] Bloom DA, Buonomo C, Fishman SJ, et al. Allergic colitis: a mimic of Hirschsprung disease. Pediatr Radiol 1999;29(1):37–41.
[185] Waldmann TA, Steinfeld JL, Dutcher TF, et al. The role of the gastrointestinal system in "idiopathic hypoproteinemia". Gastroenterology 1961;41:197–207.
[186] Parfitt AM. Familial neonatal hypoproteinaemia with exudative enteropathy and intestinal lymphangiectasis. Arch Dis Child 1966;41(215):54–62.
[187] Brice G, Child AH, Evans A, et al. Milroy disease and the VEGFR-3 mutation phenotype. J Med Genet 2005;42(2):98–102.
[188] Carver C, Brice G, Mansour S, et al. Three children with Milroy disease and de novo mutations in VEGFR3. Clin Genet 2007;71(2):187–9.
[189] Evans AL, Brice G, Sotirova V, et al. Mapping of primary congenital lymphedema to the 5q35.3 region. Am J Hum Genet 1999;64(2):547–55.
[190] Alders M, Hogan BM, Gjini E, et al. Mutations in CCBE1 cause generalized lymph vessel dysplasia in humans. Nat Genet 2009;41(12):1272–4.
[191] Shkalim V, Baris HN, Gal G, et al. Autosomal dominant syndrome of mental retardation, hypotelorism, and cleft palate resembling Schilbach-Rott syndrome. Am J Med Genet A 2009;149A(12):2700–5.
[192] Salvia G, Cascioli CF, Ciccimarra F, et al. A case of protein-losing enteropathy caused by intestinal lymphangiectasia in a preterm infant. Pediatrics 2001;107(2): 416–7.
[193] Stormon MO, Mitchell JD, Smoleniec JS, et al. Congenital intestinal lymphatic hypoplasia presenting as non-immune hydrops in utero, and subsequent neonatal protein-losing enteropathy. J Pediatr Gastroenterol Nutr 2002;35(5):691–4.
[194] Fawcett WA 4th, Ferry GD, Gorin LJ, et al. Immunodeficiency secondary to structural intestinal defects. Malrotation of the small bowel and cavernous hemangioma of the jejunum. Am J Dis Child 1986;140(2):169–72.

[195] Lee WS, John P, McKiernan P, et al. Inferior vena cava occlusion and protein-losing enteropathy after liver transplantation in children. J Pediatr Gastroenterol Nutr 2002;34(4): 413–6.
[196] Riexinger M, Galm C, Trotter A, et al. Restrictive interatrial communication with protein-losing enteropathy and coagulopathy in hypoplastic left heart syndrome after Norwood palliation. Pediatr Cardiol 2002;23(1):84–6.
[197] Stiller B. Protein-losing enteropathy in patients with Fontan operations. J Pediatr Gastroenterol Nutr 2003;37(5):528–30.
[198] Ostrow AM, Freeze H, Rychik J. Protein-losing enteropathy after fontan operation: investigations into possible pathophysiologic mechanisms. Ann Thorac Surg 2006;82(2): 695–700.
[199] Connor FL, Angelides S, Gibson M, et al. Successful resection of localized intestinal lymphangiectasia post-Fontan: role of (99m)technetium-dextran scintigraphy. Pediatrics 2003;112(3 Pt 1):e242–7.
[200] Aoyagi K, Iida M, Yao T, et al. Characteristic endoscopic features of intestinal lymphangiectasia: correlation with histological findings. Hepatogastroenterology 1997;44(13): 133–8.
[201] Wen J, Tang Q, Wu J, et al. Primary intestinal lymphangiectasia: four case reports and a review of the literature. Dig Dis Sci 2010;55(12):3466–72.
[202] Freeze HH. Disorders in protein glycosylation and potential therapy: tip of an iceberg? J Pediatr 1998;133(5):593–600.
[203] Damen G, de Klerk H, Huijmans J, et al. Gastrointestinal and other clinical manifestations in 17 children with congenital disorders of glycosylation type Ia, Ib, and Ic. J Pediatr Gastroenterol Nutr 2004;38(3):282–7.
[204] Theodore M, Morava E. Congenital disorders of glycosylation: sweet news. Curr Opin Pediatr 2011;23(6):581–7.
[205] Kristiansson B, Borulf S, Conradi N, et al. Intestinal, pancreatic and hepatic involvement in carbohydrate-deficient glycoprotein syndrome type I. J Pediatr Gastroenterol Nutr 1998;27(1):23–9.
[206] Niehues R, Hasilik M, Alton G, et al. Carbohydrate-deficient glycoprotein syndrome type Ib. Phosphomannose isomerase deficiency and mannose therapy. J Clin Invest 1998;101(7):1414–20.
[207] Murch SH, Winyard PJ, Koletzko S, et al. Congenital enterocyte heparan sulphate deficiency with massive albumin loss, secretory diarrhoea, and malnutrition. Lancet 1996;347(9011):1299–301.
[208] Westphal V, Murch S, Kim S, et al. Reduced heparan sulfate accumulation in enterocytes contributes to protein-losing enteropathy in a congenital disorder of glycosylation. Am J Pathol 2000;157(6):1917–25.
[209] Vuillaumier-Barrot S, Le Bizec C, de Lonlay P, et al. Protein losing enteropathy-hepatic fibrosis syndrome in Saguenay-Lac St-Jean, Quebec is a congenital disorder of glycosylation type Ib. J Med Genet 2002;39(11):849–51.
[210] Visser G, Rake JP, Fernandes J, et al. Neutropenia, neutrophil dysfunction, and inflammatory bowel disease in glycogen storage disease type Ib: results of the European Study on Glycogen Storage Disease type I. J Pediatr 2000;137(2):187–91.
[211] Ramaswami U, Van 't Hoff W, Clayton P, et al. Sanfilippo disease (mucopolysaccharidosis type III) presenting as transient renal tubular dysfunction. J Inherit Metab Dis 1996;19(1): 87–8.
[212] Kikuchi M, Igarashi K, Noro T, et al. Evaluation of jejunal function in Wolman's disease. J Pediatr Gastroenterol Nutr 1991;12(1):65–9.
[213] Remmele W, Beck K, Kaiserling E. Multiple lipid islands of the colonic mucosa. A light and electron microscopic study. Pathol Res Pract 1988;183(3):336–46.
[214] Brett EM, Lake BD. Reassessment of rectal approach to neuropathology in childhood: review of 307 biopsies over 11 years. Arch Dis Child 1975;50(10):753–62.

[215] Odze RD, Goldman H. Systemic and miscellaneous disorders. In: Ming SC, Goldman H, editors. Pathology of the gastrointestinal tract. Baltimore (MD): Williams & Wilkins; 1998. p. 399–432.

[216] O'Brien BD, Shnitka TK, McDougall R, et al. Pathophysiologic and ultrastructural basis for intestinal symptoms in Fabry's disease. Gastroenterology 1982;82(5 Pt 1):957–62.

[217] Hoffmann B, Schwarz M, Mehta A, et al. Gastrointestinal symptoms in 342 patients with Fabry disease: prevalence and response to enzyme replacement therapy. Clin Gastroenterol Hepatol 2007;5(12):1447–53.

[218] Mandel H, Meiron D, Schutgens RB, et al. Infantile refsum disease: gastrointestinal presentation of a peroxisomal disorder. J Pediatr Gastroenterol Nutr 1992;14(1):83–5.

[219] Cormier-Daire V, Bonnefont JP, Rustin P, et al. Mitochondrial DNA rearrangements with onset as chronic diarrhea with villous atrophy. J Pediatr 1994;124(1):63–70.

[220] Seneca S, De Meirleir L, De Schepper J, et al. Pearson marrow pancreas syndrome: a molecular study and clinical management. Clin Genet 1997;51(5):338–42.

[221] Landing BH, Nadorra R. Infantile systemic hyalinosis: report of four cases of a disease, fatal in infancy, apparently different from juvenile systemic hyalinosis. Pediatr Pathol 1986;6(1):55–79.

[222] Nezelof C, Letourneux-Toromanoff B, Griscelli C, et al. Painful disseminated fibromatosis (systemic hyalinosis): a new hereditary collagen dysplasia. Arch Fr Pediatr 1978;35(10): 1063–74 [in French].

[223] Alreheili K, AlMehaidib A, Alsaleem K, et al. Intestinal lymphangiectasia in a patient with infantile systemic hyalinosis syndrome: a rare cause of protein-losing enteropathy. Ann Saudi Med 2012;32(2):206–8.

[224] Buyukgebiz B, Ozturk Y, Arslan N, et al. A rare cause of protein-losing enteropathy and growth retardation in infancy: infantile systemic hyalinosis. Turk J Pediatr 2003;45(3): 258–60.

[225] Stucki U, Spycher MA, Eich G, et al. Infantile systemic hyalinosis in siblings: clinical report, biochemical and ultrastructural findings, and review of the literature. Am J Med Genet 2001;100(2):122–9.

[226] Geissmann F, Thomas C, Emile JF, et al. Digestive tract involvement in Langerhans cell histiocytosis. The French Langerhans Cell Histiocytosis Study Group. J Pediatr 1996;129(6): 836–45.

[227] Lee RG, Braziel RM, Stenzel P. Gastrointestinal involvement in Langerhans cell histiocytosis (histiocytosis X): diagnosis by rectal biopsy. Mod Pathol 1990;3(2):154–7.

[228] Stenzel P, Fitterer S. Gastrointestinal multicentric infantile myofibromatosis: characteristic histology on rectal biopsy. Am J Gastroenterol 1989;84(9):1115–9.

Advances in Pediatrics 60 (2013) 263–279

ADVANCES IN PEDIATRICS

# Necrotizing Enterocolitis

## Contemporary Management and Outcomes

Stephanie Papillon, MD, Shannon L. Castle, MD,
Christopher P. Gayer, MD, Henri R. Ford, MD, MHA*

Department of Surgery, Children's Hospital Los Angeles, Keck School of Medicine, University of Southern California, 4650 Sunset Boulevard, Los Angeles, CA 90027, USA

**Keywords**

• Necrotizing enterocolitis • NEC • Preterm infants • Gastrointestinal inflammation • Neonate

**Key points**

- Necrotizing enterocolitis (NEC) remains a highly lethal disease that affects predominantly preterm neonates. Infants requiring surgery face many adverse long-term sequelae.
- Several preventive strategies are under investigation and require further research before using them in preterm infants at risk for NEC.

## EPIDEMIOLOGY OF NECROTIZING ENTEROCOLITIS

Nearly 50 years after it was first described, necrotizing enterocolitis (NEC) remains the most important gastrointestinal emergency in premature infants, with a mortality rate exceeding 50% in patients with the most severe form of the disease [1]. The incidence of NEC in the United States has been estimated to be 1.1 per 1000 live births, with the highest percentage of hospitalizations reported in teaching hospitals of major cities [2]. Although there is no statistically significant difference in the incidence of NEC between boys and girls, NEC tends to affect a disproportionately higher percentage of African Americans [2,3]. Population-based studies have demonstrated that the rate of NEC is highest among very low birth weight infants weighing less than 1500 g and declines as birth weight approaches or exceeds 2500 g [2,3]. This trend in the incidence of NEC is mirrored by an equally unfavorable trend in fatality and complication rates as well as economic costs for very low birth weight infants.

*Corresponding author. Children's Hospital Los Angeles, 4650 Sunset Boulevard, Mailstop #72, Los Angeles, CA 90027. *E-mail address*: HFord@chla.usc.edu

0065-3101/13/$ – see front matter
http://dx.doi.org/10.1016/j.yapd.2013.04.011 

Indeed, very low birth weight infants typically incur exorbitant hospital costs that are exacerbated by the presence of NEC, with direct costs increasing by more than $22 000 and $13 000 for surgically and medically managed NEC, respectively [4]. Advances in neonatal care, most notably the advent of the use of surfactant and antenatal steroids, have resulted in improved survival of increasingly smaller preterm infants; thus, NEC continues to be a substantial public health concern.

## PATHOPHYSIOLOGY AND RISK FACTORS

NEC can occur anywhere along the gastrointestinal tract but most commonly involves primarily the small and large bowel [1]. The disease is characterized by the infiltration of the intestinal wall by neutrophils; submucosal edema; hemorrhage; disruption of the intestinal villus architecture; and in more advanced cases, full-thickness necrosis or perforation of the intestinal wall. Historically, immaturity of the gastrointestinal tract, abnormal bacterial colonization, and formula feeding have been implicated in the disease pathogenesis. Preterm infants often have abnormal bacterial colonization. Studies have shown decreased bacterial diversity and delayed colonization by obligate anaerobes in preterm infants [5,6]. In addition, ischemic or hypoxic insults and external or environmental stressors, in combination with poorly regulated intestinal microcirculation, can lead to mucosal injury. The resultant breach in the intestinal epithelial barrier permits bacterial invasion by opportunistic pathogens, which initiate an inflammatory cascade that ultimately leads to further mucosal injury, amplification of the inflammatory response, systemic sepsis, intestinal perforation, and other adverse sequelae that are characteristic of NEC.

## CLINICAL PRESENTATION AND DIAGNOSIS

Early signs of NEC include abdominal distention, feeding intolerance, and bloody stool. The disease can often progress rapidly resulting in abdominal wall erythema, intestinal perforation, peritonitis, and cardiopulmonary collapse. The diagnosis of NEC is largely based on the clinical presentation, radiographic findings, and laboratory data. Abdominal radiographs may reveal distended loops of bowel with or without air fluid levels during the early stages of NEC and *pneumatosis intestinalis* (Fig. 1), with or without portal venous gas, in infants with established NEC. More ominous signs, such as the presence of pneumoperitoneum, or a sentinel loop on serial abdominal radiographs, which suggests intestinal necrosis, may suggest disease progression. Although no specific laboratory value is predictive of NEC, neutropenia and thrombocytopenia are often associated with the diagnosis [7]. Severe thrombocytopenia, persistently elevated C-reactive protein, and acidosis may suggest advanced disease [8].

NEC is classified according to the modified Bell staging system, which is based on 3 broad categories that include systemic signs, gastrointestinal symptoms or findings on abdominal examination, and radiographic evaluation. Criteria for stage I, or suspected NEC, include physiologic markers consistent

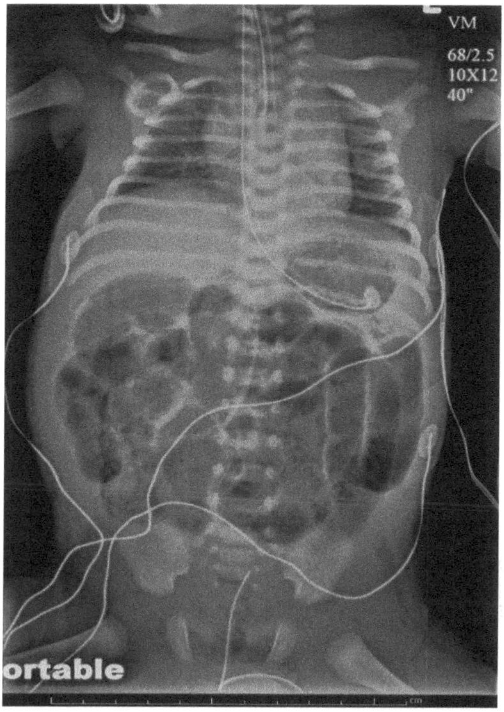


**Fig. 1.** An infant with pneumatosis intestinalis.

with the systemic inflammatory response syndrome, fecal occult blood or abdominal distention, and radiographic evidence of dilated loops of bowel or ileus. Bell stage II, or definite NEC, incorporates criteria for stage I with the addition of laboratory changes, gross fecal blood with or without abdominal tenderness, and *pneumatosis intestinalis* or portal venous gas on abdominal radiographs. Bell stage III, or advanced NEC, incorporates criteria for stage II with the addition of cardiovascular collapse, peritonitis, or pneumoperitoneum. These stages are widely used to help guide treatment.

## MANAGEMENT STRATEGIES

### Source control

The initial management of an infant with suspected NEC consists of providing supportive care, including bowel rest, volume resuscitation, and administration of broad-spectrum intravenous antibiotics following pan cultures. The stomach should be decompressed with an orogastric tube. Patients are monitored closely for signs of sepsis and progression of disease. The abdomen is regularly assessed with serial examinations and abdominal radiographs. Medical management is continued for 7 to 14 days for patients who show signs of clinical improvement. There are no randomized controlled trials that demonstrate superiority of one antibiotic regimen over another [9]. Broad-spectrum antibiotics with combinations of ampicillin, gentamicin, and metronidazole; ampicillin, cefotaxime, and metronidazole; or meropenem or piperacillin-tazobactam alone are recommended [10]. If β-lactam–resistant bacteria are suspected, then vancomycin is recommended along with an aminoglycoside [10]. Empiric antibiotic therapy should be tailored according to the hospital's antibiogram. Patients typically respond within the first 2 days of treatment [11].

The only absolute indication for surgical intervention in NEC is intestinal perforation. Deteriorating clinical status despite optimal medical management, the presence of abdominal wall erythema, or portal venous gas on abdominal radiographs are relative indications for surgery. Upwards of 40% of the patients managed medically may require subsequent surgical intervention [1]. Surgery may consist of exploratory laparotomy and resection of the necrotic or perforated bowel with either primary anastomosis or stoma creation; alternatively, patients may undergo initial peritoneal drainage.

The use of peritoneal drainage as definitive therapy for NEC remains controversial. Peritoneal drainage involves the placement of a Penrose drain in the peritoneal cavity through the lower quadrants, at times bilaterally, followed by saline irrigation to evacuate enteric contents. This approach allows for abdominal decompression and continued evacuation of enteric contents via the Penrose drains. The procedure is typically performed at the bedside under local anesthesia in critically ill, very low birth weight infants deemed too unstable to tolerate exploratory laparotomy. As such, it is often viewed as a temporizing measure to allow the patients to be resuscitated and stabilized before formal laparotomy. Although 30% of patients who undergo drainage require no further surgical intervention, no survival advantage has been shown [12]. Infants who continue to show signs of clinical deterioration after initial peritoneal drainage require formal laparotomy.

In patients undergoing exploratory laparotomy, the type of surgical intervention is largely determined by the extent of disease. The extent of disease can range from focal gangrene or perforation of a single segment of intestine to multifocal disease involving less than 50% of the bowel, diffuse intestinal necrosis, or NEC totalis, with less than 25% of the bowel remaining viable (Fig. 2) [13]. The ultimate goal is to resect frankly necrotic or gangrenous bowel while conserving questionable or viable intestine to preserve intestinal length. More extensive disease poses a greater surgical challenge. Frankly gangrenous bowel is resected with the creation of a single stoma with or without a distal mucous fistula. In general, multiple stomas should be avoided. Primary repair can be attempted in selected hemodynamically stable patients with focal intestinal perforation and minimal peritoneal soilage [13]. Currently there are no randomized studies to evaluate the benefits of primary repair compared with creation of enterostomies following bowel resection. In an effort to preserve bowel length, some investigators have proposed different approaches, such as the clip-and-drop-back technique in which clipped or stapled ends of intestine, previously abutting resected gangrenous bowel, are initially left within the peritoneal

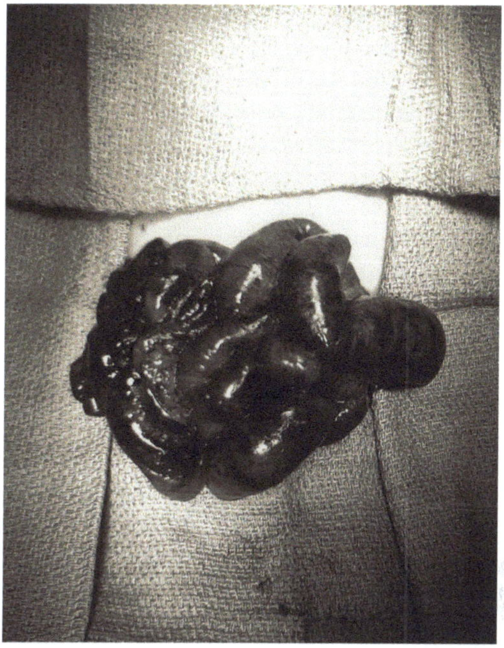

**Fig. 2.** The infant previously shown with diffuse intestinal necrosis, NEC totalis.

cavity followed by a second-look operation up to 3 days later [14]. Case reports have described other controversial techniques, such as repairing perforated segments followed by the placement of drains with re-exploration up to 8 weeks later while patients receive total parenteral nutrition [15]. Following any surgical intervention, patients must be monitored carefully and reassessed frequently for the potential need for a second-look procedure. No randomized trial has shown improved outcomes for laparotomy compared with peritoneal drainage for very low to extremely low birth weight infants (<1000 g), regardless of the extent of disease.

In a multicenter study, very low birth weight infants with NEC or focal intestinal perforation (FIP) randomized to undergo primary peritoneal drainage or laparotomy showed no difference in mortality, dependence on parenteral nutrition, or length of hospitalization at 90 days [16]. Twenty-one of 55 patients who underwent initial peritoneal drainage (16 of whom were extremely low birth weight) required laparotomy for worsening clinical status or obstructive symptoms. The investigators concluded that the type of surgical intervention does not influence outcome.

An international multicenter trial in extremely low birth weight infants with NEC or FIP randomized to primary peritoneal drainage or laparotomy demonstrated no significant difference in survival, length of hospital stay, ventilator dependence, or need for parenteral nutrition at 1 and 6 months [17]. The investigators also found no difference in median time to full feeds. Twenty-six of 35 patients who were randomized to peritoneal drainage required subsequent delayed laparotomy for clinical deterioration or signs of persistent intestinal obstruction. The investigators concluded that peritoneal drainage was not beneficial for extremely low birth weight patients.

When the results from both studies were pooled in a meta-analysis, no significant differences in survival, length of stay, or need for parenteral nutrition were observed [18]. There were also no differences in complications, such as abdominal abscesses or intestinal strictures. There was a significant difference in the need for laparotomy following primary procedure in patients who underwent peritoneal drainage. The investigators were unable to make recommendations in favor of or against either procedure. Neither of the randomized trials reached the targeted number of patients and, thus, may not have achieved statistical power to detect differences in patient outcomes. There are insufficient data on long-term postoperative complications and outcomes following laparotomy or peritoneal drainage [19].

Postoperatively, patients should continue to receive antibiotic therapy for up to 2 weeks. Patients should also receive parenteral nutrition. There are no randomized trials that have investigated appropriate timing for reintroducing enteral nutrition after the treatment of NEC [20]. The overall management has remained unchanged over the past several decades. The primary goal of treatment is to attenuate the exuberant inflammatory response that is characteristic of NEC. For the sickest patients who do not respond to medical management or surgical intervention, either peritoneal drainage or resection of diseased intestine may be required to achieve source control. Because current treatment strategies, whether medical or surgical, do not address disease prevention, NEC remains a significant source of morbidity and mortality in preterm infants.

## PREVENTIVE STRATEGIES

### Breast milk

Breast milk remains the gold standard for preventing NEC in preterm infants [21]. Earlier studies by Barlow and colleagues [22] demonstrated that when compared with formula feeding, breast-feeding reduced the incidence of NEC in newborn rats subjected to hypoxia, with or without the addition of *Klebsiella* to the feedings. The percentage of formula-fed rats that developed experimental NEC decreased when the formula was supplemented with components of breast milk, specifically immunoglobulins and probiotics, lending further credence to the protective role of breast milk.

Although the benefits of breast milk have been observed for many decades, only recently have studies revealed the exact mechanisms by which breast milk promotes intestinal health. Animal studies have revealed upregulation of proinflammatory cytokines in the intestine of formula-fed rats, which can be abrogated by the addition of transforming growth factor–β, a cytokine that is abundant in breast milk [23]. Breast milk has been shown to influence the microbial flora of the intestine, with greater diversity being found in the microbiota of breast-fed infants. Although traditional beliefs about significantly higher levels of lactobacilli and bidfidobacteria in breast-fed infants have been challenged, studies reveal consistently more *Bacteroides*, *Klebsiella*, and *Enterobacter* in formula-fed infants, whereas breast-fed infants have a greater presence of staphylococci [24,25]. Although the specific implications of these findings have yet to be determined, it is thought that components often unique to breast milk affect bacterial growth [24].

Mizrahi and colleagues [26] first described the protective role of lysozymes against the development of NEC. Lysozymes are produced by macrophages in breast milk and can digest components of the cellular wall of bacteria [27]. Immunoglobulins present in breast milk can also affect the microbial flora. In a single-center randomized controlled trial, a combination of immunoglobulin A (IgA) and IgG significantly reduced the rate of NEC in infants who weighed less than 2000 g receiving breast milk and formula [28]. These immunoglobulins were found intact in the stool of the treatment group without evidence of absorption into the serum. The investigators suggested that IgA and IgG play a role in the regulation of bacterial expansion and translocation across the intestinal barrier. Additionally, oligosaccharides present in breast milk can influence the intestinal microbial flora and regulate inflammatory pathways. Specifically, these carbohydrates have been shown to decrease neutrophil activation and the formation of platelet-neutrophil complexes [29]. Lactoferrin, a component of the innate immune system that is highly concentrated in human colostrum, has been shown to possess broad activity against microbes. Although no study has adequately assessed the role of oral lactoferrin in the prevention of NEC, it has been shown to significantly reduce the risk of late-onset sepsis in neonates [30]. Many of the goals of preventive strategies are aimed at stimulating these natural or innate defenses.

## Probiotics

With the current suspected role of the microbiota in disease pathogenesis and mounting evidence that breast milk influences the composition of the microbiota, much attention has been directed toward the use of probiotics, or live microorganisms, for the promotion of healthy intestinal microbiota. It has been suggested that probiotic bacteria may compete with potential pathogens in the intestine [31]. Beyond the "competitive exclusion" of pathogenic bacteria, probiotic bacteria also play a role in intestinal homeostasis, including the regulation of bacterial translocation and enhancement of epithelial sensitivity to IgA [31]. There have been several randomized controlled trials investigating the use of probiotics in the prevention of NEC. Two of the largest studies within the past 5 years have shown improved outcomes in infants receiving probiotics.

In a multicenter study conducted by Lin and colleagues [32], 434 very low birth weight infants were randomized to receive breast milk or a mixture of breast milk and formula, with or without a combination of *Bifidobacterium bifidum* and *Lactobacillus acidophilus,* twice daily. Mortality and the diagnosis of NEC Bell stage II or greater were significantly lower in the patients receiving probiotics. There was no difference in mortality from NEC when both groups were compared. The infants receiving probiotics were more likely to develop sepsis, although none of the blood cultures was positive for *Bifidobacterium* or *Lactobacillus.* The investigators determined that the number of infants needed to treat to prevent NEC was 20, whereas the number needed to treat to prevent death or NEC was 14 patients. The study was not powered to determine the effects of probiotics on outcomes in extremely low birth weight infants.

In a single-center randomized controlled trial, 119 preterm infants receiving breast milk with a combination of *Bifidobacterium breve* and *Lactobacillus casei* had a lower risk of developing NEC compared to a control group of 112 preterm infants receiving breast milk only [33]. These infants also achieved full enteral feeding earlier. There were no observed differences in the rate of sepsis or death between the groups.

These studies reflect the promising data available on probiotics. Although compelling, numerous uncertainties remain. The most effective probiotic preparation has yet to be determined because studies vary in the choice of species, dosage, and duration of treatment [31]. Additionally although studies differ in the selection criteria for eligible patients, most studies include patients who have a very low birth weight, thus, making it difficult to draw conclusions for extremely low birth weight infants.

## Prebiotics

Numerous authors have investigated the protective effect of prebiotics, nondigestible food ingredients that promote the growth of resident intestinal bacteria that are beneficial to human hosts, in preterm infants. Prebiotics can be digested by these beneficial bacteria, thereby improving their growth and subsequently promoting the effects of these bacteria on gastrointestinal immunity [34]. In a study by Mihatsch and colleagues [35], 20 very low birth weight infants were randomized to receive 14 days of preterm formula supplemented with galacto-oligosaccharides (short chain) and fructo-oligosaccharides (long chain) or with placebo. The investigators reported that infants in the study group had decreased stool viscosity and decreased gastrointestinal transport time at the completion of the study. The investigators concluded that prebiotics might assist in the advancement of enteral feeds. Similarly, another single-center study in which preterm infants were randomized to receive preterm formula with galacto-oligosaccharides and fructo-oligosaccharides or placebo revealed faster gastric emptying time after 15 days of prebiotic treatment [36]. There were no adverse events in either study.

Two studies investigated the effects of prebiotics on the microbial flora of preterm infants. One study used preterm formula supplemented with the combination of oligosaccharides previously described or placebo for a total of 28 days [37]. The investigators reported that although bifidobacteria increased significantly in both groups, the increase was significantly higher in patients receiving prebiotics. Infants in the study group also had significantly softer stool than controls, and this was comparable with the stool consistency observed in a reference group of breast-fed infants. The study group also had a higher frequency of stools. There was no significant difference in the number of gram-negative bacteria including *Clostridium*, *Escherichia coli*, *Klebsiella*, *Proteus*, *Citrobacter*, or *Enterobacter*. In a slightly larger randomized study in which preterm infants either received 14 days of formula with long-chain oligosaccharides or placebo, there was higher stool frequency and softer stool consistency in the study group [38]. The load of bifidobacteria in the stool and the percentage of infants colonized with bifidobacteria were significantly higher in the study group. In addition, there was a higher number of *Bacteroides* and a lower number of *E coli* in the study group. The investigators for both of these studies suggest that prebiotics stimulate the growth of bifidobacteria without any complications. They further suggest that prebiotics not only produce stool characteristics that resemble those of preterm infants receiving breast milk but they also decrease the number of potential pathogens within the intestine.

The largest trial to date that randomized preterm infants to receive preterm formula supplemented with prebiotics or placebo was also the only study to evaluate NEC as a secondary outcome; no statistically significant differences were found [39]. However, infants in both groups also received breast milk, making it difficult to assess the outcomes.

Taken together, these studies are limited by sample size, with a total of fewer than 300 patients. Furthermore, none of the studies were powered to assess outcomes for NEC or long-term outcomes. Only 2 studies limited participants to very low birth weight infants. Lastly, similar to probiotics, the ideal dosage and duration of the treatment of prebiotics have yet to be established. There are no formal recommendations regarding the use of prebiotics for the prevention of NEC. In 2010, the American Academy of Pediatrics (AAP) Section Gastroenterology, Hepatology, and Nutrition reported that there is insufficient evidence demonstrating the efficacy of prebiotic supplementation in milk [40].

### Epidermal growthlike factors

Another factor present in breast milk known to play a role in intestinal homeostasis is epidermal growth factor (EGF). In addition to breast milk, EGF is present in several endogenous fluids, including urine, amniotic fluid, bile, and saliva [41]. In the developing fetus, the presence of EGF within these endogenous fluids and intestinal epithelial and secretory cells underscores the role of EGF in intestinal maturation and homeostasis. Within the lumen of the small intestine, EGF is produced by Brunner glands and Paneth cells [41,42]. Heparin-binding epidermal growth factor (HB-EGF), another member of the EGF family, has also been under investigation for similar reasons. HB-EGF, also present in biologic fluids, may have a more pronounced effect because of its ability to bind to more than one receptor of the EGF-R family of receptors [43].

Most of the data on the mechanism of action and function of both factors stem from experimental models. These models have revealed that HB-EGF decreases intestinal injury and increases villus blood flow [44]. EGF is known to enhance epithelial cell maturation, stimulate intestinal growth, and enhance the recovery of the epithelium following injury [41,43]. The literature supporting the beneficial role of these factors in humans is less robust. The largest prospective observational study in infants greater than 23 weeks' gestation revealed that an initial low level of salivary EGF in the first week of life followed by a significant increase thereafter correlated with the development of NEC [45]. The investigators reported that low salivary EGF levels correlated with lower gestational age in a multi-regression analysis. Outside of case reports, there have been no large randomized studies investigating the use of this family of factors in the treatment of NEC in humans. The only trial to date is a single-center trial that randomized 8 infants who were less than 12 weeks of age with confirmed NEC Bell stage II or more to receive continuous intravenous infusions of EGF versus placebo. The investigators found significantly increased rectal mucosal thickness and crypt surface area in infants receiving EGF [46]. However, the study was discontinued early for administrative reasons; the results were not correlated with clinical outcomes. Thus, EGF and HB-EGF require further clinical studies to investigate their efficacy in preterm infants at risk for NEC.

### Feeding strategies

Most infants who develop NEC are fed [13]. As a result, numerous investigators have focused on various aspects of feeding that could potentially influence the development of NEC. In a study by Kamitsuka and colleagues [47], the number of low birth weight infants with NEC was significantly decreased after a standardized feeding schedule was introduced. This prospectively reviewed cohort over 3 years was compared with a retrospectively reviewed cohort of low birth weight infants for a 3-year period before the development of the feeding schedule. The investigators created a feeding regimen to address the time of feeding, rate of advancement, and concentration, which are 3 of the main considerations in the development of NEC. According to the feeding schedule, infants with weights of 1250 to 1500 g, 1501 to 2000 g, and 2001 to 2500 g were restricted to nil per os (NPO) for 72, 48, or 24 hours, respectively. Feeds were advanced by no more than 20 ml/kg daily. Infants received full-strength breast milk or half-strength formula if breast milk was not available. Half-strength formula was changed to full-strength on the fourth day of feeding. The decreased percentage of infants with NEC in the cohort receiving the feeding regimen was independent of the exposure to breast milk, birth weight, age (in days) at the first feeding, age (in days) at full feeding, exposure to prenatal steroids, or race. These findings have not yet been supported by randomized controlled trials assessing NEC as the primary outcome.

In a single-center randomized controlled trial, there was no difference in the percentage of very low birth weight infants who developed NEC Bell stage II or more while receiving slow advancement of their formula feeding (15 mL/kg daily) compared with those receiving fast advancement of their formula (35 mL/kg daily) [48]. These findings were unchanged when subgroup analysis was conducted for birth weight. The investigators also found no difference in the age at which NEC was diagnosed in the infants receiving slow or fast feeding advancements. There are several randomized trials that followed this study investigating the clinical effects of the rate of feed advancement in preterm or very low birth weight infants [49–51]. All of these studies found no significant difference in the percentage of infants who developed NEC with slow or fast advancement of feeding, ranging from 15 to 30 mL/kg/d. However, these studies may not have been powered to observe a significant difference because NEC was a secondary outcome. A meta-analysis also failed to demonstrate any significant difference in the relative risk of NEC [52].

Similar findings have been reported comparing early versus delayed enteral feeds. A multicenter randomized controlled trial found no difference in the percentage of preterm growth-restricted infants who developed NEC with early feeding, within 24 to 48 hours, when compared with those receiving late feeding, within 120 to 144 hours [53]. The investigators found that the infants who received early feeding achieved full enteral feeding sooner, had shorter exposure to parenteral nutrition, had a lower incidence of cholestatic jaundice, and a smaller degree of postnatal growth restriction on discharge. Another single-center study found no significant difference in the percentage of preterm growth-restricted infants with NEC when randomized to receive early feedings, within 5 days, or delayed feedings, after 5 days [54]. The investigators found no difference in the percentage of infants who developed feeding intolerance. They were also able to demonstrate that birth weight correlated with the risk of developing NEC. Both of these studies assessed NEC as a primary outcome. When these data were combined with smaller randomized studies from the 1980s and 1990s, there was no significant effect of timing of feedings on the development of NEC [55]. There was also no significant effect on mortality.

There have been no studies demonstrating an association between a high concentration of feedings and NEC [56]. One of the largest randomized controlled studies from 2 centers in the United Kingdom found no difference in the development of NEC as a secondary outcome in preterm infants receiving human milk enriched with a multi-nutrient fortifier compared with those receiving human milk enriched with a control supplement [57]. Nearly 20% of the patients in both groups received preterm formula. When these data were pooled with other trials in a meta-analysis, the findings were unchanged [58].

The American Pediatric Surgical Association Outcomes and Clinical Trials Committee has stated there is no evidence to support delayed enteral feedings or slow advancement of feedings for the prevention of NEC [19]. The American Society for Parenteral and Enteral Nutrition suggests that infants who weigh 1000 g or more should receive enteral feedings within the first 2 days of life and that the feedings can be advanced by 30 mL/kg daily [20]. The traditional consensus regarding the concentration of milk has been that osmolality should be no greater than 450 mOsm/kg based on expert opinion [56]. The AAP recommends fortification of human milk for preterm infants [21]. These recommendations are summarized in Box 1.

**Box 1: Recommendations for practice**

Breast milk: All preterm infants should receive fortified breast milk.

Probiotics: Current evidence is insufficient to recommend use in preterm infants.

Prebiotics: There is insufficient evidence demonstrating efficacy of prebiotic supplementation in milk.

Feeding strategies: Infants who weigh 1000 g or more should receive enteral feeds within the first 2 days of life and can be advanced by 30 mL/kg/d.

## OUTCOMES

### Short-term

Infants with NEC have a longer length of hospitalization and higher risk of death before discharge than preterm infants without NEC [2].

Immediate postoperative morbidities following surgical intervention include surgical site infections and wound dehiscence. Blakely and colleagues [59] investigated postoperative outcomes in 156 extremely low birth weight infants in a multicenter prospective observational study following laparotomy or peritoneal drainage for NEC or FIP. The investigators found no difference in the percentage of wound dehiscence, intra-abdominal abscesses, or intestinal stricture; however, 23% of the patients who underwent drainage subsequently required laparotomy.

Recurrence is estimated to occur in about 4% to 10% of patients with NEC [60,61]. In a retrospective study of 196 infants in the United Kingdom, recurrent NEC was successfully managed with supportive care [60]. The investigators found no association between initial management, timing of feedings, the type of feed, or recurrence. The investigators proposed that congenital heart disease and decreased mesenteric blood flow might contribute to recurrence. A subsequent retrospective study from the same institution 2 decades later reported that recurrent NEC often required surgery. Furthermore, there was no difference in the need for surgical intervention in patients with a single episode versus a recurrent episode of NEC [61]. The investigators found no difference in mortality between patients with a single episode of NEC and those with recurrent episodes.

### Long-term

#### *Neurodevelopmental*

Long-term outcomes have revealed a higher incidence of neurodevelopmental impairment in infants with NEC. The largest and longest-term study evaluated infants within the ORACLE children study with NEC at 7 years [62]. The study was not originally designed to evaluate outcomes for NEC. The investigators found a higher likelihood of functional impairment in patients with NEC as compared with those without. The investigators found no increased likelihood of behavioral abnormalities or educational difficulty in math, reading, or writing.

In the largest study on extremely low birth weight infants, patients with NEC managed surgically had significantly more neurodevelopmental disabilities [63]. Patients were identified from the National Institute of Child Health and Human Development (NICHD) Neonatal Research Network Registry. This registry is a multicenter registry in which infants are prospectively enrolled. Patients were followed up for 18 to 22 months. Significantly more surgical patients were found to have neurodevelopmental disabilities, including cerebral palsy, deafness, and blindness. However, NEC treated medically or surgically was not found to be an independent risk factor for cerebral palsy. There was no statistical difference in the incidence of neurodevelopmental disabilities in infants with medical NEC and those without NEC. There was a significantly higher percentage of growth failure as measured by weight, length, and head circumference in patients with NEC requiring surgery compared with those without NEC. The investigators also found a significantly higher percentage of infants with surgical NEC with markedly reduced mental developmental and psychomotor developmental indices. There was no significant difference between medical NEC and patients without NEC. All examiners were certified and blinded.

Another study by Castro and colleagues [64] examining outcomes in extremely low birth weight infants using a cohort identified from the NICHD registry about 2 years earlier similarly found a significantly increased likelihood of a psychomotor developmental index less than 70 and cerebral palsy in patients with NEC Bell stage II or more. However, using a predictive model, the investigators suggest that there may be bias toward worse outcomes in patients who are compliant with the follow-up. These patients were predicted to have significantly higher observed percentages of mental developmental indices less than 70 compared with the estimated percentage for children noncompliant with follow-up. The investigators predicted neurodevelopmental outcomes for noncompliant patients using a logistic regression model. They speculate that perhaps neurodevelopmental disability may contribute to the "perceived need for more frequent evaluation."

*Gastrointestinal*

The most common complication following both medical and surgical NEC is intestinal strictures most commonly in the left colon, followed by the terminal ileum [13]. Multiple strictures are uncommon [13]. Patients may present with obstructive symptoms, abdominal distention, feeding intolerance, failure to thrive, hematochezia, or evidence of an acute abdomen and sepsis in extreme cases. Those with clinical signs of distal bowel obstruction should undergo water-soluble contrast enema [1,13]. Definitive management involves resection of the stricture, often with primary anastomosis, although balloon dilatation and spontaneous resolution of strictures have been reported [1].

The most devastating complication of NEC is intestinal failure, most commonly caused by short bowel syndrome (SBS) following the management of surgical NEC, which is the number one cause of SBS in premature infants. Intestinal failure is estimated to occur in more than 20% of infants who undergo surgical resection [13]. Extensive resection resulting in less than 40 cm of small intestine is thought to place infants at higher risk; however, the age at the time of the operation as well as the functional capability of the remaining intestine are also critical [1,65]. In a multicenter prospective observational study, infants undergoing surgical intervention for NEC, either peritoneal drainage or laparotomy with or without resection, were found to have an increased likelihood of intestinal failure with a birth weight less than 750 g, need for mechanical ventilation on the day of diagnosis, exposure to enteral feeds before the onset of disease, and every 10-point increase in the percentage of small intestine resected [66].

## SUMMARY

NEC continues to present a formidable challenge to practitioners. The current management strategies aimed at disease control are limited and often complicated by equally devastating sequelae. There is undoubtedly a critical need for effective preventive strategies to address this vexing problem.

### References

[1] Henry MC, Moss R. Necrotizing enterocolitis. In: Holcomb GW III, Murphy J, editors. Ashcraft's pediatric surgery. 5th edition. Philadelphia: Saunders; 2010. p. 439–55.

[2] Holman RC, Stoll BJ, Curns AT, et al. Necrotising enterocolitis hospitalisations among neonates in the United States. Paediatr Perinat Epidemiol 2006;20(6):498–506.

[3] Llanos AR, Moss ME, Pinzon MC, et al. Epidemiology of neonatal necrotising enterocolitis: a population-based study. Paediatr Perinat Epidemiol 2002;16(4):342–9.

[4] Johnson TJ, Patel AL, Jegier BJ, et al. Cost of morbidities in very low birth weight infants. J Pediatr 2013;162(2):243–9.e1.

[5] Siggers RH, Siggers J, Thymann T, et al. Nutritional modulation of the gut microbiota and immune system in preterm neonates susceptible to necrotizing enterocolitis. J Nutr Biochem 2011;22(6):511–21.

[6] Johnson CL, Versalovic J. The human microbiome and its potential importance to pediatrics. Pediatrics 2012;129(5):950–60.

[7] Berman L, Moss RL. Necrotizing enterocolitis: an update. Semin Fetal Neonatal Med 2011;16(3):145–50.

[8] Lin PW, Stoll BJ. Necrotising enterocolitis. Lancet 2006;368(9543):1271–83.

[9] Shah D, Sinn JK. Antibiotic regimens for the empirical treatment of newborn infants with necrotising enterocolitis. Cochrane Database Syst Rev 2012;(8):CD007448.

[10] Solomkin JS, Mazuski JE, Bradley JS, et al. Diagnosis and management of complicated intra-abdominal infection in adults and children: guidelines by the surgical infection society and the Infectious Diseases Society of America. Clin Infect Dis 2010;50(2):133–64.

[11] Sato TT, Oldham KT. Pediatric abdomen. In: Mulholland MW, Lillemoe KD, Doherty GM, et al, editors. Greenfield's surgery scientific principles and practice. 4th edition. Philadelphia: Lippincott Williams & Wilkins; 2006. p. 1878–945.

[12] Hackam DJ, Grikscheit TC, Wang KS, et al. Pediatric surgery. In: Brunicardi CF, Andersen DK, Billiar TR, et al, editors. Schwartz's principles of surgery. 9th edition. New York: McGraw-Hill; 2010. p. 1409–57.

[13] Kim SS, Albanese CT. Necrotizing enterocolitis. In: O'Neill JA, Coran AG, Fonkalsrud E, et al, editors. Pediatric surgery, vol. 2, 6th edition. Philadelphia: Elsevier; 2006. p. 1427–52.
[14] Vaughan WG, Grosfeld JL, West K, et al. Avoidance of stomas and delayed anastomosis for bowel necrosis: the 'clip and drop-back' technique. J Pediatr Surg 1996;31(4):542–5.
[15] Moore TC, Collins DL, Nguyen M. Marked (24-fold) elevation of peritoneal cavity drainage fluid vascular endothelial growth factor after successful "patch, drain, and wait" approach for extensive midgut necrosis in a newborn. Pediatr Surg Int 2002;18(5–6):400–4.
[16] Moss RL, Dimmitt RA, Barnhart DC, et al. Laparotomy versus peritoneal drainage for necrotizing enterocolitis and perforation. N Engl J Med 2006;354(21):2225–34.
[17] Rees CM, Eaton S, Kiely EM, et al. Peritoneal drainage or laparotomy for neonatal bowel perforation? A randomized controlled trial. Ann Surg 2008;248(1):44–51.
[18] Rao SC, Basani L, Simmer K, et al. Peritoneal drainage versus laparotomy as initial surgical treatment for perforated necrotizing enterocolitis or spontaneous intestinal perforation in preterm low birth weight infants. Cochrane Database Syst Rev 2011;(6):CD006182.
[19] Downard CD, Renaud E, St Peter SD, et al. Treatment of necrotizing enterocolitis: an American Pediatric Surgical Association Outcomes and Clinical Trials Committee systematic review. J Pediatr Surg 2012;47(11):2111–22.
[20] Fallon EM, Nehra D, Potemkin AK, et al. A.S.P.E.N. clinical guidelines: nutrition support of neonatal patients at risk for necrotizing enterocolitis. JPEN J Parenter Enteral Nutr 2012;36(5):506–23.
[21] Section on Breastfeeding. Breastfeeding and the use of human milk. Pediatrics 2012;129(3):e827–41.
[22] Barlow B, Santulli TV, Heird WC, et al. An experimental study of acute neonatal enterocolitis–the importance of breast milk. J Pediatr Surg 1974;9(5):587–95.
[23] Penttila IA, Flesch IE, McCue AL, et al. Maternal milk regulation of cell infiltration and interleukin 18 in the intestine of suckling rat pups. Gut 2003;52(11):1579–86.
[24] Verhasselt V. Neonatal tolerance under breastfeeding influence. Curr Opin Immunol 2010;22(5):623–30.
[25] Adlerberth I, Wold AE. Establishment of the gut microbiota in Western infants. Acta Paediatr 2009;98(2):229–38.
[26] Mizrahi A, Barlow O, Berdon W, et al. Necrotizing enterocolitis in premature infants. J Pediatr 1965;66(4):697–706.
[27] Orlando S. The immunologic significance of breast milk. J Obstet Gynecol Neonatal Nurs 1995;24(7):678–83.
[28] Eibl MM, Wolf HM, Furnkranz H, et al. Prevention of necrotizing enterocolitis in low-birth-weight infants by IgA-IgG feeding. N Engl J Med 1988;319(1):1–7.
[29] Bode L, Rudloff S, Kunz C, et al. Human milk oligosaccharides reduce platelet-neutrophil complex formation and suppress neutrophil beta 2 integrin expression. J Leukoc Biol 2004;76(4):820–6.
[30] Pammi M, Abrams SA. Oral lactoferrin for the prevention of sepsis and necrotizing enterocolitis in preterm infants. Cochrane Database Syst Rev 2011;(10):CD007137.
[31] AlFaleh K, Anabrees J, Bassler D, et al. Probiotics for prevention of necrotizing enterocolitis in preterm infants. Cochrane Database Syst Rev 2011;(3):CD005496.
[32] Lin HC, Hsu CH, Chen HL, et al. Oral probiotics prevent necrotizing enterocolitis in very low birth weight preterm infants: a multicenter, randomized, controlled trial. Pediatrics 2008;122(4):693–700.
[33] Braga TD, Pontes da Silva GA, Cabral de Lira PI, et al. Efficacy of Bifidobacterium breve and Lactobacillus casei oral supplementation on necrotizing enterocolitis in very-low-birth-weight preterm infants: a double-blind, randomized, controlled trial. Am J Clin Nutr 2011;93(1):81–6.
[34] Mugambi MN, Musekiwa A, Lombard M, et al. Probiotics, prebiotics infant formula use in preterm or low birth weight infants: a systematic review. Nutr J 2012;11:58.

[35] Mihatsch WA, Hoegel J, Pohlandt F. Prebiotic oligosaccharides reduce stool viscosity and accelerate gastrointestinal transport in preterm infants. Acta Paediatr 2006;95(7): 843–8.
[36] Indrio F, Riezzo G, Raimondi F, et al. Prebiotics improve gastric motility and gastric electrical activity in preterm newborns. J Pediatr Gastroenterol Nutr 2009;49(2):258–61.
[37] Boehm G, Lidestri M, Casetta P, et al. Supplementation of a bovine milk formula with an oligosaccharide mixture increases counts of faecal bifidobacteria in preterm infants. Arch Dis Child 2002;86(3):F178–81.
[38] Kapiki A, Costalos C, Oikonomidou C, et al. The effect of a fructo-oligosaccharide supplemented formula on gut flora of preterm infants. Early Hum Dev 2007;83(5):335–9.
[39] Modi N, Uthaya S, Fell J, et al. A randomized, double-blind, controlled trial of the effect of prebiotic oligosaccharides on enteral tolerance in preterm infants (ISRCTN77444690). Pediatr Res 2010;68(5):440–5.
[40] Thomas DW, Greer FR. Nutrition AAoPCo, American Academy of Pediatrics Section on Gastroenterology Hp, and Nutrition. Probiotics and prebiotics in pediatrics. Pediatrics 2010;126(6):1217–31.
[41] Nair RR, Warner BB, Warner BW. Role of epidermal growth factor and other growth factors in the prevention of necrotizing enterocolitis. Semin Perinatol 2008;32(2):107–13.
[42] Coursodon CF, Dvorak B. Epidermal growth factor and necrotizing enterocolitis. Curr Opin Pediatr 2012;24(2):160–4.
[43] Dvorak B. Milk epidermal growth factor and gut protection. J Pediatr 2010;156(2):S31–5.
[44] Yu X, Radulescu A, Zorko N, et al. Heparin-binding EGF-like growth factor increases intestinal microvascular blood flow in necrotizing enterocolitis. Gastroenterology 2009;137(1):221–30.
[45] Warner BB, Ryan AL, Seeger K, et al. Ontogeny of salivary epidermal growth factor and necrotizing enterocolitis. J Pediatr 2007;150(4):358–63.
[46] Sullivan PB, Lewindon PJ, Cheng C, et al. Intestinal mucosa remodeling by recombinant human epidermal growth factor(1-48) in neonates with severe necrotizing enterocolitis. J Pediatr Surg 2007;42(3):462–9.
[47] Kamitsuka MD, Horton MK, Williams MA. The incidence of necrotizing enterocolitis after introducing standardized feeding schedules for infants between 1250 and 2500 grams and less than 35 weeks of gestation. Pediatrics 2000;105(2):379–84.
[48] Rayyis SF, Ambalavanan N, Wright L, et al. Randomized trial of "slow" versus "fast" feed advancements on the incidence of necrotizing enterocolitis in very low birth weight infants. J Pediatr 1999;134(3):293–7.
[49] Krishnamurthy S, Gupta P, Debnath S, et al. Slow versus rapid enteral feeding advancement in preterm newborn infants 1000-1499 g: a randomized controlled trial. Acta Paediatr 2010;99(1):42–6.
[50] Caple J, Armentrout D, Huseby V, et al. Randomized, controlled trial of slow versus rapid feeding volume advancement in preterm infants. Pediatrics 2004;114(6):1597–600.
[51] Salhotra A, Ramji S. Slow versus fast enteral feed advancement in very low birth weight infants: a randomized control trial. Indian Pediatr 2004;41(5):435–41.
[52] Morgan J, Young L, McGuire W. Slow advancement of enteral feed volumes to prevent necrotising enterocolitis in very low birth weight infants. Cochrane Database Syst Rev 2011;(3):CD001241.
[53] Leaf A, Dorling J, Kempley S, et al. Early or delayed enteral feeding for preterm growth-restricted infants: a randomized trial. Pediatrics 2012;129(5):e1260–8.
[54] Karagianni P, Briana DD, Mitsiakos G, et al. Early versus delayed minimal enteral feeding and risk for necrotizing enterocolitis in preterm growth-restricted infants with abnormal antenatal Doppler results. Am J Perinatol 2010;27(5):367–73.
[55] Morgan J, Young L, McGuire W. Delayed introduction of progressive enteral feeds to prevent necrotising enterocolitis in very low birth weight infants. Cochrane Database Syst Rev 2011;(3):CD001970.

[56] Pearson F, Johnson MJ, Leaf AA. Milk osmolality: does it matter? Arch Dis Child Fetal Neonatal Ed 2013;98(2):F166–9.
[57] Lucas A, Fewtrell MS, Morley R, et al. Randomized outcome trial of human milk fortification and developmental outcome in preterm infants. Am J Clin Nutr 1996;64(2):142–51.
[58] Kuschel CA, Harding JE. Multicomponent fortified human milk for promoting growth in preterm infants. Cochrane Database Syst Rev 2004;(1):CD000343.
[59] Blakely ML, Lally KP, McDonald S, et al. Postoperative outcomes of extremely low birth-weight infants with necrotizing enterocolitis or isolated intestinal perforation - a prospective cohort study by the NICHD neonatal research network. Ann Surg 2005;241(6):984–9.
[60] Stringer MD, Brereton RJ, Drake DP, et al. Recurrent necrotizing enterocolitis. J Pediatr Surg 1993;28(8):979–81.
[61] Thyoka M, Eaton S, Hall NJ, et al. Advanced necrotizing enterocolitis part 2: recurrence of necrotizing enterocolitis. Eur J Pediatr Surg 2012;22(1):13–6.
[62] Pike K, Brocklehurst P, Jones D, et al. Outcomes at 7 years for babies who developed neonatal necrotising enterocolitis: the ORACLE Children Study. Arch Dis Child Fetal Neonatal Ed 2012;97(5):F318–22.
[63] Hintz SR, Kendrick DE, Stoll BJ, et al. Neurodevelopmental and growth outcomes of extremely low birth weight infants after necrotizing enterocolitis. Pediatrics 2005;115(3):696–703.
[64] Castro L, Yolton K, Haberman B, et al. Bias in reported neurodevelopmental outcomes among extremely low birth weight survivors. Pediatrics 2004;114(2):404–10.
[65] Goulet O, Ruemmele F. Causes and management of intestinal failure in children. Gastroenterology 2006;130(2):S16–28.
[66] Duro D, Kalish LA, Johnston P, et al. Risk factors for intestinal failure in infants with necrotizing enterocolitis: a Glaser Pediatric Research Network study. J Pediatr 2010;157(2):203–8.

Advances in Pediatrics 60 (2013) 281–294

ADVANCES IN PEDIATRICS

# Historical Development of Pediatric Surgical Quality: The First 100 Years

Jennifer Bruny, MD*, Moritz M. Ziegler, MD

Department of Surgery, Children's Hospital of Colorado, University of Colorado School of Medicine, 13123 East 16th Avenue, Aurora, CO 80045, USA

**Keywords**

• Pediatric surgical quality • Pediatric surgical outcomes
• Surgical quality improvement

**Key points**

- The development of surgical quality in pediatrics began in the early 1900s when pediatric surgery began to develop as its own specialty. Around the same time, pioneering ideas about tracking surgical quality began to take shape.
- Development of collaborative efforts through organized associations and quality improvement organizations has fostered data sharing and combining of experiences, which has resulted in improved surgical outcomes for children.
- The development of a prospective database for surgical outcomes in children is currently expanding, the results of which are risk-adjusted outcome comparisons of surgical treatment between pediatric hospitals with the goal of fostering quality improvement efforts.

The history of pediatric surgery has developed sequentially and simultaneously along 4 complementary pathways. First, individual pioneering surgeons declared their interest by confining their practice to the surgical diseases of children. Second, the Boston school of Ladd and Gross provided the legacy and leadership by establishing principles for the surgical care of children and by training most of the next generation of training program leaders in pediatric surgery. The third critically important development was the evolution of organized pediatric surgery, the initiation of the *Journal of Pediatric Surgery* as a specialty journal, and the eventual evolution to a board certification process.

Disclosures: The authors have no financial relationships to disclose.

*Corresponding author. Children's Hospital of Colorado, 13123 East 16th Avenue, 323, Aurora, CO 80045. *E-mail address*: jennifer.bruny@childrenscolorado.org

0065-3101/13/$ – see front matter
http://dx.doi.org/10.1016/j.yapd.2013.04.012 

The fourth pathway was the evolution from a collection of anecdotal clinical observations to one of scientific achievement based on sound laboratory and clinical research.

On review, an analysis of pediatric surgical quality (success of operation as well as preoperative and postoperative care with subsequent long-term outcomes that satisfy the initial goals of care) occurs in parallel with the overarching history of the field itself. On assessment, it seems that both simultaneously are approaching the completion of their first century of activity. This article reviews this evolution and its associated milestones, placing them in historical perspective; in particular monitoring the quality initiatives of assessment and putative improvement that characterize this area of study is currently called clinical outcomes research.

## THE PIONEER OF AMERICAN PEDIATRIC SURGERY

William E. Ladd, MD (1880–1967) is generally considered to be the father of American pediatric surgery. Born in Milton, Massachusetts, he graduated from Harvard College and Harvard Medical School (1906). He was a surgical intern at the Boston City Hospital. Thereafter, in addition to his general surgery and gynecologic surgery practice, he joined the staff of the Boston Children's Hospital in 1910 to do an occasional surgical procedure on a child.

On December 6, 1917, the French munitions ship Mont Blanc collided with the Norwegian vessel Imo in the narrows of Halifax harbor. The result was the most powerful man-made explosion in history to that time. The resulting destruction of life and property was massive: 2000 men, women, and children were killed, 9000 injured, 6000 lost their homes, and 25,000 were left without adequate shelter. Multiple medical care teams poured into Halifax, and Ladd organized and led such a team from Boston. Witnessing the plight of burned and disabled children in this disaster so moved Ladd that he resolved to change the direction of his career and devote himself exclusively to the surgical care of the pediatric age group. Thereafter, Ladd fulfilled this resolve, and in 1927 he was named Surgeon-in-Chief at the Boston Children's Hospital, succeeding James S. Stone, MD. Over the next decade, Dr Ladd applied his meticulous operative skills and attention to detail, and he began to recruit individuals who would eventually lay the foundation for the Boston school of pediatric surgery, culminating in the recruitment of Robert Gross as resident in 1938 and fellow staff member in 1939. Ladd ascended to the first endowed chair in pediatric surgery at the Boston Children's Hospital and the Harvard Medical School in 1941, and he retired as Surgeon-in-Chief in 1945 [1].

## PIONEER IN SURGICAL QUALITY

Slightly earlier than Ladd, Ernest A. Codman, MD (1869–1940) also was a graduate of Harvard College and Harvard Medical School. From 1894 to 1895 he served as intern at Massachusetts General Hospital (MGH). Expressing an interest in the nascent field of skiagraphy (the early term for radiology), in 1899 he was appointed as the first radiologist at Children's Hospital Boston and in 1900 he was appointed as Assistant Surgeon at MGH. Although not a pediatric surgeon, his commitment to the pediatric patient occurred in radiology. However, his major historical contribution is summarized in his statement defining his commitment to surgical quality and outcomes, a position 100 years ahead of its time:

> Every hospital should follow every patient it treats long enough to determine whether or not the treatment had been successful and then to inquire, if not, why not? [2]

So committed was Codman to his leadership position on assessing surgical outcomes and surgeon competence that he jeopardized his academic surgical career. His persona was described as one-minded and manically obsessed with surgical quality and outcomes not only for the purpose of a hospital to assess its results of care but also for the purpose of judging quality and competency of the surgeon of record [3]. This latter goal separated Codman from his MGH colleagues, so much so that he was forced to resign from the staff, which he did completely by 1914. In a similar way, in a 1915 meeting of the Suffolk Medical Society on hospital efficiency, he took issue with a cartoon depicting an ostrich with its head buried in the sand. He was requested to step down from this society position as well, and he readily complied.

Codman subsequently returned to Boston and developed his own hospital, which he aptly named the End-result Hospital [4]. There his goal was to assess, measure, and share the outcomes of each and every patient admitted for care. The additional analysis of the individual surgeon's performance that Codman advocated was also the basis for his continued alienation by surgical colleagues. Other major contributions from Codman's quality legacy include the development of a tumor registry for bone sarcomas, the first of its kind. This step was continued and subsequently expanded by the Commission on Cancer of the American College of Surgeons (ACS). He is also credited with the development of the first anesthesia record. His participation in the Committee on Hospital Standardization of the ACS became the critically important forerunner of the Joint Commission on Accreditation of Hospital Organizations (JACHO), the organization that assures the quality performance of American hospitals to the present time.

Perhaps most importantly to surgical quality and safety was Codman's creation of an error assessment and classification system that, along with his development of a morbidity and mortality conference discussion forum, originally at MGH but eventually nationwide, as an almost universal routine in every surgical department's assessment system. This system and the cultural behavior that surrounds such a departmental conference have continued over these 100 years until today. In addition, it has become a required curricular mandate for training programs.

## THE FURTHER DEVELOPMENT OF PEDIATRIC SURGERY

The organization of pediatric surgery first occurred with the development of its relationship with the American Academy of Pediatrics (AAP), the so-called

Surgical Section of the AAP in 1948. This relationship produced an annual meeting forum in which pediatric surgeons could present their largely clinical research data to a group of like-minded specialists. This section also eventually offered a competitive resident research award for the best article and it has also awarded 2 prestigious honors, the Salzberg Mentorship Award and the Ladd Medal, the latter being the highest recognition attained by an American pediatric surgeon. By 1970, pediatric surgeons had developed their own independent organization, the Americana Pediatric Surgical Association (APSA), an organization that has matured to produce an annual meeting educational forum, a continuing self-assessment forum, a foundation that supports young pediatric surgical researchers, and collaboration with both international organizations of pediatric surgeons and oncologists as well as our own American Pediatric Surgical Nurses Association (APSNA). In addition, pediatric surgeons sought to collaborate with the American Board of Surgery (ABS) to develop a certification process. The effort took 20 years of persuasive negotiation beginning in 1955, and not until 1975 did the first examination occur, granting a Certificate of Special Competency in Pediatric Surgery from the ABS. In parallel with these developments there were also specialty journals (*Journal of Pediatric Surgery*, *Seminars in Pediatric Surgery*, and the *International Journal of Pediatric Surgery*) and there were further specialty textbook publications as well.

The linkage of this maturation of the specialty field of pediatric surgery to the further development of surgical quality should be self-evident. The forums of the various organizational meetings provided an opportunity to develop and exchange ideas, test hypotheses, and introduce new innovations to the field. For example, the fields of fetal surgery and minimally invasive surgery of children were innovations introduced and vetted in this way. The linkage to the ABS and a certification process proved key. It helped to standardize the pediatric surgical training process that had matured under the oversight of the Residency Review Committee of Surgery of the American College of Graduate Medical Education (ACGME) and the Association of Pediatric Surgical Training Program Directors. It also standardized the certification processes for individuals qualifying for either board certification or recertification, and it both qualified and required surgeons to participate in the maintenance of competency process as defined by the ABS. This program has further emphasized the need for continuing learning as well as self-assessment in the specialty field (Box 1).

## COLLABORATIVE QUALITY INITIATIVES

The initiation of a cooperative group system for clinical cancer research began in 1955, with a consortium focused on childhood cancer research. By the end of the 1990s this program had expanded to 4 funded cooperative groups focused specifically on childhood cancer research using varied multidisciplinary therapies and long-term outcomes assessment. The Children's Cancer Group (CCG) and the Pediatric Oncology Group (POG) studied a diverse

**Box 1: Six core competencies of the ACGME**

1. Patient care
2. Medical knowledge
3. Practice-based learning and improvement
4. Interpersonal and communication skills
5. Professionalism
6. Systems-based practice

array of childhood cancers, whereas the Intergroup Rhabdomyosarcoma Study Group (IRSG), and the National Wilms' Tumor Study Group (NWTS) were cancer specific. By the year 2000, the 4 pediatric groups voluntarily merged efforts to create the Children's Oncology Group. These efforts represented the first prospective outcomes studies for pediatric surgery, and, in selected examples (eg, outcomes with Wilms tumor), the results are continually outstanding. The organizational protocol-driven diagnostic and treatment strategy had a huge impact on the improvement in childhood cancer outcomes, and it considerably enhanced the quality of life of patients with cancer as well. Pediatric surgery representatives were, and continue to be, critical participants in these groups and their considerable improvement in disease-specific outcomes [5].

More recently, a collaborative of children's hospitals in Ohio has been a leader in a broad-reaching effort to improve the quality of pediatric medical and surgical care. The Ohio Children's Hospitals' Solutions for Patient Safety (OCHSPS) foundation started in 2006 as 8 pediatric hospitals working together to decrease hospital-acquired conditions. OCHSPS received a Center for Medicare and Medicaid Services' Hospital Engagement Network grant to expand the effort across the country. The current focus is on preventable readmissions and 9 hospital-acquired conditions, including adverse drug events, catheter-associated urinary tract infections, central line–associated blood stream infections, injuries from falls and immobility, pressure ulcers, venous thromboembolism, ventilator-associated pneumonia, surgical site infections (SSIs), and serious safety events. The collaborative hospitals agree to be transparent in their data sharing. The goal is reducing hospital-acquired conditions by 20% and preventable readmissions by 10% in 2013.

## THE INSTITUTE OF MEDICINE REPORTS

After the Codman era, his work on error analysis and classification, outcomes assessment, and the personal audit of surgeon performance, the major emphasis in surgery became an analysis of morbidity and mortality. After applying the Codman error classification system, often feared by the surgical resident who was subject to the blame mentality and who was assigned an error in judgment or an error in technique, the surgical morbidity and mortality conference spent little time on error analysis, systems failure, and process improvement. By the 1950s, such audit tools were promulgated worldwide [6] and, soon thereafter, in the 1960s and 1970s, a series of scoring techniques were developed. The advent of computer technology resulted in more readily applied systems-based mechanisms to record large volumes of data from which institutional and surgeon-specific outcomes performance could be assessed [7–10]. It was soon recognized that several shortcomings were still present: data were irregularly captured, risk-stratification of patient and disease comorbidities were incompletely assessed, and the extent of follow-up into the post-hospital discharge time frame was crucial in depicting the overall care-cycle morbidity as well as mortality, but postdischarge follow-up was not being captured [11–13]. Despite the accomplishments of Deming and the total quality improvement movement that extended to international and then American industrial management in the post–World War II recovery era, this quality initiative had little impact on health care processes.

It was not until the late 1980s that pediatric surgeon Lucian Leape, MD, at the Harvard School of Public Health and his team of investigators reported a sentinel contribution on the previously unrecognized frequency of hospital errors that could cause either significant patient injury or even hospital death [14]. This report was soon followed by a sequence of reports from the Institute of Medicine (*To Err is Human* and *Crossing the Quality Chiasm*), both confirming and responding to Leape's data [15,16]. These data revealed as many as 98,000 in-hospital deaths, as many as 200,000 incorrect pharmaceutical prescriptions, and as many as 5000 incorrect operations, all on an annual basis and also deemed preventable. The dramatic nature of these events is better described when plotted against the potential performance improvement analysis of 6 sigma (Table 1). However, health care performance does not approach 6 sigma in error frequency. Furthermore, if 6 sigma error analyses from industry are applied to such health care data, the degree of process improvement that needs to be achieved to attain best practice outcomes is considerable. It was this revelation that led to the reactive modern day response to improve the quality, safety, and outcomes of current health care diagnostic and treatment strategies. Such process improvement initiatives have included broad issues of data-driven analyses, data transparency, a culture of team and improvement (not of individual blame), and process standardization with minimization of variability. On a practical level, clinical care guidelines became popular, and application of strict patient identification strategies and application of the universal protocol

**Table 1**
Errors in medicine: what degree of excellence is achievable?

| 99% Good (3.8 Sigma) | 99.99966% Good (6 Sigma) |
|---|---|
| 5000 incorrect surgical operations per week | 1.7 incorrect operations per week |
| 200,000 incorrect drug prescriptions per year | 68 incorrect drug prescriptions per year |
| 48,000–96,000 hospital error deaths per year | 17–34 hospital error deaths per year |

became a JACHO mandate in an attempt to ensure right patient, correct side, and right operation [17].

## THE ADMINISTRATIVE DATABASE AND SURGICAL QUALITY

Until recently, automated health-record databases in the United States have generally been administrative; that is, the data are derived from requests to insurers for health care payments, or claims, for clinical services and therapies. These retrospective databases have several important advantages for surgical outcomes research: a large, population-based sample of all surgical procedures, data are already collected and inexpensive to access, and information on patient diagnoses and medical care received during the admission is recorded without the risk of physician recall bias [18]. Administrative databases are well suited for quickly and efficiently evaluating relationships between patient and hospital characteristics and disparities in surgical quality. For example, higher hospital and surgeon case volumes have repeatedly been associated with favorable surgical outcomes [19].

However, automated databases have several recognized limitations when evaluating surgical outcomes. First, there is uncertain validity of the recorded medical diagnoses, which calls into question the validity of risk-adjusted outcomes when using administrative data [18]. The magnitude of this limitation depends on the diagnosis of interest and how consistently it is routinely recorded in hospital admission records [20]. In addition, information on other important preoperative and operative risk factors not billed during the hospital stay (eg, preoperative evaluations, the American Society of Anesthesiologists classification, emergency status, operative times, estimated percent blood loss) is generally not available [21]. Although administrative data can track some process measures reflecting the quality of surgical care (eg, prophylactic antibiotic use), the information is often not recorded in sufficient detail to adequately assess adherence to specific medical recommendations (eg, the timing and duration of antibiotic use relative to the time of the surgical incision). Hospital administrative data are also limited to examining surgical outcomes occurring during the hospital admission, such as death or surgical infections, and are not a good data source for evaluating mortality and morbidity outcomes after discharge and long-term surgical success rates.

Thus, the usefulness of administrative data for assessing surgical quality depends on the measures being studied and how well they are captured in hospital administrative records. At a minimum, administrative data can be an important hypothesis-generating source for evaluating surgical performance and improving quality. The widespread adoption of electronic medical records systems will address some of the limitations of administrative data by providing a more complete record of patient risk factors while preserving the efficiency of computerized databases.

We previously reported on the varied databases available for pediatric surgical clinical research and their potential use in outcomes analysis [22]. These data are summarized in Table 2.

**Table 2**
Administrative databases and their application in pediatric surgical outcomes research

| Database | Scope of data | Applied usefulness |
|---|---|---|
| Nationwide Inpatient (NCIS) | Began 1988; all payers; 1000 hospitals; all inpatients-8 Million adult and pediatric yearly admissions | Trends over time in surgical care; tracks diffusion of new technology |
| Kids' Inpatient Database | Pediatric inpatients <age 21 y; every 3 y Since 1997; includes births; not every state | Care comparison across hospital types, eg, pediatric vs nonpediatric hospitals |
| State Ambulatory Surgical Database | — | Contrast inpatient and outpatient care for the same diagnosis |
| State Inpatients Database | — | Inpatient surgical case volume distribution by hospital type |
| Pediatric Health Information System | CHCA privately holds; 40 tertiary pediatric hospitals | Time sequence of service; outcomes and cost; readmissions; granular data |

*Abbreviations*: CHCA, Child Health Corporation of America; NCIS, Nationwide Child Information System.
*Data from* Morrato E, Dillon P, Ziegler M. Surgical Quality: from personal audits to administrative data bases to risk-adjusted outcome measures. How far have we come? Curr Opin Pediatr 2008;20:320–5.

## RISK-ADJUSTED OUTCOME ASSESSMENT IN CHILDREN'S SURGERY

### Lessons from adult surgery

The National Surgical Quality Improvement Program (NSQIP) was initiated by Khuri and colleagues [23] in 1991 in the Veterans Administration Health Administration (VAH), in which operative results of major procedures had been substandard. In a performance improvement initiative that addressed morbidity and mortality, the prospective entry of patient risk and outcome information following major surgery in the VAH system nationwide was proposed [24]. Risk assessment followed and hospitals were for the first time able to be ranked in terms of unadjusted and risk-adjusted outcome performance using the calculation of observed/expected ratios of predicted morbidity [25,26]. By 1998, a system of reliable and valid data capture was available for major surgical patients nationwide in the VAH that included presurgical risk factors, process of care factors during surgery, and 30-day morbidity and mortalities [27]. These data permitted the hospital system and its surgeons to engage in outcome performance improvement initiatives. This system emphasized administrative and management support, a uniform national informatics system, consistent clinical definitions, and data collection by a dedicated core of trained nurses [28]. By 2000, the value of this study began to be realized: there was improvement in wound infection complications [26] and, by 2002, there was a report of an aggregate system-wide 27% decrease in surgical mortality and a 45% decrease in surgical morbidity [27]. What was emphasized was the value of annual site-specific outcomes reports, self-assessment tool applications, structured site visits by an oversight body, and dissemination of best-practices methods by best-practice institutions throughout the VAH system.

Also in 2002, 3 academic health centers reported their application of the NSQIP module to the assessment of surgical outcomes. Their data collection began in 1999 and, by 2002, their analysis showed the feasibility of the NSQIP module's application to non-VAH hospitals [28].

In the interim there have been multiple studies of surgical care outcomes, either disease specific or institutional, fostered by participation in the NSQIP. Additional studies have focused on the important question of relating surgical case volumes to improved outcomes, an observation that cannot be supported by NSQIP data from VAH [29,30]. Further studies have addressed the important comparison of assessing quality with either a risk-adjusted program such as NSQIP versus the use of administrative databases for outcome assessment of postoperative morbidity and mortality. The results of such a comparison are mixed [31]. However, in urology as well as general surgery, what has been shown is that the reporting of morbidity and mortality by an NSQIP system as opposed to the voluntary reporting mechanism used in the traditional morbidity and mortality conference significantly improves the capture of adverse events both in the hospital and after discharge, and facilitates the development of corrective strategies [32,33]. Perhaps most importantly, the well-developed and rich database along with the semiannual reports of risk-adjusted surgical morbidity and mortality provides to member participants an important opportunity to foster quality and safety improvement strategies and provide a catalyst for change [34].

## Quality studies in pediatric surgery

Although specialty-specific efforts (eg, congenital heart surgery [35,36] and trauma [37,38]) exist to examine outcomes and improve results in children's surgical care, there are no broad-based, multicenter quality improvement programs capable of examining the spectrum of surgical care for children. In 2006, as a consequence of an APSA strategic planning process led by President Patricia Donahoe, MD, the APSA Outcomes Committee was directed to seek a relationship with the ACS to explore the development of a pediatric surgical real-time, risk-adjusted surgical outcomes program, an NSQIP-Pediatric (NSQIP-P).

Because of unique characteristics encountered in the surgical care of infants and children, there are major challenges to the development of a quality improvement program in children's surgery. Although the simplest approach might have been to model the pediatric NSQIP exactly after the adult NSQIP structure, while making some allowances for differing surgical procedures, procedure volumes, and outcomes, there are several features that mandate looking at quality improvement in children's surgery from a different viewpoint. First, there is marked heterogeneity in the outcomes of these surgical procedures, and most are performed infrequently in relation to adult procedures. Second, the perioperative mortalities for most noncardiac major pediatric surgical procedures are low. Third, the marked and rapid changes in physical and neurologic function that are part of normal growth and development complicate the measurement, aggregation, and interpretation of some nonfatal outcomes, such as functional status and health-related quality of life. Fourth, because of age-related cognitive limitations, the determination of preoperative comorbidities, postoperative outcomes, and any quality-of-life assessments often must be obtained through a surrogate for neonates, infants, and preschool children.

In addition, there were potential major issues that challenge the statistical analysis and modeling of the data collected. Because of the rare and specialized nature of many procedures, there were potential major differences in the type, volume, and outcome rates of procedures between the various institutions such as tertiary children's hospitals and general hospitals that care for children. Most importantly, the heterogeneity in surgical procedures, low volume, and low mortality could result in inadequate statistical power if mortality is used as the primary outcome as in the adult NSQIP.

### Goals for the development of the children's NSQIP

After 3 years of development and planning, a final test version of an NSQIP-P was readied for an alpha test to assess whether this was a feasible way to assess inpatient morbidity and mortality across the multiple pediatric surgical specialties of orthopedic surgery, urology, neurosurgery, otolaryngology, plastic surgery, and gynecology in addition to the specialty of pediatric general and thoracic surgery. Excluded from this phase of NSQIP-P were trauma, transplantation, cardiac surgery, and ophthalmology. An outcomes measure for each of these areas was already in place, except for ophthalmology.

The alpha phase was originally rolled out in 4 pediatric centers; namely Yale New Haven Children's Hospital, A.I. Dupont Children's Hospital, Milwaukee Children's Hospital, and The Children's Hospital Denver. During this initial phase of program refinement, standard NSQIP practices were implemented for patient review and data collection with the goal of collecting risk, procedural, and outcomes data in 20,000 to 30,000 children undergoing inpatient surgery.

The results of this alpha phase have been reported [39]. Data were captured from these four centers from October 2008 to May 2009, reviewing each of 114 variables along with a 30-day follow-up in 3117 patients, who themselves represented 31 states, 685 cities, and operative work done by 183 surgeons. There were 12 deaths (0.36%). There were 399 postoperative complications/occurrences in 277 patients, and these represented 8.4% of the study population. When compared by specialty, complications were most frequent for neurosurgery and least for otolaryngology. When compared across the four institutions, complications ranged from 6.8% to 10.2%. These data represented the first multi-institutional real-time assessment of morbidity and mortality in the pediatric surgical specialties. Furthermore, it became clear that the study was poised for expansion to additional institutions, data definition and patient sampling required continued refinement, and, importantly, expansion of patient enrollment would allow application of risk-adjustment methodology.

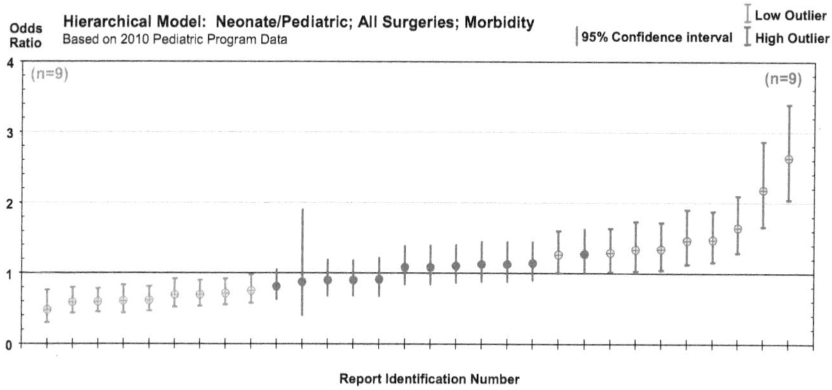


**Fig. 1.** Hierarchical model showing institutional odds ratios for outcomes in all cases for any morbidity for the year 2010. Institutional identification numbers were supplied to the participating institutions.

Beta phase NSQIP-P was then conducted in 29 institutions nationwide in 2010, with the aim of further refining variables, solidifying processes, and investigating risk-adjusted models across pediatric specialties [40]. These sites included 14 free-standing and 15 hospital-within-hospital institutions, 14 academic institutions, and 15 nonacademic institutions. Data were prospectively collected for 37,157 patients. A total of 2917 cases (7.9%) had intraoperative or postoperative occurrences/complications (other than death). There were also 94 deaths (0.25%). There were 677 SSIs (1.8%). For the 1382 neonatal cases, mortality was 2.4%, any morbidity was 18.7%, and the SSI rate was 3.0%. Risk-adjusted hospital performance models were then generated. Fig. 1 presents the risk-adjusted morbidity for all cases. Each point represents a participating institution and its relative risk of complications with 95% confidence interval. For the first time, participating children's institutions and programs had clinically relevant, rigorously risk-adjusted performance data relative to peer institutions to inform their quality improvement efforts.

The ACS NSQIP-P has now expanded into full production with more than 40 participating institutions. Higher case numbers have expanded the success of modeling, and for the first time institutions have received specialty-specific risk-adjusted comparisons, which will be reported in the literature in the near future. Refinement of variables and creation of specialty-specific outcomes continues, and pilot projects evaluating resource use as a marker of quality have begun to take place. The goal of the ACS NSQIP-P remains to ensure that the end result is an improvement in surgical outcomes for all pediatric age group patients.

## SUMMARY

The development of pediatric surgery has been closely involved with the development of surgical quality initiatives over the past 100 years. Quality surgical care for children was initiated by pioneers with the foresight to dedicate their surgical practice to children, as well as follow surgical outcomes. This overriding drive for quality care for children has resulted in the creation of multiple associations and societies for sharing of outcomes as well as collaboratives that allow data sharing and quality improvement efforts. These efforts have culminated in the development of a prospectively collected database that for the first time allows for risk-adjusted comparisons of surgical outcomes for children.

## References

[1] Ziegler MM. History of pediatric surgery. In: Operative pediatric surgery. 2nd edition. McGraw-Hill, in press.
[2] Codman EA. A study in hospital efficiency 1916 Boston: Privately printed.
[3] Berwick DM. E. A. Codman and the rhetoric of battle: a commentary. Milbank Q 1989;67(2):262–7.
[4] Donabedian A. The end results of health care: Ernest Codman's contribution to quality assessment and beyond. Milbank Q 1989;67(2):233–56.
[5] Nuchtern JD, London WB, Barnewolt CE, et al. A prospective study of expectant observation as primary therapy for neuroblastoma in young infants: a Children's Oncology Group study. Ann Surg 2012;256(4):573–80.
[6] Wright J. The history of surgical audit. J Qual Clin Pract 1995;15:81–8.
[7] Strauch G. Problem-oriented surgical audit in the community hospital. A concept in evolution. Am J Surg 1975;129:401–6.
[8] Andrus C, Daly J. Evaluation of surgical services in a large university-affiliated VA hospital: use of an in-house-generated quality assurance data base. South Med J 1991;84: 1447–50.
[9] Rageth J, Haner C, Hess P, et al. Systematic scientific quality improvement in surgical specialties. The AQS model. Swiss Surg 1999;5:62–72.
[10] Donati A, Ruzzi M, Andrario E, et al. A new and feasible model for predicting operative risk. Br J Anaesth 2004;93:393–9.
[11] Hadjianastassiou V, Tekkis P, Poloniecki J, et al. Surgical mortality score: risk management tool for auditing surgical performance. World J Surg 2004;28: 193–200.
[12] Martin R, Brennan M, Jaques D. Quality of complication reporting in the surgical literature. Ann Surg 2002;235:803–13.
[13] Hardwick R, Saltrese-Taylor A, Collins C. Need to measure outcome after discharge in surgical audit. Qual Health Care 1992;1:165–7.
[14] Leape LL, Robert E. Gross lecture. Making health care safe: are we up to it? J Pediatr Surg 2004;39(3):258–66.
[15] Kohn LT, Corrigan JM, editors. To err is human: building a safer health system. Washington, DC: National Academies Press; 2000.
[16] Institute of Medicine Committee on Quality Health Care in America. Crossing the quality chasm: a new health system for the 21st century. Washington, DC: National Academies Press; 2001.
[17] Gewande A. Complications: a surgeon's notes on an imperfect science. New York: Henry Holt and Company; 2002.
[18] Strom BL. Overview of automated databases in pharmacoepidemiology. In: Strom BL, Kimmel SE, editors. Textbook of pharmacoepidemiology. West Sussex (England): John Wiley & Sons; 2006. p. 167–72.
[19] Rogers SO. The holy grail of surgical quality improvement: process measures or risk-adjusted outcomes? Am Surg 2006;72(11):1046–50.

[20] Best WR, Khuri SF, Phelan M, et al. Identifying patient preoperative risk factors and postoperative adverse events in administrative databases: results from the department of veterans affairs national surgical quality improvement program. J Am Coll Surg 2002;194(3):257–66.
[21] Gordon H, Johnson M, Wray N, et al. Mortality after non-cardiac surgery: prediction from administrative versus clinical data. Med Care 2005;43:159–67.
[22] Morrato E, Dillon P, Ziegler M. Surgical quality: from personal audits to administrative data bases to risk adjusted outcome measures. How far have we come? Curr Opin Pediatr 2008;20:320–5.
[23] Khuri S, Daley J, Henderson W, et al. Risk adjustment of the postoperative mortality rate for the comparative assessment of the quality of surgical care: results of the National Veterans Affairs Surgical Risk Study. J Am Coll Surg 1997;185:315–27.
[24] Daley J, Khuri SF, Henderson W, et al. Risk adjustment of the post-operative morbidity rate for the comparative assessment of the quality of surgical care: results of the National Veterans Affairs Surgical Risk Study. J Am Coll Surg 1997;185:328–40.
[25] Khuri S, Daley J, Henderson W, et al. The Department of Veterans Affairs' NSQIP: the first national, validated, outcome-based, risk-adjusted, and peer-controlled program for the measurement and enhancement of the quality of surgical care. National VA Quality Improvement Program. Ann Surg 1998;228:491–507.
[26] Neumayer L, Mastin M, Vanderhoof L, et al. Using the Veterans Administration National Surgical Quality Improvement Program to improve patient outcomes. J Surg Res 2000;88:58–61.
[27] Khuri S, Daley J, Henderson W. The comparative assessment and improvement of quality of surgical care in the Department of Veterans Affairs. Arch Surg 2002;137:20–7.
[28] Fink A, Campbell DJ, Mentzer RJ, et al. The National Surgical Quality Improvement Program in non-veterans administration hospitals: initial demonstration of feasibility. Ann Surg 2002;236:344–53.
[29] Khuri SF, Daley J, Henderson W, et al. Relation of surgical volume to outcome in eight common operations: results from the VA National Surgical Quality Improvement Program. Ann Surg 1999;230:414–29.
[30] Khuri SF, Henderson WG. The case against volume as a measure of quality of surgical care. World J Surg 2005;29:1222–9.
[31] Hall BL, Hirbe M, Waterman B, et al. Comparison of mortality risk adjustment using a clinical data algorithm (American College of Surgeons National Surgical Quality Improvement Program) and an administrative data algorithm (Solucient) at the case level within a single institution. J Am Coll Surg 2007;205(6):767–77.
[32] Miller D, Filson C, Wallner L, et al. Comparing performance of Morbidity and Mortality Conference and National Surgical Quality Improvement Program for detection of complications after urologic surgery. Urology 2006;68:931–7.
[33] Hutter M, Rowell K, Devaney L, et al. Identification of surgical complications and deaths: an assessment of the traditional surgical morbidity and mortality conference compared with the American College of Surgeons-National Surgical Quality Improvement Program. J Am Coll Surg 2006;203:618–24.
[34] Rowell KS, Turrentine FE, Hutter MM. Use of national surgical quality improvement program data as a catalyst for quality improvement. J Am Coll Surg 2007;204(6):1293–300.
[35] Jenkins K, Gauvreau K, Newburger J, et al. Consensus-based method for risk adjustment for surgery for congenital heart disease. J Thorac Cardiovasc Surg 2002;123(1):110–8.
[36] Lacour-Gayet F, Clarke D. The Aristotle method: a new concept to evaluate quality of care based on complexity. Curr Opin Pediatr 2005;17(3):412–7.
[37] Tepas JI. The national pediatric trauma registry: a legacy of commitment to control of childhood injury. Semin Pediatr Surg 2004;13(2):126–32.

[38] Osler T, Vane D, Tepas J, et al. Do pediatric trauma centers have better survival rates than adult trauma centers? An examination of the National Pediatric Trauma Registry. J Trauma 2001;50(1):96–101.
[39] Raval MV, Dillon PW, Bruny JL, et al, ACS NSQIP Pediatric Steering Committee. Pediatric American College of Surgeons National Surgical Quality Improvement Program: feasibility of a novel, prospective assessment of surgical outcomes. J Pediatr Surg 2011;46:115–21.
[40] Bruny JL, Hall BL, Barnhart DC, et al. American College of Surgeons National Surgical Quality Improvement Program Pediatric: a beta phase report. J Pediatr Surg 2013;48(1): 74–80.

Advances in Pediatrics 60 (2013) 295

ADVANCES IN PEDIATRICS

# Introduction

# Parents' Perspective

John P. Moyer, MD

My wife, younger son, and I made a critical decision nearly 20 years ago.

Our 23-year-old son, Andy, lay on life support in an intensive care unit. Nearly one day after sustaining a head injury from a skiing accident, and despite the finest neurosurgical management and nursing care, the blood flow to his brain had ceased. We fully understood that he would never recover. At that point we became an organ and tissue donor family.

Vivid memories of organ donation began to surface. In medical school in the early 1960s, I witnessed a kidney transplant. In my pediatric residency, I was part of a support team that was transplanting livers into children.

Our son, Andy, was a senior in a fine university and was majoring in physics. He was planning a career in medicine or bioengineering. His close friends told us that he was a brilliant student. He often would stop and come to the aid of those who didn't catch on quite as quickly and spend time with them as a mentor and tutor. He seemed to have very positive influences on people's lives. His friendships were genuine and cemented.

Our choice to donate Andy's organs and tissues seemed to give some glimmer of sense to the tragic loss that we suffered. We were certain that we were doing the right thing by giving the transplant professionals permission to recover his organs and tissues. Donation in some mysterious manner has assuaged our grief, and the gifts have ended the suffering of other families.

The three men that received Andy's solid organs continue to live quality lives all these years later. They have seen grandchildren come into the world, build new homes, manage business ventures, teach, and generally enjoy quality lives with their families and friends.

John P. Moyer, MD
University of Colorado School of Medicine
Children's Hospital of Colorado
Morrison, CO 80465, USA

*E-mail address:* john.moyer@ucdenver.edu

0065-3101/13/$ – see front matter
http://dx.doi.org/10.1016/j.yapd.2013.04.016 

Advances in Pediatrics 60 (2013) 297–310

ADVANCES IN PEDIATRICS

# Abdominal Organ Transplantation in Children

Jonathan P. Roach, MD[a,*], Frederick M. Karrer, MD[b]

[a]Division of Transplant Surgery, University of Colorado School of Medicine, 1635 Aurora Court, C-318, Aurora, CO 80045, USA; [b]Division of Pediatric Surgery, Children's Hospital Colorado, University of Colorado School of Medicine, 13123 East 16th Avenue, B-323, Aurora, CO 80045, USA

**Keywords**

• Liver transplant • Kidney transplant • Immunosuppression • Pediatric

**Key points**

- Organ transplantation is only 50 years old, with the first kidney and liver transplants being performed in the 1950s and 1960s.
- While advances in surgical and perioperative care have been substantial, advances in immunosuppression have made possible organ transplantation with the excellent outcomes enjoyed today.
- Organ availability is the predominant limiting factor to transplanting children on the United Network for Organ Sharing waiting list.
- All patients receiving a kidney or liver transplant require long-term immunosuppression, which increases the lifetime risk of infection and malignancy.

## INTRODUCTION

Abdominal transplantation has grown dramatically since Murray performed the first kidney transplant in Boston in 1954 [1]. Starzl performed the first liver transplant on a 3-year-old girl with biliary atresia in Denver in 1963 [2]. Subsequently, there have been drastic improvements in surgical technique and anesthesia, as well as postoperative care and immunosuppression. These advances have allowed abdominal transplantation to become definitive therapy for end-stage renal disease (ESRD) or children with end-stage liver disease (ESLD). Intestinal transplantation is a viable means of treating children with short bowel syndrome, and although pancreas transplantation has been performed in children who have complications of diabetes mellitus it is rarely,

The authors report no significant financial relationships.

*Corresponding author. *E-mail address:* Jonathan.Roach@childrenscolorado.org

0065-3101/13/$ – see front matter
http://dx.doi.org/10.1016/j.yapd.2013.04.013 

if ever, performed any longer. Because these organ transplants are performed infrequently in children, they are outside the scope of this article. The reader is referred to other sources for a review of intestinal transplantation [3].

At the end of 2012 there were approximately 900 children younger than 18 years on the United Network for Organ Sharing (UNOS) kidney transplant waiting list. There were just less than 500 children on the UNOS liver transplant waiting list and 2 children awaiting a simultaneous kidney and pancreas transplant [4]. During the same year, 704 kidney transplants and 493 liver transplants were performed by transplant programs within the United States [4]. Overall, liver transplantation has good long-term outcomes for those children who would otherwise succumb to their liver disease. Kidney transplantation is also a viable, in fact preferred, therapy for most children with ESRD in comparison with long-term dialysis.

## IMMUNOLOGY AND IMMUNOSUPPRESSION

Advances in surgical technique and perioperative care have certainly allowed abdominal transplantation to progress. However, major advances in long-term allograft and patient survival can be predominantly attributed to advances in the understanding and modulation of the immune system. The immune response is a complex interaction between T cells, B cells, natural killer cells, macrophages, and dendritic cells. It is these lymphocytes that recognize the allograft as foreign and cause rejection of the transplanted organ. Antigen-presenting cells (APCs), T cells, and B cells all play a role in the rejection of a transplanted organ. Three cellular signals comprise the focus of drugs developed for immunosuppression in transplantation: signal 1, signal 2, and signal 3. Signal 1 refers to the interaction between an antigen being presented on an APC and the T cell through the T-cell receptor (TCR), also known as CD3. A costimulatory signal, signal 2, is also delivered when CD80 and CD86 on the APC interact with CD28 on the T cell. The calcium-calcineurin pathway, the RAS-mitogen activated protein kinase pathway, and the nuclear factor κB pathway are all activated by signals 1 and 2. These pathways serve to upregulate the immune response by activating transcription factors that cause the expression of many other inflammatory molecules. One of the main responses to signals 1 and 2 is the expression of interleukin (IL)-2 [5]. IL-2, among other mediators of inflammation, acts in an autocrine fashion on the T cell. This process initiates signal 3 thereby causing cellular proliferation. These molecules are recognized by cell surface receptors, which initiate cell signaling via Janus kinase 3 (JAK3), and the molecule-target-of-rapamycin (mTOR) pathway, which initiates the cell cycle [6].

In general, the goal of immunosuppression is to deplete lymphocytes and block the response pathways by blocking signals 1, 2, and 3. Although not all 3 signals must be blocked to attain adequate immunosuppression, all 3 are targets in achieving this goal. Many medications have been developed over the last 50 years to achieve the goal of adequate immunosuppression with tolerable side effects. Only the more commonly used medications are covered herein. There are 3 general categories of drugs used for immunosuppression: glucocorticoids, small-molecule drugs, and protein drugs. The mechanism of action of glucocorticoids is not fully elucidated, but in general they have an overall suppressive effect on the immune system. Small-molecule drugs, such as calcineurin inhibitors and mycophenolate mofetil, affect intracellular pathway signaling thereby causing immunosuppression. Protein drugs are generally monoclonal or polyclonal antibodies against 1 or many cell surface receptors involved in APC T-cell interaction and activation. A list of the commonly used immunosuppressive medications, their mechanisms, and side effects is presented in Table 1 [7].

## ORGAN DONATION

In 2012 there were approximately 8100 deceased organ donors and almost 6000 living donors in the United States. A deceased donor can provide organs for up to 8 different recipients. The heart, both lungs, both kidneys, the liver, pancreas, and small intestine may be transplanted, although for various reasons it is rare to have 8 recipients effected by a single donor. The availability of suitable organs has been the limiting factor in providing organs for transplant. There have been 2 strategies implemented in an attempt to increase the availability of organs for abdominal transplantation, the first being living donation. A parent, sibling, or friend can donate one of their kidneys or a part of their liver to a specific patient requiring a transplant. However, this is not without risk to the donor, and thorough preoperative workup is mandatory to ensure that the risk to the donor is minimized and that the kidney or portion of the liver being removed for transplant has appropriate function and anatomy. The second strategy for increasing organ availability is the use of donation after cardiac death (DCD) donation. This option occurs when a potential donor does not meet the criteria for brain death while there is no expectation of a meaningful recovery. In this instance, care may be withdrawn by the treating medical team and the organs rapidly recovered by a separate organ recovery team after the patient has expired. To avoid any conflict, the organ recovery team must in no way be involved in the management of the patient before the declaration of death. Although livers and kidneys from DCD donors are acceptable for transplant, the overall outcome is not as good as donation after brain death (DBD) [8,9], due to the requisite time required for a patient to expire before flushing the organs with an organ-preservative solution. DCD donors younger than 18 years account for only 1% of all DCD donors. Thus, DCD kidneys account for only 2% of all kidneys transplanted in the pediatric population, and DCD livers account for only 0.5% of all DCD livers [10].

## KIDNEY TRANSPLANTATION

### Indications

Ultimately, failure of the kidneys requiring renal replacement therapy is the only true indication for kidney transplantation. The cause of kidney failure is a secondary concern when considering a child for kidney transplant.

**Table 1**
Immunosuppressive drugs and their targets and toxicities

| Drug | Mechanism | Toxicities |
|---|---|---|
| Cyclosporin (Gengraf; Neoral) | Binds cyclophilin, inhibits calcineurin | Nephrotoxic, hemolytic-uremic syndrome, neurotoxicity, hyperlipidemia, diabetes mellitus, hypertension |
| Tacrolimus (Prograf) | Binds FKBP12, inhibits calcineurin | Effects similar to but less than cyclosporine, greater diabetes mellitus and neurotoxicity |
| Sirolimus (Rapamune) | Binds FKBP12, complex inhibits target of rapamycin and interleukin (IL)-2 driven cell proliferation | Hyperlipidemia, impaired wound healing, thrombocytopenia, delayed graft function, mouth ulcers, pneumonitis |
| Everolimus (Zortress) | Cousin of sirolimus | Similar to sirolimus |
| Mycophenolate mofetil (Cellcept; Myfortic) | Inhibits purine synthesis and thus cell proliferation | Gastrointestinal complaints, neutropenia, anemia |
| Azathioprine (Imuran) | Converted to 6-mercaptopurine, a purine synthesis inhibitor, and inhibits DNA synthesis and thus cell proliferation | Leukopenia, bone marrow depression, liver toxicity (rarely used any more) |
| Polyclonal antithymocyte globulin (Thymoglobulin) | Blocks T-cell membrane proteins causing altered function, lysis, and prolonged T-cell depletion | Significant cytokine release syndrome, thrombocytopenia, leukopenia, serum sickness |
| Alemtuzumab (Campath) | Binds to CD52 on all B and T cells, most monocytes, macrophages, and natural killer cells, causing lysis and prolonged depletion | Mild cytokine release syndrome, neutropenia, anemia, autoimmune thrombocytopenia, thyroid disease |
| Rituximab (Rituxan) | Binds CD20 and mediates B-cell lysis | Infusion reactions, hypersensitivity reactions |
| Basiliximab (Simulect) | Binds and blocks the IL-2 receptor α chain on activated T cells, which depletes them and inhibits IL-2–induced T-cell activation | Hypersensitivity reactions |

*Data from* Wiesner RH, Fung JJ. Present state of immunosuppressive therapy in liver transplant recipients. Liver Transpl 2011;17:S1–9.

Whereas complications of diabetes and hypertension are the leading causes of renal failure in adults, the etiology of pediatric renal failure is more varied. Congenital malformations of the urologic system, glomerular disease, and membranoproliferative glomerulonephritis are the most common causes of renal failure leading to a transplant in children (Box 1) [11]. Although ESRD is cured by renal transplant in many instances, there are disease processes, such as focal segmental glomerulosclerosis, hemolytic-uremic syndrome, and

**Box 1: Etiology of pediatric renal failure**

Glomerulonephritis 18%
Obstructive uropathy 16%
Dysplasia or agenesis 16%
Focal segmental glomerulosclerosis 12%
Ureteral reflux 5%
Prune belly syndrome <5%
Hemolytic-uremic syndrome <5%
Mebranoproliferative glomerulonephritis <5%
Polycystic kidney disease <5%

primary oxalosis, which can recur in the transplanted kidney and lead to graft failure.

### Evaluation

The evaluation of children being considered for a renal transplant is relatively straightforward. There are few absolute contraindications to renal transplantation. Children should be free of infection and malignancy at the time of transplant. The child should be able to tolerate anesthesia and the operation without undue cardiac or pulmonary risk. Barring any of these issues, most children with ESRD are appropriate candidates for a renal transplant. Preoperative workup is relatively basic and includes laboratory data such as a complete blood count, basic metabolic panel, urinalysis (both spot and 24-hour urine collection), culture, and sometimes renal biopsy. Any mechanical barriers or abnormalities leading to renal failure must have been previously addressed and resolved. Psychosocial circumstances and familial support are also critical components of evaluation, as noncompliance is a major cause of graft dysfunction and loss. Lastly, prolonged insurance coverage is also critical. Immunosuppressive medications are expensive and are required for the life of the graft. Loss of financial support has been identified as a major cause of noncompliance at many transplant programs across the country [12].

### Surgery and perioperative complications

When a potential organ becomes available for a child on the UNOS kidney transplant waiting list, the surgeon must consider several factors when deciding whether that particular organ is appropriate for that particular child. The size of the kidney must be taken into consideration. A kidney that is too large may not fit into the retroperitoneum or peritoneal cavity of the intended recipient. Conversely, a kidney that is too small may not provide enough filtering capability to keep the patient off dialysis, although this problem is rarely encountered in the pediatric population. Blood type, HLA-antigen match, and cross-match between the donor and recipient are also key factors in the decision. A negative cross-match is compulsory before accepting an organ for transplant. HLA antigens A, B, and DR (with 2 loci each) are used when tissue typing and matching organs and recipients. Thus, a perfect match would be a 6-antigen match, or 0 mismatch. In general, a better match confers a graft survival advantage. However, children who receive 0 antigen match organs can do quite well. The concern is that these unmatched allografts may only last 10 years, making a second or third kidney transplant necessary within the patient's life expectancy. As each successive transplant further sensitizes the recipient's immune system, starting with HLA matches of even 1 or 2 antigens may increase the success of subsequent future transplantation. However, this will not preclude subsequent transplantation, as some have shown success with desensitization protocols [13].

Living donation has evolved as a means of increasing the pool of available kidneys for transplant. Parents, siblings, and friends may all be considered for living donation, although using a first-degree relative confers the potential advantages of better HLA-antigen matching. A living-donor kidney transplant has several advantages over a deceased-donor transplant. The graft itself experiences shorter ischemic times because the graft is usually implanted immediately after it is removed from the donor. The recipient can receive the kidney transplant in an elective fashion rather than being rushed into the hospital when a suitable cadaver organ has become available. Finally, live donation allows for transplantation before the onset of dialysis, saving any potential morbidity caused by this therapy. These reasons combine to give kidney transplants from living donors better outcomes than transplants from cadaver donors [14].

Implantation of a kidney requires providing arterial inflow, venous outflow, and passage for urine evacuation. In larger children this is accomplished using the iliac vessels in the retroperitoneum, with the right being the preferred side. The ureter can then be anastomosed directly to the bladder with a neocystoureterostomy. In smaller children when the donor organ is too large to fit in the pelvis, revascularization to the aorta and vena cava for vascular inflow and outflow may be required. Nevertheless, most kidneys can still be placed in a retroperitoneal location [15]. Similarly, it may be more challenging to obtain a path for urine egress in children with previous complex bladder reconstruction or augmentation. Anastomosis of the donor ureter into either an augmented bladder or the native ureters is within the armamentarium of the transplant surgeon.

As with all vascular surgery, bleeding may be a major cause of operative morbidity. Fortunately, this is rare. Thrombosis of the artery or vein is also an infrequently seen technical complication. Unfortunately, when thrombosis occurs the most likely outcome is graft loss. Urine leak and ureteral stricture are feared technical complications.

Graft dysfunction may also occur in the perioperative period. Delayed graft function is defined as the need for dialysis within the first 7 days after kidney transplantation. The delay is thought to be a result of the ischemia-reperfusion injury experienced by all transplanted organs. Marginal donor and organ quality, prolonged warm ischemic time, and prolonged cold ischemic time all adversely affect the incidence and severity of delayed graft function. Early rejection may also occur in patients with previous immune sensitization or low levels of immunosuppression. This acute rejection is most often T-cell mediated (cellular rejection) but can also be B-cell mediated (antibody-mediated rejection). Acute rejection can be treated, but repeated episodes of rejection adversely affect long-term graft survival [16].

### Postoperative care

Immediately after surgery the child is usually admitted to the intensive care unit for at least 24 hours. Urine output from the transplanted kidney can be variable. Therefore, maintenance intravenous fluid with some sort of urine replacement is generally used. Induction of immunosuppression with a T-cell–depleting antibody such as thymoglobulin is generally used. Less than 50% of children receiving a kidney transplant will have their immunosuppression induced with a lymphocyte-depleting agent [17]. Maintenance immunosuppression with tacrolimus, mycophenolate, and steroids is preferred by the authors, but the specific immunosuppression protocol may vary slightly depending on the transplant center. A Foley catheter is maintained for 5 days to allow the neocystoureterostomy to heal. Patients are generally allowed to advance their diets as tolerated, starting on the first postoperative day. The total hospital stay is generally 5 days, with 24 hours spent in the intensive care unit.

### Long-term results, complications, and outcomes

If the child makes it through the perioperative phase of care (30 days from the day of transplant) with good graft function, the overall long-term results of kidney transplantation are excellent. Patients and their families can expect 1-, 3-, and 5-year graft survival to be 97%, 92%, and 84%, respectively, if a living-donor graft is used. If a deceased-donor graft is used, 95%, 84%, and 78% 1-, 3-, and 5-year graft survival can be expected. Patient survival rates are similarly excellent. Recipients of a live donor kidney have 98.4%, 97.7%, 96.1%, 94.2%, and 92.4% overall survival at 1, 2, 5, 7, and 10 years after transplantation, respectively. Survival rates are slightly lower with deceased-donor kidney transplants, being 97.4%, 96.5%, 93.3%, 91.1%, and 86.6% overall survival at 1, 2, 5, 7, and 10 years after transplantation, respectively [17]. These outstanding results reflect the cumulative improvements of pediatric kidney transplants over the course of the last 50 years. Perhaps the greatest contribution to long-term success has been the improvement and refinement in immunosuppression. In previous eras azathioprine and cyclosporine, along with steroids, were the mainstays of maintenance immunosuppression. In the current era, azathioprine has been largely replaced by mycophenolate mofetil, and cyclosporine has been replaced by tacrolimus. While many programs still use steroids, others are moving away from long-term steroid use. Long-term social outcomes are also good. Many children with growth retardation can make up any deficiencies [18], and patients and their parents are very happy with their overall quality of life [19].

Long-term complications of transplant are predominantly infections or side effects, as well as complications of immunosuppression. Antiviral medications are used as prophylaxis against clinically relevant cytomegalovirus (CMV) and Epstein-Barr virus (EBV) infection. If a clinically relevant viral infection is present, lowering the overall level of immunosuppression and providing treatment doses of antiviral medication are added. BK virus is a polyoma virus that is present in 80% to 100% of children by age 5 years. In the immunocompromised kidney transplant patient, BK virus can cause hemorrhagic cystitis, ureteral stenosis, and graft nephropathy. Lowering the overall level of immunosuppression as well as several antiviral medications can treat BK virus. Increased risk of malignancy is also a consequence of long-term immunosuppression. Posttransplant lymphoproliferative disorder (PTLD) and skin malignancy, most commonly basal cell carcinoma, are the most frequent malignancies associated with immunosuppression. There are, however, many malignancies that have a higher incidence in the immunosuppressed, and increased vigilance is required from those caring for such patients.

## LIVER TRANSPLANTATION

### Indications

Whereas the vast majority of adults who require liver transplant have one of several diagnoses (hepatitis C, alcoholic cirrhosis, nonalcoholic steatohepatitis, and primary sclerosing cholangitis), children present with a broader range of etiology for liver failure (Box 2). Children may present early in life with biliary atresia, metabolic disease, or vascular tumors necessitating transplantation. Others may require transplantation later in childhood, or even adolescence, for cirrhosis, metabolic disorders, or fulminant failure from ingestion of substances toxic to the liver. Regardless of the origin, a liver transplant can provide these children with good long-term outcomes and, in some cases, cure them of disease.

### Evaluation

Preoperative evaluation of liver transplant candidates must be more thorough than for kidney transplant recipients, as the operation places much more stress on the cardiopulmonary system. The anhepatic phase and the need for complete inferior vena caval cross-clamping make thorough investigation of the cardiopulmonary system compulsory, as cardiopulmonary collapse in the operating room my lead to the patient's demise.

Patients may also present with complications of portal hypertension such as esophageal varices and hypersplenism. The risk of esophageal variceal rupture must be mitigated with appropriate preoperative therapy; this may require octreotide and variceal banding. Many patients with liver failure or metabolic disease also present with suboptimal nutritional status. Enteral or parenteral feeding with vitamin supplementation may be required.

**Box 2: Etiology of liver failure requiring transplantation in children**

Biliary atresia ~50%
Fulminant liver failure 15%
$\alpha_1$-Antitrypsin deficiency 9%
Hepatoblastoma or other tumor 4%
Cryptogenic cirrhosis 4%
Alagille syndrome 3%
Tyrosemia 2%
Autoimmune hepatitis 2%
Urea cycle defects 2%
Primary sclerosing cholangitis 2%
Glycogen storage disease 1%
Neonatal hepatitis 1%
Cystic fibrosis <1%
Wilson disease <1%

*Data from* Tiao GM, Alonso MH, Ryckman FC. Pediatric liver transplantation. Semin Pediatr Surg 2006;15:218–27.

Absolute contraindications to a liver transplant include unresectable extrahepatic malignancy, progressive disease not reversible with liver transplantation, and active severe infection. Because liver failure may lead to significant and permanent neurologic damage, one must also ensure that this is not present before proceeding with transplantation.

## Surgery and perioperative complications

The limiting factor, not only in liver transplantation but in all transplants, is the availability of donor organs. This limitation is further compounded in the pediatric liver transplant community, as liver grafts of the appropriate size for an infant or small child are even scarcer. The limitation has been mitigated somewhat by the development of reduced-size or split-liver transplantation. The liver is organized into 8 anatomic segments, each with its own portal supply and hepatic vein drainage (Fig. 1). This segmentation allows for the surgical reduction of the size of a graft while maintaining complete function of the size-reduced graft. The most common reductions result in use of the right lobe (segments V–VIII), the left lobe (segments II–IV), or the left lateral segment (segments II–III). The surgeon determines which size variant is appropriate for a particular patient at the time of transplant. In some cases, the anatomy of the liver allows a whole donor organ to be split into 2 functional pieces that may be used to transplant 2 patients. Most often, the left lateral segment will go to a pediatric patient and the right lobe will go to an adult patient. The liver's ability to hypertrophy to meet the metabolic demands of the recipient allows split-liver transplantation to be successful.

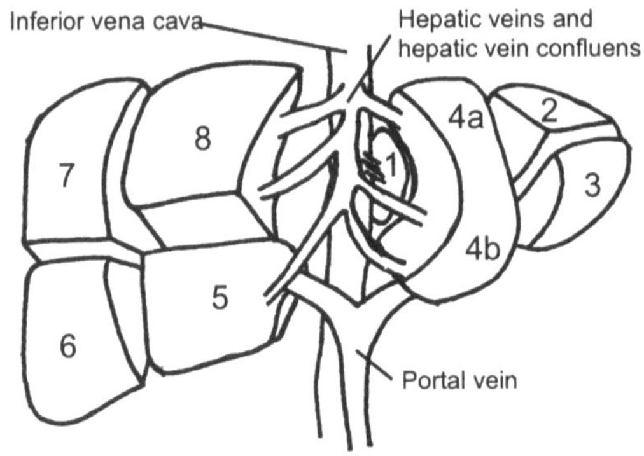


**Fig. 1.** Couinaud segments. The liver is made up of 8 anatomic sections each with its own portal triad and hepatic venous drainage. These segments allow for split and reduced-size liver allografts.

Liver transplantation is one of the most demanding operations for both patient and surgeon. Meticulous dissection and rigid adherence to surgical principles that allow for hemostasis are mandatory. Whereas kidney transplant is heterotopic, liver transplant is orthotopic and requires removal of the native liver. The native vasculature is used for inflow and outflow. Allograft implantation proceeds with the outflow anastomosis first; this is usually accomplished by anastomosis of the hepatic vein(s) to the confluence of the hepatic veins opened into a common orifice on the front wall of the inferior vena cava. Occasionally, when using a whole graft the entire retrohepatic inferior vena cava is replaced with donor vena cava. This technique requires an extra infrahepatic vena caval anastomosis (Fig. 2). Portal anastomosis occurs next, with the donor portal vein being connected directly to the recipient portal vein. Rarely, when thrombosis of the portal vein (cavernous transformation) has occurred, the portal vein must be traced back to the confluence of the superior mesenteric vein (SMV) and splenic veins, or even down to the lower SMV, to obtain splanchnic inflow. Some surgeons chose to routinely reperfuse the liver at this stage, whereas others complete the arterial anastomosis before reperfusion. Arterial anastomosis directly to the recipient hepatic artery is usually possible. In rare circumstances arterial inflow must be obtained directly from the infrarenal aorta using donor iliac artery as an aortic jump-graft. Biliary drainage is either through the native bile duct or directly into the gastrointestinal tract via Roux-en-Y choledochojejunostomy or choledochoduodenostomy. With a well-performed operation, the surgeon is given the immediate satisfaction of visible bile production before biliary anastomosis is completed.

Surgical technique and anesthetic care have progressed to the point whereby many children have excellent perioperative outcomes. Although complications may be rare, when they do occur they can be devastating. Perhaps the most

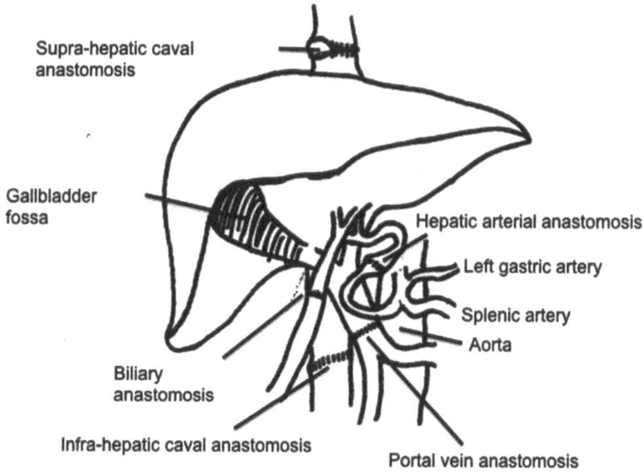


**Fig. 2.** Implantation of the transplanted liver. The liver is implanted, sewing the caval, portal, arterial, and biliary anastomoses. The gallbladder is always removed.

feared complication is primary nonfunction of the graft. Without a functioning liver, children will exhibit hemodynamic instability, recalcitrant acidosis, renal failure, severe coagulopathy, and severe neurologic deterioration resulting from cerebral edema. There is a multitude of factors that may contribute to primary nonfunction. Donors who exhibit hypotension, anemia, or other traits that may lead to organ hypoxia increase the risk for primary nonfunction. Steatosis of the donor liver may also contribute to nonfunction. Because pediatric and young adult donors are preferentially paired with pediatric recipients, the problem of graft steatosis is lessened. Cold ischemia time (the time the organ is stored) should be less than 10 to 12 hours. Warm ischemia time (the time required to implant the liver after it is removed from its ice bath) should be kept to a minimum. Hypotension on reperfusion should also be avoided. All of these factors increase the risk of primary nonfunction. If primary nonfunction occurs, immediate retransplantation may be the only option.

Hepatic artery thrombosis (HAT) is another feared postoperative complication. HAT is detected most often by loss of signal on ultrasonographic examination and when its occurrence mandates an emergent return to the operating room in an attempt to reopen the artery. If this is unsuccessful, the likely outcome becomes retransplantation, as the intrahepatic and extrahepatic bile ducts will necrose without arterial inflow. This complication also necessitates retransplantation.

Bile leak may also complicate the postoperative course. With meticulous technique this complication is rare, although it is more common with the technical variants (reduced size, splits). If bile leak does occur it is important to address the complication quickly, as bile leak is associated with long-term stenosis of the bile duct [20].

### Postoperative care

If the entire operation runs smoothly and without complication, the patient may be extubated in the operating room. More frequently, however, the patient remains intubated on transfer to the intensive care unit. Postoperative coordination of care between the transplant surgeon, hepatologist, and critical care physician is critical to success. Each discipline brings its own strengths which, when pooled, leads to the best outcome for the liver transplant recipient [21]. Liver function, coagulation, and complete blood count studies must be followed closely in the immediate postoperative period. Bleeding from the anastomoses may ensue, particularly if the graft is not functioning perfectly. Downtrending liver enzymes and improving coagulation profiles are evidence of a functional graft. At least one ultrasonogram must be checked to document the patency of the hepatic vasculature. Many programs will perform a daily liver transplant ultrasonogram such that vascular complication is caught early when it is easiest to fix [22]. As the patient recovers from surgery, extubation and feeding ensue. Liver transplant patients generally will not leave the hospital before 1 to 2 weeks after the operation.

### Long-term results, complications, and outcomes

Short-term complications such as technical failure, acute rejection, or infection will generally occur within the first 6 months after transplant. Once a child makes it through this period, one can expect prolonged graft function. Among those who survived 10 years after a liver transplant, the first graft survival was 94%, 91%, and 88% at 1, 5, and 10 years, respectively. Long-term overall survival is 87%, 84%, 82%, and 81% at 1, 3, 5, and 10 years, respectively [23,24]. All long-term survivors of liver transplants face long-term complications such as decreased renal function, hypertension, diminished bone density, and atherosclerosis. Many patients who are EBV negative at the time of transplantation will seroconvert, and most will do this with in the first 4 years. Approximately 5% of patients will be diagnosed with tissue-confirmed lymphoproliferative disorder. Long-term use of calcineurin inhibitors may also lead to renal dysfunction and failure. Some patients may require a kidney transplant.

## SUMMARY

The last half century has seen dramatic improvement in the outcomes after solid organ transplantation in children. Kidney transplantation is now the preferred therapy for renal failure over chronic hemodialysis or peritoneal dialysis. Similarly, liver transplantation has evolved to the point whereby children who previously were doomed to succumb to their disease may now go on to lead full lives after transplantation. These advances are due to improved perioperative care and surgical technique, as well as advances in the understanding of the immune system and the ability to suppress it. The future of abdominal transplantation in children will see further improvements in immunosuppression, with fewer side effects, as well as further strategies to alleviate the organ shortage that plagues all fields in transplantation. These features will combine to further increase the survival of both grafts and patients.

## References

[1] Guild WR, Harrison JH, Merrill JP, et al. Successful homotransplantation of the kidney in an identical twin. Trans Am Clin Climatol Assoc 1955–1956;67:167–73.

[2] Starzl TE, Marchioro TL, Vonkaulla KN, et al. Homotransplantation of the liver in humans. Surg Gynecol Obstet 1963;117:659–76.

[3] Nayyar N, Mazariegos G, Ranganathan S, et al. Pediatric small bowel transplantation. Semin Pediatr Surg 2010;19(1):68–77.

[4] Available at: http://optn.transplant.hrsa.gov/latestdata/rptdata.asp. Accessed February 24, 2013.

[5] Halloran PF. Immunosuppressive drugs for kidney transplantation. N Engl J Med 2004;351(26):2715–29.

[6] Coelho T, Tredger M, Dhawan A. Current status of immunosuppressive agents for solid organ transplantation in children. Pediatr Transplant 2012;16(2):106–22.

[7] Wiesner RH, Fung JJ. Present state of immunosuppressive therapy in liver transplant recipients. Liver Transpl 2011;17(Suppl 3):S1–9.

[8] Foley DP, Fernandez LA, Leverson G, et al. Biliary complications after liver transplantation from donation after cardiac death donors: an analysis of risk factors and long-term outcomes from a single center. Ann Surg 2011;253(4):817–25.

[9] de Vries EE, Hoogland PE, Wind J, et al. Transplantation of kidneys from paediatric DCD donors: a comparison with DBD donors. Nephrol Dial Transplant 2013;28:220–6.

[10] Yoo PS, Olthoff KM, Abt PL. Donation after cardiac death in pediatric organ transplantation. Curr Opin Organ Transplant 2011;16(5):483–8.

[11] Shapiro R, Sarwal MM. Pediatric kidney transplantation. Pediatr Clin North Am 2010;57(2):393–400.

[12] Evans RW, Applegate WH, Briscoe DM, et al. Cost-related immunosuppressive medication nonadherence among kidney transplant recipients. Clin J Am Soc Nephrol 2010;5(12): 2323–8.

[13] Jin MK, Cho JH, Kwon O, et al. Successful kidney transplantation after desensitization using plasmapheresis, low-dose intravenous immunoglobulin, and rituximab in highly sensitized patients: a single-center experience. Transplant Proc 2012;44(1): 200–3.

[14] McEnery PT, Stablein DM, Arbus G, et al. Renal transplantation in children. A report of the North American Pediatric Renal Transplant Cooperative Study. N Engl J Med 1992;326(26):1727–32.

[15] Furness PD 3rd, Houston JB, Grampsas SA, et al. Extraperitoneal placement of renal allografts in children weighing less than 15 kg. J Urol 2001;166(3):1042–5.

[16] Joseph JT, Kingsmore DB, Junor BJ, et al. The impact of late acute rejection after cadaveric kidney transplantation. Clin Transplant 2001;15(4):221–7.

[17] Smith JM, Martz K, Blydt-Hansen TD. Pediatric kidney transplant practice patterns and outcome benchmarks, 1987-2010: a report of the North American Pediatric Renal Trials and Collaborative Studies. Pediatr Transplant 2013;17(2):149–57.

[18] Klare B, Montoya CR, Fischer DC, et al. Normal adult height after steroid-withdrawal within 6 months of pediatric kidney transplantation: a 20 years single center experience. Transpl Int 2012;25(3):276–82.

[19] Anthony SJ, Hebert D, Todd L, et al. Child and parental perspectives of multidimensional quality of life outcomes after kidney transplantation. Pediatr Transplant 2010;14(2): 249–56.

[20] Lu CH, Tsang LL, Huang TL, et al. Biliary complications and management in pediatric living donor liver transplantation for underlying biliary atresia. Transplant Proc 2012;44(2): 476–7.

[21] Hendrickson RJ, Karrer FM, Wachs ME, et al. Pediatric liver transplantation. Curr Opin Pediatr 2004;16(3):309–13.

[22] Englesbe MJ, Kelly B, Goss J, et al. Reducing pediatric liver transplant complications: a potential roadmap for transplant quality improvement initiatives within North America. Am J Transplant 2012;12(9):2301–6.

[23] Ng VL, Alonso EM, Bucuvalas JC, et al. Health status of children alive 10 years after pediatric liver transplantation performed in the US and Canada: report of the studies of pediatric liver transplantation experience. J Pediatr 2012;160(5):820–6.

[24] Bucuvalas JC, Ryckman FC. Long-term outcome after liver transplantation in children. Pediatr Transplant 2002;6(1):30–6.

Advances in Pediatrics 60 (2013) 311–325

ADVANCES IN PEDIATRICS

# Surgical Management of Adolescent Obesity

Sean J. Barnett, MD, MS

Division of Pediatric General & Thoracic Surgery, Cincinnati Children's Hospital Medical Center, 3333 Burnet Avenue, Cincinnati, OH 45215, USA

**Keywords**

• Morbid obesity • Adolescents • Bariatric surgery • Comorbidities • Weight loss

**Key points**

- Morbid obesity continues to see a rapid increase in pediatric and adolescent populations. Morbidly obese adolescents develop significant comorbidities that continue on into adulthood. Although medical management in the overweight population of children can be helpful, morbidly obese adolescents do not show significant long-term weight reduction with lifestyle modification.
- Bariatric surgery is a safe and long-term solution in selected morbidly obese adolescents who are physically and psychosocially mature.
- Adolescent bariatric surgical patients require lifelong dietary modification and follow-up to ensure adequate nutritional supplementation. Roux-en-Y gastric bypass (RYGB) remains the gold standard operation but sleeve gastrectomy (SG) continues to gain rapid prominence, given its simplicity and reduced post-operative complication rates.
- The adjustable gastric band (AGB) in the adolescent population can be efficacious compared with medical therapy but has demonstrated significantly higher complication and reoperation rates compared with its use in adults. More long-term, longitudinal studies are necessary to firmly establish guidelines for patient selection and optimal procedure choice.

## INTRODUCTION

It has been estimated that approximately 18% of all children and adolescents meet the criteria of being overweight or obese in the United States, a rate that has almost tripled over the past 30 years [1]. Of these overweight children,

Disclosures: The author has no relevant financial relationships to disclose.

*E-mail address*: sean.barnett@cchmc.org

0065-3101/13/$ – see front matter
http://dx.doi.org/10.1016/j.yapd.2013.04.014 

50% to 77% will continue to be obese into adulthood, carrying with them all the associated comorbidities [2–4]. More alarming, however, are the approximately 4% to 7% of all children and adolescents (more than 2 million) considered morbidly obese (body mass index [BMI] >99th percentile) in this country [2,5,6]. These data parallel recent National Health and Nutrition Examination Survey (NHANES) data demonstrating that approximately two-thirds of US adults are considered overweight and more than one-third considered obese [7]. The importance of these data cannot be overlooked given the long-term health, psychosocial, and economic ramifications of childhood obesity.

Although behavioral weight management programs have been shown to have lasting effects in some children, these approaches are ineffective in those patients who are morbidly obese [8]. Of those morbidly obese children undergoing behavioral weight loss, one-third to one-half cannot even complete a program. Those who complete a program lose, on average, 5 pounds (3% weight loss), which is not maintained 7 months later [8]. These findings lend toward performing bariatric surgery on morbidly obese adolescents to provide longer-lasting overall weight loss and comorbidity reduction. This article discusses the definition of pediatric obesity and the comorbidities of morbid obesity in children and adolescents, provides guidelines for performing bariatric surgery in adolescents, discusses the procedures and their outcomes in this patient population, and provides a framework for postoperative care.

## DEFINITION

The prevailing standard for measurement of obesity in the adult population is body mass index (BMI $kg/m^2$). This is a simple way to define obesity in those who have attained their full adult height. By definition, adults are considered overweight with a BMI greater than 25 $kg/m^2$ and considered obese with a BMI greater than or equal to 30 $kg/m^2$. These numbers can be extrapolated over different ethnic groups and populations to allow for easy formation of guidelines for treatment.

In children and adolescents, the use of BMI becomes more complicated due to the physiologic changes in adiposity with height and weight changes during normal growth. Therefore, growth charts are used for most children and adolescents that are both age specific and gender specific to better define obesity throughout childhood [9]. General guidelines throughout the literature define pediatric obesity as a BMI greater than the 95th percentile for age and gender, with those greater than the 99th percentile considered severely obese (BMI >35 $kg/m^2$, consistent with the definition for adults) [10]. These definitions present unique problems in defining those individuals at the extreme categories of obesity, given the relative paucity of population-based data to calculate these percentile boundaries. This definition is compounded by the small number of children and adolescents with a BMI greater than 40 $kg/m^2$ represented in the data sets used to formulate pediatric growth charts, namely NHANES. Because most adolescents with a BMI greater than 35 $kg/m^2$ are greater than the 99th BMI percentile for current growth charts [2], it is appropriate to use adult selection criterion for the use of bariatric surgery in this patient population. Thresholds should be considered general guidelines and those with significant comorbidities should also be considered for bariatric surgery despite regard for BMI.

## COMORBIDITIES ASSOCIATED WITH MORBID OBESITY IN ADOLESCENTS

Given the relative explosion in the prevalence of pediatric obesity over the past 30 years, there has been a parallel increase in the frequency and severity of obesity-related comorbidities in morbidly obese adolescents. These disease states are frequently seen at a much younger age than previously encountered, encompass a wide range of organ systems, and carry subsequent increased risks into adulthood [11–14].

### Glucose intolerance

Although a frequent manifestation of adult obesity, it has been demonstrated that there has been a significant (more than 10-fold) increase in the prevalence of type 2 diabetes mellitus in adolescents over the past decade [15]. Even more striking is the finding that up to 25% of all obese children and adolescents have some form of impaired glucose intolerance [16]. Insulin resistance has been clearly linked with childhood obesity [17], and studies suggest that type 2 diabetes mellitus developing in childhood or in adolescence can progress more rapidly than in adults [18]. Type 2 diabetes mellitus in adolescents is considered a chronic and progressive disease associated with many other comorbidities, including dyslipidemia, hypertension, cardiac disease, and nonalcoholic liver disease [19,20]. In a recent study published by the Centers for Disease Control and Prevention, epidemiologists predict that type 2 diabetes mellitus is expected to develop in 33% to 50% of all Americans born in the year 2000 [21].

### Cardiovascular disease

Risk factors for atherosclerosis and coronary artery disease are common in obese adolescents [22–24], with approximately 60% of obese children in the Bogalusa Heart Study having 1 of these factors and 20% having 2 or more of these factors [25]. Hypertension occurs at a 9-fold increased rate in obese children [26] and is a well-known risk factor for the development of cardiac disease in adults. Furthermore, there has been a linear increase in the development of cardiovascular risk factors in relation to increased BMI in children [27]. The incidence of left ventricular hypertrophy has also been shown significantly increased in young adults as a direct consequence of comorbidities related to adolescent obesity, namely obstructive sleep apnea [28].

### Obstructive sleep apnea

Up to 20% of school-aged children with obesity are reported to have either moderate or severe sleep apnea [29]. Data associates poor school performance with sleep deprivation and disordered sleep patterns [30,31], both of which are common in obese children and adolescents,as well as placing them at increased risk for hyperactivity and learning difficulties throughout life [32]. Adolescents with sleep apnea also exhibit significant left ventricular hypertrophy [28] and abnormal ventricular dimensions [33], which have not been found improved with medical weight loss alone [34].

### Nonalcoholic fatty liver disease and nonalcoholic steatohepatitis

Approximately 38% of obese adolescents have steatosis and 9% have nonalcoholic steatohepatitis (NASH) compared with 5% and 1%, respectively, in their lean counterparts [35]. Of those undergoing bariatric surgery at Cincinnati Children's Hospital, 83% have evidence of fatty liver disease, with 20% formally demonstrating NASH [36]. The most serious consequence of liver damage associated with obesity is fibrosis coupled with accelerated cirrhosis, ultimately leading to end-stage liver disease.

### Pseudotumor cerebri

Pseudotumor cerebri is a rare progressive childhood disorder associated with increased intracranial pressure that often leads to papilledema and blindness. The relationship between obesity and symptom onset is unclear. As many as 50% of children with pseudotumor cerebri are obese [37] and, with extensive weight loss after bariatric surgery, it can improve in both adults [38] and in adolescents [39].

### Psychological aspects

A significant number of adolescents seeking treatment of their obesity present with differing stages of clinical depression [40]. Many obese adolescents have been found to have low self-esteem and can engage in high-risk behaviors [41], and obesity has been found to have a significant negative effect on their quality of life [42]. Obese adolescents also demonstrate significantly lower quality-of-life scores than lean children with scores and are comparable with pediatric cancer patients [43]. Women who were overweight as adolescents are also less likely to marry and have completed fewer years of school compared with their lean counterparts [44]. A recent longitudinal study demonstrated a significant improvement in depressive symptoms and quality of life over the first postoperative period after bariatric surgery in adolescents [45].

### Summary

The large mounting body of literature demonstrating the significant number of comorbidities associated with obesity coupled with their relative lack of resolution by medical weight loss means in the morbidly obese has led to a large body of evidence in support of the use of modern weight loss operations for selected, morbidly obese adolescents. Bariatric surgery has been shown to completely resolve type 2 diabetes mellitus in adolescents who have undergone gastric bypass [46]. It has also shown a dramatic reduction in the severity of obstructive sleep apnea symptoms in all patients, with complete resolution of symptoms in 90% [47]. A decrease in the degree of steatosis and regression of hepatic fibrosis has been found in some patients after bariatric surgery [48]. These data, coupled with the improvements in pseudotumor cerebri and psychosocial behaviors (discussed previously), support the early use of bariatric surgical procedures in the adolescent population.

## GUIDELINES FOR SURGERY

Best practice guidelines by the American Society for Metabolic and Bariatric Surgery have been recently updated and published [49]. As discussed previously, most adolescents with a BMI greater than 35 kg/m$^2$ are greater than the 99th percentile; therefore, adult criteria for selection are considered appropriate for adolescents. Current recommendations have not changed significantly since the last best practice guidelines were set in 2009 (Table 1) [50]. In summary, these include those individuals with a BMI greater than or equal to 35 kg/m$^2$ with significant major comorbidities, which include type 2 diabetes mellitus, pseudotumor cerebri, severe NASH, and moderate to severe obstructive sleep apnea (apnea-hypopnea index >15). Those individuals with a BMI greater than or equal to 40 kg/m$^2$ with less severe comorbid disease, including glucose intolerance, hypertension, dyslipidemia, mild to moderate obstructive sleep apnea (apnea-hypopnea index >5), and impaired quality of life, are also thought to meet criteria for bariatric surgery [49]. Given that these are merely guidelines for treatment, exceptions can be made in extenuating circumstances if the potential long-term health risks outweigh the risks of bariatric surgery.

Because adolescence represents an extensive period of growth, the timing for surgical treatment remains controversial and depends on the compelling needs of patients. For those adolescents who have attained the majority of linear growth (>95%), there is little reason to believe that bariatric surgery will impair growth. Physiologic maturation is generally complete by sexual maturation (Tanner stage 4) [51]. Skeletal maturation (adult stature) is normally attained by the age 13 to 14 in girls and age 15 to 16 in boys [52]. The onset of menarche is also a sign of physiologic maturity in girls, with growth usually complete within 2 years after menarche. For those patients for whom physical maturation is uncertain, bone age can be assessed by plain radiography of the hand or wrist and estimated by a radiologist via nomograms.

Coupled with physiologic factors of maturation in adolescents is the determination of a patient's psychosocial maturity level. Patients should not only be able to demonstrate a general understanding of the risks and benefits of surgery

**Table 1**
Patient selection criteria for adolescent weight loss surgery

| BMI (kg/m$^2$) | Comorbidities |
|---|---|
| >35 | Type 2 diabetes mellitus, moderate of severe obstructive sleep apnea, pseudotumor cerebri, severe NASH |
| >40 | Mild obstructive sleep apnea, hypertension, insulin resistance, glucose intolerance, dyslipidemia, impaired quality of life |

*Data from* Michalsky M, Reichard K, Inge T, et al. ASMBS pediatric committee best practice guidelines. Surg Obes Relat Dis 2012;8:1–7.

but also the long-term ramifications after bariatric surgical procedures and ability to comply with vitamin and nutritional recommendations. Although the majority of patients cannot consent for themselves, it is expected that patients provide assent for the procedure. It is paramount that a patient's parents are readily involved in the entire process in order to assess support mechanisms, determine and ensure the likelihood of postoperative compliance, and provide adequate consent for the procedure.

Specific recommendations regarding team member qualifications have been made to maximize the multidisciplinary approach required for bariatric surgery in adolescents [49]. These include, but are not limited to, the following:

- Surgeon: The surgeon performing adolescent bariatric surgery should meet the general certification requirements of the American Board of Surgery and have appropriate training and experience in performing bariatric procedures. The individual should be credentialed by the institution to perform such procedures, but it is not necessary to be boarded specifically in pediatric surgery. As an example, Cincinnati Children's Hospital has 4 board-certified surgeons (adult and pediatric) who have extensive knowledge and training in the various bariatric surgical procedures performed.
- Medical specialist: Includes at least one physician with specialty training in endocrinology, gastroenterology, nutrition, or adolescent medicine. The main responsibilities of this team member are the screening and management of a patient's comorbid conditions with the team and the patient's primary care physician. My program uses a board-certified pediatric gastroenterologist as its medical director (which comes in handy for those patients who require preoperative and postoperative endoscopy) and a board-certified adolescent medicine physician who assists with the care of the majority of female patients who experience menstrual dysfunction.
- Registered dietitian: Arguably the most important part of the overall program, the dietitian should have extensive experience in treating adolescents and their families with obesity. The dietician sets the tone during the preoperative phase of the program and helps manage patient questions and concerns throughout the postoperative phase.
- Mental health specialist: Includes a psychologist, psychiatrist, or other independently licensed metal health provider with specific training in pediatric, adolescent, and family treatment. The individual should also have experience in treating those patients with obesity and eating disorders. My psychologist plays a pivotal role during the initial assessment to ensure that patients are psychologically ready to begin the program and to help garner the necessary resources required to move past the preoperative phase.
- Program coordinator: Includes a registered nurse, social worker, or business specialist whose main responsibility is the coordinating of care to help facilitate compliance and follow-up. My coordinator also works with patients' insurance companies to ensure coverage for treatment and procedures.
- Exercise physiologist or specialist: This specialist provides safe physical activity education for morbidly obese patients.
- Social worker: A dedicated social worker is not required but is highly recommended. In my program, she monitors patients' psychosocial health as well as

communicates with patient therapists on a regular basis. She also manages the support group, access to resources, and various functions throughout the year.
- Nurse practioner: This position is not required but is an integral part of the team at Cincinnati Children's Hospital. She has an ongoing dialogue with all my patients and literally has her hands on the pulse of the program. She also helps manage many of the medical problems of the patients within the program on a daily basis.

With the various team members comes a significant commitment of the institution to provide safe and quality care for these difficult patients. A recent article, published in *Pediatrics* in 2011, sought to develop certain criteria for pediatric/adolescent bariatric surgery programs [53]. Michalsky and colleagues [53] propose 10 criteria for proposed specialty programs, including (1) institutional commitment, (2) a defined medical home for patients, (3) routine experience in laparoscopic bariatric procedures, (4) program staffing (discussed previously), (5) multidisciplinary review for each patient, (6) specialized equipment (hospital beds, patient transfer systems, operating room tables, and adequate radiologic facilities), (7) standardized care using clinical pathways, (8) follow-up care, (9) support groups, and (10) transition of care as patients move into adulthood. The ability to meet these criteria help to ensure a well-rounded program that is able to meet all the needs of morbidly obese adolescents.

## PROCEDURES AND OUTCOMES

The experience of several small series suggests that gastric bypass, AGB, and SG can be performed routinely, safely, and effectively in adolescents [54,55–65]. To date, however, adolescent bariatric surgery has not been evaluated in a longitudinal or prospective manner. To address these shortcomings in outcomes for adolescent bariatric surgery, a consortium of 5 pediatric institutions is currently involved in a National Institutes of Health–funded study, designed to collect standardized prospective preoperative and postoperative clinical data longitudinally (Teen–Longitudinal Assessment of Bariatric Surgery [Teen-Labs]). Accrual of patients for the study is complete and the initial data are being analyzed with initial results set to be published by the end of this year.

There have been many bariatric operations performed in adolescents in the past but the remainder of this section focuses on the 3 most commonly performed operations to date. These include the AGB, RYGB, and SG (Fig. 1). All the operations are performed laparoscopically. Minimally invasive bariatric surgery has significant advantages over open surgery, namely the reduction of complications, length of stay, and pain postoperatively, but is one of the most technically difficult procedures performed [66].

## ADJUSTABLE GASTRIC BAND

The Food and Drug Administration approved the use of Lap-Band (Allergan, Irvine, California) for use in adults in the United States in 2001 and the Realize Band (Ethicon, Cincinnati, Ohio) shortly thereafter. Prior to its introduction

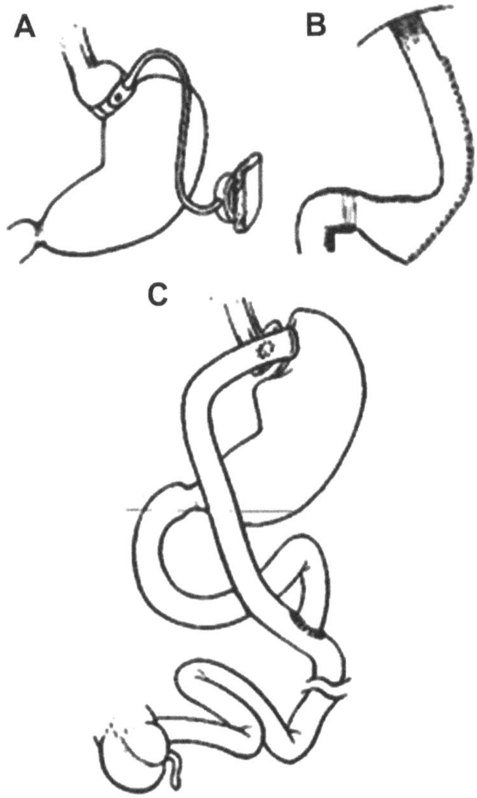


**Fig. 1.** Bariatric procedures performed in adolescents: (*A*) AGB, (*B*) SG, and (*C*) RYGB.

into the United States, the AGB procedure was the most commonly performed procedure in Europe, Latin America, and Australia. It is not currently approved for patients under age 18 by the Food and Drug Administration, with results of an ongoing national study awaiting publication. Given its current restrictions, studies in adolescents are generally found to originate from outside the United States.

The laparoscopically placed gastric band creates a small pouch in the upper portion of the stomach, acting solely as a restrictive procedure. A balloon on the inside of the band is connected to a port placed in the subcutaneous tissues of the upper abdomen (see Fig. 1A). The port can be accessed by a small-gauge needle to perform periodic adjustments by placing or removing sterile water into the system. This in turn changes the size of the balloon around the stomach, thus changing the size of the functional stoma that it creates. These periodic adjustments are critical for the overall success of the band and require as many as 10 visits over the course of the first postoperative year. The procedure generally requires 45 to 60 minutes to complete, patients are discharged on the same day or next day, and there is no cutting or stapling of the stomach or intestine. Complications include gastric prolapse, stomal obstruction, band erosion, and, most commonly, access port or tubing problems. These seem similar when comparing adolescent AGBs with their adult counterparts.

A recent study from Australia followed patients with a BMI greater than 35 for 2 years randomized to either supervised lifestyle intervention or gastric banding [57]. The main outcomes were weight loss and adverse outcomes; 24 of the 25 gastric banding patients and 18 of 25 lifestyle modification patients completed the study. A mean excess weight loss of 78.8% was seen in the banding group and 13.2% in the lifestyle modification group. The study also noted significant improvement in features of the metabolic syndrome and quality of life in the gastric banding group. Alarmingly, however, 8 reoperations (33%) were required in 7 patients, with an overall complication rate of 48% over the 2-year period [57]. Smaller studies have achieved similar results with many experiencing marked improvement of obesity-related comorbidities [63,64]. Given these studies, AGB seems more effective than lifestyle modification alone and can result in a significant reduction in comorbidities. Given the much higher complication rate in adolescents compared with adults, the surgeon must be careful when considering AGB in this population. Additional long-term data are forthcoming from industry-sponsored trials before any recommendation can be made regarding their use in patients under age 18.

## SLEEVE GASTRECTOMY

The SG is rapidly gaining acceptance as a primary operation in both adult and adolescent populations. Once considered only part of the larger duodenal switch operation, it has been shown to offer significant weight loss with fewer complications than gastric bypass [67]. This restrictive procedure involves the longitudinal resection of the stomach along a narrow 34-French bougie. The resection extends approximately 6 cm from the pylorus to the angle of His, thus creating a long gastric tube along the lesser curve of the stomach. The fundus and greater curvature of the stomach are removed (see Fig. 1B). The mechanism of weight loss is not yet understood but may be the result of both restriction and alteration of appetite and satiety signals from the gut to the brain, including changes in ghrelin and peptide YY levels [68]. Literature regarding its effectiveness in the pediatric population is growing [62,67–72] but continues to be sparse. The largest single institutional study to date reported outcomes of 108 adolescents undergoing SG in Saudi Arabia [62]. The investigators reported a significant reduction in BMI of 37% at 1 year, similar to previously reported studies in this country after gastric bypass [73], with no major complications or deaths. Significant reductions in type 2 diabetes mellitus, sleep apnea, hypertension, and dyslipidemia were also noted.

Given these promising findings, and with the help of additional longitudinal prospective studies like the current Teen-Labs study, SG seems a viable option for bariatric surgery in adolescents.

## ROUX-EN-Y GASTRIC BYPASS

RYGB is both a restrictive and malabsorptive procedure and is considered the gold standard for bariatric surgical procedures in the United States. The restrictive component is a small gastric pouch (approximately 15–20 mL in size) coupled with a small gastric outlet (2–3 cm in diameter) that results in early and sustained satiety. The malabsorptive component involves re-establishing intestinal continuity with a gastric bypass segment of varying lengths between 100 cm and 150 cm (see Fig. 1C).

Currently, there have been no procedure-related deaths reported in adolescents undergoing RYGB. Early complications include pulmonary embolism, wound infections, stomal stenosis, and marginal ulcers. Late complications have included small bowel obstruction, incisional hernias, symptomatic cholelithiasis, protein calorie and micronutrient deficiencies, and late weight regain (10%–15% incidence) [53,65,73]. These complications parallel their adult counterparts and stress the requirement of lifelong follow-up. The majority of weight can be expected to be lost within the first 18 to 24 months after surgery.

Two recent studies in adolescents have demonstrated similar postoperative outcomes compared with adults. A recent meta-analysis of 6 studies involving adolescent RYGB demonstrated a significant reduction in excess body weight with improvement in associated comorbidities [74]. A recent report from Cincinnati Children's Hospital demonstrated a significant reduction in BMI (35%–37%) within the first year after RYGB in adolescents [73]. One finding from that article showed an equal percentage of weight reduction despite the preoperative BMI. Unfortunately, those patients who started out heavier (BMI >60), despite losing a significant amount of weight, remained morbidly obese at 1 year. This demonstrates the need for earlier referral to ensure adequate weight loss to maximize comorbidity reduction. Several studies (cited previously in this review) demonstrate the resolution of numerous comorbid states in adolescents, including hypertension [74], sleep apnea [75], and type 2 diabetes mellitus [46], and psychosocial improvements [45]. Given these findings, the current literature supports the use of RYGB as a safe and efficacious means for significant weight loss and comorbidity reduction. As discussed previously, the Teen-Labs study should help strengthen the literature once outcomes are reported.

## POSTOPERATIVE MANAGEMENT

It is of the utmost importance for a bariatric patient's primary care physician to become familiar with the physiologic changes that occur after bariatric surgery. This allows for effective partnership between the bariatric team and the primary physician for the care of the patient after the operation.

Patients generally spend between 2 and 3 nights after their operation in the hospital and are discharged home on clear liquids. They are advanced fairly quickly to a high-protein liquid diet, which is usually maintained for at least 1 month after surgery. The postoperative diet is methodically advanced by introducing new food choices toward the goal of a well-balanced, small-portion (approximately 1 cup) diet, ensuring a daily intake of 1 g of protein per kilogram of ideal body weight. Patients are encouraged to eat proteins first during every meal to ensure their adequate intake. Nonsteroidal anti-inflammatory medications are generally avoided to reduce the risk of ulcer formation. Postoperative nausea is common after SG and most patients are discharged home on antinausea medications. The nausea tends to resolve within the first week after surgery. Reflux is also common after SG with approximately half of my patients requiring proton pump inhibitors for at least the first 6 postoperative months. Routine postoperative vitamin supplementation is the key for all operations, given the significant reduction in nutrients (AGB and SG) and combined malabsorption (RYGB). The typical regimen consists of 2 pediatric chewable multivitamins, a calcium supplement, and an iron supplement for menstruating women. B-complex vitamins are also supplemented beyond the typical multivitamin primarily to augment thiamine and folate supplementation (Table 2) [76]. Severe complications can arise with their deficiency, specifically in those who undergo RYGB [77].

There are 5 basic rules that are routinely emphasized with patients and family at each visit: (1) eat protein first; (2) drink 64 oz to 96 oz of water or sugar-free liquids daily; (3) no snacking between meals; (4) exercise at least 30 minutes per day; and (5) always remember vitamins and minerals.

All bariatric surgeries, to varying degrees, result in surgically enforced, low-calorie, low-carbohydrate intake, which, in turn, requires intensive attention to ensure adequate intake of important macronutrients and micronutrients. Postoperative follow-up consists of an initial visit 2 weeks after surgery. After this initial visit, patients are seen during regular intervals within my program (6 weeks, and then generally every 3 months for the first 18 months postoperatively). Patients are then generally seen on an annual basis. Serum chemistries, complete blood cell count, urine specific gravity, prothrombin time (evidence of vitamin K adequacy), and representative B-complex vitamin levels (eg, $B_1$, $B_{12}$, and folate) are obtained at regular intervals. Upper gastrointestinal series are usually obtained yearly in our SG patients and on an as-needed basis otherwise.

**Table 2**
Recommended nutritional supplementation after weight loss surgery

| Supplement | Recommendation |
|---|---|
| Multivitamin (with folic acid) | 1 to 2 Daily |
| Calcium citrate with vitamin D | 1500–1800 mg/d |
| Vitamin D | 1000 IU/d (if deficiency found preoperatiavely) |
| Vitamin $B_{12}$ | 500 μg/d Oral or 1000 μg/mo intramuscular |
| Elemental iron | 65 mg Elemental iron for menstruating women |
| Vitamin $B_1$ | Consider 50 mg daily in first 6 mo |
| Vitamins A and K | Treat if symptomatic |

Laboratory results are checked at 6 months postoperatively and then yearly unless symptoms arise.
*Data from* Xanthakos SA. Nutritional deficiencies in obesity and after bariatric surgery. Pediatr Clin North Am 2009;56(5):1105–21.

## SUMMARY

Morbid obesity continues to see a rapid increase in pediatric and adolescent populations. These patients develop significant comorbidities that continue into adulthood. Although medical management in the overweight population of children can be helpful, the morbidly obese adolescents do not show significant long-term weight reduction with lifestyle modification. Bariatric surgery is a safe and long-term solution in selected morbidly obese adolescents who are physically and psychosocially mature. Adolescent bariatric surgical patients require lifelong dietary modification and follow-up to ensure adequate nutritional supplementation. RYGB remains the gold standard operation but SG continues to gain rapid prominence, given its simplicity and reduced postoperative complication rates. AGB in the adolescent population can be efficacious compared with medical therapy but has demonstrated significantly higher complication and reoperation rates compared with its use in adults. It remains to be approved by the Food and Drug Administration only for those 18 years of age and older. More long-term, longitudinal studies are necessary to firmly establish guidelines for patient selection and optimal procedure choice.

### References

[1] Ogden CL, Carroll MD, Curtin LR, et al. Prevalence of overweight and obesity in the United States, 1999-2004. JAMA 2006;295(13):1549–55.

[2] Freedman DS, Mei Z, Srinivasan SR, et al. Cardiovascular risk factors and excess adiposity among overweight children and adolescents: the Bogalusa Heart Study. J Pediatr 2007;150:12–7.

[3] Strauss RS, Pollack HA. Epidemic increase in childhood overweight. 1986-1998. JAMA 2001;286:2845–8.

[4] Parsons TJ, Powers C, Logan S, et al. Childhood predictors of adult obesity: a systematic review. Int J Obes Relat Metab Disord 1999;23(Suppl 8):S1–107.

[5] Skelton JA, Cook SR, Auinger P, et al. Prevalence and trends of severe obesity among US children and adolescents. Acad Pediatr 2009;9:322–9.

[6] Koebnick C, Smith N, Coleman KJ, et al. Prevalence of extreme obesity in a multiethnic cohort of children and adolescents. J Pediatr 2010;157:26–31.e2.

[7] Flegal KM, Carroll MD, Kit BK, et al. Prevalence of obesity and Trends in the distribution of body mass index amoung US adults, 1999-2010. JAMA 2012;307:491–7.

[8] Levine MD, Ringham RM, Kalarchian MA, et al. Is family-based behavioral weight control appropriate for severe pediatric obesity? Int J Eat Disord 2001;30(3):318–28.

[9] Michels KB. Early life predictors of chronic disease. J Womens Health (Larchmt) 2003;12(2):157–61.

[10] Wahlqvist ML. Chronic disease prevention: a life-cycle approach which takes account of the environmental impact and opportunities of food, nutrition and public health policies—the rationale for an eco-nutritional disease nomenclature. Asia Pac J Clin Nutr 2002;11(Suppl 9):S759–62.

[11] Pi-Sunyer FX. The obesity epidemic: pathophysiology and consequences of obesity. Obes Res 2002;10(Suppl 2):97S–104S.

[12] Whitaker RC. Understanding the complex journey to obesity in early adulthood. Ann Intern Med 2002;136(12):923–5.

[13] Must A, Jacques PF, Dallal GE, et al. Long-term morbidity and mortality of overweight adolescents; A follow-up of the Harvard Growth Study of 1922-1935. N Engl J Med 1992;327:1350–5.

[14] Dietz WH. Health consequences of obesity in youth: childhood predictors of adult disease. Pediatrics 1998;101(3 pt 2):518–25.
[15] Pinhas-Hamiel O, Dolan LM, Daniels SR, et al. Increased incidence of non-insulin dependent diabetes mellitus among adolescents. J Pediatr 1996;128:608–15.
[16] Sinha R, Fisch G, Teague B, et al. Prevalence of impaired glucose tolerance among children and adolescents with marked obesity. N Engl J Med 2002;346(11):802–10.
[17] Caprio S. Insulin resistance in childhood obesity. J Pediatr Endocrinol Metab 2002;15(Suppl 1):487–92.
[18] Type 2 diabetes in children and adolescents. American Diabetes Association. Pediatrics 2000;105:671–80.
[19] Scott A, Toomath R, Boucher D, et al. First national audit of the outcomes of care in young people with diabetes in New Zealand: high prevalence of nephropathy in Maori and Pacific Oslanders. N Z Med J 2006;119:U2015.
[20] Scott A, Whitcombe S, Bouchier D, et al. Diabetes in children and young adults in Waikato Province, New Zealand: outcomes of care. N Z Med J 2004;117:U1219.
[21] Narayan K, Boyle J, Thompson T, et al. Lifetime risk for diabetes mellitus in the United States. JAMA 2003;290(14):1884–90.
[22] Daniels SR. Cardiovascular disease risk factors and atherosclerosis in children and adolescents. Curr Atheroscler Rep 2001;3:479–85.
[23] Freedman DS, Srinivasan SR, Harsha DW, et al. Relation of body fat patterning to lipid and lipoprotein concentrations in children and adolescents: the Bogalusa Heart Study. Am J Clin Nutr 1989;50:930–9.
[24] May AL, Kuklina EV, Yoon PW. Prevalence of cardiovascular disease risk factors among US adolescents, 1999-2008. Pediatrics 2012;129:1035–41.
[25] Freedman DS, Khan LK, Dietz WH, et al. Relationship of childhood obesity to coronary heart disease risk factors in adulthood: the Bogalusa Heart Study. Pediatrics 2001;108: 712–8.
[26] Rosner B, Prineas R, Daniels SR, et al. Blood pressure difference between blacks and whites in relation to body size and among US children and adolescents. Am J Epidemiol 2000;151:1007–19.
[27] Katsuren K, Nakamura K, Ohta T. Effect of body mass index-z score on adverse levels of cardiovascular disease risk factors. Pediatr Int 2012;54:200–4.
[28] Li AM, Nelson EA, Wing YK. Obstructive sleep apnea and obesity. Hong Kong Med J 2004;10:144.
[29] Verhulst SL, Schrauwen N, Haentjens D, et al. Sleep-disordered breathing in overweight and obese children and adolescents: prevalence, characteristics, and the role of fat distribution. Arch Dis Child 2007;92:205–8.
[30] Gozal D. Sleep-disordered breathing and school performance in children. Pediatrics 1998;102:616–20.
[31] Gozal D, Wang M, Pope DW. Objective sleepiness measures in pediatric obstructive sleep apnea. Pediatrics 2001;108:693–7.
[32] Chervin RD, Dillon JE, Archbold KH, et al. Conduct problems and symptoms of sleep disorders in children. J Am Acad Child Adolesc Psychiatry 2003;42:201–8.
[33] Amin RS, Kimball TR, Bean JA, et al. Left ventricular hypertrophy and abnormal ventricular geometry in children and adolescents with obstructive sleep apnea. Am J Respir Crit Care Med 2002;165:1395–9.
[34] Ippisch HM, Inge TH, Daniels SR, et al. Reversibility of cardiac abnormalities in morbidly obese adolescents. J AM Coll Cardiol 2008;51(14):1342–8.
[35] Schwimmer JB, Deutsch R, Kahen T, et al. Prevalence of fatty liver in children and adolescents. Pediatrics 2006;118:1388–93.
[36] Xanthakos S, Miles L, Bucuvalas J, et al. Histologic Spectrum of NASH in Morbidly Obese Adolescents Differs from Adults. Clin Gastroenterol Hepatol 2006;4(2): 226–32.

[37] Weisberg LA, Chutorian AM. Pseudotumor cerebri of childhood. Am J Dis Child 1977;131:1243–8.
[38] Sugarman HJ, Felton WL III, Sismanis A, et al. Gastric surgery for pseudotumor cerebri associated with severe obesity. Ann Surg 1999;229:634–42.
[39] Chandra V, Dutta S, Albanese CT, et al. Clinical resolution of severely symptomatic pseudotumor cerebri after gastric bypass in an adolescent. Surg Obes Relat Dis 2007;3:198–200.
[40] Zeller MH, Modi AC. Predictors of health-related quality of life in obese youth. Obesity (Silver Spring) 2006;14:122–30.
[41] Strauss RS. Childhood obesity and self-esteem. Pediatrics 2000;105:e15.
[42] Ball K, Crawford D, Kenardy J. Longitudinal relationships among overweight, life satisfaction, and aspirations in young women. Obes Res 2004;12:1019–30.
[43] Schwimmer JB, Burwinkle TM, Varni JW. Health-related quality of life of severely obese children and adolescents. JAMA 2003;289:1813–9.
[44] Gortmaker SL, Must A, Perrin JM, et al. Social and economic consequences of overweight in adolescence and young adulthood. N Engl J Med 1993;329:1008–12.
[45] Zeller MH, Modi AC, Noll JG, et al. Psychosocial functioning improves following adolescent bariatric surgery. Obesity (Silver Spring) 2009;17:985–90.
[46] Inge TH, Miyano G, Bean J, et al. Reversal of type 2 diabetes mellitus and improvements in cardiovascular risk factors after surgical weight loss in adolescents. Pediatrics 2009;123(1):214–22.
[47] Kaira M, Inge T. Effect of bariatric surgery on obstructive sleep apnea in adolescents. Paediatr Respir Rev 2006;7(4):260–7.
[48] Kral JG, Thung SN, Biron S, et al. Effects of surigcal treatment of the metabolic syndrome on liver fibrosis and cirrhosis. Surgery 2004;135:48–58.
[49] Michalsky M, Reichard K, Inge T, et al. ASMBS pediatric committee best practice guidelines. Surg Obes Relat Dis 2012;8:1–7.
[50] Pratt JS, Lenders CM, Dionne EA, et al. Best practice updates for pediatric/adolescent weight loss surgery. Obesity (Silver Spring) 2009;17:901–10.
[51] Tanner JM. Growth at adolescence. 2nd edition. Oxford (United Kingdom): Blackwell Scientific Publications; 1962.
[52] Tanner JM, Davies PS. Clinical longitudinal standards for height and weight velocity for North American children. J Pediatr 1985;107:317–29.
[53] Michalsky M, Kramer RE, Fullmer MA, et al. Developing criteria for pediatric/adolescent bariatric surgery programs. Pediatrics 2001;128(2):S65.
[54] Sugerman HJ, Sugerman EL, DeMaria EJ, et al. Bariatric surgery for severely obese adolescents. J Gastrointest Surg 2003;7:102–8.
[55] Rand CS, MacGregor AM. Adolescents having obesity surgery: a 6 year follow-up. South Med J 1999;87:1208–13.
[56] Barnett SJ, Stanley C, Hanlon M, et al. Long-term follow-up and the role of surgery in adolescents with morbid obesity. Surg Obes Relat Dis 2005;1:394–8.
[57] O'Brien PE, Sawyer SM, Laurie S, et al. Laparoscopic adjustable gastric banding in severeley obese adolescents; a randomized trial. JAMA 2010;303:519–26.
[58] Alqahtani AR, Antonisamy B, Alamri H, et al. Laparoscopic sleeve gastrectomy in 108 obese children and adolescents aged 5 to 21 years. Ann Surg 2012;256(2):266–73.
[59] Jen HC, Rickard DG, Shew SB, et al. Trends and outcomes of adolescent bariatric surgery in California, 2005-2007. Pediatrics 2010;126:e746–53.
[60] Zitsman JL, Fennoy I, Witt MA, et al. Laparoscopic adjustable gastric banding in adolescents: short-term results. J Pediatr Surg 2011;46:157–62.
[61] Lawson ML, Kirk S, Mitchell T, et al. One year outcomes of Roux-en-Y gastric bypass for morbidly obese adolescents: a multicenter study from the Pediatric Bariatric Study Group. J Pediatr Surg 2006;41:137–43.

[62] Al-Qahtani AR. Laparoscopic adjustable gastric banding in adolescents: safety and efficacy. J Pediatr Surg 2007;42:894–7.
[63] Dolan K, Creighton L, Hopkins G, et al. Laparoscopic gastic banding in morbidly obese adolescents. Obes Surg 2003;13:101–5.
[64] Angrisani L, Favretti F, Furbetta F, et al. Obese teenagers treated by Lap-Band System: the Italian experience. Surgery 2005;138:877–81.
[65] Strauss RS, Bradley LJ, Brolin RE. Gastric bypass in adolescents with morbid obesity. J Pediatr 2001;138:499–504.
[66] Schauer PR, Ikramuddin S. Laparoscopic surgery for morbid obesity. Surg Clin North Am 2001;81:1145–79.
[67] Rosenthal RJ. International sleeve gastrectomy expert panel consensus statement: best practice guidleines based on experience of > 12,000 cases. Surg Obes Relat Dis 2012;8:8–19.
[68] Langer FB, Reza Hoda MA, Bohdjalian A, et al. Sleeve gastrectomy and gastric banding: effects on plasma ghrelin levels. Obes Surg 2005;15:1024–9.
[69] Lee CM, Cirangle PT, Jossart GH. Vertical gastrectomy for morbid obesity in 216 patients: resport of two year results. Surg Endosc 2007;21:1810–6.
[70] Till H, Bluher S, Hirsch W, et al. Efficacy of laparoscopic sleeve gastrectomy (LGS) as a stand-alone techniwque for children with morbid obesity. Obes Surg 2008;18:1047–9.
[71] Till H, Muenstere O, Keller A, et al. Laparoscopic sleeve gastrectomy acheives substantial weight loss ni an adolescnet girl with morbid obesity. Eur J Pediatr 2008;1:47–9.
[72] Boza C, Viscido G, Salina J, et al. Laparscopic sleeve gastrectomy I obese adolescents: results in 51 patients. Surg Obes Relat Dis 2012;8:133–9.
[73] Inge TH, Jnekins TM, Zeller M, et al. Baseline BMI is a strong predictor of nadir BMI after adolescent gastric bypass. J Pediatr 2010;156:103–8.
[74] Treadwell JR, Sun F, Schoelles K. Systematic review and meta-analysis of bariatric surgery for pediatric obesity. Ann Surg 2008;248(5):763–76.
[75] Ippisch HM, Inge TH, Daniels SR, et al. Reversibility of cardiac abnormalities in morbidly obese adolescents. J Am Coll Cardiol 2008;51:1342–8.
[76] Xanthakos SA. Nutritional deficiencies in obesity and after bariatric surgery. Pediatr Clin North Am 2009;56(5):1105–21.
[77] Towbin A, Inge TH, Garcia VF, et al. Beriberi after gastric bypass surgery in adolescence. J Pediatr 2004;145(2):263–7.

Advances in Pediatrics 60 (2013) 327–332



# INDEX



*Note:* Page numbers of article titles are in **boldface** type.

0065-3101/13/$ – see front matter

http://dx.doi.org/10.1016/S0065-3101(13)00027-3

## S



## T

## U



## V



## W



## Y